Categorical Propositions

The Four Standard Forms

A: All *S* are *P*   **E**: No *S* is *P*

I: Some *S* are *P*   **O**: Some *S* are not *P*

The Traditional Square of Opposition

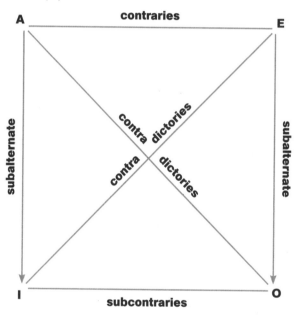

Immediate Inferences

Each statement in the left column is logically equivalent to the statement directly across from it in the right column.

CONVERSION

E: No *S* is *P*   No *P* is *S*

I: Some *S* are *P*   Some *P* are *S*

OBVERSION

A: All *S* are *P*   No *S* is non-*P*

E: No *S* is *P*   All *S* are non-*P*

I: Some *S* are *P*   Some *S* are not non-*P*

O: Some *S* are not *P*   Some *S* are non-*P*

CONTRAPOSITION

A: All *S* are *P*   All non-*P* are non-*S*

O: Some *S* are not *P*   Some non-*P* are not non-*S*

FOURTH EDITION

The Art of Reasoning

An Introduction to Logic and Critical Thinking

DAVID KELLEY

W. W. NORTON & COMPANY, INC.

NEW YORK · LONDON

W. W. Norton & Company has been independent since its founding in 1923, when William Warder Norton and Mary D. Herter Norton first published lectures delivered at the People's Institute, the adult education division of New York City's Cooper Union. The firm soon expanded its program beyond the Institute, publishing books by celebrated academics from America and abroad. By midcentury, the two major pillars of Norton's publishing program—trade books and college texts—were firmly established. In the 1950s, the Norton family transferred control of the company to its employees, and today—with a staff of four hundred and a comparable number of trade, college, and professional titles published each year—W. W. Norton & Company stands as the largest and oldest publishing house owned wholly by its employees.

Editors: Peter Simon, Ken Barton
Assistant Editor: Quynh Do
Manuscript Editor: Christopher Curioli
Project Editor: Rachel Mayer
Electronic Media Editor: Cliff Landesman
Marketing Manager, Philosophy: Michael Moss
Production Manager: Ashley Horna
Permissions Manager: Megan Jackson
Text Design: Lisa Buckley
Art Director: Rubina Yeh

Composition: Achorn International
Manufacturing: R. R. Donnelley—Crawfordsville

The text of this book is composed in Legacy Serif with the display set in AG Book Pro.

Library of Congress Cataloging-in-Publication Data

Kelley, David, 1949-
    The art of reasoning / David Kelley. — Fourth Edition.
       pages cm
    Includes bibliographical references and index.
    ISBN 978-0-393-93078-8 (pbk.)
    1. Reasoning. 2. Logic. I. Title.
    BC177.K38 2013
    160—dc23
                              2013016117

W. W. Norton & Company, Inc., 500 Fifth Avenue, New York, NY 10110-0017
wwnorton.com

W. W. Norton & Company Ltd., Castle House, 75/76 Wells Street, London W1T 3QT
1 2 3 4 5 6 7 8 9 0

About
the Author

David Kelley is Founder of The Atlas
Society in Washington, DC. He has a Ph.D. in
philosophy from Princeton University and has
taught at Vassar College and Brandeis University.

Contents
in Brief

Contents

PART TWO   Deductive Logic

CHAPTER 6   Categorical Propositions

CHAPTER 7   Categorical Syllogisms

CHAPTER 8   Reasoning with Syllogisms

PART THREE   Inductive Logic

Preface

The *Art of Reasoning* is a textbook designed for courses in introductory logic or critical thinking. In addition to the elements of formal deductive logic, it includes classification and definition, basic argument analysis, fallacies, and inductive reasoning.

My goal in the book is to make it a valuable resource for the classroom instructor. Based on my own experience as a teacher, I believe the most important means to that end is to write in a way that will hold the interest of students. Otherwise, they are not likely to do the reading assignments; they will not come to class prepared; and instructors will have to spend valuable class time reviewing the basics. I have therefore tried to explain the standards of good thinking in a clear, engaging, conversational style. On each topic, I have tried to follow an arc of learning: beginning with a clear, straightforward example; then extracting the relevant concept or principle; and then moving on to further implications, qualifications, and more complex or borderline examples. And I have kept theoretical discussion to a minimum, including only those points necessary to make the standards and techniques intelligible.

Organization

Part 1, Language and Reasoning, covers the basic linguistic tools required for thinking clearly and the basic elements of argument analysis and evaluation. The material on classification (Chapter 1) is rarely covered in other texts, but I find that a clear understanding of genus–species hierarchies makes it much easier for students to master other topics, especially definitions (Chapter 2), categorical syllogisms (Chapters 6–8), inductive generalization (Chapter 12), and statistical reasoning (Chapter 14). In addition, Chapter 3, which discusses propositions as assertions, gives students the preparatory work they need to identify the premises and conclusions of arguments.

Chapter 4 (Argument Analysis) begins the treatment of arguments and introduces key logical concepts: premise and conclusion; deduction and induction; and validity, soundness, strength, and cogency. This material has been substantially expanded for the fourth edition, including a new section on deductive and inductive arguments. The chapter presents a simple diagramming technique that can be used with arguments of any type and any degree of complexity, and it gives students guidelines on identifying assumed premises. Chapter 5 (Fallacies) focuses on the fallacies most often encountered in everyday thought and speech and indicates the contexts in which each fallacy is most likely to be committed. (This edition contains new sections on the fallacies of accident and slippery slope.)

Part 2 covers both traditional and modern deductive logic. Chapters 6 and 7 deal with categorical propositions and syllogisms. The treatment of Venn diagrams has been expanded to give students more help in diagramming propositions, immediate inferences, and syllogisms. Chapter 8 begins with the traditional versions of disjunctive and hypothetical syllogisms. It goes on to show how to identify and analyze deductive arguments as they typically occur in ordinary language, including complex arguments that involve combinations of categorical, hypothetical, and disjunctive syllogisms. The chapter will be useful for instructors who do not plan to cover the modern propositional and predicate logic.

For instructors who *do* cover modern symbolic logic, the next three chapters deal with propositional (Chapters 9 and 10) and predicate (Chapter 11) logic. For the fourth edition, these chapters have been significantly expanded in response to comments by reviewers. I have added more explanations to help students understand the connectives, truth tables, and proofs. The text breaks processes down into small sections with explanations at each step. The exercises have many real-language applications of the logic—everything from arguments in science, religion, and law to Robert Frost's poetry—and are balanced to test the items students need to master, with roughly equal representation of each method, inference rule, etc.

Chapter 9 includes a new section on tautology, contradiction, and consistency. Chapter 11 now introduces proofs in predicate logic early on. It treats rules, restrictions, and strategies contextually, moving from basic proofs, to those involving conditional and *reductio* proofs, to relational predicates and multiple quantification. For the three chapters on modern logic, moreover, I have doubled the number of exercises.

Part 3, finally, covers inductive reasoning. In addition to material on rules for inductive generalization and Mill's methods for causal inference (Chapter 12) and argument by analogy (Chapter 13), I have devoted a chapter to statistical reasoning (Chapter 14), offering students the basic concepts and standards for evaluating the kinds of statistical arguments they will frequently encounter in the media. Chapter 15 deals with the analysis and evaluation of explanations. Among other things, it shows how the same diagramming technique used for arguments can easily be extended to explanatory structures. And Chapter 16, new to this edition, covers the basics of probability.

Pedagogical Features

Throughout the book, elements of design help students assimilate the material:

- *Summary* sidebars pull together important definitions, principles, and rules.

- *Strategy* sidebars highlight procedures to follow, including heuristics and tips.
- *Summaries* at the end of each chapter condense the essential material in each chapter.
- *Key terms* following each end-of-chapter Summary give definitions of concepts introduced in the chapter and are compiled in the Glossary at the back of the book.

Each chapter also contains abundant exercises of different types and levels of difficulty. Following most sections of each chapter are exercises to let students test their understanding of the material before proceeding to the next section. Answers to every third item of these exercises and to every third item of the Additional Exercises are included at the back of the book. At the end of each chapter, Additional Exercises integrate the material in the chapter by asking students to use their skills in many different combinations on different sorts of task. There are creative exercises asking students to come up with their own definitions, arguments, and explanations, as well as critical exercises in which they evaluate those of others. Examples are drawn from works in many different disciplines—politics, science, literature, and history—so that all students will encounter at least some material from fields with which they are familiar. I have tried to use examples and exercises that have the flavor of reality to help students see how the standards of thinking apply to the sorts of issues they actually encounter in their everyday experience, in political debate, and in the other courses they take across the curriculum.

For this fourth edition of *The Art of Reasoning*, I have substantially revised the examples used in the text and exercises and have added more than 600 new exercises. In the end, however, I think variety is more important than sheer abundance. There are diminishing returns from performing the same task over and over on material of the same kind. I have tried to give students an imaginative variety of tasks that, like finger exercises for pianists, will exercise their mental muscles in different combinations, sounding different chords of understanding.

Custom Options

The Art of Reasoning has a basically modular design, allowing individual chapters to be used in various combinations, but there are a number of integrating links (such as diagrams for classification and for argument structure), and most chapters provide some exercises that ask students to use skills they have learned in earlier chapters. There is more material in the book than can be covered in a one-semester course, even at the brisk pace of a chapter a week, and many different selections are possible.

- A course in *informal logic and critical reasoning*, emphasizing basic skills in analyzing language and reasoning, might cover the five chapters in Part 1 (Language and Reasoning), Chapters 6–8 (traditional categorical logic), and Chapters 12–14 (inductive logic).
- A course in *introductory logic*, including traditional syllogistic and modern logic, might begin with Chapter 1 (Classification), Chapter 3 (Propositions), Chapter 4 (Argument Analysis), and Chapter 5 (Fallacies); and then move on to Chapters 6 and 7 (traditional syllogism), Chapters 9 and 10 (propositional logic), and Chapter 12 (Inductive Generalizations).
- A course in *modern formal logic* might include Chapter 4 (Argument Analysis) and then move on to Part 2 (Deductive Logic), including Chapter 6 (Categorical Propositions) and Chapters 9–11 (propositional and predicate logic).

These three selections are available as standard custom editions from W. W. Norton. Many other combinations are possible on request.

Supplements

In addition to the text, *The Art of Reasoning* comes with supplemental materials designed to make the instructor's job easier and to improve learning outcomes:

- *Study Space*: The companion student Web site (wwnorton.com/studyspace) includes flashcards of key terms, chapter summaries, and feature boxes, including a complete list of the rules of inference.
- *Online Homework*: A comprehensive online homework system that students can access through StudySpace gives students feedback and guidance as they work through problems. Access to this system is free with every new copy purchased of *The Art of Reasoning*. Instructors should go to wwnorton.com/logic to learn more or to set up a course.
- *Test Bank*: Extensively revised by Andrew Hill (Xavier University) and Richard Shedenhelm (University of Georgia), the test bank now includes more than 2,600 questions, all keyed and categorized according to question type and difficulty level.
- *Solutions Manual*: In this resource for instructors, I have provided solutions to all 2,400 problems found in the book, and the problems are rated by difficulty.
- *Lecture PowerPoint Slides*: These lecture slides, written by Dr. Ray Peace (Valdosta State University), are completely new to the fourth edition. With more than 30 slides per chapter (more than 500 total), these PowerPoint slides offer clear, detailed outlines to help professors prepare for lectures. Where applicable, we have included figures and diagrams from the textbook.

Instructors should contact their local W. W. Norton representative or go to wwnorton.com/logic for more information or to request access to these supplemental materials.

Acknowledgments

I am indebted to many personal friends and colleagues, past and present, who have offered advice and encouragement, sent me examples, and otherwise made my life easier. Special thanks to Audrey McKinney and Kenneth Livingston—

former colleagues at Vassar College—for many helpful discussions about teaching logic; to Roger Donway, Stephen Hicks, Andrew Hill, Richard Shedenhelm, and Susan Dawn Wake for ideas and exercise material they provided over the years.

I am grateful to the exceptional team of programmers and logicians at Carnegie Mellon University whose work has made the homework system that accompanies *The Art of Reasoning* a reality: Wilfrid Sieg, John Rinderle, Norman Bier, Dawn McLaughlin, Alexandra Drozd, and Davin Lafon.

I have also had the benefit of comments from numerous instructors who reviewed earlier drafts and editions of the text, its problem sets, or its online homework: Rod Adams (Front Range Community College), Mahesh Ananth (Indiana University, South Bend), Nathan Anderson (Eckerd College), Janet Andrews (Vassar College), Benjamin Arah (Bowie State University), Monica Aufrecht (Linfield College), Justine Baker (Pierce College), Barnard Robert (University of Mississippi), Ronald Barnette (Valdosta State University), Thora Bayer (Xavier University of Louisiana), James Beebe (University of Buffalo), Dave Beisecker (University of Nevada, Las Vegas), Bruce Bethell (University of Illinois, Urbana-Champaign), Peter Boltuc (University of Illinois at Springfield), Charles Bolyard (James Madison University), Vanda Bozicevic (Bergen Community College), Marshell Bradley (Sam Houston State University), Jurgis Brakas (Marist College), Patrick Brissey (University of South Carolina), Tom Buford (Furman University), Robert Burch (Texas A&M University), Michael Burke (St. Joseph's College, New York), Charles Byrne (University of Illinois, Urbana-Champaign), Michael Byron (Kent State University), Lloyd Carr (Rivier College), Jennifer Caseldine-Bracht (Indiana University–Purdue University, Fort Wayne), Gladys Childs (Texas Wesleyan University), Drew Christie (University of New Hampshire), Daniel Cohen (Colby College), Jay Conway (California State University, Los Angeles), Brett Coppenger (University of Iowa), Victor Cosculluela (Polk State College), Michael Coste (Front Range Community College), Steve Cowan (Louisiana College), Helen Daly (Colorado College), Raymond Darr (Southern Illinois University, Edwardsville), Julian Davies (Siena College), Peter Dendle (Pennsylvania State University), Gianluca Di Muzio (Indiana University Northwest), Jill Dieterle (Eastern Michigan University), Sarah Donovan (Wagner College), Gregory Doolan (Catholic University of America), Shane Drefcinski (University of Wisconsin, Platteville), Keith Dromm (Northwestern State University of Louisiana), Dennis Earl (Coastal Carolina University), C. E. Emmer (Emporia State University), Jonathan Evans (University of Indianapolis), Frank Fair (Sam Houston State University), Joel Feldman (Rider University), Edward Feser (Pasadena City College), Richard Findler (Slippery Rock University), Peter Fosl (Transylvania University), Martin Fowler (Elon College), Steven Gamboa (California State University, Bakersfield), John Gibson (University of Louisville), Mark Gilbertson (Texas Lutheran University), John Gist (Western New Mexico University), Ben Gorman (York College of Pennsylvania), Frank Grabowski (Rogers State University), Roger Hall (West Valley College), Liam Harte (Westfield State College), Amanda Hicks (State University of New York at Buffalo), Judith Hill (Saginaw Valley State University), James Hill (Valdosta State University), Andrew Hill (Xavier University), Charles Hornbeck (Keene State University), Charles Hughes (Chapman University), John Humphrey (Minnesota State University, Mankato), Elaine Hurst (St. Francis College), Peter Hutcheson (Texas State University), Debby Hutchins (Gonzaga University), Jeffrey Irwin (Carnegie Mellon University), Christine James (Valdosta State University), Michael Jordan (Iona College), Rebecca Kajs (Anne Arundel Community College), Holly Kantin (University of Wisconsin, Madison), Jerry Kapus (University of Wisconsin, Stout), Catherine Kemp (John Jay College), Ethan Kosmider (Stony Brook University), Adam Kovach (Marymount University), Sunita Lanka (Hartnell College), Sanford Levy (Montana State University), Kenneth Livingston (Vassar College), James Loftis (Loraine County Community College), Joseph Lombardo (St. Joseph's College of New York), Zhaolu Lu (Tiffin University), Amy MacArthur

(High Point University), Jennifer McErlean (Siena College), Timothy McGrew (Western Michigan University), Audrey McKinney (Texas State University), Vicente Medina (Seton Hall University), Andrew Mills (Otterbein College), Michael Monge (Long Beach City College), Daniel Murphy (St. Peter's College), Erica Neely (Ohio Northern University), Nathaniel Nicol (Washington State University), Elizabeth Oljar (University of Detroit, Mercy), John Olson (Normandale Community College), Michael Papazian (Berry College), Michael Patton (University of Montevallo), Ray Peace (Valdosta State University), Thomas Pearson (University of Wisconsin, Parkside), Mark Pestana (Grand Valley State University), Daniel Petersen (Hartnell College), Linda Reardan (California State Polytechnic University, Pomona), Alan Rhoda (University of Notre Dame), David Richards (Cayuga Community College), Jeffrey Roland (Louisiana State University), Michael Rombeiro (St. Joseph's College of Maine), Michael Rooney (Pasadena City College), Glenn Sanford (Sam Houston State University), Fred Seddon (Pennsylvania State University, Altoona), David Seltzer (Pennsylvania State University), Patrick Shade (Rhodes College), Richard Shedenhelm (University of Georgia), Aeon Skoble (Bridgewater State College), James Smith (Calvin College), Arnold Smith (Kent State University), Renee Smith (Coastal Carolina University), Harvey Solganik (Southwestern Baptist Theological Seminary), James South (Marquette University), George Spangler (California State University, Long Beach), Andrew Spear (Grand Valley State University), Gordon Steinhoff (Utah State University), Alfred Stewart (Midwestern State University), Peter Suber (Earlham College), Chris Surprenant (Tulane University), Mate Szabo (Carnegie Mellon University), Edward Trudeau (Catholic University of America), Matthew Turner (Francis Marion University), Russell Wahl (Idaho State University), Susan Dawn Wake (Rochester Institute of Technology), Sara Waller (Montana State University), Ronald Weed (University of New Brunswick), John Wingard (Covenant College), Mia Wood (Pierce College), Elaine Yoshikawa (Arizona State University), Jeffrey Zents (University of Texas–Pan American), and Steven Zusman (Illinois State University). Thank you all.

Needless to say, none of the people I have mentioned is responsible for the use I have made (or failed to make) of their comments, which in many cases were highly critical.

Any book is a collaboration between author and publisher, and I have been particularly fortunate in that regard. During the years I have worked on *The Art of Reasoning*, I have come to rely on the enthusiasm and professionalism of the staff at W. W. Norton. For the fourth edition, I am particularly indebted to Ken Barton, Cliff Landesman, and Peter Simon for the extraordinary thought, care, and patience they have devoted to this project. The team that worked with them to publish this edition—Kim Yi (managing editor, College Digital Media), Rachel Mayer (project editor), Christopher Curioli (copy editor), Quynh Do (assistant editor), Conor Sullivan (assistant editor), Nicole Sawa (ancillary editor), Carson Russell (ancillary editor), Zach Miller (editorial assistant), Stefani Wallace (electronic media editorial assistant), Debra Morton Hoyt (art director), Rubina Yeh (design director), and Megan Jackson (permissions manager)—was stellar. Thank you all.

Finally, I owe a huge debt to my colleague Laurie Rice, who has worked with me on every aspect of the fourth edition. Her work has improved the book immensely.

Introduction

This is a book about thinking. It's a book about *how* to think.

In a broad sense, the word "thinking" refers to anything that goes on in our minds. When I say "a penny for your thoughts," I want to know what's on your mind—whether it's a feeling, a memory, a question, an anxiety, a problem you're trying to solve, or a daydream. As long as you are conscious, there is always something going on up there. In *this* sense, you can't help thinking. You don't need this book. You just have to stay awake. In a narrower sense, however, thinking is a particular *kind* of mental activity, the kind involved in solving a problem, planning an action, studying for a test, or defending your position on a controversial issue. This is still a pretty broad concept, but we have excluded some things.

In the first place, we can distinguish thinking from feeling. Thinking is a cognitive process we use in the attempt to gain knowledge or to understand something, as distinct from our emotional responses to things. This distinction does not mean, as people too often assume, that someone with strong emotions is necessarily illogical or that a logical person must be unemotional. On the contrary, there is no reason we cannot have both: clear, logical minds and passionate feelings. But thinking and feeling do have different roles to play, different jobs to do, in our mental lives.

Second, thinking is purposive. It differs from activities such as daydreaming and fantasizing in which we simply let our minds wander where they will. Thinking is something we have to *do*, usually with some degree of effort. And because it aims at a goal, it is something that can be done with varying degrees of success. You may or may not succeed in solving a problem, forming a plan, grasping something you read, or proving your case. In this way, too, it differs from daydreaming, where the concepts of success and failure don't really apply. Thinking is a skill. It's a skill that everyone has in some degree, but it is also a skill that everyone can improve.

How can we improve this skill? Let's consider an analogy with the game of tennis. If we want to improve our skill at tennis, we need to do two things. We need to learn more about the rules and strategies of the game. And we need to practice the moves that implement those rules and strategies—to practice serving, volleying, rushing the net, and so forth. The same is true for the activity of thinking. There are certain rules and strategies of thinking, certain standards that tell us when we have achieved a clear understanding of some subject or succeeded in proving a case. Our first task is to learn what these standards are and to understand why they are correct. Our second task is to practice applying these standards to a variety of examples drawn from everyday life, from politics, and from the different subjects one studies in school. The more practice we get, the more effectively we can incorporate the standards of logic into our habits of thought. That's why this book has a lot of exercises.

Before we begin, let's get an overview of the range of standards and techniques that we're going to be learning about.

Reasoning

When we engage in thought, our goal is normally to find out something. We are trying to answer a question, solve a problem, prove a conclusion, or learn a body of material. We want to know why the car will not start, or which candidate to vote for, or what is the cheapest way to get home for the holidays, or what the man or woman of our dreams really feels about us. In all these cases, we can't acquire this knowledge by direct observation. We have to do some reasoning. Reasoning is a process of thought in which we make inferences: starting with information we already have, an inference draws some further conclusion based on that information. For example, if your car will not start but the lights still work, you can infer that the problem is not a dead battery.

Logic is the study of the methods and standards of inference. Throughout this book, we will be talking about different kinds of inferences and about which ones to use in which sorts of situations. We will study rules for evaluating inferences and learn to distinguish good inferences from bad ones. As a preview, let's look at a particular case.

Some states have passed laws requiring that seat belts be used in cars. Supporters of the law say that those who wear seat belts have a better chance, statistically, of surviving an accident than those who don't. Opponents often point to particular cases in which someone survived because he was *not* wearing a seat belt. Which is the better sort of evidence? Are the opponents making too much of the exceptions? Are the supporters making proper use of the statistics? Let's assume, just for the sake of discussion, that wearing seat belts really is safer. Is that enough to justify the law? No—not by itself. The greater safety of seat belts would justify the law only if we take the position that the government should require us to do what is safe. Some people defend that position. Others say we should be free to decide these things for ourselves. So there are really two issues here: the safety of seat belts and the proper role of government. Can the second one be settled by statistical evidence? If not, then what sort of evidence *is* relevant?

The purpose of logic is to answer the sort of questions I raised in the last paragraph. Logic alone won't tell you whether to support mandatory seat belt laws. It *will* give you a method to follow in making that decision and backing it up. It will show you how to break an issue down into subissues, so that you can be sure to consider all the relevant points. It will give you standards for deciding what sort of evidence is appropriate to a particular issue. And it will give you standards for determining how much weight to give a piece of evidence.

The value of these logical standards is not limited to political arguments. In many college courses, students are presented with competing ideas or theories and asked to discuss them critically. In a philosophy class, the issue might be the existence of free will; in literature, it might be different interpretations of *Hamlet*. Whatever the subject, discussing ideas critically means presenting reasons for or against them. Even in our personal lives we all have choices to make, major ones or minor, and here too we need to weigh the reasons on each side and try to consider all the relevant issues.

Logic can also help us develop other, more subtle skills. Most of us have been in discussions that were frustrating because they kept going around in circles. That often happens when people "talk past each other"—when they are not really addressing the same issue. Suppose someone argues that it's wrong to treat abortion merely as a medical procedure, like removing an appendix, because the fetus is a potential person. Someone else might argue that a woman should have the right to make decisions concerning her own body. These two people are both dealing with the topic of abortion, but they may not be addressing quite the same issue. The first person may be trying to show that abortion is morally wrong, while the second is denying that it should be made illegal. Whether abortion is right or wrong in moral terms and whether it should be legal or illegal are different issues. They are related (which is why they are easily confused), but not identical.

If the two people could identify the difference, they might find that they don't disagree after all. The one who says that abortion should be legal might be willing to agree that abortion is nevertheless a serious action that would be wrong to take without an equally serious reason. And the one who says that abortion is morally wrong might be willing to agree that it's still a decision that a woman should be legally free to make on her own. Of course, the argument might not work out so neatly. But we'll never know until we try, and we can't try until we know how to distinguish one issue from another. That's a skill that logic can help us develop.

In this particular case, the problem of talking past each other would be fairly easy to fix because the two different issues are signaled by two different words: "immoral" versus "illegal." A more difficult problem occurs when two people are using the same word but with two different meanings. Suppose there is an argument over whether student work should be graded. If one person is referring specifically to letter grades, while the other is referring to *any* form of evaluation, they are probably going to talk past each other. If we take the different meanings of the word into account, we would have to say that here again the people are not debating the same issue. But the problem is harder to fix because the difference in meaning lies below the surface of the language. And "grade" is a fairly concrete word. Think of the possibilities for miscommunication in words like "democracy," "freedom," "love," or "art."

This brings us to another area of logic: concepts and definitions. People often talk past each other when they use words with different meanings. Even when that is not a problem, it is always valuable to make the meaning of our words as clear and explicit as possible. Some concepts, such as "democracy," are extremely hard to define, and great minds have spent lifetimes in the effort. Logic won't guarantee success, but it can give us a method to follow, and the method will pay immediate dividends in the clarity and precision of our thinking. It will also make it easier to master new concepts and words that are introduced in most courses at school.

So far we have talked about skills involved in taking ideas apart: breaking an issue down into its components, distinguishing between closely related ideas, and analyzing the meaning of a word. But we also need to put our ideas together again. Thinking involves synthesis as well as analysis, integration as well as differentiation. To understand a line of reasoning, we need to break it down into its parts, but we also need to put it in its wider context. In working on a problem, the most creative solutions often come when we notice similarities to problems in other areas. In a college course, it's important to understand each component of the material, but it's equally important to organize the material as a whole into a logically coherent framework.

Indeed, we can often integrate ideas from different courses. In a religion or ethics class, for example, you might discuss the idea that love of money is the root of all evil. How does that relate to the economist's description of money as a medium of exchange? In a political science class on democracy, you might discuss the idea that people are capable of governing themselves. Is that supported or contradicted by what you've learned in psychology, history, and philosophy? As these examples illustrate, integration means the awareness of logical relations on a larger scale. An idea in one area may provide evidence for an idea in another, quite different area. Or the two ideas may contradict each other—in which case they cannot both be right. An understanding of logic will help you spot these relationships.

Objectivity

As you can see from our discussion so far, thinking is a complex skill. It has many component activities, each with its own methods and standards. But these methods and standards have a purpose: to help us be *objective*. Objectivity in this context means staying aligned with the facts, guiding our thought processes by a concern for truth. To some extent, objectivity is a matter of choice: the choice not to indulge in wishful thinking, not to let bias or prejudice distort our judgment, and so forth. But there's more to it than that. Objectivity also involves a skill. Even with the best will in the world, we can't really be objective unless we know how to use our cognitive equipment: how to follow and evaluate the arguments we hear, how to isolate the relevant issues clearly, how to avoid ambiguity and vagueness in the words we use.

The essence of objectivity is the ability to step back from our train of thought and examine it critically. This is a virtue because it is the only way to avoid jumping to conclusions, the only way to check the results of our thinking, the only way to make sure that we are in touch with the facts. The results of our thinking cannot be any better than the processes by which we arrive at them. There is no Book of Life with answers in the back where we can see whether we got it right. Good thinking is a self-directed, self-correcting process, and you are the only one who can take responsibility for steering your own mind in the right direction. The methods and standards we discuss in this book will give you a compass.

Objectivity also has a social aspect. It means not only presenting your own ideas logically but also listening to what others say. Objectivity does not require that you be neutral, nonpartisan, or indifferent to the issue. It does require that you try to look at the matter from the other person's perspective. Even if your view is right, it is rare that any single perspective reveals the *whole* truth. Objectivity requires that you give a fair hearing to the evidence and arguments for the other side. Even if you reject them in the end, knowing *why* you reject them will give you a better understanding of your own position.

Another aspect of objectivity is especially important in communicating with others. To get our ideas across successfully, we have to take account of the other person's context. A point so obvious to me that it hardly seems worth mentioning may not be obvious to someone else, and if I fail to mention it, he may not understand what I am saying. Objectivity is the ability to step back from our own thinking so that we can see it critically, through the eyes of someone who does not share our outlook, our context of knowledge, our preferences, or our idiosyncrasies. All that we can reasonably ask of our audience is the ability to follow logical connections. In this respect, logic, like language, is a shared framework without which we could not communicate.

This sort of objectivity is especially important in writing, where readers are not present to ask questions if the message isn't getting through. If I fail to make clear what issue I am addressing, or if I use terms in new or ill-defined ways, readers can't interrupt to ask what I am talking about. They are stuck with what I've put down on paper. If my presentation is vague, or fails to consider a relevant alternative, or makes a questionable assumption, they can't stop me to ask for an elaboration. In writing, therefore, we have to be on our best behavior, logically speaking. Many writing problems are really problems in logical thinking. Conversely, writing exercises are one of the best ways to practice the techniques of logic, and you will find many such exercises in this book.

Speaking of exercises, I want to offer a final word of advice and encouragement. There are two kinds of exercises in each of the chapters in this book. At the ends of most sections within a chapter, you will find regular Exercises. Even if you feel you understood the material in a given section as I explained it, you don't know for sure whether you have mastered the thinking skills until you try doing them yourself. That's what the Exercises are for. At the end of each chapter is a longer set of Additional Exercises that call on all the skills you learned in the chapter. These exercises ask you to use thinking skills in different combinations; they often involve "real-life" examples; and they are a bit more challenging than the in-chapter exercises. Answers for exercises with stars next to them can be found at the back of the book.

It's going to take a certain amount of effort to improve your thinking skills and to build the muscles of your mind. As the ads for health clubs used to say, "No pain, no gain." But the process can also be fun. The exercises in this book are designed to make the effort enjoyable. And you can expect to take pleasure and pride in the results of your efforts: the sense of mental clarity and mastery you will get from the ability to organize your thoughts, to make logical connections, to understand the world around you, to see past the blinders of little minds and enjoy the company of great ones.

PART ONE

Language & Reasoning

Part 1 is concerned with the basic elements and standards of reasoning. Later sections will deal with the details of specific forms of reasoning, but here we will cover the elements and standards that pertain to reasoning in general and that will be of value in all your studies as well as everyday life.

Language is the medium in which we think, communicate, and reason. Words expand the range of our senses, bring order to our experiences, allow us to learn from the experiences of others, and preserve the thoughts of preceding generations. In learning to speak, each of us has acquired an amazingly powerful and versatile set of tools. But the tools will not do what we want unless we know how to use them properly. So before we turn to reasoning per se, we need to master these tools, and that will be the focus of the first five chapters.

One of the major functions of language is to divide the world up into categories. Except for proper names, most nouns stand for *groups* of things: tigers, tables, tests, and so forth. Organizing a set of things into groups is called *classification*, and a word that stands for such a group expresses a *concept*. Chapter 1 is concerned with concepts and classification. We will learn the rules for classifying things in the most effective way, and we'll see how concepts can be arranged in hierarchies of *species* and *genus*.

To use concepts with precision and to understand the relationships among different concepts, we need to *define* them. In Chapter 2, we will learn how to evaluate and construct definitions.

Finally, we use words to make statements about things. In logic, we analyze statements in terms of the *propositions* they assert. In Chapter 3, we'll see how to identify propositions and how to tell whether two statements assert the same or different propositions.

Propositions are the units of reasoning, which is concerned with the *truth* of propositions. Its goal may be to *discover* whether a given proposition is true, or to *justify* one's belief that it is true, or to *persuade* someone else of its truth. In all of these cases, reasoning makes use of logical relationships among propositions, and we analyze and evaluate reasoning by identifying those relationships.

Chapter 4 will introduce the basic unit of reasoning, which in logic is called an *argument*. We'll learn how to identify the premises and the conclusion of an argument and begin our study of how to analyze and then evaluate its logical structure. Chapter 5 is concerned with fallacies—spurious arguments in which the premises may appear to support the conclusion but do not really support it. We are going to review some of the more common fallacies and learn how to spot them in everyday thought and speech.

Classification

Suppose that I ask you to classify the courses you've taken in college. You might classify them by subject matter: art, biology, history, etc. Or you might classify them by level: introductory, intermediate, advanced. Whichever way you choose, you are grouping together courses that have something in common and distinguishing them from other courses. In effect you are creating a set of file folders in your mind and then putting each course into the proper folder.

Classifying things together into groups is something we do all the time, and it isn't hard to see why. Imagine trying to shop in a supermarket where the food was arranged in random order on the shelves: tomato soup next to the white bread in one aisle, chicken soup in the back next to the 60-watt light bulbs, one brand of cream cheese in front and another in aisle 8 near the Oreos. The task of finding what you want would be time consuming and extremely difficult, if not impossible.

In the case of a supermarket, someone had to design the system of classification. But there is also a ready-made system of classification embodied in our language. The word "dog," for example, groups together a certain class of animals and distinguishes them from other animals. Such a grouping may seem too obvious to be called a classification, but this is only because you have already mastered the word. As a child learning to speak, you had to work hard to learn the system of classification your parents were trying to teach you. Before you got the hang of it, you probably made mistakes, like calling the cat a dog. If you hadn't learned to speak, the whole world would seem like the unorganized supermarket; you would be in the position of an infant, for whom every object is new and unfamiliar. In learning the principles of classification, therefore, we'll be learning about the structure that lies at the core of our language.

1.1 Concepts and Referents

Whenever we classify, we make use of concepts—ideas that represent classes of things we have grouped together. In classifying your courses, you used concepts such as ART,

HISTORY, and INTRODUCTORY. (We will use capital letters to indicate a concept.) To learn the word "dog," you had to acquire the concept DOG. A scientist who discovers a new phenomenon forms a concept for that class of thing and expresses the concept in a new word (e.g., "quark"). As these examples illustrate, concepts and words are intimately related. A concept is an idea; a word is the linguistic vehicle we use to express the idea. And the class of things that a concept stands for are called the **referents** of the concept. The referents of DOG, for example, are all the individual dogs in the world. We can diagram the relation between a concept and its referents as follows:

The black dots stand for individual objects. The bracketing lines indicate that certain objects (Lassie, the Hound of the Baskervilles, etc.) are included within the concept—they are the referents of DOG—while other things are excluded (my cat, the Taj Mahal, and everything else in the world that is not a dog).

Now consider the concept ANIMAL. We could diagram this separately, and the diagram would look like the one we just did for DOG. But these concepts are obviously related: dogs are a type of animal. That means we can represent both concepts in the same diagram:

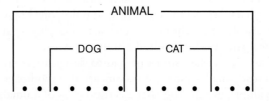

Notice that all the referents included in DOG are also included in ANIMAL, but ANIMAL includes many other things as well—cats (as the diagram indicates), squirrels, fish, and all the other types of animals. ANIMAL is a broader concept because it includes more than the narrower concept DOG. Whenever we encounter this relationship, we use the term **genus** for the broader concept and the term **species** for the narrower one. Thus, DOG and CAT are both species within the genus ANIMAL. If a species is a file folder, a genus is a file drawer containing many folders.

You may be familiar with the idea of genus and species from biology, where they are part of an elaborate system of classification with many levels: species, genus, family, etc. In logic, however, the terms "genus" and "species" have a more flexible meaning. Here, a genus can be any group to which a species belongs. That's why I said ANIMAL is a genus; in biology, it is a kingdom. And a species can be any subcategory within a given genus. "Genus" and "species" are relative terms, like "mother" and "daughter."

Your mother is also a daughter—in relation to *her* parents. In the same way, a given concept can be either a genus or a species, depending on our perspective. DOG is a species in relation to ANIMAL, but it is a genus in relation to the narrower concept BEAGLE.

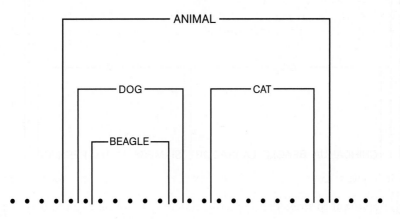

By using the genus–species relationship, we can create very complex systems of classification. For instance, the items in your house can be classified as TABLES, CHAIRS, etc.; these are species of the genus FURNITURE, which in turn is a species of the genus MAN-MADE OBJECTS or ARTIFACTS. If you classified your courses by subject matter—ART, HISTORY, ECONOMICS, PHYSICS—you might go on to classify these disciplines into wider groups, such as HUMANITIES, SOCIAL SCIENCES, and PHYSICAL SCIENCES. Indeed, *every* concept can be placed within some hierarchy of genus and species (and, as we will see, most concepts can be placed within many different hierarchies).

The referents of our concepts are *concrete*; each is a single, individual object. If we had separate names for each referent (as we do in the case of people or cities), the names would also be concrete. But a concept (such as PEOPLE or CITY) is *abstract*. The word "abstract" here means two things. It means first that a concept refers to a group of objects, not just to a single thing (as a name does). The concept PEOPLE includes all human beings; CITY includes all cities. Second, a concept is abstract because it groups together things that differ from one another. There are many differences among people, among cities, among the referents of any concept. We group them together, not because they are identical but because they are *similar*.

Abstractness is a relative property. Any concept is abstract to some degree. But a species is less abstract than the genus to which it belongs. The genus is a larger and broader group; it has more referents than the species does. And the referents of the genus are less similar to each other than are the referents of the species. There are many more differences among animals, taken as a group, than there are among dogs. Thus, as we move up a species-genus hierarchy, we are moving in the direction of greater abstractness. As we move down the hierarchy, we are moving in the direction of greater concreteness.

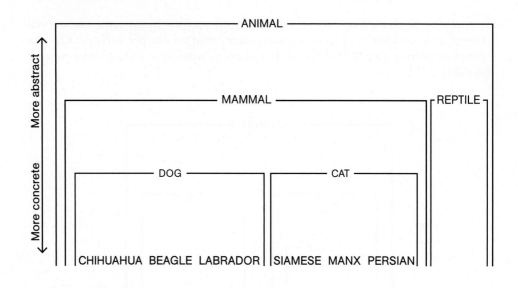

It's important to stress that the term "concrete" is not limited to physical, tangible things, nor does the term "abstract" mean "intangible." The feelings we have at a given moment, for example, are not tangible, but they are concrete: each is an individual, particular occurrence. And the concepts we use to classify feelings are measured in the same way as other concepts. The concept LOVE is more abstract than its species, such as ROMANTIC LOVE, but less abstract than its genus, EMOTION.

The distinction between abstract and concrete allows us to extend our notion of classification. So far, we have been classifying objects: animals, furniture, cities, etc. But we also have concepts for qualities, like colors, for actions, like running, and for relationships, like marriage. These concepts can also be placed in species–genus hierarchies according to their degree of abstractness. RED, BLUE, and GREEN are species of the genus COLOR, which might in turn be classified as a species of the genus PHYSICAL QUALITY (as distinct from nonphysical qualities such as intelligence). RUNNING, WALKING, and SWIMMING are species of the genus LOCOMOTION. MARRIAGE and FRIENDSHIP are species of the genus PERSONAL RELATIONSHIP. (In our society, marriage is also a legal relationship; this is an example of the way hierarchies of classification can overlap.)

You can see that in all these cases, the genus is the more abstract concept, the species the more concrete. *Every* concept, not just those for objects or entities, has some particular degree of abstractness, and every concept fits into some species–genus relationship. This fact is the basis for the technique of defining concepts, which we will study in the next chapter.

EXERCISE 1.1

A. For each of the following pairs of concepts, first determine which is the genus, which the species; and then name two other species of the same genus.

* 1. MAN, ANIMAL

   2. GARMENT, COAT

   3. VEHICLE, CAR

* 4. BASEBALL, SPORT

5. AUTOBIOGRAPHY, NONFICTION BOOK
6. MATERIAL SUBSTANCE, SOLID
* 7. COUNTRIES, EUROPEAN
8. ANGER, EMOTION
9. COURAGE, VIRTUE

* 10. ARISTOCRAT, DUKE
11. BURRITO, TORTILLA DISHES
12. TOOTH, BICUSPID
* 13. MAUSOLEUM, BURIAL PLACE
14. TIMEPIECE, WATCH
15. PERCEIVE, SMELL

B. Arrange the following lists in terms of order of increasing abstractness.

* 1. Performer, Lady Gaga, singer
2. Cattle, organism, mammal, steer, animal
3. Quadrilateral, square, figure, rectangle
* 4. Alloy, steel, mineral, metal
5. Google, corporation, multinational company, institution
6. U.S. president, Thomas Jefferson, national leader
* 7. Telephone, iPhone, mobile telephone, communication device

8. Durable good, manufactured object, refrigerator, appliance
9. *Moby Dick*, literature, novel
* 10. Brother, family member, sibling, kin
11. Tart, pie, pastry
12. Jump, leap, move
* 13. Cardigan, garment, top, sweater
14. Psychological disorders, schizophrenia, psychosis
15. Islam, Sufism, worldview, religion

1.2 Rules of Classification

Classification is the process of sorting things into categories. The set of things to be classified—animals, college courses, or whatever—constitutes a genus, and the task is to subdivide the genus into species so that each item can be assigned its place. There is usually more than one way to do this, as we noticed earlier in regard to college courses, depending on our needs, our purposes, and the kind of information we have available. But even if there is no single best way of subdividing a genus, some ways are better than others, and there are guidelines for selecting the better ones.

1.2A Consistent Principle

Suppose you tried to classify your courses into the following categories: ART, BIOLOGY, HISTORY, ECONOMICS, and INTRODUCTORY. Where would you put "Introduction to Art"? Because your categories overlap, we don't know whether to classify this as an introductory course or an art course. The first rule of classification, then, is that the species must not overlap. We express this in logic by saying the species must be **mutually exclusive**: Each species must exclude all the members of every other species. At the same time, a good classification divides up the genus completely, allowing us to assign every member of the genus to one or another of the species. We express this in logic by saying that the classification must be **jointly exhaustive**: the species taken together (jointly) must cover (exhaust) all the objects in the genus. If you had also taken a philosophy course, for example, then the classification of courses I gave earlier would not be jointly exhaustive.

A good classification should divide the genus into species that are mutually exclusive and jointly exhaustive. How do we go about creating such a classification? Let's consider first an example of how *not* to do it. In one of his stories, Jorge Luis Borges describes a mythical book called *The Chinese Emporium of Benevolent Knowledge*:

> On those remote pages it is written that animals are divided into (a) those that belong to the Emperor, (b) embalmed ones, (c) those that are trained, (d) suckling pigs, (e) mermaids, (f) fabulous ones, (g) stray dogs, (h) those that are included in this classification, (i) those that tremble as if they were mad, (j) innumerable ones, (k) those drawn with a very fine camel's hair brush, (l) others, (m) those that have just broken a flower vase, (n) those that resemble flies from a distance. [Jorge Luis Borges, *Other Inquisitions 1937–52*]

These categories are obviously not mutually exclusive. A stray dog (g) might well resemble a fly from a distance (n); an animal belonging to the Emperor (a) might also be drawn with a very fine camel's hair brush (k). The categories overlap in numerous ways. Strictly speaking, the classification *is* jointly exhaustive because of "others" (l). But that's cheating: "Others" is a "miscellaneous" category. Without it, the classification would leave out many animals.

It's not hard to see why the classification is inadequate. It does not follow any *consistent principle* for dividing up the genus. It jumps from the question of ownership (a), to condition after death (b), to training (c), and so on. Since there is no necessary relationship among these various principles, the classification is bound to be chaotic. In classifying, we should try to follow a consistent principle. If we classify college courses by subject matter, we should stick to that principle throughout and not include species like INTRODUCTORY that involve a different principle. Similarly, there are various ways to classify furniture: by function (tables, chairs, etc.), by style of design (Danish, Colonial, Mission, etc.), by material (wood, plastic, chrome, etc.). But whichever principle we choose, we should follow it consistently.

When we diagram a classification, we can represent the principle we're following by enclosing it within brackets under the name of the genus. For example:

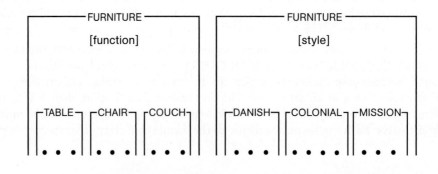

As the diagram illustrates, the principle is an attribute that all members of the genus possess, and the species are defined by the way they differ in regard to that attribute. Thus, in the diagram on the left, the concept TABLE groups together things that have the same *function* and distinguishes them from chairs and couches, which have different functions. In the diagram on the right, the concept DANISH groups together articles of furniture that have the same *style* and distinguishes them from furniture designed in other styles. We can find this same structure in any system of classification, though it may not always be so easy to name the principle explicitly.

The need for a consistent principle does not require a *single* principle. Animal species, for example, differ from each other in many ways: shape, color, and other external properties; internal anatomy and physiology; behavior; method of bearing young; and so on. Biologists use all these properties in classifying animals. It is appropriate to use multiple principles of classification whenever we are dealing with complex phenomena; in such cases, a single principle would often be artificial and not very useful.

When we use more than one principle, however, we should take extra care to make sure that the resulting categories are mutually exclusive. Suppose we try to classify people on the basis of personality into two categories: extroverts and introverts. Extroverts are outgoing, adventurous, frank, open; introverts are reclusive, cautious, reserved. Where would we put someone who is adventurous, but reserved in the presence of other people? What about someone who is outgoing and frank with people, but timid about physical danger? The problem here is that the various attributes don't always fit together according to our stereotypes of extroverts and introverts; so these categories are not mutually exclusive. We should either pick one of the attributes (e.g., outgoing vs. reserved) so that everyone would fit into one or the other category, or create more categories to handle the variety of personality types.

The first rule for classifying, then, is to use a single principle or set of principles consistently so that the resulting categories are mutually exclusive and jointly exhaustive. In many cases, however, this will leave more than one possible way to divide the genus. A second classification rule will help us select among those alternatives.

1.2B Essential Attributes

The second rule is to use a principle based on the *essential* attributes of the things we are classifying. An essential attribute is a fundamental one, an attribute that makes a thing what it is. If we divide a genus according to an essential attribute, we are grouping together things that are fundamentally similar and separating things that are fundamentally different. And because a fundamental attribute underlies and explains many of a thing's superficial attributes, things that are fundamentally similar will probably have many attributes in common; things that share a superficial, nonessential attribute may well have nothing else in common.

Let's consider the animal kingdom once again. Biologists classify animals into the categories MAMMAL, REPTILE, AMPHIBIAN, BIRD, INSECT, etc. The principles they use include mode of reproduction (does the animal lay eggs or bear its young alive?), internal physiology (vertebrate vs. invertebrate, warm-blooded vs. cold-blooded), and means of locomotion (swimming, flying, crawling). These principles are aspects of two attributes fundamental to all forms of life: An organism must maintain itself by acting on the environment, and it must reproduce itself. This classification of animals, then, is based on essential principles, and the advantages of the classification are obvious. Animals that survive and reproduce in similar ways are likely to have a great deal in common and can naturally be studied as a group.

By contrast, suppose that we classify animals according to a nonessential attribute such as color:

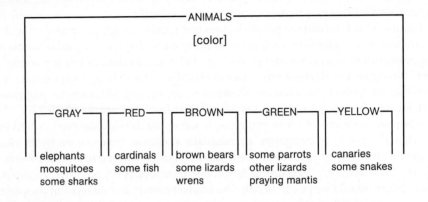

Of course this is not a complete classification of animals, but it does indicate what's wrong with classifying them according to this attribute. The items that are grouped together in each category have nothing else in common. The differences among elephants, mosquitoes, and gray sharks are much more fundamental than the superficial similarity in color. And the similarities between green and brown lizards are much more fundamental than the superficial differences in color. As a result, this classification is useless. Knowing that a certain animal belongs to one of these categories tells you almost nothing about it. Imagine having to act on the information that a gray animal was approaching, without knowing anything else about it!

How does the distinction between essential and nonessential attributes apply to other areas? Let's look at a few examples. The essential attribute of a man-made object is usually its function. Such objects are created to serve a purpose, and the purpose explains why they are designed the way they are. If you came across an unfamiliar tool in a museum, your first question would probably be: What's it for? If you knew the answer to that question, then you would understand why the tool has a certain shape and internal structure, why it is made of the material it is, and so on. The same is true for human institutions. Thus, if you were studying corporations, it would be natural to classify each according to its function: Does the corporation produce goods or services? Is it a nonprofit or for-profit organization?

In the physical sciences, essential attributes are those that underlie and explain the surface properties we can observe directly, and scientists have pushed deeper and deeper into the structure of matter in the search for these underlying causes. Ancient Greek philosophers, for example, divided matter into four elements: earth, air, water, and fire. Modern chemists have replaced that early system with the table of elements, classifying matter according to the kinds of atoms that make it up. The properties of the atoms explain many of the observable features of matter: They explain why some elements are gases at room temperature, why metals conduct electricity, and so on. The table of elements is therefore a classification by essential attributes.

SUMMARY   **Two Rules of Classification**

---

1. A single principle or set of principles should be used consistently so that the categories (species) are mutually exclusive and jointly exhaustive.

2. The principle or principles used should be essential.

In dealing with people, our standards for what is essential are too complex even to summarize here, but let's look at a case in which one of these standards is applied: the issue of discrimination. In the abstract, discrimination means noticing differences among people and classifying them into groups on the basis of those differences. We do this all the time. Teachers discriminate among students in assigning grades; employers discriminate among job applicants; everyone discriminates among people in choosing friends. What most of us object to is not discrimination (or classification) per se, but discrimination on the basis of attributes such as race or sex that are not *essentially* related to the treatment a person deserves. Thus an employer who adopts an equal opportunity policy is choosing to classify job applicants by ability, training, and character rather than by race or sex—on the ground that ability, training, and character are essentially related to job performance, whereas race and sex are not.

The word "essential" always has the sense of "fundamental" or "important." But as the preceding examples illustrate, standards for what is fundamental or important vary from case to case. Identifying essential attributes may take years of research (as in science), and it always takes a good deal of thought. Unfortunately, there is no simple, mechanical rule we can follow in distinguishing essential from nonessential principles of classification. You will have to use your judgment, and you will have to accept the possibility that reasonable people may disagree. Nevertheless, the examples also indicate the value of looking for essential attributes: They bring clarity and coherence to the organization of our knowledge.

In addition, we need to remember that classification serves a purpose, and our purpose affects what we take to be essential. So far, we have taken for granted that our purpose is to understand the nature of the things being classified, on the basis of the similarities and differences among them. That is, we are considering the things as they are in themselves. In and of itself, for example, the essential attribute of a piece of furniture is clearly its function. But an interior designer, who is concerned primarily with aesthetic issues, may need to classify furniture by style. In relation to that specialized practical purpose, it is legitimate to regard style as essential.

EXERCISE 1.2

Evaluate each of the following classifications. First determine whether it uses a consistent principle and is mutually exclusive and jointly exhaustive. If it passes that test, then determine whether the principle used is essential. If it is not, try to think of a specialized purpose for which the principle might be essential.

* 1. Books: paperbacks, hardbacks, first editions
2. Medicines: antibiotics, laxatives, pills, antihistamines
3. Foods: meats, vegetables, junk food, fruits, breads
* 4. Movies: thrillers, Westerns, pornographic, foreign
5. Students: under 5 feet tall, 5 to 6 feet tall, over 6 feet tall
6. Wine: Chardonnay, red, Merlot, French, sparkling
* 7. Sports: team, aquatic, individual, noncompetitive
8. Trees: leaf-shedding, evergreen, shade
9. Cars: economy, oversize, intermediate, compact, standard, full-size
* 10. Shoes: walking, athletic, leather, dress
11. Colors: blue, orange, warm, red, primary
12. People: those who would rather be hosts, those who would rather be guests
* 13. Jobs: clerical, sales, managerial, service, manual
14. Countries: developed, underdeveloped
15. Countries: free, unfree, partially free

1.3 Levels of Organization

So far we have treated classification as if it were always a matter of sorting things into categories or dividing a genus into species (two ways of describing the same operation). And this is indeed the task we face when we start from scratch. But we do not always start from scratch. We often deal with concepts that reflect preexisting classifications, and the task we face is to locate the concepts at the right level of a species–genus hierarchy.

Suppose you were studying religious affiliations. People describe themselves as Baptists, Methodists, Catholics, Jews, and so forth. These are indeed different religious groups, but they do not all belong on the same level of classification; they are not all species of a single genus. Jews, for example, should not be compared directly to Methodists. They should be compared to Christians—a category that I did not include in the list. And Catholics should be compared to Protestants, another term missing from the list. Thus the classification might look like this:

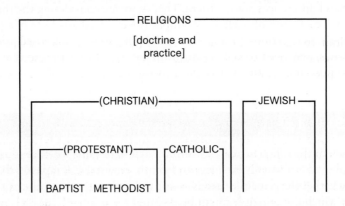

This diagram illustrates several points. First, concepts on the same level of organization should have roughly the same degree of abstractness. It is clear in this case that CATHOLIC and PROTESTANT belong on the same level and that BAPTIST and METHODIST are narrower (less abstract) subdivisions within the category PROTESTANT. Second, when it is necessary to separate levels in this way, we must often add concepts that were not given to us originally. The new concepts in this case are PROTESTANT and CHRISTIAN, and we indicate that they were not on the original list by putting them in parentheses. Finally, the diagram gives us ideas about ways in which we might want to flesh out the classification: Are there other religions besides Christianity and Judaism? Are there other branches of Protestantism? Are there categories within Catholicism and Judaism?

This sort of analysis is often required when you are learning a new subject and have to learn a new set of concepts. Separating the different levels of organization will help you understand the concepts much more clearly than if you try to master each concept as an individual, isolated unit. In a course in legal theory, for example, you might encounter concepts like FELONY, TRESPASS, MISDEMEANOR, HOMICIDE, TORT (see the diagram that follows). In order to grasp these concepts, you would need to understand that felonies and misdemeanors are the two species of *crimes* regarded as offenses against public order and prosecuted by the state; and that a tort (such as trespass) is considered a *civil wrong*, an offense for which a private individual must bring suit.

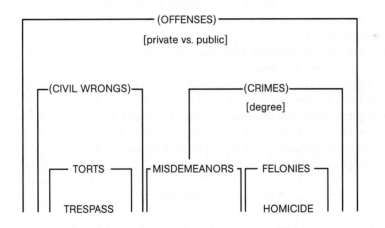

In addition to clarifying the new concepts, this diagram would provide a skeleton or outline for organizing all the other crimes and offenses you learn about.

Notice that one of the concepts we had to fill in here was the genus, OFFENSES. This is the first case we've seen in which the genus was not given at the outset, but it is not an uncommon case. When you are learning a new set of concepts or organizing an old set, you will often have to find an overarching concept for the entire domain. Such generic concepts will of course be more abstract than concepts for the corresponding species, and it may help to be familiar with some of the highest-level abstractions we use to organize our knowledge of the world. One fundamental distinction is between living and nonliving (animate vs. inanimate) objects. Another distinction is between natural objects (living or nonliving) and man-made ones. Yet another basic division is between

---

STRATEGY Organizing Concepts

To organize related concepts into a classification diagram:

1. Find the highest-level (most abstract) genus.
2. Identify concepts that are species of that genus; they should all have the same degree of abstractness.
3. Identify the principle of division that applies to the concepts in step 2; put the principle in brackets.

4. For each concept in step 2, identify any other concepts that are its species, and identify the principle of division (the single principle by which the concept has been divided into species).
5. Repeat step 4 for as many levels as necessary.

---

physical and mental phenomena: the external world of material things versus the internal world of thoughts and feelings. (Mental phenomena in turn are often divided into cognitive and affective states—thinking vs. feeling.) Perhaps the most abstract set of generic concepts is one devised by the ancient Greek philosopher Aristotle. He divided the world into things (in the sense of whole objects), actions, relations, quantities, times, and places. When you are looking for a genus, it may help to remember these fundamental concepts. You may not need anything so abstract, but if you are stuck, they may help you get oriented.

One final word of warning: Classification is the process of dividing a genus into its species. This is not the same as breaking an object down into its parts or elements. Engines and driveshafts are parts of cars, but they are not themselves types or species of cars. In this case, the point is pretty obvious, but it's easy to get confused when we are learning new concepts. Suppose you have just learned in biology that an enzyme is a type of protein, and that a protein is a large organic molecule made up of a sequence of amino acids. Because enzymes are a species of protein, you could use the diagram on the left to capture the relationship:

But the diagram on the right is fundamentally incorrect. An amino acid is *not* a species of protein. It is a component of a protein. Both the species-genus and the part-whole relations are important for our understanding of the world, but they should not be confused.

EXERCISE 1.3

A. Fill in the blanks indicated by XXX in the classification diagram below.

✳ 1.

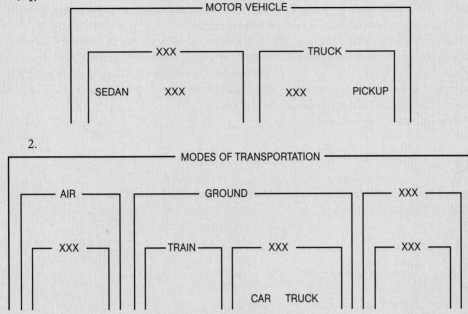

2.

B. Arrange the following concepts in a classification diagram, making sure that each concept is on the appropriate level of abstractness and adding concepts where necessary to complete the diagram.

✳ 1. CD PLAYER, AUDIO EQUIP-MENT, WALL SPEAKERS, FLOOR SPEAKERS, RADIO

2. HUMANITIES, ECONOMICS, PHILOSOPHY, SOCIAL SCIENCES, PHYSICS

3. MARXISM, LIBERALISM, CONSERVATISM, SOCIALISM, LIBERTARIANISM

✳ 4. SPRINTS, HURDLES, PARALLEL BARS, GYMNASTIC EVENTS, 100-METER BREASTSTROKE, DIVING

5. MUSIC, LITERATURE, PAINTING, POETRY, VISUAL ARTS, STILL LIFE

✳ C. The classification diagram below violates several of the principles discussed in this section. Identify the errors, and fix the diagram.

GOVERNMENTS

DEMOCRATIC   PARLIAMENTARY   DICTATORSHIP

LEGISLATIVE   EXECUTIVE   JUDICIAL   AUTHORITARIAN   TOTALITARIAN
BRANCH   BRANCH   BRANCH

Summary

Classification is the process of putting things together into groups on the basis of similarities. A concept is an idea that represents such a group. The concepts involved in a system of classification are organized into hierarchies of species and genuses. Every concept is abstract to some degree; a genus is more abstract than its species.

When we subdivide a genus into species, we should use a consistent principle, so that the species are mutually exclusive and jointly exhaustive.

We should also use essential attributes, so that the members of each species are fundamentally alike and fundamentally different from members of other species.

When we learn a new set of concepts, we need to identify genus–species relationships among the concepts. Concepts at the same level of abstractness should be placed at the same level in the hierarchy.

Key Terms

Classify—to group things into species and genuses according to their similarities and differences.

Referents—the class of things for which a concept stands.

Genus—a class of things regarded as having various subcategories (its species).

Species—a class of things regarded as a subcategory of a wider class (a genus).

Mutually exclusive—in a classification, the property that each species excludes the members of every other species.

Jointly exhaustive—in a classification, the property that the species taken together cover all the objects in the genus.

Additional Exercises

A. In each of the following sentences, replace any **boldfaced** words with more abstract ones and any *italicized* words with more concrete ones.

  ✳ 1. Joan *walked* across the room.
   2. The tall stranger **whirled** around and dashed his *drinking implement* against the fireplace.
   3. Our daughter is going out with a *nice* young man.
  ✳ 4. My **kingdom** for a **horse**!
   5. Mary expressed herself *with feeling*.
   6. Life is but a *nonobjective sensory experience*.
  ✳ 7. A **government** cannot exist without popular support.
   8. The only problem with Jeff is that he has this *thing* about math.
   9. Around the bend lay a set of *dangerous* rapids.
  ✳10. In the years ahead, our country will face *many* problems.

B. For each series of items below, first identify a genus to which all the items belong, and then turn that genus into a species by thinking of a higher-level genus.

  ✳ 1. Glider, helicopters, jets
   2. Knife, fork, and spoon
   3. Tragedy, comedy, melodrama, farce
  ✳ 4. FBI, IRS, State Department
   5. Granite, marble, slate

C. For each of the following genuses, one species has been listed. List as many more as you can. If you are not familiar with the classification of terms within any of the genuses, use a dictionary or an encyclopedia.

✳ 1. Publications: magazine, . . .
   2. Seasonings: herbs, . . .
   3. Parts of speech: noun, . . .

✳ 4. Causes of death: accidents, . . .
   5. Dishonest ways of manipulating people: flattery, . . .

D. Diagram each of the following sets of concepts. (Some are at the same level of abstraction, and some are not.) Be sure to fill in concepts where necessary.

✳ 1. FRIEND, CLIENT, RELATIVE, COLLEAGUE, AUNT, HUMAN RELATIONSHIPS
   2. HORIZONTAL, RECTANGULAR, LARGE, ROUND, INFINITESIMAL, VERTICAL

   3. LEAF-SHEDDING TREES, LETTUCE, CARROT, DANDELION, PINE, OAK
✳ 4. HONESTY, VICE, LAZINESS, INTEGRITY
   5. ANGER, WISH, MEMORY, LOVE, COGNITION

E. Each of the following passages proposes a system of classification for some domain. Identify the concepts the author is using, diagram the genus–species relationships among them, and note any points at which the passages fail to make these relationships clear.

✳ 1. "The human species, according to the best theory I can form of it, is composed of two distinct races, the men who borrow, and the men who lend." [Charles Lamb, *Essays of Elia*]

   2. "[D]igital computers operate by carrying out a number of discrete steps, each of which involves the change of one or more basic engineering components from one physical state to another. (Usually, only two states are possible.) Analog computers are not like this, because the physical parameters used to represent information are continuously variable—like voltage levels, for instance." [Margaret Boden, *Artificial Intelligence and Natural Man*]

   3. Lakes and ponds are standing bodies of water. A pond is a body of standing water that occupies a depression in the earth's surface. A lake is generally larger than a pond. A stream is any body of moving water that flows to progressively lower escalations, in a relatively narrow but clearly defined channel on the surface of the ground. Rivers and brooks are types of streams, and rivers are larger than brooks. [Adapted from: *Glossary of Geology*, R. L. Bates and J. A. Jackson (eds.), 1987, American Geological Institute, 3rd Edition]

✳ 4. "We can distinguish altogether three kinds of 'monopoly': those achieved through legal means; those achieved through means that are illegal only because of antitrust and other laws intended to make monopoly difficult; and monopolies achieved through means that are criminal by any standards—means that would be criminal whether or not they were aimed at monopolizing business." [Thomas C. Schelling, *Choice and Consequence*]

   5. The term "myth" is sometimes used broadly to refer to any traditional story about the past. But anthropologists sometimes use the term in a narrower sense to mean one specific type of story. Myths in this sense are stories about gods, including creation

myths about how the world came to be, and narratives about the interactions of the gods with each other and with human beings. Legends, by contrast, are stories about humans, including real people in the past, such as the Greek hero Odysseus and his struggle to return home after the Trojan War or the story of George Washington telling the truth after chopping down the cherry tree. Myths are also distinguished from folklore, such as fairy tales, Aesop's Fables, etc.

6. "Carbohydrates, proteins (which are made up of amino acids), fats, minerals, vitamins, and water are all nutrients—absorbable components of foods—and necessary for good health. Nutrients are necessary for energy, organ function, food utilization, and cell growth. . . .

   "Micronutrients, like vitamins and minerals, do not themselves provide energy. The macronutrients—carbohydrates, fat, and protein—do that, but only when there are sufficient micronutrients to release them." [Earl Mindell, *Vitamin Bible*]

✳ 7. "The sources of the Shariah are of two types: revealed and non-revealed. There are only two revealed sources—first, the Quran; second, the teaching and exemplary conduct (Sunna) of the Prophet Muhammad, including his sayings, acts, and tacit approval (or lack of condemnation) of the conduct of his Companions and some of the customs of Arabian society. . . .

   "Another source of Shariah is ijtihad, which literally means 'striving.' It is defined as exertion by a qualified scholar to the best of his or her ability to deduce the ruling of a particular issue from the evidence found in the sources. Unlike the revelation of the Quran and the Sunna, which ended with the Prophet's death, juristic reasoning continues to be the principal source and instrument that keeps the law consistent with the realities of social change." [Mohammad Hashim Kamali, "Law and Society: The Interplay of Revelation and Reason in the Shariah." In John L. Esposito (ed.), *Oxford History of Islam*, Oxford University Press, 2000.]

8. "From the standpoint of the individual all contributions to government are either gratuitous, contractual or compulsory. Every governmental revenue must fall within one of these three great classes. Individuals may make the government a free gift, they may agree or contract to pay, or they may be compelled to pay. . . .

   "The taxing power may manifest itself in three different forms, known respectively as special assessments, fees and taxes. These three forms are all species of taxation in the wider sense, so far as they differ on the one hand from contractual revenue, . . . and on the other hand from the remaining divisions of compulsory revenue, like expropriation and fines. What is common to all three is that they are compulsory contributions levied for the support of government or to defray the expenses incurred for public purposes. That is the essence of the taxing power. But, although they are all forms of taxation in this wider sense, the differences between fees and special assessments on the one hand, and taxes in the narrower sense on the other, are so marked that they must be put into separate categories." [Edwin R.A. Seligman, *Essays in Taxation*, 10th ed.]

F. Many colleges have a distribution requirement; students must take some courses in each area of the curriculum. In order to have such a requirement, the college must divide the curriculum into various categories. Evaluate the following system according to the principles of classification. (Or substitute the system your college uses.)

Arts	Foreign Languages and Literatures	Social Sciences	Natural Sciences
Art	Chinese	Anthropology	Astronomy
Drama	French	Economics	Biology
English	German	Education	Chemistry
Music	Greek	Geography	Computer science
Physical education	Hispanic studies	History	Geology
	Italian	Philosophy	Mathematics
	Latin	Political science	Physics
	Russian	Religion	Psychology
		Sociology	

Definitions

As we saw in the past chapter, concepts serve as mental file folders that help us organize our knowledge about classes of similar things. **Definitions** tell us what is in the folders. In the case of simple, relatively concrete concepts—such as TABLE or RUNNING—we can get along pretty well without definitions. We can tell just by sight whether something is a table, whether someone is running. But most concepts are more abstract and more complex. By telling us what they stand for, and how they relate to other concepts, definitions are an important tool of knowledge. To see more clearly *why* definitions are so valuable, let's look at some of the problems they help us to solve.

2.1 The Functions of a Definition

First, a definition can clarify the boundaries of a concept. A child who has just learned the concept PLANT can point to some obvious and clear-cut examples, such as house-plants or outdoor shrubs. Such cases are called "paradigm" or "prototypical" examples. But it will take a while before the child understands the full range of the concept PLANT, which includes trees, moss, and so on. At a more advanced level, a person might understand that the category of social sciences includes such prototypical examples as economics, but not be sure whether geography fits. One major function of definitions is to tell us what is and is not included in a concept by giving us a test or rule for membership.

Some people would argue that a concept can never have completely sharp borders. On the color spectrum, for example, orange lies on the border between red and yellow, and it isn't clear which way to classify it. Nor can we solve the problem by treating orange as a separate category between red and yellow, because then there would be colors on the borderline between red and orange. In biology, the one-celled organism *Euglena* sits on the border between plants and animals: It has chorophyll and engages in photosynthesis, like a plant, but it also has flagellae for swimming, like an animal. Fortunately, we do not have to settle the theoretical issue of whether concepts can—or should—have completely sharp borders. The important point is that there are *degrees* of precision in understanding a concept's boundaries, and definitions help us to become *more* precise.

A second function of a definition is to clarify the relationships among concepts. Concepts are not isolated, self-contained units; they form networks of interrelated ideas. We have already seen that they fit together into genus–species hierarchies. But there is more to it than that. A concept groups things together into classes on the basis of similarities. In some cases, like TABLE, the objects and their similarities are perceptible. You can literally see the similarity among tables. In such cases, we can employ what is sometimes called an *ostensive definition*: pointing and saying, "Things like *that*." More often, however, the referents of a concept and the attributes they have in common are not directly observable, and we have to learn about them by means of other concepts that we already understand.

Consider the concept GOVERNMENT. If you were trying to explain this concept to someone, what concrete objects could you point to? A police officer? The flag? The White House? These are merely symbols or instruments of government and would convey only a child's understanding of the concept. Actual examples, such as the U. S. government, are not things you can literally point to. You would have to explain in abstract language that the concept GOVERNMENT refers to an *institution*, with the *authority* to make *laws* for a *society*, to *enforce* those laws, and to protect its *citizens* against *foreign* threats. Each of the italicized words expresses a concept necessary for understanding what governments have in common; each is a link in a long chain that connects the concept GOVERNMENT to its referents in reality. If the chain is weak—if the person doesn't understand the intervening concepts—then he won't really understand the concept GOVERNMENT either.

Our ability to acquire new concepts on the basis of old ones is enormously valuable. It allows us to expand our knowledge and to profit from discoveries made by other people. But it poses the danger that we will acquire a concept only as a vague idea, without any clear understanding of the class of things it actually stands for. It also poses the danger that different people using the concept will have radically different ideas of what the concept includes. Definitions help us ward off these dangers. They keep a concept tied to its referents by relating it clearly to other concepts that serve as links in the chain.

A third function of a definition is to provide a summary statement about the referents of our concepts. If we think of a concept as a file folder where we put all the information we have about a certain class of things, then we have to realize that these folders may contain enormous amounts of information. In one way or another, for example, virtually all knowledge in the humanities and social sciences is relevant to the concept HUMAN. Definitions help us keep our filing system in order by giving us summary statements about what is in each folder. A good definition *condenses* the knowledge we have about the referents of a concept, giving us just the highlights, the key points, the essence. Because it performs this service, a definition is valuable even in cases, such as HUMAN, where we already know what class of things the concept stands for.

SUMMARY **The Main Functions of Definitions**

Definitions:

1. State the criteria for membership in the class of referents.

2. Indicate the relationship between a concept and other concepts.

3. Condense the knowledge we have about the referents of a concept.

Within the broad framework of the functions we have discussed so far, definitions can serve a variety of more specific purposes. In this chapter, we're going to be concerned primarily with definitions of concepts that we employ frequently in everyday thought and language. But for specialized purposes in science, law, and other technical fields, we may also need to introduce a new word or give a new meaning to an old word. We may need to give more precise boundaries to a concept. Or we may need to clarify the role that a concept plays in a complex theory. As we will see, however, the type of definition that works well for ordinary concepts can also be adapted to these other contexts.

This type is called a definition by genus and differentia. To understand what this means, consider a classic example: "Humans are rational animals." Notice that the definition has two parts. The term "animals" names the wider class to which humans belong; it classifies us as a species of the genus ANIMAL. A **genus** is a class of things regarded as having various subcategories (its species). The term "rational" specifies an attribute that distinguishes us from other species of the same genus. This part of the definition is called the **differentia**—it differentiates humans from other animals. A differentia can rarely be expressed in a single word, like "rational," but it always serves the same function of differentiating a concept from other species within the same genus. Thus the genus is like your last name, which indicates the family you belong to; the differentia is like your first name, which distinguishes you from other members of your family.

In light of what we have said about the functions of a definition and its genus–differentia structure, we can now define the very concept of DEFINITION itself:

> A definition is a statement that identifies the referents of a concept by specifying the genus they belong to and the essential characteristics (differentia) that distinguish those referents from other members of the genus.

2.2 Rules for Definitions

If we're looking for a definition, why not just use the dictionary? Isn't that what dictionaries are for? Well, yes and no. A dictionary is a good place to begin our search for a definition. But dictionaries are concerned with *words*. They often give nothing more than synonyms and rarely provide the full context we need to understand the *concept* that a word expresses. To define a concept, we usually have to go beyond the dictionary.

Logicians have identified six rules for constructing a type of definition that is suitable for general purposes.

1. **A definition should include a genus and a differentia.** The most common way to violate this rule is to leave out the genus. And the usual sign of this omission is the use of the word "when," as in "fear is when you think you're in danger." What's missing in this definition is the genus: Fear is the *emotion* one feels in response to the awareness of danger. The word "where" is sometimes used in the same way, as in "a denouement is where the conflict is resolved and the story ends." Here again, the genus is missing. This definition does not tell us what *kind* of thing a denouement is—namely, an element or a stage in the plot of a literary work.

Like the differentia, the genus need not be specified by a single word. If we define an automobile as a motor vehicle intended for personal transportation, the genus is contained in the phrase "motor vehicle." A definition of USER SESSION might be: "A user session at a Web site occurs when a unique user is present on a site during a specified period of time, as opposed to a hit, which occurs each time a user views a different page at a site." This definition includes a genus even though it uses the word "when," because it describes the user session as a unit of measure for usage of a Web site and contrasts it with another measure, a hit. From a logical standpoint, user sessions and hits are two species of the genus "unit of measure for Web site usage." The definition makes this clear. When we define a concept that designates an action, we often use a verb phrase, as in "to practice is to perform an activity for the sake of improving one's skill." The genus here can be restated as "an activity one performs." The English language gives us many ways to specify a genus. To identify the genus, we need to look for the element in a defining statement that refers to a wider class.

A definition by genus and differentia builds on what we have learned about classification. The genus not only helps us identify the referents of a concept, but also conveys a great deal of information about them. If you don't know what a *peso* is, for example, the most useful thing I can tell you is that it's a unit of Mexican currency. In the same way, the statement that humans are animals locates our species within the biological order and conveys a vast amount of information in summary form—that we are living beings, that we are mortal, that we have specific needs for survival and reproduction, and so on.

EXERCISE 2.2A

For each proposed definition, identify the genus (if it has one) and the differentia.

꙳ 1. Snow is precipitation consisting of flakes or clumps of ice crystals.

2. A tree is a plant with thick roots.

3. A landfill is where you take refuse.

꙳ 4. A bargain is an opportunity to buy something at an unusually low price.

5. A pen is a hand-held writing implement that uses ink.

6. To diet is to select the food one consumes for purposes of health or appearance.

* 7. A touchdown is when one team completes a run or pass across the other team's goal line.

8. Government is an institution with the authority to make laws for a society, to enforce those laws, and to protect its citizens against foreign powers.

9. Charisma is when someone can charm or influence others.

* 10. To feel alienated is to feel wrongfully detached from certain people or things.

2. **A definition should be neither too broad nor too narrow.** A definition is too broad if it includes things that are not referents of the concept. For example, the definition "Humans are two-legged animals" is too broad because the defining phrase "two-legged animal" includes birds as well as humans. We can represent this problem in a diagram:

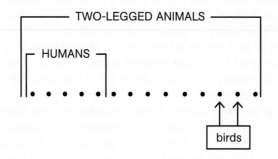

A definition is too narrow if it fails to include things that *are* referents of the concept. An example would be "Humans are religious animals." This definition is too narrow because, no matter how widespread religious belief may be, some people are atheists. We can see this by drawing a diagram

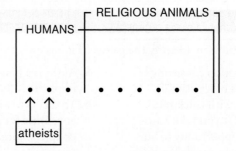

Being too narrow and being too broad are opposite flaws in a definition. But both involve the relation between the concept and its referents. One purpose of a definition

is to identify the referents of a concept. A definition that does not pick out the right referents—one that includes too much or too little—is not doing its job. It is like an incompetent doorkeeper at a party, letting in people who weren't invited or turning away people who were.

We can tell whether a definition is too broad or too narrow by looking for **counter-examples**. A counterexample is a particular instance that proves a definition wrong. If a definition is too narrow, a counterexample is something that belongs in the concept, but is excluded by the definition. Atheists are counterexamples to the definition of humans as religious animals. However, if a definition is too broad, a counterexample is something that does not belong in the concept but is included in the definition. Birds are counterexamples to the definition of humans as two-legged animals. Let's look at a few other cases. "A college is a degree-granting educational institution." A counterexample would be a law school. Law schools are degree-granting educational institutions, but they are not colleges. So this definition includes too much; it's too broad. "A cigarette is a sheaf of chopped tobacco rolled in white paper." What about the brands that are rolled in brown paper? They are counterexamples proving that the definition does not include enough; it's too narrow.

We should notice, finally, that a definition can be simultaneously too broad *and* too narrow. Suppose, for example, that we define murder as the act of killing another person outside a military context. By this definition, killing someone in self-defense would be an act of murder, but it isn't. So this definition is too broad. But it is also too narrow. Suppose a soldier kills another member of his own regiment in cold blood. This would be murder, but the definition would exclude it because it occurred in a military context. So the same definition can violate the rule in both ways: It can be both too broad and too narrow.

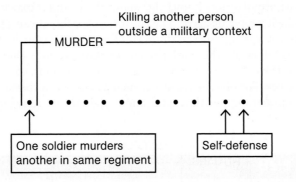

3. **A definition should state the essential attributes of the concept's referents.** The referents of a concept often have many attributes in common. Some are relatively superficial, some are essential. The term "essential" means *fundamental*: an essential attribute causes or explains the existence of other attributes. For example, the heart makes a certain thumping noise, so we might try to define it as "the organ that goes lub-dub, lub-dub." But the "lub-dub" sound is a superficial trait; it is merely a by-product of the heart's essential function, which is to circulate the blood. This essential function explains many of the heart's other properties: the way it beats, the way it is hooked up

to the veins and arteries, even the sound it makes. But explanation is a one-way street. The "lub-dub" sound does *not* explain the heart's function. Remember that one purpose of a definition is to condense the knowledge we have about the referents of a concept. Defining by essential attributes is the best way to achieve this purpose, because then you convey not only the particular attributes named in the definition, but also the ones they underlie and explain.

The rule of essentiality applies to the genus as well as the differentia. Dogs, for example, belong to various wider groups: they are animals, they are playmates, they are a means of self-defense. But ANIMAL would be the best genus to use for general purposes in defining DOG, because a dog's animal nature is more fundamental and explains more about it than does the fact that it can play with human beings or defend them.

In regard to the differentia, the rule of essentiality will help us choose among attributes when there is more than one that would differentiate a concept from other species of the same genus. Consider the concept HUMAN. Many attributes, in addition to the faculty of reason, are common and distinctive to humans: language, social institutions, the accumulation of knowledge from one generation to the next, laws, moral codes, certain complex emotions such as reverence, a sense of humor, a brain of a certain size and complexity, a certain physical shape and posture. But reason is the common element, the underlying cause, for many of these attributes. Not for all of them—reason doesn't seem to have much connection with our physical shape and posture. But it is reason that allowed us to develop abstract language and technology, to create social institutions based on general rules and laws, to pass along knowledge to the next generation, and so forth. Reason gives us a differentia that condenses the greatest amount of knowledge about the concept HUMAN.

As we saw in the chapter on classification, there is no hard and fast rule for determining which attributes are essential. Our view of what is essential to a class of objects may change as we acquire more knowledge about them, and it may involve controversial issues on which people disagree. The rule of essentiality means: pick the most essential attribute you can, given everything you know, using your best judgment. And the guidelines to follow are the ones discussed in the previous chapter: look for the attribute that explains the most. For man-made objects, actions, and institutions, look for the basic *function*. For objects in nature, such as biological species or physical substances, look for *underlying traits* that cause and explain the more superficial attributes.

EXERCISE 2.2B

Identify the rule violated by each of these definitions. If the definition is too broad or too narrow, find a counterexample.

✳ 1. A *blizzard* is when it snows sideways.
2. A *salad* is a food dish containing lettuce.
3. *Blood* is a bodily fluid that is red.
✳ 4. A *file folder* is an item of stationery designed to organize one's papers.
5. A *pleat* is a fold in the fabric of a skirt.
6. An *advertisement* is disseminated in the media to encourage people to buy or use a product or service.

* 7. A *telephone* is an electronic device that uses audio transmitting to communicate between two or more people.

8. A *watch* is a device used for telling time and worn on the wrist.

9. *Cosmetics* are substances applied to the face to alter appearance.

* 10. An *antidote* is a substance that counteracts snakebite.

11. A *pen* is a writing implement that can be clipped to a pocket.

12. *Nodding* is when you move your head forward and down, indicating assent.

* 13. A *calculator* is an electronic instrument that has replaced the slide rule.

14. A *book* is a non-periodical text.

15. A *test* is an activity in which someone demonstrates ability or knowledge according to specified standards.

4. **A definition should not be circular.** Suppose we define *ownership* as the legal relation between people and the things they own. Because this definition uses the word "own," it defines the concept OWNERSHIP in terms of itself. Instead of explaining what it means to own something, it assumes that we know this already. It tells us how the concept relates to itself, but not how it relates to other concepts or to reality. This definition doesn't go anywhere; it just moves in a circle.

The same problem arises if we use synonyms in a definition. Suppose we define ownership as the legal relation between people and things they *possess*. "Own" and "possess" are synonyms, different words that express the same concept. In terms of concepts, therefore, the definition is still circular: The concept OWNERSHIP is still being used to define itself. The same objection would apply if we define *man* as the *human* animal, *large* as the attribute possessed by something that is *big*, or *folly* as a *foolish* act. In each case, the italicized words are synonyms. To avoid such circularity, it is useful to ask: What contrast is the concept intended to draw? For example, what is the difference between owning a dress and borrowing it or trying it on in the store? How are humans different from other animals? What makes an action a folly as opposed to a wise action?

Circularity can take an even subtler form when two different concepts are used to define each other. Suppose that we define a husband as a man who has a wife. So far, so good: HUSBAND and WIFE are distinct concepts. But if we now define a wife as a woman who has a husband, then we have a circular *pair* of definitions. A better approach would be to define the relationship of marriage first; then we could define both HUSBAND and WIFE in terms of that relationship.

5. **A definition should not use negative terms unnecessarily.** At the beginning of the 20th century, the automobile was described as a "horseless carriage." That phrase certainly does describe the automobile, but it would not be a good definition. The differentia "horseless" tells us about one source of power that automobiles do *not* use. But there are many sources of power automobiles do not use; what we want to know is the source they *do* use. As another example, suppose that when I introduced the term "differentia," I defined it as the part of the definition that is not the genus. That would not have been much help to you in understanding what a differentia is. In general, negative

definitions should be avoided because knowing what a thing is *not* doesn't tell us much about what it *is*. For that reason, a negative definition usually violates the rule of essentiality as well.

Some concepts, however, are inherently negative and thus require negative terms in their definitions. A *bachelor* is a man who is not married; *failing* means not succeeding; an *empty* space is one with nothing in it. How do we know whether a concept is negative? In some cases, a suffix or prefix gives us a linguistic clue: *im*mortal, worth*less*, *a*symmetric. In the absence of such clues, you will have to use your judgment. There are no hard and fast rules, but it's a good idea to look first for a positive attribute, then fall back on a negative one only if the search fails.

6. **A definition should not use vague, obscure, or metaphorical language.** We might think of this as the "clarity" rule. The purpose of a definition is to clarify our understanding of a concept. At the very least, therefore, the language we use in a definition should not be *less* clear than the concept being defined. Unfortunately, there are too many ways of being unclear to list them all here, but vagueness, obscurity, and metaphor are the three most common.

A *vague* definition is unclear because it does not give any precise criterion for membership in the concept. Suppose we define *maturity* as the stage of psychological development in which a person becomes well-adjusted. How do we tell whether a person is well-adjusted? Does adjustment mean passive acceptance of the social environment, or can it include a critical outlook? Is it primarily a set of cognitive skills, an emotional state, or both? As these questions indicate, the term "well-adjusted" is vague. It's unclear who belongs in the class of well-adjusted people and who doesn't; the class has highly indefinite boundaries. Of course, the concept MATURITY itself has indefinite boundaries, but a definition shouldn't make the problem worse. It shouldn't have borders that are significantly less definite than those of the concept being defined.

An *obscure* definition is unclear because it uses abstract or technical language that is more difficult to understand than the concept itself. An example would be a definition of *death* as the cessation of one's participation in finitude. The problem here is not necessarily one of vagueness. In the appropriate context of a philosophical theory about human life and afterlife, this definition might have a perfectly clear and definite meaning. But that's the problem: it has a clear meaning only in a specialized context. For general purposes, the defining terms are too obscure to be useful. The same is true of many technical definitions in law, science, or other specialized areas. Such definitions may be perfectly clear to specialists, but if the concept is employed outside the specialty, then we also need a general-purpose definition that is intelligible to laymen.

A *metaphorical* definition is unclear because it doesn't convey the literal meaning of the concept, but only an analogy that we have to interpret. A famous Broadway musical maintained that "Life is a cabaret." Like any good metaphor, this one uses a simple image to convey a complex thought that would take many paragraphs to explain in literal terms. But for a definition, we need the literal terms. A metaphor leaves too many questions unanswered. In exactly what ways is life like a cabaret? How far does the analogy extend? Is this the essential truth about life or just one perspective? Metaphors are valuable tools of thought and communication, but they can't do the work of definitions.

Altogether, then, there are six rules of definition. These rules give us standards for evaluating definitions proposed by other people and guidelines for creating definitions—as we will see in the next section.

SUMMARY **Rules for Definitions**

A definition should:

1. Include a genus and a differentia.
2. Not be too broad or too narrow.
3. State the essential attributes of the concept's referents.

4. Not be circular.
5. Not use negative terms unnecessarily.
6. Not use vague, obscure, or metaphorical language.

EXERCISE 2.2C

For each of the following definitions, identify the genus (if it has one) and the differentia. Then identify which rule (or rules) it violates.

✳1. A *necklace* is a jewel worn on a pendant around the neck.
2. A *tree* is a plant with thick roots.
3. *Art* is any object or action created by an artist.
✳4. A *squirrel* is a rat in a fur coat.
5. *Garbage* is what's left when you finish eating.
6. A *conspiracy* is a collusion in machination.
✳7. A person has *integrity* when he or she plays by the rules.
8. A *bar* is a wooden counter where alcoholic beverages are served.
9. *Seeing* is visually perceiving.
✳10. A *drunk* is a person who is not sober.
11. *Education* is when someone learns something.
12. *Eloquence* is the ability to arouse emotions by means of words.
✳13. *Disappointment* is not getting what you want.
14. *Running* is an aerobic activity useful for quick weight loss.
15. An *orphan* is a person who does not have a living parent.
✳16. A *debate* is an exercise in obscuring the weakness in one's own position by browbeating one's opponent.
17. A *conservative* is a person who opposes legalized abortion.
18. A *stranger* is a friend one has yet to meet.
✳19. A *jacket* is an outer garment designed to protect the wearer from cold, wind, and rain.
20. *Liberty* is a political condition in which people are free.

2.3 Constructing Definitions

Definitions do not appear out of thin air. It's up to us to construct our own. To come up with definitions that satisfy the rules we've learned, we need a procedure we can follow— a technique for constructing definitions.

Of the six rules of definition, the first three are the most important. If you can find a genus and differentia that, together, are neither too broad nor too narrow, and that state the essential attributes of the referents of the concept, you can be pretty sure that your definition will satisfy the remaining three rules. We can think of those other rules as backup tests. To define a concept, therefore, the first step is to find the genus. Then look for a differentia that states the essential attributes of the referents and distinguishes them from other species of the same genus. Finally, double-check your definition by looking for counterexamples and by making sure that your definition is not circular, negative, or unclear. Let's look a little more closely at each step. Then we'll apply our techniques to a particular case.

If we start by finding the genus, it will make the rest of the job easier. Suppose we want to define CUP. We would use what we know about classification to locate the concept in a genus-species hierarchy:

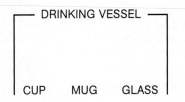

Now we know that our definition will have the form, "A cup is a drinking vessel that___." And we're in a good position to fill in the blank—to find the differentia. We know we have to distinguish cups from mugs and glasses, so we'll look for properties such as shape or function that will best do the job.

In defining a term, we are concerned only with its literal meaning, not with any metaphorical use. A metaphor typically applies a concept from one genus to things in some other genus. An army, for example, is a military organization, but the term "army" is used metaphorically to describe nonmilitary groups that are similar in one way or another, such as an army of ants. If we tried to define ARMY in such a way as to include these metaphors, we couldn't use MILITARY ORGANIZATION as the genus. Indeed, there is no genus we could use, because we could not possibly anticipate every metaphorical use of the term. But we don't need to include the metaphorical uses. The purpose of a definition is to give the *literal* meaning of a concept.

When we choose a genus, we need to consider the appropriate level of abstraction. As noted, the genus of CUP would be DRINKING VESSEL. But a drinking vessel is a kind of *utensil*, which is a kind of *tool*, which is a kind of *man-made object*. Each of these terms is more abstract than the one before and covers a wider range of things. Any of them could serve as the genus. Why choose the narrowest one, DRINKING VESSEL? The answer lies in the rule that a definition should state essential attributes. If we choose UTENSIL as the genus for CUP, then our differentia would still have to include the information that a cup is a utensil used for drinking. That's the function of a cup, and the function explains why a cup has a certain size and shape. The function is an essential attribute, so we might as well include it in the genus.

In contrast, we used ANIMAL as the genus in defining HUMAN, but this is *not* the narrowest genus. Humans are also *vertebrates*, *mammals*, and *primates*. Each of these terms is narrower, less abstract, than the one before. Again, any of them could serve as the genus. Why choose the wider genus, ANIMAL? Once again, we consider which features of humans are essential. The feature we share with other vertebrates, for example, is a spinal column. However important that feature of our anatomy may be, it is not as fundamental as the biological attributes we share with all animals: being alive, having needs for sustenance, reproducing, etc. Our similarities to other primates, mammals, or vertebrates are not as essential as our similarity to all animals. So unless we have a specialized purpose, as biologists do, there is no need to mention these other similarities. Remember that a definition is selective. Its purpose is to condense the information we have about a concept by stating only the fundamental facts.

The main thing to keep in mind when you look for a differentia is that it should distinguish the referents of the concept from the referents of other species in the same genus. It should name an attribute possessed by all the referents of the concept and not possessed by members of the other species; this will ensure that the definition is neither too broad nor too narrow (rule 2). You may be able to find many attributes shared by all the referents, but you should not include them all unless they are all necessary to distinguish the concept from other species in the genus. Once again, a definition should be selective, so look for the essential attribute (rule 3).

When we apply rule 2, we should keep in mind the possibility of borderline cases. Suppose we're defining CITY. Cities are distinguished from other municipalities mainly on the basis of population. Our definition should thus include any place large enough to be considered a city and exclude any place too small. A place with 1,000 residents is obviously a village or town, while a metropolis of 2 million is clearly a city. But there is no sharp line between a large town and a small city. So how would we define CITY?

We have two choices. If we do not have any specialized need for precision, then we should define a city simply as a *large* metropolis. The term "large" clearly includes the metropolis of 2 million, it clearly excludes the village of 1,000, and it leaves the borderline area unclear. Thus it matches the content of the ordinary concept, including the indefinite areas around the borders. In general, we can expect a definition to help clarify boundaries, but we cannot expect it to set more definite boundaries than the concept itself has. However, if we do need a concept with a precise borderline, as we may if we are taking a census or doing economic research, then we will have to specify a precise criterion of population size and turn the concept into a technical one. A definition of this type is sometimes called a "precising definition."

A precising definition is a special case of a more general type: the **stipulative definition**. A stipulative definition introduces a new word by specifying that it shall mean such-and-such. We may need to do this in the case of new technological products (e.g., compact discs), new scientific discoveries (e.g., quarks), new professions (e.g., programming), and so forth. We may also need to give a new meaning to an old word; in physics, for example, "work" is defined as the product of the force applied to an object and its displacement in the direction of that force. Stipulative definitions are not subject

sin. There's an obvious difference in meaning here: one phrase classifies the couple with sinners; the other does not.

Before we decide that two words differ merely in connotation, therefore, we should make sure that they do not also differ in literal meaning. We should ask whether they attribute different properties to their referents or classify them in different ways.

EXERCISE 3.1A

For each pair of sentences that follow, determine whether the sentences express the same proposition.

✳ 1. a. You have a lovely view from your window.
 b. You have a beautiful view from your window.

2. a. Stealing is a sin.
 b. Stealing is a crime.

3. a. It's a pleasure to meet you.
 b. It's an honor to meet you.

✳ 4. a. Wendy is a journalist.
 b. Wendy works for a newspaper.

5. a. It was a tense moment.
 b. It was an anxious moment.

6. a. Henry proposed to her.
 b. Henry asked her to marry him.

✳ 7. a. The elderly person ahead of me was doing about 25 miles per hour.
 b. The geezer ahead of me was doing about 25 miles per hour.

8. a. George is a mellow individual.
 b. George is an unmotivated slob.

9. a. Paul broke up with Diane.
 b. Paul dumped Diane.

✳ 10. a. The activist was zealous about her cause.
 b. The activist was fanatical about her cause.

11. a. The lovers were preoccupied with each other.
 b. The lovers were obsessed with each other.

12. a. The smile she gave him when he left was insincere.
 b. The smile she gave him when he left was forced.

✳ 13. a. The enemy's intelligence operative was terminated with extreme prejudice.
 b. The enemy spy was deliberately killed.

14. a. That remark was offensive.
 b. That remark was insulting.

15. a. Pat had a good time at the party.
 b. Pat didn't have a bad time at the party.

3.1B Metaphors

A special problem arises in the case of metaphors. Strictly speaking, a metaphor is a particular figure of speech in which one thing is equated to another in order to bring out some point of similarity, as in the example we discussed in the past chapter: "Life is a cabaret." In this strict sense, metaphors are distinguished from other figures of speech such as similes ("Life is like a box of chocolates"). But we will use the term "metaphor" more broadly here to include *any* nonliteral use of language.

We have seen that metaphors are not appropriate in definitions, but they are extremely valuable in other contexts, and we use them all the time. They allow us to make our language more colorful and interesting; they convey similarities and shades of meaning that would otherwise be difficult to express. For that very reason, however, it is often difficult to interpret a metaphorical sentence, to formulate in literal terms the proposition it asserts.

For example, when the poet Robert Burns said "My love is like a red, red rose," he was making a comparison. But in what respects? He wasn't making a biological comparison: he didn't mean that he was dating a form of plant life. Presumably he meant his love was beautiful—that is the literal meaning of the metaphor. Yet the two statements

> My love is like a red, red rose
> and
> My love is beautiful

do not express quite the same proposition. "Beautiful" is a very abstract word. The point of this metaphor is to convey the particular *kind* of beauty she has: the dark and delicate, regal beauty of a red rose, not the more exotic beauty of an orchid, or the sturdier, sunnier beauty of a daffodil. And roses have thorns. So perhaps the poet also means to say that his love is prickly and temperamental. You can see that it would be extremely hard to find a literal statement that asserts exactly the same proposition.

Why do we have to find a literal translation? Why can't we just say that the poet is expressing the proposition: My love is like a red rose? Well, sometimes we *can* let it go at that. We can savor the metaphor without analyzing it. In the context of reasoning, however, where we are concerned with the logical relationships among propositions, a literal translation is usually necessary. To know how a given proposition is logically related to others, we have to know exactly what the proposition does and doesn't say. If two people are using metaphorical terms in an argument, we won't know whether they are really talking about the same issue until we formulate their positions in literal terms. In these situations, we have to interpret metaphors, and the only rule we have is a fairly vague one: we should give as full, sensitive, and reasonable an interpretation as we can.

Usually it is not difficult to find a reasonable interpretation. Few of the metaphors we encounter are as rich in meaning as the ones we find in poetry. For example, to describe something as a "Band-Aid solution" is to say that it doesn't solve the underlying problem, but is only a short-term or superficial treatment. This is a one-dimensional metaphor and is easily put into literal terms. Our language is also filled with "dead" metaphors: words so often used to express an idea metaphorically that they now contain the idea as part of their literal meaning. Thus we often speak of *grasping* a fact: "Grasp" is a physical metaphor for the mental act of understanding, but it has been used so often that *understanding* is now considered one of the literal meanings of the word. In the same way, we often describe pains as *sharp*, people as *dense*, spicy food as *hot*, relationships as *stormy*, and so on. If you think about it, you can see that each of the italicized terms is based on a metaphor that is now incorporated into its literal meaning. In such cases, there is no need for interpretation at all.

STRATEGY Words in Propositions

To determine whether two sentences assert the same proposition:

1. Use techniques of classification and definition to identify the concepts the words express.

2. Ignore differences in connotation.

3. Find a literal interpretation of all metaphors.

EXERCISE 3.1B

For each of the metaphorical statements below, formulate a literal equivalent.

* 1. The teacher's announcement was electrifying.
2. Kim is not dealing from a full deck.
3. James's boss ripped his head off at a staff meeting.
* 4. The budget that the president submitted to Congress was dead on arrival.
5. They never clean their attic; it's like the bottom of a bird cage up there.

6. He had a nagging feeling that she was lying.
* 7. The article glossed over the controversy.
8. Jerry was a loose cannon.
9. Fannie Mae and Freddie Mac would have gone under if not for a government bailout.
* 10. Roger was such a good salesman; he could talk a possum out of a tree.

3.2 Propositions and Grammar

3.2A Propositions and Sentence Structure

Some people seem to think grammar is an arbitrary, conventional set of rules—a kind of verbal etiquette, with no more objective basis than the convention that the fork goes on the left side of the plate. Nothing could be further from the truth. Most grammatical rules and structures serve the purpose of maintaining clarity in thought and speech. A sentence is made up of words, but if it is to have any meaning, the words cannot be put together randomly. They must be structured in a certain way, just as building materials—bricks, beams, pipes, and shingles—must be put together in a certain way to make a house. The rules of grammar tell us how to put words together, just as a blueprint tells us how to assemble a building. A mastery of grammar allows us to formulate a thought clearly, no matter how complex or subtle it is, and to express the thought in a way that allows other people to share and appreciate it.

There is much that could be said about the cognitive role of grammar, but our concern in this chapter is specifically with the way the grammatical structure of a sentence affects the propositions it expresses. There are three basic points we need to be aware of in this regard:

1. *Two different grammatical structures can be equivalent, just as two words can be synonymous.*

We've seen that it is possible to replace a word in a sentence with a synonym for the word without changing the proposition the sentence asserts. We can also change the word order without changing the proposition. For example:

1a. The Mets beat the Red Sox. 1b. The Red Sox were beaten by the Mets.

"The Mets" is the subject of the first sentence, while "the Red Sox" is the subject of the second. The first is in the active voice, the second in the passive; but they describe the same action and express the same proposition. The same is true for

2a. Jane did better than Tom on the test. 2b. Tom did worse than Jane on the test.

In this case we reversed the order of "Jane" and "Tom" and replaced "better" with "worse," but 2a and 2b describe the same relationship between their test scores. Logically, they are equivalent; they assert the same proposition.

2. *A single sentence can assert more than a single proposition.*

This is true even of the simplest type of sentence, which contains a single subject and predicate, because we can use adjectives and other modifiers to incorporate additional information. Suppose someone says,

3. "We live in a red house near the lake."

The statement contains the following information:

3a. We live in a house.
3b. The house is red.
3c. The house is near the lake.

Each of these is a proposition asserted by the sentence, and the speaker is saying that each proposition is true.

Here is an example of a somewhat more complex sentence, along with a breakdown into its constituent propositions:

4. Samuel Morse, who invented the telegraph and made a fortune from it, was also a painter whose work is highly regarded and often exhibited.
4a. Samuel Morse invented the telegraph.
4b. Samuel Morse made a fortune from the telegraph.
4c. Samuel Morse was a painter.
4d. Samuel Morse's work is highly regarded.
4e. Samuel Morse's work is often exhibited.

Once again, the sentence asserts each of these propositions. If 4 is true, then 4a through 4e must be true as well, and vice versa. The original sentence is a much more economical way of presenting the information, but it is logically equivalent to the constituent propositions, taken as a set.

When we encounter a complex sentence like 4, how do we identify the constituent propositions? The best approach is to imagine that we are the ones making the statement and to ask: What has to be true for the statement as a whole to be true? How many distinct facts are involved? Or we can imagine that someone else has made the statement and think of all the possible ways of challenging it. Think of all the propositions that, if they were false, would undercut the statement as a whole.

3. *A sentence does not always assert every proposition that it expresses.*

So far in this chapter, we have been talking about the distinction between propositions and sentences and the relationship between them—the ways in which a sentence expresses one or more propositions. Now we need to consider another distinction and another relationship. When we use a sentence to make a definite statement, we are *asserting* the proposition: We are saying that it is true. But we can also think about possibilities that may or may not be real. In such cases, the content of the thought is a proposition, but you are not committing yourself to its truth. When you put the thought into words, you express the proposition without asserting it.

The grammar of English gives us many ways of expressing propositions without asserting them. Here's a typical example:

5. The reelection of the president depends on whether [the economy will improve by November].

The proposition in brackets—that the economy will improve by November—is contained in the statement as a whole, but the speaker is not asserting that this component proposition is true. He's only asserting that the president's reelection depends on whether or not it turns out to be true. Suppose you are the speaker, and someone walks into the room halfway through the statement; all he hears is ". . . the economy will improve by November." If he assumes that you are making a prediction and chides you later, when the prediction turns out false, you would object that you weren't actually committing yourself to the truth of the proposition. We indicate this fact by saying that the statement *expresses* the component proposition, but does not *assert* it.

In the remaining parts of this section, we will look at some of the specific grammatical structures that determine what propositions a sentence asserts and which of them are unasserted. The more you are able to see past the surface complexities of language to its propositional content, the easier you will find it to understand and apply the rules of logical inference we will cover in the rest of the book.

SUMMARY **Propositions and Sentence Structure**

1. Two different grammatical structures can be equivalent, just as two words can be synonymous.

2. A single sentence can assert more than a single proposition.

3. A sentence does not always assert every proposition that it expresses.

EXERCISE 3.2A

A. Determine whether the following pairs of sentences assert the same proposition.

❋ 1. The couch is in front of the window.
The window is behind the couch.

2. The salmon struggled to swim upstream.
The salmon fought their way upstream.

3. I spilled the coffee.
The coffee was spilled.

❋ 4. The paintings were interspersed with the drawings.
The drawings were among the paintings.

5. The man who painted my house is the brother of my best friend.
My best friend's brother painted my house.

B. List the component propositions in each example below.

❋ 1. He arrived in time but out of breath.

2. The ice on the river is thick enough to hold our weight.

3. A bald man wearing pajamas chased the tax collector down the street.

❋ 4. Beavers, which are a type of rodent, build dams that can flood a whole valley.

5. The most annoying thing about Jenny, my ex-girlfriend, is that she chewed her nails.

C. Determine whether the italicized proposition in each of the sentences below is asserted or unasserted.

❋ 1. I don't care whether *it rains*.

2. I could fly if *I had wings*.

3. The prosecution said the butler committed the murder, but in fact *the butler was out playing Bingo that night*.

❋ 4. The photos were disqualified because the judges determined that *they had been altered*.

5. The abandoned wooden church, gray and dusty, looked as if *it was built a hundred years ago*.

3.2B Connectives

A single sentence can assert more than a single proposition. We do this all the time by using the word "and." In the sentence "Jack *and* Jill went up the hill," "and" joins two subjects to make two statements: that Jack went up the hill and that Jill went up the hill. We can do the same thing with predicates, as in "Jack fell down *and* broke his crown," or with two complete sentences

6. [Jack fell down and broke his crown] and [Jill came tumbling after].

where the square brackets indicate the component propositions. When we join two complete sentences in this way, the result is a compound sentence. There are many other words that perform the same function as "and," such as:

7. [Nothing works any more] *but* [nobody cares].
8. [I went to the kitchen] *because* [I was hungry].

9. [He ran from the scene], *for* [he was afraid].
10. *After* [the storm passed], [the temperature dropped].

In grammar, these connecting words are called conjunctions. In logic, however, we use the term "conjunction" in a narrower sense, to refer specifically to "and." We refer to the whole class of words used to make compound sentences as **connectives**. Connectives always join two or more components, like the ones indicated in brackets above, which we can represent symbolically as *p, q,* etc. The result is a new compound sentence that expresses a compound proposition—*p and q; p but q; p because q; p, for q; after p, q;* etc.—that is treated as a distinct proposition, above and beyond *p* and *q*. The reason is that compound propositions normally say something more than just the sum of their parts.

In 8, for example, the statement asserts that I went to the kitchen, it asserts that I was hungry, and it asserts that there is a certain relationship between these facts: My hunger was the cause or reason for going to the kitchen. That relationship is additional information we get through the connective. Many other connectives are like "because" in asserting a relationship of dependence, including "since," "whenever," "therefore," and "so that." Connectives like "after," "before," "when," "while," and "where" assert a relationship of time or place. Connectives like "but," "although," and "even though" assert a relationship of contrast or seeming opposition.

In all these cases, the conjunction combines component propositions into a statement in which *all* components are being asserted as true. Thus in a statement with the form *after p, q,* such as "After I do the dishes, I'll go out for a walk," we are asserting *p* ("I'll do the dishes"), we are asserting *q* ("I'll go out for a walk"), and we are asserting a connection between *p* and *q*: Doing the dishes will occur before going for a walk.

This is not the case, however, with certain other connectives. Consider the following statements:

11. *If* [my cat could talk], [I'd be ruined].
12. *Either* [my cat is talking], *or* [I am hearing things].
13. *Unless* [it rains today], [the Yankees will play the Red Sox].

A statement using one of these connectives asserts that a certain relation exists between the component propositions, but does not assert the components themselves. Sentence 11 does not assert that my cat can talk, nor does it assert that I am ruined; all it says is that *if* the first were true, the second would be true as well. In the same way, 12 does not assert that my cat is talking, nor does it assert that I am hearing things; all it says is that one or the other of these propositions must be true. And 13 does not actually assert that the Yankees will play the Red Sox, since it leaves open the possibility that rain will cancel the game. In all of these examples, therefore, only one proposition, the compound one, is actually being asserted. The components themselves are being expressed but are *unasserted*.

EXERCISE 3.2B

In each example below, identify the connective and the propositions it connects. Then determine whether those component propositions are asserted (a) or unasserted (u).

* 1. His mind was racing, but his body was in the lead.
2. I'm okay, and you are a cockroach.
3. Either the clinic will be open over the holidays, or a doctor will be on call.
* 4. After the ice storm, the trees glittered in the sun.
5. If Dick and Mindy get married in Anchorage, none of their friends will come to the wedding.
6. While the bride lowered her veil, the bridesmaid fluffed her train.
* 7. If Sparky hears the car in the driveway, he runs to the back door.
8. The Becketts will move to Arizona unless Mr. Beckett is not offered the promotion.

3.2C Restrictive and Nonrestrictive Clauses

A clause is a grammatical unit containing a subject and a predicate. Every sentence, therefore, contains at least one clause. But it may contain more. We have just seen how connectives serve to combine two or more clauses. The connective relates one clause, taken as a whole, to another clause, taken as a whole. A different type of structure can be seen in the following example:

14. The Japanese, who eat lots of fish, have fewer heart attacks.

The main clause in this sentence asserts the proposition that the Japanese have fewer heart attacks. But the sentence also contains a subordinate clause—"who eat lots of fish"—that modifies a particular word in the main clause: the subject, "Japanese." As a result, the statement also asserts the proposition that the Japanese eat lots of fish.

This structure is known as a *relative clause*, because it relates one clause to a particular word in another clause. A relative clause normally begins with a *relative pronoun*: "who" or "whom," "which," or "that." And a relative clause normally asserts a proposition in addition to the one asserted by the main clause, as in the example above. But this is not always the case, as we can see by comparing example 14 with

15. The Japanese who eat lots of fish have fewer heart attacks.

What is the difference between these sentences? Well, in example 15, the relative clause restricts the reference of the term "Japanese" to a certain subclass of the Japanese people: those who eat lots of fish. As a result, we are making a single statement about that subclass, and we are not making any statement about the Japanese people as a whole. We could diagram the statement as follows:

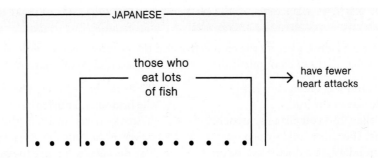

In example 14, in contrast, the commas tell us that the clause introduces a separate point and does *not* restrict the reference of the subject term. So 14 makes two statements: that the Japanese (as a whole) have fewer heart attacks and that the Japanese (as a whole, again) eat lots of fish. Thus:

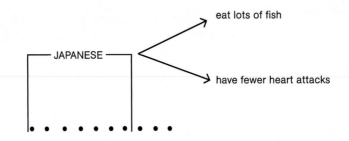

It's clear that the presence or absence of the commas makes a big difference to the meaning of these sentences, even though all the words are the same. A clause like that in 15 is called a *restrictive* clause, because it restricts the reference of the term it modifies; a clause like that in 14 is called a *nonrestrictive* clause, because it does *not* restrict that term's reference. To be clear about what proposition is being asserted, we need to know what class of things we are talking about. When a relative clause is involved, therefore, we must consider whether it is restrictive or nonrestrictive.

If we want to identify all the propositions asserted in these statements, the analysis would be as follows:

Sentence	Relative Clause	Asserted Propositions
14. The Japanese, who eat lots of fish, have fewer heart attacks.	Nonrestrictive	14a. The Japanese have fewer heart attacks. 14b. The Japanese eat lots of fish. 14c. The Japanese eat lots of fish and the Japanese have fewer heart attacks.
15. The Japanese who eat lots of fish have fewer heart attacks.	Restrictive	15. The Japanese who eat lots of fish have fewer heart attacks.

Notice that in 14c we have replaced the relative pronoun with "and" to make it clear that two distinct component propositions are being asserted.

The relative clauses in 14 and 15 modified the subject term, "The Japanese." Relative clauses can also modify a term in the predicate, and the same distinction between restrictive and nonrestrictive applies. For example:

Sentence	Relative Clause	Asserted Propositions
16. Kira hit the boy who was insulting her.	Restrictive	16a. Kira hit the boy who was insulting her.
17. Kira hit the boy, who was insulting her.	Nonrestrictive	17a. Kira hit the boy. 17b. The boy was insulting her. 17c. Kira hit the boy and the boy was insulting her.

In 16, the relative clause beginning with "who" is restrictive. It isolates the particular boy whom Kira hit from any other boys present in the situation. So the sentence asserts only one proposition: that Kira hit the boy who was insulting her. In 17, the relative clause is nonrestrictive. Presumably there is only one boy in the situation, or a particular boy has been identified by some earlier statement, so that we know to whom "the boy" refers. Then the relative clause makes an additional statement about him. In this case, the component propositions are that Kira hit the boy, and that the boy insulted her. And the statement as a whole makes the conjunctive assertion 17c. Once again we have replaced the relative pronoun with "and" to make it clear that two distinct component propositions are being asserted.

EXERCISE 3.2C

Identify the relative clause in each sentence below, and determine whether it is restrictive or nonrestrictive.

* 1. People who live in glass houses shouldn't throw stones.
2. I love jewels that are expensive.
3. I love diamonds, which are expensive.
* 4. Wars that are waged in self-defense are justified.
5. The driver behind me, who has his brights on, is a pain in the neck.
6. I prefer true/false tests, which give you a 50% chance of getting the answer.
* 7. We are looking for a person who was last seen wearing a Cleveland Indians baseball cap.
8. My accountant, who is very good, does not do his own taxes.

3.2D Noun Clauses

Suppose you are discussing a candidate for public office, and someone mentions the candidate's unusual religious affiliation. You might find yourself saying:

18. [That Johnson is a Druid] is irrelevant.

The phrase within the brackets is called a noun clause because the whole clause functions as a noun. Like any clause, it contains a subject ("Johnson") and a predicate ("is a Druid"). Unlike the relative clauses we considered earlier, however, it doesn't modify anything, neither the subject nor the predicate, in the main clause. Rather, it *is* the subject. The noun clause turns the sentence "Johnson is a Druid" into the subject of a longer, more complex sentence. As a result, you have asserted two propositions. You have asserted that Johnson is a Druid. And you have asserted that this fact is irrelevant. In contrast, suppose you had said:

19. It is irrelevant [whether Johnson is a Druid].

Once again, the bracketed words are a noun clause and the subject of the sentence. You are still expressing two propositions here and still asserting that Johnson's religion is irrelevant. But this time you are *not* asserting that Johnson is a Druid. The word "whether" implies that you are leaving this as an open question.

A noun clause can also occur in the predicate of a sentence. It will still express a proposition, but once again the proposition may or may not be asserted. Compare these two sentences:

20. The president knows that war is imminent.
    and
21. The president believes that war is imminent.

In both cases we are making an assertion about the president. In both cases we use a noun clause, "that war is imminent," to convey what it is that the president knows or believes. And in both cases the noun clause expresses a proposition. The difference is that sentence 20 asserts the proposition, while sentence 21 does not.

If we say the president *knows* that war is imminent, we imply that the imminence of war is a fact. You can't know what isn't so. In 20, therefore, we are not only attributing a certain view to the president, we are also endorsing his view as correct. So we are making two assertions: one about the president, the other about war. In 21, however, we are *not* endorsing the president's view. The word "believes" does not carry this implication. Even if we happen to agree with him, we are not committing ourselves. So in this case we are not asserting the proposition expressed by the noun clause. The only thing we're asserting is the proposition that the president does have this belief.

Notice that the difference between 20 and 21 results from the verbs we used: "knows" versus "believes." The English language contains a large class of verbs that we use to describe what people say and think. We can classify these verbs on the basis of whether or not they imply the endorsement of what is said or thought. Thus:

$$X \begin{cases} \text{believes} \\ \text{says} \\ \text{argues} \\ \text{is convinced} \\ \text{suspects} \end{cases} \text{that } p. \quad X \begin{cases} \text{knows} \\ \text{acknowledges} \\ \text{proves} \\ \text{is aware} \\ \text{realizes} \end{cases} \text{that } p.$$

STRATEGY Asserted and Unasserted Propositions

A single sentence may express more than one proposition. To identify the component propositions:

1. Ask what facts are being asserted, i.e., what claims would have to be true for the sentence as a whole to be true.
2. Distinguish nonrestrictive clauses, which introduce a distinct proposition, from restrictive clauses, which do not.

A component proposition may be either asserted or merely expressed. To determine whether a proposition is asserted, ask whether the speaker is committing himself to its truth. Remember that:

1. In sentences of the form *p or q* and *if p then q,* the component propositions *p* and *q* are not asserted.
2. In sentences with a noun clause following a verb like "believes," "says," etc., the proposition expressed by the clause is not asserted.

In the column on the left, we are making an assertion about X, but we are not asserting p. We mention p only to describe X's thought or statement. In the column on the right, however, we *are* asserting p. In addition to the statement about X, we are committing ourselves to the truth of p. In the study of argument, it is crucial to know whether a speaker is endorsing a given proposition as one of his own premises or merely reporting that someone else accepts that proposition. (This distinction is less clear when a speaker makes this sort of statement about himself or herself. If Christiane Amanpour says "I believe that war is imminent," she might well intend it as an assertion that war is imminent, not merely as an assertion about her own state of mind. In that case, there is no difference between "I believe . . ." and "I know. . . ." In such first-person statements of belief or conviction, you will have to judge from the context what the speaker intends to be asserting.)

EXERCISE 3.2D

For each of the following sentences, identify the propositions it asserts (a) and those it does not assert (u).

✳ 1. The little girl thinks that animals can talk.

2. John acknowledged that he had made a mistake.

3. I would like diamonds for Christmas, but I haven't been good this year.

✳ 4. He is convinced that two plus two equals four.

5. The dog, who loves his master, defended him against attack.

6. Gena, a dance student, decided that yoga would be a beneficial complement to her ballet training.

* 7. Samantha suspected that Zack was planning a surprise birthday party for her.

8. Many insects communicate by means of chemical substances, known as pheromones.

9. I met a man who had only one shoe.

* 10. If you buy two pairs of jeans, the third pair is free; and if your purchase is over $50, you get 30% off.

11. Graphic novels are becoming popular again, but as an art form rather than as commercial entertainment.

12. If Deborah takes the new job, she will make more money.

* 13. David was driving well above the speed limit, although he knew better.

14. People who believe in ghosts stay away from graveyards and deserted houses.

15. The Greek philosopher Democritus believed that all objects are made of atoms.

* 16. Professional baseball players, who make a lot of money, should not complain that the season is too long.

17. Samuel Taylor Coleridge, an English Romantic poet, would have finished "Kubla Khan" if he had not been interrupted.

18. The airline pilot was ready to take off, so he radioed the tower and signaled to the traffic controller.

* 19. The city planner called the zone developer because she wanted to find out whether the area had been marked and the architect had been chosen.

20. Although Miss Devon, the district attorney, did not have enough evidence to convict the thief, she knew that he was guilty.

21. After a harsh editorial appeared in the student newspaper, the president of the college said that students should be seen but not heard.

* 22. Because he is a living organism, man is mortal; because he is rational, he is aware of his mortality.

23. The politician realized that if he modified his stance on the smoking ban, he would have a better chance of winning the election.

24. The sweat glistened on the cowboy's brow as he decided whether the approaching man, who was dressed in black, was going to start a fight or leave him alone.

* 25. When we found our seats at the race track, we could hear the announcer reporting that Pardon My Dust was already ahead of Try Me, but he thought Try Me still had a chance at winning the handicap.

Summary

A proposition makes an assertion that is either true or false, and it is normally expressed in a declarative sentence containing a subject and a predicate.

To identify the proposition or propositions asserted by a sentence, we must consider the meanings of the words composing the sentence. In this context, two words are considered to have the same meaning if they express the same concept, even if they differ in connotation. And when a word or phrase is being used metaphorically, we must find a literal interpretation if we are to determine what proposition is being asserted.

We must also consider grammatical structure when identifying the proposition or propositions asserted by a sentence. It is possible to vary the grammatical structure of a sentence without changing the proposition it asserts. And grammatical devices such as connectives, restrictive and nonrestrictive clauses, and noun clauses allow us to combine more than one proposition into a single complex sentence. So to identify the propositions a complex sentence asserts, we must break that sentence down into its components, and we must differentiate between those propositions the sentence asserts and those it merely expresses.

Key Terms

Proposition—the meaning or content of a statement.

Connective—a word that creates a compound proposition from component propositions.

Additional Exercises

A. For each of the following sentences, find another sentence that will express the same proposition (or propositions). You may change the words, or the grammatical structure, or both, so long as the meaning is preserved.

* 1. Joanne and Bob met for lunch.
2. The dog fell asleep on the couch.
3. It probably won't rain today.
* 4. It is raining heavily.
5. John bought his stereo at a 50% discount.
6. Shakespeare was both a poet and a playwright.
* 7. Since Wednesday is a holiday, the mail will not be delivered.
8. All men are created equal.

9. If I move to Chicago, where my family lives, I will be able to see them more often.
* 10. John Calvin said that people are innately evil, but I don't believe him.
11. The police officer apprehended the alleged perpetrator at the crime scene, a commercial eating establishment.
12. Jane suffers from recurring bouts of acute anxiety.

B. The following statements are from accident reports that people have filed with insurance companies. Identify the propositions they assert (a) and those they do not assert (u).

* 1. "A pedestrian hit me and went under my car."

2. "I collided with a stationary truck coming the other way."

3. "I pulled away from the side of the road, glanced at my mother-in-law, and headed over the embankment."

✳ 4. "The pedestrian had no idea which direction to go, so I ran over him."

5. "As I approached the intersection, a stop sign suddenly appeared in a place where no stop sign had ever appeared before."

6. "I told the police that I was not injured but on removing my hat, I found that I had a fractured skull."

✳ 7. "An invisible car came out of nowhere, struck my vehicle, and vanished."

8. "Coming home, I drove into the wrong house and collided with a tree I don't have."

9. "The indirect cause of this accident was a little guy in a small car with a big mouth."

✳ 10. "The accident happened when the right front door of a car came around the corner without giving a signal."

C. For each word below, find two other words that express the same concept, one with a more positive connotation, the other with a more negative connotation. If you were given "elderly person," for example, you might complete the series as follows:

Positive	Neutral	Negative
senior citizen	elderly person	geezer

You may use metaphors as well as literal terms.

✳ 1. Government official
2. Disabled person
3. Deceased person
✳ 4. Overeating
5. Dirty
6. Prostitute
✳ 7. Elated
8. Businessman
9. Married
✳ 10. Mentally retarded

D. For each of the following sets of propositions, write a single sentence in which all the propositions are asserted. You may reword them so long as you do not change their meaning.

✳ 1. John ran 7 miles yesterday. John has been practicing for the marathon. John did not find the run very strenuous.

2. Opposites are usually not attracted to each other. Lauren loves opera. George hates opera. Lauren and George have been happily married for 10 years.

3. Freedom of speech is a necessary component of a democracy. Ruritania censors newspapers. If freedom of speech is a necessary component of a democracy, then a country that censors newspapers is not a democracy.

✳ 4. The law generally holds a manufacturer responsible for harm caused by its product. If the manufacturer warns a buyer that a product is dangerous, the law will not hold the manufacturer responsible for harm. If a buyer is harmed by a product through the buyer's own negligence, the law will not hold the manufacturer responsible for the harm.

5. "Elvis Presley died on August 16, 1977. He died at Graceland, his home in Memphis. Graceland is now an Elvis Presley museum. . . ."

"Yesterday, fans walked past Elvis' grave carrying candles. Many of Elvis Presley's fan clubs sent flowers. They were shaped like guitars and hearts. . . ."

"Many adults did not like Elvis Presley. They did not like the sound of his music. They thought rock'n'roll was bad for teenagers. These adults did not like the way Elvis moved when he sang. He moved his hips a lot." [*Philadelphia Daily News*, August 17, 1988. Make one sentence out of each paragraph.]

E. The following passages are very repetitive. Determine how many distinct propositions each one asserts; then rewrite it so that each proposition is asserted only once.

✳ 1. The problem with Hamlet is that he is very indecisive. He can't seem to make up his mind about anything. He's always thinking about what he should do, but he never does it. He seems unwilling to make a decision, to take a stand. He wanders around pulling his hair out, and nothing ever comes of it.

2. The soul is immortal. It does not die, but lives forever. It existed before birth, and will continue to exist after death. It is completely indestructible. There is nothing that can make it go out of existence. The soul exists forever, and cannot be destroyed. It is therefore separate from the body. The soul is one thing, the body another. The body dies; the soul lives forever. They are utterly distinct.

3. "Could you imagine your mailbox jammed with parcels every day? Free parcels of every size coming to you from all over the world direct to your doorstep. . . . All of this could be yours and more with this amazing system that jams gifts in your mailbox almost every day of the week.
"These free parcels are yours just for the asking. I absolutely guarantee that you will get parcels delivered to you almost every day of the week. . . .
"Imagine coming home to free gifts almost every day of the week. . . . Direct to your doorstep the mailman will deliver your free parcels. This is an absolute reality and can be yours with this amazing system that loads your home with different parcels from all over the world just for the asking." [Magazine advertisement]

✳ 4. "The object of this Essay is to assert one very simple principle, as entitled to govern absolutely the dealings of society with the individual in the way of compulsion and control, whether the means used be physical force in the form of legal penalties, or the moral coercion of public opinion. That principle is, that the sole end for which mankind are warranted, individually or collectively, in interfering with the liberty of action of any of their number, is self-protection. That the only purpose for which power can be rightfully exercised over any member of a civilized community, against his will, is to prevent harm to others. . . . The only part of the conduct of any one, for which he is amenable to society, is that which concerns others. In the part which merely concerns himself, his independence is, of right, absolute. Over himself, over his own body and mind, the individual is sovereign." [John Stuart Mill, *On Liberty*]

F. For each of the following passages, list all the propositions it expresses; then indicate which are asserted and which are merely expressed.

✳ 1. "Man is born free, and everywhere he is in chains." [Jean-Jacques Rousseau, *The Social Contract*]

2. "Last night I dreamt I went to Manderley again." [Daphne du Maurier, *Rebecca*]

3. "Happy families are all alike; every unhappy family is unhappy in its own way." [Leo Tolstoy, *Anna Karenina*]

✳ 4. "Blessed are the poor in spirit: for theirs is the kingdom of heaven.

Blessed are they that mourn: for they shall be comforted.
Blessed are the meek: for they shall inherit the earth." [*Gospel According to St. Matthew*]

5. "It is a truth universally acknowledged, that a single man in possession of a good fortune, must be in want of a wife." [Jane Austen, *Pride and Prejudice*]

6. "I come to bury Caesar, not to praise him.
  . . . The noble Brutus
  Hath told you Caesar was ambitious;
  If it were so, it was a grievous fault,
  And grievously hath Caesar answer'd it."
  [William Shakespeare, *Julius Caesar*]

* 7. "But not only has the bourgeoisie forged the weapons that bring death to itself; it has also called into existence the men who are to wield those weapons—the modern working class—the proletarians." [Karl Marx and Friedrich Engels, *Manifesto of the Communist Party*]

8. "Men fear Death, as children fear to go in the dark; and as that natural fear in children is increased with tales, so is the other." [Francis Bacon, "Of Death," *Essays*]

9. "I went to the woods because I wished to live deliberately, to front only the essential facts of life, and see if I could not learn what it had to teach. . . ." [Henry Thoreau, *Walden*]

* 10. "We hold these truths to be self-evident, that all men are created equal, that they are endowed by their Creator with certain un-alienable Rights, that among these are Life, Liberty, and the pursuit of Happiness. That to secure these rights, Governments are instituted among Men, deriving their just powers from the consent of the governed. . . ." [Declaration of Independence]

* G. Suppose that you are an attorney representing a plaintiff (X) who is suing a defendant (Y) for fraud, and suppose that the legal definition of fraud is as follows:

Fraud consists of a misrepresentation of existing fact upon which the defendant intends that the plaintiff will rely and upon which the plaintiff justifiably relies to his detriment.

How many distinct propositions would you have to prove in order to win your case?

Argument Analysis

There are some things we can know simply by observation. You can tell whether it is raining simply by looking outside. You can tell whether the bath water is warm by putting your hand in it. Your own experience, including the memory of things you perceived in the past, is your basic window on the world. But no matter how much you've seen and done, only a small portion of the world has passed before your window. For every fact you have observed directly, you know a great many things that you haven't observed.

For example, how do you know what year you were born? Obviously you did not witness your own birth. You were told about it by your parents, who did experience the event, and you trust what they told you. In the same way, you know that George Washington was the first president of the United States because you learned it from a history teacher or textbook. In this case, neither the teacher nor the writer of the textbook witnessed Washington's presidency, any more than you did. But they learned about it from other people, who learned it from still others, extending back in a chain to people who were alive in 1788 and kept records of events at that time. A great deal of our knowledge comes from other people in this way. Because we can communicate what we experience, human beings can merge their separate windows into one giant window.

Still, much of the world lies beyond even that window. We have knowledge that transcends the collective experience of human beings in general. We know things about the origins of our planet, the reaches of outer space, the inner life of atoms—none of which has been directly observed by anyone. We make judgments about right and wrong, about character, about the rights of citizens—none of which is a matter of simple observation. In such cases, we proceed by means of reasoning. When we reason, we use relationships among propositions to push our knowledge beyond the limits of what we can experience directly. In this chapter, we will begin our study of the reasoning process.

4.1 Elements of Reasoning

Consider the proposition:

1. Rivers in Taiwan flow downhill.

We know that this proposition is true. But how do we know? Few of us have actually been to Taiwan to observe the rivers there or have even talked to people who have seen them. But we can establish the truth of sentence 1 by reasoning. We know from experience that the fluid nature of water makes it flow in the direction of the forces acting on it, and we know that the primary force is gravity, which pulls water downhill. These are general principles that apply everywhere, and they imply that rivers in Taiwan must behave like rivers in our own environment.

Here is another statement that calls for reasoning:

2. The government should restrict ownership of handguns.

This is one side of a controversial political issue. In this case, unlike the previous one, people tend to have strong opinions for or against the proposition, and they often argue about it. For that very reason, questions of truth and falsity may seem inappropriate here. But they are appropriate. When people argue about gun control, they are not merely voicing personal preferences, as if they were talking about flavors of ice cream. They are trying to show that their position is true—and they will offer reasons. An *advocate* of gun control might argue that government should pursue the goal of reducing crime, and that restricting ownership of handguns would reduce crime. An *opponent* of gun control might argue that restricting ownership of handguns would violate the right of self-defense.

4.1A Premise, Conclusion, and Argument

These examples involve different types of reasoning, but they also illustrate a common pattern. In each case we are concerned with evidence for the truth of some proposition. In logic, this proposition is called a **conclusion**. The evidence in support of the conclusions consists of other propositions called **premises**. Thus each of our examples involves the use of premises to support a conclusion:

Rivers in Taiwan

Premise 1: Water flows in the direction of the forces acting on it.
Premise 2: The primary force acting on rivers in Taiwan is gravity.
Premise 3: Gravity pulls downward.
Conclusion: Rivers in Taiwan flow downhill.

Gun control—for

Premise 1: Restricting ownership of handguns would reduce crime.
Premise 2: Government should pursue the goal of reducing crime.
Conclusion: The government should restrict ownership of handguns.

<u>Gun control—against</u>

Premise 1: Restricting ownership of handguns would violate the right of self-defense.

Conclusion: The government should not restrict ownership of handguns.

For each conclusion, we have identified the premises that provide the evidence for that conclusion, and we have formulated those premises as distinct propositions.

A set of premises together with a conclusion is called an **argument**. In everyday speech, this term is often used to mean a quarrel between two people. But it is also used to mean an appeal to evidence in support of a conclusion. In logic, we use the term *argument* in the latter sense. It means a set of propositions in which some propositions (the premises) are asserted as support or evidence for another (the conclusion). Another way to put this is to say that the conclusion is *inferred* from the premises. Thus an argument can also be described as an inference, and we will use those terms interchangeably.

Each of the examples above is an argument. By contrast, consider the following exchange:

John: The government ought to ban handguns.

Mary: That's not a good idea.

John: Why not? I think it's a good idea.

Mary: Well, I don't.

In everyday speech, we might say that John and Mary are arguing about gun control. But neither of them is offering an argument in the logical sense; they are just expressing their views without giving reasons.

In this chapter, we will study the basic techniques for analyzing and evaluating arguments. Before we turn to this topic, however, let's consider how we can *recognize* an argument.

4.1B Recognizing Arguments

When we listen to someone speak, or read a written text, we expect there to be some relationship among the statements, some organizing principle or structure. There are various structures, not all of them arguments. In a narrative, for example, there is usually no argument; instead, the author simply describes a sequence of events, and the organizing principle is the order of their occurrence, as in the following passage from George Orwell's *1984*:

Winston Smith, his chin nuzzled into his breast in an effort to escape the vile wind, slipped quickly through the glass doors of Victory Mansions, though not quickly enough to prevent a swirl of gritty dust from entering along with him.

A descriptive passage states a series of facts about something; the series may be organized in various ways, but again there is usually no argument, as in another passage from *1984*:

The Ministry of Truth was startlingly different from any other object in sight. It was an enormous pyramidal structure of glittering white concrete, soaring up, terrace after terrace, 300 metres into the air.

STRATEGY Indicator Words

To identify premises and conclusions, look for the following indicator words:

Premise indicators	Conclusion indicators
Since	Therefore
Because	Thus
As	So
For	Consequently
Given that	As a result
Assuming that	It follows that
Inasmuch as	Hence
The reason is that	Which means that
In view of the fact that	Which implies that

What distinguishes an argument from these other patterns is the effort to support a statement logically. The author doesn't just tell us something that he takes to be true; he also presents *reasons* intended to convince us that it *is* true. This intention is usually signaled by certain verbal clues. For example, the word "therefore" indicates that a statement is intended as a conclusion. The word "because" usually indicates a premise. There are many such indicator words and phrases in English. The more common ones are listed in the Strategy box.

When you encounter such words, it is a good sign that you are in the presence of an argument and you can use the indicators to distinguish the premises from the conclusion.

But you cannot use them mechanically. Some of the words are used in contexts other than argument. In the statement "Since I arrived in Dry Gulch, I haven't seen a single green thing," the word "since" indicates a temporal relation, not a logical one. However, the absence of indicator words does not necessarily mean the absence of an argument. If I say "Dry Gulch is an arid place—I haven't seen a single green thing," I am offering evidence in support of a conclusion, even though I used no indicator words.

A final point to keep in mind is that many of the words listed above can be used to indicate an *explanation* rather than an argument. In an argument, we are trying to show that some proposition—the conclusion—is true. In an explanation, we are trying to show *why* it is true. To see the difference, compare the following two statements:

1. It will probably rain tomorrow, because a cold front is moving in.
2. It rained yesterday because a cold front moved in.

In both cases, the word "because" indicates a relationship between the cold front and rain. But the relationship is not the same in both cases. In sentence 1, we are using the presence of a cold front as evidence that it will rain; we are offering an argument. In sentence 2, we already know that it rained. We don't have to offer an argument for that proposition; we know it is true because we observed the rain directly. What we are doing instead is stating the *cause* for the rain; we are offering an explanation. In an argument, we reason forward from the premises to the conclusion; in an explanation, we reason backward from a fact to the cause or reason for that fact.

To recognize an argument, the most important technique is to read carefully, asking what point the author is trying to make, isolating the propositions asserted, and identifying the relationships among them.

Let's look at an example from a speech by President Ronald Reagan in 1984:

> "The truth is," Mr. Reagan said, "politics and morality are inseparable, and as morality's foundation is religion, religion and politics are necessarily related. We need religion as a guide." [*New York Times*, August 24, 1984]

There are three propositions here: (1) politics and morality are inseparable; (2) morality's foundation is religion; and (3) religion and politics are necessarily related. The final sentence—"We need religion as a guide"—is essentially a restatement of 3. Do we have an argument? Well, the word "as" indicates that 2 is intended as a premise. The word "necessarily" suggests that 3 is a conclusion. It means: If you accept 1 and 2, you should accept 3 as well. So in essence Mr. Reagan was saying: Politics depends on morality, morality depends on religion, therefore politics depends on religion. That's an argument.

Let's consider one more example.

> The rule of law means that people should be punished only for a breach of a law, not by the arbitrary discretion of government. It means that laws should be clearly stated and made known to the public. And it means that laws should be applied uniformly to everyone—everyone is equal before the law.
>
> The rule of law is a worthy ideal. To the extent that it can be achieved, it allows people to know which actions will and will not get them in trouble with the law. It is also fair in treating all people without discrimination.

The first paragraph is a description of the rule of law. Though it describes an ideal, and is cast in positive terms, it does not actually make a case for the ideal. It is not an argument. The second paragraph does provide an argument. No indicator words are used, but the paragraph clearly makes a case for the conclusion that the rule of law is a worthy ideal by offering two premises in support of it.

So far I have asked you to distinguish arguments from nonarguments in a basically intuitive way, with some help from indicator words. The distinction will become easier to draw as you learn more about the inner workings of arguments—a topic we will turn to next.

EXERCISE 4.1

For each of the following paragraphs, determine whether it contains an argument. If so, identify the premises and the conclusion.

＊ 1. We parked at the trailhead and began our hike up Mt. Washington, walking through a dense forest. After 2 hours we reached the halfway point and stopped to eat lunch.

2. It's important to have sturdy boots for this hike, because the trail is very rocky.

3. There are streams to cross and some muddy places, so it is good to have waterproof boots.

* 4. From the top of the mountain, we could see other mountains to the north and the south. None were as high as Washington. A cold wind blew across the entire chain.

5. Since these peaks are above the tree line, hikers are totally exposed to the weather.

6. Cable television can provide the viewer with more channels than broadcast television, and it usually delivers a higher quality picture. For these reasons, the number of cable subscribers will probably continue to grow rapidly.

* 7. The first cable companies served remote rural communities. These communities were too far from any broadcast station to receive a clear signal over the air. Tall towers, usually located on hills, picked up the signals and distributed them to individual homes.

8. Since cable companies are now serving the suburbs and cities, they pose a competitive challenge to broadcast television.

9. More than half the homes in the country subscribe to cable television. Basic cable service usually includes local TV channels, such as the three networks, and one or more news channels. For an additional fee, subscribers can also receive movie channels and other specialized programs.

* 10. It is rarely economical for two companies to lay cables in the same area and compete directly. This suggests that cable television is a natural monopoly, which should be regulated by the government.

11. Cable competes with broadcast TV, satellite TV, and other media. And as a medium of communication, it is protected by the First Amendment. So it should not be regulated.

12. Depression is a condition characterized by changes in appetite, sleep patterns, and energy levels. Depressed individuals often have trouble concentrating and finding pleasure in activities they used to enjoy.

* 13. In an experiment involving twins raised in different families, psychologists found that the children had significantly similar rates of depression. This indicates that depression is more strongly affected by one's genetics than by one's environment.

14. Treating depression with medication is the same as treating any illness with medication. Therefore, the patient should not stop taking the medication just because his symptoms have gone.

15. Although depression is an undesirable experience, it can sometimes serve a useful function. Some researchers believe that depression, like pain, signals damaging behavior and thought patterns. So, people with depression can potentially improve their condition by becoming more aware of their emotions and habitual attitudes.

4.2 Diagramming Arguments

We can think of the premises as the raw materials for an argument and the conclusion as the final product. To understand an argument, we need to know what happens in between—on the factory floor, so to speak. We need to analyze the inner workings of the argument, the individual steps that lead from premises to conclusion. Once we have *analyzed* the argument, we can go on to *evaluate* it: Is it a good argument? Does it provide a good reason to accept the conclusion? Analysis and evaluation are the two basic tasks we are going to discuss in this chapter. We will begin with analysis in this section and move on to evaluation in later sections.

To analyze an argument, we can use a diagramming method that employs just two symbols but is flexible enough to handle arguments of any complexity. One symbol is an arrow pointing from premise to conclusion. This arrow represents a single step in reasoning—the relationship between a premise and the conclusion. Suppose you argued against gun control on the ground that it would violate the right of self-defense. Then your reasoning could be diagrammed as follows:

Restricting handgun ownership violates the right of self-defense.

$$\downarrow$$

The government should not restrict handgun ownership.

This is an extremely simple argument. It has a single premise, and there is a single step in the reasoning. So the structure of the argument is fully represented by a single arrow.

But what if there is more than one premise? Then we have a decision to make. In some cases, the premises are dependent on one another: Two or more premises work together to make a single argument for a conclusion. In other cases, the premises are independent: They do not work together; each one offers a separate line of support for the conclusion. These two patterns are diagrammed in different ways, so we have to decide which pattern is present in a given argument. To illustrate the distinction, let's reexamine two arguments that we have already discussed.

The first is Ronald Reagan's argument about politics and religion. In essence, he said: (1) politics depends on morality, and (2) morality depends on religion, therefore (3) politics depends on religion. This argument illustrates the first pattern—an argument with dependent premises. Premises 1 and 2 must be combined in order to have an argument for 3. The premise that politics depends on morality, taken by itself, does not tell us anything about religion, so it doesn't give us any reason to think that politics depends on religion. In the same way, the premise that morality depends on religion, taken by itself, does not tell us anything about politics, so again we would have no reason to think politics depends on religion. It is only when we put the premises together that we have an argument. We represent this fact by using a second symbol, the plus (+) sign, to join the premises. Using the numbers to stand for the individual propositions, we would diagram the argument like this:

$$\frac{1 + 2}{}$$
$$\downarrow$$
$$3$$

We use a single arrow, drawn from the line joining the premises, to represent the fact that the premises together make up a single argument.

By contrast, consider the argument about the rule of law. In this case, the conclusion is stated first, so we give it the number 1. In diagramming arguments, it does not matter how we number the premises and conclusion, as long as we give each proposition its own number. So it is easiest to number them in the order they are stated.

> (1) The rule of law is a worthy ideal. To the extent that it can be achieved, (2) it allows people to know which actions will and will not get them in trouble with the law. (3) It is also fair in treating all people without discrimination.

This argument illustrates the second pattern: premises 2 and 3 *independently* support the conclusion. If the rule of law allows people to know the legal consequences of their actions, as stated in 2, that gives us some reason to think the rule of law is a worthy ideal, regardless of whether it is also fair. And the fairness of the rule of law, as stated in 3, provides a reason for considering it a worthy ideal, regardless of premise 2. So in diagramming this argument, we don't use the plus sign. We use two arrows to join each premise to the conclusion separately:

To tell whether a set of premises is dependent or independent, we look at each premise separately and ask whether the kind of support it offers to the conclusion depends on the other premises. A good way to pose the question is to suppose that the other premises are unknown or even false. If that would significantly affect the logical impact of the premise in question, then the relationship among the premises is one of mutual dependence, and a plus sign should be used in the diagram. In contrast, if the premise in question would still give us a reason for accepting the conclusion, then it is independent of the other premises and should be diagrammed with a separate arrow. The goal is to put together those premises that form a single line of thought and separate them from premises that represent distinct lines of thought. But this is not always easy. If the relationship between premises is unclear, it is a good idea to treat them as dependent. As we learn more about specific types of argument, we'll learn more about what sorts of premises must be combined to support a conclusion.

In an argument with independent premises, two (or more) arrows will converge on the conclusion. But can we have the opposite situation? Can we have arrows diverging from a single premise to two or more different conclusions? That is, can a single fact serve as evidence for more than one conclusion? Certainly—as we noticed earlier, the law of gravity implies that water flows downhill, but the law of gravity has many other implications: that the roof of a building needs to be supported, that a rocket needs a certain velocity to go into orbit around the earth, and so on. These would be distinct arguments, but because they rely on the same premise, we can combine them in a single diagram. If we numbered all these different propositions, starting with the law of gravity itself, the diagram would look like this:

In all the arguments we have examined so far, a given proposition served as either a premise or a conclusion, but not as both. But that's only because we have been dealing with very simple arguments. In everyday thinking, as well as in science and other academic subjects, we often find chains of inferences: A premise gives us evidence for a certain conclusion, which in turn supports a further conclusion, and so on. Or conversely, we look for a premise to back up our position, and then look for a further premise to back up the first premise, and so on. For example, if someone opposes gun control on the ground that it violates the right of self-defense, we might ask: Why assume that people have such a right? The person might answer: Because people have a right to life, and therefore have a right to defend themselves. So we have four propositions to deal with:

1. People have a right to life.
2. People have a right to defend their lives.
3. Gun control violates the right of self-defense.
4. The government should not restrict gun ownership.

And the argument would be diagrammed.

1
↓
2+3
↓
4

STRATEGY Diagramming Arguments

1. An argument must have at least one premise and one conclusion; use an arrow to represent the link between them.

2. A single conclusion may be supported by more than one premise; use a plus sign and a single arrow for dependent premises, convergent arrows for independent ones.

3. A single premise may support more than one conclusion; draw divergent arrows.

4. An argument may have more than one step, so that a given proposition can be both a conclusion (of one step) and a premise (of another step); use separate arrows to represent each step, with the final conclusion on the bottom line.

This argument has two steps, and proposition 2 serves both as the conclusion of the first step and as a premise of the second. An argument can have any number of premises, any number of steps.

Point 1 in the Strategy box is true of all arguments; indeed, it is true by the very definition of an argument. Points 2 through 4 describe the various ways in which arguments can differ in structure, and for each one we have a way of representing it in a diagram. So no matter how complex an argument is—no matter how many steps it has, or how many conclusions each premise supports, or how many premises support each conclusion—we should now be able to represent it in a diagram.

Now let's use the diagramming method to construct an argument of our own. Consider the proposition that extremely sarcastic people feel inadequate. Let's see whether we can find an argument to support the claim. We might notice that chronic sarcasm, especially when it is not provoked, seems to express hostility. And why would someone express unprovoked hostility all the time? Isn't it usually because the person feels inadequate in some way? Let's write these ideas down in a list. And since the order in which we number the propositions in an argument is arbitrary, we'll start with the conclusion this time:

1. Extremely sarcastic people feel inadequate.
2. Extreme sarcasm is a form of unprovoked hostility.
3. Unprovoked hostility results from feelings of inadequacy.

Sentences 2 and 3 are clearly dependent premises; neither one alone supports the conclusion. So when we diagram the argument, we get:

$$\begin{array}{c} 2 + 3 \\ \downarrow \\ 1 \end{array}$$

Now suppose someone challenges us on premise 2—or suppose we ourselves wonder why it strikes us as true. Can we offer any further argument for it? After all, sarcasm can be playful and witty. It can be an indirect way of expressing fondness or any number of other feelings. Yes, we might answer, that's true in small doses. But chronic and extreme sarcasm always seems to have the goal of undercutting or belittling another person. And the desire to undercut someone, when it isn't provoked, is a kind of hostility So now we have two further premises:

4. Extreme sarcasm is an effort to undercut someone.
5. The desire to undercut someone is a kind of hostility.

Like 2 and 3, these are dependent premises, so we can expand the diagram thus:

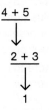

$$\begin{array}{c} 4 + 5 \\ \downarrow \\ 2 + 3 \\ \downarrow \\ 1 \end{array}$$

Now we have an argument in two steps. If we were to discuss the issue thoroughly, we would have to look for reasons to support premise 3, and we would want to consider other lines of evidence as well. The diagram would get more and more complex. But we would proceed in the same fashion, listing premises and adding them to the diagram as we go.

EXERCISE 4.2

A. For each of the following arguments, you are given the structure of the diagram; fill in the numbers at the appropriate places.

✳1. (1) I shouldn't go home this week-end not only because (2) I have too much studying to do, but also (3) because I can't afford the trip.

2. (1) Cheating on schoolwork is wrong because (2) it is dishonest.

( )
↓
( )

3. (1) Cheating on schoolwork is wrong because (2) it means rely-ing on someone else's knowledge, whereas (3) the purpose of educa-tion is to learn how to rely on your own knowledge.

( )   +   ( )
        ↓
      ( )

✳4. (1) Regular exercise strengthens muscles, (2) strengthens the car-diovascular system, and (3) lowers cholesterol. For all those reasons, (4) one should exercise regularly.

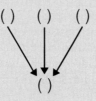

5. Since (1) my car won't start, (2) I will have to take the bus, so (3) I need to take exact change for the fare.

( )
↓
( )
↓
( )

B. In each of the following arguments, identify the conclusion. Then determine whether the premises are dependent or independent.

✳1. (1) To be a lawyer, you need to be good at keeping track of details, and (2) Lenny is terrible at that, so (3) he shouldn't go into law.

2. (1) Molly is a very bright child. (2) She began speaking on her first birthday, whereas (3) most children do not begin to speak until later.

3. (1) At the trial, Harris said he was in Milwaukee that night, but (2) he later told me that he was in Chicago. One way or another, then, (3) he is a liar.

✳ 4. (1) Edward prefers Frigidaire to Amana. (2) Edward always buys Frigidaire appliances, even though (3) the Amana store is cheaper and (4) closer to his home.

5. (1) Thomas Jefferson had a profound effect on America, inasmuch as (2) he drafted the Declaration of Independence, (3) served as ambassador to France during a crucial period in the young country's history, and (4) negotiated the Louisiana purchase.

6. (1) We cleaned out all the water that flooded the basement before and (2) all the windows were shut the last time it rained. (3) Now there's water in the basement again, so (4) there must be a leak somewhere.

✳ 7. (1) Governor Baldacci originally told the press that a civil union was an appropriate alternative to gay marriage. (2) He has since signed a bill to legalize gay marriage, which means that (3) he changed his mind.

8. (1) When a pencil is put into water, it remains straight. (2) But our eyes perceive it as bent. Therefore, (3) our senses are flawed.

9. (1) The military must invade the city. (2) It needs supplies, and (3) if it moves ahead without taking the city, there will be enemies both behind and in front of it.

✳ 10. (1) He sat next to me in class today, and (2) the other day he smiled when I ran into him at the library. (3) I think he is interested in me.

C. Diagram each of the following arguments. (For further practice, diagram the examples in Exercise 4.1 on pages [71–72] that you have determined are arguments.)

✳ 1. Annette must be wealthy. Last week she bought a diamond choker for her ocelot.

2. That movie was terrible. The plot was incoherent, the theme was trite, and the acting was not very good.

3. Johnson finished his last project in only 4 days. Because he's such an efficient worker, he deserves a promotion.

✳ 4. I don't think it would be a good idea to take the American Revolution course this term, because it conflicts with a course I need for my major, and my schedule would have more balance if I took a science course instead.

5. Everyone needs to understand how the structure of language can affect the way we think. But since this is difficult to appreciate in the case of our native language, it is valuable to study a foreign language.

6. Key West, the southernmost city in the continental United States, is located at the tip of the Florida peninsula. This means not only that it enjoys year-round warm weather, but also that it is vulnerable to Caribbean hurricanes.

✳ 7. Business conditions will improve over the next year, and when they do so, corporate profits will increase. Increasing profit levels will drive up stock prices. So I am confident that investing in the stock market is a good idea.

8. Government regulation tends to delay the introduction of new drugs. If a drug is harmful, regulators get blamed for approving it;

but if it is beneficial, they get no reward for approving it. So regulators have an incentive to be excessively cautious.

9. An encyclopedia is a valuable possession for a family to have and well worth the family's money. For adults, it is a quick reference tool. For children, it provides a form of learning that complements what they get in school. Why? Because in school they have to follow a structured program, whereas an encyclopedia lets them go from topic to topic following their own curiosity.

✳ 10. Raising the age of retirement would both decrease an expenditure and generate revenue for the government. It would reduce the number of years that citizens drew money from their pensions, and people would continue to pay income and social security taxes during their additional years of employment.

4.3 Evaluating Arguments

A diagram is a valuable tool of analysis. It is like an X-ray picture of an argument, revealing its internal structure. Once we understand that structure, the next step is to *evaluate* the argument, to determine how good an argument it is. How do we measure that value? What standards shall we use? The basic standard is that an argument is good to the extent that it provides evidence for the truth of its conclusion. That, after all, is the goal of reasoning: to determine the truth or falsity of propositions that we are not in a position to verify directly by sense perception.

To provide evidence for a conclusion, an argument must have two essential attributes. First, its premises must be true. An argument is an attempt to establish the truth of a proposition by relating it to facts we already know. So we have to start from facts; false premises don't prove anything. Second, the premises must be logically related to the conclusion in such a way that if the premises *are* true, the conclusion is likely to be true as well. In other words, it is not enough that the premises be true; they must also support the conclusion. They must provide evidence that the conclusion is true.

These two standards of evaluation are largely independent. On the one hand, we can have premises that are true but provide no support for an unrelated conclusion. It is certainly true that dogs bark and that dogs are animals, but those propositions do not support the conclusion that cats make nice pets. On the other hand, we can have premises that are false but that are still logically related to a conclusion in such a way that, if they *were* true, they *would* support that conclusion. Consider the argument

(1) All fish breathe through gills, and (2) whales are fish. Therefore (3) whales breathe through gills.

Premise 2 is false. Nevertheless, the conclusion follows from the premises; if both premises were true, the conclusion would have to be true as well.

For any given conclusion, different arguments can provide different degrees of support. Suppose, for example, that Lenny Lightfinger is accused of stealing Mary Mobil's car. Compare the following two bodies of evidence:

A. Lenny Lightfinger was once convicted of auto theft; therefore he stole Mary Mobil's car.
B. Lenny Lightfinger was seen by several witnesses entering Mary's car and driving it away; the car was later found one block from his home, and his fingerprints were on the steering wheel; therefore he stole her car.

Let's assume that the premises in both A and B are all true. Nevertheless, it is clear that the premise in A provides very little evidence for the conclusion; it might justify a slight suspicion of Lenny, but nothing more. In B, however, we have solid evidence of Lenny's guilt. The conclusion that he was the thief is the only conclusion that seems consistent with the premises.

One of the most important goals of logic is to provide standards for measuring the degree to which a given set of premises supports a conclusion. These standards are extremely valuable, even when we aren't sure whether the premises are true. When we encounter an argument that strikes us as wrong, the standards will help us locate the problem and state our objections precisely. When we encounter an argument whose conclusion we agree with, the standards will help us resist the temptation to put more weight on the argument than it deserves. And if we're not sure whether a proposition is true or false, the standards will tell us what sort of evidence would be relevant.

To illustrate the different degrees of support, consider the types of evidence we might use to support the conclusion that someone named Harry is a lousy driver. At the bottom end of the continuum is the argument that he got a parking ticket. This premise gives no support whatever to the conclusion. Now suppose we learned that Harry once dinged his door in a parking lot. That is not much evidence, but it's something. It's enough to raise a question in our minds. If we acquired the additional information that he failed Drivers' Ed three times and was involved in a major accident, we would have much better support for the conclusion; this evidence makes it probable that he is not a good driver. Finally, if we knew that his vision was 20/200 and that he had trouble telling the brake pedal from the accelerator, our premises would make the conclusion virtually certain.

The general principle illustrated by the preceding example is that we assess the degree of support by seeing how much free play there is between premises and conclusion. The technique is to assume that the premises are true and then ask whether there could still be reasonable doubt as to whether the conclusion is true. Assuming that the premises are true, are there rival conclusions that would be equally consistent with the premises? In the case of Harry the driver, the argument that he once dinged his door provides very little support for the conclusion that he is a lousy driver. That is because even a good driver can have such a minor accident if, for example, he was in a hurry to make an appointment, or was trying to park in a tight spot. The argument does not rule out these rival conclusions.

This method of assessing degree of support relies on your general ability to assess how much free play there is between the premises and the conclusion of an argument. As we proceed in the study of logic—starting with the next section of this chapter—we will discuss further techniques for evaluating specific kinds of arguments. These techniques will help sharpen your ability to distinguish degrees of support.

EXERCISE 4.3

Each pair of arguments that follow has the same conclusion. Determine which one has the greater logical strength. Remember that your assessment should depend not on whether you agree with the premises or the conclusion but on whether the relationship between the premises and the conclusion is strong.

✳ 1. a. It's probably going to rain to-night; my trick knee is aching.
  b. There's a cold front moving in from the west, and the barometer is falling, so it's probably going to rain tonight.

2. a. Cross-country skiing is one of the best forms of exercise: My sister is a cross-country skier, and she's in great shape.
  b. Cross-country skiing uses all the major muscle groups and gives the cardiovascular system a good workout, so it is an ideal form of exercise.

3. a. Business conditions will improve over the next year, and when they do so, corporate profits will increase. Increasing profit levels will drive up stock prices. So I am confident that investing in the stock market is a good idea.
  b. Investing in stocks is a good idea. My cousin Vinny, who's a broker, says the market is going up.

✳ 4. a. Gelato is a better product than ice cream because it's popular with young, progressive people who are concerned about politics and the arts.
  b. Gelato is a better product than ice cream because it has fewer calories, less fat, and a richer taste.

5. a. The fact that average wages of manufacturing workers increased by a factor of 5 since 1900 indicates that the standard of living has improved a great deal since then.
  b. In 1900 there were no laptop computers, no Papa John's pizza, no Disneyland. Our standard of living has certainly improved since then.

6. a. Marriage is a good institution because it creates jobs for people in the bridal industry.
  b. Marriage is a good institution because all married people are happy.

✳ 7. a. John must have been lying when he said he was home Saturday night, because in the past he has never stayed home on a Saturday night.
  b. I saw John at McGinty's Bar Saturday night, so he was lying when he said he stayed home.

8. a. Weaver is guilty of the murder of Taylor. The evidence: The murder weapon was found in Weaver's possession, and a witness testified that he was at the scene of the crime.
  b. Weaver is guilty of the murder of Taylor. The evidence: The murder weapon was found in his possession.

9. a. Affirmative action programs increase the amount of record-keeping and red tape that a school or business has to deal with, which makes these programs very expensive. They should be abolished.

b. People should be treated the same regardless of race and sex, but affirmative action programs require that people be treated differently depending on their race and sex. Such programs should therefore be abolished.

✳ 10. a. The government's banning Muslim women from wearing a burqa in public spaces is detrimental to individual liberty. Wearing the burqa is an instance of religious expression, and freedom of religion is crucial to individual liberty.

b. The government's banning Muslim women from wearing a burqa in public spaces is detrimental to individual liberty. The ban is xenophobic in motivation, it causes tension within the Muslim community, and it makes Muslim women feel uncomfortable.

4.4 Induction and Deduction

So far we have treated all arguments as a single class, defined by the use of premises to support a conclusion. But there are many different types of argument, different patterns of reasoning. These narrower classes have distinctive structures, and in later chapters we will learn specific methods for analyzing and evaluating them. It is important now, however, to understand the broad distinction between two basic types of argument: induction and deduction.

The following arguments illustrate the difference:

A. A detective investigating a murder notices that nothing was taken from the victim's wallet. He might reason as follows: (1) If robbery was the motive, the money would have been taken, but (2) the money was not taken, so (3) robbery was not the motive.

B. A scientist investigating an outbreak of disease examines a random sample of the victims. She discovers (1) that all of them had recently eaten strawberries from California, and, as far as she can tell, (2) that the people in the sample had nothing else in common. The scientist concludes (3) that something in the strawberries was causing the disease in all the victims.

Argument A is an example of a **deductive argument**. The conclusion (3) simply makes explicit the information implicit in premises 1 and 2. If those premises are true, they guarantee the truth of the conclusion: It would be impossible for the conclusion to be false. Argument B is an **inductive argument**. The conclusion is certainly supported by the premises, but it does not merely draw out the information contained in them. The conclusion applies not just to the particular victims in the sample, but to all cases of the disease: The scientist is inferring that the strawberries (or food containing the same chemical elements) causes the disease in people she has not examined. Logicians sometimes describe this feature of induction by saying that it is *ampliative*: The conclusion amplifies—it goes beyond—what the premises state. As a result, the truth of the premises does *not* guarantee the truth of the conclusion; there is some possibility, however small, that the conclusion is false.

Both deductive and inductive arguments have certain common forms. We will explore these forms in detail in Part 2 (Deductive Logic) and Part 3 (Inductive Logic). As a preview, let us consider a few of the more common ones.

Some deductive arguments have compound premises with more than one component proposition. Among the most common are those with premises of the form *if p then q* and *p or q*. Neither type of statement asserts the component propositions *p* and *q* as being true; what *is* asserted is a relationship between *p* and *q*. But in combination with other premises, such statements allow us to make deductive arguments. In the following examples, beginning with the detective's argument, notice how the premises, if true, would guarantee the truth of the conclusion. (Instead of diagrams, we use the standard form for deductive arguments: The propositions are put on separate lines, with an underscore separating premises from conclusion.)

A. If robbery was the motive, then the victim's money would have been taken.
   The victim's money was not taken.
   Therefore, robbery was not the motive.

C. If robbery was the motive, then the victim's money would have been taken.
   If the victim's money was taken, then the bills will have the perpetrator's fingerprints.
   Therefore, if robbery was the motive, then the bills will have the perpetrator's fingerprints.

D. The motive for the murder was either robbery or vengeance.
   The motive was not robbery.
   Therefore, the motive was vengeance.

In each of these examples, the conclusion follows because of the repetition of the component propositions (*p* and *q*). Another type of deductive argument involves noncompound statements, and the conclusion follows because of the repetition of subject and predicate *terms* in the statements. Here are a few examples of this type, beginning with an inference we discussed previously.

E. All water flows downhill.
   All rivers in Taiwan are water.
   Therefore, all rivers in Taiwan flow downhill.

F. Any driver convicted of three moving violations will have his or her license suspended.
   Roxanne has been convicted of three moving violations.
   Therefore, Roxanne will have her license suspended.

In all these forms of deductive argument, the conclusion simply makes explicit the information contained in premises, so there is no gap between premises and conclusion. If the premises are true, the conclusion *must* be true as well. If you accept the premises but deny the conclusion, you contradict yourself. This property is known as **validity**. A deductive argument is valid when it is impossible for the premises to be true and the conclusion false. If an argument is intended as deductive but does not meet this criterion, it is invalid. Suppose, for example, that our detective found that money *was* taken from the victim's wallet and then reasoned as follows:

G. If robbery was the motive, then the victim's money would have been taken.
   The victim's money was taken.
   Therefore, robbery was the motive.

This argument is somewhat similar in form to argument A, so we would classify it as deductive, but it is invalid because the premises could be true and the conclusion false. For example, the murderer might have killed for revenge but taken the money to cover his tracks. The following deductive arguments are likewise invalid:

H. The woman just appointed CEO at Megacorp is either very smart or very ambitious.
   <u>She is very ambitious.</u>
   Therefore she is not very smart.

I. All voters are citizens.
   <u>Some citizens are not taxpayers.</u>
   Therefore, some taxpayers are not voters.

A deductive argument is either valid or invalid. Validity does not come in degrees. It is either possible or impossible for the premises to be true and the conclusion false. In the first case the argument is invalid, period; in the second it is valid.

Inductive arguments also have various common forms. One common form is generalization: drawing a general conclusion about a class of things by observing a sample of the class. Inductive generalizations are pervasive in science as well as everyday common knowledge. For example, you know that fire burns, not because you have observed every case of fire burning, worldwide, but because you have observed enough cases to draw the general conclusion. Argument B given earlier is another example. From information about a sample of people who got sick after eating the strawberries, the scientist infers that any person who eats strawberries with the same chemical composition would get the disease.

Another kind of inductive argument moves in the opposite direction, drawing a conclusion about some particular thing or event from a generalization about that type of thing or event. For example:

J. Cold fronts usually bring rain.
   <u>A cold front is moving in.</u>
   Therefore, it will rain tomorrow.

If the first premise stated that *all* cold fronts bring rain, this would be a deductive argument. But the premise says only that cold fronts *usually* bring rain, not that they always do, so it is possible for the conclusion to be false even if the premises are true. The argument provides reasonably good support for the conclusion, depending on exactly what percentage of cold fronts bring rain, but the truth of the premises would not guarantee the truth of the conclusion.

Yet another common form of induction is called argument by analogy. We draw a conclusion about one thing because of its similarity to something else that we know more about. Here's an example from pop music:

K. Lady Gaga is like Madonna in a lot of ways. She's edgy and iconoclastic, she keeps reinventing her persona, she's a talented performer and has a huge talent for self-promotion. Madonna has had a long and successful career, so Lady Gaga probably will, too.

The premises assert several points of similarity between the two singers. Together with the further premise that Madonna had a successful career, the similarities provide evidence for Lady Gaga's future success, though the premises do not guarantee the truth of that conclusion. We use argument by analogy frequently in thinking about people, as in the example; in using history to predict future political and economic outcomes; and in problem-solving, when we compare the problem at hand to other problems that we know how to solve.

These forms of arguments illustrate the ampliative nature of induction. Even in a good inductive argument, the conclusion goes beyond the information given in the premises. The distinction between valid and invalid is therefore not applicable. Instead, we evaluate such arguments in terms of their **strength**. Unlike the qualitative distinction between valid and invalid deductive arguments, inductive strength comes in degrees. When the scientist in argument B infers that the strawberries caused the disease, the argument has some strength. But the victims might have had something else in common, something that the scientist has not yet checked out. Or the victims might have reacted to the strawberries for diverse, idiosyncratic reasons that would not apply to people in general. Thus the argument could be made stronger by examining more cases of the disease, by testing other possible factors and ruling them out, and by finding the underlying mechanism by which something in the strawberries affects the body. For induction, in other words, there is a continuum from relatively weak support to very strong support. As we move along the continuum by gathering more evidence, we increase the likelihood that the conclusion is true.

As we noted in the previous section, we evaluate arguments by two basic standards: 1. Are the premises true? 2. How well do the premises support the conclusion?
In logic, we are mainly concerned with the second standard. To meet that standard, a deductive argument must be *valid*; an inductive argument must be *strong*. We also have special terms for arguments that meet both standards. If a deductive argument is valid and its premises are true, we say that the argument is **sound**. If an inductive argument is strong and its premises are true, we say that it is **cogent**. In other words:

Deduction: Sound = Valid + True premises

Induction: Cogent = Strong + True premises

Induction and deduction normally work together. Deductive arguments typically apply general knowledge that we have already acquired to new instances. But we first had to acquire that general knowledge by inductive reasoning. Each individual step in an argument will be either inductive or deductive, but the argument as a whole—the case for believing the conclusion is true—normally requires that the premises of any deductive step be supported by induction. In argument A, the detective's deductive conclusion rests on the premise that if robbery had been the motive, then something would have been taken from the victim's wallet. How does the detective know this? He learned it by observing human nature in general and the behavior of criminals in particular. On the basis of these observations, he drew the inductive generalization that people normally carry money in wallets, that thieves know this, and that robbery is a common motive for murder but not the only one.

As another example, consider an argument we diagrammed earlier: that extreme sarcasm is a form of unprovoked hostility, which results from feelings of inadequacy. This argument would best be construed as deductive. To make its deductive character clear, we might formulate it as follows:

SUMMARY **Induction and Deduction**

1. A deductive argument attempts to show that its conclusion makes explicit the information implicit in the premises, so that the conclusion must be true if the premises are.

2. A deductive argument is either valid or invalid. If it is valid, then it is impossible for all of its premises to be true and its conclusion to be false. Otherwise it is invalid. If it is valid and all of its premises are true, the argument is sound.

3. An inductive argument attempts to show that the conclusion is supported by the

premises even though the conclusion amplifies—it goes beyond—what the premises state.

4. Inductive arguments have degrees of strength, and a given argument can be strengthened or weakened through additional evidence. If the argument is strong and all of its premises are true, it is cogent.

Deduction: Sound = Valid + True premises

Induction: Cogent = Strong + True premises

All extremely sarcastic people are acting from unprovoked hostility.
All people who act from unprovoked hostility feel inadequate.
Therefore, all extremely sarcastic people feel inadequate.

In this argument as stated, the conclusion necessarily follows from the premises. Now suppose that we want to provide evidence for the second premise. We might consider the people we know who tend to act from hostility. If they all tend to feel inadequate, then we have some inductive evidence for the generalization about human psychology. We could strengthen the evidence by doing psychological experiments that use larger samples of people and objective measures for hostility and inadequacy. But the evidence would still be inductive because it involves a generalization from the sample of people in the experiment to the class of all humans.

Conversely, inductive arguments often involve deductive steps, at least implicitly. In argument B given earlier, the scientist looking for a common factor among the victims of the disease probably did not ask whether they all rooted for the same baseball team. Why not? Because she knows that only biochemical processes in the body cause disease; being a Yankees fan is not a biochemical process, so it could not cause the disease. That's a deductive inference.

EXERCISE 4.4

Determine whether each of the following arguments is inductive or deductive. If it is deductive, is it valid or invalid?

✳ 1. No Greek philosopher taught in a university, but some Greek philosophers were great thinkers.

Therefore, some great thinkers have not taught in a university.

2. Barbara is a liberal. She's a strong advocate of environmentalism, and most environmentalists are liberals.

3. All Romans are Italians; all Italians are Europeans; so Romans are Europeans.

✳ 4. Two flowers of the same cultivar were planted in adjacent plots. The first was fertilized with Miracle-Gro and it flourished; the second was not and it didn't. Therefore, Miracle-Gro stimulates plant growth.

5. If a triangle has angles of 30° and 60°, then its third angle is 90°. If an angle in a triangle is 90°, then it is a right triangle. So if a triangle has angles of 30° and 60°, then it is a right triangle.

6. Thanks to St. Patrick, no snake lives in Ireland. Since snakes are reptiles, that means no reptiles live in Ireland.

✳ 7. Xavier is a student at Orchard College, where 80% of students complete their undergraduate degree within 5 years. So Xavier has a good chance of getting his degree.

8. No machine is capable of perpetual motion, because every machine is subject to friction, and nothing that is subject to friction is capable of perpetual motion.

9. Either Jesus was telling the truth when he said he was the son of God or he was insane. But he wasn't insane, so he was actually the son of God.

✳ 10. The plan to build a new factory does not have a provision for construction delays, so its cost estimates are likely to be too low. Experienced contractors know that most building projects on this scale do have delays, which add to the expense of the project.

11. If the tectonic plates under the Atlantic Ocean are moving apart, there will be volcanic activity in Iceland—and there is volcanic activity there. So the tectonic plates are separating.

12. Everything we know about was created at a certain point in time, as a result of causes that existed before. So the universe itself must have been created by a being that existed before the universe.

✳ 13. The fossil record shows that certain dinosaurs, like birds, were capable of winged flight. Although the birds that exist today are different in many ways, they do share a number of anatomical features with that class of dinosaurs, including scales, hollow bones, expanded pneumatic sinuses in the skull, 3-fingered opposable hands, and 4-toed feet. We can conclude that birds evolved from those dinosaurs.

14. Either health care is a right or it is something that individuals have to earn. Since health care is something that has to be earned, it isn't a right.

15. The economic crisis of 2008-2009 is like the panic of 1873 in that it was caused by a bubble in real estate, after which banks severely tightened their lending practices, and both consumers and businesses were hobbled by the inability to get loans. The recession of the 1870s lasted more than 3 years, so today's economy will likely take that long to recover.

4.5 Implicit Premises

People rarely express in all words *all* the premises they are using in an argument. Most arguments contain some premises that are assumed but not stated. We refer to these as **implicit premises** to distinguish them from the explicit premises that are actually stated. Suppose we are planning a hiking trip, and I tell you that Sally can't come because she has a broken leg. My argument clearly assumes that people with broken legs can't go hiking, but I didn't state that premise, because it was too obvious. Everyday speech would be horribly stilted and tedious if we stated all our premises explicitly. It makes sense to state only the new, the substantive, the controversial premises of an argument.

But sometimes it is the substantive and controversial premise that goes unspoken, making an argument seem more plausible than it really is. Suppose I argue that since bungee-jumping is dangerous, there ought to be a law against it. This argument relies on the implicit premise that the government should ban things that are dangerous. This is not an assumption that everyone would accept; it relies on a particular view about the proper role of government, and really should be supported logically before one uses it to derive a further conclusion.

So when we analyze an argument, it is important to identify the implicit premises. They can then be labeled—using letters instead of numbers to distinguish them from explicit premises—and included in the diagram. The argument about Sally, for example, would be diagrammed as follows:

1. Sally has a broken leg.
a. No person with a broken leg can go hiking.
2. Sally can't go hiking.

$$\frac{1 + a}{}$$
$$\downarrow$$
$$2$$

Notice that 1 and *a* are dependent premises. This will always be the case when we fill in implicit premises. Our justification for reading an implicit premise into an argument is that the assumption is necessary in order to link a stated premise with the conclusion. By the very nature of the case, the implicit premise has to work together with some explicit premise. If we supply a new *independent* premise, we are adding a new line of argument and not merely analyzing the argument at hand. Notice, too, that the argument is now a deductive one. If premises 1 and *a* are both true, then the conclusion must be true as well. This will not always be the case when we fill in implicit premises, however, for reasons that we will discuss in a moment.

In the argument above, it was easy to identify the implicit premise. It is not always so easy, and it will be helpful to have certain rules to follow. To understand these rules, we have to keep in mind what our goal is. Identifying implicit premises is a means to the goal of analyzing an argument. The point of argument analysis is to understand what the premises of an argument are and how they relate to the conclusion. In the case of implicit premises, however, we also need to consider what assumption would be necessary for the argument to provide good support for the conclusion. Identifying implicit premises is also a means, therefore, to the goal of evaluating an argument. In light of these goals, there are two basic rules we should follow:

1. The premise we supply should narrow the logical gap between the stated premise and the conclusion, and
2. The premise we supply should not commit us to more than is necessary.

Let's see how these rules apply to a specific case. Suppose you are taking French, and you learn that some of your classmates are failing; you infer they do not enjoy the subject. In diagram form:

> 1. Some students are failing French.
>
> ↓
>
> 2. Those students are not enjoying French.

What is the implicit premise in your argument? Consider the following candidates:

a. French is a Romance language.
b. Paris is beautiful in the springtime.
c. People never enjoy something that they find difficult.
d. Students never enjoy subjects in which they are failing.

Using rule 1, we can eliminate candidates *a* and *b*, both of which are irrelevant to the conclusion. Neither of them will help close the gap in the argument as stated. Rule 2 will help us choose between the remaining candidates. Both *c* and *d* would close the gap in the argument. Indeed, each of them would eliminate the gap entirely by making the argument deductive. But notice that *c* is a much more sweeping generalization than *d*; *c* applies to all people and all activities, whereas *d* applies only to students and the subjects they are studying. Since premise *d* serves our purpose without committing us to as much as *c* would, it is the one we should choose.

Sometimes we have to supply more than one premise in order to make sense of an argument. Consider the earlier example about gun control:

> 1. Restricting ownership of handguns will reduce crime.
>
> ↓
>
> 2. The government should restrict ownership of handguns.

To connect the premise with the conclusion, we need to say something about the government's responsibility for reducing crime. Is the assumption that the government should take every means possible to reduce crime? No. That assumption would commit us to far more than is necessary. It would imply that the government should put troops in armored cars on every street corner, force people to ask permission before they leave their homes, and engage in all manner of other police-state tactics. For the argument to have any plausibility, the real assumption must be that the government should take any measures that will reduce crime without unduly sacrificing other values (such as liberty). But now we must introduce an additional implicit premise to the effect that restricting handgun ownership will not unduly sacrifice other values. The complete argument now goes like this:

1. Restricting handgun ownership will reduce crime.

a. The government should take any measures that will reduce crime without unduly sacrificing other values.

STRATEGY Finding Implicit Premises

To identify the implicit premise in an argument, look for a premise that:

1. Closes the logical gap between the stated premises and the conclusion.

2. Does not commit the speaker to more than is necessary.

---

b. Restricting handgun ownership will not unduly sacrifice other values.

2. The government should restrict handgun ownership.

In diagram form, it looks like this:

$$1 + a + b$$

$$2$$

In all the examples we have discussed so far, we supplied an implicit premise that made the argument deductive. Doing so has the advantage of eliminating any gap between premises and conclusion, so that we can then focus our attention exclusively on whether the premises are true. In some cases, however, it is more reasonable to supply a premise that makes the argument inductive. Consider an example from the previous section: *It will probably rain tomorrow, because a cold front is moving in and cold fronts usually bring rain.* Suppose that second premise had been left unstated. In that case, we would need to choose between two possible implicit premises:

a. Cold fronts usually bring rain.
b. Cold fronts always bring rain.

Premise *a* is true, and it gives us an inductive argument that is pretty strong. Premise *b* gives us a deductive argument, but only at the cost of a premise that is false. The trade-off isn't worth it.

EXERCISE 4.5

Identify the implicit premise(s) in each of the following arguments.

✳ 1. Tom is a very successful salesman, so he must be an outgoing person.
  2. The doorbell just rang. Someone must be at the door.

  3. Cheating is dishonest and therefore wrong.
✳ 4. This sample of copper melted at 1063°C in the laboratory.

Therefore, all copper has a melting point of 1063°C.

5. Politicians who are convicted of crimes should not be returned to office, so Congressman Jones should not be re-elected.

6. The arresting officer had not read Johnson his Miranda rights, so the judge had to let him go, even though he confessed to the Pine Street burglary.

* 7. The traditional wax record, played on top-of-the-line equipment, can reproduce the spatial features of music such as the positions of the instruments in an orchestra. So in that respect it is superior to most compact disc recordings.

8. The government should continue to deregulate the telecommunications industry, because we need an industry that can act quickly and flexibly to exploit the new communications technology.

9. The plays attributed to Shakespeare exhibit a profound intelligence, but Shakespeare himself never went to college, and therefore could not have been very intelligent. So someone else wrote his plays.

* 10. When testing the effects of a new drug, it's important to isolate the physical effects of the drug from the psychosomatic effects of taking it. Therefore, one must use a placebo.

4.6 Distilling Arguments

In order to analyze the structure of an argument, we have to identify its premises and conclusion. So far, we have done this simply by going through the statement of the argument and numbering the propositions. But this technique works only for short arguments and only when the argument is presented in a fairly condensed and straightforward way. It works well for newspaper editorials and letters to the editor, and for paragraphs in which an author summarizes his argument. But some arguments are presented over the course of an entire essay or book. Such arguments are normally more complex than the ones we have considered up to this point, and they may not contain a summary statement. The reader may be left to extract the main argument from a mass of illustrations, historical background, explanatory material, dramatic narratives, digressions, and so on. In these cases, it would be tedious at best to number every statement in the essay or book, since we would have to ignore most of them. At the same time, an important premise or conclusion might not be stated explicitly—it might be present only as the central point or drift of a passage—and the numbering system would fail to include it.

Before we can analyze or evaluate such an argument, therefore, we have to *distill* it from the work as a whole. In effect, we have to write our own summary statement of the argument. (It is often a good idea to do this literally: Write out a paragraph summarizing the argument concisely, and then use the paragraph as the basis for diagramming.) This requires that we step back from the text of the argument and ask ourselves some questions. What is the author's basic purpose? What conclusion does he want us to accept? What evidence does he offer for that conclusion? Why does he think this evidence proves his case? As we answer these questions, we can write down the propositions—the premises and the conclusion—as we identify them and put them into a diagram of the argument.

When we restate an argument in our own words, the distinction between explicit and implicit premises becomes blurred. Instead of a clear distinction, we have a continuum, from propositions that the author clearly endorses, to those that are suggested but not stated in so many words, to those that are entirely implicit and unspoken. As a result, it may be very difficult to tell which propositions should be given numbers (as explicit statements) and which should be given letters (as implicit ones). The safest approach in this context is to number all of them, and then to apply to all of them the rules for identifying implicit premises. Because we are putting the argument in our own words, we have to be especially careful not to commit the author to more than is necessary for him to make his case.

Arguments of the kind that we need to distill are usually complex. They often have multiple steps from premises to intermediate conclusions to the final conclusion. And they often have multiple lines of argument converging on a single conclusion. The diagramming method gives us a way to analyze arguments of any degree of complexity. To *evaluate* arguments of this kind, we need to qualify a distinction we drew in discussing deduction and induction. A deductive argument is either valid or invalid; the premises either do or do not guarantee the truth of the conclusion. We evaluate inductive arguments, however, in terms of strength: the degree to which the premises support the conclusion. But now we are dealing with complex arguments that may include both deductive and inductive components, and the strength of the argument as a whole is a function of the strength of all its components. To evaluate such an argument as a whole, we will use the term "strength" in a broader sense, even if the argument includes deductive components.

Let's look at several examples that will illustrate the process of distillation. The first is an argument for population control, based on the idea that material resources, like a pie, have to be divided among people:

> There is only so much pie. We may be able to expand the pie, but at any point in time, the pie *is* finite. How big a piece each person gets depends in part on how many people there are. At least for the foreseeable future, the fewer of us there are, the more there will be for each. [Johnson C. Montgomery, "The Island of Plenty," *Newsweek*, December 23, 1974]

This is a brief argument, formulated rather clearly. It might seem we could analyze it by the technique set forth earlier in this chapter, numbering the propositions as stated and diagramming the structure. But there is a problem. The core of the argument is presented in the form of a metaphor, and we have to extract its literal meaning.

At one level, the metaphor is easy to interpret. The pie represents a society's material wealth: the sum total of goods and resources. And each person's share of that wealth is a piece of the pie. So we could go through the passage, translating into literal terms, and the result would be:

1. The world is finite.
2. At any point in time, there is a fixed amount of wealth.

3. At any point in time, the fewer people there are, the larger each person's share of the wealth will be.
4. For the foreseeable future, reducing the number of people will increase each person's share of wealth.

But our analysis is not yet complete. Notice that proposition 3 pertains to a given moment in time, whereas 4 refers to the foreseeable future. This creates a gap in the argument. If we have a fixed amount of wealth being divided up at a certain moment, it's a mathematical certainty that fewer people would mean larger shares for each. But if we are talking about the foreseeable future, we have to consider how wealth is produced. In particular, we have to consider whether reducing the number of people might reduce the total amount of wealth and, conversely, whether more people might produce more wealth. If each new person produces as much as he consumes, a 10% rise in population might bring a 10% rise in wealth; a 10% fall in population would bring an equivalent decline in wealth. Either way, each person's share would remain the same.

The metaphor of a pie serves to exclude this possibility. We picture the pie already baked, and of course its size does not depend on the number of people waiting at the table. For a full analysis of the argument, then, we must translate this dimension of the metaphor into literal terms. We must extract from it proposition 5: For the foreseeable future, the amount of wealth does not depend on the number of people. And 5 must be combined with 3 in order to bridge the gap between the present and the foreseeable future:

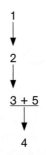

We have now distilled the author's argument. Our analysis identifies the premises implicit in the metaphor and their logical relationships. To evaluate the argument, we assess the strength of each step, on the principle that an argument with more than one step can be no stronger than its *weakest* step. As we saw in analyzing the argument, the steps from 1 to 2 and from 2 to 3 are very strong. Indeed, we could cast those steps in mathematical terms, which would make them deductive. In the initial diagram, however, the step from 3 to 4 is weak. That's why we supplemented it with premise 5 as an implicit premise. As we have seen, analysis and evaluation work hand-in-hand when we are dealing with implicit premises. With 5 in place, we now have a fairly strong argument overall. Notice, though, that the gain in strength does not come free. We paid for it by adding a premise whose truth is far from obvious. To back it up, the author would need to add much more evidence and deal with the objections of economists who reject it.

Let's turn now to a second example. This is a longer passage from the British writer G. K. Chesterton, and it will bring out other aspects of distilling an argument.

> It is not fashionable to say much nowadays of the advantages of the small community. . . . There is one advantage, however, in the small state, the city, or the village, which only the wilfully blind can overlook. The man who lives in a small community lives in a much larger world. He knows much more of the fierce varieties and uncompromising divergences of men. The reason is obvious. In a large community we can choose our companions. In a small community our companions are chosen for us. Thus in all extensive and highly civilized societies groups come into existence founded upon what is called sympathy, and shut out the real world more sharply than the gates of a monastery. There is nothing really narrow about the clan; the thing which is really narrow is the clique. The men of the clan live together because they all wear the same tartan or are all descended from the same sacred cow; but in their souls, by the divine luck of things, there will always be more colours than in any tartan. But the men of the clique live together because they have the same kind of soul, and their narrowness is a narrowness of spiritual coherence and contentment. . . . A big society exists in order to form cliques. A big society is a society for the promotion of narrowness. It is a machinery for the purpose of guarding the solitary and sensitive individual from all experience of the bitter and bracing human compromises. [G. K. Chesterton, *Heretics* (New York: John Lane Company, 1905)]

This is an arresting argument because it is paradoxical. Chesterton is saying that life in a small village is, in a sense, more cosmopolitan than life in a large city. And he flaunts the paradox by restating it in a variety of ways. This makes the passage colorful as a piece of writing, but somewhat redundant in logical terms, and we need to boil the argument down to its essence.

As usual, our first step is to identify the conclusion. Chesterton is defending the small community by describing a trait that he considers advantageous, and the passage is an effort to persuade us that small communities do have this trait. The point is put most concisely in the sentences: "The man who lives in a small community lives in a much larger world. He knows much more of the fierce varieties and uncompromising divergences of men." What are these "varieties" and "divergences"? Chesterton does not give us any detailed analysis, but it is clear that he is talking about psychological differences among people—differences in character, opinion, values, personality. If we use the term "personality" to include all these factors, we can formulate his conclusion as:

1. A person who lives in a small community acquires a deeper knowledge of the variety in human personality than does a person who lives in a large community.

The essential argument for this conclusion is presented in the next few sentences. In a large community we can select our companions—the people we interact with. And we tend to choose people who are similar to ourselves, so that our companions are likely to represent a single type of personality. In a small community, however, we have to interact with the people who happen to be our neighbors. Since we do not choose them, the laws of probability ("the divine luck of things") make it likely that they will represent a wider range of human personalities. We can formulate this argument as follows:

2. A person in a large community can select his companions.
3. People tend to select companions who are similar to themselves in personality.
4. A person in a large community will be exposed primarily to a single type of personality.
5. A person in a small community cannot select his companions.
6. Unchosen companions are likely to be diverse in personality.
7. A person in a small community will be exposed to many types of personality.

Propositions 4 and 7 will have to be combined to support the conclusion, because the conclusion makes a comparison between large and small communities. But notice that those propositions refer to the types of personalities with which we have actual experience, whereas the conclusion is a statement about our knowledge of human variety. There is a gap here, and it is bridged by an assumption that is implicit in the passage, though very close to the surface. This assumption is:

8. Knowledge of personalities depends on actual experience with them.

So the second step of the argument can be diagrammed:

$$\frac{4 + 7 + 8}{} \\ \downarrow \\ 1$$

Now that we have distilled the argument, drawing chiefly on the first half of the paragraph, we can see that the rest of the paragraph is repetition and embellishment. Chesterton restates the general argument in terms of the particular case of the clan, which allows him to contrast the clan with the clique, which allows him to talk about the narrowness of a big society. All of this adds color and drama, but it does not add anything substantive to the logical structure of the argument. To evaluate the strength of the argument, we would examine each of the component arguments and ask whether there is a significant gap between its premises and conclusion. In the inference from 2 and 3 to 4, for example, we assume that the premises are true: People in a large community can select their companions, and tend to select other people like themselves. But the conclusion, 4, is about the range of personalities people are *exposed to*, and that is a larger class. People who live in a city interact not only with their friends but with shopkeepers, co-workers, people attending the same concert or sports event, etc. Is it reasonable to think that these groups will be as homogeneous as one's friends? That is the kind of question we need to raise about each step in Chesterton's argument in order to arrive at an overall assessment of its strength.

These two examples illustrate the process of distilling an argument from a text in which it is not laid out for us step by step. The interpretation of such arguments is inherently more difficult, more subject to uncertainty and alternative readings, than was the case for the arguments treated earlier in this chapter. But once we have distilled an argument, the basic tools of analysis and evaluation are the same.

EXERCISE 4.6

Distill and diagram the following arguments—a scene from "The 'Gloria Scott'" by Arthur Conan Doyle, and an argument against online classroom courses adapted from *The Chronicle of Higher Education* (July 10, 2009).

✳ 1. "Come now, Mr. Holmes," said he, laughing good-humoredly. "I'm an excellent subject, if you can deduce anything from me."

"I fear there is not very much," I answered; "I might suggest that you have gone about in fear of some personal attack within the last twelvemonth."

The laugh faded from his lips, and he stared at me in great surprise.

"Well, that's true enough," said he, . . . "though I have no idea how you know it."

"You have a very handsome stick," I answered. "By the inscription I observed that you had not had it more than a year. But you have taken some pains to bore the head of it and pour melted lead into the hole so as to make it a formidable weapon. I argued that you would not take such precautions unless you had some danger to fear."

2. Students are more likely to cheat in online courses than in classroom courses. When students take an exam in an online course, there is no one to monitor them. With the Internet at their fingertips, students can look up answers online. Also, students might ask more advanced students to answer a particular question or take their exams for them—taking an introductory biology exam would be no trouble for someone 3 years into a biochemistry major. There are simply more ways to cheat in online courses, without being caught, than there are in classroom courses. And although they might not admit it, many students will cheat or help others cheat if they can do so without being caught.

Summary

Reasoning is the process of providing evidence for the truth or falsity of a proposition by relating it logically to other propositions. An argument is a set of propositions in which some (the premises) are asserted as support or evidence for another (the conclusion). Arguments are usually, though not always, signaled verbally by indicator words.

To analyze an argument is to identify its logical structure: the logical relationships between premises and conclusion. The various possible relationships can be diagrammed using arrows and plus signs. This technique allows us to distinguish between dependent and independent premises and to identify the individual steps in an argument.

To evaluate an argument, we must determine whether the premises are true, and we must assess the degree to which the premises, if true, support the conclusion. To determine the truth of the premises, we normally depend on our own experience or on information provided by other disciplines; logic is primarily concerned with methods of assessing the degree of support that the premises provide the conclusion. The primary method is to estimate the size of the gap between premises and conclusion. Another method is to find the assumed premise that would close the gap and to estimate the plausibility of that premise. In either case, the strength of an argument containing more than one component is a function of the strength of the components. An argument with more than one step is only as strong as its weakest step.

Arguments can be divided into two broad categories: deductive and inductive. A deductive argument attempts to make explicit the information implicit in the premises. In a valid argument, it would be impossible for the premises to be true and the conclusion false. In an inductive argument, the conclusion goes beyond what the premises state. Inductive arguments have degrees of strength, and a given argument can be strengthened or weakened through additional evidence.

Many arguments are not stated in brief, concise form, but are presented over the course of longer works such as an entire essay or book. In these cases, we need to distill the core argument and put it in our own words by identifying what conclusion the author is trying to prove and what premises are used to support it.

Key Terms

Conclusion—a proposition whose truth an argument seeks to establish.

Premise—a proposition used in an argument to provide evidence for another proposition (the conclusion).

Argument—a unit of reasoning in which one or more propositions (the premises) purport to provide evidence for the truth of another proposition (the conclusion).

Deductive argument—an argument that attempts to show that its conclusion makes explicit the information implicit in the premises, so that the conclusion must be true if the premises are.

Inductive argument—an argument that attempts to show that its conclusion is supported by the premises even though the conclusion amplifies—it goes beyond—what the premises state.

Validity—the property of a deductive argument in which it is impossible for the premises to be true and the conclusion false.

Strength—the degree to which the premises of an inductive argument support the conclusion.

Sound—the property of a deductive argument that is valid and whose premises are true.

Cogent—the property of an inductive argument that is strong and whose premises are true.

Implicit premise—a premise that is assumed by an argument but is not stated.

Additional Exercises

A. Diagram each of the following arguments.

✳ 1. You have to be very quiet to see deer in the woods. Deer tend to run when they hear noise.

2. Consciousness cannot be explained by the laws of physics and chemistry, so it is not a physical phenomenon.

3. I'm sure now that Richard and Lisa are in love. They both have that dreamy look, and besides, I just saw them talking together.

✳ 4. You shouldn't ask a friend to keep a secret from his or her spouse. Marriage is a more intimate relationship than friendship, and one should not ask someone to compromise a more intimate relationship for the sake of a less intimate one.

5. It is extremely dangerous to carry a can of gasoline in the trunk of your car. Gasoline is highly flammable, and it has tremendous explosive power. After all, when it is burned in your engine, a gallon of gas is capable of propelling 2 tons of metal for 20 miles or more.

6. We shouldn't give in to the demands of terrorists when they take hostages. That will only convince them that their tactic works and thus encourage them to use it again.

✳ 7. Without welfare, some poor people would have no means of support, so we must not eliminate welfare. The government has a duty to provide everyone with at least the essentials of life.

8. Welfare is a form of expropriation: It takes money out of one person's pocket and puts it into someone else's. Since the function of government is to protect individual rights, including property rights, it should not be running welfare programs.

9. Welfare programs are intended to help poor people, but existing programs are not helping: They encourage poor unmarried women to have babies, they discourage poor people from seeking jobs, and they create a habit of dependence. The welfare system should therefore be reformed.

✳ 10. People are allowed to vote when they are 18, and males have to register for the draft then. Since 18-year-olds are considered old enough to have these responsibilities, surely they are old enough to decide whether to have a drink. The drinking age should not be 21.

11. Religious cults typically demand that followers regard the leader's life as more valuable, and his judgment more reliable, than their own. A person with high self-esteem would not find either demand acceptable, so you won't find many people with high self-esteem as members of cults.

12. The case against playing baseball on artificial turf is unassailable. Fake turf makes the ball bounce unnaturally and intensifies high temperatures, often by as much as 20 or 30° during summer day games. Players tend to injure their legs more often and more seriously on artificial turf. And it has contributed to the decay of many traditional baseball skills, such as bunting and the positioning of fielders.

✳**B.** Evaluate each of the arguments in Exercise A. Consider whether alternative conclusions would be consistent with the premises as stated, and identify implicit premises in the arguments.

C. Identify the implicit premises in the arguments below.

✳ 1. "Robbery had not been the object of the murder, for nothing was taken." [Arthur Conan Doyle, *A Study in Scarlet*]

2. "A cat knows how to anticipate. If they didn't, they could never hunt birds or mice or other sportingly fleet prey." [Roger A. Caras, *A Cat is Watching*]

3. "You see, we don't believe that any of the investment information you can get in financial newsletters, magazines and newspapers will ever make you rich. That's because mass publications, by definition, are written for the masses. They've got to be somewhat trite and conventional." [promotional letter, Royal Society of Lichtenstein]

✳ 4. "No man is allowed to be a judge in his own cause, because his interest would certainly bias his judgment. . . ." [James Madison, *Federalist Papers,* No. 10]

5. "All languages are the product of the same instrument, namely, the human brain. It follows, then, that all languages are essentially the same in their deep structure, regardless of how varied the surface structure might be." [National Council of Teachers of English, "Students' Right to Their Own Language"]

6. "How often have I said to you that when you have eliminated the impossible, whatever remains, however improbable, must be the truth? We know that he did not come through the door, the window, or the chimney. We also know that he could not have been concealed in the room, as there is no concealment possible. Whence, then, did he come?"
"He came through the hole in the roof!"
"Of course he did. He must have done so."
[Arthur Conan Doyle, *The Sign of Four*]

✳ 7. "Since everyone has some understanding [of what life is all about]—some world view, no matter how limited or primitive or inaccurate—everyone has a religion." [M. Scott Peck, *The Road Less Traveled*]

D. Determine whether each of the following passages contains an argument. If it does, diagram the argument.

✳ 1. "For some years the suspicion had existed among the more inspired geneticists that viruses were a form of naked genes. If so, the best way to find out what a gene was and how it duplicated was to study the properties of viruses." [James Watson, *The Double Helix*]

2. "The more complicated the forms assumed by civilization, the more restricted the freedom of the individual must become." [Benito Mussolini, Grand Fascist Council Report, 1929]

3. "The balance of nature is preserved through the deaths of countless individual organisms which come into conflict with others. The lion lives at the expense of the antelope, zebra, and giraffe, whom it kills in order to sustain its own life. The snake lives at the expense of rodents, and if the snakes were eliminated the rodent population would explode until most of them died of starvation." [John Hospers, "Humanity vs. Nature," *Liberty*, March 1990]

✳ 4. ". . . there's something inherently repugnant about judging people by their skin color. Partly it's because it seems wrong to punish or reward people for something over which they have no control. Partly it's because race is almost never relevant to a person's suitability for anything. Partly it's that the very ethic of individualism demands that we treat people as individuals, not as members of a group." [Alex Kozinski, "Color and Caution," *New Republic*, February 1, 1993]

5. "We should frankly recognize that there is no side of a man's life which is unimportant to society, for whatever he is, does, or thinks may affect his own well-being, which is and ought to be a matter of common concern, and may also directly or indirectly affect the thought, action, and character of those with whom he comes in contact." [L. T. Hobhouse, *Liberalism*]

6. "There are three possible parts to a date, at least two of which must be offered:

entertainment, food, and affection. It is customary to begin a series of dates with a great deal of entertainment, a moderate amount of food, and the merest suggestion of affection. As the amount of affection increases, the entertainment can be reduced proportionally. When the affection is the entertainment, we no longer call it dating. Under no circumstances can the food be omitted." [Judith Martin, *Miss Manners' Guide to Excruciatingly Correct Behavior*]

✳ 7. "The 2010 oil spill from the Deepwater Horizon drill in the Gulf of Mexico released some 200,000 tons of methane into the waters of the Gulf. Within a few months, the methane had disappeared. A team of ocean-ographers concluded that it was consumed by methanotrophs, bacteria that ingest methane. The waters surrounding the drill head were depleted of oxygen, which the bac-teria burn when they consume methane. 'If the methane had just traveled someplace else and was hiding, we wouldn't see any reduc-tions in dissolved oxygen,' [oceanographer John] Kessler said. 'But if it were consumed by microbes, we should see some reductions in dissolved oxygen, which we did.'" [Brian Vastag, "Methane-gobbling bacteria were hard at work in gulf oil spill, scientists say," *Washington Post*, January 7, 2011]

8. "The existence of biological predispositions [toward crime] means that circumstances that activate criminal behavior in one person will not do so in another, that social forces cannot deter criminal behavior in 100 percent of a population, and that the distributions of crime within and across so-cieties may, to some extent, reflect underly-ing distributions of constitutional factors." [James Q. Wilson and Richard Herrnstein, *Crime and Human Nature*]

9. "Neither parole nor probation are justifi-able. . . . They are a demonstrable failure in reducing inmate recidivism. They under-mine the deterrent impact of the law on criminals, while demoralizing crime victims

with their outrageous leniency. Most important, they jeopardize public safety." [Robert James Bidinotto, *Criminal Justice: The Legal System vs. Individual Responsibility*, 86]

✳ 10. "I'm a sick man . . . a mean man. There's nothing attractive about me. I think there's something wrong with my liver. . . .
"I've been living like this for a long time, twenty years or so. I'm forty now. I used to be in government service, but I'm not any more. I was a nasty official. I was rude and enjoyed being rude. . . .
"When petitioners came up to my desk for information, I snarled at them and felt indescribably happy whenever I managed to make one of them feel miserable." [Fyodor Dostoyevsky, *Notes from Underground*]

11. "To the outsider, the chief reason [for believing that Morelly was the author of *Le Code de la Nature*] seems to be that Le Code contains . . . somewhat fulsome praise of a bad allegorical political poem, La Basiliade, published two years earlier; and as it seems to be agreed that no one but the author of La Basiliade could possibly praise La Basiliade, it follows that the author of Le Code was the author of La Basiliade, who was Morelly." [Alexander Gray, *The Socialist Tradition*]

12. "To a plant, breathing involves a built-in cost-benefit analysis. The wider the gas-exchanging pores on the leaf surface are open, the greater the supply of carbon di-oxide for photosynthesis. But wide-open pores also allow evaporation of water, so the plant must balance the benefits of increased carbon dioxide against the cost of water loss." [J. A. Miller, "Plant 'Sight' from Pores and Pumps," *Science News*, November 30, 1985]

✳ 13. "A foolish consistency is the hobgoblin of little minds, adored by little statesmen and philosophers and divines. With consistency a great soul has simply nothing to do. He may as well concern himself with his shadow on the wall. Speak what you think now in hard words and to-morrow speak what tomorrow thinks in hard words again, though it contradict every thing you said to-day." [Ralph Waldo Emerson, "Self-Reliance"]

14. "This month is the 600th anniversary of the famous Boar's Head Dinner at Queen's College, Oxford.

"It was around this time of year in 1395 that a student wandering in Shotover Forest was attacked by a wild boar.

"He managed to strangle the beast with the volume of Aristotle he had been reading, and it was brought back to the college with the book still in its mouth.

"In commemoration, Queen's College has held a Boar's Head dinner in November ever since.

"By tradition, the boar is always served with something in its mouth, like a lemon or an apple (but not a book)." [Associated Press, November 1995]

15. "There are good reasons to believe that polyphony existed in Europe long before it was first unmistakably described. It was probably used chiefly in nonliturgical sacred music; it may have been employed also in folk music, and probably consisted of melodic doubling at the third, fourth, or fifth." [Donald Jay Grout, *A History of Western Music*]

*16. "[M]ost of the basic elements of structure and function of all organisms, from bacteria to humans, are remarkably similar—in some cases, identical. We all use the same sorts of proteins made up of an identical set of twenty amino acids; we all use the same nucleic acids made up of the same four bases as genetic material. We all have similar machinery for oxidizing our food and producing our energy and for doing our cellular work, including the building of ourselves. We store, replicate, and use genetic information in the same way. The genetic code, the cipher for translating inherited information into living

substance, is the same in all of us. These truths are pillars of support for evolution's first premise—that we all had a common origin. [Mahlon Hoagland, *Toward the Habit of Truth: A Life in Science*]

17. "A tree trunk does not grow from the bottom up, as some people think, lifting its branches as it grows. A tree develops vertically only at the top while increasing its girth below to support the weight of its growing crown; the points at which the branches spring from the trunk stay at the same levels. You can see this fact demonstrated if you drive along a country road where pastures are fenced with barbed wire nailed to trees. The fencing may have been nailed up so long ago that the trunks now envelop the wire, but it is still at the height at which it was originally placed, as you can verify from the height of wires on nearby fence posts." [James Underwood Crockett, *Trees*]

18. "Let me now re-emphasize . . . the extreme looseness of the structure of all objects. . . . [T]here is no perceptible object that does not consist of a mixture of matter and vacuity. In the first place, we find that in caves the rocky roofs exude moisture and drip with trickling drops. Similarly in our own bodies sweat oozes from every surface; hairs grow on the chin and on every limb and member; food is suffused through every vein, building and sustaining the most outlying parts even to the nails. . . . The stone partitions of houses are pervious to voices and to scent and cold and heat of fire, which penetrates also through hard iron." [Lucretius, *The Nature of the Universe*, translated by Ronald Latham]

*19. The title of Master Bladesmith is awarded by the American Bladesmith Society. To earn the title, according to an article in the *New Yorker* (2008), a knife-maker must create a knife that can "accomplish four tasks, in this order: cut through an inch-thick piece of Manila rope in a single swipe; chop through a two-by-four, twice; place the blade on his forearm and shave a swath of arm hair; and finally, lock the knife in a vise and permanently bend it ninety degrees." [Todd Oppenheimer, "Sharper," *New Yorker*, November 24, 2008]

20. "A struggle for existence inevitably follows from the high rate at which all organic beings tend to increase. Every being, which during its natural lifetime produces several eggs or seeds, must suffer destruction during some period of its life, and during some season or occasional year, otherwise, on the principle of geometrical increase, its numbers would quickly become so inordinately great that no country could support the product. Hence, as more individuals are produced than can possibly survive, there must in every case be a struggle for existence, either one individual with another of the same species, or with the individuals of distinct species, or with the physical conditions of life." [Charles Darwin, *The Origin of Species*]

E. For each of the following propositions, first, construct an argument to support it, and then construct an argument against it. Diagram your arguments, and make them as strong as possible (even if that means using premises you don't actually agree with).

1. The athletes at a college or university should have to meet the same academic standards as other students.
2. The government should pay tuition for anyone who wants a college education.
3. Anyone caught cheating on a final exam should be expelled from school.
4. Public high-school officials should not have the right to search students' lockers for drugs.
5. Before the age of 21, everyone should have to spend a year in mandatory national service, working in the military or in domestic government programs.

F. Use each of the following propositions as a premise in an argument. You may look for a conclusion that will follow from the proposition directly, or you may combine the proposition with other premises to support some conclusion (the latter approach is recommended). Make your argument as strong as possible, and diagram it as you go. When you are finished, write a paragraph expressing the argument as clearly and persuasively as you can.

1. Los Angeles is located near a fault line.
2. It's a warm and sunny day.
3. Fraud is a form of theft.
4. People with radically different standards of personal hygiene rarely find each other attractive.
5. Rock stars make much more money than philosophy professors.
6. Adults are responsible for their actions.
7. Men and women have the same basic capacities for productive work in every field.
8. No one is going to live forever.
9. War is the most destructive of human activities.
10. Freedom is worth risking one's life for.

CHAPTER 5

Fallacies

In the broadest sense of the term, a **fallacy** is any error in reasoning. But the term is normally restricted to certain patterns of errors that occur with some frequency, usually because the reasoning involved has a certain surface plausibility. To the unwary, the premises of a fallacious argument seem relevant to the conclusion, even though they are not; or the argument seems to have more strength than it actually does. This is why fallacies are committed with some frequency.

We are going to study fallacies now for two reasons. The first is to help you avoid them in your own thinking and identify them when they are used

against you in debate. Forewarned is forearmed. The second reason is that understanding why these patterns of argument are fallacious will help us understand the nature of good reasoning. Just as doctors increase their understanding of health by studying diseases, we can gain clarity about good arguments by seeing what is wrong with bad ones.

The fallacies discussed in this chapter should not be regarded as a complete list. The varieties of bad reasoning are too numerous to catalog here. For one thing, as we saw in the previous chapter, there are invalid forms of deductive argument. For example:

If robbery was the motive, then the victim's money would have been taken.	If p, then q
The victim's money was taken.	q
Therefore, robbery was the motive.	Therefore, p

The abstract form of this argument is indicated on the right, and any argument with the same form is invalid. Such errors are called formal fallacies, and we will examine them when we study deduction. This chapter is concerned with informal fallacies, in which the error is not simply a matter of the argument's form. Even so, I have included only those informal fallacies that are most common in everyday discussion and that illustrate something about the nature of good reasoning. Many of these fallacies were identified and labeled by medieval logicians and thus have Latin names, but we will use the English names for most of them.

I have grouped the fallacies into four categories based on their similarities to and differences from each other.

You should be aware, however, that this is not a standard, widely accepted classification. In fact, there is no standard classification. Logicians debate about the best way to classify these errors, and each textbook has its own system. This may seem surprising. Of all people, you might think, logicians would have worked out a proper system of classification by now. The explanation is partly that bad reasoning is often bad in more than one way, and even experts can disagree about which specific errors are the most important. In addition, fallacies differ along two essential dimensions: They involve an error of reasoning and they have the capacity to deceive us. While the first dimension is a matter of logic, the second is a matter of psychology. Just as optical illusions occur because of the way our visual system works, psychologists have found that we are more vulnerable to certain errors than to others because of the way our minds work. But the logical and psychological dimensions do not always match up exactly.

My classification of fallacies is the one that I have found most natural and most useful for students in learning about fallacies. In the end, though, the important thing is to understand the fallacies themselves.

5.1 Subjectivist Fallacies

The cardinal virtue in reasoning is objectivity: a commitment to thinking in accordance with the facts and interpreting them logically. The fallacies we'll examine in this section involve the violation of objectivity in one way or another.

5.1A Subjectivism

The first and most straightforward violation of objectivity is the fallacy of **subjectivism**. This fallacy is committed whenever we hold that something is true merely because we *believe* or *want* it to be true. Thus, if *p* is the proposition in question, subjectivism has the form:

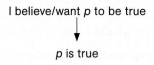

In an argument of this sort, a subjective state—the mere fact that we have a belief or desire—is being used as evidence for the truth of a proposition. But the thoughts and feelings that pass through our minds may or may not correspond to reality. That's why we need a logical method of *discovering* whether they are true; that's why objectivity is a virtue in the first place.

The fact that someone prefaces a statement with the words "I think" or "I feel" does not necessarily imply subjectivism. This is a conventional way of expressing a view, and the person may go on to offer a perfectly objective argument. Nor are statements *about* our thoughts and feelings necessarily subjective. Suppose I am trying to tell whether the emotion I am feeling is resentment or justifiable anger. My thought process may be either objective or subjective: objective if I am open to the evidence, subjective if I decide that it is justifiable anger merely because I can't bear to think of myself as resentful. In other words, subjectivism is not an issue of what a statement or conclusion is about; it's an issue of the kind of evidence one uses to support a conclusion. The fallacy is committed only when someone uses the mere fact that he believes or feels something as a reason for thinking it to be true.

It is unlikely that you will ever hear someone commit the fallacy of subjectivism in the pure form diagrammed earlier. As with most fallacies, the pure, textbook cases are too obviously fallacious for anyone to fall for them. In real life, the fallacies take more subtle and disguised forms. Here are some examples:

1. *"I'll think about that tomorrow."* This is Scarlett O'Hara's line from *Gone with the Wind*. It is her way of dealing with unpleasant facts. The point, of course, is that tomorrow never comes: She is simply putting the facts out of mind, on the implicit assumption that they will then cease to exist. Subjectivism is not only a way of *adopting* conclusions on subjective grounds, but also—and probably more often—a way of *evading* them. Some people have perfected the skill of ignoring what they don't want to see, and most of us indulge this habit occasionally. If the habit were put into words, it would take the form "I don't want to accept *p*, therefore *p* isn't true." That's subjectivism.

2. *"I was just brought up to believe in X."* This statement typically occurs when people encounter challenges to their basic convictions. In a discussion of premarital sex, for example, someone might respond to arguments condoning this practice by saying "Well, I was just taught to believe it's wrong." The fact that one was brought up to believe something may explain how one came to have that belief, but it doesn't explain why one *ought* to believe it; it does not provide any reason for thinking that the belief is true. It simply reinforces the claim that one has that belief. This is not to say that you are irrational if you refuse to abandon a long-held belief just because you've heard an argument against it that you can't answer on the spot. Many of our beliefs—especially on fundamental issues of religion, ethics, and politics—are rooted in a lifetime of experience and reflection. We can't always put that experience and reflection into words right away, and we shouldn't throw out a well-rooted belief on the basis of a single counterargument. But we shouldn't ignore the counterargument, either. To dismiss it on the grounds that it's easier and less threatening not to reexamine our convictions is a type of subjectivism.

3. *"That may be true for you, but it isn't true for me."* Suppose two people are discussing man's biological origins. Pat argues that our species arose by evolution; Mike, a creationist, says, "Well, that may be true for you, but it's not for me." What does Mike mean when he says that something is (or is not) true for him? Perhaps he means simply that he does (or does not) believe it. In that case, the statement means: You may believe in evolution, but I don't. There's no fallacy here, just the recognition that a disagreement exists, without any claim as to which side is right. But if this is what he means, he should say so directly and not introduce the concept of truth. The point of introducing the concept of truth is usually to give an objective gloss to a belief without having to provide evidence for it; or to paper over a disagreement

by suggesting that both sides are legitimate, even though they contradict each other and cannot both be true. In either case, the concept of something as "true for me" contains an element of subjectivism: It attributes objective status to a proposition merely because one happens to believe it. At the very least, the phrase ought to be a warning flag to keep an eye out for the fallacy.

5.1B Appeal to Majority

People have criticized the Roman Catholic Church for opposing birth-control measures even though many Catholics do not believe birth control is wrong. This criticism is an appeal to majority belief, which is a fallacy for essentially the same reason that subjectivism is. The argument has the form:

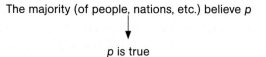

The majority (of people, nations, etc.) believe *p*

p is true

In this case, the subjective state of large numbers of people, not just a single person, is being used as evidence for the truth of a proposition. But the argument is still subjectivistic—and still fallacious. At various times, majorities have believed that the earth is flat, that bathing is unsanitary, and that certain women should be burned as witches.

The fallacy of **appeal to majority** is committed whenever someone takes a proposition to be true merely because large numbers of people believe it (regardless of whether those people actually constitute a majority). This fallacy probably occurs more often in political debate than in any other area. One version is the argument from tradition—as in "I oppose socialized medicine because it is inconsistent with our tradition of private medical practice." To say that a principle or policy is traditional is merely to say that it was widely accepted by our predecessors. The mere fact that they accepted it does not prove it correct. Another version of the fallacy might be called the "wave of the future" argument—as in "Every other progressive nation has already adopted a program of government-provided health care; the United States likewise should abandon its outmoded system of private medicine." To say that some principle or policy is the wave of the future is merely to say that many people or countries have already accepted it; so an appeal to their preferences in support of that principle or policy is, once again, an appeal to majority. The only difference between these opposing arguments is that they appeal to *different* majorities.

The fact that such an appeal is fallacious doesn't mean we should ignore majority opinion. Objectivity requires a willingness to consider the views of others. If large numbers of people have accepted a principle or policy, it may well be because the principle is true, the policy a good one. The possibility is certainly worth exploring. When we explore it, however, we should look for objective evidence; mere popularity doesn't count.

5.1C Appeal to Emotion

This fallacy is the attempt to persuade someone of a conclusion by an **appeal to emotion** instead of evidence. A person who commits this fallacy is hoping that his listeners will adopt a belief on the basis of a feeling he has instilled in them: outrage, hostility, fear, pity, guilt, or whatever. In effect, he is hoping that *they* will commit the fallacy of subjectivism. The appeal to emotion may be quite explicit. More often, however, the appeal is less direct. It may take the form of rhetorical language that is heavily laden with emotive connotations, as in propaganda and other sorts of incendiary political speech. The fallacy may also take the form of visual images that have a strong emotional impact. On television, for example, you can find examples of the fallacy not only in advertising but also in news and documentary programs that use images to sway the viewer.

Rhetoric and other emotive devices are not fallacious per se. If you have a logical argument to back up a conclusion, there is nothing wrong with stating it in such a way that your audience will endorse it with their feelings as well as their intellects. Good writers and speakers combine logic and rhetoric to produce exactly that effect. Even in advertising, the emotional pitch may be accompanied by a bona fide reason to buy the product. The fallacy occurs only when rhetoric *replaces* logic, only when the intent is to make an audience act on emotion *instead* of rational judgment.

How can we tell when this intent is present? A good test is to translate the argument into neutral language. If the translation leaves a large gap between premises and conclusion, then there is reason to suspect that the emotive language (or visual image, as the case may be) was intended to make a nonrational appeal to the audience. Let's apply this test to some examples.

In a famous speech, Martin Luther King, Jr., said:

> I have a dream that one day this nation will rise up and live out the true meaning of its creed: "We hold these truths to be self-evident—that all men are created equal." . . . I have a dream that one day even the state of Mississippi, a desert state sweltering with the heat of injustice and oppression, will be transformed into an oasis of freedom and justice. I have a dream that my four little children will one day live in a nation where they will not be judged by the color of their skin but by the content of their character. [Quoted from *Let the Trumpet Sound*, by Stephen B. Oates]

This passage certainly makes an appeal to the emotions. But it is not fallacious because we can distill a logical argument implicit in what King says. The argument starts by invoking the principle that all men are created equal. As stated in the Declaration of Independence, it is the political principle that all people have equal rights and should be equal before the law. But King is using the principle in a broader moral sense to mean that people should be judged by morally relevant traits, not by accidents of birth that have no moral relevance. Since skin color is not a morally relevant trait, but character is, King has a strong argument for his conclusion. In diagram form:

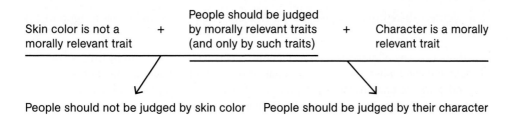

The emotional devices in King's speech—the repetition of "I have a dream," the description of Mississippi as a "desert state," the reference to his children—do not compete with or replace his argument. They simply make the meaning of the abstract principles more concrete and vivid.

By way of contrast, let's look at an argument that does commit the fallacy. The following example is taken from a political advertisement by a state employees' union:

> THE RETURN OF THE PRIVATEERS
> A long time ago, politicians hired private companies to do government work. They were mercenary ships, called privateers.
> *We know them as pirates.*
> Today, right here in New York State, politicians are trying to hoist the same old idea. This time around, calling it privatization.
> Let them get away with it, and privateers will be loose again.

Privatization is a policy adopted by some state governments of hiring private companies to collect garbage, maintain parks, and so forth, rather than having these jobs performed by state employees. Some people argue that private companies do the job more efficiently and thus save the government money. Some people argue the opposite. But the passage quoted above can hardly be considered an argument at all. It relies solely on the negative emotions associated with the privateers, who were private sea-captains authorized by their governments to attack and loot the merchant ships of their enemies. In neutral language, the argument would be

> Governments once contracted with private
> interests to loot the ships of other nations.
> ↓
> New York State should not contract with private
> companies to collect garbage, maintain parks, and so forth.

This is an extremely weak argument, as we can see by noting the implicit premise required to link the stated premise with the conclusion. The implicit premise is that what was wrong with the privateers was that they were private. But surely what was wrong was that they engaged in looting. And looting would have been wrong even if done by the governments with their own ships and sailors. The authors of the advertisement are obviously hoping that the emotionally laden image of pirates will keep us from raising such objections.

5.1D Appeal to Force (*Argumentum ad Baculum*)

The eighteenth-century essayist Joseph Addison once wrote (with his tongue in his cheek):

> There is a way of managing an Argument . . . which is made use of by States and Communities, when they draw up a hundred thousand Disputants on each side, and convince one another by dint of sword. A certain grand Monarch was so sensible of his strength in this way of Reasoning, that he writ upon his great Guns—Ratio Ultima Regum, The Logick of Kings. [*The Spectator*, No. 239, December 4, 1711]

Addison's remark is sarcastic: The use of force is *not* a type of reasoning, but is actually its antithesis. A threat is not an argument; a club (in Latin, *baculum*) is not a reason. If I "persuade" you of something by means of threats, I have not given you a reason for thinking the proposition is true; I have simply *scared* you into thinking, or at least into saying, it is true. In this respect, the appeal to force might be regarded as a form of the appeal to emotion.

An **appeal to force** may well involve direct coercion. When a government engages in censorship, for example, it uses force to prohibit the expression of certain ideas and to compel agreement with other ideas. The point of this control over verbal expression is to influence what people believe. But the fallacy need not involve actual *physical* force or violence. It is committed whenever *any* sort of threat is used, and nonphysical threats are probably more common than physical ones. When parents threaten to withdraw their support unless a child adopts their religious beliefs, when a teacher threatens a dissenting student with a lower grade, when someone "persuades" a friend by threatening the loss of affection—they are committing forms of this fallacy. As the examples illustrate, the fallacy is usually committed in the effort to breed conformity in belief, and society has many nonphysical means of intimidating people into accepting the conventional views. Dissenters may be held up to ridicule, threatened with moral disapproval ("Only a pig would believe *that*"), told they aren't "cool," and so on. Whenever intimidation of this sort replaces logic in an effort to persuade, it is no less fallacious than the use of actual force.

SUMMARY Subjectivist Fallacies

Subjectivism: using the fact that one believes or wants a proposition to be true as evidence of its truth.

Appeal to majority: using the fact that large numbers of people believe a proposition to be true as evidence of its truth.

Appeal to emotion (*argumentum ad populum*): trying to get someone to accept a proposition on the basis of an emotion one elicits.

Appeal to force (*argumentum ad baculum*): trying to get someone to accept a proposition on the basis of a threat.

EXERCISE 5.1

Identify which of the fallacies discussed in this section—subjectivism, appeal to majority, appeal to emotion, or appeal to force—is committed in the statements below.

❋ 1. Of course Jane is going to be successful. Everyone says so.

2. "Hank is a really sharp dresser."
   "What about the purple plaid pants he wore last night?"
   "I don't want to think about that."

3. Boy: "It's *my* milk money. Stealing is wrong, you shouldn't take it."
   Bully: "Well I'm bigger and stronger, and I think that I should take it."

✳ 4. "Fine. Go ahead and marry him. Why should you care about breaking your mother's heart? I guess you love him more than me—but why should I care? Who am I to complain? I'm only your mother. I only spent twenty years trying to make a good match for you, a nice boy, and now you run off . . ."

5. You can argue all you want that democracy gives us only the illusion of control over the government, but I don't buy it. I was brought up to believe in the democratic system.

6. Our video series "The Key to Life" will vastly improve your career, your relationship, and your emotional well-being—just ask the thousands of people who have made it work for them!

✳ 7. I think you will find that this merger is the best idea for our company, especially because disagreement may indicate that this company is not the right place for you.

8. Teacher to student: "and finally, in reconsidering your position, you might remember who gives the grades in this course."

9. After the accident I was in, I was so upset I couldn't sleep for weeks; I'd wake up with my heart pounding, hearing the sound of the other car crushing the metal of my car door. Cars should be built more solidly than they are.

✳ 10. "He's clearly not qualified for the job—I get a bad feeling just talking to him."

11. How can you believe that John is innocent? I don't see how we can go on being friends if you believe that.

12. People in favor of leaving health care to the private sector have suggested that those with preexisting conditions get loans to cover their costs, instead of insurance. But this idea is completely ridiculous! Are you telling me that we're going to take a young man, suffering from chronic diabetes or muscular dystrophy, struggling every day with his disease, and make him spend his life as an indentured servant to a bank?

✳ 13. The most effective way to increase government revenues would be to raise the corporate income tax, since opinion polls show widespread support for this approach.

14. Foreign imports are wrecking our economy and savaging our workers, the backbone of this country. Buy American! Before you put your money on that Honda, think of the guy in Detroit whose kids may not eat tomorrow. Before you buy those Italian pumps, ask yourself whether a little glamour is worth the job of the shoemaker in Boston who's worked all his life to make an honest living.

15. The Golden Rule is a sound moral principle, for it is basic to every system of ethics in every culture.

5.2 Fallacies Involving Credibility

We noticed at the beginning of Chapter 4 that we rely on information passed on by other people for much of what we know. Most of us lack firsthand knowledge of the evidence for the theory of relativity, the DNA model of genes, the link between smoking and lung cancer; we accept these and other scientific ideas because we accept the authority of experts in the various fields. We know about historical events largely through the records and memoirs left by our predecessors. We learn about current events from reading newspaper accounts by journalists. Courts of law rely on eyewitness testimony and expert witnesses. Indeed, we can extend the legal concept of *testimonial evidence* to cover all of these cases.

To evaluate such evidence, we must weigh the *credibility* of the witness. When we accept a conclusion on the basis of someone's testimony, our reasoning can be diagrammed as follows:

X says p

$\downarrow$

p is true

If such an argument is to have any strength, two assumptions must be true. First, X must be competent to speak on the subject. If p is a statement in some technical area, then X must have some expertise in that area. If it is a statement about some event, X must be someone who was in a position to know what happened. Second, X must be reporting what he knows objectively, without distortion or deceit. In other words, X must be someone who not only *knows* the truth, but who also *tells* the truth. Both conditions are essential for credibility. Ideally, we should have a positive reason to think that X is competent and objective. At the very least, we must not have any evidence that X is *in*competent or *non*objective.

In this section, we'll look at two fallacies that involve a misuse of the standards for credibility.

5.2A Appeal to Authority (*Argumentum ad Verecundiam*)

An authority is someone whose word carries special weight, someone who can speak *with* authority because of expertise in some area of knowledge such as law, science, or medicine. It is perfectly appropriate to rely on the testimony of authorities if the conditions of credibility are satisfied. If they are not satisfied, however, the **appeal to authority** is fallacious.

The first condition is that the alleged authority be competent—an expert on the subject matter in question. It is typically violated when people speak outside their fields of expertise. For example, advertisers often use celebrity endorsements—a basketball star praises his favorite brand of orange juice, a famous actor extols the virtues of a luxury car. If the role of the celebrity is merely to add glamour, there's no fallacy involved, because there's no attempt at logical argument. But the advertiser's point is usually to persuade you that the product is good because someone you respect says so. That's a fallacy. Skill on the basketball court does not imply a discriminating taste in orange juice, nor does acting ability give one expertise in judging cars. When people of talent or expertise speak on matters outside their fields, their opinion carries no more weight than that of any layman.

How can we tell whether someone is an expert in a given field? No one standard applies to all the countless fields of human expertise, but the following are at least a start:

- *Education*: Degrees and other credentials indicate that someone has completed a systematic course of education and training in the field. This includes academic degrees such as a Ph.D. in a scientific field; professional degrees in medicine, law, and other fields; and certificates from training programs in software, automobile maintenance, plumbing, etc. Credentials aren't everything, but it is no accident that the word "credential" has the same Latin root as "credibility."
- *Position*: The fact that someone is hired for a position indicates that he inspired confidence in those who hired him. The fact that someone has kept a position over time is evidence that he is performing competently and gaining more and more experience.
- *Achievement*: Significant achievement in a field—such as a scientific discovery, a successful business start-up, or a new medical procedure—is obviously a sign of expertise. But a record of achievement on any scale reflects a proportionate degree of expertise.
- *Reputation*: People in a given field earn recognition not only through their position and achievements but also through interactions with others in the field—collaborating on projects, reviewing each other's work, etc. Someone who has earned a good reputation among his peers is likely to have earned it, at least in part, by their judgment of his ability in the field.

None of these factors is decisive. But each of them can provide inductive evidence for a person's expertise, and the strength of the evidence depends on the particular case.

It often happens that experts disagree. A criminal defendant is said to be insane by one psychiatrist, sane by another. One economist says that a change in the tax code will eliminate jobs, another says that it will create jobs. Across a wide array of issues—from the safety of nuclear power plants, to the causes of inflation, to the historical origins of human beings—specialists disagree. What should we do when we encounter such disagreements? The first thing to do, of course, is to make sure that we are dealing with a genuine dispute among experts and not simply an effort by some non-expert to challenge well-established principles or theories. If the dispute is a genuine one, then we have to take both sides into account. An argument that appeals only to one group of experts is fallacious.

The second condition for credibility is that the alleged authority be objective. Obviously, we cannot peer into a person's mind to see whether he is thinking objectively. But there are certain red flags that should at least raise a question about objectivity. Vested interests are an obvious example. When people stand to gain money or other personal benefit from making an assertion, it is reasonable to consider whether that benefit is biasing their judgment. Since celebrities are paid to appear in advertisements, for example, they have an obvious motive for praising the product regardless of what they really think about it. Emotional commitments are another red flag. When a jury is being picked for a trial, potential jurors are typically excused if they have personal connections with anyone involved in the case. For the same reason, doctors do not operate on members of their own family, and lawyers say that an attorney who represents himself in court has a fool for a client.

Political agendas are yet another kind of red flag. Government policies, and debates about those policies, depend on a wide range of specialized knowledge, from physics to medicine to economics to military strategy. Like the rest of us, experts in these fields can have political views that sometimes bias their judgment about the facts. A climate scientist who strongly favors government environmental regulation may overstate the evidence for global warming; a scientist who opposes such policies may be too quick to dismiss the evidence. In addition, much of the research we find in the media is conducted by advocacy groups whose very mission is to advance a political cause. Good reporters are careful to acknowledge the orientation of such groups.

We should be careful, however, to weigh these factors fairly. A red flag is merely a warning sign; it raises a question but does not answer it. With enough imagination, and enough cynicism, we can find a reason to impugn anyone's objectivity. If we go to that extreme, however, then we ourselves are not being objective: We are ignoring the fact that a genuine commitment to the truth can override the incentives for distortion or deceit. We would also lose the advantages of having specialists in different fields; we lose the advantages of cooperation in the pursuit of knowledge. The cognitive division of labor, like any other social arrangement, depends to some extent on mutual trust. So it seems more reasonable to presume an expert innocent until proven guilty—that is, to presume he is objective unless we have good reason to doubt it. In any case, we should be even-handed. On economic issues, for example, government and industry experts should be judged by the same standard, regardless of whether we favor more or less government regulation.

5.2B *Ad Hominem*

An ***ad hominem*** argument rejects or dismisses another person's statement by attacking the person rather than the statement itself. As we will see, there are many different forms of this fallacy, but all of them involve some attempt to avoid dealing with a statement logically, and in each case the method is to attempt to discredit the speaker by citing some negative trait. An *ad hominem* argument has the form:

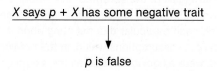

This is a fallacy because the truth or falsity of the statement itself, or the strength of an argument for it, has nothing to do with the character, motives, or any other trait of the person who makes the statement or argument.

This principle is true even when we are concerned with testimonial evidence, but we have to keep a certain distinction in mind. If someone defends a position by citing an authority, as we have seen, then it is legitimate to consider evidence regarding the authority's competence and objectivity. When a jury is asked to accept the testimony of a witness, it is certainly legitimate for the opposing side to introduce evidence that the witness is dishonest or biased. But discrediting witnesses or authorities does not provide evidence that what they say is actually false; it merely eliminates any reason for thinking that what they say is true. So we go back to square one: We are left with no evidence one way or the other. In other contexts, where there is no issue of relying on authorities, the use of discrediting evidence about the person is always fallacious. If someone offers an argument for his position, then his character and motives do not matter. We have to evaluate the argument on its merits.

In its crudest form, the *ad hominem* fallacy involves nothing more than insults—calling one's opponent an idiot, slob, lowlife, airhead, fascist, pinko, nerd, fairy, bleeding heart, wimp, Neanderthal, and so on through the rich vocabulary of abuse our language offers. Unlike the other fallacies, moreover, this one is committed fairly often in its crude form. In personal disputes, disagreement often breeds anger, and angry people hit below the belt. In politics, *ad hominem* arguments are a common technique of propaganda and a common device of politicians who try to enlist support by attacking their enemies. But the fallacy can also take more sophisticated forms. Let's look at a few.

Suppose that someone criticizes you for telling a white lie. If your critic is himself a notorious liar, you would probably be tempted to say, "Look who's talking!" This response is certainly understandable—no one enjoys being censured by a moral inferior—but it is fallacious. It's a species of *ad hominem* known as the *tu quoque* ("you're another") argument. The fact that someone else is guilty of an accusation doesn't prove that you are innocent. It may be unseemly for the pot to call the kettle black, but the kettle is black nonetheless.

A related version of the *ad hominem* fallacy occurs when we attack someone's position by claiming that it is inconsistent with his practice or with his other positions. The classic example is the patient who says to his doctor: "How can you tell me I should stop smoking when you still smoke yourself?" The fact that a doctor doesn't take his own advice hardly means that it isn't good advice; a hypocrite may still say something true or make a valid argument.

A final version of *ad hominem* attempts to impugn someone's objectivity by alleging a vested interest, emotional commitment, or political agenda. Except in the case of someone being cited as an authority (as we discussed earlier), this tactic is fallacious, and it is usually done in a sneaky way. Here's an academic example:

> In the constitutional struggles of the seventeenth century, the modern theory of natural law—the theory of individual rights—was eventually perfected. Stripped of the trappings which each particular theorist hung upon it, the bare theory was a simple pattern of . . . assumptions which, in the opinion of the men whose interests they served, were as obviously true as the axioms of Euclid. [Richard Schlatter, *Private Property*]

The natural law theory in politics said that individuals had certain inalienable rights that government could not violate, including the right to acquire and dispose of private property. This passage describes one aspect of the theory: that such rights were held to be self-evident, like axioms of geometry. The author clearly does not agree with this view. But instead of presenting a reasoned argument against it, he takes a shortcut: He implies that the principle of property rights seemed self-evident only because it served the political interests of those who were wealthy. This tactic is sometimes called "poisoning the well," and it is obviously fallacious. The fact that someone might have a nonrational motive for supporting a position does not mean the position is false, and it certainly does not mean we can decide ahead of time that all his arguments for the position can be dismissed.

In face-to-face disputes, poisoning the well usually takes the form of the statement, "You're just saying that because . . . ." For example: "You're only supporting Julie for class president because she's your friend," or "You're just defending the draft because you know you'd get a medical exemption." If you have given an argument for the draft, or in favor of Julie's candidacy, the strength of your argument is unaffected by the existence of other motivations you may have for your position. Such statements are insulting. They say, in effect, "I won't even listen to what you have to say because I know ahead of time that you can't be objective; your reasoning is nothing more than a mouthpiece for your emotions and your vested interests." This is a particularly insidious form of the *ad hominem* fallacy because it can undercut your confidence in your ability to think objectively; it breeds self-doubt and timidity. It's true that we have to be careful not to let our judgment be biased by subjective factors. But we should not accept undeserved accusations that we are guilty of this (or any other) logical sin.

SUMMARY **Fallacies Involving Credibility**

Appeal to authority (*argumentum ad verecundiam*): using testimonial evidence for a proposition when the conditions for credibility are not satisfied or the use of such evidence is inappropriate.

Ad hominem: using a negative trait of a speaker as evidence that his statement is false or his argument weak.

EXERCISE 5.2

Identify which of the fallacies discussed in this section—appeal to authority or *ad hominem*—is committed in the each of statements below.

✳ 1. To solve our transportation problems, we have to put more money into mass transit. CBS News said so last night.

2. My son says he's ready to get married, but I don't think so. I'm his mother, and I know him best.

3. Why should Congress consult the Joint Chiefs of Staff about military funding? They are military men, so obviously they will want as much money as they can get.

✳ 4. How can you say that animals have rights and should not be killed, when you eat meat?

5. I think America should be more careful about the international organizations we join and the treaties we sign. After all, wasn't it George Washington himself

who warned against "foreign entanglements"?

6. Television commentators are always attacking big business for making "obscene profits," but the media companies they work for have higher profits than almost any other industry.

✳ 7. John Stuart Mill says that happiness is the oscillation between tranquillity and excitement. But he spent years dealing with terrible depression, so he can't really know what happiness is.

8. I will vote for whoever the Democrat Party chooses as its candidate. If these experienced politicians think that someone is fit to represent them in office, then that person must be a good leader.

9. Nicole advised me that it was best to be totally honest in a relationship, but her love advice can't be very good: She's been divorced twice.

✳ 10. Mayor McPherson says that homelessness is a social problem, but that's always the mantra of a bleeding-heart liberal.

11. The committee for education showed that budget cuts to the art and music departments did not diminish the academic performances of students in the past, and so argued that upcoming cuts wouldn't either. But Mrs. Jensen says the budget cuts will diminish academic performances, and I think a teacher who's in the classroom every day knows a lot more about education than a committee.

12. Mike Tepp tried to convince the board that it would be most profitable to invest in the advertising department. That seems like a convenient position for someone who's up to take over the advertising department next month.

5.3 Fallacies of Context

Fallacies in this category include arguments that "jump to conclusions." Although some of these fallacies can be cast in the form of deductive arguments, what makes them fallacious is a weak inductive component. As we saw in the previous chapter (Section 4.4), the logical strength of an inductive argument is a matter of degree, depending on how thoroughly we have taken account of the factors relevant to the conclusion. The fallacies in this section all involve a significant logical gap because they fail to consider a wide enough context of relevant information. The problem is not the premises per se. Unlike the subjectivist fallacies, the premises of these arguments do provide genuine evidence. But the evidence is simply inadequate or incomplete in ways that the argument overlooks. We could just treat such arguments as weak. But the patterns of argument we're going to study in this section have features that make them appear to be stronger than they actually are. As with other kinds of fallacy, learning to see past the appearance will help us avoid poor reasoning.

5.3A False Alternative

Suppose you tell me that Diane is not rich, and I infer that she is poor. I have obviously failed to take account of other alternatives. Rich and poor are the extremes on a scale that contains many intermediate degrees of wealth. Again, suppose you say that you do not identify with political conservatives and I infer that you are a liberal. I am ignoring the other political positions that you might hold, along with the possibility that you have not adopted *any* position. Such inferences have the general form

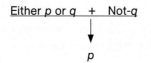

That is a deductively valid form of argument. But the soundness of any such inference depends on whether the premises take account of *all* the relevant alternatives. The fallacy of **false alternatives** occurs when we fail to do so, when we exclude relevant alternatives without justification.

Another name for this fallacy is "false dichotomy," because the premises of such arguments often posit just two alternatives, as in the examples above and in premises such as the following:

1. Either you are with us or you are against us.
2. Either we reduce Social Security benefits or government spending will wreck the economy.
3. Either we increase Social Security benefits or elderly people will starve in the streets.

The essence of the fallacy, however, is not the number of alternatives but the fact that they do not exhaust the possibilities. That can occur whether an argument posits two, three, or any number of alternatives. If the list is incomplete—if it excludes a further alternative that is relevant to the issue—the argument is fallacious. For example, a man in an unsatisfying marriage might try to justify cheating on his wife by appealing to the premise

4. I can (a) stay with her and be unfulfilled, or (b) leave and be lonely, or (c) stay but have affairs on the side.

This assumption ignores other possibilities, such as discussing the problem with his wife or seeking therapy. If the man chooses (c) on the grounds that (a) and (b) are unacceptable, he has committed the same fallacy as in arguments based on 1–3.

As these examples illustrate, considering a range of alternatives plays a major role in reasoning. When we reason about the truth or falsity of a conclusion, we rarely consider the conclusion in a vacuum. Instead, we have in mind a range of other possible conclusions. When we think about whether to take a certain action, we weigh it against other options. When we consider a hypothesis to explain why something happened, we test it against other hypotheses. In short, thinking often involves a choice among alternatives. For that reason, it is important to be alert to the fallacy of false alternative.

The best safeguards against this fallacy are an open mind and a good imagination. No matter how certain we are of our conclusions and our arguments, it is always worthwhile to stop and ask: Is there anything I've overlooked? Could there be some other explanation for these facts? Is there some other perspective one might take? When we can't find the solution to a problem, it is often because we are making an assumption that excludes alternative approaches. If we are not satisfied with any of the standard positions on a given issue, it may be because they all make some assumption that should be called into question, thus opening up other possible positions.

5.3B *Post Hoc*

The Latin name of this fallacy is short for *post hoc ergo propter hoc*: "after this, therefore because of this." The fallacy has to do with causality, and it has the structure:

A occurred before *B*

↓

A caused *B*

Such reasoning is fallacious because many events that precede a given event have nothing to do with it, as in the old joke: "Why are you whistling?" "To keep the elephants away." "But there aren't any elephants around here." "See? It works."

The **post hoc** fallacy is probably the source of many superstitions. Someone, somewhere, had a run of bad luck and attributed it to breaking a mirror, walking under a ladder, stepping on a crack, or some other previous action. A student does well on an exam and thereafter always wears the same "lucky" sweater on exam days. More serious examples of the fallacy occur in situations where causal relationships are extremely complex and difficult to identify. Stock market advisers, for instance, sometimes make predictions on the basis of a few indicators that happened to precede a previous rise or fall in prices. *Post hoc* reasoning can also occur in speculation about the causes of historical events such as the Civil War, the causes of economic phenomena such as the Great Depression, or the causes of sociological trends such as crime rates.

It's certainly true that if we want to know what caused an event or phenomenon *B*, we have to *start* by identifying the factors that preceded it. But we can't stop there. To show that some particular factor *A* was the cause, we have to find evidence that there is some stronger connection between *A* and *B* than just a temporal relationship. When we study inductive reasoning in Part 3, we will study in detail the types of argument that provide such evidence. For now, we will have to rely on our intuitive judgment. When someone presents an argument that *A* caused *B*, ask yourself: Could it be merely a coincidence that *A* happened just before *B*? Is *A* the *kind* of thing that could have an effect on *B*? Has the person offered any explanation of *how A* affected *B*?

5.3C Hasty Generalization

Each of the following is a general proposition, or generalization:

1. Water always flows downhill.
2. Large breeds of dogs have shorter life spans than smaller ones.
3. People in France are not very friendly to tourists.
4. Italians are quick-tempered.

5. Stockbrokers drive BMWs.
6. Bill never gets anywhere on time.

General propositions make a claim about a category of things (water, dogs, Italians, etc.), attributing some characteristic to all members of the category. As statement 6 illustrates, however, a generalization may be about a particular individual; what makes it a generalization is that it attributes a general pattern of behavior to that individual.

General propositions play a vital role in reasoning. They allow us to reap the advantages of having concepts: We form a concept for a type of thing, and then generalize about the attributes and patterns of action shared by things of that type. This saves us the trouble of having to discover from scratch the features of every particular thing we encounter. Knowing about the life spans of large versus small dogs, for example, can help us in choosing a pet.

General propositions are normally supported by observing a sample of particular cases. But we often draw conclusions too quickly, on the basis of insufficient evidence. This fallacy, known as **hasty generalization**, can take many forms. A single bad experience while traveling can prejudice our view of an entire city or country (as in 3 above). Most of us have stereotypes about ethnic groups, professions, or people from different regions of the country, based on our exposure to a few individuals (as in 4 and 5 above). Even a judgment about the character or personality of an individual is a generalization drawn from our observation of that person on specific occasions; here, too, we often jump to conclusions. And we can jump to conclusions about ourselves: We make a mistake, fail a test, have a problem in a relationship, and then draw a sweeping conclusion about our inadequacies.

In Part 3, we are going to study the proper methods and precautions for generalizing from particular cases. But the essence of the method is to ask ourselves whether we have considered a wide enough context. Two contextual factors are especially important if we want to avoid hasty generalization: the *number* and the *variety* of cases in the sample from which we generalize. It is rarely if ever possible to draw a legitimate generalization from a single instance, or even from a few; we should consider a larger sample. I may have met a few stockbrokers who drive BMWs, for example, but if I asked around I would quickly find some who don't. We should also look at a *variety* of instances. For example, we might observe that Bill is late for work not just on one occasion but on many. It would still be hasty to conclude that he never gets *anywhere* on time. Is he also late for parties, dates, ball games? If so, we have much stronger evidence that his problem has to do with time in general rather than with work.

Of these two factors, variety is usually the more important one. If you liked a certain novel and wanted to know whether you might like all the author's works, it would obviously be useless to read another copy of the same novel; you would want to sample other novels by that author. To take a more realistic situation, suppose you are buying a car and want to know whether a certain dealer offers good service on the cars it sells. You might ask other customers of that dealer. If you ask people who are very similar, you run the risk that they are not representative of the dealer's clientele. If those customers are all friends of the dealer, for example, or if they are all lawyers who are good at negotiating service contracts, then the generalization that this dealer offers good service might well not be true for other people—including yourself. To avoid hasty generalization, we want to base our generalization on a sample of particular cases that are representative of the wider group. Seeking variety in our sample is the best way to get a representative sample.

5.3D Accident

Hasty generalization is a fallacy that can occur in moving from particular cases to a generalization. There is also a fallacy, called **accident**, that can occur when we move in the opposite direction by applying a generalization to a particular case. This fallacy consists in applying a generalization to a special case without regard to the circumstances that make the case an exception to the general rule. Accident is the fallacy of hasty application.

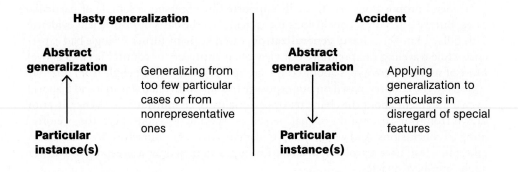

For example, matches are made to light when they are struck correctly, so I can infer that the next match I strike will perform as advertised. But what if the match is wet? If I disregard that fact and expect the match to light, I am committing the fallacy. Again, consider the generalization that birds fly. What does this imply about penguins? If we infer that penguins must be able to fly because they are birds, or conversely that they can't be birds because they can't fly, we commit the fallacy of accident. Penguins are properly classified as birds for anatomical and evolutionary reasons, even though the adaptation of their wings to swimming, and the heavy layer of body fat to insulate them from the cold, prevents them from flying.

In everyday speech, "accident" refers to something that is unexpected or happens by chance. In logic, however, the word retains the older meaning: "a nonessential property . . . of an entity or circumstance" (*Merriam-Webster's Collegiate Dictionary*, 10th ed.). Generalizations typically apply to things in virtue of the things' essential properties. When a generalization has an exception, it's usually because of some accidental (i.e., nonessential) feature of that particular thing. Matches are designed to be used dry; if my matches got soaked in the rain, that's an accidental feature. Penguins evolved from birds and they adapted to finding food in the cold waters of the Antarctic; their inability to fly is a by-product, and thus in a sense is accidental.

The classic examples of accident involve the application of moral principles to particular situations. Take the principle that one should always tell the truth. What if a mugger on the street asks you where you live? Applying the principle mechanically to this situation by answering the question truthfully would be a rather dangerous case of fallacious thinking. Even if you lie but feel guilty about doing so, the feeling of guilt presumes that you *should* have told the truth to the mugger. Drawing that conclusion is fallacious whether you act on it or not. As an exercise for yourself, you might take other moral principles and imagine exceptional cases in which applying the principle would commit the fallacy. When we apply a given principle to a particular situation, we need to take account of other principles that may also apply and take account of any unusual consequences that might arise from applying the principle. It will not always be clear what the best decision is, and reasonable people may disagree. The point is not to apply the principle mechanically without considering the context.

Another common form of accident is extrapolating a generalization beyond the range in which we established its truth. For example, we have all learned that water boils at 212°F. But that measurement was made at sea level. It would be fallacious to assume that the generalization is true for all locations. That's not the case, as you have probably also learned. At higher altitudes, where the atmospheric pressure is lower, water boils at lower temperatures.

Not all generalizations have exceptions. In mathematics, there is a principle that if you have two equal quantities and subtract the same amount from both, the quantities will still be equal. That principle is true in all cases. In any area, on any topic, a strictly universal generalization has the form "All P are Q," and "all" means *all*, without exception. If even one P is not Q, then the generalization is false. But if the generalization is true, we can safely infer that any particular instance of P will be Q. (This is one of the major forms of deductive inference, and we will examine it at length in Part 2.) If a generalization does have exceptions, moreover, and if we know exactly how and why the exceptions occur, we can qualify the generalization and restore it to strict universality. For example, we can qualify the generalization "water boils at 212°F" by adding "at sea level."

For many generalizations, however, we may not know all the qualifications that would be needed to make them exception-proof. Or the exceptions may be so rare that we don't bother to add the qualification. The fact is that in wide areas of knowledge—including ethics, law, and politics and the properties and behavior of living species, to name a few—many of the generalizations we rely on have exceptions, and we need to avoid the fallacy of accident.

5.3E Slippery Slope

You have probably heard the phrase "slippery slope." It's a cliché, but it is a pretty good metaphor for the kind of situation in which, once you take the first step in a certain direction, circumstances will pull you further in that direction whether you like it or not, and you may slide too far down the slope. We have a number of other common expressions for asserting that one decision, action, or event will set off a train of causes leading on to some result beyond what we intended—usually an undesirable one.

1. "If you give him an inch, he'll take a mile."
2. The Marxist takeover in country X had "a domino effect" of inciting rebellions in neighboring countries.
3. Giving in to small temptations leads you down "the primrose path" to immorality.
4. Changing the grading standards had "a ripple effect" throughout the college.
5. The antitrust laws were "the camel's nose in the tent" (or "the thin edge of the wedge") leading to further government regulation of business.

6. The collapse of the sub-prime mortgage market "snowballed" into a crisis in all financial markets.

There's no question that the kind of causal sequence described by these expressions actually occurs. We can all think of slippery slopes in our past experience, and historians can provide us with many examples of how nations started down slippery slopes from the decisions of their leaders. But our concern is with arguments. A slippery slope *argument* is the attempt to show that some action or policy *will* lead on to a series of further consequences and should be avoided for that reason. Such arguments are usually directed against something that might otherwise seem desirable, or at least harmless, by trying to show that it would be the first step onto a slippery slope. People who defend free speech, for example, sometimes argue as follows:

> We should oppose any effort by government to censor obscene books, movies, or other forms of expression, no matter how offensive we may find such material. The reason is that once government has the power to ban obscenity, that precedent will open the door to further controls on speech: banning racist remarks, then speech that the majority finds offensive, then speech that opposes government policies, and so on until no one is free to say anything without government permission.

The argument assumes that such a loss of freedom would be very bad, so we should not take the first step of censoring obscenity. Thus the general form of slippery slope arguments is

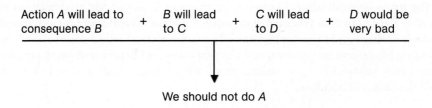

(There need not be exactly four items in the series of projected consequences; there could be any number.)

The **slippery slope** fallacy occurs when we posit a sequence of effects without good reason for thinking they will actually follow. This often happens in the heat of debate, when people exaggerate the likelihood of further consequences; or when people imagine dangers down the road, where their imagination is driven more by fear than by objective evidence. For example, suppose a teenager comes home an hour late one night, and a parent argues that that is the first step down a slippery slope:

> First it's staying out late, then it's not calling home, then it's a few drinks with friends, then wild parties, and before you know it, your life will be completely out of control. Someday you'll be glad that you had a curfew.

Unless the teenager has a history of being grossly irresponsible, the parent's argument seems exaggerated, not to say paranoid.

Slippery slope arguments can be good ones if the slope is real—that is, if there is good evidence that the consequences of the initial action are highly likely to occur. The strength of the argument depends on two factors. The first is the strength of each link in the causal chain; the argument cannot be stronger than its weakest link. The second is the number of links; the more links there are, the more likely it is that other factors could alter the consequences. The argument for free speech, for example, posits a series of steps by which government would expand its control over more and more kinds of speech, once the precedent of censoring pornography was established. The argument assumes that government seeks to expand its power over people. Even if that is true, however, it does not mean that government can expand its power indefinitely without provoking opposition. So we can't assume that a ban on obscenity—the first step down the slope—will lead inexorably to censorship of all speech. Since each step is more intrusive than the one before, it is plausible that each step would provoke more opposition and thus become less likely. At best, therefore, this is a weak argument. Because it assumes that government power will expand inexorably, without recognizing any other factor, I would say that it is also fallacious.

Slippery slope arguments are very common in discussions of social and political issues. At the same time, such arguments are often used to persuade other people of a conclusion that the arguer has accepted for other, deeper reasons. For example, some people who use the slippery slope argument against censoring pornography are opposed to censorship primarily because it inherently abridges individual freedom, not because it may have further consequences. That does not affect the strength of the slippery slope argument itself; people can have multiple arguments for a given conclusion, and each argument is what it is—it has whatever strength it has—regardless of how important it may be to a given person. But putting forward a slippery slope argument when it is not the main reason one accepts a conclusion *is* rather disingenuous. And, in such cases, refuting a slippery slope argument may do nothing to change the arguer's mind.

5.3F Composition and Division

The fallacy of **composition** consists in inferring that what is true of a part must be true of the whole. Of course, parts and wholes sometimes do have the same properties. Every page in a newspaper is flammable, and so is the newspaper as a whole. But not every property is like this. We commit the fallacy of composition when we jump to a conclusion about the whole without considering whether the nature of the property in question makes it reasonable. The radio in my car was made by Motorola, but that does not imply that Motorola made my car as a whole. Every snowflake on my lawn is star-shaped and fell from the sky, but the snowball I make has neither of those properties. The fallacy of **division** is the mirror image of composition: It is the inference that what is true of the whole must be true of the parts. The fact that my car gets 25 miles to the gallon does not mean that the radio gets 25 miles to the gallon—a statement that hardly even makes sense. The fact that my car was made by General Motors does not mean that GM made every part.

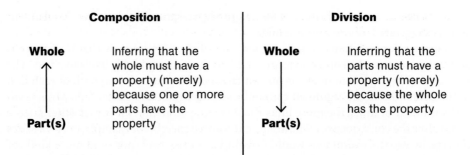

As the diagram suggests, composition has a certain similarity to hasty generalization. But hasty generalization applies to individual things and the *general classes* to which they belong, whereas composition applies to the parts of an individual thing and that *individual* thing as a whole. To see the difference, consider again the radio in my car. The radio is a member of the general class of audio equipment. It would be hasty to generalize that all audio equipment is made by Motorola, just because my car radio is. That is a different error from composition: inferring that Motorola made my car just because it made the radio. In the same way, the fallacy of division has a certain similarity with accident, but the latter involves a hasty application of a generalization about a class of things, whereas division is an inference from an individual thing to its parts.

The fallacies of composition and division can also occur in thinking about groups as well as individual things—when we are treating the group as a single whole. Suppose, for example, that every member of a college football team is a senior. We obviously cannot infer that the football team itself is a senior; that would be composition. Conversely, the team has properties as a team (e.g., a budget of $X from the college) that do not apply to individual players; inferring that the left guard Harold has a budget of $X would be a case of division. The same distinction applies to statements about general classes. Compare the statements:

1. Human beings are animals.
2. Human beings evolved 100,000 years ago.

The first is a general statement about humans. It applies to each and every one of us. If we have the additional premise that X is a human being, we can validly infer that X is an animal. But 2 is a statement about the human species as a whole, as a single biological unit. It does *not* apply to individual humans as members of the species. The fact that the species evolved 100,000 years ago does not imply that you or I evolved—came into existence—back then.

It isn't likely that anyone would make the absurd inferences I have used so far to illustrate composition and division. So let us turn to cases in which these fallacies are more likely to be committed. One case is the use of statistics. Compare the statements:

3. American steel companies are profitable.
4. The average American steel company is profitable.

Statement 3 is like 1 above, a generalization about each instance of a class. You could therefore infer that any given company is profitable. But an average is a statistical fact about a class as a whole. So 4 does not support the inference that a given company is profitable, and we would commit the fallacy of division if we made that inference. The controversial issue of racial differences in intelligence provides another example of the same error. If such differences do exist, they are differences in the average IQ of racial groups. To infer that a given individual in one group is more intelligent than another individual in another group, just because his group's average is higher, would be a fallacy of division. Averages are computed from the scores of individuals who are distributed along the whole continuum of intelligence, so the group average tells us nothing about any individual.

People also commit the fallacy of composition with statistical information. Treatment for mental disorders is less expensive per-person than treatment for cancer. But it would be composition to infer that total spending on mental disorders is less than total spending on cancer treatment. That depends on the number of patients who seek treatment for these conditions. As it happens, there are many more people being treated for mental disorders than for cancer, so that total spending is roughly the same.

Political issues are another area in which these fallacies occur. A society is made up of individual people. What is true of individuals may or may not be true of society as a whole, and vice versa, so we have to be careful to avoid composition and division. For example, a newspaper editorial argues for government economic planning by asking, "Why is planning considered a good thing for individuals and business but a bad thing for the national economy?" The fact that individuals need to plan how they are going to earn a living and spend their income does not imply that society as a whole should plan how wealth should be produced and distributed throughout the economy. Whether national planning is a good idea depends on a host of other questions, such as whether government planners are capable of performing this task, and whether they have the right to supersede the decisions that individuals and businesses make about how to use their resources. Because the editorial ignores these issues and makes a simple inference to parts to the whole, the argument is a case of composition.

SUMMARY Fallacies of Context

False alternative: excluding relevant possibilities without justification.

Post hoc: using the fact that one event preceded another as sufficient evidence for the conclusion that the first caused the second.

Hasty generalization: inferring a general proposition from an inadequate sample of particular cases.

Accident: applying a generalization to a special case in disregard of qualities or circumstances that make it an exception to the generalization.

Slippery slope: arguing against a proposed action or policy by claiming, with insufficient evidence, that it will lead to a series of increasingly bad consequences.

Composition: inferring that a whole has a property merely because its parts have that property.

Division: inferring that a part has a property merely because the whole has that property.

EXERCISE 5.3

Identify which of the fallacies discussed in this section—false alternative, *post hoc*, hasty generalization, composition, division—is committed in the statements below.

✳ 1. Don't go down to River Road. I was down there once and got mugged. They're all thieves down there.

2. If she loved me, she would have called me back tonight. She didn't, so she must hate me.

3. Flowers require soil, water, and sunlight to grow. Foxglove grows in the shade, so it must not be a flower.

✳ 4. Although I'm happy about the raise I got today, I'm also a little worried. The last time I got a raise my car got stolen the next morning.

5. Tell your representative that you don't want health care reform! If the health care reform is passed, private insurance companies won't be able to compete with the public option. With the private companies out of the picture, individuals will only be able to turn to the public option, and then it will be up to the government to decide whether we should live or die.

6. I'm sure this outfit will look great. It's got leopard print, zebra print, plaid, and polka dots, and I like each of those patterns.

✳ 7. On the basis of the rambling speech Madeleine gave at the school assembly last week, I would say she's not a good public speaker.

8. How can you say that you washed the car? Did you wash every part—under the hood, around the muffler, under the seats?

9. One should always keep appointments. So even though Joe is an hour late, we should continue to wait for him.

✳ 10. Congressman Jones denies that he's a liberal, so he must be a conservative.

11. Twenty-five years after graduation, Harvard alumni have incomes much higher than that of the average college graduate. A Harvard education must be the road to riches.

12. Everyone on the Dream Team is the best player in his position, so the Dream Team is the best team around.

✳ 13. If their band accepts this mainstream record deal, they'll be selling out! Next they'll get corporate sponsors for their tour, and then we'll be hearing their songs redone as commercial jingles for toothpaste.

14. A pile of stones will topple if it is not stacked vertically. So it is impossible to build a stone arch.

15. Either Tom was telling the truth when he said his grade average was 3.7 or he was lying. But he wasn't telling the truth, since his average is actually 3.6, so he was lying.

✳ 16. It's good to put water in your body, so it must be good to put water in your lungs.

17. I've seen my daughter's teachers underestimate her ability in math and science. This just goes to show that educators in America are sexist.

18. Stock prices fell dramatically 2 years ago, after Congress raised tariffs, and they just raised tariffs

again, so expect another crash in the market.

* 19. Dr. Kingston should not have given that choking man the Heimlich maneuver. He cracked one of his ribs, and a doctor's first principle is to "do no harm."

20. If pharmaceutical companies aren't monitored by the government, then individual consumers will have to be completely responsible for learning every detail about the medicines that they take. The majority of people don't have enough time or expertise to take on this responsibility, so we should leave it to the government.

21. University admissions departments should not be allowed to give preference to the children of alumni. This will lead to the perpetuation of a predominantly white upper class, which will make it increasingly difficult for minorities to achieve upward mobility.

* 22. The last time I stretched my arms first and my legs second, I won my race. So that stretching sequence must have increased my speed.

23. The catalog said it was a gold figurine, but these accents are made of silver! So it is not actually a gold figurine.

5.4 Fallacies of Logical Structure

In the previous sections, we examined arguments that are fallacious either because they introduce irrelevant considerations into the reasoning process (emotions, threats, personal traits) or because they fail to consider a wide enough context of information. In this section, we'll examine fallacies that involve more subtle logical errors within the argument itself.

5.4A Begging the Question (Circular Argument)

Begging the question is the use of a proposition as a premise in an argument intended to support that same proposition. The point of reasoning is to throw light on the truth or falsity of a proposition (the conclusion) by relating it to other propositions (the premises) that we already have some basis for believing to be true. If our reasoning does nothing more than relate p to itself, then it hasn't gained us anything. It has not given us a *reason* to think p is true. Circular arguments are no more productive than circular definitions.

The most obvious way to commit the fallacy would be simply to restate the conclusion as a premise, in an argument of the form:

$$p$$
$$\downarrow$$
$$p$$

This usually occurs only when the proposition is formulated in two different ways, so that it is not immediately apparent that the person is simply restating the conclusion. For example: "[l] Society has an obligation to support the needy, because [2] people who cannot provide for themselves have a right to the resources of the community." Statement 2 expresses the same proposition as 1: "society" means the same thing as "community," "the needy" are the same class of people as "those who cannot provide for themselves," and the obligation mentioned in 1 is merely another way of expressing the right mentioned in 2. Both statements, therefore, should be given the same number, and the diagram would be

$$1$$
$$\downarrow$$
$$1$$

People typically beg the question in this way when a proposition seems so obvious to them that they aren't sure what further evidence could be given for it, so they keep restating it in the hope that some formulation will strike the listener as plausible and lead him to agree.

A more subtle form of the fallacy occurs when the circle is enlarged to include more than one step: The conclusion p is supported by premise q, which in turn is supported by p (though there could be any number of intervening steps). Suppose I am arguing with an atheist about the existence of a supreme being. He asks why I believe that God exists, and I say, "Because the Bible says so." If he then asks why he should take the Bible's word for it, and I answer that the Bible is trustworthy because it is the Word of God, I am arguing in a circle: My premise assumes the existence of God, which was precisely the question at issue. As this example illustrates, circular reasoning of this type often occurs in debates when we try to answer an objection by falling back on the conclusion we are trying to establish.

An indirect form of begging the question is known as the *complex question* or *loaded question*. Suppose I accuse you of having cheated on a test, and when you deny it I say, "Why are you lying to me?" Any answer you give will imply that you were indeed lying, and thus that you did cheat. The reason for this is obvious. Despite its appearance, the question is not simple but complex; it is loaded with an implicit assumption. There are really two questions here: "Are you lying?" and "If so, why?" We can't even raise the second question, much less answer it, until we have answered the first one. By not asking the first question, I have simply assumed that the answer to it is "Yes"—I have begged that question. Strictly speaking, it is not the question itself— "Why are you lying" —that is fallacious. A question is not an assertion or an argument. But such questions rest on certain assumptions. In asking the question, I am implicitly asserting that you did lie (i.e., that you did cheat). I am thus assuming the very thing I need to prove.

5.4B Equivocation

We have seen that an argument links one or more propositions used as premises with a proposition that serves as the conclusion. We have also seen that what a proposition asserts depends (in part) on the words used to express it. The fallacy of **equivocation** occurs when a word switches meaning in the middle of the argument—when it expresses one concept in one premise and another concept in another premise or in the conclusion.

Consider the following argument:

> [Letter] grades are a crude and mechanical device that does not measure the nuances of student performance
>
> ↓
>
> Student work should not be graded [evaluated]

The conclusion is not supported by the premise because the term "grade" has shifted its meaning. The claim that letter grades are a poor evaluation device hardly implies that student work should not be evaluated at all; if anything, it implies that we should find a better means for measuring performance.

In this example, the equivocation occurred because a word was used in both a narrower sense, to designate a species (letter grades), and in a wider sense to designate a genus (evaluation as such). This illustrates a common pattern in which a word's meaning is broadened in the course of an argument.

Another way in which this happens is by the metaphorical extension of a concept. The term "censorship," for example, refers to a restriction on someone's freedom of speech by a government, using the coercive threat of fines, jail, or worse. But the term is sometimes used metaphorically for other constraints on the ability to express oneself. It would be equivocation to switch between these meanings, as in the following argument:

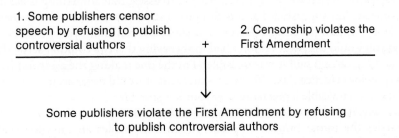

1. Some publishers censor speech by refusing to publish controversial authors   +   2. Censorship violates the First Amendment

Some publishers violate the First Amendment by refusing to publish controversial authors

In premise l, the term "censor" is used in the metaphorical sense, since the newspapers are merely choosing not to publish certain authors rather than literally threatening them with legal sanctions. But in premise 2, the term is used in its literal meaning, so the conclusion does not follow.

As an argument employs more complex and abstract concepts, equivocation becomes more of a danger. The best way to avoid the danger is to use the techniques for clarifying and defining concepts that we studied in Chapter 2.

5.4C Appeal to Ignorance (*Argumentum ad Ignorantiam*)

Suppose I claim that politician X is having an affair with an aide. "Prove it," you say. "Can you prove that he's not having an affair?" I ask—and thereby commit the fallacy of **appeal to ignorance**. This fallacy consists in the argument that a proposition is true because it hasn't been proven false. To put it differently, it is the argument that a proposition is true because the *opposing* proposition hasn't been proven true. Using the symbol –*p* to stand for the denial or negation of *p*, the fallacy has the structure:

–*p* has not been proven true

↓

p is true

This is a fallacy because a lack of evidence for –*p* does not imply that there is evidence for *p*. All it means is that we do not know that –*p* is true. I can't; prove that a storm is not brewing in the atmosphere of Jupiter, but that would hardly count as evidence that a storm *is* brewing. The absence of evidence usually means that we simply don't know enough to make a judgment. Such ignorance cannot be transmuted into knowledge, any more than brass can be transmuted into gold.

In the preceding examples of the fallacy, the proposition *p* was a positive claim: that X is having an affair, that a storm is brewing on Jupiter. But the fallacy can also be committed when *p* is a negative claim. The absence of evidence that X *is* having an affair does not prove that he isn't; the absence of evidence that a storm *is* brewing doesn't prove that one *isn't*. In the diagram above, *p* may be either negative or positive, and –*p* will have the opposite quality; the structure of the fallacy is the same in either case. Strictly speaking, there is a logical symmetry between positive and negative claims.

In practice, however, the fallacy is normally committed by those who assert the positive. The reason is that we rarely have occasion to assert that something is *not* the case until someone has suggested that it *is*. Suppose I suddenly announced that there is an invisible leprechaun hovering over your left shoulder. Naturally, you would be skeptical, and you would ask what reason I had for believing this (we couldn't settle the matter by looking, since I said it was invisible). I'm the one making the assertion here, so I have to provide evidence. Apart from my statement, it would never occur to you to deny that there is an invisible leprechaun over your left shoulder.

As a rule, it is the positive claim that puts the ball in play and the positive claim that carries the initial burden of proof. If someone makes an unsupported statement, therefore, the proper response is not to make an equally unsupported denial. Nor should you accept the burden of disproving the person's statement; if you do, you are cooperating in an implicit appeal to ignorance. (This is a trap that paranoid people often spring on their listeners: They make an arbitrary claim about a conspiracy against them and then take their claim to be vindicated unless others can disprove it.) The proper response is simply to point out that the claim is unsupported and ask the person to provide some evidence for it. If evidence *is* forthcoming, then the ball is in your court; if you do not find the evidence convincing, it is your responsibility to explain why.

One application of this rule is the legal principle that a person is innocent until proven guilty. To assert that someone is guilty is to make a positive claim: that the person committed a certain act. Thus in a court of law, the burden of proof rests with the party who brings the charges. But we need to be careful here. The prosecution's failure to establish guilt on the part of the defendant does not prove that the defendant didn't commit the crime. We would commit the fallacy of appealing to ignorance if we thought so. In this respect, the legal rule goes beyond the burden of proof principle. It also reflects the ethical principle that it is better to let a guilty person go free than to punish an innocent one.

5.4D Diversion

The fallacy of **diversion** consists in changing the issue in the middle of an argument. A prosecutor in a child abuse case might go on and on about the horrors of child abuse—the child's suffering and future psychological problems, statistics showing that the problem is a growing one, and so forth—when the real issue is whether the defendant is guilty of the crime. The argument would run:

1. The defendant is guilty of child abuse.
2. Child abuse is an awful crime.
3, 4, ... *n*. Statements concerning immediate and long-term effects on children, statistics on the extent of the problem, and other evidence.

The prosecutor's strategy is obvious. He is diverting attention from 1 to 2, because 2 is much easier to prove. Who could deny that child abuse is awful? At the same time, however, he is hoping that the jury will not notice the diversion and that the strength of the argument for conclusion 2 will carry over in their minds to 1, even though the defendant's guilt is a completely separate question. As the example illustrates, diversion often works hand in glove with the appeal to emotion: Diversion works best when the nonrelevant conclusion arouses powerful emotions. For this reason, a nonrelevant issue is sometimes called a *red herring*—herring turns red when it is smoked, and a smoked fish has such a powerful smell that dragging it across the ground will throw a dog off the scent.

A common form of diversion occurs in regard to human actions and their consequences. Virtually any action has some effects that are not intended, and often not even foreseen. The fact that your action had a certain consequence, therefore, does not necessarily mean that you intended it, and I would commit the fallacy of diversion if I tried to prove your intent solely by showing that the action did have that consequence. Suppose you go to the library one evening and miss a call from your mother. There may have been no way to anticipate the call. Even if there was, you may have felt that doing work at the library was more important and that missing the call would have to be an unfortunate by-product of going there. To prove that you were deliberately trying to avoid the call, we would need some positive evidence of that intent. It would be diversion to argue that you wanted to miss the call if the only evidence is that you did go to the library. In the same way, it would be fallacious to argue that the U.S. Labor Department is controlled by labor unions just because some decision turns out to be of benefit to union members; once again, we need evidence of intent, not merely of consequence.

Another form of diversion is called the *straw man* argument. This fallacy occurs in debate when someone distorts an opponent's position, usually stating it in an oversimplified or extreme form, and then refutes the distorted position, not the real one. For example, suppose you are a student in my class, and you come to me with the suggestion that I allow more class discussion. I would commit the straw man fallacy if I replied: "I don't want to give the entire class period over to an aimless bull session, because no one would learn anything." This may be an excellent argument against giving the entire class period over to an aimless bull session, but that is not what you suggested. (If you diagram this example, you will see that it fits the pattern of diversion.) Straw man arguments occur most often when issues are complex and emotions run high. Look for them especially in politics and in quarrels between friends and lovers.

Before we leave the subject of fallacies, a word about the term *non sequitur*, a Latin phrase whose literal meaning is "It does not follow." In everyday discourse, the term is often used to describe a wild leap or disconnect in a conversation or narrative, sometimes for deliberate comic effect. When an argument is described as a *non sequitur*, it is often because the premises seem completely unrelated to the conclusion.

> She: Why are you wearing your shirt backward?
> He: Because there's going to be lunar eclipse tonight.
> [Pause]
> She: That's it? That's your reason?

In logic, the term has been given various meanings. It is sometimes used broadly to mean any argument in which the conclusion does not follow from the premises. In that sense every fallacy is a *non sequitur*. It is sometimes used more narrowly as another name for diversion (and its special forms red herring and straw man). Because the premises in a case of diversion are used to support a conclusion that is different from the intended one, this fallacy is a particularly clear case of an argument in which the conclusion simply does not follow from the premises. In yet another sense, *non sequitur*s are a miscellaneous category of bad arguments that do not fit the specific patterns of any of the named fallacies.

In light of these different meanings, I have not used the term in classifying and describing the fallacies in this chapter, nor in the exercises that ask you to identify the fallacy committed by a given argument. Nevertheless, it is a useful term to have at your disposal. When you encounter an argument whose conclusion just doesn't follow, and you aren't sure or can't remember which specific fallacy it commits, it is safe to describe it as a *non sequitur*.

SUMMARY **Fallacies of Logical Structure**

Begging the question (circular argument): trying to support a proposition with an argument in which that proposition is a premise.

Equivocation: using a word in two different meanings in the premises and/or conclusion.

Appeal to ignorance (*argumentum ad ignorantiam*): using the absence of proof for a

proposition as evidence for the truth of the opposing proposition.

Diversion: trying to support one proposition by arguing for another proposition.

EXERCISE 5.4

Each of the following arguments commits one or more of the fallacies of logical structure discussed in this section; identify them.

✳ 1. No one has proved that global warming is actually occurring, so I'm sure it isn't.

2. It would be a crime to let that dessert go to waste. Since I am a law-abiding citizen, I'd better eat it.

3. Why are you so skeptical about ESP? Can you prove that it doesn't exist?

✳ 4. No one has shown that aliens did not create the crop circles. So the crop circles must have been made by aliens.

5. Only short poems, not long ones, can be good. Of course, many so-called poems, such as *Paradise Lost*, take up a large number of pages. But if they are any good, they must really be collections of short poems, because a long poem as such cannot be of any great value.

6. The safety inspector has suggested that American Traveler airlines delay the introduction of its new fleet for another year because of engine problems. But it has been

widely shown that air travel is safe. You are seven times more likely to get in a car accident than an airplane accident, not to mention that airport security measures have increased dramatically in the past 10 years, lowering the risk of people bringing weapons aboard a plane.

✳ 7. George's coaches say he has a real gift for football. So because his skill is a gift, he doesn't deserve any credit for it.

8. Abortion should be illegal because it's criminal to deliberately kill another human being.

9. There can't be a law without a law-giver. But nature operates in accordance with laws, like the law of gravity, so there must be a Law-Giver above nature.

✳ 10. Mary says she loves me. I don't know whether to believe her or not, but I guess I do, because I don't think she would lie to someone she loves about something that important.

11. Hard-core pornography is disgusting and offensive to any civilized person, so it cannot be included in the right to free speech.

12. "I don't see how you can support distribution requirements. Don't you want students to have any choice about their courses?"

*13. The federal government should save New York City from default, for New York deserves such aid.

14. Helping someone who is in trouble is the right thing to do. So if you don't help someone who's in trouble, you're violating his rights.

15. The layoffs at Acme Corporation were obviously racist in intent, since more than 60% of the people laid off were black or Puerto Rican.

Summary

A fallacy is an argument in which the premises appear to support the conclusion but actually provide little or no support. This chapter covered four categories of fallacies that occur fairly often in everyday thought and speech:

- Subjectivist fallacies involve the attempt to support a conclusion by appealing to nonobjective, nonrational factors.
- Fallacies of credibility involve a misuse of the standards of credibility for evaluating testimonial evidence.
- Fallacies of context jump to a conclusion without considering a large enough context of evidence.

- Fallacies of logical structure involve errors in the relation between premises and conclusion.

The 17 common fallacies we studied are listed and defined in the Key Terms section.

This is not an exhaustive list of errors in reasoning; it includes only the more common and more significant ones. It should also be emphasized that a given argument may commit more than one fallacy. If you encounter such an argument, in the exercises at the end of this chapter or in real life, you should try to identify all the fallacies it commits.

Key Terms

fallacy—an argument in which the premises appear to support the conclusion but actually provide little or no support.

SUBJECTIVIST FALLACIES

subjectivism—using the fact that one believes or wants a proposition to be true as evidence of its truth.

appeal to majority—using the fact that large numbers of people believe a proposition to be true as evidence of its truth.

appeal to emotion (*argumentum ad populum*)—trying to get someone to accept a proposition on the basis of an emotion one induces.

appeal to force (*argumentum ad baculum*)—trying to get someone to accept a proposition on the basis of a threat.

FALLACIES OF CREDIBILITY

appeal to authority (*argumentum ad verecundiam*)—using testimonial evidence for a proposition when the conditions for credibility are not satisfied or when the use of such evidence is inappropriate.

ad hominem—using a negative trait of a speaker as evidence that the speaker's statement is false or the argument weak.

FALLACIES OF CONTEXT

false alternative—excluding relevant possibilities without justification.

post hoc—using the fact that one event preceded another as sufficient evidence for the conclusion that the first caused the second.

hasty generalization—inferring a general proposition from an inadequate sample of positive instances.

accident—applying a generalization to a special case in disregard of qualities or circumstances that make it an exception to the generalization.

slippery slope—arguing against a proposed action or policy by claiming, with insufficient evidence, that it will lead to a series of increasingly bad consequences.

composition—inferring that a whole has a property merely because its parts have that property.

division—inferring that a part has a property merely because the whole has that property.

FALLACIES OF LOGICAL STRUCTURE

begging the question (circular argument)—trying to support a proposition with an argument in which that proposition is a premise.

equivocation—using a word with two different meanings in the premises and/or conclusion of an argument.

appeal to ignorance (*argumentum ad ignorantiam*)—using the absence of proof for a proposition as evidence for the truth of the opposing proposition.

diversion—trying to support one proposition by arguing for another proposition.

Additional Exercises

A. Identify the fallacy (or fallacies) committed by each of the following arguments.

✳ 1. The Beatles were the best rock group of the 1960s—they sold more records than any other group.

2. "That was a great movie."
"Why do you think so?"
"Well, I just loved it."

3. The seatbelt law should be repealed. It starts with the government making citizens do small things, like wearing seatbelts and helmets for biking, then it's curfews and policemen asking to see your papers, and then people will be afraid to do anything without seeking government approval first.

✳ 4. We can maintain our military strength by bringing back the draft and increasing the military budget, or we can cut spending and become a militarily weak nation. Which option do you favor?

5. How can you deny that the belief in an afterlife is universal? After all, everyone believes in it.

6. I just broke up with my boyfriend—it just goes to show I'll never make a relationship work.

✳ 7. If we pass a law to require that guns be registered with the government, it will be easier for the government to take the next step of confiscating guns. So we must oppose gun registration now.

8. This must be an important event. The *New York Times* gave it four columns on the front page.

9. Opinion poll question: Do you favor more money for welfare programs, or do you feel we should let people starve in the streets?

✳ 10. The spokesman for Wild West cigarettes says that advertisements do not get people addicted to cigarettes. But in a recent poll, 45% of Americans agreed that smoking advertisements affect whether people smoke or not, and 67% think that advertisements increase the amount of cigarettes that smokers have.

11. Both President Bush and President Obama have allowed their religious views to influence the government policies they support, and this is not right. Next there will be a national religion, and the government will persecute dissenters.

12. Salesman to customer: "I think you'll find that those shoes are the ones you want. Shall I wrap them up, or would you prefer to wear them?"

✳ 13. No one can criticize the Freudian theory unless he has been psychoanalyzed, for opposition to the theory is normally caused by unconscious resistance, arising from the Oedipal complex, which distorts one's thinking.

14. My logic teacher says it's a fallacy to appeal to authority, but I noticed in class today that she cited Aristotle in answering an objection we had.

15. Six months after President Hoover took office in 1929, the stock market crashed and

the Great Depression began. He is therefore responsible for this tragic episode in our nation's history.

✳ 16. Elephants live in tropical climates where there is plenty of vegetation. So we probably won't see any at the Chicago zoo.

17. The U.S. federal government should enact polices to provide day care for families who cannot afford it. Governments in all other industrialized nations have taken steps toward national child care.

18. Because she couldn't find a position as a teacher, Jackie was forced to take a job in data entry. But no one should be forced to work, so the police should investigate Jackie's situation.

✳ 19. I'm shocked to hear you preaching atheism. Does your father know you believe that?

20. Eight out of ten doctors support a woman's right to have an abortion. How can you deny that this is a genuine right?

21. This dish ought to be delicious, since I love everything that goes into it.

✳ 22. Mr. Miller said there was to be no talking during the test. So it's fair that Jamie had points deducted for asking to go to the bathroom because she felt sick.

23. "C'mon, spend the night with me."
"Why should I?"
"Why shouldn't you?"

24. Interviewer: "Senator, you voted for the new missile defense system. Would you explain your reasons, particularly in light of criticisms about the effectiveness of the system?"
Senator: "I'd be glad to. America needs a strong defense. We'd all like to live in peace with the other nations of this world, but we deceive ourselves if we think we can do that without being prepared to defend ourselves and our allies, our rights and our interests. It's a dangerous world out there, and I'd be derelict in my duty to the people of this nation if I allowed us to lie down and cry 'Uncle.'"

✳ 25. Wilson used abusive language toward the child who threw a stone at his car. Since child abuse is a crime, he should be reported to the authorities.

26. Studies show that most men who are married live longer, happier lives than men who do not get married. Therefore, if Troy wants a long happy life, he should marry Jennifer.

27. "The poor nations of the world will have to learn to produce their own food if they are to solve the problem of hunger in the long run."
"That's a heartless position. You wouldn't say that if you had ever really been hungry."

✳ 28. Democracy is the best political system. Therefore Iraq should adopt a democratic system now.

29. Many people say that Picasso was a great artist, but are we supposed to admire a man who beat his mistresses?

30. Bill Smith has lived all his life in Maplewood. From his schoolboy days, when he was a wrestling champ, to his service as a church deacon and downtown merchant, he has always been ready with a friendly smile and a helping hand. With his wife Mary, he has raised a family here. He has deep roots in our community and wants to make it an even better place to live. Vote for him for town council.

✳ 31. You weren't in class today, and you weren't in your room when I called. Why are you avoiding me?

32. The percentage of whites who are on welfare is higher than the percentage of Asians who are. Whites therefore make up a larger portion of the welfare population.

33. As a determinist, I believe that none of our actions results from free choice and that all of them are determined by the strongest motive acting upon us. To be sure, it sometimes does seem that we choose to act on the weaker of two motives. But if so, it only shows that the motive that seemed weaker

was really the stronger of the two, since it determined our action.

✱34. Human life depends on an environment that includes the existence of a large number of diverse species of plants and animals. Therefore we must do everything possible to prevent the extinction of any species.

35. Student to teacher: "How can you give me a C in this course? I've been getting Bs from all my other teachers. Maybe your grading standards are too high."

B. Taking each of the propositions that follow as a conclusion, make up an argument that commits the fallacy named in brackets. Try not to make the fallacy too blatant; instead, make it as subtle and persuasive-sounding as you can.

✱ 1. Mary lied when she said she saw a ghost. [False alternative]

2. Children should not be spanked. [Appeal to authority]

3. I'll pass this course. [Subjectivism]

✱ 4. The United States should adopt regulatory policies favoring entrepreneurs. [Appeal to majority]

5. Megadoses of vitamin C can cure cancer. [*Post hoc*]

6. Many crimes result from television violence. [Appeal to ignorance]

✱ 7. Capitalism exploits the working class. [Appeal to emotion]

8. *Moby Dick* is the greatest novel ever written. [Diversion]

9. U.S. savings bonds are a good investment. [Appeal to force]

✱10. Logic is worth studying. [Begging the question]

C. Identify any fallacies committed in the following passages.

✱ 1. "Received the Amulet at 2:00 p.m. on Friday. Went to Bingo at 6:00 p.m. and won $50.00. The next day I won $300.00! I'm very happy because I was about to give up Bingo, cause I wasn't winning." [Testimonial for Magic Square Amulet]

2. "I think in my country, in my family, I think that I believe that a marriage should be between a man and a woman. No offense to anybody out there, but that's how I was raised." [Carrie Prejean, 2009 Miss USA pageant. Fox News, May 11, 2009. http://www.foxnews.com/story/0,2933,519795,00.html]

3. Sister James: I don't think Father Flynn did anything wrong.
Sister Aloysius Beauvier: You just want things to be resolved so you can have simplicity back. [*Doubt* movie. http://www.imdb.com/title/tt0918927/quotes]

✱ 4. "After deciding to sell his home in Upland, California, novelist Whitney Stine pounded a 'For Sale' sign into his front yard. But he deliberately waited to do so until 2:22 p.m. one Thursday. "The house sold three days later for his asking price—$238,000. And Mr. Stine credits the quick sale to the advice of his astrologer, John Bradford, whom he has consulted for 12 years in the sale of five houses.

"'He always tells me to put out the sign according to the phases of the moon, and the houses have always sold within a few months,' Mr. Stine says." [Kathleen A. Hughes, "Thinking of Buying or Selling a House? Ask Your Astrologer," *Wall Street Journal*, October 12, 1986]

5. A pre-med student to her sculpture professor: "My lowest grade last year was in your class. It brings down my grade point average, and then I may not get into medical school. I'm taking sculpture to expand my horizons, and it shouldn't affect my life."

6. "[New York Mayor Ed Koch] dismisses *I, Koch* with a wave of the hand: 'It is not a

good book, it did not sell well.'" [Nicholas Lemann, "Koch as Koch Can," *New Republic*, January 20, 1986]

✳ 7. "Finally, in finding the $5 billion punitive award [against Exxon Corporation for the Valdez oil spill] justified, you are applying a different standard from the one you apply to yourself. Last year *The Times* joined in a brief that argued that a $10 million punitive damage verdict against another news medium should be set aside." [Letter to the Editor (from the chairman of Exxon), *New York Times*, November 3, 1994]

8. "Nothing is more irritating than taking a bottle of wine to someone's house and having them put it away, unopened. There are only two possible messages there: 1) This stuff is so bad, I'd never be caught dead serving it, or 2) This stuff is so good, I certainly wouldn't want to share it with *you*." [Dorothy J. Gaiter and John Brecher, "When You're Asked to Bring the Wine," *Tastings, Wall Street Journal*, October 23, 1998]

9. "Abortion is America's modern day holocaust. The taking of innocent human life has inflicted incalculable misery. The human suffering and the spiritual blindness caused by abortion are beyond comprehension. God is a compassionate and a just God, but His justice will not sleep forever. We must not—we cannot—remain silent when millions of innocent unborn children are killed every year." [Mathew Staver endorsing *40 Days For Life*. http://www.40daysforlife.com/about.cfm?selected=endorsements]

✳ 10. "[The classical liberals] put forward their ideas as immutable truths good at all times and places; they had no idea of historic relativity . . . The tragedy is that although these liberals were the sworn foes of political absolutism, they were themselves absolutist in the social creed they formulated." [John Dewey, *Liberalism and Social Action*, pp. 33–34]

11. "But don't wrangle with us so long as you apply, to our intended abolition of bourgeois property, the standard of your bourgeois notions of freedom, culture, law, etc. Your very ideas are but the outgrowth of the conditions of your bourgeois production and bourgeois property . . ." [Karl Marx and Friedrich Engels, *Communist Manifesto*]

12. Father Brendan Flynn: You haven't the slightest proof of anything!
Sister Aloysius Beauvier: But I have my certainty! And armed with that, I will go to your last parish, and the one before that if necessary. I'll find a parent. [*Doubt*. http://www.imdb.com/title/tt0918927/quotes]

✳ 13. "White House spokesman Robert Gibbs defended Obama's all-out campaign for Chicago's Olympics bid by claiming America will see a "tangible economic benefit." But as is always the case with sports corporate welfare disguised as "economic development," an elite few will benefit more than others." [Michelle Malkin, "All President's Cronies Are Going For Gold," *Investors Business Daily*. http://www.investors.com/NewsAndAnalysis/Article.aspx?id=50754]

14. "[Rev. Wieslaw Jankowski] cited the case of a woman who asked for a divorce days after renewing her wedding vows as part of a marriage counseling program. What was suspicious, he said, was how the wife suddenly developed a passionate hatred for her husband. 'According to what I could perceive, the devil was present and acting in an obvious way,' he said. 'How else can you explain how a wife, in the space of a couple of weeks, could come to hate her own husband, a man who is a good person?'" ["Ritual of Dealing With Demons Undergoes a Revival," *Washington Post*, February 28, 2008]

15. "Tall and handsome, [Karl Marx's collaborator Friedrich] Engels had a taste not just for ideas but for the good life—wine,

women, riding with the Cheshire hunt—and seems to have felt little sense of irony that all these things were paid for by the proletariat's back-breaking labor." ["A very special business angel," *Economist.com*. © 2009 The Economist Newspaper and The Economist Group.]

* 16. "Sen. Rudman advanced a 'pizza theory' to resolve disputes; budget negotiators were stalled for five hours but reached agreement 20 minutes after Rep. Aspin had pizza delivered." [*Wall Street Journal*, December 13, 1985]

17. "Voting 'yes' for the new Iranian constitution will satisfy the will and wrath of God Almighty." [Ayatollah Kohmeini, quoted on ABC News, December 2, 1979]

18. ". . . the concourse [in Heathrow airport] was temporarily immobilized by a hundred or more Muslim pilgrims, with 'Saracen Tours' on the luggage, who turned to face Mecca and prostrated themselves in prayer. Two cleaners leaning on their brooms . . . viewed this spectacle with disgust.

   "'Bloody Pakis,' said one. 'If they must say their bloody prayers, why don't they go and do it in the bloody chapel?'

   "'No use to them, is it?' said his companion, who seemed a shade less bigoted. 'Need a mosque, don't they?'

   "'Oh yerse!' said the first man sarcastically. 'That's all we need in 'Eathrow, a bloody mosque.'

   "'I'm not sayin' we ought to 'ave one,' said the second man patiently. 'I'm just sayin' that a Christian chapel wouldn't be no use 'em. Them bein' in-fi-dels.'. . .

"'I s'pose you think we ought to 'ave a synagogue an' a 'Indoo temple too, an' a totem pole for Red Indians to dance around?. . .'" [David Lodge, *Small World*]

* 19. ". . . we do not believe that any [telephone] service efficient, progressive and permanent can be given by companies not making fair profits. No community can afford to be served by unprofitable or bankrupt companies which are bound to give inefficient, unprogressive service." [Theodore M. Vail, *AT&T Annual Report*, 1914]

20. "Though Kornbluth concedes that [financier Michael] Milken did commit certain crimes, he basically swallows the line that Milken was the victim of an excessively ambitious prosecutor and a pair of excessively ambitious journalists. Apparently, Kornbluth thinks the world would be a whole lot safer if it was filled with unambitious prosecutors and diddling, passive reporters. Like him." [Joe Queenan, "Prose and Con: Separating Gems from Junk in the Milken Book boom," *Barrons*, November 30, 1992]

21. ". . . the insurance companies and [the Republicans] will fight the inclusion of a public option with every bit of power they can muster. They'll call it 'socialized medicine'—but by now we should all have realized that Republicans will call any health care reform Democrats propose socialized medicine.'" [Paul Waldman, "The Public Option and the Hope of Health Care Reform," *American Prospect*, December 23, 2008. http://www.prospect.org/cs/articles?article=the_public_option_and_the_hope_of_health_care_reform]

D. Diagram each of the following arguments, and assess it for logical strength. Identify any fallacies you think it commits.

* 1. ". . . an individual obviously is created at conception, because everyone was once a zygote, but no one was ever an unfertilized ovum or a sperm." [Letter to the editor, *New York Times*, June 5, 1989]

2. It's appalling that many of our young soldiers have to spend second and third tours in Iraq and Afghanistan, fighting for our nation, while we at home fuss over sports and the affairs of celebrities. If we're

going to fight this war, we ought to institute a draft. That way, there will be enough soldiers that none have to spend more than one tour in risky combat zones unless they want to. The institution of a draft is the only just way to proceed. [Adapted from a letter to the editor in *Boston Globe*, December 6, 2009]

3. "For tire consumers who can barely afford to replace a worn tire, an increase [in price due to tariffs on tires imported from China] . . . would be dramatic. This would increase the risk that some consumers will not replace worn tires when they should. It is an invitation to have more tire-related accidents on our roads." [Roy Littlefield, "Where Rubber Hits The Roadblock," *Washington Times*, August 21, 2009. http://www.washingtontimes.com/news/2009/aug/21/where-rubber-hits-the-roadblock/?feat=article_related_stories]

✳4. "If the task of the painter were to copy for men what they see, the critic could make only a single judgment: either that the copy is right or that it is wrong . . . No one who has read a page by a good critic . . . can ever again think that this barren choice of yes or no is all that the mind offers." [Jacob Bronowski, *Science and Human Values*]

5. "The fact that a majority of the States, reflecting after all the majority sentiment in those States, have had restrictions on abortions for at least a century seems to me as strong an indication there is that the asserted right to an abortion is not 'so rooted in the traditions and conscience of our people as to be ranked fundamental.'" [*Roe v. Wade*, J. Rehnquist, dissenting]

6. "William Butler, chief counsel for the Environmental Defense Fund, which led the attack on DDT between 1966 and 1972, repeats the argument today: 'You can't prove a negative,' he said when I called him in April. 'You can't say something doesn't exist because there's always a chance that it does exist but nobody has seen it. Therefore you can't say something doesn't cause cancer because there's always the chance that it does cause cancer but it hasn't showed up yet. . . .'" [William Tucker, "Of Mice and Men," *Harpers Magazine*, August 1978]

PART TWO

Deductive Logic

In Chapter 4, we identified the two broad kinds of inference, deductive and inductive. The role of a deductive argument is to draw a conclusion that is contained implicitly in the premises. A deductive argument is either valid or invalid; there are no intermediate degrees of partial validity. If the argument is valid, then the conclusion follows necessarily from the premises. In an inductive argument, by contrast, the conclusion amplifies—it goes beyond—what the premises state. Inductive arguments have degrees of strength, depending not only on the relationship between premises and conclusion but also on the context of other information available.

We now begin our study of deduction, which is the subject of Part 2. We are going to examine two approaches, two different ways of analyzing deductive arguments and evaluating them for validity. In the first half of Part 2 (Chapters 6–8), we will examine the traditional approach, first developed by the ancient Greek philosopher Aristotle. In the second half of Part 2 (Chapters 9–11), we will turn to the modern approach, developed mainly in the 20th century. While both approaches use symbols to represent certain aspects of deductive arguments, the traditional method is more closely related to ordinary language and is still valuable for analyzing and evaluating the forms of deductive reasoning we use most often. The modern approach is more thoroughly symbolic. It's more like algebra, which means that we have to invest in learning the symbolic notation. But the reward is the ability to analyze and evaluate a wider range of deductive arguments.

Categorical Propositions

At a certain point in our understanding of the natural world, we learned that whales are mammals. Since we also know that all mammals breathe by means of lungs, we can infer that whales breathe by means of lungs. Using the method of argument analysis we learned in Chapter 4, we would diagram this inference as follows:

1. Whales are mammals.
2. All mammals breathe by means of lungs.
3. Whales breathe by means of lungs.

<u>1 + 2</u>

↓

3

This is an example of the inference pattern known as the categorical syllogism. A categorical syllogism is a deductive argument with two premises, in which the premises and the conclusion are categorical propositions. In this chapter, we will examine the basic structure of categorical propositions. We will turn to the syllogism itself in the next chapter.

6.1 Standard Form

6.1A Components of Categorical Propositions

A **categorical proposition** can be regarded as an assertion about the relations among classes. This is easy to see in the example above. Whales are a species of animal; mammals

145

are the genus to which that species belongs. The proposition "Whales are mammals" says that the first class is included in the second. Every categorical proposition says that a certain relationship exists between two classes. The parts of the proposition that refer to the classes are called the *terms* of the proposition, and there are two terms: the *subject* and the *predicate,* symbolized by S and P. In our example, the subject is "whales" and the predicate is "mammals."

It isn't always so obvious that we are talking about classes of things. In the proposition "Whales breathe by means of lungs," the phrase "breathe by means of lungs" indicates a property that some objects have. But for any property there's a class of things that have property—in this case, things that breathe by means of lungs. So we would rewrite the proposition as "Whales are things that breathe by means of lungs," in order to make it clear that we are talking about two classes. In the same way, we would rewrite the proposition "Whales are large" as "Whales are large things." In general, we revise each proposition (without changing the meaning) so that it has the form "S is P" or "Ss are Ps."

The subject and predicate are not always single words. In fact, that is rarely the case. More often, one or both of the terms is a complex phrase. But phrases can designate classes of things just as well as individual words can. In each of the following examples, the subject and predicate terms are set off by parentheses.

1. (Computers) are (electronic machines that can be programmed to follow a sequence of instructions).
2. (Soldiers who have won the Medal of Honor) are (heroes).
3. (Commodities such as corn and wheat) are (economic goods subject to the law of supply and demand).

In 1, the subject is a single word, but the predicate is not. The opposite is true in 2. And in 3 neither term is a single word. But all three have the same basic form: Ss are Ps.

In addition to the subject and predicate, there is a third element of categorical propositions, indicated by the words "is" or "are." This element—called the **copula**—links subject and predicate. In all the examples so far, the copula has been *affirmative.* We said that S is P. But the copula can also be *negative,* as in the propositions:

4. Whales *are not* fish.
5. Copper *is not* a precious metal.
6. Businesses with fewer than 20 employees *are not* required to have a pension plan.

In terms of classes, we can make both the affirmative statement that S is included in P and the negative statement that S is excluded from P. The affirmative or negative character of a proposition is called its **quality**.

The fourth and final element of a categorical proposition, **quantity**, is a little less obvious than the others. The subject of "Whales are mammals" is "whales," and it is clear that we are talking about all of them. But sometimes we make statements about only *some* members of a class: Some whales are fish-eating carnivores, some politicians are crooks, some of Woody Allen's movies are not comedies. In ordinary language, we often do not say "all" or "some" explicitly; the context makes it clear which we mean. But the difference is crucial in logic, and we need to make it explicit.

A proposition with the form "All S are P" is **universal** in quantity. A proposition with the form "Some S are P" is **particular**. The distinction between universal and particular also applies to negative as well as affirmative propositions. Thus, "Some good tablet computers are not Apple products" is a particular negative proposition. "No freshman is a varsity player" is a universal negative proposition. Notice that the word "No" does double duty: It indicates both the negative quality and the universal quantity of the proposition.

A categorical proposition, then, has four components: (1) a subject term; (2) a predicate term; (3) a copula, which is either affirmative or negative in quality; (4) one or more words indicating quantity, universal or particular. The quality and quantity, taken together, determine the logical *form* of a proposition; the subject and predicate determine its *content*. Thus, the two statements "All whales are mammals" and "All snakes are reptiles" have the same logical form—affirmative and universal—although their content is quite different. Since there are two possible qualities, and two possible quantities, there are altogether just four standard logical forms for categorical propositions, no matter how complex their subject and predicate terms may be. These four forms are

	Affirmative	Negative
Universal	All *S* are *P*	No *S* is *P*
Particular	Some *S* are *P*	Some *S* are not *P*

Each of these standard forms has a traditional label that we will use as a shorthand reference to the form. The two affirmative forms are A and I, the first two vowels of the Latin word *affirmo* ("I affirm"). The negative forms are E and O, the vowels in *nego* ("I deny").

	Affirmative	Negative
Universal	A	E
Particular	I	O

EXERCISE 6.1A

For each of the following propositions, identify the subject and predicate terms, the quality, and the quantity. Then name the form (A, E, I, O).

 ✳ 1. Some movie stars are good actors.

 2. Some movie stars are not good actors.

 3. Some baseball players are not golfers.

 ✳ 4. All graduate students are broke people.

 5. All phones are communication devices.

 6. Some phones are cordless devices.

* 7. No phones are CD players.

8. Some people who have Ph.D.s are airheads.

9. No self-respecting person is a liar.

*10. No one who laughs at my teddy bear is a friend of mine.

11. All discoveries are additions to the stock of human knowledge.

12. No person over the age of 60 is an Olympic marathon champion.

*13. Some arguments in the works of great philosophers are fallacies.

14. All paintings are works of art.

15. Some works of art are not beautiful things.

6.1B Translating into Standard Form

To work with a categorical statement, we need to formulate it as one of the four standard forms: A, E, I, or O. The quantity must be explicitly indicated by a quantifier—a word such as "all," "no," or "some." The subject and predicate terms must be words or phrases designating a class of objects. And the copula must always be some form of the verb "to be": "is," "are," "was," "were," "will be" (and their negative forms).

Quantifier	Subject Class	Copula	Predicate Class
[All]		[Are, were, will be]	
[No]	S	[Is, was]	P
[Some]		[Are, are not]	

If a categorical statement is already in standard form, then all we need to do is look for words that indicate logical form. But in most cases we have to rework the sentence a bit in order to get it into standard form. If the predicate of a sentence is not a term designating objects, we have to turn it into one. "All whales are large," as we saw, must be rewritten as "All whales are large things." Similarly, "Some blondes have more fun" becomes "Some blondes are people who have more fun"; "No mammal can breathe under water" becomes "No mammal is a thing that can breathe under water"; and so on. The goal is always to arrive at the basic form: *[quantifier] S [copula] P*, where S and P are nouns or phrases referring to things, types of things, or classes of things.

As we go along, I will point out other problems connected with putting statements in standard form, as well as the techniques for dealing with them. But let's take care of some of the easier problems now.

Subject–predicate order. In English, the subject normally comes first in a sentence, with the predicate following it. But there are exceptions. In the statement "Tender is the night," for example, "the night" is the subject; that is what the statement is about. Similarly, the subject of the sentence "In the middle of the table were some pears" is "pears." In both of these cases, the order of subject and predicate is simply reversed. But consider another nonstandard statement: "No code has been made that cannot be broken." What is the subject term? "Codes." But which codes? "Codes that cannot be broken." The subject has been split in half, with the predicate ("has been made") coming in between the two halves of the subject. In standard form, this statement would be "No code that cannot be broken is a thing that has been made." In all cases of nonstandard order, you can identify the subject by asking what the statement is about.

Singular terms. Some categorical propositions have subject terms referring to a single person, place, or thing rather than to a class. For example,

7. New York is a large city.
8. Tom is a good basketball player.
9. I am not a coward.
10. The third car in the lot is a clunker.

In logic, a statement of this sort is called a **singular proposition**. The mark of a singular proposition is that the subject term is a name, pronoun, or phrase standing for a single object. Even though these propositions do not refer to classes, they have traditionally been treated as having universal quantity, and in this chapter we will follow that tradition. Thus an affirmative singular statement is an A proposition, and a negative one is an E proposition. The rationale is that a singular term may be thought of as naming a class with one member, and so of course the statement is about all the members of that class. To make this explicit, we could recast the examples above:

7. All cities identical to New York are large cities.
8. All people identical to Tom are good basketball players.
9. No person identical to me is a coward.
10. All cars identical to the third car in the lot is a clunker.

Such rephrasing is cumbersome, though. From here on out, we will leave singular statements as is, but remember that they are to be treated as universal.

Nonstandard quantifiers. Words that indicate quantity are called **quantifiers**. So far we have considered only the standard ones: "all," "some," and "no." But English (like any other language) has many nonstandard quantifiers in addition to the standard ones. Here are some of the ways to indicate universal quantity, with the quantifier indicated in bold:

Universal Propositions

Affirmative	Negative
11. **All** whales are mammals.	12. **No** dinosaur ate sushi.
13. **A** cat is a predator.	14. Not **a** creature was stirring.
15. **Every** president faces unexpected challenges.	16. **None** of the telephone is working.
17. **Each** item on the menu must has a price.	
18. **Any** student using the gym must show an ID.	

Particular propositions can also be expressed in various ways:

Particular Propositions

Affirmative	Negative
19. **Some** apples are good for baking.	20. **Some** apples are not good for baking.
21. **A** car is parked outside.	22. **A** wire is not plugged in.

Notice that the indefinite article "a" can mean either universal or particular quantity, depending on the context. It can mean any instance of a category such as cats, but it can also mean some instance, as in our example: "A car is parked outside."

As we noticed before, statements do not always contain an explicit quantifier, so we often need to determine from the context which one to insert. The statement that whales are mammals, for example, is clearly meant as a universal statement. So is the statement "Objects heavier than air must fall when unsupported"; if such objects *must* fall, then all of them do. In contrast, when you stay at a friend's house and he says, "Beer is in the refrigerator," it's a safe bet he means some beer, since the refrigerator has not been built that would hold all the beer that exists.

A special problem arises with statements that have the form "All *S* are not *P*." Despite its appearance, this is not a standard form. It is ambiguous. Consider the statement "All politicians are not crooks." Does this mean that no politicians are crooks (an E proposition) or that some politicians are not crooks (an O proposition)? It could mean either. So when you encounter a statement with that form, you will need to decide from the context whether an E or an O statement is intended and translate it accordingly.

In regard to particular quantifiers, remember that "some" means "at least one." "Some" is an extremely unspecific quantifier. It says, in effect: I know that at least one *S* is/is not *P*, but I don't know (or I'm not saying) how many are. Certain other nonuniversal quantifiers are much more specific than "some"—for example, "few," "several,"

STRATEGY Putting Propositions in Standard Form

To put a categorical proposition in standard form:

1. Identify the subject and predicate terms. Remember that the subject does not always come first in ordinary language.
2. If necessary, reformulate the subject and predicate terms so that they refer to classes.

3. Identify the quantity of the proposition.
   1. Singular propositions about an individual thing are treated as universal.
   2. Nonstandard quantifiers like "every," "few," and "any" must be translated into the standard quantifiers: "all," "some," and "no."

"many," "most." But they should all be translated as "some," and the statements containing them should be treated as particular propositions. To be sure, this can change the meaning of the statement; sometimes important information is lost. But the logic of the syllogism recognizes only two degrees of quantity: all and less than all. Reasoning that depends on the more specific degrees of quantity will be treated in Part 3.

EXERCISE 6.1B

Put each of the following statements into standard form; identify the subject and predicate terms, the quality, and the quantity; and name the form (A, E, I, or O).

* 1. All human beings are rational.
2. No mushrooms that grow in this forest are edible.
3. Some men are born great.
* 4. Some men do not achieve greatness.
5. Some men have greatness thrust upon them.
6. None of the students in my fourth hour class failed the exam.
* 7. Foolish is the man who seeks fame for its own sake.
8. Some of the members of the Capitol Rotunda Exercise and Reducing Club have not been pulling their weight.
9. The political party that wins a presidential election can expect to lose congressional seats 2 years later.
*10. Some of the greatest authors in literature did not attend college.
11. Some skiers are out of control.
12. Blessed are the meek.
*13. Some houses in the area were not affected by the storm.
14. Nobody's perfect.
15. Every rise in the stock market is followed by a fall.
*16. John F. Kennedy was not successful in his domestic policy.
17. Not a single doctor can figure out what is wrong with my son.
18. A family that plays together stays together.
*19. Some of the furniture is not on sale.
20. The window in my study is open.

6.2 The Square of Opposition

If you are given a subject term *S* and a predicate term *P*, there are four possible categorical propositions you can form with them: the four standard forms A, E, I, and O. Each of these propositions is logically related to the others, and traditional logicians organized these relationships into what they called the square of opposition. In this section, we will explore the traditional square of opposition. In the next section, we will consider a modern challenge to it.

6.2A Contraries

Let's start with the two universal propositions, A and E. Consider "All bread is nutri-tious" and "No bread is nutritious." Obviously, these are opposing statements. They cannot both be true. Even if you don't know what *S* and *P* stand for, you can tell in the abstract that "All *S* are *P*" and "No *S* is *P*" cannot both be true. But notice that they could both be false. If some types of bread are nutritious and others are not—if some *S* are *P* and some *S* are not *P*—then both universal statements would be false. In general, an A proposition and an E proposition that have the same subject and predicate terms cannot both be true, but they could both be false. We identify this relationship in logic by calling A and E **contrary** propositions. We can enter this relationship on a diagram that has the four standard forms of proposition arranged in a square:

A: All *S* are *P* ←————— contraries —————→ E: No *S* is *P*

I: Some *S* are *P*   O: Some *S* are not *P*

6.2B Contradictories

Our discussion of contraries suggests another possible relationship: statements that cannot both be true *and* cannot both be false. Does this relationship exist in our square? Yes. Look at A and O. If you accept the O proposition "Some bread is not nutritious," then you cannot also accept the A, "All bread is nutritious," and vice versa. They can-not both be true. But they cannot both be false, either. A can be false only if there is at least one *S* that is not *P*—some bread that is not nutritious—and in that case O is true. (Remember that "some" means "at least one.") Similarly, O can be false only if all *S* are *P*—all bread, every loaf without exception, is nutritious. So A and O cannot both be true, and they cannot both be false. If one is true, the other is false, and vice versa. Propositions that have this relationship are called **contradictories**.

It should be easy to see now that E and I are also contradictories. They cannot both be true and they cannot both be false. If it is false that no bread is nutritious, this could only be because at least some bread is nutritious, in which case I is true. In contrast, if I is false, that means not even one *S* is *P*, and thus it would be true to say that no *S* is *P*—E would be true. So our diagram now looks like this:

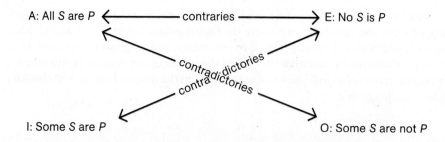

It's important to be clear about the difference between contrary and contradictory propositions. If you want to challenge a universal statement that someone else has made, you do not have to prove the contrary statement; you just have to prove the contradictory. Suppose someone says that all men are male chauvinists, and you object. You don't have to show that *no* man is a male chauvinist, only that *some* men are not. For the same reason, if you're the one claiming that all men are male chauvinists and someone else objects, you can't say, "Oh, you think no man is a male chauvinist?" You would be committing the fallacy of false alternatives, because you would be ignoring the possibility that some men are not chauvinists—a claim that is more limited, but still incompatible with your own assertion.

6.2C Subalternates

Let's consider now the relationship between A and I, a vertical relation on the diagram. Both A and I are affirmative propositions; they differ only in quantity. A is the more sweeping statement, because it makes a claim about all Ss. I is more cautious: When we say that some S are P, we are not committing ourselves to any claim about the whole class of Ss. We can see from this that if A is true, I must be true as well. If *all* Ss are P, then it is safe to say that *some* Ss are P—though we usually wouldn't bother to say it.

What about going in the opposite direction? Here we have to be careful. Normally when a person says "Some S are P," we take him to mean also that some Ss are not P. If *all* S were P, we assume he would have said so. Thus, in everyday speech, an I proposition is often taken to imply that the corresponding O proposition is true, and the corresponding A false. But in logic we do not make this assumption. We take the I proposition quite literally as a statement that at least one S is P. That leaves it an open question whether the other Ss are P or not. It might turn out that the others are not P (in which case the O proposition would be true). But it also might turn out that all the others *are* P, in which case the A proposition would be true. We don't know. So the truth of the I proposition leaves the truth or falsity of the corresponding A and O propositions *undetermined*.

In logic, the I proposition is called a **subalternate** to the A. This technical term is drawn from the military hierarchy, where "subaltern" means "lower in rank," and this gives us a good analogy. A general can issue orders to a private, but not vice versa; in the same way, the truth of an A proposition implies the truth of the I, but not vice versa. For exactly the same reasons, the O proposition is subalternate to the E. In this case, both propositions are negative, but that doesn't matter; the universal one always implies the particular, but not vice versa.

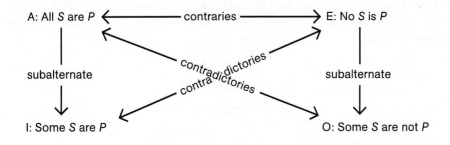

Before we leave the subalternate relation, notice what happens when we consider false statements instead of true ones. Now the tables are turned. If the I proposition is false, then the A must be false as well. If not even one *S* is *P*, then it is certainly false that all *S* are *P*. In the same way, on the negative side of the square, if not even one *S* is *not P*, then it is certainly false that no *S* is *P*: if O is false, E is false as well. But suppose that A is false. Does that mean I must be false, as well? No. Even if it isn't true that all politicians are honest, it might still be true that some are. Similarly, the falsity of an E proposition leaves the truth or falsity of the O undetermined. It would be false, for example, to say that no natural substances cause cancer, but it is still possible that some do not.

6.2D Subcontraries

There is only one relationship we haven't considered yet: the relationship between I and O. Can they both be true? Yes—that happens quite often. Some movie stars are good actors; some are not. Some clothes are made of wool; some are not. But can they both be false? No. Any given object in the class of *S*s must either be *P* or not be *P*. If it is *P*, that makes the I proposition true. If it is not *P*, that makes the O proposition true. So I and O cannot *both* be false. Notice that this is the mirror image of the relationship between A and E, which cannot both be true but can both be false. A and E are contraries, so I and O are called **subcontraries.**

When we add this relationship to our diagram, we have the full traditional square of opposition.

In laying out the square of opposition, I have used fewer examples than usual, and I've generally explained the logical relationships in a more abstract way as relationships among *S* and *P*. This was deliberate, and the reason can best be conveyed by an analogy. When you learned arithmetic, you learned a set of rules about specific numbers: 1 + 1 = 2, 3 × 7 = 21, 8 – 5 = 3, and so forth. When you went on to algebra, you had to master the idea of variables (*x, y, z*), which stand for any number, so that you could learn rules applying to all numbers: $x + x = 2x$, $x + y = y + x$, and so on. A number like 4 is abstract because it can stand for anything that has four units or members. But the variable *x* represents a higher level of abstraction, because it can stand for any number.

In the same way, a specific proposition is abstract because it contains concepts: WHALES, MAMMALS, etc. As we saw in Chapter 2, these are abstract terms. But *S* and *P* represent a higher level of abstraction because they are variables: *S* stands for a class of things, any class, just as *x* in algebra stands for a number, any number. What we are doing now is the algebra, not the arithmetic, of concepts. And the relationships in the square of opposition are like the laws of algebra, not like the rules for adding or subtracting specific numbers. Thus, in order to grasp these relationships, you need to be able to think at the higher level of abstraction, in terms of the variables *S* and *P*. The more you practice this, the easier it will be for you to spot logical relationships in concrete examples.

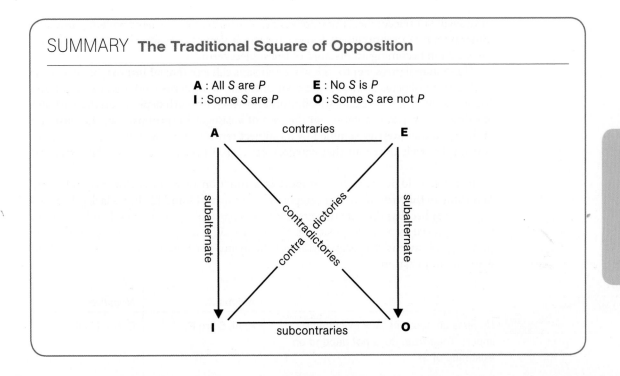

SUMMARY **The Traditional Square of Opposition**

A : All *S* are *P*   **E** : No *S* is *P*
I : Some *S* are *P*   **O** : Some *S* are not *P*

EXERCISE 6.2

For each pair of propositions, given that the first one is true, determine whether the second is true, false, or undetermined, in accordance with the traditional square of opposition.

✻ 1. All *S* are *P*. Some *S* are *P*.
  2. All *S* are *P*. No *S* is *P*.
  3. No *S* is *P*. All *S* are *P*.
✻ 4. Some *S* are *P*. All *S* are *P*.
  5. Some *S* are not *P*. All *S* are *P*.
  6. No *S* is *P*. Some *S* are *P*.
✻ 7. Some *S* are not *P*. No *S* is *P*.
  8. All *S* are *P*. Some *S* are not *P*.
  9. Some *S* are *P*. Some *S* are not *P*.
✻10. Some *S* are *P*. No *S* is *P*.
  11. Some *S* are not *P*. Some *S* are *P*.
  12. No *S* is *P*. Some *S* are not *P*.

6.3 Existential Import

In discussing the relationships that make up the square of opposition, we have been assuming that subject and predicate terms stand for categories of things in reality. But some terms, such as "unicorn" and names of other mythological beings, are vacuous: They do not have any referents in reality. How does this affect the truth or falsity of categorical statements involving these terms? It seems natural to say that the A proposition "All unicorns have horns" is true, at least as a statement about mythology. In the same way, when a teacher issues the warning, "All students who miss three or more classes will fail the course," the statement may be true even if there aren't any students who miss three or more classes. Indeed, the whole point of the warning is to discourage anyone from becoming an instance of the subject term.

These statements seem to lack what logicians call **existential import**, because their truth doesn't depend on the existence of unicorns or students who miss three or more classes. A statement has existential import only when its truth depends on the existence of things in a certain category—in the case of a categorical proposition, the existence of things in the category signified by its subject term. A statement with existential import implies that things in that category exist, so if they do not exist, the statement is false.

In modern logic, existential import is a function of a statement's logical form. According to this view, universal categorical statements (A and E) always lack existential import, just because they are universal, whereas particular statements (I and O) always have existential import. Propositions of the form *All S are P* and *No S is P* do not imply that there are any Ss, but propositions of the form *Some S are P* and *Some S are not P* do have that implication.

	Affirmative	Negative
Universal statements *lack* existential import: Their truth does *not* depend on existence of Ss	A: All S are P	E: No S is P
Particular statement *have* existential import: Their truth *does* depend on existence of Ss	I: Some S are P	O: Some S are not P

Because this distinction is based on logical form, it doesn't matter what the subject term is. The principle that universal propositions lack existential import is not limited to statements like "All unicorns have horns." It also applies to statements like "All dogs are animals," which is clearly about a class of existing things. According to the modern view, however, the statement does not *logically* imply their existence; it would be true even if there were no dogs. In contrast, the statements "Some dogs are animals" and "Some unicorns have horns" do have existential import because of their logical form. Since dogs exist but unicorns don't, the first statement is true but the second is false. The same distinction applies to negative propositions. The universal E proposition "No perpetual motion machine has been patented" is true, even though there are no perpetual motion machines. But the particular O statement "Some perpetual motion machines have not been patented" is false.

The issue of existential import has major implications for the square of opposition. The traditional square presupposes that the terms of any categorical proposition do have referents. If we adopt the modern doctrine about existential import, however, then some of the relations in the traditional square no longer hold. Let's start with subalternation. On the traditional view, an A proposition of the form *All S are P* entails the corresponding I proposition *Some S are P*. Now suppose there are no Ss. On the modern view, the I proposition would be false, but the A proposition could still be true. So the truth of the A proposition does not imply the truth of the corresponding I. The same is true for E and O. Subalternation must therefore be removed from the square.

The next casualty is the relation between A and E. On the traditional view, these propositions are contraries: They cannot both be true. If all *S*s are *P*, then it cannot also be true that no *S* is *P*. On the modern doctrine, however, neither of these universal statements has existential import, so they could both be true in the case where there are no *S*s. For example, "All unicorns have horns" and "No unicorns have horns" are both true by default because there are no unicorns.

Finally, the I and O propositions no longer fit the definition of subcontraries. Two statements are subcontraries if, in virtue of their logical form, they could both be true but could not both be false. If no *S*s exist, however, then both particular statements are false. To stay with our mythological example, the absence of unicorns means that both "Some unicorns have horns" and "Some unicorns do not have horns" are false statements.

The only relationship that survives in the modern square of opposition is that of contradictories. If there exists a single thing that is both *S* and *P*, then the I proposition is true and the E is false. But if nothing is both *S* and *P*, then the I proposition is false and the E is true—even if the absence of things that are both *S* and *P* is due to the fact that there aren't any *S*s at all. The same reasoning applies to the A and O propositions. So E is true if and only if I is false, and A is true if and only if O is false.

The modern square of opposition, then, is quite different from the traditional square. All of the horizontal and vertical relationships in the traditional square are removed, leaving only the diagonal relationship between contradictory statements.

Which version of the square of opposition—the traditional or the modern—should we adopt? Our answer depends on which is the correct view of existential import, and that remains a controversial issue. Something can be said on both sides. Against the modern doctrine, it can be argued that it's unfair to deprive all universal statements of existential import just because of a few unusual cases. Normally, we do take such statements to be about a class with real members. For example, if I said that everyone convicted of terrorism last year was sentenced to life in prison, you would feel cheated if I

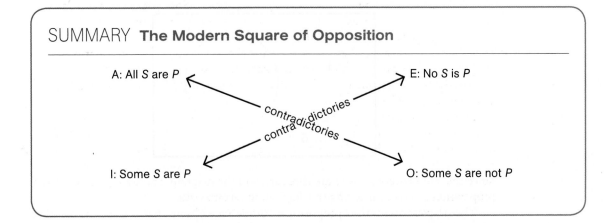

SUMMARY **The Modern Square of Opposition**

A: All *S* are *P*   E: No *S* is *P*

contradictories
contradictories

I: Some *S* are *P*   O: Some *S* are not *P*

went on to claim that the statement is true only because no one was convicted of terror-ism last year. However, the exceptions do exist—there are statements that lack existen-tial import—and we want our principles of logical form to be true without exception.

In light of this unresolved theoretical issue, it is useful for you to be familiar with both the traditional and the modern square of opposition. If you are dealing with a universal statement that clearly refers to class of actual things, it is safe to use the tradi-tional version of the square in deriving implications. But if there is any question about the existence of *S*s or *P*s, then you should rely on the modern version of the square.

EXERCISE 6.3

For each pair of propositions, given that the first one is true, determine whether the sec-ond is true, false, or undetermined, in accordance with the modern square of opposition.

✻ 1. All *S* are *P*. Some *S* are *P*.
  2. All *S* are *P*. No *S* is *P*.
  3. Some *S* are not *P*. All *S* are *P*.
✻ 4. Some *S* are *P*. All *S* are *P*.
  5. No *S* is *P*. Some *S* are *P*.
  6. Some *S* are not *P*. Some *S* are *P*.

✻ 7. All *S* are *P*. Some *S* are not *P*.
  8. Some *S* are *P*. Some *S* are not *P*.
  9. Some *S* are *P*. No *S* is *P*.
✻10. No *S* is *P*. Some *S* are not *P*.
  11. Some *S* are not *P*. No *S* is *P*.
  12. No *S* is *P*. All *S* are *P*.

6.4 Venn Diagrams

It is often helpful to think of a term in a proposition as a circle containing the members of the relevant class. There is in fact a systematic way of doing this: the method of Venn diagrams, invented by the English mathematician John Venn. This method gives us a way to represent each of the different forms of categorical proposition.

Venn diagrams use two overlapping circles, representing the subject and predicate terms:

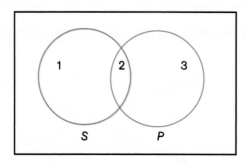

Since the circles overlap, there are three areas in the diagram, and we represent what a proposition asserts by marking the diagram in certain ways.

The simplest case is the I proposition. "Some *S* are *P*" says that at least one member of *S* is also a member of *P*. We can represent this by putting an X in area 2, where the *S* and *P* circles overlap, to mark the existence of at least one *S*:

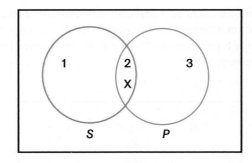

In the same way, the O proposition "Some *S* are not *P*" means that at least one member of *S* is not a member of *P*, so we put the X in area 1:

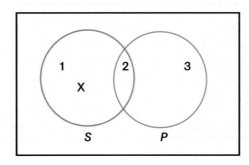

The representation of the universal propositions is a little different. For the A proposition "All *S* are *P*," we can't just add more Xs to area 2. That would not capture the universality of the proposition because it would leave open the possibility that some *S*s are not *P*. To capture the universality of the proposition, we need to rule out that possibility. We do so by shading out area 1 to indicate that it is empty:

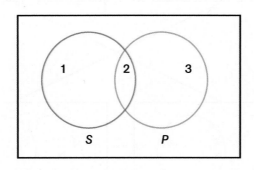

What this diagram tells us is that if there are any *S*s, they will be in area 2 (i.e., they will be *P*). But does the diagram say that there *are* any *S*s? No. Venn diagrams are based on the modern view of existential import, which holds that universal propositions do not imply the existence of any referents for the subject term.

In the same way, the E proposition "No *S* is *P*" is represented by shading out area 2 to indicate that it is empty:

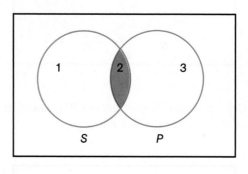

This diagram says that if there are any *S*s, they will be in area 1 (i.e., they will not be *P*), but it does not assert that there are any *S*s. Once again, in accordance with the modern doctrine of existential import, the universal E proposition does not imply the existence of referents for its subject term.

When the diagrams for the four categorical propositions are arranged in a square, they show very clearly the logical relationships in the modern square of opposition:

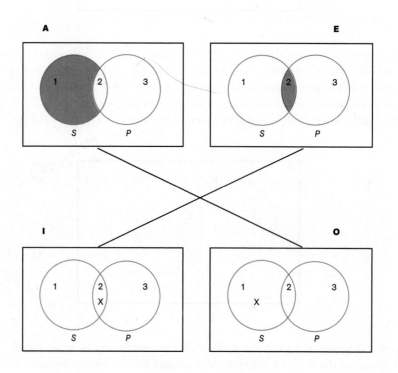

The diagrams for the A and O propositions are exact opposites, as they should be, since these propositions are contradictories: The diagram for the O proposition says there is something in area 1, while the A proposition says there is nothing there. The same relationship clearly exists between the E and I propositions.

On the modern view of existential import, A and E are not contrary propositions, since they can both be true if there are no Ss. The Venn diagrams make this clear: If both A and E are true, the entire S circle is shaded out, meaning that there are no Ss at all. Similarly, I and O can both be false: If there are no Ss, then we cannot put an X in either area of the S circle. Finally, the truth of an A proposition does not imply the truth of the I. By shading area 1 to represent "All S are P," we indicate that that area is empty. The absence of anything in that area does not imply the presence of anything in area 2. The same reasoning applies to the E and O propositions.

STRATEGY Using Venn Diagrams

To construct a Venn diagram for a categorical proposition:

1. Draw two overlapping circles, representing the subject and predicate terms.

2. If the proposition is universal, shade out the area of the S circle that must be empty if the proposition is true.

3. If the proposition is particular, put an X in the area of the S circle where something must exist for the proposition to be true.

EXERCISE 6.4

A. Put each of the following statements into standard form as a categorical proposition. Then construct a Venn diagram for the proposition. (Instead of labeling the circles S and P, you can use letters appropriate to the actual subject and predicate terms.)

* 1. Some cats are friendly.

2. No lie detector is perfect.

3. There are some fast turtles.

* 4. All policemen do their best to protect us from criminals.

5. No man can lift a ton.

6. There are no gilled mammals.

* 7. All clocks tell time.

8. Some cities are infested with crime.

9. Some stores don't charge high prices for trendy clothes.

*10. Some actors don't know how to act.

B. For each pair of Venn diagrams, determine whether the propositions represented by the diagrams are consistent or inconsistent—that is, if one of the propositions is true, could the other be true as well?

❋ 1.

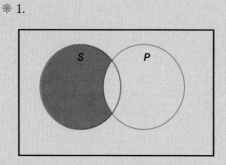 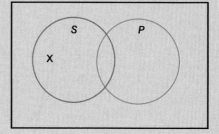

2.

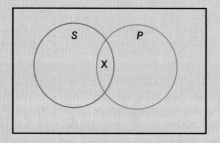 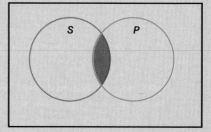

3.

 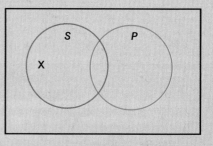

❋ 4.

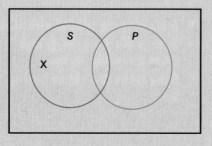 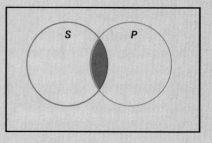

5.

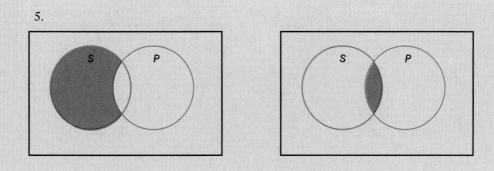

6.5 Immediate Inference

The square of opposition expresses the relationships of compatibility or incompatibility among the four standard forms of categorical proposition. These propositions have the same subject and predicate terms, but they make different assertions about the relationship between the subject class and the predicate class. For any two of the propositions, the question is: Are they compatible? Could they both be true? Could they both be false? But there are also relationships of logical equivalence among categorical propositions.

Equivalence is the relationship two propositions have when they say the same thing. In Chapter 4, we saw that statements can be equivalent if they use synonymous words (e.g., "Sally bought a car" and "Sally purchased a car") or if they differ only in grammatical structures such as active versus passive—"Sally purchased a car" and "A car was purchased by Sally." Now we are going to consider some of the ways categorical propositions can be equivalent in virtue of their logical form rather than the specific meaning of words or the grammar of English. In logic, two propositions are equivalent if the truth of each necessarily implies the truth of the other, and the falsity of each necessarily implies the falsity of the other. Logically equivalent propositions, in other words, must be either both true or both false. Categorical propositions can be transformed into logically equivalent propositions by means of various operations. Three particular operations—*conversion*, *obversion*, and *contraposition*—have traditionally been singled out for special attention. An understanding of these operations—known as *immediate inferences*—will give you a better feel for the logical features of categorical statements.

6.5A Conversion

The first immediate inference is called conversion, or taking the **converse**. The converse of a proposition is the result of switching its subject and predicate terms. Thus the converse of the I proposition "Some Englishmen are Scotch drinkers" is "Some Scotch drinkers are Englishmen"—another way of saying the same thing. The changes required for conversion are highlighted in this table:

	Quantity	Subject	Quality	Predicate
Proposition	Some	Scotch drinkers	are	Englishmen
Converse	Some	Englishmen	are	Scotch drinkers

Notice that the converse is itself an I proposition. Taking the converse of a proposition does not alter its quality or quantity, so the form of the proposition remains the same.

If the first proposition is true, the second must be true as well, and vice versa. Venn diagrams help make this equivalence clear. If two propositions are equivalent, their diagrams must be the same, and that's exactly what we find when we diagram an I proposition and its converse:

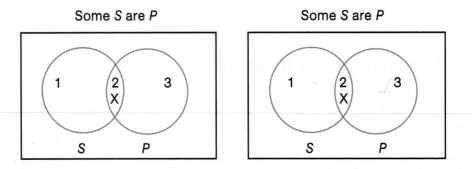

You might have thought that, to diagram the converse, we have to switch the S and P circles, since the P term is now the subject of the proposition. You could do that, but you don't have to; and keeping the circles in the same place makes it easier to use the diagrams as a test for equivalence. But that policy requires a small change in the way we approach the diagram. To diagram the standard form proposition "All S are P," we start with the S circle and ask: What does this proposition assert about things in the class of Ss? To diagram the converse, we follow the same process of thought. But since P is now the subject of the proposition, we start with that circle and ask: What does this proposition assert about things in the class of Ps?

The converse of the E proposition "No women have been U.S. presidents" is "No U.S. presidents have been women." Once again, the converse has the same form as the original proposition, and once again the statements are equivalent. An E proposition says that S is excluded from P, which implies that P is excluded from S.

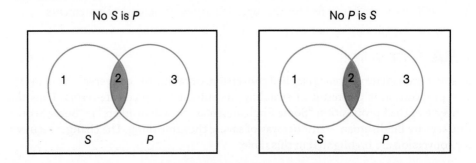

Since an E proposition is equivalent to its converse, it is legitimate to infer one from the other.

It is not legitimate, however, to infer the converse of an A proposition. The converse of "All pickpockets are criminals" would be "All criminals are pickpockets." As you can see, the converse here is not equivalent: The first statement is true, but its converse is false. *All S are P* does not imply *All P are S*, because saying that *S* is included in *P* does not imply that *P* is included in *S*.

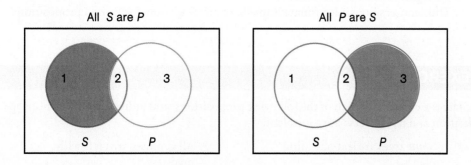

"All *S* are *P*" might seem to imply "All *P* are *S*" when *S* and *P* are terms standing for the same class. Consider the definition of "human beings" we discussed several chapters ago. Both of the following propositions are true: (1) "All human beings are rational animals," and (2) "All rational animals are human beings." The fact remains, however, that 2 does not logically follow from 1. If it seems to follow, that is because we know that there are no rational animals other than human beings. But that information is not contained in 1; it is extra information we happen to have in this case.

Taking the converse of an A proposition is sometimes called the fallacy of *illicit conversion*. Have you ever heard someone say, when he was being ridiculed for a new or unconventional idea, "Yeah, well they laughed at Columbus, too"? In saying that, he is appealing to the proposition "All brilliant new ideas were ridiculed," which may well be true. But he is implicitly inferring the converse, namely, "Any idea that is ridiculed is a brilliant new idea," and that proposition is almost certainly false. In any case, it does not follow. Be careful, then, to avoid illicit conversion. As we will see in the next chapter, it is a common error in syllogistic reasoning.

Finally, let's look at the O proposition. Venn diagrams tell us that the converse is not equivalent.

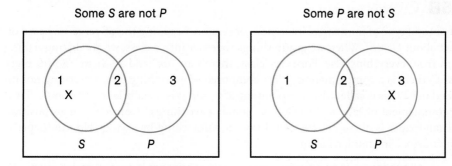

It often happens that an O proposition and its converse are both true. For example: some officers are not gentlemen and some gentlemen are not officers; some teachers are not gifted people and some gifted people are not teachers. Nevertheless, an O proposition is not logically equivalent to its converse, as we can see from another example: "Some human beings are not Americans" does not imply "Some Americans are not human beings." You can generate other examples like this if you use a genus as the subject term and a species as the predicate term. (Try it with "Some animals are not dogs," "Some legislators are not senators.")

Thus conversion is a legitimate immediate inference only for E and I propositions.

EXERCISE 6.5A

State the converse of each of the following propositions, and indicate whether the proposition and its converse are equivalent.

* 1. Some trees are leaf-shedding plants.
2. All stickers are scented.
3. All shrimp are crustaceans.
* 4. All green vegetables are things that contain beta carotene.
5. Some books are not hardbacks.
6. Some poor neighborhoods are safe areas.
* 7. No candidates for the legislature this year were adherents of Zoroastrianism.
8. All passenger trains are enterprises that depend on government subsidies.
9. All geniuses struggle with madness.
*10. Some videogames are not violent.
11. Some tornadoes move in a straight line.
12. Some copiers do not work properly.
*13. Some poor neighborhoods are not safe areas.
14. None of my children is a married person.
15. Nothing you read on the Internet is trustworthy.

6.5B Obversion

The second type of immediate inference—obversion, or taking the **obverse**—is based on a fact about classes. When we group things together into a class, we are distinguishing them from everything else. For every class, there's an "us" and a "them." So for every class C, there is a complementary class composed of everything else, everything not included in C. This is called the **complement** of C, and it is usually labeled "non-C." Thus the complement of "abrasive things" is "nonabrasive things." Consider the proposition "All sandpaper is abrasive." We could say the same thing by saying "No sandpaper is nonabrasive." In standard form:

All sandpaper is an abrasive thing.   No sandpaper is a nonabrasive thing.

The second proposition is called the obverse of the first.

We arrive at the obverse of a proposition by making two changes: We replace the predicate term with its complement, and we change the quality of the proposition—affirmative to negative or negative to affirmative. Thus the obverse of an A proposition, "All *S* are *P*," is always an E proposition, "No *S* is non-*P*." The changes required for obversion are highlighted in this table:

	Quantity	Subject	Quality	Predicate
Proposition	All	sandpaper	is	an abrasive thing
Obverse	No	sandpaper	is	a nonabrasive thing

Notice that the subject term remains unchanged and that the quantity also stays the same. (Remember that in a universal negative proposition, "No" does double duty; it signifies both universal quantity and negative quality. So when we take the obverse of the A proposition, "No *S* is non-*P*" changes the quality of the A proposition but the quantity remains universal.) If the predicate term already has the form "non-*P*," we follow the same rule: "Non-*P*" is changed to its complement, which is "*P*." Thus the obverse of "All heavy elements are unstable things" is "No heavy element is a stable thing."

For all four types of proposition, obversion results in an equivalent proposition. In each case, the obverse follows logically. The two changes we make—replacing *P* with non-*P* and switching the quality—cancel each other.

Proposition	Obverse
A: All sandpaper is an abrasive thing.	E: No sandpaper is a nonabrasive thing.
I: Some people are kind persons.	O: Some people are not unkind persons.
E: No machine is a conscious being.	A: All machines are nonconscious beings.
O: Some chemicals are not toxic substances.	I: Some chemicals are nontoxic substances.

To diagram these equivalences, we first need to understand how to diagram the complement of a term. The complement of *P*, non-*P*, includes everything outside the *P* circle. That includes not only area 1 in the *S* circle, but also the region outside both circles, which I have labeled area 4.

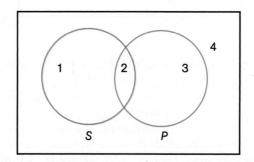

So let's take the A proposition "All *S* are *P*." Its obverse is "No *S* is non-*P*." Since this is an E proposition, we diagram it by shading out the area of overlap between subject and predicate. The subject term is represented by areas 1 and 2. The predicate term, non-*P*, is represented by areas 1 and 4. The area of overlap is obviously area 1, so we shade it out.

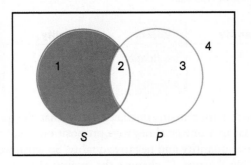

You can see that this Venn diagram is identical to the standard diagram for the A proposition, which means the proposition and its obverse are equivalent.

Let's try this with one of the particular propositions: "Some *S* are *P*" and its obverse "Some *S* are not non-*P*." The obverse is an O proposition, so we will need to put an X in the subject circle outside its overlap with the predicate. Once again, the subject term *S* is represented by areas 1 and 2 and the predicate term non-*P* by areas 1 and 4, so the overlap is again area 1. That leaves area 2 as the only part of *S* that is outside the area of non-*P*, so that's where we put our X. The result is identical with the standard diagram for I propositions.

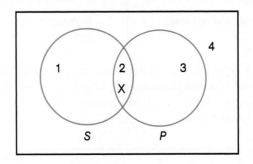

Having seen how to prove equivalence of the obverse for the A and I propositions, you should now be able to apply the technique to E and O.

When you take the obverse of any categorical proposition, you need to be careful about how you formulate the complement of the predicate term. Strictly speaking, the complement of a term refers to everything in the universe not included under the term. A term and its complement divide the entire universe into two mutually exclusive and jointly exhaustive categories. Now consider the words "mature" and "immature."

These do not divide the universe exhaustively. They apply only to living things that pass through stages of development before they reach an adult form. A six-penny nail is neither mature nor immature. Strictly speaking, therefore, "immature things" is not the complement of "mature things." The complement is "nonmature," which refers to anything—even six-penny nails—that is outside the class of mature living things. The same point applies to many words that have the prefix "im-," or similar prefixes such as "a-" and "un-."

Nevertheless, when we take the obverse of the proposition "All the dogs in Fleabite Kennels are mature things," it would be acceptable to use "None of the dogs in Fleabite Kennels are immature things." That's because the subject term, "dogs in Fleabite Kennels," restricts the universe of discourse to a genus that *can* be exhaustively divided into mature and immature members. Since we're talking about dogs, we can be sure that if they are all mature, then none are immature. In general, we can use obversion whenever *P* and non-*P* exhaustively divide the class of *S*s.

We do need to distinguish carefully, however, between terms that are complementary, even in this extended sense, and terms that are opposed in other ways. The obverse of "All logic students are smart," for example, is not "No logic student is stupid." The class of stupid people does not include everyone outside the class of smart people; it leaves out the middle range of average intelligence. "Smart" and "stupid" are opposites, but not complements. The real obverse would be "No logic student is non-smart." You need to be careful about this wherever you are dealing with terms at opposite ends of a spectrum—black and white, tall and short, fat and thin. The fallacy of false alternatives is often committed in such cases. "No one in that family is thin," says Joe. "You mean," says Martha, "everyone in the family is fat?" No. All Joe said is that everyone in the family is non-thin.

When you take an obverse, finally, be sure to distinguish between the word "not" and the prefix "non-." "Not" is a mark of quality and is part of the form of a proposition. "Non-" is part of the predicate term. With the I proposition, it is easy to forget that we need both: *P* must become non-*P* and "is" must become "is not." Notice also that the obverse of an O proposition is an I proposition. "Some *S* are non-*P*" is affirmative, even though it sounds negative, because the "non-" is part of the predicate term and does not indicate negative quality.

EXERCISE 6.5B

State the obverse of each of the following propositions. Make sure that you use genuinely complementary terms.

* 1. None of the athletes is an injured person.
2. Some of the beans are cooked foods.
3. All of the dishes are washed things.
* 4. All of Alister's friends are students.
5. Some gamblers are lucky people.
6. Some criminals are not insane people.
* 7. Some policies are wise things.
8. No sighting of a UFO is a thing that has been confirmed.
9. All of the campers were happy people.

＊10. Some companies were not enterprises that made a profit this year.

11. Some proponents of the legaliza-
tion of marijuana are unkempt
people.

12. Some snakes are not poisonous
beings.

＊13. No one in this room is a suspect.

14. All of the rooms with an ocean
view are reserved places.

15. Some of the planes are things unable to take off.

6.5C Contraposition

Suppose you did not know anything about the Ismaili religion but were told that
Ismailis are Muslims. You could infer immediately that any non-Muslim is a non-
Ismaili. That would be an example of contraposition, or taking the **contrapositive**. The
contrapositive of a proposition is formed by two steps: switching the subject and predicate terms, as in taking the converse, and replacing both the subject and the predicate
terms with their complements. The quality and quantity of the proposition remain as
they were.

	Quantity	Subject	Quality	Predicate
Proposition	All	Ismailis	are	Muslims
Contrapositive	All	non-Muslims	are	non-Ismailis

It is always legitimate to take the contrapositive of an A proposition. "All *S* are *P*" is
equivalent to "All non-*P* are non-*S*." You can see why by thinking once again in terms
of classes. The A proposition says that the class of *S*s is included within the class of *P*s.
So anything outside the class of *P*s (i.e., all the non-*P*s) must also be outside the class of
*S*s (i.e., it must be a non-*S*). Switzerland is in Europe, so if you're not in Europe, you're
not in Switzerland.

Diagramming the equivalence can be challenging because we have to deal with the
complements of both the subject and the predicate terms. So let's start by listing the
areas that represent the terms and their complements:

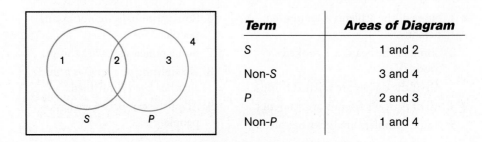

Term	Areas of Diagram
S	1 and 2
Non-*S*	3 and 4
P	2 and 3
Non-*P*	1 and 4

Using the table on the right as our guide, we diagram "All non-*P* are non-*S*" in the usual way by looking first to the subject of the proposition, non-*P*. Since this is an A proposition, we must shade out the area of non-*P* that is not included in the predicate term, non-*S*. Of the two areas that make up the class of non-*P*s, area 4 is the one that it shares with non-*S*—4 is the area of overlap between non-*P* and non-*S*—which leaves area 1 as the area of non-*P* outside non-*S*. That's the area we can now shade out.

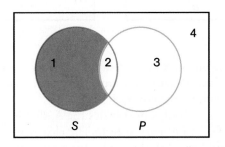

This diagram is identical to the standard diagram for the A proposition, which means the proposition and its contrapositive are equivalent.

Contraposition is not a legitimate operation for E and I propositions. For example, the E proposition "No primate is an aquatic animal" is clearly not equivalent to its contrapositive, "No nonaquatic animal is a nonprimate," because the first is true and the second false (cows are nonaquatic animals but they are nonprimates). Venn diagrams reveal why an E proposition is not equivalent to its contrapositive:

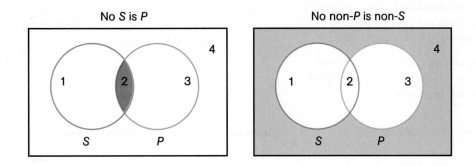

The diagram on the left is the standard one for the E proposition, with the area of overlap between *S* and *P*—area 2—shaded out. In the diagram on the right, for the contrapositive, the shaded area of overlap between non-*P* and non-*S* is not area 2 but area 4.

Similarly, the I proposition, "Some humans are giraffes," is clearly not equivalent to its contrapositive, "Some nongiraffes are nonhumans." In this case the first is false while the second is true (monkeys are nongiraffes and also nonhumans).

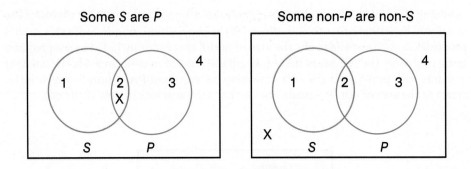

For an I proposition, we put an X in the area of overlap between subject and predicate. In the diagram for the contrapositive, the area of overlap is 4, not 2. Once again the difference in diagrams illustrates the nonequivalence.

The O proposition is the only one, besides the A, that is equivalent to its contrapositive. It is rarely used in ordinary speech. The closest we can come to a natural-sounding example would be something like the following. If we were considering

---

SUMMARY Immediate Inferences

The table that follows summarizes the key information about the three immediate inferences. For the converse and contrapositive, the nonequivalent propositions are crossed out. In order to test your understanding, try to reproduce the table without looking at it. List the converse, obverse, and contrapositive for each of the four types of propositions (12 items in all), and determine whether they are equivalent or not.

Converse: the proposition that results from switching the subject and predicate terms in a categorical proposition.

Obverse: the proposition that results from changing the quality of a categorical proposition and replacing the predicate term with its complement.

Contrapositive: the proposition that results from replacing the subject term in a categorical proposition with the complement of the predicate and the predicate with the complement of the subject.

Standard Form Proposition	Converse	Obverse	Contrapositive
A: All S are P	~~All P are S~~	No S is non-P	All non-P are non-S
E: No S is P	No P is S	All S are non-P	~~No non-P is non-S~~
I: Some S are P	Some P are S	Some S are not non-P	~~Some non-P are non-S~~
O: Some S are not P	~~Some P are not S~~	Some S are non-P	Some non-P are not non-S

candidates for some job or office, we might say with a sigh, "Some talented candidates are not acceptable." The contrapositive would be "Some unacceptable people are not untalented." (You can test this equivalence yourself by constructing the Venn diagrams.) The A proposition, however, is far and away the most common case in which we use the contrapositive.

EXERCISE 6.5C

For each proposition below, find the converse, obverse, or contrapositive as indicated in parentheses, and determine whether the resulting proposition is the equivalent of the original.

✳ 1. Some *S* are *P*. (contrapositive)

2. All *S* are *P*. (converse)

3. No *S* is *P*. (converse)

✳ 4. Some *S* are not *P*. (obverse)

5. Some *S* are not *P*. (converse)

6. All *S* are *P*. (obverse)

✳ 7. Some *S* are *P*. (contrapositive)

8. No *S* is *P*. (obverse)

9. Some *S* are non-*P*. (obverse)

✳10. Some non-*S* are *P*. (converse)

11. All non-*S* are non-*P*. (obverse)

12. Some *S* are non-*P*. (converse)

✳13. No non-*S* is non-*P*. (contrapositive)

14. All non-*S* are *P*. (converse)

15. All *S* are non-*P*. (contrapositive)

✳16. Some non-*S* are not non-*P*. (contrapositive)

17. No non-*S* is *P*. (conversion)

18. Some non-*S* are non-*P*. (obverse)

✳19. No *S* is non-*P*. (contrapositive)

20. Some *S* are not *P*. (contrapositive)

Summary

In this chapter, we have studied the structure of categorical propositions and some of the logical relations among them. A categorical proposition has a subject and a predicate term, which give it its content. It also has an affirmative or negative quality and a universal or particular quantity. The quality and quantity together determine the form of the proposition—A, E, I, or O. In traditional logic these four standard forms can be arranged in a square of opposition, which exhibits the following logical relationships: contraries, contradictories, subalternates, and subcontraries. If we hold that A and E propositions lack existential import, however, then all these relationships except contradictories are omitted from the square.

Each term (*S* and *P*) also has a complementary term (non-*S*, non-*P*). Some forms of categorical propositions can be transformed into equivalent propositions through immediate inferences, but we must be careful to avoid illegitimate transformation. Only I and E propositions can legitimately be transformed through conversion; only A and O propositions can legitimately be transformed through contraposition; all four forms of the propositions can legitimately be transformed through obversion.

If we accept the view that universal propositions lack existential import, we can use Venn diagrams, in which the subject and predicate terms of a proposition are represented by overlapping circles, to represent the meaning of any categorical proposition and to determine whether two propositions are equivalent or not.

In the next chapter, we'll use what we've learned about these propositions to analyze and evaluate categorical syllogisms.

Key Terms

categorical proposition—a proposition containing a subject and a predicate term and asserting that some or all of the referents of the subject term are included in or excluded from the class designated by the predicate term.

copula—a verb of being ("is," "are," etc.) that links the subject and the predicate in a categorical proposition.

quality—the affirmative or negative character of a categorical proposition.

quantity—the particular or universal character of a categorical proposition.

universal proposition—a categorical proposition that makes an assertion about all members of the class designated by its subject term. (A and E are universal propositions.)

particular proposition—a categorical proposition that makes an assertion about at least one but not all members of the class designated by its subject term (I and O are particular propositions).

singular proposition—a categorical proposition whose subject term designates a specific thing rather than a class.

quantifier—the element in a statement's logical form that indicates whether the predicate term is asserted of all or some of the referents of the subject term.

contraries—in the traditional square of opposition, a pair of categorical propositions that, in virtue of their logical form, could not both be true but could both be false (A and E).

contradictories—in the traditional and modern squares of opposition, a pair of categorical propositions that, in virtue of their logical form, could neither both be true nor both be false (A and O, E and I).

subalternate—in the traditional square of opposition, the relationship between a universal and a particular proposition of the same quality (A and I, E and O): If the universal is true, the particular must be true, and if the particular is false, the universal must be false.

subcontraries—in the traditional square of opposition, a pair of propositions that, in virtue of their logical form, could both be true but could not both be false (I and O).

existential import—a property of categorical propositions: A proposition has existential import if its truth depends on the existence of things of the kinds specified by terms in the proposition.

converse—the proposition that results from switching the subject and predicate terms in a categorical proposition.

obverse—the proposition that results from changing the quality of a categorical proposition and replacing the predicate term with its complement.

complement—a term designating the class of all things excluded by another term.

contrapositive—the proposition that results from replacing the subject term in a categorical proposition with the complement of the predicate and the predicate with the complement of the subject.

Additional Exercises

A. The following statements are in standard form. Name the form of the proposition (A, E, I, or O). Then reformulate them so that they are more concise (see how many words you can eliminate) and less awkward.

＊ 1. Some large corporations are not things that paid any income tax last year.

2. No Spanish playwright is a person who has won the Nobel Prize in Literature.

3. All planets are things whose motion is governed by the gravitational attraction of the sun.

＊ 4. Some statistics that indicate economic growth are statistics that can be misleading.

5. All persons who chronically tell lies are persons who feel insecure about their ability to succeed on the basis of the truth.

6. Some academic subjects are branches of study that require the use of mathematical techniques.

＊ 7. Some proponents of radical economic change are not thinkers who have carefully considered the consequences of their ideas.

8. Some fast-food restaurants are establishments in which you are permitted to have a hamburger prepared "your way."

9. No automobile produced in the United States as a standard factory model is a vehicle that can safely be driven at over 200 miles per hour.

＊10. No Friday is a day on which my family ate meat.

B. Translate each of the following statements into standard form and identify the form. Then find the logically related proposition mentioned in the parentheses.

＊ 1. All sonnets have 14 lines. (contrary)

2. Some metals rust. (converse)

3. That man in the corner is drunk. (obverse)

＊ 4. Some fish are not carnivores. (obverse)

5. Nobody knows the trouble I've seen. (subalternate)

6. At the edge of the clearing were some deer. (subcontrary)

＊ 7. Big girls don't cry. (contrary)

8. "War is hell"—General Sherman. (contradictory)

9. Sugar is sweet. (subalternate)

＊10. So are you. (obverse)

11. "Men at work"—highway sign. (contradictory)

12. Alice doesn't live here any more. (contrary)

✳13. Real men don't eat quiche. (converse)

14. Students who return after midnight are required to sign in. (obverse)

15. No one has run a mile in less than 3:40. (contradictory)

✳16. Every country with the word "Democratic" in its official name is a dictatorship. (contrapositive)

17. Someone is knocking at my door. (subcontrary)

18. Some criminals don't come from poor families. (contrapositive)

✳19. No law is just that forces a person to act against his judgment. (contrapositive)

20. Some proposals put forward for the control of nuclear arms would not affect the levels of submarine-based missiles. (contradictory)

C. For each Venn diagram below, name the categorical proposition it represents.

✳ 1.

2.

3.

✳ 4.

5.

6.

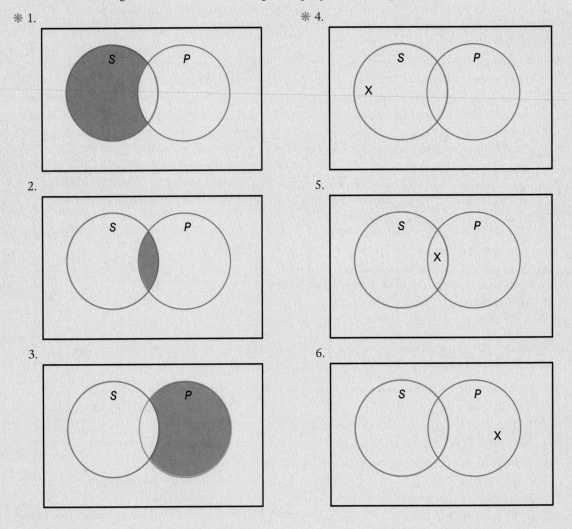

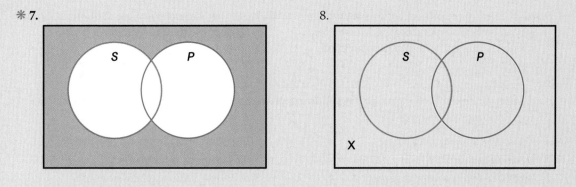

* 7.

8.

D. Name the logical relationship that exists between each pair of propositions below. Then state whether the second one is equivalent to the first. In any case where existential import makes a difference, give both the traditional and the modern interpretation.

* 1. No man is an island. Some men are not islands.
2. Some water is not fit to drink. Some water is unfit to drink.
3. All sailors are swimmers. All swimmers are sailors.
* 4. Some cases of cancer are conditions hard to diagnose. Some cases of cancer are not conditions hard to diagnose.
5. Some people are persons unlucky in love. Some people are not persons lucky in love.
6. None of my acquaintances is in trouble with the law. No one who is in trouble with the law is an acquaintance of mine.

* 7. No dishonest person is a happy person. No unhappy person is an honest person.
8. Some of the union members were not pleased with the new contract. Some people who were pleased with the new contract were not union members.
9. All voluntary actions are actions for which we can be held responsible. All actions for which we cannot be held responsible are involuntary actions.
*10. All medical expenses are deductible items. Some deductible items are medical expenses.

E. For each pair of propositions in Exercise D, use Venn diagrams to determine whether they are equivalent. In both diagrams, the *S* circle represents the subject of the first proposition and the *P* circle represents the predicate of the first proposition.

* 1. No man is an island. Some men are not islands.
2. Some water is not fit to drink. Some water is unfit to drink.
3. All sailors are swimmers. All swimmers are sailors.
* 4. Some cases of cancer are conditions hard to diagnose. Some cases of cancer are not conditions hard to diagnose.
5. Some people are unlucky in love. Some people are not lucky in love.

6. None of my acquaintances is in trouble with the law. No one who is in trouble with the law is an acquaintance of mine.
* 7. No dishonest person is a happy person. No unhappy person is an honest person.
8. Some of the union members were not pleased with the new contract. Some people who were pleased with the new contract were not union members.

9. All voluntary actions are actions for which we can be held responsible. All actions for which we cannot be held responsible are involuntary.

✳10. All medical expenses are deductible. Some deductible items are medical expenses.

F. Find a literal translation for each of the following proverbs. Your translation should be a universal categorical proposition (A or E).

✳ 1. Every cloud has a silver lining.

2. Nothing ventured, nothing gained.

3. Birds of a feather flock together.

✳ 4. Rome wasn't built in a day.

5. People in glass houses shouldn't throw stones.

6. A penny saved is a penny earned.

✳ 7. Forewarned is forearmed.

8. A rolling stone gathers no moss.

9. Uneasy lies the head that wears a crown.

✳10. Money talks.

G. The passages below contain immediate inferences. Put the premise and conclusion in standard form, and determine whether the conclusion is a legitimate inference.

✳ 1. "[A]ll revolutionaries in the domain of thought, from Galileo and Columbus to Wagner and Manet, have been for a time persecuted and derided. Ergo, since the Post-Impressionists have provoked a vast amount of scornful mirth, they are necessarily great men." [Art critic Royal Cortissoz speaking ironically, "The Post-Impressionist Illusion," *Century* magazine, April 1913]

2. "He said he would acquire no knowledge which did not bear upon his object. Therefore all that knowledge which he possessed was such as would be useful to him." [Arthur Conan Doyle, *A Study in Scarlet*]

3. "The East Coast was hammered by its second snowstorm in a week yesterday. . . . Most intriguing of all was the word out of Washington, D.C., possibly the most snow-fearing town anywhere in the U.S. . . . All 'nonessential federal workers' were allowed to go home. So that means those who lashed themselves to their desks during the 10-inch 'blizzard' are essential. Did anyone make the list?" [*Wall Street Journal*, January 27, 1987]

✳ 4. "The chief foundations of all states, new as well as old or composite, are good laws and good arms; and as there cannot be good laws where the state is not well armed, it follows that where they are well armed they have good laws." [Niccolo Machiavelli, *The Prince*]

5. Just as my fingers on these keys
Make music, so the selfsame sounds
On my spirit make a music, too.

Music is feeling, then, not sound;
And thus it is that what I feel,
Here in this room, desiring you,

Thinking of your blue-shadowed silk,
Is music.
[Wallace Stevens, "Peter Quince at the Clavier." Copyright 1921, renewed 1951 by Wallace Stevens. Reprinted from *The Collected Poems of Wallace Stevens* by permission of Alfred A. Knopf.]

✳ **H.** The operation of contraposition can be deconstructed into a sequence of simpler operations. If we take the obverse of a proposition, and then apply conversion to the result, and then take the obverse again, we will arrive at the contrapositive of the original proposition. Use this to explain why contraposition is legitimate for A and O propositions, but not for E and I.

Categorical Syllogisms

Now that we understand the logical structure of categorical propositions, we can turn to the categorical syllogism, which is one of the basic types of deductive argument. In this chapter, we will learn how to analyze and evaluate arguments of this type. The first section will review the logical structure of syllogisms, and the remainder of the chapter will describe two different methods for evaluating them.

7.1 The Structure of a Syllogism

Let's begin with an example from the previous chapter—the inference that whales breathe by means of lungs because they are mammals. When we put the premises and conclusion into standard form as categorical propositions, the argument may be expressed as follows:

1. All whales are mammals.
2. All mammals are animals that breathe by means of lungs.
3. All whales are animals that breathe by means of lungs.

If we were diagramming this argument using the techniques we learned in Chapter 4, we would join the premises with a plus sign. But in deductive reasoning the premises always work together, so we don't need a special symbol to represent that fact. All we need is the line between the premises and the conclusion.

This argument is a **categorical syllogism**. The term **syllogism** refers to various types of deductive argument that have two premises and a conclusion. In a *categorical* syllogism, both of the premises and the conclusion are categorical propositions. Since every categorical proposition has two terms, there could be six distinct terms here. But there aren't. There are only three, "whales," "mammals," and "animals that breathe by means of lungs"—each term occurring twice. This pattern exists in every categorical syllogism, and each of the three terms has a distinct name.

The term that occurs in the predicate of the conclusion ("animals that breathe by means of lungs") is called the **major term** of the syllogism. This term also occurs in one of the premises (2), which is therefore called the **major premise**. The term that occurs in the subject of the conclusion ("whales") is called the **minor term**. This term occurs as well in the other premise (1), which we therefore label the **minor premise**. That leaves "mammals," which is not part of the conclusion, but occurs once in each of the premises. It is called the **middle term**, because it links together the major and minor terms. Schematically, the pattern of repetition is

Major premise	All *M* are *P*	All mammals are animals that breathe by means of lungs.
Minor premise	<u>All *S* are *M*</u>	<u>All whales are mammals.</u>
Conclusion	All *S* are *P*	All whales are animals that breathe by means of lungs.

Notice that we have switched the order of the premises. This makes no difference in the logic of the argument, but it is a convention that when we put a categorical syllogism into standard form, we always put the major premise first. The schematic argument on the left is the logical form of the argument on the right; the left side represents the structure of the right side, in the same way that "All *S* are *P*" represents the structure of any universal affirmative proposition. We always use *S* and *P* to stand for the terms in the conclusion—*S* for the minor term (the subject of the conclusion), *P* for the major term (the predicate). And we always use *M* for the middle term.

An argument need not have exactly this structure in order to be a categorical syllogism. Suppose that you didn't know whether moose were predators or not, but you did know that horned animals are not predators. Then you might reason as follows:

No *M* is *P*	No horned animal is a predator.
<u>All *S* are *M*</u>	<u>All moose are horned animals.</u>
No *S* is *P*	No moose is a predator.

In this argument, the conclusion and one of the premises are E propositions, but it is still a categorical syllogism, for we can still identify a major, a minor, and a middle term.

The premises and conclusion of a categorical syllogism, in fact, can have any of the standard forms: A, E, I, or O. A categorical syllogism also has a form, as a syllogism. To identify its form, we start by listing the letters that identify the forms of the propositions in the syllogism in the following order: major premise, minor premise, conclusion. This list is called the **mood** of the syllogism. The mood of the argument about whales is AAA; the mood of the argument about moose is EAE.

Syllogisms can also vary in the way their terms are arranged. Notice the arrangement in the following argument:

No *P* is *M*	No Marxist is an advocate of private property.
<u>All *S* are *M*</u>	<u>All conservatives are advocates of private property.</u>
No *S* is *P*	No conservative is a Marxist.

The mood of this argument is also EAE. But the terms are arranged differently: The middle term is now the predicate in both premises, whereas in the argument about moose it was the subject of the major premise.

The position of the middle term in the premises is called the **figure** of the syllogism. Since there are two premises, and two possible positions for the middle term in each premise, there are four figures They are identified by number, as follows:

Figures of Categorical Syllogisms

	1st	2nd	3rd	4th
Major	*M* *P*	*P* *M*	*M* *P*	*P* *M*
Minor	*S* *M*	*S* *M*	*M* *S*	*M* *S*
Conclusion	*S* *P*	*S* *P*	*S* *P*	*S* *P*

Within each figure, the premises and the conclusion can have any of the standard forms for categorical propositions. That is, within each figure, a syllogism can have any mood. Conversely, any given mood describes four different syllogisms, one in each figure. To identify a syllogism completely, therefore, we must indicate figure as well as mood. The argument about whales is AAA-1, the argument about moose is EAE-1, and the argument about private property is EAE-2. In this way mood and figure together uniquely identify the form of any categorical syllogism, just as the letters A, E, I, and O uniquely identify the form of a single categorical proposition.

In each figure, the middle term serves as a link between major and minor terms. But in everyday reasoning, the different figures are typically used to express different kinds of links. The first figure, for example, is a natural way to express a species–genus relationship. Thus we inferred that whales have a certain property (they breathe by means of lungs) because they belong to a genus (mammals) that has the property. And we inferred that moose do not have a certain property (they are not predators) because they belong to a genus (horned animals) that lacks the property. In both cases, the minor term *S* was the species, the middle term *M* its genus.

In the second figure, the middle term is the predicate of both premises. It is therefore commonly used when we try to find out the relation between two classes, *S* and *P*, by seeing whether there is some property *M* that one has and the other lacks. In the example above, we inferred that conservatives (*S*) cannot be Marxists (*P*) because one group believes in private property and the other doesn't.

In the third figure, the middle term is the subject of both premises. Thus it can be used to show that there is some overlap between two classes, *S* and *P*, by pointing out that *M*s are members of both groups. Suppose we were wondering whether any great plays (*S*) had been written in blank verse (*P*). We might think of Shakespeare, and reason thus:

All *M* are *P*	All of Shakespeare's dramas are plays written in blank verse.
Some *M* are *S*	Some of Shakespeare's dramas are great plays.
Some *S* are *P*	Some great plays are plays written in blank verse.

The form of this argument is AII-5

The fourth figure is somewhat odd. In structure it is the mirror image of the first figure, and perhaps because the first figure strikes us as a natural way to reason, the fourth seems very unnatural. You will probably not encounter it often in everyday speech. Nevertheless, it can be a valid mode of inference, as in the following syllogism:

Some *P* are *M*	Some crimes against property are frauds.
All *M* are *S*	All frauds are felonies.
Some *S* are *P*	Some felonies are crimes against property.

This has the form IAI-4.

Of course, these examples are merely the typical uses of the different figures. In each figure there are also many atypical examples. Moreover, in all the examples we've considered so far, the conclusion followed from the premises, but this is not always the case. In the next section, we will discuss the standard for evaluating syllogistic arguments.

STRATEGY Identifying a Syllogism's Form

A categorical syllogism is a deductive argument containing two categorical premises, a categorical conclusion, and three terms—major, minor, and middle—with each term occurring in two propositions. To identify the logical form of a syllogism:

1. Put each of the propositions into standard form as a categorical proposition.

2. Determine which proposition is the conclusion; the other two are the premises.

3. Arrange premises and conclusion in the standard order:
   a. On the first line, put the major premise: the premise containing the predicate term of the conclusion (i.e., the major term).

   b. On the second line, put the minor premise: the premise containing the subject term of the conclusion (i.e., the minor term).

   c. On the third line, put the conclusion.

4. Mood: Identify the logical form of the premises and conclusion as A, E, I, or O propositions. Write down the letters in order: major premise, minor premise, conclusion.

5. Figure: Determine whether the syllogism is first, second, third, or fourth figure by noting the location of the middle term in the two premises. Write the figure down after the mood.

EXERCISE 7.1

A. For each mood and figure, write out the syllogism it describes. Hint: Start with the figure, and lay out the positions of S, M, and P; then use the mood to fill in the quantifier and copula for each proposition.

✱ 1. AII-1
2. AEE-2
3. IAI-1
✱ 4. EAE-1
5. EIO-3

6. IEO-2
✱ 7. IOO-4
8. AAI-4
9. AOO-3
✱10. AEO-2

B. Put each of the following syllogisms into standard form (remember to put the major premise first), and then identify the mood and figure.

✱ 1. Any ambitious person can learn logic, and anyone reading this book is ambitious. So anyone reading this book can learn logic.

2. No Greek poet was a genius, because no Greek poet was eccentric, and all geniuses are eccentric.

3. Some kids who play videogames have poor language skills. No person with poor language skills does well in school. So some kids who play videogames do poorly in school.

✱ 4. Some books about vampires are not great works of literature. After all, no *Twilight* book is a work of great literature, and all the *Twilight* books are about vampires.

5. Some dresses with tulle are red. No red dress is a wedding dress, so some dresses with tulle are not wedding dresses.

6. Some promilitary advertisements are not propaganda, because some of them are truthful, and no truthful advertisement is propaganda.

✱ 7. Some essential nutrients are not organic, because no mineral is an organic substance, and some minerals are essential nutrients.

8. Some bureaucrats are not chosen on the basis of their ability, and all bureaucrats are civil servants. Therefore some civil servants are not chosen on the basis of their ability.

9. No machine is capable of perpetual motion, because every machine is subject to friction, and nothing that is subject to friction is capable of perpetual motion.

✱10. Any good poem is worth reading, but some good poems are difficult to interpret. Thus some things worth reading are difficult to interpret.

7.4B The Rules

Now that we understand the concept of distribution, we can examine the rules for determining whether a categorical syllogism is valid.

1. The middle term must be distributed in at least one of the premises.
2. If either of the terms in the conclusion is distributed, it must be distributed in the premise in which it occurs.
3. The premises cannot both be negative.
4. If either premise is negative, the conclusion must be negative; and if the conclusion is negative, one premise must be negative.

If a syllogism complies with all four, it is valid; if it violates even one of the rules, it is invalid. Let's examine each of these rules in turn.

1. In a valid syllogism, the middle term must be distributed in at least one of the premises.

   This rule means that at least one of the premises in a syllogism must make a statement about the entire class designated by the middle term M. If M is undistributed in both premises, it will not provide a strong enough link between the other two terms, S and P, to guarantee that the conclusion follows from the premises.
   Consider the following argument, which has the form AAA-2:

All P are M	All conservatives believe in private property.
All S are M	All people who defend capitalism believe in private property.
All S are P	All people who defend capitalism are conservatives.

If we look at the abstract form on the left, we can see that in each premise, M is the predicate of an affirmative proposition. M is therefore undistributed in both premises, and the argument violates the rule. If we look at the example on the right, we can see why an argument of this form is invalid. The fact that conservatives believe in private property does not mean that they are the *only* people who do. So the fact that people who defend capitalism believe in private property does not necessarily mean that they are conservatives. They may or may not be. The premises locate the two classes. P (conservatives) and S (procapitalists), within the wider class (M) of believers in private property. But that doesn't tell us whether S is included in P, or P in S, or whether there is any overlap at all. Again, there may or may not be.
   A syllogism that violates rule 1 commits the fallacy of the undistributed middle, and AAA-2 is the classic example, one that occurs fairly often. The reason that people often take such an argument to be valid is probably that they switch M and P in the major premise. They hear "All P are M," but switch it to "All M are P." They hear "All conservatives believe in private property" but take it to mean "Any one who believes in private property is a conservative"—treating the belief as a defining trait of conservatives. If this transformation were legitimate, it would change the argument from the invalid form AAA-2 to the valid form AAA-1:

AAA-2	*AAA-1*
All P are M	All M are P
All S are M	All S are M
All S are P	All S are P

But this transformation is not legitimate. The major premise on the right is the *converse* of the major premise on the left, and we know that an A proposition and its converse are not equivalent.

The fallacy of the undistributed middle is often committed when people attribute guilt by association—for example, the accusation that someone is a terrorist because he supports the same causes as some terrorists. The fallacy is clear when we put this inference into standard form:

> Some terrorists support an independent Palestinian state.
> <u>So-and-so supports an independent Palestinian state.</u>
> So-and so is a terrorist.

This syllogism has the logical form IAA-2 (remember that singular propositions are treated as universals). The middle term (people who support an independent Palestinian state) is not distributed, so the conclusion doesn't follow.

2. If either of the terms in the conclusion is distributed, it must be distributed in the premise in which it occurs.

Once again, the rationale for this rule is based on the nature of distribution. If the predicate of the conclusion (the major term) is distributed, then the conclusion is making a statement about all the members of that class. If that term is not distributed in the major premise, then the premise is not making a statement about the entire class. So the conclusion is making a stronger claim than the premise can support—it goes beyond the information given in the premise. The same reasoning applies to the minor term: If the minor term is distributed in the conclusion, it must be distributed in the minor premise as well. A syllogism that violates this rule is said to have an *illicit major* or *illicit minor*, depending on which term is at fault.

The following argument has an illicit minor:

> All *M* are *P*   All vertebrates reproduce sexually.
> <u>All *M* are *S*</u>   <u>All vertebrates are animals.</u>
> All *S* are *P*   All animals reproduce sexually.

S is distributed in the conclusion, but not in the minor premise. The minor premise says that vertebrates are a species of the genus animals, and it is not valid to assume that what is true of all vertebrates (that they reproduce sexually) must be true of other species in the same genus, such as lower invertebrates. At most we can conclude that *some* animals reproduce sexually. That is, we must keep *S* undistributed in the conclusion.

The classic example of an illicit major is the syllogism AEE-1, and it occurs often in political debate. Here's an example:

> Supporters of national health insurance want to make medical care more widely available.
> <u>None of the doctors I know supports national health insurance.</u>
> None of the doctors I know wants to make medical care more widely available.

Here the major term (people who want to make medical care more widely available) is distributed in the conclusion but not in the major premise. The argument boils down to the claim that if you don't agree with my policies (e.g., that national health insurance is a good idea), then you don't accept my goals (making medical care more widely avail-able). And of course that isn't true. People can share a goal but disagree about the best means of achieving it.

It is important to remember that rule 2 applies only if a term in the conclusion is distributed. If the term is undistributed in the conclusion, then it doesn't matter whether or not it is distributed in the premise.

3. No valid syllogism can have two negative premises.

In syllogistic reasoning, two negatives don't make a positive. They don't make any-thing. If both premises are negative, they tell us that both the major and the minor term are excluded, wholly or in part, from the middle term. And that won't tell us how the major and minor terms are related to each other. Thus knowing that no chiro-practor has sung for the Metropolitan Opera and that no one who has sung for the Metropolitan Opera has been in Kuala Lumpur will not tell us that no chiropractors have been in Kuala Lumpur or that some have, or anything else. You can see this for yourself by substituting different terms for this example.

4. If either premise of a valid syllogism is negative, the conclusion must be negative; and if the conclu-sion is negative, one premise must be negative.

If a premise is negative, it tells us that one class (either S or P, depending on which premise it is) is excluded from another class (M). From this information, we might be able to infer that S is *excluded* from P—if the other rules are satisfied. But we could not correctly infer that S is *included* in P. Conversely, if the conclusion is negative, it says that S is excluded from P. The only information that would justify this conclusion is the information that S is excluded from M (which is included in P) or that S is included in M (which is excluded from P). In either of those cases, we have one negative premise.

Violations of rules 3 and 4 occur much less often than violations of 1 and 2. In most cases, syllogisms that commit either of the fallacies of negation are so obviously invalid that we avoid them instinctively. But there are a few contexts in which syllogisms that violate rules 3 or 4 do seem plausible, and we have to be careful. Here's an example:

No *P* is *M*	No one who competes for money is an amateur.
No *S* is *M*	No member of the Bush League is an amateur.
All *S* are *P*	All members of the Bush League compete for money.

This syllogism violates both rules 3 and 4: It has two negative premises and an affirma-tive conclusion. By our rules, it is hopelessly invalid. Yet the conclusion does seem to follow. Why is that?

Well, for one thing, we assume that members of the Bush League are involved in some competitive sport and are thus either amateur or professional players. But that information is not actually given in the minor premise; it is merely suggested by the name "Bush League." We also assume that competing for fun (or whatever) rather than money is the defining trait of an amateur, so that any nonamateur competitor must be competing for money. That, too, is not given or implied by the premises. What makes the argument seem valid, therefore, is that in our minds we substitute for it the follow-ing syllogism, which is valid (it is our old friend AAA-l):

All *M* are *P*	All nonamateur competitors compete for money.
All *S* are *M*	All members of the Bush League are nonamateur competitors.
All *S* are *P*	All members of the Bush League compete for money.

As always, it is important to focus on what the premises actually say and to be careful not to read into them any background knowledge we happen to possess.

When we apply the rules of negation, finally, we need to remember a point from the last chapter: We need to watch out for complementary terms, such as *S* and non-*S*. Suppose someone says that Ruth does not make friends easily because she is not communicative, and uncommunicative people do not make friends easily. We might represent this syllogism as follows:

> No uncommunicative people make friends easily.
> <u>Ruth is not communicative.</u>
> Ruth does not make friends easily.

Intuitively, this argument seems valid, and indeed it is. Yet both premises are negative, and so you might conclude that it is invalid. The problem is that the syllogism is not in standard form, so we can't apply the rules just yet.

Since "communicative" and "uncommunicative" are complementary terms—logically related, to be sure, but still distinct—the argument has four terms altogether, whereas a syllogism can have only three. Because those two terms are logically related, however, we can change one into the other by using an immediate inference. What we do in this case is take the *obverse* of the minor premise, so that we now have the syllogism in standard form:

> No uncommunicative people make friends easily.
> <u>Ruth is uncommunicative.</u>
> Ruth does not make friends easily.

We now have just three terms, so the argument is in standard form. And the minor premise is now affirmative, so that the syllogism satisfies all the rules. When you encounter complementary terms, you will have to use the obverse, or occasionally the contrapositive, to change one of them into the other before you can apply the rules.

The four rules we have discussed provide a complete test for the validity of categorical syllogisms—with one caveat. Consider the following syllogism:

> All cars are designed for personal transportation.
> <u>All cars are motor vehicles.</u>
> Some motor vehicles are designed for personal transportation.

This syllogism satisfies all of our rules. But notice that its conclusion is particular, while both premises are universal. This raises the issue of existential import, discussed in the previous chapter. If we adopt the traditional view, which presupposes referents for all terms in categorical propositions, there is no problem here. But if we adopt the modern view, which says that universal propositions lack existential import while particular ones have it, then the conclusion makes an assertion not justified by the premises. The premises do not actually assert the existence of any motor vehicles, while the conclusion does.

The logicians who identified the rules of validity usually held the traditional view of existential import. As a method of determining whether a syllogism is valid, the rules are indeed better suited to the traditional view. Conversely, if we adopt the traditional view of existential import, the rules provide the most natural way to assess validity. It is not difficult, however, to adapt this method for the modern view. Since existential import is a function of quantity—universal versus particular—we just need to add a fifth rule dealing with quantity:

5. If the conclusion of a valid syllogism is particular, one premise must be particular.

In effect, the rule says that if the conclusion has existential import—if it implies the real existence of things in the class of Ss—it must get that import from one of the premises. Otherwise the conclusion makes a claim that goes beyond what is given in the premises. The syllogism about cars obviously violates the rule, so it would be invalid on the modern view. When you include this rule in order to test for validity on the modern view, it is best to start by applying the first four rules. If a syllogism violates any of them, it is invalid on both the traditional and the modern view of existential import. If it satisfies those rules, then check whether it has a particular conclusion; if it does, then it must have a particular premise in order to be valid on the modern view.

The syllogism about cars has the form AAI-1. It is one of nine forms that are valid on the traditional view of existential import but invalid on the modern view:

1st figure	2nd figure	3rd figure	4th figure
AAI-1	AEO-2	AAI-3	AAI-4
EAO-1	EAO-2	EAO-3	EAO-4
			AEO-4

SUMMARY **Rules for Testing Validity**

	Rule	**Violation**
Distribution	1. The middle term must be distributed in at least one of the premises.	Undistributed middle term
	2. If either the major or the minor term in the conclusion is distributed, it must be distributed in the premise in which it occurs.	Illicit major term, illicit minor term
Negation	3. The premises cannot both be negative.	Two negative premises
	4. If either premise is negative, the conclusion must be negative; and	Negative premise, affirmative conclusion
	If the conclusion is negative, one premise must be negative.	Affirmative premises, negative conclusion
Quantity	5. If the conclusion is particular, one premise must be particular. [Required only on the modern view of existential import.]	Universal premises, particular conclusion

EXERCISE 7.4B

A. Use the rules to test the validity of the following syllogisms. (These are the same syllogisms you evaluated intuitively in Exercise 7.2.) If the syllogism is invalid, state the reason.

✳ 1. All *P* are *M*
   No *S* is *M*
   No *S* is *P*

2. All *M* are *P*
   No *S* is *M*
   No *S* is *P*

3. All *M* are *P*
   Some *S* are *M*
   Some *S* are *P*

✳ 4. No *M* is *P*
   Some *M* are *S*
   Some *S* are not *P*

5. No *P* is *M*
   No *S* is *M*
   No *S* is *P*

6. All *P* are *M*
   Some *S* are *M*
   Some *S* are not *P*

✳ 7. All *M* are *P*
   No *M* is *S*
   Some *S* is not *P*

8. Some *M* are not *P*
   All *M* are *S*
   Some *S* are not *P*

9. All *P* are *M*
   All *M* are *S*
   All *S* are *P*

✳10. Some *M* are not *P*
   All *S* are *M*
   Some *S* are not *P*

B. First put each of the following syllogisms into standard form, and identify its mood and figure. Then use the rules to determine whether it is valid or invalid. If it is invalid, state the rule that it violates.

✳ 1. It's obvious that Tom has something to hide. He pled the Fifth Amendment in court last week; people with things to hide always plead the Fifth.

2. Protestant churches do not accept the authority of the pope. Since the United Church of Christ does not accept the pope's authority, it must be a Protestant church.

3. Some of the students in this class are freshmen, and of course no freshman will graduate this year. So none of the students in this class will graduate this year.

✳ 4. Some things that are well made are not expensive, for paperback books are inexpensive, and some of them are well made.

5. Some developing countries that need AIDS medication are places with poor manufacturing standards, because no developing country that needs AIDS medication can produce it and no country that can produce the medication has poor manufacturing standards.

6. No one who makes a profit cares about people, and lots of pharmaceutical companies make a huge profit. So those companies must not care about people.

✳ 7. None of the developing countries can afford the AIDS medications that they need. Many countries that can afford AIDS medicines are capitalist, so some of the developing countries must not have a capitalist system.

8. Any tax that discourages productive activity harms the economic growth of the country. Hence a tax on income, which obviously discourages productive activity, harms the country's economic growth.

9. All journalists are people with low salaries, and some people with low salaries are freelance writers, so at least some journalists must be freelancers.

✳10. Some of the proposals before this committee, I have to conclude, are not inspired. All of the proposals are reasonable, but some inspired ideas are not reasonable.

11. Some flowers that bloom all season flourish in the shade, and thus some shade-loving flowers are not perennials (since no perennial blooms all season).

12. Pharmaceutical companies that aid developing countries give their products as charity, and they will raise their prices. So some of the companies that are giving their products as charity will raise their prices.

✳13. Some countries that can participate in the global market flout drug patent laws, and all countries that can participate in the global market get the imports that they need. So some countries that get the imports they need are countries that flout drug patent laws.

14. Some countries whose people need AIDS medications have illegitimate governments, and no legitimate government neglects the needs of its poor populations. So some countries that neglect the needs of their poor are countries whose people need AIDS medication.

15. No country that can afford preventative medicines is a country where the number of people with AIDS will increase, but many countries with an AIDS population can't afford preventative medicine, so these countries will see an increase in the numbers of their people with AIDS.

7.4C Enthymemes and Rules

We can use the four rules of validity to help us analyze enthymemes. When we are given a syllogism with a missing premise, as we have seen, we can always determine what terms must be involved in the missing premise. For example, suppose a literature professor says, "Some works of epic narrative are poetry because they are in rhymed stanzas." Putting this inference into standard form, we have a conclusion and one premise:

(?)	(?)
<u>Some works of epic narrative are works written in rhymed stanzas</u>	<u>Some S are M</u>
Some works of epic narrative are poetry	Some S are P

Since the missing premise is the major one, it must be a proposition relating P (poetry) and M (works written in rhymed stanzas). In this case, we can see that M is not distributed in the minor premise: That premise does not make a claim about all works in rhymed stanzas. So rule 1 requires that the term be distributed in the major premise. Since the conclusion is affirmative, rule 4 requires that the major premise be affirmative as well. There is only one way to have M distributed in an affirmative premise: the proposition "All works written in rhymed stanzas are poetry (All M are P)."

Let's try another example. Someone observes that since all banks have government-insured deposits, no hedge fund is a bank. Once again we start by putting the conclusion and the stated premise into standard form:

All banks are institutions with government-insured deposits	All P are M
(?)	(?)
No hedge fund is a bank	No S is P

In this case, the missing premise is the minor one, involving the terms S (hedge funds) and M (institutions with government-insured deposits). Since the major premise is affirmative but the conclusion is negative, the minor premise must be negative as well (rule 4). And both terms in that premise must be distributed, M because it is not distributed in the major premise (rule 1) and S because it is distributed in the conclusion (rule 2). Only two premises satisfy all these conditions:

No S is M No hedge fund is an institution with government-insured deposits.
No M is S No institution with government-insured deposits is a hedge fund.

Each of these E propositions is the converse of the other and thus they are equivalent. Either one would give us a valid syllogism.

EXERCISE 7.4C

For each of the following enthymemes, use what you have learned about the rules of validity to supply the missing premise or conclusion that will result in a valid syllogism.

＊ 1. Trees need water because they are plants.

2. No one who is dishonest will be happy, since a dishonest person lacks character.

3. Because all government agencies are spending other people's money, none can be truly entrepreneurial.

＊ 4. Some water is unsafe to drink, because anything containing coliform bacteria is unsafe.

5. Some exceptional people are not eligible to vote, since everyone eligible to vote is a citizen.

6. Not one of the union demands deserves any serious consideration, since none of them is compatible with the labor contract that is still in effect.

＊ 7. No creature whose actions are wholly determined by heredity and environment is a moral agent. Thus no animal other than man is a moral agent.

8. The plan to build a new factory is flawed because it does not have a provision for construction delays.

7.5 Venn Diagrams

7.5A Diagramming Syllogisms

In the past chapter, we learned how to draw Venn diagrams for categorical propositions. These diagrams provide another test for validity. To create a Venn diagram for a syllogism, we do not need three separate diagrams for the premises and conclusion. We can represent the argument as a whole in a single diagram using *three* overlapping circles, one for each term. We always use the following structure:

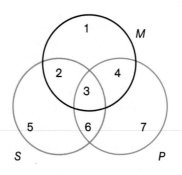

The three circles divide the space into seven different areas, instead of the three areas in the simpler diagrams we used to represent individual propositions. But any two of these circles overlap in the same way as the simpler diagrams. That means we can diagram any of the propositions in a syllogism by focusing just on the relevant pair of circles and ignoring the third one.

The technique of Venn diagrams is based on the fact that in a valid syllogism, the conclusion asserts no more than what is already contained, implicitly, in the premises. If the conclusion asserts more than that, it does not follow from the premises, and the syllogism is invalid. The technique is to diagram the premises, and then see whether anything would have to be added in order to diagram what the conclusion asserts. If so, the syllogism is invalid; if not, it is valid.

Let's take an example we've used before:

No horned animal is a carnivore.	No M is P
All moose are horned animals.	All S are M
No moose is a carnivore.	No S is P

The first step is to diagram the major premise, using just the circles representing *M* (horned animals) and *P* (carnivores). So we shade out the area of overlap between *M* and *P*, which includes areas 3 and 4.

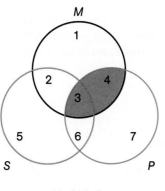

No M is P

The second step is to add the minor premise to our diagram, using the circles representing *S* (moose) and *M*. Since this is an A proposition, we shade out the region of *S* outside *M*—areas 5 and 6.

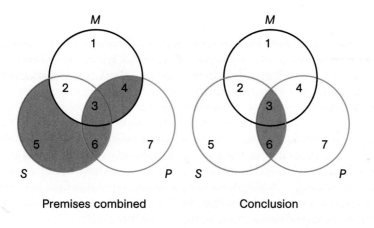

Premises combined   Conclusion

The final step is to examine the completed diagram of the premises and determine whether it contains the information asserted by the conclusion. The conclusion, *No S is P*, requires that the overlap between *S* and *P* (areas 3 and 6) be shaded out. The premises taken together do shade out that region: 3 was shaded by the first premise, 6 by the second. So the syllogism is valid. For a syllogism to be valid, the combined diagram must contain all the information asserted by the conclusion. It may contain more information, but it cannot omit anything.

Now let's try a syllogism with a particular premise:

No privately held company is listed on stock exchanges.   *No M is P*
Some privately held companies are large corporations.   *Some M are S*
Some large corporations are not listed in stock exchanges.   *Some S are not P*

First we diagram the premises:

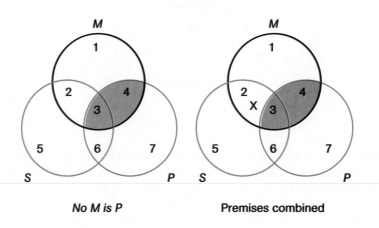

No M is P   **Premises combined**

Notice that we diagrammed the major premise first. This is not required logically, but whenever there is a particular and a universal premise, it is best to diagram the universal one first because that will usually help us in placing the X for the particular premise. Suppose we had started with the particular premise. The diagram for *Some M* (privately held companies) *are S* (large corporations) requires an X in the region of overlap between *M* and *S*. But that region is divided into two areas, 2 and 3, by the *P* circle. Taken by itself, the premise tells us that at least one thing is both *M* and *S*, but it doesn't tell us whether that thing is in area 2 or area 3—which means it doesn't tell us whether that thing is *P* (listed on stock exchanges) or not. So we would have to put a tentative X on the line between 2 and 3. By diagramming the universal premise first, however, we have shaded out area 3, so now we know that the X for the other premise must go in area 2, outside the *P* circle. And that is vital information; it means that at least one *S* is not a *P*. Since that is what the conclusion asserts, the argument is valid.

If a syllogism is invalid, a Venn diagram will reveal that fact in one of two ways. The combined diagram for the premises will either fail to shade out an area excluded by the conclusion or fail to put an X where the conclusion requires one. Let's look at an example of each.

Consider a syllogism of form AAA-2:

All athletes are people in good physical condition.   *All P are M*
All fitness instructors are people in good physical condition.   *All S are M*
All fitness instructors are athletes.   *All S are P*

The Venn diagram reveals the invalidity by failing to shade out the right areas:

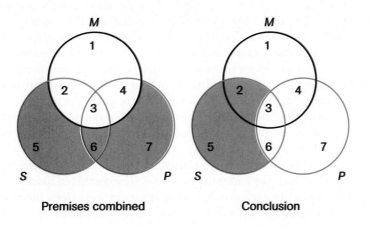

Premises combined   Conclusion

In the combined diagram, areas 6 and 7 have been shaded to represent the major premise, *All P* (athletes) *are M* (people in good physical condition). To diagram the minor premise, *All S* (fitness instructors) *are M*, we need to shade out the region of *S* outside *M*; since area 6 is already shaded, we just need to shade out area 5. But one area in the region of *S* outside *P*, area 2, has not been shaded. Thus the premises leave open the possibility that some *S* are not *P*; they do not guarantee that all *S* are *P*. So the conclusion does not follow; the syllogism is invalid.

Now let's examine a case in which the problem is revealed by the placement of Xs:

No member of the Green Party was elected to Congress.	No M is P
Some candidates who favor strong environmental regulation are not members of the Green Party.	Some S are not M
Some candidates who favor strong environmental regulation were elected to Congress.	Some S are P

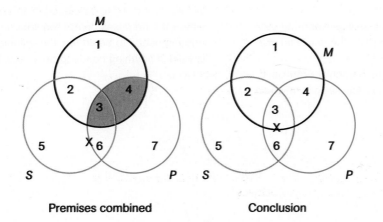

Premises combined   Conclusion

The conclusion requires an X in the overlap between *S* (candidates who favor strong environmental regulation) and *P* (people elected to Congress). It could be either in area 3 or in area 6, so we put it on the line between the areas. But the premises do not justify putting an X in either area. The major premise, *No M* (member of the Green Party) *is P* (a person elected to Congress), tells us that area 3 is empty, so it has been shaded out. To justify the conclusion, the minor premise would therefore need to give us an X in area 6. But the minor premise does not give us that information. It tells us that some *S* are not *M*, which means there is at least one such candidate in either area 5 or area 6. We cannot put the X inside area 6. It has to go on the line between 5 and 6. Locating the X on the line means: We know that some *S* is not an *M*, but we don't know whether that *S* is also a *P*. All that the premises tell us is: There's an *S* that may or may not be a *P*. The conclusion doesn't follow.

Remember that the premises of a valid syllogism may contain more information than the conclusion, but they cannot contain less. The combined diagram may shade out areas that the conclusion leaves open, but it cannot leave open the areas that the conclusion says are shaded out. In the same way, the combined diagram may locate an X inside an area while the conclusion says merely that the area *may* contain one. But if the conclusion requires an X inside an area, the premises must put one there; otherwise the syllogism is invalid.

STRATEGY Testing Validity by Venn Diagrams

1. Draw three overlapping circles, representing the major, minor, and middle terms.
2. Diagram each of the premises:
   a. Using just the two circles representing the terms in that premise, diagram the proposition as you would on a two-circle diagram.
   b. If one premise is universal and the other is particular, diagram the universal one first.
   c. In diagramming a particular premise, if there are two possible regions in which to put the X, put it on the line separating the regions.
3. Determine whether anything would have to be added to the diagram to represent the claim made by the conclusion: Would any additional areas need to be shaded out? Would an X need to be placed in an area where the premises do not require one? If nothing needs to be added, the syllogism is valid. If anything needs to be added, it is invalid.

EXERCISE 7.5A

For each of the following syllogisms, diagram the premises and the conclusion to determine whether the syllogism is valid.

* 1. No *M* is *P*
     Some *M* are not *S*
     Some *S* are *P*

2. No *M* is *P*
   All *M* are *S*
   All *S* are *P*

3. All *P* are *M*
   No *M* is *S*
   No *S* is *P*

* 4. Some *P* are *M*
     No *M* is *S*
     Some *S* are not *P*

5. Some *P* are not *M*
   No *S* is *M*
   Some *S* are *P*

6. Some *P* are not *M*
   Some *S* are not *M*
   Some *S* are not *P*

* 7. Some *M* are *P*
     All *M* are *S*
     Some *S* are *P*

8. Some *M* are *P*
   All *S* are *M*
   Some *S* are not *P*

9. Some *P* are not *M*
   All *S* are *M*
   Some *S* are not *P*

*10. All *M* are *P*
     All *S* are *M*
     All *S* are *P*

11. No *P* is *M*
    Some *M* are *S*
    Some *S* are not *P*

12. All *P* are *M*
    Some *M* are *S*
    Some *S* are *P*

*13. No *M* is *P*
     Some *S* are *M*
     Some *S* are not *P*

14. All *P* are *M*
    No *S* is *M*
    No *S* is *P*

15. All *M* are *P*
    Some *M* are *S*
    Some *S* are *P*

7.5B Enthymemes and Venn Diagrams

Now that we know how to construct Venn diagrams, we can put them to a further use: finding the missing premise (or conclusion) in an enthymeme. Remember that to find the missing element, our goal is to make the syllogism valid if possible. Since Venn diagrams test for validity, they can reveal what the missing element must be.

The first step is to diagram the premise that is given and compare it with the conclusion. Suppose we have an argument of the form "Since no *S* is *M*, no *S* is *P*." To diagram the premise, we shade out the region of overlap between *S* and *M*:

Now we look at the conclusion. If "No *S* is *P*" is true, then the region of overlap between *S* and *P* must be shaded out. Area 3 has already been shaded out by diagramming

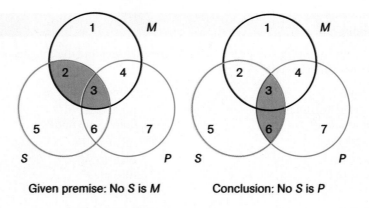

Given premise: No *S* is *M*   Conclusion: No *S* is *P*

the premise we were given. The missing premise, therefore, must be one that will let us shade out area 6. The missing premise involves the terms *M* and *P*. Of all the possible propositions involving these terms, "All *P* are *M*" is the only one that allows us to shade out area 6:

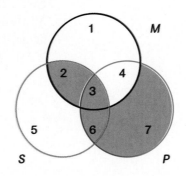

Combined diagram: No *S* is *M* + All *P* are *M*

Thus the syllogism is

    (All *P* are *M*)
    <u>No *S* is *M*</u>
    No *S* is *P*

Let's try this strategy with an enthymeme that has a particular conclusion: "Some *S* are not *P*, because no *M* is *P*." Once again, we diagram the premise that we are given:

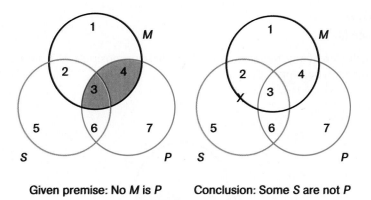

Given premise: No *M* is *P*   Conclusion: Some *S* are not *P*

The conclusion requires an X in the region of *S* that is outside *P*, either in area 2 or in area 5. Is there a missing premise that could give us an X in either area? We know that the missing premise must involve the terms *S* and *M*. And since it must give us an X to put in the diagram, we know that it must be a particular proposition. The obvious candidate is "Some *S* are *M*." Since area 3 has already been shaded out, the X for this premise must go in area 2. Since this is one of the regions of *S* outside *P*, the premise makes the syllogism valid.

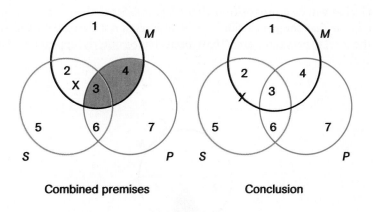

Combined premises   Conclusion

We would get the same result if we used the converse proposition, "Some *M* are *S*." But the premise "Some *S* are not *M*" would *not* give us a valid syllogism. The X for that proposition would go on the line between areas 5 and 6, which means we have not established the existence of any *S*s that are not *P*.

Occasionally, as we saw in discussing enthymemes previously, we will be given the premises, and the conclusion will be left unstated. Suppose we are given the premises:

No *P* is *M*
<u>All *S* are *M*</u>

What conclusion, if any, follows validly from these propositions? To answer that question, we diagram both premises:

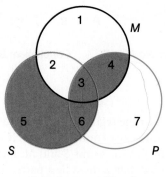

Premises combined
No *P* is *M* + All *S* are *M*

The conclusion will be a proposition about *S* and *P*. Since there are no Xs in the diagram, we know that the conclusion will be universal, not particular. And since both areas in the overlap between *S* and *P* have been shaded out, the appropriate conclusion is "No *S* is *P*."

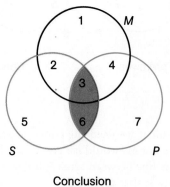

Conclusion
(No *S* is *P*)

EXERCISE 7.5B

For each of the enthymemes that follow, use what you have learned about Venn diagrams to find the missing element and to prove that the resulting syllogism is valid.

✳ 1. Some *S* are *P*, because some *S* are *M*

2. All *S* are *M*, and all *M* are *P*, so . . .

3. All *M* are *P*, so some *S* are *P*

✳ 4. Since some *M* are S, some *S* are *P*

5. Since no *P* is *M*, some *S* are not *P*

6. Since no *P* is *M*, no *S* is *P*

✳ 7. No *S* is *P*, because all *S* are *M*

8. Some *S* are *P*, since all *M* are *P*

9. All *M* are *S* and some *M* are not *P*, which means that . . .

✳10. Some *S* are not *P*, because no *P* is *M*

7.5C Venn Diagrams and Existential Import

As we learned in Chapter 6, Venn diagrams reflect the modern view that universal propositions do not have existential import. For example, the diagram for an A proposition, *All S are P*, shades out the region of the *S* circle outside the *P* circle but does not put an X in the region of overlap. The diagram does not indicate that there are any Ss. Nevertheless, Venn diagrams for syllogisms can be adapted for use with the traditional view of existential import—just as we can adapt the method of rules for the modern view.

When we discussed how to adapt the method of rules, we used the following example:

All cars are designed for personal transportation.	*All M are P*
All cars are motor vehicles.	*All M are S*
Some motor vehicles are designed for personal transportation.	*Some S are P*

The standard Venn diagrams for premises and conclusion would be

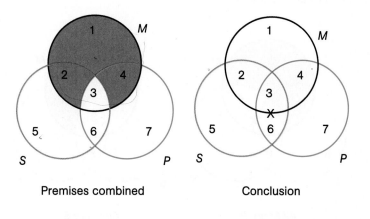

Premises combined   Conclusion

The conclusion requires an X in the overlap between S and P; it goes on the line between areas 3 and 6 because the existence of an S in either area would make the conclusion true. But the premises do not give us an X anywhere in the diagram. They shade out areas 1, 2, and 4, but that is all they do.

To reflect the traditional view, we need to modify the way universal propositions are diagrammed. On both the traditional and the modern views of existential import, a proposition of the form *All S are P* excludes the possibility of Ss that are not P. It is this negative aspect of the universal propositions that we represent by shading out area 1 in the diagram on the left. On the traditional view, however, the universal proposition also has a positive aspect: It implies that some Ss exist and that those Ss are P. In addition to shading out area 1, therefore, we need to put an X in area 2.

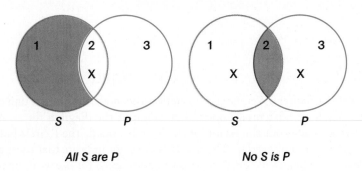

All S are P   *No S is P*

Exactly the same reasoning applies to a proposition of the form *No S is P*, which requires an X in area 1. But a proposition of this form is equivalent to its converse, *No P is S*. That means we are assuming the existence of Ps as well as Ss, and we need a second X in area 3.

How does this work in a diagram for a syllogism? Let's return to our example. The diagram on the left represents the major premise, *All M are P*. The X would have to go on the line between areas 3 and 4 because the premise says there are Ms in the overlap with P, but it does not tell us whether those Ms are S (area 3) or non-S (area 4). In the same way, the diagram on the right represents the minor premise, *All M are S*, with an X on the line between areas 2 and 3.

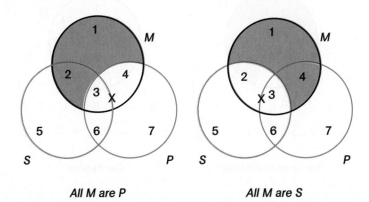

All M are P   *All M are S*

When we combine the premises into a single diagram, however, areas 2 and 4 are shaded out, so the Xs that indicate existential import have to go in area 3. Since that area is in the overlap between *S* and *P*, we know that some *S* are *P*—exactly what the conclusion says. The diagram tells us that the syllogism is valid, as it is on the traditional view.

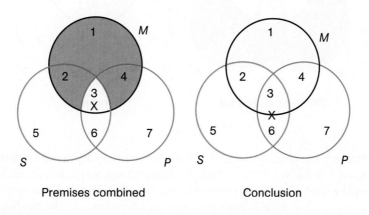

Premises combined   Conclusion

The issue of existential import is relevant to validity only when both premises of a syllogism are universal and the conclusion is particular. In all other cases, standard Venn diagrams yield the same results on both the traditional and the modern views, without having to put in Xs for universal propositions. When you do have universal premises with a particular conclusion, it is best to do the shading for both premises before trying to locate the Xs. As our example illustrated, the shading will often allow us to put the X in a particular area rather than on the line between areas. Thus to use Venn diagrams with the traditional view of existential import, we should test them first by the standard procedure. If a syllogism is invalid by that procedure and has two universal premises and a particular conclusion, it may still be valid on the traditional view of existential import. In this case, insert Xs in the appropriate regions of the diagram and reapply the standard procedure.

Of course, not every syllogism with two universal premises and a particular conclusion is valid, even on the assumption of existential import. Here's an example:

All rock stars are skilled musicians.	*All P are M*
<u>All band leaders are skilled musicians.</u>	<u>*All S are M*</u>
Some band leaders are rock stars.	*Some S are P*

By this point in our study of syllogisms, you can probably see what's wrong with this one. The Venn diagram makes the problem clear.

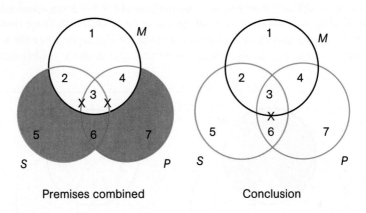

Premises combined   Conclusion

The conclusion that some band leaders (*S*) are rock stars (*P*) requires an X in the overlap between *S* and *P*. It doesn't matter whether it is in area 3 or area 6. But area 6, along with 5 and 7, will be shaded out by the two universal premises. So the premises are going to have to give us an X in area 3. Both premises are affirmative, so the Xs that represent their existential import will go in the areas of overlap: 3 and 4 for the major premise *All P are M*, 2 and 3 for the minor premise *All S are M*. Since none of these areas has been

---

STRATEGY Testing Validity by Venn Diagrams—with Existential Import

1. Draw three overlapping circles, representing the major, minor, and middle terms.

2. Diagram each of the premises:
   a. Using just the two circles representing the terms in that premise, diagram the proposition as you would on a two-circle diagram.
   b. If one premise is universal and the other is particular, diagram the universal one first.
   c. In diagramming a particular premise, if there are two possible regions in which to put the X, put it on the line separating the regions.

3. Determine whether anything would have to be added to the diagram to represent the

claim made by the conclusion: Would any additional areas need to be shaded out? Would an X need to be placed in an area where the premises do not require one? If nothing needs to be added, the syllogism is valid. If anything needs to be added, it is invalid.

4. If the syllogism is invalid by the preceding test but has two universal premises and a particular conclusion, it may still be valid on the traditional view of existential import. In this case: For each universal premise, add an X to the diagram in the appropriate region. Then repeat step 3.

shaded out, both Xs have to go on the lines dividing area 3 from the adjacent areas. And that means the conclusion does not follow. The band leaders (*S*) who are skilled musicians (*M*) are represented by the X on the line between 2 and 3. Since we don't know whether they are in area 3, we can't infer that those band leaders are also rock stars (*P*), which is what the conclusion asserts. In the same way, rock stars who are skilled musicians are represented by the X on the line between 3 and 4. Since we don't know whether they are in area 3, we can't infer those rock stars are also band leaders.

EXERCISE 7.5C

Use Venn diagrams to determine whether each of the following syllogisms is valid (a) on the modern view of existential import and (b) on the traditional view.

* 1. No *P* is *M*
   All *S* are *M*
   Some *S* are not *P*

2. All *M* are *P*
   No *S* is *M*
   Some *S* are not *P*

3. No *P* is *M*
   All *S* are *M*
   Some *S* are *P*

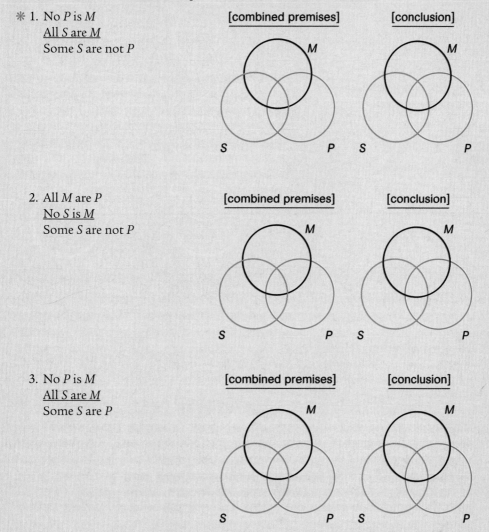

✳ 4. All *P* are *M*
    <u>No *M* is *S*</u>
    Some *S* are not *P*

5. All *P* are *M*
   <u>All *M* are *S*</u>
   Some *S* are *P*

6. All *P* are *M*
   <u>No *S* is *M*</u>
   No *S* is *P*

✳ 7. Some *M* are not *P*
    <u>All *S* are *M*</u>
    Some *S* are not *P*

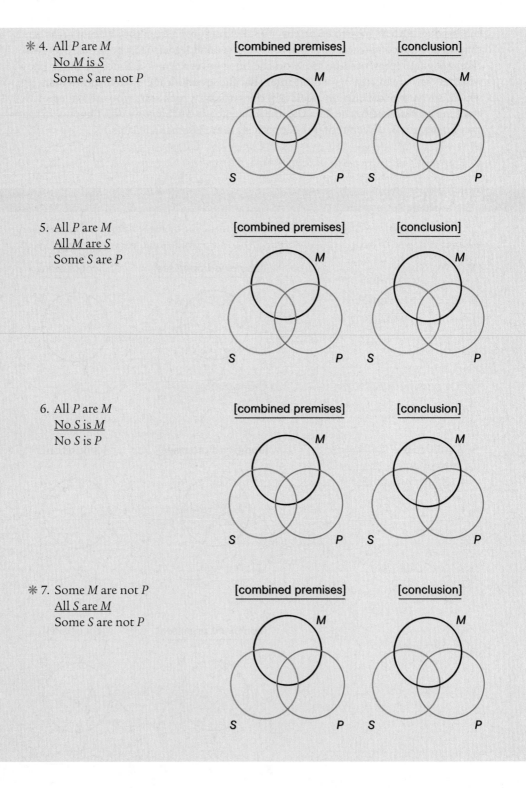

8. All *M* are *P*
   <u>All *M* are *S*</u>
   Some *S* are *P*

9. No *M* is *P*
   <u>Some *M* are *S*</u>
   Some *S* are not *P*

*10. No *M* is *P*
   <u>No *S* is *M*</u>
   Some *S* is *P*

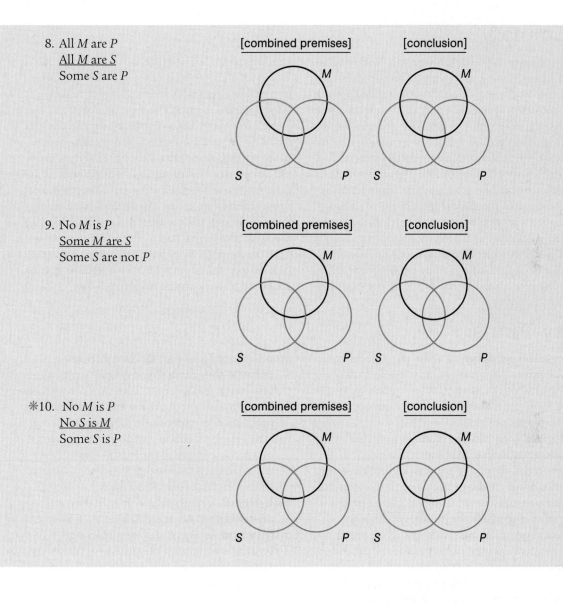

Summary

This chapter covered the analysis and evalua-tion of categorical syllogisms. The two premises and the conclusion of a categorical syllogism are categorical propositions, and they contain three terms: the major, the minor, and the middle. We analyze a categorical syllogism by identifying its logical form, which is determined by its mood and figure. The mood identifies the logical form of the component propositions, and the figure identifies the position of the middle term in the premises. A syllogism with a premise or the conclusion left un-stated is called an enthymeme; to analyze such an argument, we must identify the missing element.

We evaluate a syllogism by testing for validity. A syllogism is valid if the truth of the premises would guarantee the truth of the conclusion. A syllogism is either valid or invalid; there are no in-termediate degrees of strength. Validity depends on the logical form of the argument. We can test for validity in two ways. The first uses a set of rules that a syllogism must satisfy to be valid. If we as-sume the traditional view of existential import, we use four rules regarding distribution and nega-tion; for the modern view, we need an additional rule regarding quantity. The second method uses Venn diagrams with three overlapping circles to represent the terms. Basic Venn diagrams presup-pose the modern view that universal propositions lack existential import, but the diagrams can be adapted for use with the traditional view.

Key Terms

categorical syllogism—a deductive argument containing two categorical premises, a cat-egorical conclusion, and three terms—major, minor, and middle—with each term occurring in two propositions.

syllogism—a deductive argument with two premises and a conclusion.

major term—in a categorical syllogism, the term that occurs in the predicate of the conclusion.

major premise—in a categorical syllogism, the premise in which the major term appears.

minor term—in a categorical syllogism, the term that occurs in the subject of the conclusion.

minor premise—in a categorical syllogism, the premise in which the minor term appears.

middle term—in a categorical syllogism, the term that appears in both premises and links together the major and minor terms.

mood—the order of the standard forms that make up the premises and conclusion of a categorical syllogism.

figure—the position of the middle term in the premises of a categorical syllogism.

validity—the property of a deductive argument in which, in virtue of the logical form of the argument, it is impossible for the premises to be true and the conclusion false.

enthymeme—a categorical syllogism with an unstated premise or conclusion.

distribution—a term is distributed in a cat-egorical statement if the statement makes an assertion about all members of the class desig-nated by the term.

Additional Exercises

A. Using any of the methods discussed in this chapter, determine whether the following argument forms are valid.

✳ 1. All M are P
   <u>Some S are M</u>
   Some S are P

2. No M is P
   <u>Some S are not M</u>
   Some S are P

3. No *M* is *P*
   Some *M* are not *S*
   Some *S* are *P*

∗ 4. All *P* are *M*
   Some *S* are not *M*
   Some *S* are *P*

5. Some *M* are *P*
   Some *M* are not *S*
   Some *S* are not *P*

6. Some *P* are *M*
   No *S* is *M*
   Some *S* are not *P*

∗ 7. No *P* is *M*
   All *S* are *M*
   No *S* is *P*

8. All *M* are *P*
   Some *S* are not *M*
   Some *S* are not *P*

9. All *P* are *M*
   Some *M* are *S*
   Some *S* are *P*

∗10. No *P* is *M*
   All *M* are *S*
   No *S* is *P*

11. Some *M* are *P*
   No *M* is *S*
   Some *S* are not *P*

12. No *P* is *M*
   Some *S* are *M*
   Some *S* are not *P*

∗13. Some *M* are not *P*
   All *M* are *S*
   Some *S* are not *P*

14. Some *M* are *P*
   All *S* are *M*
   Some *S* are *P*

15. No *M* is *P*
   All *M* are *S*
   Some *S* are not *P*

B. Put each of the following statements into standard form as a categorical proposition, and determine whether the subject and predicate terms are distributed.

∗ 1. Some children broke the dishes.
2. Every toy under the tree was wrapped.
3. Some people don't like hot food.
∗ 4. Some of the president's nominees were not confirmed.
5. No warrant is issued without a judge's order.
6. Some evenings are enchanted.
∗ 7. There are no stupid questions.
8. Some restaurants that serve liquor do not have a license.
9. Dead men tell no tales.
∗10. All terms in the subject position of a universal categorical proposition are distributed.

C. Put each of the following syllogisms into standard form, supply the missing proposition if it is an enthymeme, and determine whether it is valid or not.

∗ 1. Walleyes are fish, so they live in the water.
2. Amy must have done all her studying at the last minute, for anyone who crams like that does poorly on the final exam, and Amy certainly did poorly.
3. Amoebas are not plants, because they are capable of locomotion, and no plant has that capacity.
∗ 4. No friend of mine is a friend of Bill's, but Mary is not a friend of Bill's, so she is a friend of mine.
5. Every economist understands how markets work, but some economists advocate socialism. Some advocates of socialism, therefore, understand how markets work.

6. Any office equipment worth buying will make workers more productive, but some computers do not do so. Some computers, therefore, are not worth buying.

✳ 7. Some democracies are tyrannies, because any country that ignores human rights is tyrannical, and some democracies do just that.

8. Those who supported the Voting Rights bill were opposed to racial discrimination. So conservatives, who did not support the bill, do not oppose discrimination.

9. A person who overreacts to the charge that he is motivated by envy invariably is envious. But people with a strong sense of justice are not motivated by envy, and so they don't overreact that way.

✳10. No nonprofit organization sells stock, but some hospital organizations do sell stock, and are therefore for-profit.

11. No building constructed before 1850 is earthquake-proof, because all of them were built without steel, and no structure built without steel is earthquake-proof.

12. Any syllogism of the form AAA-3 has an illicit minor term, and any syllogism with such a form is invalid. Thus any syllogism with an illicit minor term is invalid.

✳13. Some actions that are expedient in the short term are not moral. We can see this from the fact that some dishonest means of gaining wealth, which are immoral by nature, are expedient in the short term.

14. All depression involves a profound sense of loss, but this patient's condition does not involve any such sense. It is therefore not a case of depression.

15. No job providing health care benefits is unacceptable to me, but some white collar jobs do not provide such benefits. So some white collar jobs are not acceptable to me.

✳16. Some international conflicts arise from just motives, but no aggressive war arises in that way. Hence some aggressive wars are not international conflicts.

17. All great orchestra conductors are flamboyant, but none of them is careless. Thus some flamboyant people are not careless.

18. Some politicians are dishonest, for politicians by nature depend on reputation for their offices, and some people who depend on reputation are not honest.

✳19. We should never confuse music and noise: Music is an orderly progression of sounds, noise a disorderly one.

20. Some philosophy courses are graded objectively, for while any course in which the grade is based exclusively on essays is graded nonobjectively, some of those courses, at least, are not in philosophy.

D. Put each of the following statements into standard form as a categorical proposition. Then devise a valid syllogism that uses the statement as a premise.

✳ 1. "No Civil War picture ever made a nickel." [Irving Thalberg to Louis B. Mayer, advising him not to make *Gone with the Wind*. Otto Friedrich, *City of Nets*.]

2. "He that speaks much, is much mistaken." [Benjamin Franklin, *Poor Richard's Almanac*]

3. "Not all who have vices are contemptible." [La Rochefoucauld, *Maxims*]

✳ 4. "Some books are undeservedly forgotten; none are undeservedly remembered." [W. H. Auden, *Apothegms*. Find two syllogisms, one for each part of the sentence.]

E. For each mood and figure, write out the syllogism in standard form using *S*, *M*, and *P* as terms. Then devise a syllogism with that form. Try to find terms for *S, P,* and *M* that give you a plausible argument.

✳ 1. AAA-1   ✳ 4. EAE-1
   2. AEE-2   5. EIO-3
   3. IEO-3

F. Put each of the propositions below into standard form, and identify the subject and predicate terms. Then use either a genus or a species of the subject as the middle term in a syllogism that supports the given proposition as a conclusion. For example, if the given proposition is "Bears are warm-blooded," the subject term is "bears," a possible genus is "mammals," and a possible syllogism using that genus as a middle term is

All **mammals** are warm-blooded.
<u>All bears are **mammals**</u>.
All bears are warm-blooded.

✳ 1. Some bonds yield tax-free interest.
   2. Trees need water.
   3. Women have rights to life, liberty, and the pursuit of happiness.
✳ 4. Some blue-collar workers are highly paid.
   5. Electrons do not travel faster than the speed of light.
   6. No car trip is free of the risk of an accident.
✳ 7. Some relationships are lifelong.
   8. Some methods of doing research are not ethical.

G. Put each of the following syllogisms into standard form, filling in the missing premise or conclusion if it is an enthymeme; identify mood and figure; and determine whether it is valid or invalid.

✳ 1. "Thus, a minimum wage is nothing more than a price control. Price controls have always been disastrous, so a minimum wage must be harmful." [Stephan Kinsella, "Simple Economics Goes Against It," *Morning Advocate*, March 25, 1989]

   2. "Dear Connoisseur:

   "Like me, you probably first came across the 'syllogism' in an introductory course on logic.

   "Let me share with you one of our favorites:
   " 'You appreciate the finer things in life. The Glenlivet is one of the finer things. Therefore, you will appreciate The Glenlivet.' " [Glenlivet advertisement]

   3. "First, there is an argument from the universality of physical laws. It runs: All material systems are governed by the laws of physics. All living systems are material. Therefore, all living systems are governed by the laws of physics." [Marjorie Grene, "Reducibility: Another Side Issue?" in *Interpretations of Life and Mind*]

✳ 4. "That man must be tremendously ignorant: he answers every question that is put to him." [Voltaire, *Dictionnaire Philosophique*]

   5. "A member of a free democracy is, in a sense, a sovereign. He has no superior." [William Graham Sumner, *What the Social Classes Owe to Each Other*]

   6. "I want to believe I'm losing my mind. But I can't believe it. Then I say that people who are crazy can never believe they are, and that means I . . . am." [John D. MacDonald, *The Turquoise Lament*]

✻ 7. "He who would rejoice loudly of his victories cannot expect to thrive in the world of men, for he who rejoices over victory does so at the expense of other men." [*Tao Te Ching*]

8. "... the Constitution suggests that what must be proscribed as cruel [punishment] is (a) a particularly painful way of inflicting death, or (b) a particularly undeserved death; and the death penalty, as such, offends neither of these criteria and cannot therefore be regarded as objectively 'cruel.' [William F. Buckley, "Capital Punishment," in *Execution Eve and Other Contemporary Ballads*]

9. "Because no man by merit has a right to the grace of God, I, having no merit, am entitled to it." [C. S. Lewis, *The Four Loves*]

✻10. "Certainly some individuals who suffer organic abnormalities or psychoses that produce rage attacks can properly be diagnosed as insane; they do not, for one thing, revert to normalcy after a violent episode." [Carol Tavris, *Anger*]

11. "There was no wound upon the dead man's person, but the agitated expression upon his face assured me that he had foreseen his fate before it came upon him. Men who die from heart disease, or any sudden natural cause, never by any chance exhibit agitation upon their features." [Arthur Conan Doyle, *A Study in Scarlet*]

12. "My contention is that no good thing harms its owner, a thing which you won't gainsay. But wealth very often does harm its owners. ..." [Boethius, *Consolation of Philosophy*]

✻13. "Observation implies movement, that is locomotion with reference to the rigid environment, because all observers are animals and all animals are mobile." [James J. Gibson, *The Ecological Approach to Visual Perception*]

14. "No nation can be a power in a nuclear world without nuclear weapons, and Japan and West Germany won't be allowed by others to have such weapons." [Richard Nixon, quoted in *New York Times,* January 23, 1989]

15. "... we yield, of course, to this short syllogism. Man was created for social intercourse; but social intercourse cannot be maintained without a sense of justice; then man must have been created with a sense of justice." [Thomas Jefferson, *On Civil and Natural Rights*]

H. For each of the following propositions, (a) create a valid syllogism with the proposition as its conclusion; (b) create an invalid syllogism with the proposition as its conclusion; (c) create a valid syllogism with the contradictory proposition as its conclusion; and (d) create an invalid syllogism with the contradictory proposition as its conclusion.

1. All women should have careers.

2. Some lies are morally permissible.

3. Some courses should not be graded.

4. No dictatorship is truly benevolent.

5. All true art is representational.

I. Using what you know about categorical syllogisms, particularly the rules of validity, explain why each of the following statements is true.

✻ 1. A valid syllogism in the second figure must have a negative conclusion.

2. In a valid syllogism of the first figure, the minor premise must be affirmative.

3. In a valid syllogism of the third figure, the conclusion must be particular.

✻ 4. No valid syllogism has two particular premises.

5. If either premise of a valid syllogism is particular, the conclusion must be particular as well.

Reasoning with Syllogisms

The categorical syllogism is a form of deductive reasoning that we use fairly often, as should be clear from all the examples we considered in the previous chapter. But those examples were carefully chosen to illustrate the logical form of the syllogism, and we studied each form in isolation. It is time now to leave the laboratory, so to speak, and observe the behavior of these arguments in their natural environment: the context of everyday reasoning. In addition, not all syllogisms are categorical. There are other types of syllogism that we use frequently in everyday reasoning, and we need to understand how they work.

In the first two sections, we'll learn about non-categorical syllogisms that have disjunctive or hypothetical propositions as premises. Then, in Section 8.3, we'll learn more about how to spot the logical form of a syllogism beneath the verbal dress it is wearing. This is similar to the process of distilling an argument, which we studied in Chapter 5, but here we'll need to incorporate what we've learned about deductive logic. In the final section, we will examine deductive arguments that have more than a single step—extended arguments that involve *chains* of syllogisms.

To introduce the new forms of syllogism that we will examine in the first two sections, compare these three propositions:

1. Whales are mammals.
2. Whales are mammals or they are very large fish.
3. If whales are mammals, then they cannot breathe under water.

The first is a categorical proposition, but the other two are not. They are compound propositions. As we learned in Chapter 4, a compound proposition combines two or more component propositions by means of a connective. Compound propositions that use the connective *or*, as in 2, are called **disjunctive propositions**. Compound propositions that use the connective *if . . . then*, as in 3, are called **hypothetical propositions**.

Both 2 and 3 contain 1 as a component, but neither asserts that 1 is true. These are statements in which the components are expressed but *not* asserted. What the compound statement asserts is that a certain relationship exists between the components. The disjunctive proposition says that whales belong to one or the other of two wider classes—without saying which one. The hypothetical proposition tells us what the implication would be if whales are mammals—without actually saying that they are. When we use compound propositions in our reasoning, it is the relationship among the components that is important.

To put these propositions into standard form, therefore, we don't need to break down the component propositions into subject and predicate terms. We use single letters to represent the components, along with the connective:

	Compound Proposition	Logical Form
2	Whales are mammals or they are very large fish.	*p* or *q*
3	If whales are mammals, then they cannot breathe under water.	If *p*, then *q*

Notice that we use lowercase letters to stand for the components, whereas we used uppercase letters to stand for the subject and predicate terms in categorical propositions. That is a convention logicians have adopted to make it clear whether a letter stands for a term within a proposition (uppercase letters) or for whole component propositions (lowercase letters).

As in the case of categorical reasoning, our goal is to identify the logical *forms* of compound propositions and then to identify which propositions are *equivalent,* and which arguments are *valid,* in virtue of their logical forms. Traditional logic never developed a systematic theory of equivalence or validity for compound propositions; for a systematic theory, we must turn to modern propositional logic, the subject of Chapters 9 and 10. But there are certain forms of reasoning with disjunctive and hypothetical premises that we're going to study here because they are easily grasped and are frequently encountered in everyday thought and speech. We will see that even though these arguments use compound propositions, the corresponding syllogisms are simpler to analyze and evaluate than are categorical syllogisms.

8.1 Disjunctive Syllogisms

The components of a disjunctive proposition—*p* and *q*—are called **disjuncts**. Such a statement does not actually assert that *p* is true, or that *q* is, but it does say that one or the other (or both) of them is true. So if we know independently that one of the disjuncts is *not* true, we can infer that the other must be true. If you know that the meeting will be either in room 305 or in room 306, and you find that it is not in 305, you can infer that it is in 306.

The meeting is in room 305 or the meeting is in room 306.	*p or q*
<u>The meeting is not in room 305.</u>	<u>*not-p*</u>
The meeting is in room 306.	*q*

This argument is a **disjunctive syllogism**: a deductive argument with a disjunctive premise, a premise negating one of the disjuncts, and a conclusion affirming the remaining disjunct. You can see that the argument is valid. If the premises are both true, then the conclusion must be true as well. It does not matter which disjunct we deny in the second premise. If we checked the other room first and found it empty, we could have reasoned: either *p* or *q*, but *not-q*, therefore *p*. This too is valid.

It is important to understand that *p* and *not-p* are contradictory propositions. If one is true, the other is false; they cannot both be true, nor can they both be false. Since we will be dealing with such negations frequently in this chapter, let's pause to clarify how to state them correctly.

1. If we negate a proposition that is itself a negation, the strict formulation is a double negative: *not-not-p*. In modern propositional logic (see Chapters 9 and 10), we insist on strictness. But as with numbers, two negatives make a positive. So for our purposes here, we will treat the negation of a negative proposition as affirmative. Thus:

Proposition	Negation
p	*Not-p*
It is raining.	It is not raining.
It is not snowing.	It is snowing.

2. In compound propositions, the component propositions *p* and *q* are usually categorical. For example, in the proposition "Whales are mammals or they are very large fish," the first disjunct is implicitly about all whales; it is an A (universal affirmative) categorical proposition. Its negation is "Some whales are not mammals," not "No whales are mammals." In other words, we need to remember what we learned about contradictories versus contraries and subcontraries (see Chapter 6).

Quantity	Proposition	Negation
Universal	All whales are mammals. No whales are fish.	Some whales are not mammals. Some whales are fish.
Particular	Some mushrooms are hallucinogens. Some cats are not pets.	No mushrooms are hallucinogens. All cats are pets.
Singular	Tom is a rich man.	Tom is not a rich man.

A disjunctive syllogism, then, is a deductive argument with a disjunctive premise, a premise negating one of the disjuncts, and a conclusion affirming the remaining disjunct. Is it equally valid to argue by *affirming* a disjunct?

p or *q*

p

Not-*q*

No. Affirming a disjunct is not a valid form of inference. The reason is that a disjunctive statement, in claiming that at least one of the disjuncts is true, does not rule out the possibility that they are both true. The truth of one does not entitle us to deny the other. Of course, we do sometimes use "or" in what is called the *exclusive* sense to mean "*p* or *q* but not both," as in "Tom is either asleep or reading." We also use "or" in the *inclusive* sense to mean "*p* or *q* or both," as in "She's either tired or confused." An argument that denies a disjunct is valid in either case, but when an argument that affirms a disjunct seems valid, it is because of the specific content of the disjunctive premise, not the logical form of the argument. Consider the arguments

Argument 1	*Argument 2*
Tom is asleep or Tom is reading. Tom is asleep. Tom is not reading.	The meeting is in room 305 or the meeting is in room 306. The meeting is in room 305. The meeting is not in room 306.

In argument 1, we know that a person cannot be asleep and reading at the same time. That's a fact about the nature of sleep. In argument 2, we know that meetings are normally held in a single place where people can see and hear each other, so this meeting is not in both rooms. That's a fact about human conventions. In both cases, what makes the argument seem valid is a fact that is not actually stated and is not a matter of logical form. For logical purposes, therefore, we always assume that "or" is used inclusively, so that affirming a disjunct is fallacious.

In cases where such an argument seems valid intuitively, it is easy to translate the argument into a different form that makes the validity clear. Suppose someone has just given birth. We know the child is either a boy or a girl. If we find out that it is a girl, can we infer that it is not a boy? Of course we can. But that's because we know that male and female are mutually exclusive possibilities. A child cannot be both a boy and a girl—which means it is either not a girl or not a boy. That's a disjunctive proposition, and it is the real premise at work in our inference:

The child is not a girl or the child is not a boy.	*p* or *q*
The child is a girl.	not-*p*
The child is not a boy.	not-*q*

This is a case of denying a disjunct and therefore is valid.

There's another lesson to be drawn from this example. When we say that a child cannot be both a boy and a girl, the statement has the logical form

not-(p and q)

which is always equivalent to

not-p or not-q.

A proposition of the form *p and q* is true if and only if both components are true. So if we *deny* such a proposition, then we are saying that at least one component must be false. There's an old saying that "You can't have your cake and eat it, too." What this means is that you can keep the cake (i.e., have it on hand) only if you don't eat it, but that if you eat the cake, you no longer have it. Thus the proverb can be put into standard disjunctive form as: "Either you don't have the cake or you don't eat it."

In ordinary reasoning, disjunctive syllogisms often have more than two disjuncts. It is simpler to deal just with two, but this is a game that any number can play. Suppose we have four: We know that either *p* or *q* or *r* or *s*. Then we could reason:

> *p* or (*q* or *r* or *s*)
> not-*p*
> *q* or *r* or *s*
>   *q* or (*r* or *s*)
>   not-*q*
>   *r* or *s*
>   *r* or *s*
>   not-*r*
>   *s*

As long as we eliminate all the disjuncts but one, that one must be true—assuming, of course, that the disjunctive premise is true to begin with.

We use the disjunctive syllogism when we know that there is a certain range of possibilities and we want to find out which one is actual. If we want to know who committed a crime, for example, we might start out with a list of suspects and then cross them off the list one by one, as we acquired more evidence, until we were left with just one. As Sherlock Holmes said, when you have eliminated the impossible, what is left, however improbable, must be true. Again, in making a personal decision, we might start with a set of alternatives and then, by a process of elimination, narrow the set down to one. We also use disjunctive reasoning when we try to explain something: a person's behavior, a rise in the stock market, or a rise or fall in average temperatures. Various theories are proposed, and the process of establishing one particular theory usually involves the use of evidence to rule out its rivals.

It is quite common with the disjunctive syllogism, as with the categorical, to leave one of the premises unstated. If you are looking for a book and decide that it must be at the library because it isn't in your bag, you are using a disjunctive syllogism with an implicit premise:

> (Either my book is in my bag or I left it in the library.)
> My book is not in my bag.
> I left it in the library.

It is usually the disjunctive premise, as in this example, that is left implicit. Indeed, the fallacy of false alternatives is often committed because we rely implicitly on a disjunctive premise that does not identify all the possible alternatives. In the argument above, for example, it might occur to you, once you have identified the implicit assumption, that there are other places you might have left the book.

EXERCISE 8.1

Put each of the following disjunctive syllogisms into standard form, identify the disjuncts and any implicit elements, and determine whether the syllogism is valid.

＊1. Either I'm hearing things or someone is out in the hall singing "Jingle Bells." I know I'm not hearing things. So there's someone out there singing.

2. Either the circuit is broken or the light bulb is dead. But I know the bulb isn't dead, so the circuit must be broken.

3. I have to get the book here in town or else in New York next weekend. But I can't get it here; therefore I will have to get it in New York.

＊4. There are only two possible responses to this threat: We send in the troops or we negotiate. Negotiation is out of the question, so we must send in the troops.

5. I can't both go to the movies with you tonight and study for the exam, and I have to study for the exam. So I can't go.

6. We need Brody or Emily to play for the Red Team. Brody can't play, so Emily will.

＊7. Either marriage is sacrosanct or gays can get married. Gays can get married, so marriage isn't sacrosanct.

8. Jackson must be a liberal because he certainly isn't a conservative.

9. According to the union contract, either we have to close the plant on Labor Day or we have to pay the workers twice the regular wage. But we have too much work to close the plant, so we'll have to pay the workers double-time.

＊10. Either Paul will win this case or he won't be promoted to partner. He wasn't promoted to partner, so he must have lost the case.

11. Either human beings have free will or they are not responsible for their actions. But they are responsible, so they do have free will.

12. NASA and the private sector are the only viable options for space travel. NASA has shown that it's capable of piloting missions into space, so it looks like the commercial firms are out.

＊13. Kids shouldn't ever have access to guns. So if we're choosing between kids being around guns or kids being able to play violent videogames, then I guess they can play all the violent games they want.

14. Either I'm out of money or I made a mistake in my checkbook. I'm sure I made a mistake, though, so I'm not out of money.

15. I only have two hands: I can't make dinner and take out the trash, too. Since I'm making dinner, I am not going to take out the trash.

＊16. I only have two alternatives: I work hard or I fail this course. But I am working hard, so I won't fail.

17. Some economists believe that we can't have both low inflation and low unemployment. If that assumption is true, inflation must be low, because unemployment is high.

8.2 Hypothetical Syllogisms

Hypothetical propositions have the form "If p, then q," and they serve as premises in several types of inference that we use quite often. In this section, we will look first at the structure of hypothetical propositions and some of the differing ways they can be expressed in language. We will then turn to the inferences—the forms of hypothetical syllogism—and distinguish the valid ones from the invalid.

8.2A Hypothetical Propositions

Like a disjunctive proposition, a hypothetical proposition has two components that we represent with lowercase letters. But in this case they are not called disjuncts. The "if" component is called the **antecedent** and the "then" component is the **consequent**. Thus, in the statement

1. If it rains, then the graduation will be held in the gym,

the antecedent is "it rains" and the consequent is "the graduation will be held in the gym." In a hypothetical proposition, we are not actually asserting the truth of the antecedent or the consequent. We are saying that the truth of the first would be sufficient to guarantee the truth of the second. Until we know that it actually is raining, the possibility that the graduation will be held in the gym is merely hypothetical. It is not something we can assert categorically.

Hypothetical propositions are used pervasively in ordinary speech to identify relationships of dependence among facts, events, or possibilities. The statement "If you leave your bike out in the rain, it will rust" identifies the consequence of a certain action. The statement "If it's four o'clock, then I'm late for class" says that the existence of one fact ("It's four o'clock") implies the existence of another ("I'm late"). The statement "If I want to pass the course, then I need to study" expresses my recognition that achieving a goal ("I will pass the course") depends on a certain means ("I will study").

A hypothetical proposition is similar to an A categorical proposition. We have seen that the proposition "All S are P" is not equivalent to its converse, "All P are S," so we cannot infer one from the other. In the same way, "If p, then q" is not equivalent to "if q, then p." Consider the statements:

2. If I were president of the United States, I would be a politican.
3. If I were a politician, I would be president of the United States.

These are clearly not equivalent; 2 is true by definition (anyone who holds elective office must be a politician), whereas 3 is dubious to say the least.

Another point of similarity between A categorical propositions and hypothetical propositions is that both have a valid contrapositive. "All S are P" is equivalent to "All non-P are non-S." In the same way, "if p, then q" is equivalent to "if not-q, then not-p." For example:

4. If it rained last night, then the ground is wet this morning.
5. If the ground is not wet this morning, then it did not rain last night.

These propositions are clearly equivalent, and it's easy to see why the equivalence holds as a general rule. A hypothetical proposition says that the truth of p is sufficient to guarantee the truth of *q*. If that's the case, then the only way *q* could fail to be true is for *p* to be false as well.

Hypothetical propositions can be expressed in a variety of nonstandard forms. The easiest of the nonstandard cases to translate occurs when the consequent is stated first, the antecedent second, as in:

6. I'll stay home tomorrow if I still feel sick.

The component proposition "I still feel sick" is the antecedent, even though it comes second, because it is the "if" component. Thus, in standard form the proposition is: "If I still feel sick, then I will stay home tomorrow." In general "*p* if *q*" should be translated "If *q*, then *p*."

What about a statement with the form "*p* only if *q*," such as:

7. I'll stay home tomorrow only if I'm sick.

Does 7 say the same thing as 6? Am I saying that if I am sick I will stay home tomorrow? No—I am saying that if I am *not* sick, then I will *not* stay home. Being sick is the only thing that would keep me home. Think of 7 as a promise I've made to you. Now suppose I am sick, but I show up anyway. Have I broken my promise? No—but I would break the promise if I stayed home and was not sick. Thus the statement "*p* only if *q*" can be translated in either of two equivalent ways:

> *p* only if *q*   a. if not-*q*, then not-*p*
> b. if *p*, then *q*

Translation *a* will sound more natural in some contexts, *b* in others. But since they are contrapositives, they are logically equivalent. Note also that *b* is the converse of 6 above. We have already seen that a hypothetical proposition is not equivalent to its converse.

When we want to claim that the truth of either *p* or *q* implies the truth of the other, we combine the preceding forms: *p* if and only if *q*. As the word "and" suggests, we are making two statements:

$$ p \text{ if } q \longrightarrow \text{ if } q, \text{ then } p $$
$$ \text{and} $$
$$ p \text{ only if } q \longrightarrow \text{ if } p, \text{ then } q $$

The analysis on the right makes it clear that in the "if and only if" construction, both *p* and *q* serve as antecedents, and both also serve as consequents. But that's because we have two statements, not one.

Another nonstandard hypothetical statement has the form "*p* unless *q*." For example, "The plant will die unless you water it." This means the plant will die if you do not water it: "Unless" means "if not." Thus the following three propositions are equivalent:

> *p* unless *q*
> *p* if not-*q*
> if not-*q*, then *p*

Does "*p* unless *q*" also imply "if *q*, then not-*p*"? Are we also saying that if you do water it, the plant will not die? No—in some contexts it might be assumed that we are also saying this, but it is not asserted by the original statement. Once again, think of the statement as a promise I have made to you. If you water the plant and it still dies, I haven't broken my promise, strictly speaking; I didn't promise that water alone would keep the plant

---

STRATEGY Putting Hypothetical Propositions into Standard Form

The standard form of hypothetical propositions is

    If [antecedent], then [consequent].

The antecedent and consequent are component propositions that we represent by lowercase letters: p, q, r, . . . not-p, not-q, not-r, . . .

Nonstandard hypothetical propositions can be put into standard form according to the following equivalences:

Nonstandard Form	Standard Form
p if q	If q, then p
p only if q	If p, then q
p if and only if q	If q, then p and If p, then q
p unless q	If not-q, then p
Without X, q	If X does not exist (occur), then q

---

alive, only that the absence of water would kill it. Consequently, "p unless q" is exactly equivalent to "if not-q, then p" and should be translated that way.

Finally, consider a statement like the following:

"Without distribution requirements, most students would take too narrow a range of courses."

Here we do not have two component propositions: The phrase beginning "without" does not contain a whole statement. Yet it is easy to turn that phrase into a whole statement—"distribution requirements do not exist"—which can be made the antecedent in a standard-form hypothetical statement:

8. If distribution requirements did not exist, then most students would take too narrow a range of courses.

In general, "Without X, q" can be translated "If X does not exist (or occur), then q."

Of course there are other nonstandard ways of expressing disjunctive and hypothetical propositions. Our language is far too rich and subtle for us to capture every possibility in a small set of rules. But the rules we've just learned will allow us to put a great many statements occurring in everyday speech into standard form.

EXERCISE 8.2A

Identify the antecedent and consequent in each of the following statements, then put the statement into standard form (if it is not in standard form already).

⁎1. If you miss your first serve in tennis, then you get a second try.

2. You lose the point if you miss the second try.

3. If a categorical syllogism has two negative premises, then it is not valid.

⁎4. A married couple filing a joint return may deduct certain child-care expenses if they itemize their deductions.

5. People will want to protect animals in nature only if they can form a connection to animals at the zoo.

6. Prices rise if demand increases.

✳7. Without the presence of antibodies in the patient, doctors cannot detect a virus.

8. Average levels of education in Ethiopian villages will increase if and only if the people have access to clean water.

9. If you don't start saving now, then you will not be able to buy a car when you're 16.

✳10. Without a cooling mechanism, a car's engine would rapidly overheat.

11. I'll call you unless you call me first.

12. You may not take this course unless you have satisfied the prerequisites.

✳13. Without an understanding of deductive validity, we would probably commit fallacies in our reasoning.

14. If we don't punish the use of cell phones with fines and tickets, then drivers won't pay attention to simple safety reminders.

15. I will go to the party only if you go.

✳16. I'll only go out with you tonight if you promise not to wear your Nehru jacket.

17. The subject term of a categorical proposition is distributed if and only if the proposition is universal.

18. We will lower the occurrence of STDs in teenagers if and only if we teach them about using condoms.

✳19. People will not buy a product unless it is safe.

20. We cannot change the fashion industry's presentation of impossibly thin bodies unless consumers do not value thinness.

8.2B Forms of Hypothetical Syllogism

Now that we understand the logical form of hypothetical propositions, let us turn to the inferences we can make with them. The first is the **pure hypothetical syllogism**, in which the conclusion and both of the premises are hypothetical propositions. For example,

Logical Form	Example
If *p*, then *q*	If my wallet is not in my apartment, then I lost it.
If *q*, then *r*	If I lost my wallet, then I will have to cancel my credit cards.
If *p*, then *r*	If my wallet is not in my apartment, then I will have to cancel my credit cards.

Notice that the component proposition *q*—in our example, "I lost my wallet"—plays the same role as the middle term in a categorical syllogism. It serves to link the other components, *p* and *r*, which appear together in the conclusion. Any argument with the same logical form is valid.

It's essential to the validity of the pure hypothetical syllogism that the component occurring in both premises be the consequent in one premise and the antecedent in the other. If it is the antecedent in both premises, or the consequent in both, the conclusion will not follow. Thus each of the following argument forms is invalid:

1.	Logical Form	Example
	If *q*, then *p* If *q*, then *r* If *p*, then *r*	If I lost my wallet, then it is not in my apartment. If I lost my wallet, then I will have to cancel my credit cards. If my wallet is not in my apartment, then I will have to cancel my credit cards.

Suppose you are away from your apartment but your wallet is in your pocket or purse. The conclusion is false, but both premises could be still be true, which could not be the case if the argument were valid. The same applies if *q* occurs in the consequent of both premises:

2.	Logical Form	Example
	If *p*, then *q* If *r*, then *q* If *p*, then *r*	If the wind blows hard, then my hair will get mussed. If Dad pats my head, then my hair will get mussed. If the wind blows hard, then Dad pats my head.

We often use pure hypothetical syllogisms in describing chains of events in which each event causes the next. For example, if we asked an economist how government deficits are related to inflation, he might say: "If the government runs a deficit, then the Federal Reserve Bank creates more money; if the Federal Reserve Bank creates more money, prices will eventually rise; so if the government runs a deficit, prices will eventually rise." We also use these syllogisms in thinking about what implication a state of affairs might have for our lives, as in the example above; and in planning strategies to achieve our goals in games or in real life. A chess player, for example, might reason: "If I move my queen here, he will move his rook there. But if he moves his rook there, I will have to sacrifice a pawn. So if I move my queen there, I will have to sacrifice a pawn."

In a pure hypothetical syllogism, both premises are hypothetical, and so is the conclusion. At no point do we assert that *p, q,* or *r* is actually the case. Our reasoning is, so to speak, purely hypothetical. But there is another sort of inference that allows us to derive a non-hypothetical conclusion:

If *p*, then *q*	If you play with fire, you will get burned.
p	You played with fire.
q	You got burned.

In an argument of this form, the second premise is categorical; it affirms the antecedent of the hypothetical premise. This entitles us to infer the consequent, which is also categorical. Such inferences are called **mixed hypothetical syllogisms**.

Any argument of this form is valid because it merely unfolds what is implicit in the meaning of the hypothetical premise. That premise says that the truth of *p* would be sufficient for the truth of *q*. If we then assume that *p* is true, we may conclude that *q* is true as well. We can also work this in the opposite direction. If we assume that *q* is false, we can infer that *p* is false—for if *p* were not false (i.e., if it were true), then *q* could not have been false either. Thus the following mixed hypothetical syllogism is valid:

If p, then q	If God had wanted us to fly, He would have given us wings.
not-q	He has not given us wings.
not-p	He did not want us to fly.

In this case, we denied the consequent, and that allowed us to deny the antecedent. Once again, the conclusion is a categorical proposition.

Thus there are two valid mixed hypothetical syllogisms. The medieval logicians called the first one *modus ponens*: the method of **affirming the antecedent**. They called the second one *modus tollens*: the method of **denying the consequent**. Both are valid for the same reason: They spell out the implications of the hypothetical premise. Indeed, by using contraposition, we can transform any *modus tollens* argument into *modus ponens*:

Modus tollens (denying the consequent)		Modus ponens (affirming the antecedent)
If p, then q	$\longleftarrow$ contrapositive $\longrightarrow$	If not-q, then not-p
not-q		not-q
not-p		not-p

Merely by taking the contrapositive of the hypothetical premise, but leaving everything else the same, we have changed the *modus tollens* argument on the left into the *modus ponens* argument on the right.

There are two other possible forms of mixed hypothetical syllogism, both of them invalid:

Denying the antecedent	If p, then q not-p not-q	If my car is out of gas, it will stop running. My car is not out of gas. It will not stop running.
Affirming the consequent	If p, then q q p	If my car is out of gas, it will stop running. My car stopped running. It is out of gas.

In each case, the hypothetical premise says that being out of gas is sufficient to make my car stop running. Both arguments assume, however, that being out of gas is the *only* thing that can do so. That is not true, of course, and it is not implied by the hypothetical premise. Suppose I have a full tank but my battery is dead. That would make the premises of both arguments true, but the conclusion in each case would be false. A valid deductive argument cannot have true premises and a false conclusion.

There are circumstances in which these inferences may *seem* valid. Suppose someone says "If I get a C on the next exam, then I'll pass the course." Someone else who is skeptical of the first person's chances might reason:

If he gets a C on the exam, he will pass the course.
But he won't get a C.
So he won't pass.

This is a case of denying the antecedent, and it is invalid as stated. What makes it seem valid is the background knowledge that if he *does not* get a C, he will not pass. If we used this premise, then the argument would be a case of affirming the antecedent, which is valid. But this premise is not contained in or implied by the one that was actually asserted; it is extra information.

SUMMARY   Mixed Forms of Hypothetical Syllogisms

Valid		Invalid	
Affirming the antecedent (*modus ponens*)	If p, then q, <u>p </u> q	Affirming the consequent	If p, then q <u>q </u> p
Denying the consequent (*modus tollens*)	If p, then q <u>not-q</u> not-p	Denying the antecedent	If p, then q <u>not-p</u> not-q

We have now covered all the possibilities for mixed hypothetical syllogisms. There are two valid forms and two invalid ones. We don't need a separate set of rules for testing validity; we just need to remember these forms, which are summarized in the box above.

Like the other types of syllogism, a hypothetical syllogism may leave a premise unstated. Suppose you are indoors and cannot see the sky, but you infer that the sun isn't shining because there are no shadows on the ground outside. Your reasoning contains an implicit hypothetical premise:

(If the sun were shining, there would be shadows.)
<u>There are no shadows.</u>
The sun is not shining.

In other cases, both premises are given but the conclusion is left implicit; this is more common with the hypothetical than with other syllogisms. If you can find an example of this, you have grasped the material in this section—and I'm sure you *can* find an example.

EXERCISE 8.2B

Put each of the following hypothetical syllogisms into standard form, identify any implicit premise or conclusion, identify what type of hypothetical syllogism it is, and determine whether the syllogism is valid.

*1. If he had even mentioned her name, I would have hit him. But he didn't, so I didn't.

2. If children are deprived of affection as infants, they will learn not to expect it; and if they learn not to expect it, they won't seek it out later in life. So if children are deprived of affection early in life, they won't look for it later on.

3. I don't think you really do want to marry him. If you did, you wouldn't be running around with other men the way you have been.

*4. If I take the new job, I'll have a longer commute, and if I have a longer commute, I will need a new car. So I'll need a new car if I take the new job.

5. I knew I would be late if I didn't hurry, but I did hurry, so I wasn't late.

6. "There's milk in the refrigerator if you want some."
"But I don't want any, Mom."
"Then there isn't any milk there, wise guy."

*7. If you leave the milk out of the refrigerator, it will sour. The milk soured, so you must have left it out.

8. Jan made it to her appointment, if the train was running on time. The train was running on time, so Jan made it to her appointment.

9. If we don't complete the project on schedule, we will pay a penalty; and if we pay a penalty, the project will not be profitable. So making a profit requires that we finish on schedule.

*10. If salmon reliably return from the ocean to the streams in which they were spawned—and they do—then they must have some means of detecting subtle differences in the chemical composition of the water of those streams at the point where they flow into the ocean.

11. If I wait until Wednesday to take my suit to the cleaners, it will not be ready until Saturday. If so, I will not be able to wear it to the wedding on Thursday. So if I wait until Wednesday to take the suit to the cleaners, I will not be able to wear it to the wedding.

12. Frank must be jealous of Cindy. He was following her around yesterday with a sour expression,

which is exactly what he *would* do if he were jealous.

*13. If the time it takes Mercury to rotate around its axis (its period of rotation) is the same as the time it takes to revolve once around the Sun (its period of revolution), it always presents the same side to the Sun. And if it always presents the same side to the Sun, then that's the only side we can see. So if Mercury's period of rotation equals its period of revolution, we can see only one side.

14. If you install an electrical outlet with a grounding wire, you reduce the risk of shorting the circuit. You also comply with the building code. In other words, if you comply with the building code, you reduce the risk of shorting the circuit.

15. Unless we reduce the interest rate by 2%, it doesn't make sense to refinance the mortgage, and there's no way we're going to get a rate that is lower by that much.

*16. If the plan to build grocery stores in low-income areas is successful, then deaths from heart disease will decrease. Deaths from heart disease have decreased, so the plan to build grocery stores was successful.

17. Anarchy would be a fine and beautiful system for society to adopt—if men were angels. Alas, they are not.

18. If someone had been snooping around here last night, there would be footprints, right? Well there are. So someone was snooping around here last night.

*19. The battery can't be dead—the lights are still working.

20. If God had wanted man to fly, He would not have given us Buicks.

But He has given us Buicks;
therefore . . .

21. Our visual system must have some
way of detecting edges. If we did
not have such a capacity, we would
not perceive objects.

✻22. Unless we adopt this proposal, the
company will go bankrupt. So we
must adopt the proposal.

23. If Rome had been cohesive enough
in the fourth century to enlist the
efforts of all its citizens, it would
have repelled the barbarian invad-
ers. But by that time Rome had
lost all its cohesion, and so it could
not resist invasion.

24. You won't be able to master logic
unless you are serious about it. But
if you have read this far, you must

be serious. So if you have read this
far, you will be able to master logic.

✻25. If the errors and distortions in
television news were not the result
of political bias, but merely sloppy
reporting, they would be randomly
distributed across the political
spectrum. But in fact they are all
slanted in a particular direction.

26. If beauty pageants for young
girls allow tight outfits, then this
encourages girls to be sexual at too
young an age. If pageants encourage girls to be sexual at too young
an age, the girls who participate
will develop low self-esteem. So if
the girls who participate in beauty
pageants develop low self-esteem,
the beauty pageants allowed tight
outfits.

8.3 Distilling Deductive Arguments

Like any other language, English offers an endless variety of ways to express our
thoughts. By choosing words carefully, we can capture subtle shades of meaning that
do not affect the logic of an argument but are important in other ways. By varying the
grammatical structure of our sentences, we can focus attention on different parts of
the same argument. These resources of our language often enable us to convey our
reasoning more powerfully—and sometimes more clearly—than if we put it into standard form. But those same resources can make it difficult to evaluate the validity of an
argument, and they can be used to disguise poor reasoning. To analyze and evaluate a
deductive argument, therefore, we need to distill the logical form of the argument from
the words used to express it. Distilling the logical form requires that we identify what
kind of syllogism it is—disjunctive, hypothetical, or categorical. And, in the case of categorical syllogisms, it requires that we identify the *quantity* of the premises and conclusion: universal or particular. In this section, we are going to discuss the challenges you
may face in these tasks.

8.3A Identifying the Form of a Syllogism

The syllogisms we encounter in everyday thought and speech do not wear labels identifying themselves as disjunctive, hypothetical, or categorical. But we need to know this
in order to know which standard form is appropriate. To distinguish among the types

of syllogism, we rely on two basic criteria. We use *linguistic* clues: connectives like "if . . . then" and "either . . . or," quantifiers like "all" and "some," and so on. And we look at the *substance* of the argument, its content. What is it about? What kinds of facts does it use as premises? What kind of conclusion is it trying to establish?

To see how this works, let's begin with the disjunctive syllogism, which is the easiest to spot. The abstract logical form of this syllogism, as we saw, is

> *p* or *q*
> not-*p*
> *q*

If the disjunctive premise in such an argument is stated explicitly, it is easy to identify. We have seen that there are just a few nonstandard ways in which to express a disjunctive proposition. If the disjunctive premise is not stated explicitly, there's another linguistic feature to look for. A disjunctive syllogism usually has a negative premise and a positive conclusion. So we can look for the pattern "not-*p*, therefore *q*." In a mixed hypothetical syllogism, by contrast, the second premise and the conclusion are usually either both positive or both negative. Suppose, for example, that you are driving on a highway at night and see a vehicle with a single light approaching. Here are two deductive inferences you might make:

1. I don't hear engine noise from the vehicle, so it is not a motorcycle.
2. The vehicle is not a motorcycle, so it must be a car with a headlight missing.

In 1, both the stated premise and the conclusion are negative, whereas 2 has a negative premise but a positive conclusion. That's an indication that 1 is a mixed hypothetical syllogism, whereas 2 is a disjunctive syllogism, and we would fill in the implicit premises accordingly:

1. If the vehicle were a motorcycle, I would hear engine noise   If *p*, then *q*
   from the vehicle.
   <u>I don't hear engine noise from the vehicle.</u>   <u>not-*q*</u>
   The vehicle is not a motorcycle.   not-*p*
2. The vehicle is either a motorcycle or a car with a headlight   *p* or *q*
   missing.
   <u>The vehicle is not a motorcycle.</u>   <u>not-*p*</u>
   The vehicle is a car with a headlight missing.   *q*

Hypothetical and categorical syllogisms come in a greater variety of nonstandard forms, but the same kinds of criteria will help distinguish between them. The hypothetical syllogism is used primarily to deal with relationships of dependence among facts, events, and possibilities. We typically use it in reasoning about cause and effect or means and ends. The categorical syllogism is used primarily to deal with relationships among classes of things. We typically use it in applying a general rule to a specific instance and in connection with genus–species hierarchies.

Corresponding to that substantive distinction is a linguistic one: the pattern of repetition in the argument. In a hypothetical syllogism, *propositions* are repeated as units, as wholes: *p, q,* not-*p,* not-*q.* In a categorical syllogism, in contrast, the *terms—S, P,* and *M*—are repeated.

Suppose a parent says to a teenager,

> You can go to Zelda's party as long as you're home by midnight. And you understand—right?—that to get home by then, you'll have to catch the 11:15 bus from Glendale.

The parent is saying that going to the party depends on the child's being home at a certain time, which in turns depends on catching a certain bus. The obvious conclusion to be drawn is that the child can go to the party only if he or she agrees to catch the bus home. Since we are dealing here with relationships among actions, we might expect that the inference is a hypothetical syllogism. But what kind of hypothetical syllogism? The parent's instruction does not contain any of the forms of the *if–then* connective we have studied. In the first sentence, what connects the component propositions *p* ("You can go to Zelda's party") and *q* ("You are home by midnight") is the expression *as long as*. This is clearly equivalent to *only if*, and we have seen that *p only if q* is equivalent to *if p then q*. In the same way, the second sentence asserts that *q* ("You are home by midnight") *only if r* ("You catch the 11:15 bus"). So we would put the inference into standard form as a pure hypothetical syllogism with an implicit conclusion:

> If you go to Zelda's party, then you will be home by midnight.
> <u>If you will be home by midnight, then you will catch the 11:15 bus.</u>
> (If you go to Zelda's party, then you will catch the 11:15 bus.)

By contrast, consider an argument that you might hear in a courtroom:

> Some of the witnesses who have testified so far on behalf of the accused cannot be considered reliable—not because they are dishonest, but because reliability in a matter as complex as this requires a level of training and experience that some of the witnesses do not possess.

No proposition is repeated in this argument, but there is a repetition of the terms "witnesses" and "reliable [people]."

This argument also contains a second linguistic mark of a categorical syllogism: the explicit use of a quantifier, "some." As we have seen, the quantity of a proposition is an essential element in a categorical syllogism, but does not play an essential role in a hypothetical syllogism. This is not a criterion that works in every case. For one thing, the quantifier in a categorical proposition may be implicit (e.g., "Whales are mammals"). In addition, a hypothetical proposition has categorical components, and those components may contain explicit quantifiers (e.g., "if all whales are mammals, then they cannot breathe under water"). But a categorical syllogism is more likely to mention and stress the quantity of its premises than is a hypothetical syllogism.

In order to put a categorical syllogism into standard form, it is best to begin with statements that contain an explicit quantifier. Thus, in our example, the first part of the sentence, which is the conclusion, is the easiest to put into standard form: "*Some* of the witnesses are not reliable." A quantifier also appears in the last clause, which tells us that *some* of the witnesses do not possess an adequate level of training and experience. In standard form:

(?)

Some witnesses do not possess an adequate level of training and experience.

Some witnesses are not reliable.

The remaining part of the sentence—"reliability in a matter as complex as this requires a [an adequate] level of training and experience"—must be the major premise. This statement contains no quantifier. And it is a statement about attributes—reliability, training, and experience—whereas the minor premise and conclusion are about classes of people. But if attribute A (reliability) depends on attribute B (training and experience), then all people who have A must have B. So the major premise can be formulated:

All reliable people possess an adequate level of training and experience.

In the same way, a statement to the effect that attribute A is incompatible with attribute B can be translated as a universal negative proposition: No thing with A is a thing with B. Thus the statement "Good teaching is incompatible with ideological indoctrination" might be recast as "No good teacher engages in ideological indoctrination."

When you distill an argument with a hypothetical premise, you may need to restate that premise as a categorical statement before you can put the argument into standard form. Consider the following argument:

If a dog's tail is between its legs, it is fearful. Well, look at Spot. He must be scared of something.

We might try to put the argument into standard form as a mixed hypothetical syllogism—*modus ponens*, or affirming the antecedent:

If *p*, then *q*	If a dog's tail is between its legs, then it is fearful.
p	Spot's tail is between his legs.
q	Spot is fearful.

STRATEGY Identifying the Form of a Syllogism

The following strategies are useful for identifying the form of a syllogism:

1. If any of the statements in the argument are compound, try to cast the argument as a disjunctive or hypothetical syllogism.

2. Look at the patterns of repetition. If terms are repeated, the argument is likely to be a categorical syllogism; if propositions are repeated, it is likely to be a disjunctive or hypothetical syllogism.

3. Look for the presence of explicit connectives such as "or" and "if."

4. Look for the presence of explicit quantifiers such as "all" and "some," which are signs of a categorical syllogism.

5. If the argument applies a generalization to a particular case, it is likely to be a categorical syllogism.

In order to connect the hypothetical statement with the conclusion, we filled in an implicit premise that Spot's tail is between his legs. But that premise will not actually make the connection. In a *modus ponens* syllogism, the categorical premise *p* must be the same as the antecedent of the hypothetical premise. In this case, the categorical premise is about Spot, while the hypothetical premise is about dogs in general. In making the argument about Spot, we are applying a generalization about the behavior of dogs to the case of a particular dog. To capture the logic of the argument, it should be recast as a categorical syllogism:

> All dogs who have their tails between their legs are fearful.
> <u>Spot is a dog who has his tail between his legs.</u>
> Spot is fearful.

8.3B Nonstandard Quantifiers

In distilling the logical form of an argument, the presence of quantifiers is an important clue that the argument is a categorical syllogism. But English contains many quantifiers in addition to the standard ones: "all," "some," and "no." In Chapter 6 we looked at a few nonstandard quantifiers:

	Affirmative	Negative
Universal	**All** whales are mammals. **A** cat is a predator. **Every** president faces unexpected challenges. **Each** item on the menu has a price. **Any** student using the gym must show an ID.	**No** dinosaur ate sushi. Not **a** creature was stirring. **None** of the telephones is working.
Particular	**Some** apples are good for baking. **A** car is parked outside. A **few** people at the conference got sick.	**Some** apples are not good for baking. **A** wire is not plugged in.

We also learned that a singular proposition, about a particular person or thing (e.g., Spot), is to be treated as universal. But there are other nonstandard ways to indicate quantity. Let's look at three.

1. The subject term in English normally comes at the beginning of a sentence, before the verb. But when a sentence begins "There is . . . ," the subject is not "there." In the sentence "There is soot in the fireplace," the subject is "soot," so in standard form this would be "Some soot is (a thing that is) in the fireplace." The quantity in such sentences is usually particular, as in this example, but not always. The statement "There are no snakes in Ireland" is universal: "No snakes (is a thing that) exist in Ireland." Once

you have identified the subject term in such sentences, the quantity will normally be obvious.

2. There is a set of words indicating quantity pertaining to time: "always," "never," "sometimes," "occasionally," and so on. In some cases, the reference to time is not really essential, and the statement can easily be put into standard form. "Triangles always have three sides" means "all triangles have three sides." "Syllogisms in the fourth figure are never easy to analyze" means "no syllogism in the fourth figure is easy to analyze."

In other cases, however, the reference to time is essential. Suppose it occurs to you that your friend Sally won't be coming to the party because it's –20°F outside, and she never leaves home when the temperature falls that low. What you are doing here is applying a generalization about Sally's behavior. To put the inference into standard form, we need to state the generalization in terms of classes of times or occasions:

> All times when it's extremely cold are times when Sally does not leave home.
> <u>Now is a time when it's extremely cold.</u>
> Now is a time when Sally won't leave home.

This formulation of the major premise is rather awkward and pedantic, but it's necessary in order to convey the logical form of the inference. Note that the minor premise and conclusion are singular propositions because the subject term, the pronoun "now," refers to a unique time. These propositions are thus to be treated as universal in quantity.

We would use the same technique for statements like "He is never willing to admit he made a mistake," or "My car sometimes won't start when it's cold." In standard form:

> No time is a time when he is willing to admit he made a mistake.
> Sometimes when it's cold are times when my car won't start.

And we can use the same technique for quantifiers relating to place instead of time, quantifiers like "everywhere," "anywhere," "nowhere," "somewhere." For example, the complaint "You can't find a decent meal anywhere in this town" would be put into standard form as

> No place in this town is a place where you can find a decent meal.

In all of these examples of quantifiers for time and place, we are of course dealing with categorical propositions. In some cases, however, a statement with this kind of quantifier could equally well be treated as a hypothetical proposition. Consider the following argument:

> It rains whenever a mass of hot, humid air collides with a high-pressure mass of colder air. Since it has been hot and muggy, and a cold front is moving in from the west, I expect it will rain.

The component proposition "It rains/will rain" is contained in each sentence. And saying that a hot, humid air mass collides with a mass of colder air describes the same situation as saying that it has been hot and muggy and that a cold front is moving in. So the argument looks like a hypothetical syllogism. But the word "whenever" in the first sentence is a universal quantifier, and the statement is about a certain kind of weather condition that can occur at various times; whereas the second sentence is about the specific weather condition at the moment. This is a subtle example of the issue we discussed a few pages ago, with the argument that Spot is fearful because his tail is between his legs. A general proposition about the weather is being applied to a particular situation. So we might analyze the argument as either a categorical or a hypothetical syllogism.

Categorical	**Mixed hypothetical**
All times when a mass of hot, humid air collides with a high-pressure mass of colder air are times when it rains.	If a mass of hot, humid air collides with a mass of cold air, then it rains.
Now is a time when a mass of hot, humid air is colliding with a high-pressure mass of colder air.	A mass of hot, humid air is colliding with a mass of cold air.
Now is a time when it will rain.	It will rain.

I prefer the mixed hypothetical version of the argument. It captures the essential logic of the inference, and it is simpler. But either version would be correct.

3. We have seen that the word "only" is used in hypothetical propositions of the form "*p* only if *q*." "Only" is also used to indicate quantity in categorical propositions such as:

   a. Only a fool would believe that story.
   b. Only people with self-esteem are happy.

These propositions have the form "Only *S* are *P*." This is not the same as saying that all *S* are *P*. Proposition *a* does not mean that all fools believe the story: Some may never have heard it. Proposition *b* does not say that everyone with self-esteem is happy: There may be other factors that are also necessary for happiness. Instead, we must translate such statements in one of two equivalent ways.

In cases like *a*, the most natural translation is "All people who believe that story are fools": All *P* are *S*. In cases like *b*, the most natural translation is "No one who lacks self-esteem is happy": No non-*S* is *P*. These two modes of translation are logically equivalent, as we can prove by immediate inferences:

   All *P* are *S*.
   No *P* is non-*S* (taking the obverse).
   No non-*S* is *P* (taking the converse).

In distilling a categorical syllogism, however, it's a good idea to use the "all *P* are *S*" translation in all cases, even if it seems less natural. Some other proposition in the argument is likely to contain the term *S*, and this way you won't have to translate *S* into non-*S* or vice versa.

In examples *a* and *b*, the word "only" occurred at the beginning of the sentence. But it can occur elsewhere in a sentence, and in those cases you need to make sure you understand what the sentence means—what statement is being made—before you try to put it into standard form. By the rules of English grammar, "only" normally modifies the word or phrase that follows it, and that makes a difference in what the sentence means. To illustrate, consider the rules that a recreational center might have for using the various swimming pools. The following statements differ only in the placement of "only," but they do not have the same meanings.

Statement	Meaning	Standard Form
c. **Only** children under 5 may swim in the kiddie-pools.	No one 5 or older may swim in the kiddie-pools.	All people who may swim in the kiddie-pools are children under 5.
d. Children under 5 may swim **only** in the kiddie-pools.	Children under 5 may not swim anywhere else (e.g., the big pool).	All places where children under 5 may swim are the kiddie-pools.
e. Children under 5 may **only** swim in the kiddie-pools.	Children under 5 may not do anything in the kiddie-pools except swim (e.g., they can't fight, eat, throw balls, . . .)	All things that children under 5 may do in the kiddie-pools are (acts of) swimming.

Sentence *c* is like *a* and *b*. "Only" occurs at the beginning, so we apply our formula: *Only S are P* becomes *All P are S*. In standard form:

c. All people who may swim in the kiddie-pools are children under 5.

The next sentence, *d*, makes a very different statement because "only" modifies the pools rather than the children. To put it into standard form, we can begin by recasting the sentence so that "only" occurs at the beginning: "Only kiddie-pools are places where children under 5 may swim." We can then apply our formula to put the statement into standard form:

d. All places where children under 5 may swim are kiddie-pools.

Statement *e* might be taken as equivalent to *d*; in causal speech, that would be a reasonable interpretation. Strictly speaking, however, "only" modifies the verb "swim," and thus quantifies things one can do in kiddie-pools rather than the pools themselves, as in *d*. It means that swimming is the only thing that children under 5 may do in the pools; they are not allowed to do anything else, such as fighting, eating, throwing balls, or whatever. So once again we recast the sentence to put "only" at the beginning—"only swimming is a thing that children under 5 may do in kiddie pools"—and then apply our formula to put it in standard form:

e. All things that children under 5 may do in the kiddie-pools are (acts of) swimming.

The guidelines for distilling syllogisms we discussed in this section do not cover all the problems you will encounter. The resources of our language are too rich and varied for us to list all the possible nonstandard ways of expressing a deductive argument. We have discussed only the major ones. But if you understand these, you should be able to handle the others by common sense.

EXERCISE 8.3

Put each of the following syllogisms into standard form, and determine whether each is valid. Be sure to identify any implicit premises.

✳1. Only computers with at least 1 gigabyte of internal memory can run Microsoft Windows 7, and my computer doesn't have that much memory. So I can't run Windows.

2. Were the earth's crust a single rigid layer, the continents could not have shifted their positions in relation to each other, but such "continental drift" has clearly occurred.

3. Only U.S. citizens can vote in U.S. elections. Since you're a citizen, you can vote.

✳4. Without some mechanism of natural selection, there would be no way for new species of organisms to arise—as they have. So clearly there is a mechanism of natural selection.

5. It's raining today, and whenever it rains, the traffic slows to a crawl.

6. You can't get a decent meal anywhere in this town, but we have to eat here somewhere, so let's forget about a decent meal.

✳7. Anyone who can strike a log with an ax in just the right place can split it with one blow. But it takes a good eye to hit the log just right, so only someone with a good eye can split logs in a single blow.

8. Photosynthesis must occur as far down as 250 meters below the surface of the ocean, for there are algae that live at those depths.

9. Many immigrants are here illegally! In order to preserve the law, we need to expel them, make them pay fines, or grant them amnesty. We can't possibly expel them, and we can't grant them all amnesty, so we'll have to fine them.

✳10. I'd be willing to take statistics only if I could take it in the morning, when my brain is functioning. But it isn't offered in the morning, so I won't take it.

11. Current will not flow unless the circuit is unbroken, and this circuit is broken. So the current isn't flowing.

12. The book cannot be published. The agreement was that it would not be published unless there was no objection from the review committee, and the review committee did object.

✳13. Under the "bubble" concept of air pollution regulation, a new factory in a given area can emit a given quantity of pollutants into the air only if it purchases the right to emit that quantity from some other factory, and another factory is willing to sell the right only if it is willing to reduce its emissions by the same quantity. So if a new factory emits a given quantity of pollutants, some other factory is emitting less of that pollutant by the same quantity.

14. Robin wasn't really embarrassed, because the blotch she gets whenever she's embarrassed wasn't there.

15. If we don't allow drilling in the Alaska National Wildlife Reserve, we'll remain dependent on foreign oil. And we can no longer afford to depend on foreign oil.

8.4 Extended Arguments

In our study of argument structure in Chapter 4, we saw that arguments often involve more than a single step. Premises combine to support an intermediate conclusion, which is then used as a premise to support an ultimate conclusion. Or, moving in the opposite direction, a conclusion is supported by premises that are themselves supported by further premises. When such an extended argument is deductive, we can use what we know about syllogisms to analyze it in more depth than was possible in Chapter 4.

Consider the following argument:

> A nervous system contains many individual cells, so no one-celled animal, by definition, could have one. But only something with a nervous system could be conscious, so no one-celled animal is conscious.

This is certainly a deductive argument, and it has the marks of a categorical syllogism. There's an explicit quantifier, "no," and various terms are repeated: "one-celled animal," "conscious [beings]," and so on. Notice, however, that the argument has two conclusions, both introduced by the word "so." It is clear that the first one (no one-celled animal has a nervous system) is an intermediate conclusion, because a further inference is drawn from it. The ultimate conclusion of the argument is "no one-celled animal is conscious." The argument, then, has more than one step and must be analyzed accordingly.

We begin our analysis by isolating and numbering the propositions that play a role in the argument. Thus:

> (1) A nervous system contains many individual cells, so (2) no one-celled animal, by definition, could have one. But (3) only something with a nervous system could be conscious, so (4) no one-celled animal is conscious.

Before we start looking for syllogisms in an argument like this, it's a good idea to step back and try to get a feel for the flow of the argument as a whole. It seems clear that 1 is a premise used to support 2, and that 2 and 3 together support the ultimate conclusion. So we would diagram this argument as follows:

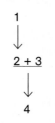

As the diagram reveals, the argument has two steps: from 1 to 2 and from 2 + 3 to 4. So now we need to look at each step individually. It doesn't matter which one we do first, but since the second step has two premises and looks as if it is a syllogism, let's start there. Putting everything into standard form, we have:

3. All conscious organisms have nervous systems.
2. <u>No one-celled animal has a nervous system.</u>
4. No one-celled animal is conscious.

Let's go back to the first step, from 1 to 2. The apparent subject term in 1 is "nervous systems," but the argument is clearly about classes of organisms that do or do not have them, so we would put 1 in standard form accordingly:

1. <u>All organisms that have nervous systems have many cells.</u>
2. No one-celled animal has a nervous system.

This is clearly an enthyrneme, and the missing premise is: *a*. No one-celled animal has many cells. (Since we are using the numbering technique of Chapter 4, we use letters instead of parentheses to indicate implicit premises.)

The argument as a whole then looks like this:

1. All organisms with nervous systems have many cells.
a. <u>No one-celled animal has many cells.</u>
2. No one-celled animal has a nervous system.

3. All conscious organisms have nervous systems.
2. <u>No one-celled animal has a nervous system.</u>
4. No one-celled animal is conscious.

What we have done here is to break up a single chain of reasoning into its component syllogisms, so that we can evaluate each step for validity. This process is like that of addition. To add a column of numbers, you first add two of them, then add their sum to the third, and that sum to the fourth, and so on. Similarly, in an extended argument, we combine two premises in a single syllogism to derive a conclusion, then combine that conclusion with the next premise to yield a further conclusion, and so on until we reach the ultimate conclusion. Just as we can add a column of numbers of any length, so we can have an argument with any number of steps. And just as we must add each pair of numbers correctly for the final sum to be correct, so each step must be valid if an argument as a whole is to be valid.

But the analogy is not perfect. When you are given a column of numbers, the intermediate sums are never part of the column itself, whereas intermediate conclusions are often given in the statement of an argument. Thus we need to distinguish premises from intermediate conclusions. Moreover, you can add numbers in any order and get the same final sum, but in an argument you have less freedom: To break it down into the correct individual steps, you must put the premises together in the right order.

So analyzing extended arguments is a little more difficult than adding numbers. No single procedure will work in every case. What we need is a set of procedures from which we can pick and choose, adapting our method to the circumstances of the particular case. In the remainder of this section, therefore, we will look at a variety of specific arguments that illustrate common problems and the techniques we can use to solve them.

8.4A Categorical Syllogisms in Extended Arguments

In the example we just analyzed, the intermediate conclusion was stated explicitly. Let's look at a somewhat more difficult example in which the intermediate conclusions are *not* stated:

> Since (l) values are nothing more than our own evaluations of the facts, (2) they are not objective. (3) Knowledge of the facts is based on empirical evidence, and (4) anything based on such evidence is objective. But (5) evaluating facts is different from knowing them.

The ultimate conclusion here is 2: "No values are objective." Four premises are used to support the conclusion, whereas a single syllogism can have only two premises, so we know that this is an extended argument. Premise 1 is directly related to the conclusion, but the others aren't, so where do we go from here?

Let's try working backward from the conclusion. Since 1 contains the minor term ("values"), we will assume that it is the minor premise of a syllogism. What major premise would be needed to complete the syllogism? It must contain the major term "objective (state of mind)" and the middle term "evaluation of the facts." None of the other statements in the argument contains these two terms, so we need to supply a major premise that makes this step of the argument valid. Using the techniques we learned for enthymemes, and labeling the new premise as *a*, we have:

a. No evaluation of the facts is objective.
1. <u>All values are evaluations of the facts.</u>
2. No values are objective.

If this were an enthymeme—that is, if 1 were the only premise we were given—then we would treat *a* as an implicit premise, and our job would be done. But since there are other premises in the argument—3, 4, and 5—we should see whether they provide support for *a* as an intermediate conclusion. We cannot combine these premises in a single step. But 3 and 4 look like the premises of a syllogism, so let's see what conclusion we get by putting them together.

4. All things based on empirical evidence are objective.
3. <u>All knowledge of the facts is based on empirical evidence.</u>
b. All knowledge of the facts is objective.

The conclusion (*b*) is not explicitly stated, so we have to give it a letter, but it follows validly from 3 and 4, which were stated.

We are almost done now. Working down from the top (from premises 5 and 4), we found that *b* followed as an intermediate conclusion. Working up from the bottom (from the ultimate conclusion), we saw that we would have to get to *a* as an intermediate conclusion. So the question is whether *b*, together with the remaining premise 5, will support *a*. That is, we now know that the argument has the structure:

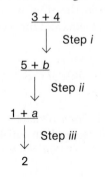

We identified *b* as the intermediate conclusion that follows from 3 and 4, so we know that step *i* is valid. Likewise, we supplied *a* as a premise that would make step *iii* valid. So everything turns on the middle step. Writing it out as a standard-form syllogism, we have:

b. All knowledge of the facts is objective.
5. <u>No evaluation of the facts is knowledge of the facts.</u>
a. No evaluation of the facts is objective.

This syllogism is invalid. In terms of the rules of validity for categorical syllogisms, it has an illicit major term, "objective (states of mind)," distributed in the conclusion but not in the major premise. You can easily confirm its invalidity by using Venn diagrams. The argument tries to show that no evaluation of the facts is objective by distinguishing evaluation from knowledge of the facts. For that line of argument to work, we would need the additional premise that *only* knowledge of the facts is objective. In accordance with the rule we learned earlier in the chapter, this "only" statement means: "All objective states of mind are knowledge of the facts." This statement is not equivalent to premise *b*. (It is the converse of *b*, and the converse of an A proposition is not equivalent to it.) Nor can the statement be derived from premises 3 and 4. So the argument as a whole is invalid.

8.4B Hypothetical Syllogisms in Extended Arguments

Extended arguments need not be categorical. Hypothetical syllogisms can also be combined into longer arguments. Suppose that during a shortage of consumer goods, the government issued this statement:

> As unpleasant as the current shortage is, it means (1) we are consuming less. And so (2) in the long run our standard of living will rise. For (3) in order to improve our standard of living, we must save, and (4) in order to save, we must forgo current consumption.

If this argument sounds fishy to you, that's because it is. Let's see why.

The speaker here is trying to convince us that because we are consuming less at the moment, our standard of living will rise in the long run: 1 is being offered as a reason for 2. The link between them is provided by 3 and 4, both of which are hypothetical propositions about means and ends and can easily be combined in a pure hypothetical syllogism:

3. If we are to improve our living standards, we must save.
4. <u>If we are to save, we must forgo current consumption.</u>
a. If we are to improve our living standards, we must forgo current consumption.

The question now is whether *a*, together with 1, will support the conclusion. The statement that we are consuming less is categorical, and it is just another way of saying what the consequent of *a* says. So these premises together give us a mixed hypothetical syllogism:

a. If we are to improve our living standards, we must forgo current consumption.
1. <u>We are forgoing current consumption.</u>
2. We will improve our living standards.

And since it isn't valid to affirm the consequent, as this step does, the argument as a whole is invalid.

Notice that for this example, I did not use a diagram. That's because it would not have been much help. It would have told us that 1 + 3 + 4 support 2, but it would not have told us how to break the argument down into steps. Once we put the two hypothetical premises together, however, the analysis was straightforward. Remember that diagrams are like maps. They are useful for keeping track of where we are in an argument, and in many cases we would be lost without them. But just as you don't always need a map to reach your destination, you won't always need a diagram to see how to reach a conclusion.

8.4C Extended Arguments with Elements of Different Types

It is possible to combine hypothetical with categorical elements in an argument—indeed, this is quite common. Consider the following:

> (1) Certainty would be possible in human knowledge only if some method of ascertaining the facts were infallible. But (2) all of our methods are subject to the influence of emotion, bias, peer pressure, and other subjective factors. Hence (3) certainty is impossible.

At first glance, the structure of this argument is simple: 1 and 2 together support 3. But the structure is actually a little more complex. Premise 1 is a hypothetical proposition of the form *p only if q*, which we put into standard form as *if p, then q*. Since the conclusion is categorical, let's try to formulate it as a mixed hypothetical syllogism:

1. If certainty is possible, then some method is infallible.
   (?)
3. Certainty is not possible.

Since the conclusion is the negation of the antecedent in 1, it looks as if the argument is an instance of denying the consequent (*modus tollens*). Thus the second premise must be the negation of "some method is infallible," which would be the E proposition "no method is infallible." And that is not what premise 2 says. But premise 2 can be used in a categorical syllogism to establish the E proposition as an intermediate conclusion. Thus the argument as a whole would be

a. No method subject to the influence of emotion, etc., is infallible.
2. <u>All of our methods are subject to emotion, etc.</u>
b. No method is infallible.

1. If certainty is possible, then some method is infallible.
b. <u>No method is infallible.</u>
3. Certainty is not possible.

So the actual structure of the argument consists of one categorical syllogism and one mixed hypothetical syllogism, both valid.

Let's work through another example, drawn from the Sherlock Holmes novel *A Study in Scarlet*, in which Holmes is trying to solve a case of murder. In the following passage, he explains why he came to believe that the killer's motive was revenge for a personal wrong, presumably involving a woman.

> And now came the great question as to the reason why. [1] Robbery had not been the object of the murder, for [2] nothing was taken. Was it politics, then, or was it a woman? That was the question which confronted me. I was inclined from the first to the latter supposition. [3] Political assassins are only too glad to do their work and to fly. [4] This murder had, on the contrary, been done most deliberately, and the perpetrator had left his track all over the room, showing that he had been there all the time. [5] It must have been a private wrong, and not a political one, which called for such a methodical revenge.

The conclusion is stated in 5, which we can state more simply as the proposition

5. The murderer was someone seeking private revenge.

Holmes reaches this conclusion by excluding the other possible motives, robbery and assassination. So let's start at the top and analyze his arguments for excluding these motives.

The case against robbery as the motive is contained in the first two statements:

a. [?]
2. <u>No thing was taken.</u>
1. The murderer was not a robber.

The implicit premise *a* is clearly that if the murderer had been a robber, something would have been taken. Premise 2 denies the consequent: "No thing was taken" is the contradictory proposition to "Some thing was taken." So in standard form we have a *modus tollens* syllogism:

a. If the murderer had been a robber, then something would have been taken.
2. <u>No thing was taken.</u>
1. The murderer was not a robber.

To explain why he ruled out political assassination, Holmes makes a general claim about assassins (3) and then applies it to the murderer (4). So we would formulate his argument as a categorical syllogism:

3. All political assassins work quickly.
4. <u>The murderer did not work quickly.</u>
b. The murderer was not a political assassin.

So far, then, we could diagram the first steps of the argument as follows:

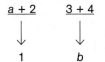

The question now is how we get from 1 and *b* to the conclusion, 5. Both 1 and *b* are negative statements, whereas the conclusion is the positive claim that the murder was someone seeking private revenge. As we observed in the previous section, that pattern is a mark of a disjunctive syllogism. And indeed, when we step back from the details of Holmes's argument and consider the basic flow, it is clear that he is considering various possibilities and ruling out all but one. The disjunctive premise is partially suggested by the question in the middle of the paragraph ("Was it politics, then, or was it a woman?"), but we need to add robbery as a further disjunct. So the final step of the argument is

c. The murderer was a robber, or a political assassin, or someone seeking private revenge.
1. The murderer was not a robber.
b. <u>The murderer was not a political assassin.</u>
5. The murderer was someone seeking private revenge.

(Remember that a disjunctive proposition can have more than two disjuncts, but then it needs more categorical premises to rule out all but one of the disjuncts.)

You can confirm for yourself that each step of this argument, and thus the argument as a whole, is valid. You can also see the value of analyzing the argument as we have, for in doing so we found that it depends crucially on the disjunctive premise *c*. And once we have made that assumption explicit, we can go on to ask whether it is true—whether there really are just three possible motives for murdering someone. Sherlock Holmes may be guilty of the fallacy of false alternative. At the very least, the argument loses some of its plausibility when it is spelled out in full.

8.4D Compound Components

When we discussed disjunctive and hypothetical propositions, we assumed that their components, *p* and *q*, were categorical propositions. That is not always the case. The components can themselves be compound, as in the following examples, where the compound component is indicated by parentheses:

1. If it rains or is cold, we will cancel the camping trip.   If (*p* or *q*), then *r*
2. If interest rates rise, then if corporate profits remain the same, their stocks will decline.   If *p*, then (if *q*, then *r*)
3. Some people are frightened if a dog approaches.   Some *S* are (if *P*, then *Q*)
4. All of the therapists at LiveWell Clinic are either psychologists or psychiatrists.   All *S* are (*P* or *Q*)

Statements 1 and 2 are hypothetical propositions; in 1 the antecedent is a disjunctive proposition, while in 2 the consequent is an embedded hypothetical proposition. Statements 3 and 4 are categorical rather than compound propositions, but they have compound predicate terms, and arguments involving such propositions may require that we take account of the disjunctive or hypothetical structure of the predicate.

To see how this works, consider an argument involving 4:

> All of the therapists at LiveWell Clinic are either psychologists or psychiatrists.
> Tess, a therapist at LiveWell, must be a psychologist since she isn't a psychiatrist.

The conclusion is that Tess is a psychologist. To derive that conclusion, we first have to apply the universal statement about therapists at LiveWell clinic to Tess. That will be a categorical syllogism:

> All therapists at LiveWell Clinic are either psychologists or psychiatrists.
> <u>Tess is a therapist at LiveWell Clinic.</u>
> Tess is a psychologist or she is a psychiatrist.

Once we have that intermediate conclusion, the rest of the argument is obvious: Tess is not a psychiatrist, so she is a psychologist.

Here's another example, drawn once again from a Sherlock Holmes story. In the following passage, Holmes is trying to find out who was with the murdered man on the night of his death; he already knows that the two drank rum together in the victim's cabin.

> You remember that I asked whether whiskey and brandy were in the cabin. You said they were. How many landsmen are there who would drink rum when they could get these other spirits? Yes, I was certain it was a seaman. [Arthur Conan Doyle, "Black Peter"]

The conclusion is that (1) the visitor was a seaman—a sailor. The first two sentences together tell us that (2) whiskey and brandy were available in the cabin. What about the rhetorical question in the third sentence? The most accurate way to formulate Holmes's assumption here would be as a compound hypothetical proposition:

3. If whiskey and brandy were available in the cabin, then if the visitor were a landsman, he would not have had rum.

This proposition has the form: if p, then (if q, then r)—a hypothetical proposition in which the consequent is itself hypothetical. And since premise 2 affirms the antecedent of 3, we can formulate the first step of the argument as a mixed hypothetical syllogism:

3. If whiskey and brandy were available in the cabin, then if the visitor were a landsman, he would not have had rum.
2. <u>Whiskey and brandy were available.</u>
a. If the visitor were a landsman, he would not have had rum.

Since Holmes has already established that (4) the visitor *did* drink rum, the consequent of *a* is false, so we can formulate the second step of the argument as another mixed hypothetical syllogism (in this case, denying the consequent):

a. If the visitor were a landsman, he would not have had rum.
4. <u>The visitor had rum.</u>
1. The visitor was not a landsman.

The conclusion here is the obverse of the conclusion as stated in the passage—on the assumption that landsmen and seamen are complementary classes. If we want to make this assumption explicit, we would have to add a disjunctive premise. But we need not bother with that here.

STRATEGY **Analyzing Extended Arguments**

1. Identify the conclusion.
2. Label as many of the premises in the passage as you can.
3. Diagram as much of the structure as possible.
4. If this is not sufficient to identify the whole structure, then use what you know about syllogisms to find missing premises and intermediate conclusions. Work up from the ultimate conclusion or down from the premises. Remember that the individual steps of the argument need not all be syllogisms of the same type.
5. Evaluate each step for validity. The argument as a whole is valid if—but only if—every step is valid.

EXERCISE 8.4A–D

Analyze each extended argument that follows. Identify the structure of the argument, formulate each step as a syllogism, adding assumed premises or conclusions where necessary, and determine whether the argument is valid.

✳1. The killer left fingerprints all over the place, so he couldn't have been a pro. A pro would not have been so sloppy.

2. It isn't true that only conscious beings can manipulate symbols, because some computers can do that, and computers aren't conscious—only living organisms are.

3. If Jones was not at the meeting, then all the witnesses have been lying. But some of the witnesses, at least, have been clergymen.

✳4. Any metal that can oxidize at normal temperatures will rust. But some steel contains chromium and is therefore rustproof.

5. Lower animals do not have a sense of humor, because humor presupposes a rational faculty, which only human beings possess.

8.4E Distilling an Extended Argument

The examples we have discussed illustrate the basic method for analyzing extended deductive arguments. But these examples have been fairly self-contained and easy to follow. In everyday speech and thought, extended arguments are normally embedded in a context of descriptions, examples, rhetorical asides, disclaimers, and other material that is not directly relevant to the argument itself. In order to analyze such arguments, you need to extract them from this context. So as our final illustration, let's look at a more realistic case. The two passages below are from a key chapter in John Kenneth Galbraith's *The Affluent Society*. Together they constitute his central argument for the claim that, in our society, private production is no longer urgent and that more resources should be transferred to the public sector (government).

If the individual's wants are to be urgent, they must be original with himself. They cannot be urgent if they must be contrived for him. And above all, they must not be contrived by the process of production by which they are satisfied. For this means that the whole case for the urgency of [private] production, based on the urgency of wants, falls to the ground. One cannot defend production as satisfying wants if that production creates the wants.

The even more difficult link between production and wants is provided by the institutions of modern advertising and salesmanship. These cannot be reconciled with the notion of independently determined desires, for their central function is to create desires—to bring into being wants that previously did not exist.

Let's go through each of these passages in turn, trying to follow the drift of Galbraith's argument. In the first passage, he is criticizing the economists who say that an increase in production is highly valuable ("urgent") because it will satisfy consumer desires. Even though Galbraith doesn't say it in so many words, his conclusion is clearly that increased production is not highly valuable. And his basic reason is indicated by the first three sentences: An increase in production is valuable only if the desires it will satisfy are "original with" the consumer—that is, only if the consumer has those desires independently, not because they have been "contrived" for him by the producers of the goods. Galbraith does not say whether he is talking about all desires or only some, but the latter is the more plausible interpretation of his argument.

So far, then, we have a hypothetical premise and a conclusion:

1. If an increase in production is valuable, then some of the desires it satisfies must be original with the consumer.
2. <u>None of the desires it satisfies are original with the consumer.</u>
3. An increase in production is not valuable.

Galbraith does not actually assert premise 2 in the first passage, but it is necessary for his argument, and it seems clear that he is gearing up to try to prove it.

Let's turn, then, to the second passage, which introduces his discussion of advertising. Advertising is the key "link between production and wants"; its "central function is to create desires" that did not exist before. Galbraith takes it as obvious that no desire instilled by advertising is "original with" the consumer. And he assumes that any desire that an increase in production *would* satisfy would have to be instilled by advertising. Thus he is giving us a categorical syllogism in support of 2:

4. No desire instilled by advertising is original with the consumer.
5. <u>All desires that would be satisfied by increased production must be instilled by advertising.</u>
2. No desire that would be satisfied by increased production is original with the consumer.

As a result of our analysis, then, we can see that Galbraith's argument is an inference in two steps. The analysis required that we read between the lines, distilling the essential points he was making to a much greater extent than in previous examples. (And of course I performed part of the "distillation" for you by isolating those two passages; had you been given the whole chapter to analyze, you would have had to pick them out yourself.) A good deal of interpretation was involved here, which means that you might have come up with a different wording for some of the premises. This will generally be the case with extended arguments in real life. But different formulations will not affect the basic logic of the argument.

This example illustrates the value of identifying the basic logic. Both steps of Galbraith's argument are valid. So the soundness of the argument depends on the truth or falsity of the premises—specifically on 1, 4, and 5. (Statement 2 is an intermediate conclusion.) Knowing that those are the key premises would help you in reading the text, because you would then be on the lookout for the evidence he offers in support of those premises. In addition, Galbraith's argument has been criticized by many other writers, so if you know the basic structure of his argument, you can organize and evaluate the counterarguments by asking which premises they are directed against.

EXERCISE 8.4E

Analyze each extended argument that follows: Identify the structure of the argument, formulate each step as a syllogism, adding implicit premises as needed, and determine whether the argument is valid.

✳1. Roy's temperature is over 100°F. If a person's temperature is above 100°F, he either is sick or has been recently engaged in some strenuous activity. Roy isn't sick, so he must have been doing something strenuous.

2. Price controls will not work in controlling inflation. They would work, perhaps, if every law of economics were false, but some of those laws are supported by overwhelming evidence.

3. Liberals believe in government support for academic research. Since no one who favors liberty can accept interference by the state in the realm of ideas, liberals do not really favor liberty.

✳4. If the direction of the flow of time, from past to present to future, depends on the expansion of the universe, then time will reverse its direction if the expansion stops and the universe begins contracting—as current evidence from astrophysics suggests it will.

5. The law that requires that one have a driver's license in order to drive in this state implies that illiterates cannot drive, since they would obviously fail the test one must pass to get a license.

6. In the early 1770s, the American colonies came to a crisis point: They would obtain full and fair representation in the English Parliament, or else they would seek independence. But they would receive full representation only if the existing Parliament was willing to accept a diminution of its power, and it was not. So the outcome was rebellion.

Summary

In order to analyze deductive arguments as they occur in ordinary language, we need to identify the kind of syllogism involved. In addition to the categorical syllogisms discussed in Chapter 7, there are disjunctive and hypothetical syllogisms.

A disjunctive syllogism employs a disjunctive proposition *p or q* as a premise. It is valid to deny one disjunct and infer that the other is true. Because we interpret the conjunction "or" in the inclusive sense, however, it is not valid to affirm one disjunct and infer that the other is false.

A hypothetical syllogism employs a hypothetical proposition *if p, then q* as a premise. In a pure hypothetical syllogism, both premises and the conclusion are hypothetical propositions. In a mixed hypothetical syllogism, one premise is hypothetical; the other premise either affirms or denies one of the components, and the conclusion affirms or denies the other. A syllogism that affirms the antecedent or denies the consequent is valid, and a syllogism that denies the antecedent or affirms the consequent is invalid.

To determine whether a given argument is a categorical, hypothetical, or disjunctive syllogism, we rely on linguistic criteria of various kinds, such as the presence or absence of explicit quantifiers and connectives. We also rely on substantive criteria: Disjunctive syllogisms typically deal with alternative possibilities, hypothetical syllogisms with relationships of dependence, categorical syllogisms with relationships among classes. Moreover, deductive arguments in everyday thought and speech are normally extended. To analyze and evaluate them, we need to break the arguments down into component steps, identifying implicit premises and intermediate conclusions.

This completes our study of the traditional approach to deductive reasoning. Even though the essential feature of deduction is that the conclusion is already contained implicitly in the premises, it should be clear by now that such reasoning is enormously valuable. It is indispensable for clarifying our thoughts, enlarging our understanding of the issues, and bringing order to complex material. It is used pervasively in politics, law, ethics, and the sciences, as well as in everyday thinking. It allows us to apply the knowledge embodied in all of our concepts for classes of things; to draw conclusions about cause and effect, means and ends; and to find our way among the alternatives set by a given situation. The traditional approach, however, did not offer a complete account of deduction; there were certain problems it was unable to solve. In the next three chapters, we will see how modern deductive logic addresses those problems. In the end, moreover, deductive reasoning is only as good as the premises on which it relies, and those premises ultimately depend, in one way or another, on *inductive* reasoning, which we will examine in Part 3.

Key Terms

Disjunctive proposition—a compound proposition that uses the connective "or."

Hypothetical proposition—a compound proposition that uses the connective "if . . . then."

Disjunct—a component of a disjunctive proposition.

Disjunctive syllogism—a syllogism with a disjunctive premise, other premises denying all but one of the disjuncts, and a conclusion affirming the remaining disjunct.

Antecedent—the "if" component in a hypothetical proposition.

Consequent—the "then" component in a hypothetical proposition.

Pure hypothetical syllogism—a syllogism in which the conclusion and both of the premises are hypothetical propositions.

Mixed hypothetical syllogism—a syllogism with a hypothetical premise, a categorical premise, and a categorical conclusion.

Affirming the antecedent (*modus ponens*)—a valid mixed hypothetical syllogism in which the categorical premise affirms the antecedent of the hypothetical premise and the conclusion affirms the consequent.

Denying the consequent (*modus tollens*)—a valid mixed hypothetical syllogism in which the categorical premise denies the consequent of the hypothetical premise and the conclusion denies the antecedent.

Denying the antecedent—an invalid mixed hypothetical syllogism in which the categorical premise denies the antecedent of the hypothetical premise and the conclusion denies the consequent.

Affirming the consequent—an invalid mixed hypothetical syllogism in which the categorical premise affirms the consequent of the hypothetical premise and the conclusion affirms the antecedent.

Additional Exercises

A. Determine whether the following argument forms are valid.

✳ 1. If *p*, then *q*
   q
   p

2. *p* or *q*
   not-*q*
   p

3. If *p*, then *q*
   not-*p*
   not-*q*

✳ 4. If *p*, then *q*
   p
   q

5. *p* if *q*
   not-*q*
   not-*p*

6. *p* unless *q*
   not-*p*
   q

✳ 7. *p* or *q*
   q
   p

8. *p* or *q*
   p
   not-*q*

9. *p* only if *q*
   p
   q

✳10. not (*p* and *q*)
   not-*p*
   q

11. *p* unless *q*
   q
   not-*p*

12. *p* only if *q*
   not-*p*
   not-*q*

B. Creating arguments: Follow the instructions for each of the problems below.

1. Construct a *modus ponens* syllogism to support this conclusion: The economy will go into a recession next year.

2. Construct an invalid mixed hypothetical syllogism with this conclusion: Jane does not speak Spanish.

3. Use a pure hypothetical syllogism to explain why pushing down the accelerator makes the car go faster.

4. Construct a valid disjunctive syllogism to support this conclusion: Honesty is the best policy.

5. Construct the most plausible argument you can that commits the fallacy of affirming the consequent.

C. Put each of the following arguments into standard form and determine whether it is valid.

✳ 1. "If the Moral Law was one of our instincts, we ought to be able to point to some one impulse inside us which was always what we call good . . . But [we] cannot . . . The Moral Law is not any one instinct." [C.S. Lewis, *Mere Christianity*]

2. "Faith is not reason, else religion would be . . . a part of philosophy, which it assuredly is not." [Richard Taylor, "Faith"]

3. "How often have I said to you that when you have eliminated the impossible, whatever remains, however improbable, must be the truth? We know that he did not come through the door, the window, or the chimney. We also know that he could not have been concealed in the room, as there is no concealment possible. Whence, then, did he come?"

   "He came through the hole in the roof!"

   "Of course he did. He must have done so." [Arthur Conan Doyle, *The Sign of Four*]

✳ 4. "At present, then, there is no evidence on the effects of imitation [on language learning] that is very conclusive. This in itself is somewhat surprising in view of the importance that many theorists have attributed to imitation. If it is an important factor in language development, it should be relatively easy to find evidence of its importance. We are forced to conclude that imitation . . . does not contribute importantly to language development." [Donald J. Foss and David T. Hakes, *Psycholinguistics*]

5. The tax benefit [for energy-related investments by businesses] only helps if you're paying taxes, and you're only paying taxes if you're making money. [National Public Radio, "Marketplace," March 15, 2010]

6. "The Air Force has a saying that if you're not catching flak, you're not over the target. I'm catching the flak, I must be over the target." [Mike Huckabee, Republican primary debate, 2008]

✳ 7. "For if we cannot be sure of the independent existence of objects, we cannot be sure of the independent existence of other people's bodies, and therefore still less of other people's minds, since we have no grounds for believing in their minds except such as are derived from observing their bodies. Thus if we cannot be sure of the independent existence of objects, we shall be left alone in a desert—it may be that the whole outer world is nothing but a dream, and we alone exist." [Bertrand Russell, *Problems of Philosophy*]

D. An article in a science magazine ("Neutrino Astronomy Born in a Supernova," *Science News*, March 21, 1987) contained the following statement:

   "If neutrinos have a small rest mass, they will have a small magnetic moment, a small intrinsic magnetism. (The converse is not true, so a zero magnetic moment does not necessarily mean no mass.)"

A letter to the editor in a subsequent issue (April 11, 1987) took issue with the statement:

   "Let 'neutrino has non-zero rest mass' be statement A, and 'neutrino has non-zero magnetic moment' be statement B. You are saying that 'A implies B' does not necessarily imply 'non-B implies not-A.' But that is wrong. 'A implies B' does necessarily imply 'non-B implies not-A.' Particle physics may be counterintuitive at times, but it doesn't overthrow the rules of logic.

   "I think you probably meant 'A implies B' does not necessarily imply 'B implies A,' which is certainly true. . . ."

The author of the original article then replied:

"The statement was in error. It should have read: 'If the neutrino has a magnetic moment, it will also have mass. But it can have mass without having a magnetic moment."

Use what you have learned in this chapter to identify the logical error of which the original article was accused. Was the letter to the editor correct in what it says about logic? Is the author's reply correct?

E. Put each of the following statements into standard form as a categorical, hypothetical, or disjunctive proposition.

✳ 1. Pride goeth before a fall

2. "Separate educational facilities are inherently unequal." [Chief Justice Warren, Opinion of the Court, *Brown v. Board of Education*, 1954]

3. "A man who does not think for himself does not think at all." [Oscar Wilde]

✳ 4. "Curiosity is one of the permanent and certain characteristics of a vigorous mind." [Samuel Johnson, *Rambler*]

5. "Where there's marriage without love, there will be love without marriage." [Ben Franklin, *Poor Richard's Almanack*]

6. "Were we faultless, we would not derive such satisfaction from remarking the faults of others." [La Rochefoucauld, *Maxims*]

✳ 7. "Not to know what happened before one was born is to remain a child." [Cicero, *De Oratore*]

8. "The whole of science is nothing more than a refinement of everyday thinking." [Albert Einstein, *Physics and Reality*]

9. "You can't think and hit at the same time." [Yogi Berra]

✳10. "The people never give up their liberties but under some delusion." [Edmund Burke, *Speech at County Meeting of Buckinghamshire*]

F. The syllogisms that follow are taken from previous exercises. Each is in standard form (or very close to it). Translate it into ordinary language. Use what you have learned in this section to express the argument in a more natural, idiomatic way: Reformulate the propositions, leave an obvious premise unstated, but above all make them sound like things people would actually say!

1. Some bureaucrats are not chosen on the basis of ability.
   All bureaucrats are civil servants.
   Some civil servants are not chosen on the basis of ability.

2. All geniuses are eccentric.
   No Greek poet was eccentric.
   No Greek poet was a genius.

3. If the circuit is broken, current will not flow.
   The circuit is broken.
   The current will not flow.

4. Any state that ignores human rights is a tyranny.
   Some democracies ignore human rights.
   Some democracies are tyrannies.

5. If children are deprived of affection early in life, they will learn not to expect it.
   If children learn not to expect affection, they will not seek it out later in life.
   If children are deprived of affection early in life, they will not seek it out later in life.

G. Put each of the following arguments into standard form as a categorical, hypothetical, or disjunctive syllogism, supplying any missing premise or conclusion. Then determine whether it is valid.

✳ 1. "The wound upon the dead man was, as I was able to determine with absolute confidence, fired from a revolver at the distance of something over four yards. There was no powder-blackening on the clothes." [Arthur Conan Doyle, "The Reigate Puzzle"]

2. " . . . If we look at the actual tasks of working science, we shall find that not all prediction is scientific—or horserace tipsters would be scientists—and not all science is predictive, or evolutionary biologists would not be scientists. [Stephen Toulmin, "From Form to Function: Philosophy and History of Science in the 1950s and Now"]

3. "Saccadic eye movements occur whenever the eyes move without a [moving] target to follow. In reading, of course, there is no moving target to follow; so reading involves saccadic eye movements." [Donald J. Foss and David T. Hakes, *Psycholinguistics*]

✳ 4. "As it is impossible for the whole race of mankind to be united in one great society, they must necessarily divide into many." [William Blackstone, *Commentaries on the Laws of England*]

5. "The fish which you have tattooed immediately above your wrist could only have been done in China . . . . That trick of staining the fishes' scales of a delicate pink is quite peculiar to China." [Arthur Conan Doyle, "The Red-Headed League"]

6. "In all the world, only mammals have true hair and produce milk, so [duckbills] have been classified as mammals. [Isaac Asimov, "What Do You Call a Platypus?" in *National Wildlife Magazine*, March–April 1972]

✳ 7. "It is only about the things that do not interest one, that one can give a really unbiased opinion; and this is no doubt the reason why an unbiased opinion is always absolutely valueless." [*More Letters of Oscar Wilde*, ed. Rupert Hart-Davis]

8. "Had we but world enough, and time, This coyness, lady, were no crime . . . But at my back I always hear Time's winged chariot hurrying near; . . ." [Andrew Marvell, "To His Coy Mistress"]

9. "This gain [in entropy] occurs every time heat flows from a higher to a lower temperature, and since nothing interesting or useful happens unless heat does make this descent, all interesting and useful things are accompanied by an irreversible increase in entropy." [Jeremy Campbell, *Grammatical Man*]

✳10. "A prince should therefore have no other aim or thought, nor take up any other thing for his study, but war and its organization and discipline, for that is the only art necessary to one who commands." [Niccolo Machiavelli, *The Prince*]

11. " . . . If a moving object does possess acceleration, that is, if *a* in formula (1) [*F* = *ma*] is not zero, then the force *F* cannot be zero. Now an object falling to Earth from some height does possess acceleration. Hence some force must be acting." [Morris Kline, *Mathematics in Western Culture*]

12. "It is well known that quantitative differences ultimately pass into qualitative differences. This is true everywhere, and is therefore true in history." [George Plekhanov, *Essays in Historical Materialism*]

✳13. "A clown is someone who stands before a crowd and gestures wildly to get their attention. So is a politician." ["Today's Chuckle"]

14. "Some philosophers have, in the past, leaped . . . to what they take to be a proof that the mind is *essentially non-physical* in character . . . No physical object can, in itself, refer to one thing rather than to another; nevertheless, *thoughts in the mind* obviously do succeed in referring to one thing rather than another. So thoughts . . . are of

an essentially different nature than physical objects." [Hilary Putnam, *Reason, Truth, and History*]

15. "Observation implies movement, that is locomotion with reference to the rigid environment, because all observers are animals and all animals are mobil. [Gibson, *Ecological Approach to Visual Perception*]

H. For each of the statements that follow, (a) find a syllogism to support the statement, (b) find a syllogism to support one of the premises of the syllogism in (a), and (c) write out the complete argument in a short paragraph.

1. Mary will win the election for student body president.

2. Dancing is good exercise.

3. If interest rates decline, stock prices will rise.

4. Cheating is wrong.

5. Nothing ventured, nothing gained.

I. Analyze each of the arguments that follow: Identify the structure of the argument, formulate each step (there may be one or more) as a syllogism, and determine whether the argument is valid.

✳ 1. "Appellant's conduct is not a nuisance unless it is unreasonably noisy for an industrial area. What a reasonable amount of noise will be depends on the character of the neighborhood. Although appellant produces more noise in the area of the industrial park than any other source, it has not been shown that the level of noise it produces is out of keeping with the character of its location. Since it has not been shown that the noise from appellant's operation is out of keeping with its industrial location, it cannot be found to be a nuisance." [Legal brief]

2. "Since happiness consists in peace of mind, and since durable peace of mind depends on the confidence we have in the future, and since that confidence is based on an understanding of the nature of God and the soul, it follows that true happiness requires that understanding." [Gottfried Leibniz, *Preface to the General Science*]

3. "[Milton] identifies four reasons why [censorship will not work]. First, the decisions of the censor cannot be trusted unless the censor is infallible and beyond corruption. No mortal possesses such grace; therefore no mortal is qualified to be a censor."

[Irving Younger, "What Good Is Freedom of Speech?" *Commentary*, January 1984]

✳ 4. Touchstone: . . . Wast ever in court, shepherd?
Corin: No, truly.
Touchstone: Then thou art damned. . . .
Corin: For not being at court? Your reason.
Touchstone: Why, if thou never wast at court, thou never saw'st good manners; if thou never saw'st good manners, then thy manners must be wicked; and wickedness is sin, and sin is damnation. Thou art in a parlous state, shepherd. [Shakespeare, *As You Like It*]

5. "Anything that changes over time has, by definition, a history—the universe, countries, art and philosophy, and ideas. Science also, ever since its emergence from myths and early philosophies, has experienced a steady historical change and is thus a legitimate subject for the historian." [Ernst Mayr, *The Growth of Biological Thought*]

6. "But the secular power has no legal right to coerce heretics unless heresy is a crime. And heresy is not a crime, but an error; for it is not a matter of will." [J.B. Bury, *A History of Freedom of Thought*]

✳ 7. Robespierre's opponents accused him of having treated his personal enemies as enemies of the state. "I deny the accusation," he answered, "and the proof is that you still live."

8. "The fifth way [of proving that God exists] is taken from the governance of the world. We see that things which lack knowledge, such as natural bodies, act for an end, and this is evident from their acting always, or nearly always, in the same way, so as to obtain the best result. Hence it is plain that they achieve their end, not fortuitously, but designedly. Now whatever lacks knowledge cannot move towards an end, unless it be directed by some being endowed with knowledge and intelligence as the arrow is directed by the archer. Therefore some intelligent being exists by whom all natural things are directed to their end; and this being we call God." [Thomas Aquinas, *Summa Theologica*]

[NOTE: The last sentence is included for the sake of completeness, but it raises problems for analysis that we have not yet discussed. For the purposes of this exercise, therefore, assume that Aquinas's conclusion is "some things are directed by a being with knowledge and intelligence."]

9. "Between these alternatives there is no middle ground. The constitution is either a superior paramount law, unchangeable by ordinary means, or it is on a level with ordinary legislative acts, and, like other acts, is alterable when the legislature shall please to alter it.

"If the former part of the alternative be true, then a legislative act contrary to the constitution is not law: if the latter part be true, then written constitutions are absurd attempts, on the part of the people, to limit a power in its own nature illimitable." [Chief Justice John Marshall, Opinion of the Court, *Marbury v. Madison*, 1803]

✳10. "... Every man has a property in his own person. This nobody has any right to but himself. The labour of his body and the work of his hands, we may say, are properly his. Whatsoever, then, he removes out of the state that nature hath provided and left it in, he hath mixed his labour with it, and joined to it something that is his own, and thereby makes it his property.... For this labour being the unquestionable property of the labourer, no man but he can have a right to what that is once joined to...." [John Locke, *Second Treatise of Civil Government*]

Propositional Logic—Propositions

The principles of deductive reasoning that we have studied so far represent a portion of traditional logic, as it was developed by ancient and medieval logicians. We've seen that these principles allow us to analyze and evaluate many of the arguments we encounter every day. But they are incomplete in certain respects.

Consider the following argument:

> If there is a recession this year or a foreign affairs fiasco, then the president will not be reelected.
> <u>There will be a recession.</u>
> The president will not be reelected.

This is a deductive argument. It's rather simple, and it's obviously valid. But it does not fit any of the argument forms we studied in Chapter 8. It has the logical form:

> If p or q, then r
> $\dfrac{p}{r}$

This may look like an example of *modus ponens* (affirming the antecedent), but the antecedent is the disjunctive proposition *p or q*, and the second premise affirms *p*, not the disjunction as a whole. In Chapter 8 we learned to recognize disjunctive and hypothetical arguments in isolation, but we didn't learn how to analyze arguments that *combine* disjunctive and hypothetical elements. Since these arguments involve more complex relationships among propositions than we are used to, we need a more elaborate system of rules. Logicians have devised such a system, called *propositional logic*.

Propositional logic is one main branch of what is known as symbolic logic. In earlier chapters, we used symbols such as p and q to represent propositions, regardless of their content. But we did not symbolize the logical forms of propositions; we used words like "all," "some," "if . . . then," and "or." Modern symbolic logic replaces all of these with symbols. In this respect it is like mathematics, which not only uses variables to represent numbers but also uses special symbols for operations like addition or multiplication that we can perform on numbers. Logicians have introduced the new symbols and rules to serve many purposes. The analysis of complex arguments is only one of these purposes. But it's the one that concerns us, given the focus of this book on thinking skills. In this chapter and the next, we will study propositional logic, and we'll see that the patterns of inference we learned in Chapter 8 are part of a larger system. As you go through these chapters, you will notice that the term "statement" is used more often than "proposition." For most purposes, the terms are interchangeable (see Chapter 3). Both terms designate the content of a complete thought. But now we will be concerned with the symbolic expression of such contents, so "statement" will usually be the better term.

9.1 Connectives

Propositional logic is the logic of compound statements—statements that are made up of other, simpler propositions. Here are some examples:

1. My sister is happy, and she's throwing a party.
2. My brother is *not* coming to the party.
3. The Democrats will win *or* the Republicans will win.
4. *If* the Democrats win, *then* my sister will be happy.
5. The party will be fun *if and only if* Buzz shows up.

Each of these statements has one or more component statements along with an italicized expression, called a **connective**, which tells us how the components are related.

In 1, the connective is "and"; statements of this form are called **conjunctions**. Statement 2 is a **negation**. Here there is only one component statement ("My brother is coming to the party"), but the negation word "not" is still called a connective because it transforms the component into a more complex proposition. We're already familiar with statements like 3 and 4: 3 is a disjunctive statement, or **disjunction**; 4 is a hypothetical statement, or **conditional**, as it is usually called in symbolic logic. In 5, the connective "if and only if" is called a **biconditional**.

These are the basic types of compound statements in propositional logic, and each of the connectives has a special symbol, indicated in the box below. Let's look a little more closely at each of them.

between the component propositions, but the sentence still asserts both components; the sentence is true as long as the components are both true. Each of these sentences, therefore, has the logical form of a conjunction.

Second, remember that the conjuncts in a statement of the form $p \bullet q$ must be separate statements. The word "and" can be misleading in this respect. Compare the following statements, which are grammatically similar:

10. Renee and Tom took logic.
11. Tony and Sue got married.

Statement 10 is a normal conjunction: It is shorthand for "Renee took logic and Tom took logic." But 11 is different. It does not mean merely that Tony got married (to someone) and that Sue also got married (to someone). It means that Tony and Sue got married to each other. So the sentence makes a single statement about a pair of people; it is not a pair of statements that can be joined by conjunction or represented by the truth table for the dot.

NEGATION   Imagine the tail end of the classic children's quarrel: "It is." "It isn't." "It is so." "It is not." We don't know from this excerpt what the children are arguing about, but one is asserting something that the other is denying. We represent the denial of a proposition by the negation sign ~, called the "tilde." If T is the statement "The temperature is rising," then ~T could be expressed in any of the following ways:

12a. It's not the case that the temperature is rising.   ~T
12b. It's false that the temperature is rising.   ~T
12c. The temperature is not rising.   ~T

Since T and ~T are contradictory propositions, they cannot both be true, and they cannot both be false. It can't be raining *and* not raining—not at the same time and same place. But it must be *either* raining *or* not raining. The truth table for negation therefore has just two lines:

	p	$\sim p$
Negation:	T	F
	F	T

If p is true, then $\sim p$ is false, and vice versa.

Since a negation sign reverses truth value, two negation signs cancel out. For example, the statements:

13a. It's not the case that Larry will not come.   ~~L
    and
13b. Larry will come.   L

are equivalent. In other words, a double negation has the same truth value as the original proposition. Negation is an on/off switch; flip it twice and you're back where you started.

DISJUNCTION A disjunctive statement asserts that either p or q is true. The component statements p and q are called the *disjuncts*, and the connective "or" is represented by $\lor$—the "vee" or "wedge" sign. It is used to symbolize statements such as the following:

14. We will grow corn in our field or we will let it lie fallow.	G $\lor$ L
15. Chelsea got a job with Goldman Sachs or Morgan Stanley.	C $\lor$ J
16. Either the Yankees or the Twins will win the American League pennant.	Y $\lor$ T

In 14, we have two component statements joined by the connective "or," and the symbolic formula mirrors the structure of the English sentence. In 15, the disjunction occurs in the predicate of a sentence with a single subject, so we have to do a bit of revising before we put it into symbolic notation. The two components in 15 are

15a. Chelsea got a job with Goldman Sachs.
15b. Chelsea got a job with Morgan Stanley.

In 16, the disjunction occurs in the subject, and again we revise to extract the component statements:

16a. The Yankees will win the American League pennant.
16b. The Twins will win the American League pennant.

As with conjunction and negation, the truth value of $p \lor q$ is determined by the truth values of its components. The disjunction is true as long as at least one of the disjuncts is true. The truth table for disjunction, therefore, is as follows:

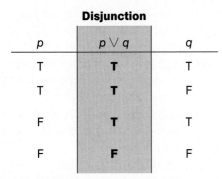

Disjunction

p	$p \lor q$	q
T	**T**	T
T	**T**	F
F	**T**	T
F	**F**	F

Notice how this truth table is different from the one for conjunction. A conjunction is true for only one pair of component truth values and false for all the others. A disjunction is *false* for only one pair of component truth values and *true* for all the others.

The second, third, and fourth lines of the table are pretty obvious. If p and q are both false, then $p \lor q$ is false. If only one of them is true (it doesn't matter which one), then the disjunction is true. What about the first line, where both components are true? Disjunction is normally used to state alternatives, such as alternative actions you can choose (go the party or watch television at home), or alternative explanations for someone's behavior (she is mad because I'm late or because I said something wrong). In some cases, the alternatives are mutually exclusive. When you tell someone "I will go to the party or I will watch television at home," part of what you mean to say is that it's one or the other but not both; you have to choose. The same is true in 14 earlier, where the choice is between one use of a farm field and another, incompatible use. So it seems odd to say that the disjunctive statement would be true if both disjuncts were true. In other cases, however, the alternatives are *not* mutually exclusive, but rather inclusive. For example, she could be mad because I'm late *and* because of something I said. Similarly, a case of emphysema can be caused both by smoking *and* by inhaling coal dust. In everyday thought and speech, it is usually clear from the context whether we are dealing with exclusive or inclusive alternatives. But in propositional logic, we abstract from the specific content of statements in order to isolate their logical form. To avoid any ambiguity, the disjunctive connective is always treated as inclusive. If we need to assert that *p* and *q* are not both true, we can add a statement to that effect.

EXERCISE 9.1A

For each of the following statements, identify the component propositions and the connective. Then put the statement in symbolic form, using the letters indicated in parentheses.

＊1. Roses are red, and violets are blue. (R, V)

2. I am not a crook. (C)

3. Mickey heard the story, and he is angry. (M, A)

＊4. I can pay the rent or I can buy groceries. (R, G)

5. It's not the case that time is on my side. (T)

6. She's either a lunatic or a genius. (L, G)

＊7. Jerry will either win the race or take second place. (W, S)

8. War is not the solution. (S)

9. Either we pay the fine now or we pay a larger fine later. (N, L)

＊10. The Cucumber County seed-spitting contest is not a world-class event. (C)

11. The campers were tired, but they were happy. (T, H)

12. The Batman action figure has two accessories, while the Spider-man toy has only one. (B, S)

＊13. Either the guest of honor wore brown or he fell in the mud on the way to the party. (B, M)

14. Color film is good for outdoor shots, but black-and-white is best for portraits. (C, B)

15. He is an excellent cook, although he hates food. (C, F)

9.1B Conditional and Biconditional

CONDITIONAL A conditional statement has the form *if p then q*. In such a statement *p* is called the *antecedent* and *q* the *consequent*. The connection between them, the if-then relationship, is represented by the symbol ⊃, called the "horseshoe." A statement involving this connective says that if the antecedent is true, the consequent is true as well. The statement does not assert that the antecedent is true, nor does it assert that the consequent is true. All it asserts is that there's a relationship between the two. Conditional statements are used to describe various relationships, such as means and ends (if you study hard, you will pass the test); cause and effect (if the Jet Stream shifts to the north, there will be drought in the Midwest); policy and consequence (if the city imposes rent control, there will be a housing shortage); or moves in a game (if I expose my king, my opponent will attack). But just as we use the letters *p* and *q* to abstract from the particular content of individual propositions, we use the symbol ⊃ to abstract from the particular nature of the relationship between them, in order to study the logical form of conditional statements. Thus the horseshoe would be used to translate each of our examples into symbolic notation:

17. If you study hard, you will pass the test.   S ⊃ P
18. If the Jet Stream shifts to the north, there will be drought in the Midwest.   J ⊃ D
19. If the city imposes rent control, there will be a housing shortage.   R ⊃ S
20. If I expose my king, my opponent will attack.   E ⊃ A

In propositional logic, the horseshoe connective is defined by a truth table:

Conditional

p	*p* ⊃ *q*	*q*
T	T	T
T	F	F
F	T	T
F	T	F

The important line in the table is the second one. To see why, let's work with 17. When I make this statement to someone, I am not asserting that the person actually will study hard or pass the test. But I am committing myself to the claim that studying hard will result in passing the test. If the person does study hard and yet fails, then my statement is false. That's what the second line of the truth table means: If *p* is true but *q* is false, the conditional statement itself is false. Now suppose that the person studies hard and passes the test, the situation represented in the first line of the table. That's certainly consistent with the truth of the conditional. Likewise if he doesn't study hard and doesn't pass—the last line of the table. What about the third line? Suppose he doesn't study hard but still passes. Would that prove my conditional statement false? No: The statement doesn't say that studying hard is the *only* way to pass; perhaps the exam was easy or perhaps the person already knew the material well.

In other words, every combination of truth values for *p* and *q* is consistent with the truth of *p* ⊃ *q* except for the case represented on line 2, where *p* is true and *q* false. The fact that the other combinations of truth values are *consistent* with *p* ⊃ *q* may not seem enough to establish that the conditional *has* to be true in these cases, rather than having an undetermined truth value. There is a real issue here, and we will discuss it soon. For now, we will have to treat it as a simplifying assumption in propositional logic that a conditional statement is regarded as true in these cases.

When we discussed conditional statements in Chapter 8 (where we called them hypothetical statements), we noted that *if p then q* is not equivalent to *if q then p*, and neither one implies the other. For example, suppose we reverse the antecedent and consequent in statement 19:

19. If the city imposes rent control, there will be a housing shortage.   R ⊃ H
19′. If there is a housing shortage, the city has imposed rent controls.   H ⊃ R

Statement 19 states that rent control will result in a housing shortage. It does not state that rent controls are the *only* cause of shortages. But that's exactly what 19′ says. If a shortage occurs in the absence of rent controls, 19′ is false, but 19 may still be true.

We can now use truth tables to understand why any statement of the form *p ⊃ q* is different from the corresponding statement *q ⊃ p*.

p	p ⊃ q	q		q	q ⊃ p	p
T	**T**	T		T	**T**	T
T	**F**	F		F	**T**	T
F	**T**	T		T	**F**	F
F	**T**	F		F	**T**	F

p ⊃ q is false only on the second row, where *p* is true and *q* is false. But for those truth values of the components, *q ⊃ p* is true. *q* is now the antecedent and *p* the consequent, and in that case the conditional is true. *q ⊃ p* is false only on the third row, where *q* is true and *p* false; and on that row *p ⊃ q* is true. This asymmetry in conditional statements makes them different from conjunctions and disjunctions, which are symmetrical: *p • q* and *q • p* always have the same truth value, as do *p ∨ q* and *q ∨ p*.

Conditional statements in English need not take the form *if p then q*. Each of the following is also a conditional:

21a. I will go camping this weekend if I finish my work.
21b. I will go camping this weekend only if I finish my work.
21c. I will go camping this weekend unless it rains.

In 21a, the "if" component is placed second in the sentence rather than first. But it is still the antecedent, and so in standard form, it is

21a. If I finish my work, then I will go camping this weekend.   F ⊃ C

Statement 21b looks similar, but the word "only" changes everything. To see the difference, suppose you have invited me to go camping this weekend. If I tell you "I'll go if I finish my work" (21a), and I do finish it, then my promise commits me to going with you; not going would mean breaking a promise; my statement to you would be proven false. But if I tell you "I'll go *only if* I finish my work" (21b), and I do finish it, does this promise commit me to going? No. Finishing is a necessary condition for going, but perhaps there are factors I didn't mention. All that I actually promised is that not finishing my work would guarantee I don't go. So if I *do* go, then I have finished my work:

STRATEGY Putting Conditional Statements into Standard Form

Conditional statements can be put into standard form according to the following rules of equivalence:

Nonstandard form	*Standard form*	
p if *q*	If *q*, then *p*	$q \supset p$
p only if *q*	If *p*, then *q*	$p \supset q$
p unless *q*	If not-*p*, then *q*	$\sim q \supset p$
	If not-*p*, then *q*	$\sim p \supset q$

21b. If I go camping this weekend, then I will have finished my work.   C ⊃ F

In 21c, finally, the component statements "I will go camping this weekend" (C) and "It is raining (this weekend)" (R) are joined by the word "unless." As a general rule, *p unless q* can be taken to mean *if not-q, then p*. Thus I am saying that I will go camping if it does not rain. I am not saying that rain will necessarily keep me from going; I'm leaving myself that option. But I *am* saying that in the absence of rain, I will definitely go; and that if I do not go, then it is raining. If it doesn't rain and I still do not go camping, then my statement was false. So we can put the statement into standard form as a conditional in either of two equivalent ways:

21c. If it does not rain this weekend, I will go camping.   ~R ⊃ C
21c'. If I do not go camping this weekend, it is raining.   ~C ⊃ R

(In the final section of this chapter, we will learn how to prove that statements of the forms $\sim q \supset p$ and $\sim p \supset q$ are indeed equivalent.)

BICONDITIONAL   The fifth and final connective, the biconditional, is illustrated by the statement that I will teach a certain class if and only if 10 or more students enroll. The symbol for *if and only if* is a "triple bar":

22. I will teach the class if and only if 10 or more students enroll.   T ≡ E

This statement can be understood as a conjunction of two conditional statements, one of them indicated by the "if," the other by the "only if":

22a. If 10 or more students enroll, then I will teach the class ("if").   E ⊃ T
22b. If I teach the class, then 10 or more students are enrolled ("only if").   T ⊃ E

We typically use the biconditional to state

- A "go/no go" criterion for an action or a decision, as in our example.
- The criteria for inclusion in a category (the platypus is a mammal if and only if it is warm blooded and produces milk for its young).

- The terms of a contract (the renter's security deposit will be returned at the end of the lease if and only if the apartment is left in good repair).
- The causal factors governing an event (a match will ignite if and only if it is struck in the presence of oxygen).

The triple bar is not the same as the equals sign, which we do not use as a connective in propositional logic, but there is a similarity. A biconditional statement is true when the two components have identical truth values; they are either both true or both false. Suppose it turns out that I teach the class but fewer than 10 students have enrolled. That would prove the statement false. And if 10 or more students do enroll but I don't teach the class, that too would prove the statement false. Thus the truth table for the biconditional is

Biconditional

p	$p \equiv q$	q
T	T	T
T	F	F
F	F	T
F	T	F

EXERCISE 9.1B

For each of the following statements, identify the component propositions and the connective. Then put the statement in symbolic form, using the letters indicated in parentheses.

⁎1. If these shoes go on sale, I'll buy two pairs. (S, B)

2. If the cat's away, the mice will play. (C, M)

3. If you put your hand in the candle flame, you will get burned. (C, B)

⁎4. I'll scratch your back if and only if you'll scratch mine. (I, Y)

5. You will succeed only if you work hard. (S, W)

6. I'll get an A for the course if I get 90% or better on the final exam. (A, F)

⁎7. I'm ready if you are. (I, Y)

8. If you're in a jam, I'm your man. (J, M)

9. The polar ice caps will start melting if average temperatures on earth rise by 5°. (P, T)

⁎10. We will launch the new Web site next month if and only if the shopping cart function passes the security test. (W, S)

11. If terrorists sabotage the Niger Delta oil pipeline, Nigerian oil shipments will be reduced by half. (T, O)

12. If you wait in line a long time, there is a good chance you are in the wrong line. (W, C)

*13. The litmus paper in the beaker will turn red if the liquid is acidic, and only if it is. (L, A)

14. You and I can be friends unless you take advantage of me. (F, A)

15. He'll go away if you ignore him. (G, I)

*16. The plant will die unless you water it. (P, W)

17. Only if oxygen is present will iron rust. (O, R)

18. Unless the Braves put their best starting pitcher in the first game of the World Series, they will lose the series. (B, L)

*19. I'll go swimming only if I can wear my water wings. (S, W)

20. I'll stand by what I said unless you prove I'm wrong. (S, P)

9.1C Truth Functions

We have defined each of the connectives in terms of a truth table. Compound statements involving these connectives are therefore *truth-functional*. That is, the truth or falsity of the compound statement is a function solely of the truth values of its components and does *not* depend on any other connection between the components. We need to appreciate the implications of this way of defining the connectives, including some of the problems it poses.

We saw that a statement of the form $p \bullet q$ is true as long as p and q are both true, even if those component statements have no other relationship. In real life, we would be puzzled if someone said something like:

23. Apples are red and the United Nations was formed in 1945.

The word "and" carries at least the suggestion that the elements it joins have some relevance to each other, however remote. But if we treat this compound statement truth-functionally, then the truth of the components is all that matters. This is not much of a problem with conjunction. The statement above is odd, but if someone pressed us, we would acknowledge that it is true. An "and" statement is nothing more than the sum of its parts, and both parts in this case are true.

A disjunctive statement in ordinary language, however, is not merely the sum of its parts, and the truth-functional interpretation is less natural here. We have already discussed the fact that the connective ∨ is inclusive rather than exclusive: The disjunction is true if p and q are both true as well as when just one of them is true. That's one point of difference from at least some uses of "or" in everyday speech. But the truth-functional definition raises additional questions. When we assert a statement of the form *p or q*, it's normally because p is related to q in some way that makes them alternatives in a given situation. We also assume that p and q are both genuine possibilities. But the truth-functional connective ∨ is not bound by these constraints. We can take any true statement and combine it with any other statement whatever to form a true disjunction. Thus

24. Napoleon was French ∨ Caffeine is addictive

is true even though the components are not related in any way that makes them alternatives to each other. And

25. Earth is spherical $\lor$ 2 + 2 = 5

is true even though the second disjunct is mathematically impossible. These statements would seem more than odd if we encountered them outside a logic text; we might well hesitate to call them true.

We would be even more hesitant about comparable examples of conditional statements. As we noted, the connective $\supset$ is a way of abstracting from the particular nature of the connection—causal, logical, means–end, etc.—between p and q. As a truth-functional connective, however, it does not require the existence of any connection between the propositions. Let's look at the truth table again:

p	$p \supset q$	q
T	**T**	T
T	**F**	F
F	**T**	T
F	**T**	F

The table shows that $p \supset q$ is true in both cases where p is false: the third and fourth rows. Thus a conditional with a false antecedent is true even if there is no connection between antecedent and consequent, as in:

26. If grass is red, then humans can breathe under water.   R $\supset$ B

The table also shows that $p \supset q$ is true in both cases where q is true. So a conditional with a true consequent is true, again regardless of any connection, as in:

27. If water runs uphill, then grass is green.   W $\supset$ G

Examples 26 and 27 are bizarre statements. They are extreme cases that illustrate the purely formal nature of the truth-functional connective. But even in cases closer to ordinary thought and speech, the same issues arise. In our initial discussion of conditionals, we considered the statement

17. If you study hard, then you will pass the exam.

S	S $\supset$ P	P
T	**T**	T
T	**F**	F
F	**T**	T
F	**T**	F

We saw that the statement is clearly false in the case where you have studied hard but do not pass (line 2 of the table). In every other case, the truth values of S and P are consistent with the truth of the conditional. Intuitively, though, the fact that they are consistent does not seem to guarantee the truth of the conditional, not in the way that the truth values on line 2 guarantee that the conditional is false. In line 1, for example, you study hard and pass the test. Does that make the conditional statement true? What if the instructor intended to give you a passing grade no matter how you did? Would the conditional statement still seem true?

In all of these examples, the hesitation to say that the statements are true arises from the sense that what makes a conditional true is some real connection between the conditions referred to by the component propositions. Since the truth-functional analysis of conditionals does not require any such connection, it seems to miss something relevant to their truth. It is only when the antecedent is true and the consequent false that the truth-functional analysis is clearly in line with our normal understanding of what makes conditional statements true or false. For on that line of the truth table, the truth values imply the absence of the connection that would make the conditional true.

The examples we have used so far have been indicative statements—the kind that purport simply to state what *is* the case. In English and other languages, however, we also make subjunctive statements about what *would be*, or *would have been*, the case. To see the difference, consider an earlier example:

26a. If grass is red, then humans can breathe under water.
26b. If grass were red, then humans could breathe under water.

Statement 26a is indicative, 26b subjunctive. The first seems odd because there's no apparent connection between the color of grass and human respiratory abilities. But statement 26a does not explicitly assert such a connection. Statement 26b does. The subjunctive form states what would be true if some fact or circumstance were different from what it is, and we can make such a statement only on the assumption that there's some real connection between antecedent and consequent. So the mere fact that the antecedent is false is not enough to make a statement like 26b true. Subjunctive statements, which are also called *contrary-to-fact* or *counterfactual* statements, are not truth-functional and can't be symbolized by ⊃.

All of these points regarding conditionals apply equally to the biconditional, which is also a truth-functional connective. The symbol ≡ stands for a relationship among truth values; it does not imply any further connection between the components. The statement

28. Squirrels eat nuts if and only if London has a subway   S ≡ L

is true because both components are true. And

29. Tom Clancy wrote *Hamlet* if and only if triangles have four sides   C ≡ T

is true because both components are false. The lack of any connection in either case is irrelevant. But a subjunctive statement like

30. I would have won the Olympic marathon if and only if I had had Wheaties every morning for breakfast

is clearly false even though both components have the same truth value (false).

So you can see there's a problem with interpreting compound statements, especially conditionals, in a truth-functional way. The problem is quite complex; it touches on a number of basic issues concerning logic and language; and there is no consensus among specialists who have explored these issues in depth. We can't go into all the issues and theories in an introductory text, but we can say this: The if–then structure in language is used to make various types of statements, all of which are truth-functional in one respect: If the antecedent is true and the consequent false, then the conditional must be false—the situation described in line 2 of the truth table. On the other lines, where the antecedent is false or consequent true—their truth values are at least consistent with the truth of the conditional. For most of the things we are concerned with in propositional logic, consistency is enough. When we study propositional inferences, for example, as we will do in the next chapter, we will be concerned with how to tell whether an inference is valid or invalid and how to derive conclusions from premises in a valid way. Validity, as we know, means that if the premises of an argument are true then the conclusion must be true as well, and the test for whether an inference is valid or invalid is whether we could consistently affirm the premises and deny the conclusion.

So even if conditional statements in ordinary language assert something more than the truth-functional analysis captures, this "something more" is not relevant for most inferences. We can regard it as a simplifying assumption that the conditional is true on lines 1, 3, and 4 of the truth table for conditionals. This assumption allows us to use truth tables as a systematic and powerful device for argument analysis. In the vast majority of cases, it is a reliable test for the validity of propositional inferences.

With these caveats about truth functions in mind, let us go on now to look at more complex statements involving the connections.

EXERCISE 9.1C

Identify the components and the connective in each of the following statements. Then put the statement into symbolic form. For this exercise, it will be up to you to pick appropriate letters to stand for the components.

✳1. Holly or Dexter will take your call.

2. Either Spitball Harry gets his act together or we're going to lose this game.

3. If Brazil was settled by aliens, water runs uphill.

✳4. Winning isn't the important thing.

5. If God is dead, everything is permitted.

6. Jackson will work on Saturday if and only if he is paid overtime.

✳7. You can't hide your lying eyes, and your smile is a thin disguise.

8. I love Karen and Karen loves Abdul.

9. If it is raining in Seattle, copper conducts electricity.

✳10. Although the beach was beautiful, the water was shark-infested.

11. Water freezes at 50°F or Canada is in North America.

12. Starting the charcoal with napalm is not a good idea.

✳13. Art is long but life is short.

14. A bank will lend you money only if you're able to repay it.

15. The French Revolution was either an act of liberation or an act of destruction.

✳16. If Morley won the lottery, he is being unusually quiet about it.

17. Swallows are nesting in the barn if and only if Congress is in session.

18. You should insert the disk if and only if you are ready to proceed.

✳19. I'll ask his advice if and only if I consider him to be a worthy sage.

20. The penny-stock market is thinly traded and will soon collapse.

21. Gainor is a brilliant scholar of ancient languages, though she is so absentminded she needs business cards to remember her own name.

✳22. The doctors X-rayed my head and did not find anything.

23. The defendant was not gone from his desk long enough to have killed the victim and returned to work.

24. If you come to a fork in the road, [you should] take it.

✳25. I will definitely come to your party, unless something better comes along.

9.2 Statement Forms

So far we have dealt chiefly with statements containing a single connective and two components (or just one in the case of negation). We can also put together much more complex statements, involving any number of connectives and components. Indeed, that is one of the chief advantages of a symbolic notation for connectives. To do so, however, we first need to talk about a distinction that has been implicit in what we have covered so far.

You may have noticed that we use capital letters as well as the lowercase letters p and q to represent statements. The capital letters are abbreviations for actual statements, so that we don't have to keep writing them out. We use lowercase letters when we want to talk about statements in general, so that we can identify the logical forms that compound statements can take. Consider the statement

1. Either the car is out of gas or the fuel line is blocked.   C ∨ F
                                                                  p ∨ q

If we represent 1 as C ∨ F, we are symbolizing this particular statement, and the letters C and F stand for its particular component statements. However, we would use $p ∨ q$ when we want to talk about this or any other disjunctive statement, with any pair of components. In logic we refer to the lowercase letters as **statement variables** and to a compound formula like $p ∨ q$ as a **statement form**. Like the variable x in a mathematical equation, which can stand for any number, the statement variables p, q, r, etc., stand for any actual or possible statement. Together with the connectives, they are used to represent the abstract logical form of compound statements. An actual statement like 1 is a particular instance or example of the abstract form. The distinction between a statement form and its instances is like the distinction between a concept and the things it stands for. The concept DOG represents any and all particular dogs, abstracting from the differences among them in order to identify what they have in common as a type of animal. In the same way, a statement form abstracts from the differences among a class of actual statements in order to identify the logical form they have in common.

When we are dealing with simple components like C and F as instances, the distinction doesn't make much difference for understanding the logical form of statements. But it is vital when we deal with statements whose components themselves are complex. Consider the two statements:

2. **Either I'll go home and watch television or I'll think about the election.**
3. **I'll go home, and I'll either watch television or think about the election.**

These statements involve the same component propositions: I'll go home; I'll watch television; I'll think about the election. We can abbreviate them with the letters H, T, and E, respectively. And both have the same connectives: one conjunction and one disjunction. But they don't say the same thing. Statement 3 implies that H is true (i.e., that I will go home), while statement 2 does not imply this.

That's a substantial difference. The reason for it becomes clear when we identify the logical form of each statement.

Statement 2			Statement 3		
H • T	∨	E	H	•	T ∨ E
p	∨	q	p	•	q

Like statement 1 earlier, 2 has the basic logical form of a disjunction; like 1, it is an instance of $p \lor q$. Unlike 1, the first disjunct in 2 is itself compound, with its own internal connective linking H and T. But disjunction is the *main* connective, and anything true of disjunction as such will be true of 2. However, as shown in the columns on the right, the main connective in 3 is conjunction. Statement 3 is an instance of $p \bullet q$, in which the q conjunct is itself compound.

So far we have identified the *core* logical form of these statements. But since the components are themselves compound and include internal connectives, we need to do more to capture the fully specific logical form. To do so, we need two rules of punctuation to avoid ambiguity. The first rule is to use parentheses so that the connectives •, ∨, ⊃, and ≡ join two and only two components, where one or both components may themselves be compound statements marked off by parentheses. The main connective stands outside all parentheses. Thus statements 2 and 3, and their fully specific logical forms, become

2. (H • T) ∨ E   3. H • (T ∨ E)
   (p • q) ∨ r   p • (q ∨ r)

In 2 and 3, the grouping makes a difference because the statements involve different connectives. If the connectives are all the same, it doesn't always matter how we group the components or which connective we treat as the main one. For example,

4. I'm going home, and I'm going to bed, and I'm going to sleep until Wednesday.

We could represent this statement either as H • (B • S) or as (H • B) • S. The statement forms

$$p • (q • r) \quad and \quad (p • q) • r$$

are equivalent. Just as you can add three numbers in any order and still get the same sum, you can group three conjuncts in any order and get equivalent statements. The same is true for disjunction: (p ∨ q) ∨ r is equivalent to p ∨ (q ∨ r). But it isn't true for conditionals. Compare the following statements:

5. If I have a million dollars, then if I am happy, I have   M ⊃ (H ⊃ C)
   nothing to complain about.

6. If it's true that if I have a million dollars, I am happy,   (M ⊃ H) ⊃ C
   then I have nothing to complain about.

These are clearly not equivalent. Even when the grouping does not make a difference, however, as with conjunction and disjunction, we must still group the components one way or the other, in accordance with the strict rule that connectives (other than negation) connect two and only two components.

The second rule of punctuation has to do with negation. A negation sign in front of a component statement is a denial of that component only, while a negation sign in front of a compound statement marked off by parentheses is a denial of the compound statement as a whole. The difference is illustrated by the following examples:

7. Either Leslie is not sad or she's a good actor.   ~S ∨ A
8. Leslie is neither sad nor a good actor.   ~(S ∨ A)

In 8, notice that negation is the main connective, applied to the component S ∨ A as a whole. So when you are translating from English into symbolic notation, you'll need to decide whether the verbal indicators of negation ("not," "isn't," "neither . . . nor," etc.) apply to individual component statements or to compound ones.

Since we are now dealing with compound statements whose components can be internally complex, we need a way of referring specifically to the simple components that we represent with letters. Traditionally they are called **atomic statements**, by analogy with the atoms that make up molecules. Atomic statements do not have any internal connectives. They are the building blocks from which we can assemble compound statements by using connectives, and then use those compound statements in turn as components to build more complex statements. Using statement 5 as an example, we can illustrate the terminology in a diagram. Each element in the symbolic formulation is labeled by the kind of element it is (top row) and by the role it plays in the statement (bottom row):

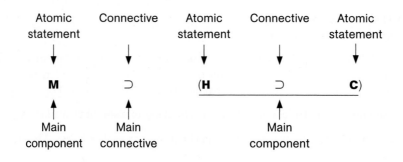

When you are given a complex statement to translate into symbolic form, you will need to rely on common sense and your knowledge of the English language. Your goal is to be able to answer three questions:

  i. What are the atomic statements, the ones that will be assigned capital letters?
 ii. What is the main connective?
iii. What are the other connectives, and how should they be grouped with the atomic statements?

Let's work through a few examples.

9. If the new videogame is a big seller, we will make a lot of money; but if not, we will still have learned something about the market, and we will be able to use many of the techniques we invented for other products.

At first glance, it may look as if the main connective is a conditional, since the statement begins with "If." When we get to the semicolon, however, we can see that there's a second conditional, and that it is joined to the first one by conjunction. As a first step toward identifying the logical form, we can recognize that 9 is saying "If X happens, then Y; but if ~X, then Z." The main connective is "but," which we know to translate as conjunction. Now let's identify and label the atomic components:

V The new videogame is a big seller.
M We will make a lot of money.
L We will learn something about the market.
I We will be able to use many of the techniques we invented for other products.

Having answered questions (i) and (ii), it's pretty clear how to put it all together:

$$(V \supset M) \bullet [\sim V \supset (L \bullet I)]$$

Notice that we use square brackets around the second conjunct because we used parentheses around one of its components. This is a convenience to help us keep our groupings clear. If we needed to group bracketed statements together, we would use braces: { }.
Let's try another:

10. If the seller delivers the goods to the purchaser's warehouse by May 1, and either the purchaser or an authorized agent of the purchaser signs an invoice for said goods, then purchaser owes seller a sum of $1,000 unless said goods are found to be defective within 30 days.

In this case, the "If" at the beginning is not misleading: The statement does have the overall form of a conditional; in essence it says that if delivery is made, then money is owed. If you can see that right away, you can follow the same top-down strategy as in the previous example. But here the antecedent has a number of components, and we don't get to the consequent for quite a while. So you might find it easier to follow a bottom-up strategy, identifying and grouping the components as they come. Initially we can isolate three components:

G The seller delivers the goods to the purchaser's warehouse by May 1.
P The purchaser signs an invoice for said goods.
A An authorized agent of the purchaser signs an invoice for said goods.

What this part of the statement says is "G and either P or A." The meaning makes it clear how this should be punctuated:

$$G \bullet (P \lor A)$$

Now we can deal with the rest of the sentence, beginning with "then." There are two more simple components:

O The purchaser owes seller a sum of $1,000.
D The goods are found to be defective within 30 days.

This part of the statement says "O unless D." As we have seen, p unless q is to be translated if not-q then p. So the consequent is a conditional and would be symbolized: $\sim D \supset O$. Finally, we put the pieces together: Having analyzed the two halves of statement 10 separately, it should be clear that the statement as a whole is a conditional, so the main connective is a horseshoe:

10. $[G \bullet (P \lor A)] \supset (\sim D \supset O)$

Now, what is the logical form of 10? One answer is

10b. $[p \bullet (q \lor r)] \supset (\sim s \supset t)$

This answer is certainly correct. Statement 10a is the fully specific logical form of 10. Each atomic statement has been replaced with a statement variable, and all of the connectives are included—the main connective as well as the connectives within the compound component statements. Any statement with the same structure would have the same logical properties, no matter what simple statements we substitute for p, q, r, s, and t. But it would also be true to say that 10 has the logical form:

10b. $p \supset q$

Statement 10b is the core logical form of 10, including only the main connective and using the variables p and q to stand for the main components. Statement 10 is an instance of 10b as well as 10a.

The formula in 10b helps us to realize that 10 has the logical properties common to all conditionals, regardless of the fact that its antecedent and consequent are themselves compound. Suppose we want to know whether the following argument is valid:

$[G \bullet (P \lor A)] \supset (\sim D \supset O)$
$\underline{G \bullet (P \lor A)}$
$\sim D \supset O$

If we start by looking for the main connective in the first premise, we can see that the premise has the form $p \supset q$. It then becomes obvious that the argument as a whole is a case of *modus ponens*,

$p \supset q$

$\underline{p}$

q

which is a valid argument form. The internal structure of the antecedent and the consequent is irrelevant to the validity of the argument.

In the next chapter, we're going to learn how to analyze arguments involving rather complex propositions. Our tools of analysis, however, will be some fairly simple rules like *modus ponens*. So it's important that you learn to spot these simple patterns even when they are embedded within a more complex structure. The way to do that is to keep in mind the difference between actual statements and statement forms.

STRATEGY Punctuation Rules

1. Use parentheses, brackets, and braces so that the connectives •, ∨, ⊃, and ≡ join two components, where one or both of the components may themselves be compound statements marked off by parentheses or brackets.

2. To negate a compound statement, enclose the compound statement within parentheses (or brackets) and place the negation sign in front of the left parenthesis (or bracket).

EXERCISE 9.2

A. Identify the main connective in each of the following statements.

✳1. (H • R) ≡ T

2. (N ∨ Q) ∨ Z

3. ~B ⊃ C

✳4. ~(B ⊃ C)

5. (J ∨ T) ∨ (K • G)

6. [(J ∨ T) ∨ K] • G

✳7. [(C • W) ⊃ I] • Q

8. L ⊃ [(U • T) ∨ (F ⊃ G)]

9. [(~J ⊃ K) ≡ (R ∨ B)] ≡ (R • K)

✳10. ~{[(J ⊃ K) ≡ (R ∨ B)] ⊃ (R • K)}

B. Put each of the following statements into symbolic notation, using appropriate letters to abbreviate atomic components.

✳1. You may have a dog only if you get straight A's this year.

2. Publicity stunts are effective only if they are comprehensible.

3. If you have to ask, then you'll never know.

✳4. If the model is ready and the cameras are working, we should start shooting the photo.

5. You'll have fun if you just relax.

6. If you work hard and long, you'll find success in the end.

✳7. If Brooklyn is in California, then either California has become larger or Brooklyn has moved.

8. The woods are lovely, dark and deep. But I have promises to keep.

9. We may lose or we may win, but we will never be here again.

✳10. Government is not the solution; it's the problem.

11. The wedding will be perfect unless it rains or the groom doesn't show.

12. Your package will be there on Wednesday morning or my company isn't the best mailing service on the West Coast.

✳13. Either you'll come to the barbecue and enjoy yourself or you'll stay at home and be depressed all day.

14. If nominated I will not run, and if elected I will not serve.

15. It's not the case that if men were angels, government would not be necessary.

✳16. I'll tell it to a priest or I'll tell it to a bottle, but I won't go to see a shrink.

17. It isn't true that he quit his job, but if he did I'd be the first to know.

18. It's my party and I'll cry if I want to.

✳19. If you don't feel guilty about lying, then either you have a good reason for lying or you don't have a conscience.

20. The stock market will go up or it will go down, but if we can't know in advance which way it will move, it is better to stay invested.

21. If a subatomic particle has a charge, the charge is either positive or negative.

✳22. If you stand I will stand with you, and if you fall I will trip over you.

23. If deuterium did change to helium, then fusion did take place, and we have discovered a new source of energy.

24. If you convinced me and I convinced you, then there would still be two points of view.

✳25. If the weather is good and we leave early, then if we don't hit any bad traffic, we will arrive on time.

26. We can visit your family on Christmas or we can visit my family in summer, but I won't go to Iowa in the winter or Arizona in the summer.

27. You should fill out either the singles' form or the married form, but not both.

✳28. The fire will be put out only if a fresh water supply is found, but it won't be found if we don't have more men searching.

29. If an object is dropped, it will fall unless some other force counteracts gravity.

30. He's either a knave or a fool, but he isn't both a knave and a fool.

✳31. If you violate the law, you will go to jail, unless you are very rich or a politician.

32. A labor is not worth doing unless it is worth doing passionately.

33. If ticket offices are open or ticket vending machines are available, and you buy your ticket on the train, you will be charged an additional $1.00, but you will not be charged the additional dollar if the station is not open.

✳34. This liquid is water if and only if it will freeze if we chill it to 32°F and will boil if we heat it to 212°F.

35. This visit is covered by your insurance if the doctor is in the network and you have paid your deductible, unless you've exceeded 40 visits or it's a new year.

36. If the apartment allows pets and has a fitness room, we will take it today, unless it doesn't have on-site parking, in which case we'll have to wait until next month.

9.3 Computing Truth Values

We have learned that a compound statement is truth-functional: Its truth or falsity is a function of the truth or falsity of its component statements. Now we will learn how to compute the truth value of a statement from information about the truth values of its components. For a statement with just one connective, the truth table column for that connective tells us how to make the computation. But we can also construct truth tables for more complex statements, with more than one connective, like the ones we discussed in the previous section. Knowing how to do this will enhance your understanding of complex statements and lay the ground for the next chapter, where we will learn how to construct and evaluate arguments involving such statements.

Let's begin by revisiting a previous example:

9. If the new videogame is a big seller, we will make a lot of money; but if not, we will still have learned something about the market, and we will be able to use many of the techniques we invented for other products. $(V \supset M) \bullet [{\sim}V \supset (L \bullet I)]$

Suppose it turns out that the game was not a big seller, but that it still made a lot of money; and that, while the company did not learn anything about the market, it did use the invented techniques for other products. In other words, M and I are true, V and L are false. What do these facts tell us about the truth or falsity of 9?

To answer that question, let's create an abbreviated truth table and put in the truth values for the atomic statements. Notice that V occurs twice, so it has to have the same truth value in both places.

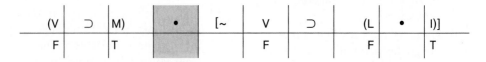

(V	⊃	M)	•	[~	V	⊃	(L	•	I)]
F		T			F		F		T

This truth table has a different format from the ones we have used previously. For simple compound statements with only one connective, we used columns for the atomic statements and put the compound statement at the head of its own column. For example,

p	p • q	q
T		T
T		F
F		T
F		F

With longer compound statements, it is easier to put just the relevant connective at the head of the column rather than repeating the whole statement. Thus in the abbreviated table above, the highlighted column with the main connective represents the truth value of the whole statement.

To compute the truth value of the whole statement, we must first compute the truth values of the components, starting with the connectives that apply directly to the atomic statements, putting T or F under those connectives. The first component, V ⊃ M, is true because V is false and M is true. Thus we put T under the horseshoe for that component. The second main component is internally complex, so the procedure is to work from the inside out, establishing truth values at each level of grouping before going on to higher levels. The conjunctive component L • I is false, since L is false. That conjunction is the consequent of a conditional statement whose antecedent, ~V, is true; so the conditional statement is false.

(V	⊃	M)	•	[~	V	⊃	(L	•	I)]
F	**T**	T		T	F	**F**	F	**F**	T

We have now computed the truth values of the two main components of the statement, so we can take the final step of determining the truth value of the statement as a whole. The statement has the core logical form of a conjunction, p • q; since q is false, the conjunction is false.

(V	⊃	M)	•	[~	V	⊃	(L	•	I)
F	**T**	T	**F**	T	F	**F**	F	**F**	T

In this case, we knew whether each of the components is true or false. But what if we don't know? Then we need to expand the truth table to include all the possible combinations of truth values for the atomic statements. Consider the conditional statement A ⊃ (A • B). Since the statement includes two atomic statements, we need four lines:

A	⊃	(A	•	B)
T		T		T
T		T		F
F		F		T
F		F		F

As in the previous example, the next step is to compute the truth value of the compound component (A • B in this case), but to do it for each line of the table, as indicated in bold below. We can then compute the truth value of the statement as a whole, as indicated under the main connective, ⊃.

A	⊃	(A	•	B)
T	**T**	T	**T**	T
T	**F**	T	**F**	F
F	**T**	F	**F**	T
F	**T**	F	**F**	F

Because this example involved just two atomic components, A and B, we could work with the familiar four-line truth table. But now we need to understand how to construct truth tables for statements with more atomic components. Remember that a truth table must represent every possible combination of truth values. Since each atomic statement can be either true or false, every additional atomic component requires that we double the number of lines in the table:

Atomic Statements	Rows in Truth Table
1	2
2	4
3	8
4	16
. . .	. . .
n	2^n

To ensure that we represent every possible combination of truth values, without repeating any combination or leaving any out, we fill in the truth values systematically. To illustrate the procedure, let's take a statement with three atomic components: ~A ⊃ (B ∨ C). The truth table will have eight rows.

~	A	⊃	(B	∨	C)
	T		T		T
	T		T		F
	T		F		T
	T		F		F
	F		T		T
	F		T		F
	F		F		T
	F		F		F

In each column for an atomic statement, the cells where we put T are highlighted. We start on the right, with the last statement, C, and alternate T and F in its column. Then we move left to the previous statement, B, and alternate two rows of T and two rows of F. Finally, in the column for A, we put T in the first four rows, F in the last four. If we had a compound statement with four atomic components, we would follow the same procedure, starting on the right with alternating rows of T and F, and moving left until we reached the first atomic statement. With four atomic components, the table will have 16 rows, so the column under the first component will have eight rows of T followed by 8 rows of F.

Now let's use the truth table to determine whether ~A ⊃ (B ∨ C) is true or false for each combination of atomic truth values.

~	A	⊃	(B	∨	C)
F	T	**T**	T	**T**	T
F	T	**T**	T	**T**	F
F	T	**T**	F	**T**	T
F	T	**T**	F	**F**	F
T	F	**T**	T	**T**	T
T	F	**T**	T	**T**	F
T	F	**T**	F	**T**	T
T	F	**F**	F	**F**	F

The main connective is a conditional, and both antecedent and consequent are compound, so we start by computing their truth values. The column under ~A is determined by the column under A together with the rule for negation. The column under (B ∨ C) is determined by the columns under B and under C together with the rule for disjunction. And the column under the horseshoe, representing the truth value of the statement as a whole, is determined by the columns under ~A and under (B ∨ C), together with the rule for conditionals, as shown in the shaded column.

Now let's look at the other punctuation rule from the preceding section, the one concerning negation. When the negation sign is attached to an atomic statement, it negates that statement only, but when it is outside the parentheses indicating a compound statement, the truth value under the negation sign in the table will be the opposite of the truth value under the connective in the compound component. To see the difference this makes, consider the statements ~(A • B) and ~A • B:

~	(A	•	B)
F	T	T	T
T	T	F	F
T	F	F	T
T	F	F	F

~	A	•	B
F	T	**F**	T
F	T	**F**	F
T	F	**T**	T
T	F	**F**	F

You can see from the columns under the main connectives that the placement of the negation sign results in different truth values for the two statements in the second and fourth rows.

STRATEGY Constructing Truth Tables

To construct the truth table for a statement with more than one connective:

1. Write the statement at the top of a table.
   a. Make enough rows to include every possible combination of truth values for the atomic component statements: for 1 atomic statement, 2 rows; for 2 statements, 4 rows; for 3 statements, 8 rows; etc.
   b. Make a column under each atomic statement and each connective, including negation signs.
2. In the column under the atomic statement farthest to the right, fill in alternating T and F from the first to the last row. In the column under the next atomic statement to the left, put T in the first two rows, F in the next two, and so on to the last row. Under the next atomic statement to the left, put T in the first four rows, F in the next four,

and so on to the last row. Continue in this fashion until you have put truth values in the columns under each atomic statement.

3. On each row, identify the connectives that apply directly to the atomic statements. Determine the truth value of the compound components involving just that connective, and put T or F in the column under that connective.

4. Identify the connectives that apply to the compound components identified in step 3. Determine the truth value of the higher-level compound components involving just *that* connective, and put T or F in the column under that connective. Repeat this step with each level of compound components until you reach the main connective (the one outside all parentheses). The truth values in its column are the truth values of the statement as a whole.

EXERCISE 9.3

For each statement below, classify the statement by identifying the main connective and construct a truth table.

＊1. A ∨ (B ∨ A)
 2. ~C ≡ D
 3. ~(E ∨ F)
＊4. G • ~G
 5. H ⊃ (I ⊃ H)
 6. J ⊃ (K • L)
＊7. (M ∨ N) ≡ O
 8. (P ⊃ Q) ≡ (~Q ⊃ ~P)

 9. (R ⊃ ~S) ∨ (T • R)
＊10. [(U ⊃ V) • (~V ∨ W)] ≡ (U ⊃ W)
 11. (A • B) ⊃ (C ∨ D)
 12. ~(F • G) ⊃ (H ∨ I)
＊13. ~[K ∨ (L ⊃ ~M)]
 14. ~[(~N ∨ ~O) ∨ (N ∨ O)]
 15. (P • Q) ⊃ ~(R • S)

9.4 Formal Properties and Relationships

So far in this chapter we have learned about the connectives that bind atomic statements into compound statements. We have learned how to use these connectives to translate English sentences into symbolic form. We have seen that the connectives are truth-functional: The truth or falsity of a compound statement is determined solely by the truth values of its atomic components; for each combination of those truth values, the connectives specify whether the compound statement is true or false. The connectives determine the logical form of a statement, and we have seen how statements with the same logical form have certain features in common. In this final section of the chapter, we are going to learn about some additional features that truth-functional statements have in virtue of their logical form.

9.4A Tautologies, Self-Contradictions, and Contingencies

In a truth table for a compound statement, each row represents a specific combination of truth values for the atomic statements, and the rows taken together represent every possible combination of atomic truth values. In the examples we have considered so far, the compound statement is true on some rows, false on others. But now we need to identify two special cases.

Consider the statements below:

A	≡	A
T	**T**	T
F	**T**	F

A	•	~	A
T	**F**	F	T
F	**F**	T	F

Both statements have a single atomic statement, A, so there are just two rows in the truth tables. The statement on the left, A ≡ A, has to be true by the very nature of the bi-conditional connective, regardless of what statement A says, and regardless of whether A is true or false. In other words, A ≡ A is true in virtue of its logical form, independently of the truth or falsity of its component. For example, you may not know how many floors there are in the Empire State Building, but you do know that the statement

1. The Empire State Building has 97 floors if and only if the Empire State Building has 97 floors.

is true. A statement that has this property is called a **tautology**. A tautology is a compound statement that is true for every combination of truth values of its atomic components. In the truth table for a tautology, therefore, the column under the main connective will have only T's, no F's.

The statement on the right has the opposite property. It is false on each row of the table. By the very nature of negation, A and ~A cannot both be true, so the statement contradicts itself. Statement A may be true or it may be false, but A • ~A *has* to be false. For example, you may not know whether vinegar is an acid, but you do know that the statement

2. Vinegar is an acid and vinegar is not an acid

is false. Statements that have this property are called **self-contradictions**. As with tautologies, a statement is self-contradictory in virtue of its logical form, regardless of the truth values of its components. In the truth table for a self-contradiction, the column under the main connective will have only F's, no T's.

Tautologies and self-contradictions are not always so easy to identify. Let's consider a few more examples. (Since we are dealing with issues of logical form, our examples will be statement forms, using statement variables p, q, r, etc.).

3.	p	⊃	$(q$	∨	$p)$
	T	**T**	T	**T**	T
	T	**T**	F	**T**	T
	F	**T**	T	**T**	F
	F	**T**	F	**F**	F

If you think about the truth-functional character of the connectives, you can see why a statement of this form will always be true. Since the statement is a conditional, it could be false only if the antecedent p is true and the consequent $q \lor p$ is false. But in every row where p is true in the antecedent, it is true in the consequent as well, which guarantees that $q \lor p$ is true. So there's no way the statement as a whole could be false. Statement 3 is a tautology.

Now, consider this statement:

4.	(p	⊃	q)	•	(p	•	~	q)
	T	**T**	T	**F**	T	**F**	F	T
	T	**F**	F	**F**	T	**T**	T	F
	F	**T**	T	**F**	F	**F**	F	T
	F	**T**	F	**F**	F	**F**	T	F

As you can see from the column under the main connective, a statement of this form is a self-contradiction. The main connective in 4 is conjunction, so both conjuncts would have to be true for the statement as a whole to be true. But there is no row in which that is the case, and once again you can see why. The first conjunct states that if p is true, then q is true as well. In other words, it denies that p • ~q is true. But that is exactly what the other conjunct affirms, making 4 a self-contradiction.

Compound statements that are neither tautologies nor self-contradictions are called **contingent statements** (or contingencies). Contingent statements are true for some combinations of atomic truth values, false for others. Their truth value, in other words, is contingent on the truth or falsity of their atomic components as well as their logical form, so they are true on some rows of their truth table but false on others.

EXERCISE 9.4A

Identify whether each of the statements below is a tautology, a self-contradiction, or contingency by creating a truth table for the statement.

✳1. (A • B) ∨ A
2. (A ∨ B) ∨ ~A
3. (A ∨ B) ∨ A
✳4. ~A ⊃ (B ⊃ ~A)
5. (D • ~E) ⊃ E
6. (A ⊃ B) ∨ ~B
✳7. (A ⊃ B) • (A • ~B)
8. (A ⊃ B) • ~ (~A ∨ B)

9. ~(A ⊃ B) • B
✳10. (~A ∨ B) ∨ (~B • A)
11. (A ≡ B) ⊃ (A ∨ ~B)
12. [(A ⊃ B) • (A ⊃ ~B)] ≡ (A • B)
✳13. [(A ⊃ B) • (B ⊃ C)] ≡ (A ⊃ C)
14. ~(A ∨ C) ≡ [(A ∨ B) • (B ⊃ C)]
15. [(A ≡ B) • (C ⊃ A)] • (C ⊃ ~B)

9.4B Equivalence, Contradiction, and Consistency

In addition to revealing certain properties of individual statements, truth tables can reveal certain formal *relationships* between compound statements. The first of these relationships is **equivalence**, and we will see in the next chapter that it is extremely important for analyzing arguments. Two statements are equivalent when they have exactly the same truth values on each row of their respective truth tables (i.e., the same truth values in the column under their main connectives). For example, we have observed time and again that conditional statements are true whenever the antecedent is false or the consequent is true. We can now express that observation in terms of equivalence: $p \supset q$ is equivalent to $\sim p \vee q$.

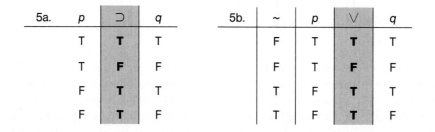

5a.	p	⊃	q
	T	**T**	T
	T	**F**	F
	F	**T**	T
	F	**T**	F

5b.	~	p	∨	q
	F	T	**T**	T
	F	T	**F**	F
	T	F	**T**	T
	T	F	**T**	F

Any statement with the disjunctive form of 5b is false in the second row, where both disjuncts, $\sim p$ and q, are false—and that is the one row on which the conditional statement 5a is false. The two statements are true on all other rows. Because the main connectives of these two statements have the same set of truth values, the statements are equivalent.

In Chapter 8, we discussed another case of equivalence: *not both p and q* is equivalent to *not-p or not-q*. We can now put these statement forms into symbolic notation and show their equivalence in a truth table:

6a.	~	(p	•	q)
	F	T	T	T
	T	T	F	F
	T	F	F	T
	T	F	F	F

6b.	~	p	∨	~	q
	F	T	**F**	F	T
	F	T	**T**	T	F
	T	F	**T**	F	T
	T	F	**T**	T	F

The opposite relationship to equivalence is **contradiction**. Two statements are contradictory when they have *opposite* values on every row of their respective truth tables (i.e., opposite truth values on each row under their main connectives). Here's a simple example:

7a.	~	p	∨	q
	F	T	**T**	T
	F	T	**F**	F
	T	F	**T**	T
	T	F	**T**	F

7b.	p	•	~	q
	T	**F**	F	T
	T	**T**	T	F
	F	**F**	F	T
	F	**F**	T	F

The truth table shows that 7a and 7b have opposite values on all rows. If $\sim p \lor q$ is true, then $p \bullet \sim q$ has to be false. Once again, this is true in virtue of the logical form of the statements. Any pair of statements with the same logical forms as 7a and 7b will be contradictory.

Let's try one more example, this one with three atomic components:

8a. $(p \bullet q) \supset r$
8b. $\sim r \supset (\sim q \lor \sim p)$

To determine whether these statement forms are equivalent, contradictory, or neither, we will need a truth table with eight rows:

8a.	(p	•	q)	⊃	r		8b.	~	r	⊃	(~	q	∨	~	p)
	T	T	T	**T**	T			F	T	**T**	F	T	**F**	F	T
	T	T	T	**F**	F			T	F	**F**	F	T	**F**	F	T
	T	F	F	**T**	T			F	T	**T**	T	F	**T**	F	T
	T	F	F	**T**	F			T	F	**T**	T	F	**T**	F	T
	F	F	T	**T**	T			F	T	**T**	F	T	**T**	T	F
	F	F	T	**T**	F			T	F	**T**	F	T	**T**	T	F
	F	F	F	**T**	T			F	T	**T**	T	F	**T**	T	F
	F	F	F	**T**	F			T	F	**T**	T	F	**T**	T	F

Both statement forms are conditionals. In 8a, the antecedent is a conjunctive statement that is true only in the first two rows. On the first row, where r is true, the conditional statement as a whole is true; on the second row, where r is false, the conditional is false. On all the remaining rows, the conditional is true simply because the antecedent is false. In 8b, each of the atomic statement variables is negated, so the first step is to fill in the columns under the negation signs. In the four rows where the antecedent $\sim r$ is false, the conditional statement is true. In the other four rows, where $\sim r$ is true, the conditional is true in all the rows where the consequent, $\sim q \lor \sim p$, is true. And that is the case in all the rows except the second. So 8b is false only in that row, as is 8a. The columns under the main connective of each statement are identical; the statements are equivalent.

To understand equivalence and contradiction, it is useful to consider how they relate to tautology and self-contradiction. Tautology and self-contradiction are features of individual statements, whereas equivalence and contradiction are relationships between two statements. Nevertheless, there's an important connection between equivalence and tautology and a similar connection between contradiction and self-contradiction.

If two statements are equivalent, we can connect them in a single biconditional statement that will be a tautology. A biconditional statement is true on a given row of its truth table when its components have the same truth value. If its components have the same truth values on *every* row of the truth table, then it is a tautology—and that will be the case whenever those components are equivalent. Thus, to take our examples 5a and 5b, the following statement is a tautology:

5c.	p	⊃	q	≡	~	p	∨	q
	T	**T**	T	**T**	F	T	**T**	T
	T	**F**	F	**T**	F	T	**F**	F
	F	**T**	T	**T**	T	F	**T**	T
	F	**T**	F	**T**	T	F	**T**	F

In the same way, connecting two contradictory statements into a single biconditional statement results in a self-contradiction. A biconditional statement is false on any row of its truth table where its components have different truth values. If the components are contradictory statements, they have opposite truth values on every row of their truth tables. So the biconditional must be false on each row, and that makes it a self-contradiction, as we can see by combining previous examples 7a and 7b into a single biconditional:

7c.	~	p	∨	q	≡	p	•	~	q
	F	T	**T**	T	**F**	T	**F**	F	T
	F	T	**F**	F	**F**	T	**T**	T	F
	T	F	**T**	T	**F**	F	**F**	F	T
	T	F	**T**	F	**F**	F	**F**	T	F

There are two other relationships among statements that we need to understand: consistency and inconsistency. Like equivalence and contradiction, these are relationships that hold in virtue of the logical forms of the statements involved. Two statement forms are **consistent** if it is possible for instances of those forms to both be true. When statements are consistent, they do not contradict each other—the truth of one statement does not rule out the possibility that the other is true as well. As with the other relationships, we test for that possibility by means of truth tables. Each row of a truth table represents a possible combination of atomic truth values. For statements to be consistent, there must be at least one row on which both statements are true. Here's an example:

9a.	q	∨	(p	•	~	q)
	T	**T**	T	F	F	T
	T	**T**	F	F	F	T
	F	**T**	T	T	T	F
	F	**F**	F	F	T	F

9b.	p	•	q
	T	**T**	T
	T	**F**	F
	F	**F**	T
	F	**F**	F

Statement 9a and 9b are both true in the first row, where their atomic components p and q are both true, so these statement forms are consistent. By contrast, the following statements are inconsistent:

10a.

p	≡	q
T	**T**	T
T	**F**	F
F	**F**	T
F	**T**	F

10b.

p	•	~	q
T	**F**	F	T
T	**T**	T	F
F	**F**	F	T
F	**F**	T	F

For 10a to be true, p and q must both be true or both be false—the possibilities represented on the first and last rows of the table. For 10b to be true, p must be true and q false, as represented on the second row. Whatever actual statements we substitute for p and q, the logical forms of the compound statements make it impossible for them both to be true. Note that 10a and 10b are not contradictory: They could both be false, as on the third row, but they cannot both be true. However, two contradictory statements will necessarily be inconsistent. Because contradictory statements have opposite truth values on each row of their truth tables, there cannot be any row on which both statements are true.

As formal relationships among statements, consistency and inconsistency differ from equivalence and contradiction in several ways:

1. The criteria for equivalence and contradiction involve every row of the truth tables for the statements: The statements must have the same truth value (for equivalence) or opposite truth values (for contradiction) on *all* rows of the tables. By contrast, the criterion for consistency can be met if the statements are both true on *some* rows (i.e., at least one).

2. For equivalence and contradiction, it does not matter whether the statements are true or false on any row of their truth tables; what matters is whether they have the same truth value (for equivalence) or opposite truth values (for contradiction) on every row. For consistency and inconsistency, by contrast, truth is precisely what matters. The criterion for consistency is not merely that the statements have the same truth value on at least one row, but that that value be T.

3. Unlike equivalence and contradiction, consistency and inconsistency are relationships that apply not only to pairs of statement forms but to sets of three or more. For any set of statements, it is possible to construct truth tables like the ones we have used so far, and then determine whether there is any row where all the statements are true. As an example, let's take the statements 9a and 9b, which we saw were consistent. Notice what happens when we add a third statement:

9a.

q	∨	(p	•	~	q)
T	**T**	T	F	F	T
T	**T**	F	F	F	T
F	**T**	T	T	T	F
F	**F**	F	F	T	F

9b.

p	•	q
T	**T**	T
T	**F**	F
F	**F**	T
F	**F**	F

9c.

p	⊃	~	q
T	**F**	F	T
T	**T**	T	F
F	**T**	F	T
F	**T**	T	F

These three statements are inconsistent, since there is no combination of truth values for which they are all true. Though 9c is consistent with 9a, it is not consistent with 9b, so the set of statements is inconsistent.

When you are given a pair of statements and want to know which of these relationships applies, the first step is to create the truth tables for the statements. Looking at the columns under the main connectives in each statement, you can then use the three points in the numbered paragraphs above, as well as the definitions of the relationships

STRATEGY Identifying Formal Relationships

To identify the relationships among pairs of statements:

1. Create truth tables for the statements and examine the truth values under their main connectives.
2. Check for the formal relationships in the following order:

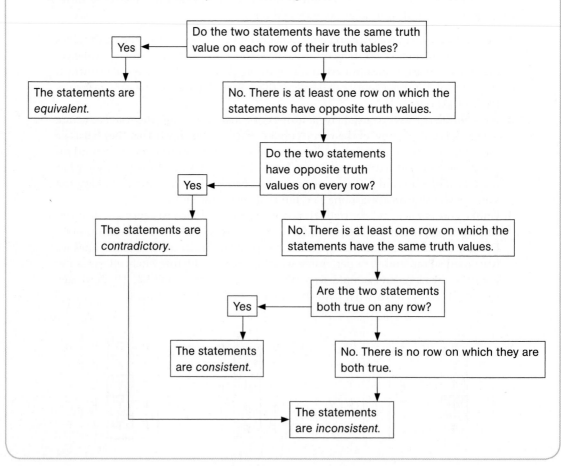

in the Summary box. A good strategy to follow is first to check for equivalence and contradiction; if the statements have neither of those relationships, you can then check for consistency and inconsistency. The Strategy box spells out the procedure as a kind of flowchart.

SUMMARY **Formal Relationships Among Statements**

Two statements are

- equivalent if and only if they have the *same* truth values for *all* combinations of their atomic truth values;
- contradictory if and only if they have *opposite* truth values for *all* combinations of their atomic truth values.

Two or more statements are

- consistent if and only if there is *some* combination of their atomic truth values that makes all of them true;
- inconsistent if and only if there is *no* combination of truth values for their atomic component statements that makes all of them true.

EXERCISE 9.4B

Determine whether the statements in each of the following sets are equivalent, contradictory, consistent, or inconsistent by creating truth tables for the statements.

　✳1. ~(A • B)　　　　　　(~A ∨ ~B)
　　2. ~(A • B)　　　　　　~ (~A ∨ ~B)
　　3. ~(A • B)　　　　　　A ∨ B
　✳4. ~(A ∨ B)　　　　　　~(~A • ~B)
　　5. C ⊃ D　　　　　　　~(C • ~D)
　　6. C ⊃ D　　　　　　　C • ~D
　✳7. C ⊃ D　　　　　　　C ∨ ~D
　　8. Y ⊃ Z　　　　　　　~Z ⊃ ~Y
　　9. ~ (Y ⊃ Z)　　　　　~(Z ∨ Y)
　✳10. Y ⊃ (Z • W)　　　　~(Z • W) ⊃ ~Y
　　11. (Y ∨ W) ⊃ (Z • W)　~(Z ~ W) ⊃ ~(Y ∨ W)
　　12. ~(A ⊃ C)　　　　　　A ⊃ (C • B)
　✳13. E • (F ∨ G)　　　　(E • F) ∨ (E • G)
　　14. E ∨ (F • G)　　　　(E ∨ F) • G
　　15. J ≡ K　　　　　　　~ [(J ⊃ K) • (K ⊃ J)]
　✳16. (J ⊃ K) • (K ⊃ J)　(J • K) ∨ (~J • ~K)

17. $(L \bullet M) \supset N$ .... $L \supset (M \supset N)$

18. $(L \lor M) \supset N$ .... $L \lor (M \supset N)$

✱19. $(A \supset B) \lor (C \bullet A)$ .... $\sim(A \supset B) \bullet \sim(C \bullet A)$

20. $\sim[(Z \lor Y) \supset W]$ .... $\sim W \supset \sim(Z \lor Y)$

21. $\sim[(C \supset E) \lor (D \bullet E)]$ .... $\sim[(C \supset E) \bullet \sim (D \bullet \sim E)]$

✱22. $(A \bullet B) \supset C$ .... $B \bullet \sim C$ .... $A \equiv C$

23. $E \bullet [F \lor (G \bullet H)]$ .... $(E \bullet F) \lor [E \bullet (G \bullet H)]$

Summary

Propositional logic is the logic of compound statements. Compound statements are made up of atomic statements linked together by connectives. We defined five basic forms of compound statement, involving five different connectives: $p \bullet q$ (conjunction), $\sim p$ (negation), $p \vee q$ (disjunction), $p \supset q$ (conditional), and $p \equiv q$ (biconditional). From these basic forms, together with rules of punctuation, we can construct more-complex compound statements. The truth value of a compound statement, whether it is a basic form or a more-complex one, is a function of the truth values of its components, in accordance with the truth table for the connectives involved.

We can construct more-complex truth tables for compound statements involving more than one connective. These truth tables show whether the statement is true or false for each combination of truth values of its atomic components.

Two special types of compound statement have truth values determined by their logical form, regardless of the truth values of their atomic components. Tautologies are true for every combination of atomic truth values; self-contradictions are false for every combination. There are also relations that hold among statements in virtue of their respective logical forms: equivalence, contradiction, consistency, and inconsistency.

Key Terms

connective—a word or symbol that creates a compound proposition from component propositions.

conjunction—a compound proposition asserting that two or more component propositions (the conjuncts) are all true.

negation—a compound statement whose truth value is the opposite truth of its component statement.

disjunction—a compound proposition containing two or more component propositions (the disjuncts) and asserting that at least one of them is true.

conditional—a compound proposition containing two component propositions (the antecedent and the consequent) and asserting that the truth of one component would be sufficient for the truth of the other.

biconditional—a compound proposition asserting that one component proposition is true if and only if the other component is true.

truth value—the truth or falsity of a proposition.

truth table—a diagram displaying the truth or falsity of a compound proposition as a function of the truth or falsity of its atomic statements and connectives.

statement variables—symbols (p, q, r, etc.) used to represent any actual or possible statement.

statement form—an expression using statement variables and connectives to state the logical form of an actual or possible statement.

atomic statement—a statement with no internal connectives.

tautology—a compound statement that is true for every assignment of truth values to its atomic components.

self-contradiction—a compound statement that is false for every assignment of truth values to its atomic components.

contingent statement—a compound statement that is true for some assignments of truth values to its atomic components and false for other assignments.

equivalence—a relation between two or more statements that have the same truth value for every assignment of truth values to their atomic components.

contradiction—a relation between two or more statements that have opposite truth values for every assignment of truth values to their atomic components.

consistent—a relation between two or more statements that are both true on at least one assignment of truth values to their atomic components.

Additional Exercises

A. Put each of the following statements into symbolic form, replacing English words and punctuation with connectives and parentheses.

⁕1. *p* if *q*

 2. Either *p* or *q*

 3. It's not the case that *p*

⁕4. *p* and either *q* or *r*

 5. Not both *p* and *q*

 6. *p* unless *q*

⁕7. Neither *p* nor *q*

 8. If *p* and *q*, then not *r*

 9. Either *p* or *q*, although if *p* then not *r*

⁕10. *p* or *q* if and only if *r*

 11. If *p* and either *q* or *r*, then *s*

 12. If neither *p* nor *q*, then if *r* or *s*, *t*

⁕13. It's true that if *p*, then *q*, if and only if it's also true that if *r*, then *s*

 14. If not *p* and not *q*, then *r*, *s*, and *t*

 15. If not both *p* and *q*, then *r*, and if *p* or *q*, then *s*

B. Find statements in English that have the following logical forms.

⁕1. ~*p* ∨ *q*

 2. *p* • *q*

 3. *p* ⊃ *q*

⁕4. *p* • (*q* ∨ *r*)

 5. ~(*p* ∨ *q*)

 6. (*p* ∨ *q*) • *r*

⁕7. *p* ⊃ (*q* ∨ ~*r*)

 8. (*p* •*q*) ∨ (*r* •*s*)

 9. (*p* • ~*q*) ⊃ *r*

⁕10. (*p* ∨ *q*) • (*r* ∨ *s*)

 11. *p* ⊃ (*q* ⊃ *r*)

 12. ~*p* ⊃ (*q* ∨ *r*)

⁕13. *p* ⊃ ~(*q* • *r*)

 14. ~(*p* • *q*) ⊃ (*r* ⊃ *s*)

 15. [*p* ⊃ ~(*q* ∨ *r*)] • *s*

C. Each of the following statements is taken from a legal document. Translate the statement into symbolic notation.

⁕1. *Employee handbook*: Employees must work their scheduled work day before and after the holiday if he or she is to be paid for the holiday, unless he or she is absent with prior permission from a supervisor.

 2. *Publishing contract*: If the Author shall not have delivered the final manuscript by the date stipulated, and if within six months of written notice from the Publisher to the Author said delivery shall not have been made or a new delivery date mutually agreed to, the Publisher may terminate this agreement and recover any advances made to the Author hereunder.

 3. *U.S. Constitution (I, 7)*: If any Bill shall not be returned by the President within ten

Days . . . , the Same shall be a Law . . . unless the Congress [has adjourned], in which Case it shall not be a Law.

⁕4. *Credit card agreement*: If we find that we made a mistake on your bill, you will not have to pay any finance charges related to any questioned amount. If we didn't make a mistake, you may have to pay finance charges, and you will have to make up any missed payments on the questioned amount. In either case, we will send you a statement of the amount you owe and the date that it is due. (Treat this as a single conjunctive statement.)

 5. *State penal code*: A person is guilty of murder in the first degree when [i.e., if and only if]:

a. With intent to cause the death of another person, he causes the death of such person; and

   i. The defendant was more than eighteen years old at the time of the commission of the crime; and . . .

   ii. Either:

      1. the victim was a police officer . . . who was killed in the course of performing his official duties, and the defendant knew . . . that the victim was a police officer; or

2. the victim was an employee of a correctional institution . . . who was killed in the course of performing his official duties, and the defendant knew . . . that the victim was an employee of a correctional institution; or

3. at the time of the commission of the crime, the defendant was confined in a state correctional institution . . . upon a sentence for the term of his natural life . . . , or at the time of the commission of the crime, the defendant had escaped from such confinement.

D. For each of the following, classify the statement by identifying the main connective and construct a truth table.

*1. ~A • B

  2. ~(A ≡ B)

  3. ~(A ⊃ ~B)

*4. (C ∨ D) • ~E

  5. (F • G) ⊃ ~H

  6. J • (K ⊃ L)

*7. (M • N) ⊃ O

  8. P ≡ ~(Q ∨ R)

  9. S ⊃ (T ∨ ~U)

*10. (V ∨ W) • ~(V • W)

Propositional Logic—Arguments

In the past chapter, we learned how to put compound statements in symbolic form, using letters to represent the atomic component statements and connectives to represent the relationships among them. In this chapter, we will learn how to analyze and evaluate *arguments* involving compound statements. Here's an example of such an argument:

If Shakespeare did not write the plays attributed to him, scholars would have discovered the real author by now. But they haven't done so. Therefore, Shakespeare did write those plays.	~W ⊃ D ~D W

The first sentence is a conditional statement involving the atomic statements W (Shakespeare wrote the plays attributed to him) and D (scholars have discovered the real author of those plays). The second sentence denies the consequent of the conditional. Those two statements function as premises in support of the conclusion, W.

As in traditional deductive logic, we evaluate arguments by the standard of validity. An argument is valid when the conclusion follows necessarily from the premises; that is, you cannot accept the premises as true but deny the truth of the conclusion without contradicting yourself. Conversely, an argument is invalid when the premises could be true while the conclusion is false. In deductive logic, whether traditional or modern, arguments are either valid or invalid: There is no middle ground; validity doesn't come in degrees.

In modern deductive logic, however, we can establish an argument's validity by methods that apply to more complex arguments than traditional logic was capable of handling. We're going to learn two of these methods. The first uses truth tables to find out whether the premises of an argument could all be true while the conclusion is false.

The second uses rules of inference to prove, step by step, that the conclusion follows from the premises.

10.1 Truth Table Test of Validity

In Chapter 9, we learned how to construct a truth table to compute the truth or falsity of a compound statement for all possible combinations of truth values of its atomic component statements:

- Create a column under each atomic statement and each connective.
- Create just enough rows to include every possible combination of truth values for the atomic statements: for 1 atomic statement, 2 rows; for 2 atomic statements, 4 rows; for 3 atomic statements, 8 rows; etc.
- Insert truth values for the atomic statements systematically, with alternating T and F in the column under the right-most atomic statement, alternating TT and FF under the next statement to the left, and so on.

We can adapt this procedure to test for the validity of an argument. Let's work with the argument about Shakespeare:

~W ⊃ D
~D
 W

If we were creating a truth table for the first premise alone, it would look like this:

~	W	⊃	D
F	T	**T**	T
F	T	**T**	F
T	F	**F**	T
T	F	**F**	F

To create a truth table for the *argument*, we create additional columns to represent the second premise and the conclusion, with a forward slash before the conclusion in order to separate it from the premises:

		Premise 1			Premise 2		/	Conclusion
	~	W	⊃	D	~	D	/	**W**
1		T		T		T		
2		T		F		F		
3		F		T		T		
4		F		F		F		

As with truth tables for individual statements, each atomic component that appears more than once must have the same truth value on each row. So in the columns under premise 2 and the conclusion, the atomic statements D and W must have the same truth values on each row that each has in premise 1.

We now compute the truth values of each premise and of the conclusion, putting the result under the main connective for each statement. The procedure is exactly the same as with truth tables for single statements, except that now we have three different statements, whose truth values are represented in the three shaded columns.

		Premise 1				Premise 2	/		Conclusion
	~	W	⊃	D	~	D	/		W
1	F	T	**T**	T	**F**	T			T
2	F	T	**T**	F	**T**	F			T
3	T	F	**T**	T	**F**	T			F
4	T	F	**F**	F	**T**	F			F

The test for validity is whether the conclusion can be false while the premises are both true. So the first step is to look at the column under the conclusion and flag the rows on which it is false—rows 3 and 4:

		Premise 1				Premise 2	/		Conclusion
	~	W	⊃	D	~	D	/		W
1	F	T	**T**	T	**F**	T			T
2	F	T	**T**	F	**T**	F			T
3	T	F	**T**	T	**F**	T			F
4	T	F	**F**	F	**T**	F			F

Now we check the premises on those rows in order to see whether they are both true.

		Premise 1				Premise 2	/		Conclusion
	~	W	⊃	D	~	D	/		W
1	F	T	**T**	T	**F**	T			T
2	F	T	**T**	F	**T**	F			T
3	T	F	**T**	T	**F**	T			F
4	T	F	**F**	F	**T**	F			F

In row 3, the premise ~D is false, and in line 4 the premise ~W ⊃ D is false. Since the truth table shows us every combination of possible truth values, we have just established that there's no way this argument could have true premises and a false conclusion, which is the standard for validity. So this argument is valid.

When we use truth tables to determine whether an argument is valid or invalid, we are concerned only with the truth values of the premises and conclusion as whole statements—the truth values in the shaded columns. For compound statements such as premises 1 or 2 in the previous argument, we disregard the truth values of their components and take account only of the columns under their main connectives. It's not that the truth values of the components are irrelevant: We had to take account of them in computing the truth value of the compound statement. But once we have done so, it is only the truth value of the statement as a whole that matters for validity; the truth values of the components have no further relevance.

Let's see how the truth table test identifies an invalid argument:

If Iran is enriching uranium in order to make a bomb, it will hide the enrichment facility from satellite observation. That's exactly what Iran is doing, so its goal is to make a bomb.

B ⊃ H
H
B

This argument is a case of affirming the consequent, which is fallacious. The truth table shows why. As before, we write the premises at the top, with the conclusion marked off by the slash; and we fill in the truth values on each row:

	B	⊃	H	**H**	/	**B**
1	T	**T**	T	**T**		**T**
2	T	**F**	F	**F**		**T**
3	F	**T**	T	**T**		**F**
4	F	**T**	F	**F**		**F**

The conclusion is false in the third and fourth rows, and in row 3, both premises are true. It only takes one such case to show that the argument is not valid.

The truth table test for validity will work with arguments of any complexity. Let's try the argument:

A ⊃ B

C ⊃ B

A ⊃ C

We have three atomic components here (A, B, and C), so to represent all the possibilities we need a truth table with eight lines:

	A	⊃	B	C	⊃	B	/	A	⊃	C
1	T	**T**	T	T	**T**	T		T	**T**	T
2	T	**T**	T	F	**T**	T		T	**F**	F
3	T	**F**	F	T	**F**	F		T	**T**	T
4	T	**F**	F	F	**T**	F		T	**F**	F
5	F	**T**	T	T	**T**	T		F	**T**	T
6	F	**T**	T	F	**T**	T		F	**T**	F
7	F	**T**	F	T	**F**	F		F	**T**	T
8	F	**T**	F	F	**T**	F		F	**T**	F

The conclusion is false on rows 2 and 4. On row 4, the first premise is false, so there is no problem. But on row 2, both of the premises are true. So that row establishes that the premises could be true while the conclusion is false. The argument is not valid.

So far we have been working back from the conclusion to the premises. We can also work forward from premises to conclusion: We flag the rows on which all the premises are true, and then check to see whether the conclusion is false on any of those rows. We will reach the same result regardless of where we start, but sometimes it is easier to work forward. Consider the argument

(A ∨ B) ⊃ C

A ___

C

	(A	∨	B)	⊃	C	A	/	C
1	T	T	T	**T**	T	**T**		**T**
2	T	T	T	**F**	F	**T**		**F**
3	T	T	F	**T**	T	**T**		**T**
4	T	T	F	**F**	F	**T**		**F**
5	F	T	T	**T**	T	**F**		**T**
6	F	T	T	**F**	F	**F**		**F**
7	F	F	F	**T**	T	**F**		**T**
8	F	F	F	**T**	F	**F**		**F**

There are just two rows on which the premises are both true, and the conclusion is true on both rows. So the argument is valid. To double-check that it's valid, notice that the conclusion is false on four other rows, and on each of those rows at least one premise is false.

STRATEGY Truth Table Test of Validity

To determine whether a propositional argument is valid:

1. Create a truth table for the argument.
   a. Put the premises and the conclusion in the top row of a truth table, with a forward slash before the conclusion.
   b. Make columns under each connective and each atomic statement contained in the premises and conclusion.
   c. Create just enough rows to include every possible combination of truth values for the atomic statements that are components of the premises and conclusion: for 1 atomic statement, 2 rows; for 2 atomic statements, 4 rows; for 3 atomic statements, 8 rows; etc.
   d. Insert truth values for the atomic statements systematically, with alternating T and F in the column under the right-most atomic statement, alternating TT and FF under the next statement to the left, and so on, until you have inserted truth values in every column under an atomic statement.

2. Test for validity:
   a. Identify each row in which the conclusion is false. If there is at least one false premise in every such row, the argument is valid. If the premises are all true in any row where the conclusion is false, the argument is invalid.

   OR

   b. Alternative: Identify each row in which the premises are all true. If the conclusion is false in any such row, the argument is invalid. If the conclusion is true in all rows where the premises are all true, the argument is valid.

EXERCISE 10.1

For each of the following arguments, construct a truth table to determine whether it is valid. If it is invalid, indicate which row or rows have true premises and a false conclusion.

✳ 1. A ⊃ B
    B
    A

2. C ∨ D
    B
    ~C

3. E ⊃ F
    ~E
    ~F

✳ 4. F ≡ G
    F ∨ G
    F • G

5. ~A ≡ ~B
    B ∨ A
    ~A

6. A • B
    B ∨ A

* 7. <u>G ⊃ H</u>
    G ⊃ (G • H)

8. A ⊃ ~A
    <u>(B ⊃ A) ⊃ B</u>
    A ≡ ~B

9. J ⊃ K
    <u>K ⊃ L</u>
    J ⊃ L

* 10. ~(M ∨ N)
    <u>~N</u>

11. D ⊃ E
    <u>E ⊃ D</u>
    (D • E) ∨ (~D • ~E)

12. P • Q
    <u>Q • R</u>
    P ⊃ R

* 13. S ⊃ (T • V)
    <u>~V</u>
    ~S

14. A ⊃ ~(B ⊃ C)
    <u>A</u>
    B

15. (J ⊃ K) ⊃ J
    <u>(K ⊃ J) ⊃ K</u>
    ~J ∨ ~K

10.2 Truth Table Test: Short Form

It's rather cumbersome to work with an eight-row truth table, and for every additional atomic component statement, we double the number of rows we need. The problem gets worse exponentially: For an argument with n components, we need a table with 2^n lines. Fortunately, there's a shorter and more efficient way to use the truth table test of validity. Since we want to know whether the conclusion can be false while the premises are true, we can try to *construct* a row where that is the case, instead of writing out the whole table and looking for it. That is, we try to find a set of truth values for the atomic components of the premises and conclusion that makes all the premises come out true and the conclusion false. If we can find even one such line, the argument is invalid; if there is no such line, the argument is valid.

Let's do this for an argument that has four atomic components, for which the complete truth table would require 16 lines.

(G ⊃ H) • (J ⊃ K)

<u>G ∨ J</u>

H ∨ K

We start in the usual way, putting the premises and conclusion in a row. We put the letter T under the main connective in each premise and F under the main connective in the conclusion to indicate our goal: We are looking for a way to assign truth values to individual components that will make the premises true and the conclusion false. In other words, we are going to work back from the truth values under the main connectives in order to see whether any assignment of truth values to the components could give rise to that result. It's a bit like doing a crossword or Sudoku puzzle.

	(G	⊃	H)	•	(J	⊃	K)	G	∨	J	/	H	∨	K
1				**T**					**T**				**F**	

We will begin with the conclusion since it is a disjunctive statement, and a disjunction is false only if both disjuncts are false. So we put an F under H and K in the conclusion—and then under those letters wherever else they occur, since we must assign truth values to letters consistently.

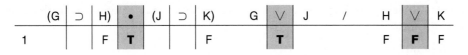

	(G	⊃	H)	•	(J	⊃	K)	G	∨	J	/	H	∨	K
1			F	**T**			F		**T**			F	**F**	F

Notice that the first premise is a conjunction, so it can be true only if each conjunct is true. And each conjunct is a conditional statement with a false consequent (H in the first case, K in the second), so it will be true only if the antecedents (G and J) are also false.

	(G	⊃	H)	•	(J	⊃	K)	G	∨	J	/	H	∨	K
1	F	T	F	**T**	F	T	F		**T**			F	**F**	F

To be consistent, of course, we need to put an F under G and J in the second premise. But that would make the premise itself false. So we can see that there is simply no way to make both premises true and the conclusion false. We have established that the argument is valid without needing to lay out all 16 lines of the truth table.

The short method worked out very easily with this argument because there is only one pair of truth values for H and K that makes the conclusion false. This will not always be the case. In the argument

A ∨ C
C ⊃ D
D • B
A • B

the conclusion is a conjunction, which can be false in three different ways. If we start there, we have three lines to consider. It would be more efficient to start with the third premise. It too is a conjunction, but since it is a premise, we are trying to make it true. There's only one way to do that:

	A	∨	C	C	⊃	D	D	•	B	/	A	•	B
1		**T**			**T**	T	T	**T**	T			**F**	T

Since B is true, the only way to make the conclusion false is to make A false:

	A	∨	C	C	⊃	D	D	•	B	/	A	•	B
1	F	T			T	T	T	T	T		F	F	T

Now we can see that the only way to make the first premise true is to make C true, and that makes the second premise true as well. So we have found a set of component truth values that make all the premises true and the conclusion false—which proves that the argument is invalid.

It will not always be possible to test validity by considering only a single line. Sometimes it is necessary to examine several possible sets of component truth values. Here's an example:

(L ∨ M) ⊃ N

~N ∨ O

(O • L) ⊃ M

M ≡ N

Each of the premises can be true with more than one combination of component truth values, and the conclusion can be false with more than one combination. So we will have to try more than one set of truth values. Let's start with the conclusion. A biconditional statement is false if its components have opposite truth values. We need two lines in the table to capture both of the ways that can happen:

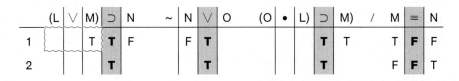

	(	L	∨	M	)	⊃	N	~	N	∨	O	(	O	•	L	)	⊃	M	)	/	M	≡	N
1				T		T	F		F	T							T	T			T	F	F
2						T				T							T				F	F	T

In row 1, we can see right away that if M is true and N false, there is no way to make the first premise true:

	(	L	∨	M	)	⊃	N	~	N	∨	O	(	O	•	L	)	⊃	M	)	/	M	≡	N
1				T		T	F		F	T							T	T			T	F	F
2						T				T							T				F	F	T

Since that premise is a conditional with a false consequent (N), it can be true only if the antecedent is false. Since M is true on this line, however, the disjunctive antecedent is true, which makes the premise false. We need not go further. No matter what values O and L have, we have established that there's no way to make both premises true in row 1.

So we can turn to row 2, where M is false and N true. We can start with the second premise: For the disjunction to be true, O must be true.

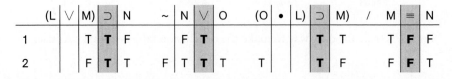

	(	L	∨	M	)	⊃	N	~	N	∨	O	(	O	•	L	)	⊃	M	)	/	M	≡	N
1				T		T	F		F	T							T	T			T	F	F
2				F		T	T	F	T	T	T		T				T	F			F	F	T

The third premise is a conditional whose consequent, M, is false. So the premise will be true only if we can make the antecedent of the conditional false. Since O is true, L must be false. And that makes the antecedent of the first premise false and the premise itself true.

	(L	∨	M)	⊃	N	~	N	∨	O	(O	•	L)	⊃	M)	/	M	≡	N
1			T	**T**	F		F	**T**					**T**	T		T	**F**	F
2	F	F	F	**T**	T	F	T	**T**	T	T	F	F	**T**	F		F	**F**	T

The result is that all the premises are true on this line. Since we have this one case in which the premises are true and the conclusion false, the argument is invalid. Even though we had to consider two different cases, the short method was easier and faster than constructing the entire truth table for this argument.

STRATEGY **Truth Table Test: Short Form**

To use the short form of the truth table test for validity:

1. Put the premises and the conclusion in the top row of a truth table, with a slash mark before the conclusion. Make columns under each atomic statement and each connective.

2. Put T under the main connective in each premise and F under the main connective in the conclusion.

3. Identify each combination of truth values for the atomic components of the conclusion that will make it *false*. Create a row for each combination. If there are more than a few such combinations, then try to identify one of the premises that can be made *true* by fewer combinations of atomic truth values.

4. In either case, put each combination of truth values in its own row, making sure that in each row, each atomic component has the same truth value wherever it occurs in the argument.

5. Determine whether any combination of truth values is consistent with the truth of the premises and the falsity of the conclusion. If so, the argument is invalid. If not, the argument is valid.

EXERCISE 10.2

Test each of the following arguments for validity by using the short form of the truth table test. (If you are uncertain of your answer, create a full truth table for the argument.)

✳ 1. A • B
C ∨ B
~C

2. D ∨ (E • F)
~E
D

3. F ⊃ (G ⊃ H)
F • H
G

✳ 4. J ⊃ K
K ⊃ L
~L
~J

5. (C ⊃ D) ⊃ (D ⊃ B)
D
C ⊃ B

6. (M • N) ∨ (N • O)
N ⊃ ~M
O

✳ 7. W ⊃ Y
(W ⊃ Z) ∨ (Y ⊃ Z)
~Z
~(W • Y)

8. ~Q
P ⊃ (Q ∨ R)
R
P

9. (J ⊃ K) ⊃ J
(K ⊃ J) ⊃ K
~J ∨ ~K

✳10. (A • C) ∨ (B ⊃ C)
~C ∨ B
~B ∨ C

11. S ⊃ T
V ⊃ W

S ∨ V
~W
T

12. (A ∨ B) ⊃ (C • D)
~B • C
~A ∨ D

✳13. (E ⊃ F) ∨ [E ⊃ (G • H)]
H ⊃ (F ∨ G)
E ⊃ H

14. (J ⊃ K) • (L ⊃ M)
~K ∨ ~M
~J ∨ ~L

15. [(J • T) • Y] ∨ (~J ⊃ ~Y)
J ⊃ T
T ⊃ Y
Y ≡ T

✳16. ~[A ∨ ~(B ∨ ~C)]
D ⊃ (A ⊃ C)
~A ≡ ~B

17. (R • C) ⊃ ~E
~(C • R) ⊃ S
~F ⊃ ~S
E ⊃ F

18. (A ⊃ B) • ~C
~B • (C ∨ D)
D • A

✳19. N ∨ O
P ∨ Q
~Q ∨ N
P ⊃ (N ∨ R)
O

20. (A ∨ B) ⊃ [C • (D ⊃ E)]
A
D ⊃ E

10.3 Proof

For arguments that involve complex statements or more than a few premises, even the short version of the truth table method can be cumbersome. An alternative is to look for a proof by which the conclusion can be derived from the premises. Proof in logic is like proof in geometry. It is a series of small steps, each of which is itself a valid inference. If we can get from premises to conclusion by valid steps, then we have shown that the conclusion follows necessarily from the premises, and thus that the argument as a whole is valid. In this section, we will learn how to establish validity by constructing proofs. It often takes some ingenuity to come up with a proof, so the fact that you haven't found one for a given argument does not establish that the argument is invalid. Perhaps you haven't looked hard enough. Unlike the truth table method, therefore, the method of proof won't establish that an argument is invalid. If an argument *is* valid, however, a proof will often reveal why the conclusion follows from the premises more clearly than the truth table method does.

10.3A Rules of Inference

To understand the method of proof, we need to begin with the rules for taking a single step. The basic rule is that each step must itself be a valid inference. In principle, we could use *any* valid form of inference to take an individual step in a proof. But it would be impossible to remember all the valid forms, even the simpler ones. It is better to work with a small set that is easily memorized. We are going to work with nine argument forms that are commonly used in propositional logic as individual steps in proofs. Each of these forms will serve as a rule for taking a single step in a proof. They can all be proven valid by the truth table method, and you are already familiar with most of them.

Let's start with four hypothetical and disjunctive forms of inference.

Modus ponens (MP)

$p \supset q$

p

q

Modus tollens (MT)

$p \supset q$

$\sim q$

$\sim p$

Hypothetical syllogism (HS)

$p \supset q$

$q \supset r$

$p \supset r$

Disjunctive syllogism (DS)

$p \lor q$ $p \lor q$

$\sim p$ or $\sim q$

q p

It's important to understand that these are argument *forms* rather than actual arguments. The difference is the same as the difference between a statement form and an actual statement. As we saw in the previous chapter, a statement form is an abstract way to represent the logical form that a class of actual statements have in common, using variables (p, q, r, etc.) for the component statements. Any actual statement in that class is an instance of the statement form. The same distinction carries over to arguments—as you might expect, since arguments are made up of statements. An argument form is an abstract way to represent a certain logical structure that a whole class of actual arguments have in common, and any actual argument in that class is an instance of the form. Thus the argument

That fabric is either silk or rayon.	S ∨ R
It is not silk.	~S
It is rayon.	R

is an instance of the argument form DS.

For statement forms, as we saw, the instances of the variables p, q, r, etc., need not be simple component statements. The same is true for argument forms. Each of the following arguments, for example, has the form *modus ponens*:

A ⊃ (B ∨ C)   (G • H) ⊃ (J • K)
A   G • H
B ∨ C   J • K

(N • O) ⊃ [(P ∨ (Q ⊃ R)]   [(S ⊃ (T ∨ ~U)] ⊃ ~V
N • O   S ⊃ (T ∨ ~U)
P ∨ (Q ⊃ R)   ~V

In the same way, each of the following arguments is an instance of one of the other argument forms:

(E ≡ F) ⊃ (F ⊃ G) (F ⊃ G) ⊃ ~H (E ≡ F) ⊃ ~H	HS
P ⊃ (L ∨ M) ~(L ∨ M) ~P	MT
(W • Q) ∨ (S • T) ~(S • T) W • Q	DS

To use these argument forms in building proofs, you will need to be able to spot the argument form embodied in complex instances like these.

So how do we build a proof? Let's work through a simple example that will give you an overview, and then look at each of the elements in the process.

Interest rates have increased (I). If so, according to economic theory, then either demand for credit has increased (D) or the supply of credit has decreased (S). The supply would have fallen only if people were saving less (L). But savings have not declined. So the demand must have gone up.

1. I
2. I ⊃ (D ∨ S)
3. S ⊃ L
4. ~L
5. D

The argument is not a simple instance of any of the four argument forms above. It is an extended argument in which we will need to apply several of the inference rules in separate steps to get from premises to conclusion, as we can see if we construct an argument diagram by the method of Chapter 4:

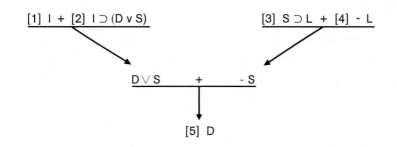

Premises 1 and 2 can be combined by *modus ponens* to infer the intermediate conclusion D ∨ S, and premises 3 and 4 can be combined by *modus tollens* to infer ~S. Those intermediate conclusions, finally, can be combined in a disjunctive syllogism to yield our ultimate conclusion.

Diagrams can sometimes be useful as an aid in constructing a proof, but in symbolic logic we represent the steps in a proof in a different notation that is more explicit. We start by listing the premises, as before, but we don't give the conclusion a number; instead, we put it on the same line as the last premise, separated by a slash mark, as in the truth table method. The slash mark indicates that we have listed the conclusion merely as a note to ourselves that D is the statement we are trying to derive from premises 1–4.

1. I   Premise
2. I ⊃ (D ∨ S)   Premise
3. S ⊃ L   Premise
4. ~L   / D   Premise / Conclusion

Now we put in the three steps of the proof:

5. D ∨ S   1,2 MP
6. ~S   3,4 MT
7. D   5,6 DS

Line 5 is our first inference from the premises, our first intermediate conclusion. To show that we inferred it from premises 1 and 2, we don't use an arrow. We just name those premises off to the right, where we also state the argument form we used. We do the same for the two other steps. When we reach the line that states the conclusion, we're done.

Thus, a proof consists entirely in statements. Each line is either a premise, an intermediate conclusion, or the final conclusion. As in a board game, we have a starting position (the premises) and we take one step at a time, in accordance with a rule, until we reach the goal. The basic argument forms serve as inference rules. Since the argument forms are valid, any line that we derive from previous lines in accordance with the rules is a valid inference from the premises—up to and including the final line, the conclusion.

There is also one overarching rule: The inference rules must be applied to the whole statement on a given line, not to a component of the statement. Thus the following "proof" is incorrect:

If the weather report is accurate (W), it is either raining (R) or snowing (S) outside. It isn't raining. Therefore it is snowing.	1. W ⊃ (R ∨ S)	Premise
	2. ~R / S	Premise / Conclusion
	3. S	1,2 DS [error]

We cannot use a disjunctive syllogism to infer S from ~R and R ∨ S because we are not given the latter as a premise; it is the consequent of a conditional statement. And you can see why the "proof" does not establish the conclusion: Until we know that the weather report was accurate (i.e., that W in premise 1 is true), we have no basis for saying that rain and snow are the only alternatives.

Two other things you need to know about proofs can be illustrated by the following example:

1. A ⊃ B		Premise
2. B ⊃ C		Premise
3. C ⊃ D	/ A ⊃ D	Premise

Since the premises give us a series of conditional statements from A to D, it is obvious that the conclusion A ⊃ D follows by the rule of hypothetical syllogism. But we cannot derive the conclusion in a single step. That would not result in a fallacious "proof," as was the case when we tried to apply an inference rule to part of a statement. But it is still an error because HS applies to two statements at a time. So our proof will need two separate steps:

| 4. A ⊃ C | 1,2 HS |
| 5. A ⊃ D | 3,4 HS |

A second lesson to draw from this example is that there may be more than one path from premises to conclusion. Instead of drawing our first intermediate conclusion from 1 and 2, we might have started from 2 and 3:

| 4. B ⊃ D | 2,3 HS |
| 5. A ⊃ D | 1,4 HS |

As we add more rules to the four we have learned so far, and as we work with proofs requiring a larger number of steps, the possibility of multiple paths from premises to conclusion will only increase.

EXERCISE 10.3A

A. Each of the following arguments is an instance of one of the four inference forms we have learned (MP, MT, HS, DS). Identify the form.

* 1. C ∨ D
   <u>~C</u>
   D

2. E ⊃ F
   <u>~F</u>
   ~E

3. M ⊃ N
   <u>M</u>
   N

* 4. H ⊃ K
   <u>K ⊃ J</u>
   H ⊃ J

5. M ⊃ ~D
   <u>~~D</u>
   ~M

6. A ∨ B
   <u>~B</u>
   A

* 7. (D ∨ E) ⊃ F
   <u>D ∨ E</u>
   F

8. (N • O) ∨ M
   <u>~M</u>
   N • O

9. (A • B) ⊃ (C • D)
   <u>A • B</u>
   C • D

*10. (H ∨ J) ⊃ K
   <u>~K</u>
   ~(H ∨ J)

11. ~M ⊃ [(N • O) ∨ P]
   <u>~M</u>
   (N • O) ∨ P

12. (H ∨ J) ∨ K
   <u>~(H ∨ J)</u>
   K

*13. A ⊃ (B ≡ C)
   <u>~(B ≡ C)</u>
   ~A

14. A ⊃ (B • C)
   <u>(B • C) ⊃ (D ∨ E)</u>
   A ⊃ (D ∨ E)

15. (E • F) ⊃ (G ∨ H)
   <u>~(G ∨ H)</u>
   ~(E • F)

*16. (M ⊃ N) ⊃ (L • N)
   <u>(L • N) ⊃ (L ⊃ O)</u>
   (M ⊃ N) ⊃ (L ⊃ O)

17. [~(N • O) ⊃ L] ∨ (M • N)
   <u>~[~(N • O) ⊃ L]</u>
   M • N

18. [(H • ~J) ⊃ K] ⊃ (L • ~M)
   <u>(L • ~M) ⊃ (J ∨ K)</u>
   [(H • ~J) ⊃ K] ⊃ (J ∨ K)

*19. [~M • (N ⊃ ~K)] ⊃ [N ≡ ~(M ∨ J)]
   <u>~M • (N ⊃ ~K)</u>
   N ≡ ~(M ∨ J)

20. (A • B) ⊃ (C ≡ A)
   <u>(C ≡ A) ⊃ D</u>
   (A • B) ⊃ D

B. For each of the following arguments, complete the proof using the four inference rules we have learned (MP, MT, HS, DS). Be sure to include the justification. (For 1–5, the numbered lines following the final premise/conclusion indicate the number of steps required for the proof. For 6–16, you will need to determine that on your own.)

＊1. 1. A ⊃ B
　　 2. ~A ⊃ C
　　 3. ~B / C
　　 4. _____　　_____
　　 5. _____　　_____

2. 1. A ∨ B
　　 2. A ⊃ C
　　 3. ~C / B
　　 4. _____　　_____
　　 5. _____　　_____

3. 1. D ∨ ~E
　　 2. E ∨ ~B
　　 3. ~D / ~B
　　 4. _____　　_____
　　 5. _____　　_____

＊4. 1. E ⊃ D
　　 2. ~D
　　 3. ~E ⊃ C / C
　　 4. _____　　_____
　　 5. _____　　_____

5. 1. J ∨ K
　　 2. ~J
　　 3. K ⊃ L / L
　　 4. _____　　_____
　　 5. _____　　_____

6. 1. B ⊃ C
　　 2. D ⊃ B
　　 3. A ⊃ D / A ⊃ C

＊7. 1. B ≡ C
　　 2. (B ≡ C) ⊃ ~A
　　 3. A ∨ D / D

8. 1. (B • C) ⊃ D
　　 2. (B • C) ∨ A
　　 3. ~D / A

9. 1. (A ⊃ B) ⊃ (C ∨ D)
　　 2. ~(C ∨ D)
　　 3. ~(A ⊃ B) ⊃ E / E

＊10. 1. ~D
　　 2. D ∨ (A ⊃ D)
　　 3. B ⊃ A / ~B

11. 1. H ⊃ I
　　 2. J ⊃ K
　　 3. H ∨ J
　　 4. ~K / I

12. 1. (A ∨ B) ⊃ (C • D)
　　 2. ~(C • D)
　　 3. ~(A ∨ B) ⊃ E / E

＊13. 1. G ⊃ H
　　 2. ~H
　　 3. I ⊃ G / ~I

14. 1. ~B ⊃ ~C
　　 2. (~B ⊃ ~D) ⊃ ~A
　　 3. ~C ⊃ ~D / ~A

15. 1. A ⊃ B
　　 2. ~B
　　 3. ~A ⊃ ~D
　　 4. D ∨ E / E

＊16. 1. (A ∨ B) ∨ (B ⊃ C)
　　 2. (A ∨ B) ⊃ (~H ≡ ~J)
　　 3. C ⊃ ~D
　　 4. G ⊃ B
　　 5. ~(~H ≡ ~J) / G ⊃ ~D

10.3B Rules of Inference (Continued)

The first four inference rules are not enough to construct proofs for all valid arguments. We will need some additional rules. We can begin with three rules that involve basic operations with conjunction and disjunction:

Simplification (Simp)	**Conjunction** (Conj)	**Addition** (Add)
$\underline{p \bullet q}$ or $\underline{p \bullet q}$	p or p	$\underline{p}$ or $\underline{q}$
p q	$\underline{q}$ $\underline{q}$	$p \lor q$ $p \lor q$
	$p \bullet q$ $q \bullet p$	

As argument forms, simplification and conjunction are based on the fact that a conjunction is true if and only if both conjuncts are true. So if we already have a conjunctive statement, then of course we can infer either of its component statements (Simp). Conversely, if we already have both conjuncts independently, then of course their conjunction follows (Conj). In the context of proof, Simp is useful when we need to eliminate a conjunction. For example, we might be given a conjunction as a premise and can see that one conjunct is not relevant to the conclusion. Conj, on the other hand, allows us to introduce a conjunction, putting together two statements into a single conjunctive statement.

Addition allows us to introduce a new statement by adding it, in the form of a disjunction, to a statement we already have. This rule may be a little less obvious than the other two because we start with a given statement p and can add any other statement whatever, regardless of whether it has any relationship to p. But remember the truth table for disjunction: A disjunctive statement is true as long as one or the other of the disjuncts is true (or both). This means that if we are given p as a premise or have derived it by a series of valid steps in a proof, then we can infer the disjunction of p with any other statement.

An example of how Add is used in proof is the argument at the very beginning of the previous chapter:

If there is a recession this year or a foreign affairs fiasco, the president will not be reelected. Since there will be a recession, the president will not be reelected.

1. (R ∨ F) ⊃ ~P
2. R / ~P

From premise 2, we would use Add to infer R ∨ F, which can then be combined with 1 to derive the conclusion by *modus ponens*:

1. (R ∨ F) ⊃ ~P		Premise
2. R	/ ~P	Premise / Conclusion
3. R ∨ F		2 Add
4. ~P		1,3 MP

Simp, Conj, and Add are often used in proofs when we need to break a compound statement down into its components and then reassemble the components in a new compound statement. Here's an example:

1. A • B		Premise
2. C	/ (A ∨ D) • C	Premise / Conclusion

Notice that the conclusion includes a disjunctive component, but there is no disjunction in the premises, nor any occurrence of D. That suggests we will need to use Add to infer A ∨ D from A. But A is conjoined with B in premise 1, so we will first need to use Simp to extract it. Once we have A ∨ D, finally, we can use Conj to combine it with C from premise 2. Thus, the proof will use all three of our new rules:

3. A	1 Simp
4. A $\lor$ D	3 Add
5. (A $\lor$ D) • C	2,4 Conj

The last two inference forms are called dilemmas. Argument by dilemma is a common tactic in debates, and we sometimes use inferences of this form in thinking about alternative courses of action. Here's an example:

> If I go to bed early (E), I'll be unprepared for the test (U); but if I stay up late studying (L), I'll be too tired to do well (T). Those are my choices: either I go to bed early or I stay up late studying. So either I'll be unprepared for the test or I'll be too tired to do well.

If we put this into symbolic notation, we can see that it involves a combination of conditional and disjunctive elements:

(E $\supset$ U) • (L $\supset$ T)

E $\lor$ L

U $\lor$ T

The first premise conjoins two conditional statements; the second premise says that at least one of the two antecedents is true; and the conclusion is that at least one of the two consequents is true. This argument is an instance of a form called **constructive dilemma** (CD).

Destructive dilemma (DD) is the parallel form in which we argue that one of the two consequents is *false* and therefore that one of the two antecedents is false, as in the example below:

> If conservatives are right (C), welfare breeds dependency (D); while if liberals are right (L), it is merely a temporary transition to self-supporting work (T). But either welfare does *not* breed dependency or it is *not* merely a temporary transition. So either the conservatives or the liberals are not right.

(C $\supset$ D) • (L $\supset$ T)

~D $\lor$ ~T

~C $\lor$ ~L

Generalizing from the examples, the inference forms are

Constructive dilemma (CD)	Destructive dilemma (DD)
$(p \supset q) \bullet (r \supset s)$	$(p \supset q) \bullet (r \supset s)$
$p \lor r$	~$q \lor$ ~s
$q \lor s$	~$p \lor$ ~s

As with the first set of inference rules, each of the rules we have just learned identifies a form of valid inference, using the letters p, q, etc., for the component propositions. We must remember that instances of these components may themselves be compound statements. Thus, each of the following arguments is an instance of the argument form indicated beside it in the table below:

(A • B) (A • B) ∨ C	Add
(D ⊃ E) • [(F ∨ G) ⊃ H] ~E ∨ ~H ~D v ~(F v G)	DD
(J ⊃ K) • L M ≡ N [(J ⊃ K) • L] • (M ≡ N)	Conj
[(P • R) ⊃ S] • (S ⊃ ~W) (P • R) ∨ S S ∨ ~W	CD
(A ⊃ B) • [D ∨ (~E • F)] D ∨ (~E • F)	Simp

As with the first set of inference rules, moreover, each of the rules we have just learned must be applied to the whole statement on a given line of a proof, not to a component of the statement. This overarching rule is very important to remember; applying an inference rule to a component of a statement is one of the most common errors in constructing proofs. Here's another example of the error:

> If I got the breaks and had the talent, I'd be a Hollywood star. But I'm not a star, so obviously I haven't had the breaks.

1. (B • T) ⊃ S			Premise
2. ~S		/ ~B	Premise / Conclusion
3. B ⊃ S			1 Simp [error]
4. ~B			2,3 MT

In line 3, simplification is being applied to the antecedent of premise 1, in an effort to reduce B • T to the simpler component B, and thus replace (B • T) ⊃ S with B ⊃ S, so that a *modus tollens* inference in line 4 will yield the conclusion. But B • T is not itself stated as a premise. It is only one component of a conditional statement, and inference rules like simplification may not be applied to a component of a previous line in a proof. You can see why the result is an invalid argument. I'm admitting at the outset that becoming a Hollywood star depends on two factors: having talent and getting the breaks. In blaming my lack of stardom on not getting breaks, however, I am conveniently forgetting the talent factor. This is illicit simplification.

SUMMARY Nine Basic Inference Rules

Modus ponens (MP)

$p \supset q$

p

q

Modus tollens (MT)

$p \supset q$

$\sim q$

$\sim p$

Hypothetical syllogism (HS)

$p \supset q$

$q \supset r$

$p \supset r$

Disjunctive syllogism (DS)

$p \vee q$		$p \vee q$
$\sim p$	or	$\sim q$
q		p

Simplification (Simp)

$p \bullet q$	or	$p \bullet q$
p		q

Conjunction (Conj)

p	or	p
q		q
$p \bullet q$		$q \bullet p$

Addition (Add)

p	or	q
$p \vee q$		$p \vee q$

Constructive dilemma (CD)

$(p \supset q) \bullet (r \supset s)$

$p \vee r$

$q \vee s$

Destructive dilemma (DD)

$(p \supset q) \bullet (r \supset s)$

$\sim q \vee \sim s$

$\sim p \vee \sim r$

EXERCISE 10.3B

A. Each of the arguments below is an instance of one of the basic inference forms we learned in this section (Simp, Conj, Add, CD, DD). Identify the form in each case.

✴ 1. A • B
    B

2. (G ⊃ H) • (I ⊃ J)
    ~H ∨ ~J
    ~G ∨ ~I

3. K
    K ∨ L

✴ 4. D
    E
    D • E

5. (F ⊃ G) • (H ⊃ I)
    F ∨ H
    G ∨ I

6. A • (B ∨ C)
    A

✴ 7. (A ⊃ B) • (C ⊃ ~D)
    ~B ∨ ~~D
    ~A ∨ ~C

8. K
    G • H
    K • (G • H)

9. (A ⊃ B) • (C ⊃ B)
    C ⊃ B

✴10. (G ⊃ H) • (I ⊃ J)
    G ∨ I
    H ∨ J

11. (K • L) • M
    M

12. (F ⊃ G)
    (F ⊃ G) ∨ H

*13. [H ⊃ (I ∨ K)] • (J ⊃ L)
    H ∨ J
    (I ∨ K) ∨ L

14. I ∨ J
    K ∨ L
    (I ∨ J) • (K ∨ L)

15. (A ⊃ B) • (C ⊃ D)
    ~B ∨ ~D
    ~A ∨ ~C

*16. (A ⊃ B) • (B ⊃ C)
    A ∨ B
    (A ∨ B) • [(A ⊃ B) • (B ⊃ C)]

17. M ∨ (L ⊃ N)]
    (~O • M) ∨ [M ∨ (L ⊃ N)]

18. [(A ≡ B) ⊃ F] • [D ⊃ (B ∨ E)]
    ~F • ~ (B ∨ E)
    [~(A ≡ B) ∨ ~D]

*19. J ∨ K
    (J ∨ K) ∨ ~(L ⊃ M)

20. [N ⊃ (O • P)] • (N ⊃ ~S)
    N ∨ N
    (O • P) ∨ ~S

B. Construct a proof for each of the following arguments using *only* the inference rules you learned in this section (Add, Simp, Conj, CD, DD).

* 1. 1. A / (A ∨ B) ∨ C
  2. 1. (A • B) • C / A
  3. 1. A • B / A ∨ C
* 4. 1. A
     2. (A ⊃ B) • (C ⊃ D) / B ∨ D
  5. 1. (A ⊃ B) • (C ⊃ D)
     2. A / B v D
  6. 1. (A ⊃ C) • (B ⊃ D)
     2. (A ∨ B) • (B ∨ D) / C ∨ D
* 7. 1. (A ⊃ C) • (B ⊃ D)
     2. ~C / ~A ∨ ~B
  8. 1. A
     2. B
     3. C / (C • A) • B
  9. 1. (A ⊃ B) • (D ⊃ E)
     2. A ∨ D / (B ∨ E) ∨ D
*10. 1. (D ⊃ E)
     2. (F ⊃ G)
     3. D ∨ F / E ∨ G

11. A ∨ C
    (A ⊃ B) • (C ⊃ D)
    (B ⊃ E) • (D ⊃ G)
    E ∨ G
12. 1. A • D
    2. B / (D • B) ∨ A
*13. 1. B • C
    2. ~A • D / ~A • B
14. 1. B
    2. A / (A ∨ D) • (B ∨ C)
15. 1. (D ⊃ B) • (C ⊃ A)
    2. (E ⊃ D) • (B ⊃ C) / (E ⊃ D) • (D ⊃ B)
*16. 1. A ⊃ D
    2. B ⊃ C
    3. B ∨ A / C ∨ D
17. 1. A ⊃ B
    2. ~E ⊃ D
    3. (~E ∨ A) • (~E ∨ B) / D ∨ B
18. 1. B ⊃ (A ∨ C)
    2. D ⊃ E
    3. B / (A ∨ C) ∨ E

*19. 1. (A ⊃ C) • (B ⊃ D)
  2. ~C ∨ ~D
  3. [(~A ∨ ~B) ⊃ E] • (~E ⊃ F) /
        E ∨ F

20. 1. A ⊃ B
  2. C ⊃ D
  3. C • A / B ∨ D

21. 1. ~C • E
  2. A ⊃ C
  3. B ⊃ D / ~A ∨ ~B

*22. 1. (D ∨ A) ⊃ ~C
  2. (D • B) ⊃ A
  3. D • ~B / ~C ∨ A

10.3C Constructing a Proof

We have now learned all nine of the inference rules that we will use to take individual steps in a proof. Each rule is an argument form that we know to be valid, ensuring that each line we add to a proof follows validly from statements on previous lines. The more familiar you are with these rules, the easier you will find it to recognize patterns in the arguments you are given, and that will make it easier to find the steps by which you can derive the conclusion from the premises.

We have also learned two overarching rules about constructing proofs. First, an inference rule must be applied to the entire statement on a previous line. For example, *modus tollens* is used correctly in the argument on the left but not in the argument on the right:

1. D ⊃ E
2. ~E
3. ~D   1,2 MT

1. (D ⊃ E) ∨ F
2. ~E
3. ~D   1,2 MT [error]

Second, inference rules must be applied one at a time. For example, in the argument

1. H ⊃ J
2. K ⊃ L
3. H ∨ K   /   J ∨ L

you may be able to see right away that 1, 2, and 3 will allow us to infer the conclusion by constructive dilemma. But the argument form CD requires a premise that is a conjunction of conditionals, so you must first use Conj with 1 and 2, and then use CD as a separate step:

4. (H ⊃ J) • (K ⊃ L)   1,2 Conj
5. J ∨ L   3,4 CD

With the inference rules and the overarching rules in hand, we can now consider the strategies for constructing proofs. The difference between rules and strategies is the same as in a game: The rules are fixed; they define the activity, and you must comply with them. Strategies, however, are guidelines you can use to best achieve the goal. The process of constructing a proof is not mechanical. You have to think about what steps, in what order, will get you to the conclusion. But there are two broad strategies to follow: You can work forward from the premises or backward from the conclusion.

Working forward from the premises: If one premise is a conditional statement and another premise affirms the antecedent (or denies the consequent), try drawing the appropriate conclusion by *modus ponens* (or *modus tollens*), and see whether that gets you any closer to the conclusion. If the premises include several conditional statements, you may be able to use two of them in a hypothetical syllogism, or conjoin them as a basis for a constructive dilemma (as we just did in the example earlier). If a premise is a conjunction, you know right away that you can extract each conjunct by Simp and use it as a basis for further inferences. A disjunctive premise can be used in a disjunctive syllogism if another premise negates one of the disjuncts.

Every proof has to begin with the premises. Sometimes there is only one inference you can draw directly from the premises, one step you can take by applying an inference rule. As the number of premises increases, however, there will normally be more than one possible inference. In that case, the order in which you draw the inferences does not matter, as long as you put each statement you derive on its own numbered line and indicate the justification. Nor does it matter if you make an inference that turns out not to be of any further use in the proof. It may be a "false start" in terms of reaching the conclusion, but it is not actually false if it follows from the premises. Having unnecessary lines makes a proof less elegant than it might be, but it does not invalidate the proof.

Working backward from the conclusion: With simple proofs, you may be able to derive the conclusion in a few steps by applying inference rules directly to the premises. But with longer, more complex proofs, you will normally have to make a series of inferences, using each intermediate conclusion as a premise for a further inference in a sequence that gets you to the conclusion. The strategy of working backward from the conclusion means asking yourself what intermediate steps would enable you to derive the conclusion, and then asking how those intermediate statements themselves could be derived. The strategy is like planning a trip. If you wanted to get to Los Angeles, for example, you might reason: "If I can get to Denver, I know how to get from there to Los Angeles. So how can I get to Denver?"

Here are some ways of applying the strategy:

- If the conclusion is the atomic statement A, you could derive it by simplification from a conjunction, A • X (where X is some other atomic statement). Or you could derive it by *modus ponens* from prior statements X and X ⊃ A. If the conclusion is a *negated* atomic statement, ~A, look for a way to derive it by *modus tollens* from A ⊃ X and ~X.
- If the conclusion is a conditional statement, A ⊃ B, you could derive it by hypothetical syllogism if you could first derive A ⊃ X and X ⊃ B.
- If the conclusion is a conjunction, A • B, you could try to derive each conjunct separately and then use the rule of conjunction.
- If the conclusion is a disjunction, A ∨ B, look for a way to derive either of the disjuncts and then use the rule of addition. You could also look for a way to derive it by constructive dilemma from intermediate conclusions (X ⊃ A) • (Y ⊃ B) and X ∨ Y.

These two broad strategies—working forward from the premises and backward from the conclusion—are not mutually exclusive. On the contrary, we normally use them together. The following proof will illustrate the process:

1. A ⊃ B		Premise
2. C • ~B		Premise
3. (C ∨ D) ⊃ E		Premise
4. E ⊃ F	/ ~A • F	Premise / Conclusion

We might notice first that the conclusion is a conjunction, which suggests that we try to establish ~A and F separately, each by its own sequence of steps. Until we can identify those steps and put them down as numbered lines, it helps to use a kind of scratch pad to keep track of what we are doing:

1. A ⊃ B		Premise
2. C • ~B		Premise
3. (C ∨ D) ⊃ E		Premise
4. E ⊃ F	/ ~A • F	Premise / Conclusion
…		
…		
i. ~A		?
…		
…		
ii. F		?
iii. ~A • F		i,ii Conj

The conclusion will of course be the last step, and we will try to find steps that will give us ~A and F. (We number them with small Roman numbers because we won't know the actual number of these lines until we have worked out the whole proof.) To derive ~A, we need to begin with premise 1, the only premise in which A is a component. Since it is the antecedent of a conditional, we could derive ~A by *modus tollens* if we could first establish ~B. We can do that from premise 2, where ~B is one conjunct. So we have achieved our first intermediate goal, and we can turn the first part of our scratch pad into a proof of ~A:

1. A ⊃ B		Premise
2. C • ~B		Premise
3. (C ∨ D) ⊃ E		Premise
4. E ⊃ F	/ ~A • F	Premise / Conclusion
5. ~B		2 Simp
6. ~A		1,5 MT

Now we can turn to our other task, deriving F. Since it is the consequent in premise 4, perhaps we can first derive E and then use *modus ponens*. Since E is the consequent of premise 3, we might use *modus ponens* here as well, if we can derive the antecedent, C ∨ D. Let's add these points to our scratch pad:

1. A ⊃ B		Premise
2. C • ~B		Premise
3. (C ∨ D) ⊃ E		Premise
4. E ⊃ F	/ ~A • F	Premise / Conclusion

5. ~B	2 Simp
6. ~A	1,5 MT
...	
i. C ∨ D	?
ii. E	3,i MP
iii. F	4,ii MP
iv. ~A • F	6,iii Conj

The missing link is the derivation of C ∨ D. D is not a component of any premise other than 3, but C occurs in premise 2 as part of a conjunction. So we can use simplification to derive C and then addition to derive C ∨ D. That gives us everything we need to complete the proof:

1. A ⊃ B			Premise
2. C • ~B			Premise
3. (C ∨ D) ⊃ E			Premise
4. E ⊃ F	/ ~A • F		Premise / Conclusion
5. ~B			2 Simp
6. ~A			1,5 MT
7. C			2 Simp
8. C ∨ D			7 Add
9. E			3,8 MP
10. F			4,9 MP
11. ~A • F			6,10 Conj

Since we have derived ~A and F, we can use Conj to reach our conclusion.

STRATEGY Constructing Proofs

The following strategies are useful in constructing proofs:

1. Working forward from the premises:
   a. Look for pairs of premises to which the rules of *modus ponens, modus tollens,* disjunctive syllogism, hypothetical syllogism, or constructive or destructive dilemma can be applied.
   b. Observe whether the result can be combined with a further premise in a way that takes you closer to the conclusion.

2. Working backward from the conclusion:
   a. If the conclusion is an *atomic* statement, identify the premise(s) in which that statement occurs and look for ways to get from that premise(s) to the conclusion.
   b. If the conclusion is a *compound* statement, identify the main connective and the elements it connects.
   c. If the main connective is a conditional, look for a way to derive it by hypothetical syllogism.

(continued)

d. If the main connective is conjunction, look for ways to derive each conjunct separately.

e. If the main connective is disjunction, look for a way to derive one of the disjuncts and then use the rule of addition. Or look for a way to derive it by constructive or destructive dilemma.

EXERCISE 10.3C

A. For each of the following proofs, state the justification for each step.

✳ 1.

1. A ⊃ B	Premise
2. ~A ⊃ C	Premise
3. ~ B / C	Premise / Conclusion
4. ~A	_____
5. C	_____

2.

1. A ∨ B	Premise
2. A ⊃ C	Premise
3. ~C / B	Premise / Conclusion
4. ~A	_____
5. B	_____

3.

1. (F • G) ∨ H	Premise
2. H ⊃ I	Premise
3. ~(F • G) / I ∨ G	Premise / Conclusion
4. H	_____
5. I	_____
6. I ∨ G	_____

✳ 4.

1. (M • O) ⊃ (L ∨ K)	Premise
2. O • (L ∨ B)	Premise
3. M • ~H / (L ∨ K)	Premise / Conclusion
4. M	_____
5. O	_____
6. M • O	_____
7. (L ∨ K)	_____

5.

1. (E ⊃ F) • (~F ∨ ~G)   Premise
2. H ⊃ I   Premise
3. I ⊃ G / ~E ∨ ~H   Premise / Conclusion
4. H ⊃ G   _____
5. E ⊃ F   _____
6. (E ⊃ F) • (H ⊃ G)   _____
7. ~F ∨ ~G   _____
8. ~E ∨ ~H   _____

B. Show that each of the following arguments is valid by constructing a proof.

✳ 1. A
    A ⊃ ~B
    <u>B ∨ C</u>
    C

2. E ⊃ (F ∨ G)
    <u>~ (F ∨ G)</u>
    ~E ∨ G

3. D ⊃ E
    F ⊃ G
    <u>D ∨ F</u>
    E ∨ G

✳ 4. D ⊃ E
    D ∨ A
    <u>~E</u>
    A

5. [(B • A) • (C • D)] • [(E • ~D) ∨ G]
    B

6. ~B
    <u>(~B ∨ ~C) ⊃ ~D</u>
    ~D

✳ 7. (A ∨ B) ⊃ C
    E ⊃ (A ∨ B)
    <u>C ⊃ D</u>
    E ⊃ D

8. (A ∨ B) ⊃ [C • (D ⊃ E)]
    <u>A</u>
    D ⊃ E

9. (P ∨ K) ⊃ ~H
    <u>P • M</u>
    ~H

✳ 10. A ⊃ B
    C ⊃ D
    <u>~B</u>
    ~A ∨ ~C

11. A ∨ (B ∨ C)
    (B ⊃ E) • (C ⊃ G)
    <u>~A</u>
    E ∨ G

12. (B ⊃ G) • (A ⊃ ~E)
    C
    <u>C ⊃ (B ∨ A)</u>
    G ∨ ~E

✳ 13. B ⊃ C
    B ∨ (A • E)
    <u>~C</u>
    A • E

14. [B ∨ (A • E)] • [C ⊃ (B ∨ A)]
    <u>~B</u>
    A • E

15. (~A ∨ G) ⊃ (B • D)
    ~C
    <u>C ∨ (~A ∨ G)</u>
    B

✳16. ~(A ⊃ B)
(A ⊃ B) ∨ C
<u>G ⊃ (A ⊃ B)</u>
~G • C

17. ~E
~D
<u>B ⊃ D</u>
(~E ∨ ~C) • ~B

18. (~B ⊃ A) • (~C ⊃ D)
~A
<u>~B</u>
D

✳19. E ⊃ B
B ⊃ C
A ⊃ E
<u>C ⊃ G</u>
A ⊃ G

20. A ⊃ B
E ⊃ G
(A ⊃ B) ⊃ (C ⊃ D)
<u>E ∨ C</u>
G ∨ D

21. H ⊃ I
J ⊃ K
H ∨ J
<u>~K</u>
I

✳22. ~C
B ⊃ C
B ∨ A
<u>A ⊃ E</u>
E

23. (A ≡ B) ⊃ [B ⊃ (C ⊃ D)]
B
A ≡ B
<u>C</u>
D

24. (A ≡ B) ⊃ (E ∨ C)
~E
A ≡ B
<u>C ⊃ D</u>
D

✳25. (A ≡ B) ⊃ (E ∨ C)
(B ⊃ D) ⊃ (A ≡ B)
(E ∨ C) ⊃ ~G
<u>~G ⊃ A</u>
(B ⊃ D) ⊃ A

26. A ⊃ B
(A ⊃ ~C) ⊃ ~D
B ⊃ ~C
<u>E ⊃ D</u>
~E

27. J ⊃ H
~C ⊃ D
J ∨ ~C
<u>~H</u>
D

✳28. E ⊃ A
B ⊃ E
A ⊃ ~C
<u>B</u>
~C

29. (J ⊃ K) ⊃ (L • M)
(N ∨ O) ⊃ (J ⊃ K)
<u>N</u>
L

30. ~A ⊃ (~B ⊃ ~C)
~B
C ∨ D
<u>A ⊃ B</u>
D

✳31. A ∨ B
C ⊃ D
<u>~A • ~D</u>
B • ~C

32. A
    $(B \lor C) \lor (D \lor \sim E)$
    $A \supset \sim(B \lor C)$
    $\underline{A \supset \sim D}$
    $\sim E$

33. $A \supset B$
    $A \lor C$
    $B \supset D$
    $\underline{\sim C}$
    $E \lor D$

✱34. $(B \bullet A) \supset (C \bullet D)$
    $E \equiv F$
    $(\sim C \supset \sim G) \supset [F \supset (D \supset H)]$
    $[F \supset (D \supset H)] \supset [(E \equiv F) \supset (B \bullet A)]$
    $\underline{\sim C \supset \sim G}$
    $C \bullet D$

35. $F \supset G$
    $G \supset H$
    $\sim I$
    $H \supset I$
    $\underline{F \lor J}$
    J

36. $(A \lor B) \bullet \sim C$
    $\underline{\sim B \bullet (C \lor D)}$
    $D \bullet A$

✱37. $D \supset B$
    $C \supset A$
    $E \supset D$
    $B \supset C$
    $\underline{E \lor B}$
    $(B \lor A) \bullet (D \lor C)$

38. $B \lor (D \bullet E)$
    $(G \lor C) \supset \sim B$
    $(D \lor H) \supset J$
    $\underline{G}$
    J

39. $A \lor (B \lor C)$
    $D \supset \sim E$
    $\sim A \supset (C \supset F)$
    $B \supset D$
    $\underline{\sim A}$
    $\sim E \lor F$

✱40. $(A \lor D) \supset [(B \supset G) \bullet (C \supset E)]$
    $A \supset \sim D$
    $A \bullet \sim G$
    $\sim C \supset D$
    $\underline{B \lor E}$
    E

41. $A \supset (B \supset)$
    $A \lor D$
    $(D \supset E) \bullet (E \supset F)$
    $G \supset (\sim F \bullet \sim C)$
    $\underline{G}$
    $\sim B$

10.4 Equivalence

The inference rules are the basic tools we use in constructing proofs. In this section, we will acquire some additional tools that involve logical equivalence. As we saw in the previous chapter (Section 9.4), two statements are logically equivalent when they have the same truth value for every combination of truth values their atomic component statements can have. We show that two statements are equivalent by constructing truth tables for each of them. If both statements are true on the same rows and false on the same rows, then they are equivalent; if their truth values differ on even a single row, then they are not equivalent. The statement forms $p \bullet q$ and $q \bullet p$ provide a simple example:

p	•	q
T	**T**	T
T	**F**	F
F	**F**	T
F	**F**	F

q	•	p
T	**T**	T
F	**F**	T
T	**F**	F
F	**F**	F

So how do we use equivalent statements in proof? Consider the following argument:

(B • A) ⊃ C

A • B

C

This looks like a simple case of *modus ponens*, but it isn't, because the second premise is not identical to the antecedent of the first. We need to replace the second premise with the equivalent statement B • A. We could do so using the inference rules simplification and conjunction:

1. (B • A) ⊃ C   Premise
2. A • B   / C   Premise / Conclusion
3. A   2 Simp
4. B   2 Simp
5. B • A   3,4 Conj
6. C   1,5 MP

We could accomplish the same thing more easily if we could just replace A • B with B • A in one step:

1. (B • A) ⊃ C   Premise
2. A • B   / C   Premise / Conclusion
3. B • A   2 [?]
4. C   1,3 MP

The replacement does not affect the validity of the argument, but it does make the proof much easier.

10.4A Rules of Equivalence

How shall we describe our justification for step 3? We could adopt a general rule allowing any statement to be replaced by any other statement equivalent to it. But there are many such equivalences, too many to remember. So once again, as with inference rules, it is customary to work with a limited set. Each equivalence rule specifies a pair of equivalent statement forms, and the rule authorizes us to replace any instance of one statement form with the corresponding instance of the other. We are going to use 10 equivalence rules altogether.

The equivalence we used in the proof above is called commutation:

Commutation (Com): $(p \bullet q) :: (q \bullet p)$

$(p \vee q) :: (q \vee p)$

The double colon, ::, is the symbol we use to assert the logical equivalence of two statement forms. As the name implies, this equivalence is like the commutative law for numbers: *x times y = y times x* and *x plus y = y plus x*. In the argument above, we used the conjunctive form of commutation, and we would put "Com" as our justification on line 3. Another equivalence rule that you may recognize from mathematics is

Association (Assoc): $[p \bullet (q \bullet r)] :: [(p \bullet q) \bullet r]$

$[p \vee (q \vee r)] :: [(p \vee q) \vee r]$

Whereas the commutation rules say that the *order* of conjuncts or disjuncts makes no difference in truth value, the association rules say that the *grouping* makes no difference, either. Note that Com and Assoc apply only to conjunction and disjunction, not to conditionals: $p \supset q$ is not equivalent to $q \supset p$, and $p \supset (q \supset r)$ is not equivalent to $(p \supset q) \supset r$.

The third equivalence rule is an obvious one known as tautology. When Robert Frost says he has "miles to go before I sleep, and miles to go before I sleep," the repetition is merely for dramatic effect. The conjunction of a statement with itself, $p \bullet p$, says nothing more or less than p. The same is true for the disjunction of a statement with itself: $p \vee p$. (Imagine a child being offered the following "choice" by a parent: You can clean your room, or you can clean your room.) So the rule is

Tautology (Taut): $p :: (p \bullet p)$

$p :: (p \vee p)$

The next equivalence is one we've seen before:

Double negation (DN): $p :: {\sim}{\sim}p$

As we noted, negation is an on/off switch, so the two signs on the right cancel out. You'll need to use DN more often than you might think. If you had the two premises ~A ∨ B and A, for example, it would be natural to infer B by disjunctive syllogism. Strictly speaking, however, DS can be applied only when you have the negation of one of the disjuncts. The negation of ~A is ~~A, so you cannot use the inference rule DS until you have used the equivalence rule DN to replace A with ~~A.

Disjunctive syllogism	Proof		
p ∨ q	1. ~A ∨ B		Premise
~p	2. A	/ B	Premise / Conclusion
q	3. ~~A		2 DN
	4. B		1,3 DS

The next two rules are a little trickier, because they involve more than one kind of connective, but they should be obvious when you think them through. One is called distribution, and it may also be familiar from mathematics. The distributive law for numbers is that

$$a \times (b + c) = (a \times b) + (a \times c)$$

for example,

$$8 \times (5 + 7) = (8 \times 5) + (8 \times 7) = 96.$$

The multiplier a distributes across both of the numbers in the sum. A parallel principle equivalence holds for the connectives conjunction and disjunction, and (unlike with numbers) it works both ways.

Distribution (Dist): $[p \bullet (q \lor r)] :: [(p \bullet q) \lor (p \bullet r)]$

$[p \lor (q \bullet r)] :: [(p \lor q) \bullet (p \lor r)]$

We can illustrate the first distributive rule with an earlier example:

1a. I'll go home and either watch television or think $H \bullet (T \lor E)$
about the election.

1b. I'll go home and watch television or I'll go home $(H \bullet T) \lor (H \bullet E)$
and think about the election.

The two statements are obviously equivalent; they are just different ways of saying the same thing.

Another very important pair of equivalences are named after the nineteenth-century logician Augustus De Morgan:

De Morgan's law (DM): $\sim(p \bullet q) :: \sim p \lor \sim q$

$\sim(p \lor q) :: \sim p \bullet \sim q$

An example of the first equivalence is the statement "You can't have your cake and eat it too," $\sim(H \bullet E)$, which means that either you don't have your cake or you don't eat it: $\sim H \lor \sim E$. The second De Morgan equivalence is equally obvious. A statement of the form $\sim(p \lor q)$ would normally be expressed in English by "neither . . . nor," as in

2a. Cheating is neither honest nor smart. $\sim(H \lor S)$
2b. Cheating is not honest, and cheating is not smart. $\sim H \bullet \sim S$

De Morgan's law is useful because it allows us to get rid of a negated compound statement, which is often hard to work with in a proof.

Equivalence rules are based on the equivalence of two statement forms, using p, q, and r for the component propositions. As with the forms of inference we learned in the previous section, the instances of these components may themselves be compound rather than atomic statements. Thus, each of the following equivalences is an instance of the rule beside it in the list below:

$(A \lor B) \bullet C$ :: $C \bullet (A \lor B)$		Com
$[F \lor (G \supset H)] \lor K$ :: $F \lor [(G \supset H) \lor K]$		Assoc
$E \equiv M$ :: $(E \equiv M) \bullet (E \equiv M)$		Taut
$L \supset (N \lor P)$ :: $\sim\sim[L \supset (N \lor P)]$		DN
$(A \bullet B) \lor (C \bullet D)$ :: $[(A \bullet B) \lor C] \bullet [(A \bullet B) \lor D]$		Dist
$\sim[(O \supset R) \lor (O \supset S)]$ :: $\sim(O \supset R) \bullet \sim(O \supset S)$		DM

When we use equivalence rules in a proof, the basic procedure is the same as when we use inference rules: We add a new line to the proof and state the justification. For example:

1. (G ⊃ K) • (G ⊃ L)   Premise
2. ~L ∨ ~K   / ~G   Premise / Conclusion
3. ~K ∨ ~L   2 Com
4. ~G ∨ ~G   1,3 DD
5. ~G   4 Taut

Before we could draw a destructive dilemma inference from the two premises, we had to switch the order of disjuncts in premise 2, replacing ~L ∨ ~K with ~K ∨ ~L. The latter is entered as a new line (3), with the notation that it was derived from 2 by the equivalence rule of commutation. Similarly, we replaced ~G ∨ ~G in line 4 with ~G, noting that it was derived by the equivalence rule of tautology.

Despite that broad similarity in the procedures for using inference and equivalence rules, however, there are two very important differences.

The first difference is that an inference rule is a one-way street. It authorizes a step from premises to conclusion but not in the other direction. If we have the premises A ⊃ B and A, we can derive B by *modus ponens*, but from B alone we obviously cannot derive A ⊃ B or A. By contrast, an equivalence rule is a two-way street. If we have the statement K • (L ∨ M) on some line in a proof, we can use distribution to replace it with (K • L) ∨ (K • M). But if we have the latter, distribution allows us to replace it with the former.

The second difference is that we can apply equivalence rules to components of a statement on a previous line in a proof as well as to the statement as a whole. We cannot do this with inference rules. As we saw in the previous section, applying an inference rule to a component does not guarantee a valid inference. When we use an equivalence rule, however, we are simply replacing one statement with its equivalent. Whether we apply the rule to the whole statement on a previous line or to a component of a statement, the new statement has exactly the same truth conditions as the statement it replaces, and it will thus have all the same logical implications. Here is a simple example:

1. A • ~(C ∨ D)   / ~D   Premise / Conclusion
2. A • (~C • ~D)   1 DM
3. (A • ~C) • ~D   2 Assoc
4. ~D   3 Simp

In step 2, we used De Morgan's law to replace the component ~(C ∨ D) in premise 1 with ~C • ~D. Since these are equivalent, and thus have the same truth values, we are guaranteed that the whole statement on line 2 has the same truth values as the whole statement on line 1. Replacing one with the other cannot affect the validity of the argument as a whole (as we could easily confirm by the truth table test of validity). But the replacement does enable us—with the help of association in step 3—to use the inference rule simplification to derive ~D.

EXERCISE 10.4A

A. For each of the following statements, find a statement that is equivalent by the specified rule. Since equivalence rules apply to component parts of a statement as well as to the statement as a whole, there may be more than one right answer.

✳ 1.	B	Taut	8.	(J ⊃ L) • (~J ⊃ M)	DN
2.	A ∨ D	Com	9.	(F ⊃ G) • (H ⊃ I)	Com
3.	C ∨ (F ∨ G)	Assoc	✳10.	~[(A ≡ B) • O]	DM
✳ 4.	~E • ~N	DM	11.	(B ∨ F) ∨ [(E ⊃ ~G) •	
5.	H ⊃ J	DN		(E ⊃ H)]	Dist
6.	~A • (D ⊃ J)	Taut	12.	(K ∨ L) • [K • (M ≡ N)]	Assoc
✳ 7.	A • (K ∨ M)	Dist			

B. Each of the following statements is an instance of one of the equivalence rules we've examined so far. Identify the rule.

✳ 1. (A ∨ B) :: (B ∨ A)

2. [C ∨ (D • E)] ::
   [(C ∨ D) • (C ∨ E)]

3. ~(F • G) :: (~F ∨ ~G)

✳ 4. H :: ~~H

5. [J ∨ (K ∨ L)] :: [(J ∨ K) ∨ L]

6. A :: (A • A)

✳ 7. (A • B) :: (B • A)

8. [(M ⊃ N) • O] :: [O • (M ⊃ N)]

9. [B • (C • D)] :: [(B • C) • D]

✳10. [F • (G ∨ H)] :: [(F • G) ∨ (F • H)]

11. (H ∨ I) :: ~~(H ∨ I)

12. (A • B) :: [(A • B) ∨ (A • B)]

✳13. [~H • ~(G ≡ I)] :: ~[H ∨ (G ≡ I)]

14. [(A ∨ ~B) ⊃ (C • D)] ::
   [(A ∨ ~B) ⊃ (~~C • D)]

15. [~C • ~(D ∨ E)] :: ~[C ∨ (D ∨ E)]

✳16. {~~D ∨ [(A • B) ≡ ~C]} ::
   {[(A • B) ≡ ~C] ∨ ~~D}

17. {~L • [(M ⊃ N) ∨ (M ⊃ ~N)]} ::
   {[~L • (M ⊃ N)] ∨ [~L • (M ⊃
   ~N)]}

18. {[(H • J) ∨ ~K] ∨ (G ⊃ K)} ::
   {(H • J) ∨ [~K ∨ (G ⊃ K)]}

✳19. [(F ⊃ E) ∨ ~(C ∨ E)] ::
   {[(F ⊃ E) ∨ ~(C ∨ E)] • [(F ⊃ E) ∨
   ~(C ∨ E)]}

20. ~{[(K ∨ L) ⊃ (M • ~N)] • O} ::
   {~[(K ∨ L) ⊃ (M • ~N)] ∨ ~O}

21. {(E ⊃ H) • [(F ⊃ I) ∨ G]} ::
   {[(E ⊃ H) • (F ⊃ I)] ∨ [(E ⊃ H)
   • G]}

C. Construct a proof for each of the following arguments, using the rules of equivalence we learned in this section (Com, Assoc, Taut, DN, Dist, and DM) along with the rules of inference from Section 10.3.

✳ 1. (A • A) ∨ ~~B
   A ∨ B

2. ~(A ∨ B)
   ~B • ~A

3. A ∨ (D ∨ C)
   C ∨ (A ∨ D)

✳ 4. ~(D ∨ E)
   ~D

5. D ∨ (E • G)
   <u>D ∨ E</u>

6. ~(~D ∨ E)
   <u>D • ~E</u>

∗ 7. A • (B ∨ C)
   <u>~(A • B)</u>
   A • C

8. ~~[A • (B ∨ C)]
   (A • B) ∨ (A • C)

9. (A • B) ∨ (C • D)
   (A • B) ∨ C

∗10. C ∨ ~D
   ~(~C • D)

11. A • [(B • B) ∨ C]
   (A • B) ∨ (A • C)

12. ~[A • ~(B • C)]
   (~A ∨ B) • (~A ∨ C)

∗13. (B ∨ C) ∨ D
   <u>~B   </u>
   C ∨ D

14. ~P ∨ (Q • R)
   <u>~Q   </u>
   ~P

15. (A • B) ∨ (C • D)
   C ∨ A

∗16. A • G
   <u>~G ∨ B</u>
   B ∨ F

17. A ⊃ B
   ~B ∨ C
   <u>A   </u>
   C

18. ~A ∨ ~C
   ~B ⊃ C
   <u>A   </u>
   B

∗19. E ∨ F
   ~G ∨ H
   <u>~(E ∨ H)</u>
   F • ~G

20. (D • E) ∨ (F • G)
   <u>(D ⊃ H) • (F ⊃ I)</u>
   H ∨ I

21. (D ⊃ C) ∨ (B ⊃ C)
   ~(E • A) ⊃ ~(D ⊃ C)
   <u>~E • ~C</u>
   ~B

10.4B Rules of Equivalence (Continued)

The preceding equivalence rules dealt with conjunction, disjunction, and negation. Another group of rules we're going to use pertains to conditionals and biconditionals. The first is

Contraposition (Contra):   (p ⊃ q) :: (~q ⊃ ~p)

We dealt with contraposition in Chapter 8, and you may recall our example:

3a. If it rained last night, the ground is wet.   R ⊃ W
3b. If the ground is not wet, it did not rain last night.   ~W ⊃ ~R

These statements are obviously equivalent. We use contraposition in proofs when it is easier to work with the contrapositive of a statement than with the statement itself. Suppose, for example, that we want to derive the statement R ⊃ S, either as the conclusion or as a step on the way to the conclusion. And suppose that earlier lines in the proof included the statements W ⊃ S and ~W ⊃ ~R. We could use contraposition to set up a hypothetical syllogism:

i.	W ⊃ S	Premise or already derived from premises
ii.	~W ⊃ ~R	Premise or already derived from premises
iii.	R ⊃ W	ii Contra
iv.	R ⊃ S	i, iii HS

Another rule was mentioned in connection with the truth-functional character of the conditional. We noticed that a conditional statement is true if either the antecedent is false or the consequent true. In other words, $p \supset q$ is equivalent to $\sim p \lor q$. An example of this equivalence in ordinary language would be

4a. If I stay for dinner, I'll have to listen to my uncle   S ⊃ L
doing his Elvis Presley impression.

4b. Either I don't stay for dinner or I'll have to listen   ~S ∨ L
to my uncle doing his Elvis Presley impression.

Notice what happens now when we apply double negation and De Morgan's law to the disjunction in 4b:

  ~S ∨ L
  ~S ∨ ~~L   DN
  ~(S • ~L)   DM

In terms of our example, the last line says

4c. I cannot stay for dinner *and* not listen to my uncle doing his Elvis Presley impression.

The equivalence of 4a and 4c reflects the fact that a conditional cannot be true if its antecedent is true and its consequent false. The equivalence rule therefore has two forms.

    Implication (Imp): $(p \supset q) :: (\sim p \lor q)$
                                        $:: \sim(p \bullet \sim q)$

The rule is so named because "implication" (or "material implication") is another name for the conditional.

Next we have two rules telling us how to transform a biconditional into equivalent statements.

    Biconditional (Bicon): $(p \equiv q) :: [(p \supset q) \bullet (q \supset p)]$
                                        $:: [(p \bullet q) \lor (\sim p \bullet \sim q)]$

The first rule captures the meaning of the biconditional: *p if and only if q*. The second rule follows from the way we introduced the connective "≡": A biconditional is true only if both components have the same truth values. These rules are essential when we encounter a biconditional statement in a proof because (as you may have noticed) none of the basic inference forms include biconditional statements. So to work with a biconditional statement in a proof, whether it is a premise or the conclusion, we normally have to replace it with one of the equivalent statements. Here's an example:

A ∨ (D ≡ C)

~A

~C ⊃ ~D

It is easy to see that the two premises can be used in a disjunctive syllogism to derive D ≡ C. But then what do we do? We need to use the biconditional equivalence rule to replace the biconditional connective. Which version of the rule should we use? Since the conclusion is a conditional statement, the natural choice is the first one. That will give us D ⊃ C, from which we can derive a conclusion by using contraposition:

1. A ∨ (D ≡ C)		Premise
2. ~A	/ ~C ⊃ ~D	Premise / Conclusion
3. D ≡ C		1,2 DS
4. (D ⊃ C) • (C ⊃ D)		3 Bicon
5. D ⊃ C		4 Simp
6. ~C ⊃ ~D		5 Contra

Our final rule is:

Exportation (Exp):   [(p • q) ⊃ r] :: [p ⊃ (q ⊃ r)]

This looks a little strange, but it makes sense when you think about it. Here is an example we have used before:

5a. If I got the breaks, and had the talent, I'd be a   (B • T) ⊃ S
Hollywood star.

The same statement in a different form would be

5b. If I got the breaks, then if I had the talent I'd be   B ⊃ (T ⊃ S)
a Hollywood star.

If we have a statement of the form (p • q) ⊃ r in a proof, exportation allows us to isolate p as an antecedent; if we have already derived p, we can then infer q ⊃ r. Conversely, if we have a statement of the form p ⊃ (q ⊃ r), exportation allows us to isolate r as a consequent; if we have already derived ~r, we can infer ~(p • q); or, if we have derived p • q, we can infer r.

We now have nine inference rules and 10 equivalence rules with which to construct proofs. As with the inference rules, the more familiar you are with the equivalence rules, the easier you will find it to recognize patterns in the arguments you are given, and that will make it easier to find the steps by which you can derive the conclusion from the premises. For both kinds of rules, the most important thing is to understand the logic of the rule—to understand why it allows a valid step in a proof. The deeper your understanding, the easier you will find it to construct proofs. The equivalence rules we have learned in this section do not change the basic strategy for constructing proofs that we discussed in connection with inference rules: to work forward from the premises and backward from the conclusion we are trying to reach. What equivalence rules add to

Hypothetical syllogism (HS)

$p \supset q$

$q \supset r$

$p \supset r$

Disjunctive syllogism (DS)

$p \lor q$ $p \lor q$

$\sim p$ or $\sim q$

q p

Simplification (Simp)

$p \bullet q$ or $p \bullet q$

p q

Conjunction (Conj)

p or p

q q

$p \bullet q$ $q \bullet p$

Addition (Add)

p or q

$p \lor q$ $p \lor q$

Constructive dilemma (CD)

$(p \supset q) \bullet (r \supset s)$

$p \lor r$

$q \lor s$

Destructive dilemma (DD)

$(p \supset q) \bullet (r \supset s)$

$\sim q \lor \sim s$

$\sim p \lor \sim r$

<u>Equivalence Rules</u>

Tautology (Taut)

$p :: (p \bullet p)$

$:: (p \lor p)$

Double negation (DN)

$p :: \sim\sim p$

Commutation (Com)

$(p \bullet q) :: (q \bullet p)$

$(p \lor q) :: (q \lor p)$

Association (Assoc)

$[p \bullet (q \bullet r)] :: [(p \bullet q) \bullet r]$

$[p \lor (q \lor r)] :: [(p \lor q) \lor r]$

Distribution (Dist)

$[p \bullet (q \lor r)] :: [(p \bullet q) \lor (p \bullet r)]$

$[p \lor (q \bullet r)] :: [(p \lor q) \bullet (p \lor r)]$

De Morgan's law (DM)

$\sim(p \bullet q) :: (\sim p \lor \sim q)$

$\sim(p \lor q) :: (\sim p \bullet \sim q)$

Contraposition (Contra)

$(p \supset q) :: (\sim q \supset \sim p)$

Implication (Imp)

$(p \supset q) :: (\sim p \lor q)$

$:: \sim(p \bullet \sim q)$

Biconditional (Bicon)

$(p \equiv q) :: [(p \supset q) \bullet (q \supset p)]$

$:: [(p \bullet q) \lor (\sim p \bullet \sim q)]$

Exportation (Exp)

$[(p \bullet q) \supset r] :: [p \supset (q \supset r)]$

Additional Exercises

A. Use the truth table method, either the full or the short form, to determine whether the following arguments are valid.

✳ 1. $A \supset B$

$\sim B \lor C$

$\sim A \lor C$

2. $D \bullet (E \lor F)$

$\sim F$

$D \supset E$

3. G ⊃ H

   ~G ⊃ H

   H

✳ 4. (M • N) ∨ (M • O)

    N ≡ O

    M

5. A ≡ B

   (A • C) ⊃ D

   B ∨ E

   D ∨ E

6. [(K ∨ L) • M] ⊃ N

   (L • M) ⊃ O

   ~O ⊃ K

✳ 7. (K ⊃ L) ⊃ (M ⊃ N)

    (K ⊃ M) ⊃ (L ⊃ N)

8. (A • B) ≡ (C • D)

   ~B ∨ ~D

   ~A • ~C

9. (F • G) ⊃ [H ⊃ (I • J)]

   G ⊃ H

   F ⊃ ~J

   ~F ∨ ~G

✳10. E ⊃ (F • G)

    H ⊃ (I ∨ J)

    F ⊃ (~I • ~J)

    ~(E • H)

11. A ⊃ [B ⊃ (C ⊃ D)]

   (C ⊃ D) ⊃ E

   F ∨ A

   F ∨ (B ⊃ E)

12. (G ⊃ H) • [(I ∨ J) ⊃ K]

   (G • I) ∨ (G • J)

   H • K

✳13. [A ∨ (B • C)] ⊃ D

    ~(D • E)

    A ⊃ E

    B • C

14. {F • [(G ∨ H) ⊃ (I • J)]} ⊃ (F ∨ G)

   F • I

   G ⊃ ~L

   ~K ⊃ (H ∨ ~J)

B. Each of the following is an instance of one of the basic inference forms. Identify the form.

✳ 1. (A ≡ B) • [C ⊃ (D • ~E)]

    A ≡ B

2. [(F ⊃ G) ∨ H] ∨ (G • I)

   ~[(F ⊃ G) ∨ H]

   G • I

3. [J ∨ (K • L)]

   [J ∨ (K • L)] ∨ (J ⊃ L)

✳ 4. ~I ⊃ [J • (K ∨ L)]

    J ⊃ (K ∨ I)

    {~I ⊃ [J • (K ∨ L)]} • [J ⊃ (K ∨ I)]

5. (A ∨ B) ⊃ ~(C ∨ D)

   ~(C ∨ D) ⊃ (A ∨ E)

   (A ∨ B) ⊃ (A ∨ E)

6. [(A • B) ⊃ C] • [(C ∨ D) ⊃ B]

   [(A • B) ∨ (C ∨ D)]

   C ∨ B

✳ 7. ~(E • F) ⊃ [(E ⊃ G) • (F ⊃ H)]

    ~(E • F)

    (E ⊃ G) • (F ⊃ H)

8. (M • N) ⊃ [(M ∨ O) • (N ∨ O)]

   ~[(M ∨ O) • (N ∨ O)]

   ~(M • N)

9. [(F ∨ G) ⊃ (G ∨ H)] • [(H • I) ⊃ J]

   ~(G ∨ H) ∨ ~J

   ~(F ∨ G) ∨ ~(H • I)

✳10. (K • L) ⊃ [M • (N ∨ O)]

    (K • L) ⊃ (M ⊃ O)

    {(K • L) ⊃ [M • (N ∨ O)]} • [(K • L) ⊃ (M ⊃ O)]

11. (A • B) ∨ [(A • C) ⊃ (B • C)]

   ~[(A • C) ⊃ (B • C)]

   A • B

12. $[(D \bullet E) \lor (D \bullet F)] \bullet [(E \bullet F) \lor (E \bullet D)]$
$\underline{}$
$(E \bullet F) \lor (E \bullet D)$

＊13. $[G \supset (H \bullet I)] \supset [J \bullet (I \supset K)]$
$\underline{[J \bullet (I \supset K)] \supset [(K \bullet G) \supset I]}$
$[G \supset (H \bullet I)] \supset [(K \bullet G) \supset I]$

14. $\{(L \lor M) \supset [N \supset (O \supset M)]\} \bullet [(L \bullet N) \supset \sim O]$
$\underline{(L \lor M) \lor (L \bullet N)}$
$[N \supset (O \supset M)] \lor \sim O$

15. $[(A \lor B) \bullet (C \lor D)] \supset \{A \supset [D \bullet (E \lor C)]\}$
$\underline{\sim\{A \supset [D \bullet (E \lor C)]\}}$
$\sim[(A \lor B) \bullet (C \lor D)]$

C. Each of the inferences below can be justified by one of the rules of equivalence. (The rule may have been applied to the whole premise or only to a component of the premise.) Name the rule.

＊ 1. $\underline{(A \bullet B) \lor C}$
$\sim\sim[(A \bullet B) \lor C]$

2. $\underline{[(D \lor E) \lor F] \supset G}$
$[D \lor (E \lor F)] \supset G$

3. $\underline{\sim\{(H \supset I) \lor [J \bullet (K \lor L)]\}}$
$\sim(H \supset I) \bullet \sim[J \bullet (K \lor L)]$

＊ 4. $\underline{[(A \lor B) \supset C] \supset (D \lor E)}$
$\sim[(A \lor B) \supset C] \lor (D \lor E)$

5. $\underline{[(F \bullet G) \bullet H] \supset (I \bullet J)}$
$\sim(I \bullet J) \supset \sim[(F \bullet G) \bullet H]$

6. $\underline{(K \lor L) \bullet [M \supset (N \bullet O)]}$
$[M \supset (N \bullet O)] \bullet (K \lor L)$

＊ 7. $\underline{(A \lor B) \supset (C \supset D)}$
$[(A \lor B) \supset (C \supset D)] \lor [(A \lor B) \supset (C \supset D)]$

8. $\underline{[(E \lor F) \bullet G] \supset [(H \bullet I) \supset (I \supset J)]}$
$[(E \lor F) \bullet G] \supset [\sim(H \bullet I) \lor (I \supset J)]$

9. $\underline{[(A \lor B) \supset C] \equiv (C \lor D)}$
$\{[(A \lor B) \supset C] \supset (C \lor D)\} \bullet \{(C \lor D) \supset [(A \lor B) \supset C]\}$

＊10. $\underline{[(E \bullet F) \bullet G] \supset [(E \lor H) \bullet (E \lor I)]}$
$(E \bullet F) \supset \{G \supset [(E \lor H) \bullet (E \lor I)]\}$

11. $\underline{(K \bullet L) \lor [(M \supset N) \bullet O]}$
$[(K \bullet L) \lor (M \supset N)] \bullet [(K \bullet L) \lor O]$

12. $\underline{\{(J \supset K) \supset [L \equiv (M \lor N)]\} \supset [J \supset (N \lor K)]}$
$\{(J \supset K) \supset [(L \bullet L) \equiv (M \lor N)]\} \supset [J \supset (N \lor K)]$

＊13. $\underline{[(A \bullet B) \lor C] \bullet [(A \lor C) \bullet (C \lor D)]}$
$[(A \bullet B) \lor C] \bullet [(C \lor A) \bullet (C \lor D)]$

14. $\underline{[(E \bullet F) \lor (G \bullet H)] \bullet [(E \bullet F) \lor (I \supset J)]}$
$(E \bullet F) \lor [(G \bullet H) \bullet (I \supset J)]$

15. $\underline{\sim\{[(K \lor L) \supset M] \bullet (N \lor O)\} \bullet [(L \bullet M) \supset N]}$
$\{\sim[(K \lor L) \supset M] \lor \sim(N \lor O)\} \bullet [(L \bullet M) \supset N]$

D. For each of the following proofs, state the justification for each line, giving the line(s) from which it was derived and the inference or equivalence rule by which it was derived.

＊ 1. 1. $A \supset (B \lor C)$ — Premise
2. $\sim B / \sim(A \bullet \sim C)$ — Premise / Conclusion
3. $\sim A \lor (B \lor C)$ — $\underline{}$
4. $\sim A \lor (C \lor B)$ — $\underline{}$
5. $(\sim A \lor C) \lor B$ — $\underline{}$
6. $\sim A \lor C$ — $\underline{}$
7. $\sim A \lor \sim\sim C$ — $\underline{}$
8. $\sim(A \bullet \sim C)$ — $\underline{}$

2. 1. (H • J) ⊃ K   Premise
   2. ~H ⊃ L   Premise
   3. ~(J ⊃ L) / J ⊃ K   Premise / Conclusion
   4. ~~J • ~L)   _____
   5. J • ~L   _____
   6. ~L   _____
   7. ~~H   _____
   8. H   _____
   9. H ⊃ (J ⊃ K)   _____
  10. J ⊃ K   _____

3. 1. (D ⊃ E) • (F ⊃ G)   Premise
   2. D ≡ ~G   Premise
   3. D / E • ~F   Premise / Conclusion
   4. (D ⊃ ~G) • (~G ⊃ D) _____
   5. D ⊃ ~G   _____
   6. ~G   _____
   7. F ⊃ G   _____
   8. ~F   _____
   9. D ⊃ E   _____
  10. E   _____
  11. E • ~F   _____

✱ 4. 1. (A • B) ⊃ ~C   Premise
   2. (C ⊃ E) ⊃ D   Premise
   3. ~D • B / ~A   Premise / Conclusion
   4. ~D   _____
   5. ~(C ⊃ E)   _____
   6. ~~(C • ~E)   _____
   7. C • ~E   _____
   8. C   _____
   9. ~~C   _____
  10. ~(A • B)   _____
  11. ~A ∨ ~B   _____
  12. B   _____
  13. ~~B   _____
  14. ~A   _____

5. 1. (M ∨ N) ∨ (P • R)   Premise
   2. S ⊃ ~P   Premise
   3. M ⊃ R   Premise
   4. N ⊃ Q / S ⊃ (R ∨ Q)   Premise / Conclusion
     5. S   _____
     6. ~P   _____
     7. ~P ∨ ~R   _____
     8. ~(P • R)   _____
     9. M ∨ N   _____
   10. (M ⊃ R) • (N ⊃ Q)   _____
   11. R ∨ Q   _____
   12. S ⊃ (R ∨ Q)   _____

E. Translate each of the arguments below into symbolic notation, and test it for validity by the truth table method. If it is valid, construct a proof.

✳ 1. It's possible that the earth's continents were once joined in a single giant landmass. The reason is that the earth's crust is divided into separate tectonic plates. If earthquakes occur, and they do, then the plates must be moving. If the crust is divided into separate plates and the plates are moving, then it's possible that the continents were once joined in a single giant landmass.

2. The patient reported headaches, fatigue, and loss of interest in normal activities. When these symptoms occur, the condition is either sleep deprivation or depression. If he is sleep-deprived, sleeping pills would eliminate his symptoms; but they did not. Therefore he is depressed.

3. If the boss snaps at you if you make a mistake, he's irritable. So, if he's irritable and you make a mistake, he'll snap at you.

✳ 4. Smith is guilty of burglary if and only if he took the goods from Jones's residence and she did not consent to their removal. Smith did take the goods, but Jones consented. So Smith is not guilty of burglary.

5. Either human beings as a species evolved in Africa and later dispersed in migration to various other regions or their precursors migrated at an earlier time and modern humans evolved independently in various regions. If the precursors of humans migrated at an earlier time, then it should not be the case—and it is—that we find their remains only in Africa. Therefore humans evolved in Africa.

6. Identical twins are formed 5 days after conception, when the cell cluster divides in two and each half attaches separately to the uterine wall. If personhood begins at conception, then there is a person present before the cell division. If so, that person either (a) is identical with both of the persons who come to exist after cell division; or (b) dies and is replaced by those two persons; or (c) is identical with one but not the other of those persons. But none of those alternatives can be the case. Therefore personhood does not begin at conception.

✳ 7. Either human choices are determined by antecedent factors or they are free. If human choices are determined by antecedent factors, then we cannot act in any way different from the way we do act. If so, then we are not morally responsible for our actions. But we *are* morally responsible for our actions, so our choices must be free.

8. Either human choices are determined by antecedent factors or they are free. If human choices are free, then they are uncaused; if they are uncaused, they are random; and if they are random, then we are not responsible for them. Since we are responsible for our choices, they must be determined by antecedent factors.

9. Gravity is solely an attractive force. If so, then if the universe is not expanding, it is contracting due to gravitational attraction. But if the universe were contracting, the average density of matter in space would be increasing, and it isn't. So the universe is expanding.

*10. At the trial of Ken Giscan for the murder of Alice Lovelace, the judge instructed the jury that Giscan is guilty if and only if he had a motive, he possessed the murder weapon, and he was not with Sally Alibi at the time of the murder. The facts established at trial were these: Lovelace had ended her relationship with Giscan; Giscan was with Alibi at the time of the murder only if Alibi was telling the truth; if Alibi is jealous, she was not telling the truth; if Lovelace ended the relationship, then Giscan had a motive and Alibi was jealous; Giscan possessed the murder weapon. Therefore, Giscan is guilty.

11. It's a sure bet that the antacid division of the Hi-5 corporation is going to be sold. Hi-5 stock is going to decline unless the company improves its profits or the economy as a whole improves. The company will not improve its profits unless it sells the antacid division. However, if Hi-5 stock declines, the company will be taken over and its antacid division will be sold.

12. Maritania has threatened to attack our commercial vessels in the shipping lanes off its shores. If we take preventive action and the threat is not real, we will be denounced for aggression. If the threat is real and we do not take preventive action, the attack will succeed; and if it succeeds, lives will be lost and further attacks will be encouraged in the future. None of these consequences is acceptable. We shall not be denounced for aggression, and we shall neither lose lives nor encourage future attacks. Therefore we will take preventive action if and only if the threat is real.

*13. Why read books? Either a book repeats what is in the Bible, in which case, if you read it, you are wasting your time; or it contradicts what is in the Bible, in which case, if you read it, you are committing a sin. One should neither waste time nor commit a sin. Therefore one should not read a book.

14. If the traditional religious view is correct, God is both omnipotent and perfectly benevolent. If God is omnipotent, He is capable of preventing evil, and if He is perfectly benevolent, he would want to prevent evil. But if God wanted to prevent evil, and was capable of doing so, then there would be no evil, and there is. So the traditional religious view is not correct.

15. If I take his pawn with my knight, he will either take my knight or move his bishop to the space my knight is now guarding. If he takes my knight, I'll lose a valuable piece, but his queen will be exposed. If he moves his bishop to that space, *my* queen will be exposed. But if I don't take his pawn with my knight, my queen will be exposed anyway. I'm going to either take his pawn or not take it. So either his queen or mine will be exposed.

F. Show that each of the following arguments is valid by constructing a proof.

✳ 1. ~C
   C ⊃ D

2. (A ≡ B) • C
   (A ≡ B) ∨ C

3. ~(A ∨ B)
   ~B

✳ 4. B ⊃ D
   B ⊃ (B ⊃ D)

5. A ⊃ B
   B ∨ ~A

6. D ∨ E
   ~D ⊃ E

✳ 7. A ⊃ ~F
   F ⊃ ~A

8. B • {[~(D ≡ E) • (B ≡ C)] ∨ (G ⊃ A)}
   B ∨ (A • E)

9. H ⊃ (I • G)
   I ⊃ (G ⊃ F)
   H ⊃ F

✳10. (A ⊃ C) • (B ⊃ C)
   A ∨ B
   C

11. C
   D ⊃ C

12. ~B ∨ (C • D)
   B ⊃ C

✳13. E ⊃ (F ⊃ G)
   F ⊃ (E ⊃ G)

14. ~D
   (A • B) ∨ (C ∨ D)
   (A • B) ∨ C

15. (A ≡ B) • C
   D
   (A ≡ B) • D

✳16. ~C ∨ ~D
   C
   ~D

17. ~(D • G)
   ~~G
   ~D

18. (D ∨ E) ∨ H
   (D ∨ H) ∨ E

✳19. [~(D ≡ E) • (B ≡ C)] ∨ (G ⊃ A)
   ~[~(D ≡ E) • (B ≡ C)]
   G
   A

20. A ⊃ (B ≡ C)
   ~(D ≡ E)
   A
   ~(D ≡ E) • (B ≡ C)

21. (A • B) ∨ (C ∨ D)
   ~A
   C ∨ D

✳22. W ⊃ X
   ~Y ⊃ ~X
   W ⊃ Y

23. (D • E) ⊃ F
   (D ⊃ F) ⊃ G
   E ⊃ G

24. (H ∨ I) ⊃ [J • (K • L)]
   I
   J • K

✳25. A ⊃ B
   (C ⊃ D) • (E ≡ G)
   A ∨ C
   B ∨ D

26. ~[(A • B) ∨ C]
   (A • B) ∨ (C ∨ D)
   D

27. D
   ~D ∨ (E ≡ F)
   ~E ⊃ ~F

✳28. A ⊃ (B • C)
   ~(A ⊃ D)
   B

29. (E ∨ F) ⊃ G
   ~H ⊃ F
   <u>~G   </u>
   H • ~E

30. A ⊃ (B ⊃ C)
   (~D ∨ E) ⊃ (F ∨ G)
   <u>~(D ⊃ E) ⊃ (B • ~C)</u>
   A ⊃ (F ∨ G)

∗31. (H • I) ⊃ J
   <u>(I ⊃ J) ⊃ (K ∨ L)</u>
   ~L ⊃ (H ⊃ K)

32. A • (B ⊃ C)
   <u>(B • ~A) ∨ (B • D)</u>
   C • D

33. [(A ∨ B) • C] ⊃ [(A ∨ D) • (A ∨ E)]
   <u>C • ~A</u>
   B ⊃ (D • E)

∗34. (~E • F) ⊃ G
   (H • J) ⊃ (E ∨ J)
   <u>~E • (F ∨ ~J)</u>
   H ⊃ (J ⊃ G)

35. (F • G) ⊃ [H ⊃ (I • J)]
   G ⊃ ~J
   <u>F ⊃ H</u>
   ~F ∨ ~G

36. ~(A • B) ⊃ [C ⊃ (D ⊃ E)]
   [(A • B) ∨ F] ⊃ (G • H)
   [(C • D) ⊃ E] ⊃ I
   <u>J ⊃ (G ⊃ ~H)</u>
   J ⊃ I

∗37. <u>[K ⊃ (L ⊃ K)] ⊃ (~M ⊃ M)</u>
   M

38. [(G • H) ⊃ (I ∨ J)] ⊃ ~G
   <u>(K ∨ G) ⊃ (I • L)</u>
   ~G

39. (A ⊃ B) • ~(C ⊃ D)
   ~A ⊃ D
   <u>[(A • C) ∨ B] ⊃ E</u>
   G ⊃ E

∗40. [(A • B) ∨ C] ⊃ [D ⊃ (E • F)]
   <u>B • ~(A ⊃ E)</u>
   D ⊃ F

41. (G • H) ∨ [(I ∨ J) • (K ⊃ L)]
   (J ⊃ M) • ~I
   <u>G ≡ N</u>
   M ∨ N

42. A ≡ B
   [(C ⊃ D) • ~D] ∨ [A • ~(C • ~D)]
   <u>(B ∨ E) ⊃ F</u>
   C ⊃ F

∗43. (A ∨ B) ⊃ [~(C • D) ⊃ E]
   B • C
   E ⊃ (F ∨ G)
   <u>(B ⊃ ~F) • (C ⊃ ~G)</u>
   D

44. H ≡ {I • [(J • K) ∨ (L • M)]}
   <u>[I • (K ∨ L)] ⊃ N</u>
   H ⊃ N

45. (A • ~B) ⊃ (C • D)
   E • ~F
   (G • E) ⊃ ~(A ≡ B)
   <u>(B • ~A) ⊃ F</u>
   G ⊃ C

∗46. H ⊃ {I • [(J • K) ⊃ (L • M)]}
   <u>K ⊃ ~(I • L)</u>
   J ⊃ ~(H • K)

47. (H ≡ J) ∨ (H ≡ K)
   J ⊃ (L • M)
   K ⊃ (N • M)
   <u>H   </u>
   M

Predicate Logic

Propositional logic allows us to analyze arguments that depend on logical relationships among propositions. The units of analysis are component propositions—p, q, r, etc.—along with the truth-functional connectives that create compound propositions. But some arguments require a finer-grained analysis. An obvious example is the categorical syllogism:

No herbivore eats meat.
All horses are herbivores.
No horse eats meat.

Neither the premises nor the conclusion of this argument are compound, so the representation of the argument in propositional logic would be

p
q
r

which gives no clue that the argument is valid. To understand its validity, we need to break the propositions down into their elements, and this is the function of *predicate logic*.

Like the traditional logic of categorical syllogisms (see Chapter 7), predicate logic breaks a proposition down into a subject and a predicate. The subject is what the statement is about; the predicate is what the statement says about the subject. But predicate logic analyzes the subject–predicate relationship in a way that is different from traditional logic. In the first three sections of this chapter, we'll go over the symbolic notation that is used to represent the inner structure of propositions. Then we'll go on to learn a few new rules of inference and see how to use them (along with the propositional rules from the past chapter) in constructing proofs. Finally, we will see how predicate logic can handle statements about relationships among things.

11.1 Singular and Quantified Statements

11.1A Singular Statements

To understand how to analyze statements in predicate logic, we begin by distinguishing the subject of a statement from the predicate. The subject is the part of the sentence that specifies what the statement is about; the predicate is the part that specifies what we are saying about the subject. In the following examples, the subject is in boldface, and the rest of the sentence is the predicate.

1. **London** is a city.
2. **Jane** got married last Saturday.
3. **Our family** lives in a white house.
4. **Our house** is the last one on the right.
5. **The Civil War** was caused by many factors.
6. Totally unprepared am **I**.
7. **The Milky Way galaxy** is immense.
8. Down the chimney came **Santa**.
9. **Cyprus** was a major source of copper in the Bronze Age.
10. On my left is **Mr. Keith Richards**.

In English, the subject normally comes first, but that is not always the case. In 6, the phrase "totally unprepared" is not the subject; it designates a property of the actual subject, "I" (actually, Leisl in *The Sound of Music*). In the same way, the subject comes last in 8 and 10. Nevertheless, "Santa" and "Mr. Keith Richards," respectively, are the subjects of the statements because they name the thing that we're talking about. In each of the examples, the rest of the statement is the predicate, whose function is to say something about what is named. The predicate may indicate a category to which the thing belongs (as in 1), an attribute of the thing (as in 4, 6, 7, 9, and 10), an action (as in 2, 3, and 8), or a causal explanation (as in 5)—there are many kinds of statements we can make about things.

Every statement has a subject–predicate structure. But each of our examples belongs to the subcategory of **singular statements**. A singular statement is about a single thing, as opposed to a general statement about a class of things. The thing can be a person (Jane, Keith Richards), a place (London, Cyprus), an event (the Civil War), or an object (our house). It can be a group that is treated as a single unit, like "our family" in 3. Even 7 is a singular statement; although our galaxy contains a great many things, the statement treats it as a single unit, as opposed to a general statement about galaxies (e.g., galaxies tend to have spiral shapes). And even if the thing does not actually exist, as in 8 (you knew that, right?), the statement at least purports to refer to an individual.

To represent singular statements symbolically, we need two symbols, one for the subject, and one for the predicate. It is conventional to use capital letters for predicates, lowercase letters for subjects, with the predicate letter given first. Thus our examples would be put into predicate notation as follows:

	Subject	Predicate	Symbolic
1.	**l**ondon	is a **C**ity.	Cl
2.	**j**ane	got **M**arried last Saturday.	Mj
3.	**w**e	**L**ive in a white house.	Lw
4.	our **h**ouse	is the last one on the **R**ight.	Rh
5.	the **c**ivil war	was **C**aused by many factors.	Cc
6.	**i**	am totally **U**nprepared.	Ui
7.	the **m**ilky way	is **I**mmense.	Im
8.	**c**yprus	was a major source of **C**opper in the Bronze Age.	Cc
9.	**s**anta	**C**ame down the chimney.	Cs
10.	mr. **k**eith richards	is on my **L**eft.	Lk

This notation may seem foreign at first, since it reverses the order of English grammar. It's a bit like Yoda-speak in *Star Wars* ("Strong am I with the Force"). It may help to think of the symbolic formula as saying that the predicate is true of the subject: Being a city (C) is true of London (l); getting married last Saturday (M) is true of Jane (j), and so on.

In the 10 examples of actual statements, we used letters keyed to the subject and predicate. When we are working with statement *forms* rather than actual examples, it is customary to use *a, b, c, . . .* as subjects and *P, Q, R, . . .* as predicates. Thus we can say that singular statements have the form "*a* is *P*," where *a* is the name of something and *P* is what we're saying about it, so the statement will look like this: *Pa*. These subject–predicate pairs are the atomic statements in predicate logic, just as *p, q, r*, etc., are the atomic statements in propositional logic. And, as in propositional logic, singular statements can be combined into compound statements by means of propositional connectives. Indeed, everything we learned about propositional logic applies to them. Here are some examples:

	Statement	Symbolic
11.	If London is a city, it has a mayor.	Cl ⊃ Ml
12.	Scotland is not a city.	~Cs
13.	If Cyprus was a major source of copper in the Bronze Age, then Egypt imported copper.	Cc ⊃ Ie
14.	Jane got married last Saturday and so did Tamara.	Mj • Mt
15.	Harry's car is an orange convertible.	Oc • Cc
16.	I will be either at home or in New York.	Hi ∨ Ni
17.	If the moon is out tonight and the sea is calm, I'll go for a sail or a walk on the beach.	(Om • Cs) ⊃ (Si ∨ Wi)

Note that the atomic components in these compound statements may have the same subject, as in 11, 15, and 16. The atomic components can also have the same predicate, as in 14, or differ in both subject and predicate, as in 13. In 15, we could have treated "orange convertible" as a single predicate, but since the color and the type of car are independent characteristics, we can also make them separate predicates ascribed to the car. These differences in structure would not be evident if we represented the statements simply as propositions—*p, q, r*, etc. The predicate notation includes more of the statement's structure than does the propositional notation we studied in the preceding two chapters. We will make use of that additional structure in a moment. But for now the important point is that everything we learned about using connectives to combine atomic statements applies to predicate as well as propositional notation.

EXERCISE 11.1A

Put each of the following statements into symbolic notation.

＊1. Tobias is bored.

2. Governor Smith is a crook.

3. The solar system is billions of years old.

＊4. London Bridge is falling down.

5. Tom's car is a Volkswagen but Sally's car is a Rolls.

6. I'm confused and she is not helping.

＊7. Randy Newman is not a short guy but Napoleon was.

8. The ninja kicked and spun.

9. Monaco is either a big city or a small nation.

＊10. Jim Jones is either crazy or thirsty.

11. I am sick and tired.

12. If the paint is dry, the wall is finished.

＊13. Luminous beings are we, not this crude matter. (—Yoda)

14. The printer works but the fax is broken.

15. If we win, we'll either go dancing or go to a movie.

＊16. Macbeth was a tyrant with a conscience.

17. I am firm, you are stubborn, and he is obstinate.

18. If I fail this course or get a low grade, I will change my major.

＊19. If Saudi Arabia lowers the price of oil or the Iraq war ends, then Obama will be reelected.

20. If Julius Caesar crosses the Rubicon and maintains his popular support, then Pompey will rally his forces if he has Senate support.

21. If Sofia didn't answer my e-mail, she didn't receive it or she is mad.

＊22. If the streets are clear, I'll drive, but if not, I'll take the train.

23. If Angelina Jolie retires or has a baby, then she will not make movies.

24. If Ashwin runs any faster, he'll break the record or at least win.

＊25. Whether the baby is a boy or a girl, its name will be Jamie.

11.1B Quantified Statements

Suppose we want to make a statement about a class of things rather than an individual object—for example, "All cities have mayors." How can we formulate that statement in the notation of predicate logic? We can't take the predicate C ("is a city") and make it the subject: MC. The literal translation of this would be "is a city has a mayor," which doesn't make any sense. Instead, predicate logic uses a device called the bound variable. In this section, we will see how the device works. In Section 11.2, we will see how it applies to statements like "All cities have mayors."

Suppose someone says, "It is a city." The subject term "it" is a pronoun without an antecedent. We would assume that "it" stands for something, but we wouldn't know what; it could stand for anything. In logic, we would represent such an "it" by the letter x, and the statement "it is a city" would be symbolized Cx. The letter x functions as a **variable**, as in an algebraic equation. In the equation $x + x = 2x$, for example, x stands for *any* number, without specifying which number. In the same way, the x in Cx can stand for any individual thing without specifying which thing.

The formula Cx—"x is a city"—is not a complete statement. A statement has to say something that is either true or false, but that is not the case with Cx (imagine seeing "x is a city" on a true–false test—quick, which is it, true or false?). The variable x can stand for anything that exists, so we at least need to specify whether our statement concerns everything that exists or only some things. We can accomplish this by introducing a **quantifier**, which tells us whether Cx is being asserted of all x (everything in the world) or of some x (at least one thing in the world).

In the first case, we use a **universal quantifier**, symbolized by an x in parentheses at the front of the statement: $(x)Cx$. Any of the following would be a literal translation of this formula:

> For all x, x is a city.
> Take anything whatever: it is a city.
> "It is a city" is true of everything.

All of these are ways of saying that everything is a city. Of course this statement is quite false. You and I and the Liberty Bell are all individual things in the world, and none of us is a city. At most we can say that some things are cities. To make this statement, we use the **existential quantifier**, symbolized by a backward E and placed, once again, in parentheses at the front of the statement: $(\exists x)Cx$. Any of the following would be a literal translation:

> For some x (one or more), x is a city.
> There exists something such that it is a city.
> "It is a city" is true of at least one thing.

All of these are equivalent to the statement in ordinary English that something is a city.

An expression of the form Px is called an **open sentence**, and its variable is said to be a **free variable**. When we preface the sentence with a quantifier, the variable is said to be a **bound variable**. The quantifier binds the variable by telling us how to interpret it, and the result is a **closed sentence** or statement. The use of a quantifier, then, completes a statement containing a variable. It turns an open sentence, which has no truth value, into a statement that is either true or false.

The universal and existential quantifiers are the only ones used in the basic-level predicate logic we are studying. As with the traditional logic of syllogisms, predicate logic recognizes only two degrees of quantity: all, and at least one. In ordinary language, of course, we have terms for many intermediate degrees, such as "few," "many," or "most." But statements involving such terms must be put into symbolic form using the existential quantifier.

It is important to distinguish both kinds of quantified statement from singular statements. A singular statement is about a particular thing, and we refer to the subject by name or by a description such as "our house," "the dog," or "that man I met last night." In symbolic notation, we use a lowercase letter as the subject of the statement, and we do not use a quantifier of either kind. In a quantified statement, by contrast, the subject is a variable that can stand for anything. So we must use a quantifier to specify whether the statement applies to everything or only to some things. Thus, predicate logic uses three types of statement:

Type	Example	Symbolic Notation	Quantifier	Predicate	Subject
Singular	My father is alive.	Af	None	A	f
Quantified					
Existential	Some things are alive. There are living things.	$(\exists x)Ax$	$(\exists x)$	A	x
Universal	Everything is alive.	$(x)Ax$	(x)	A	x

In principle, we could use any letter in the alphabet as a variable. To avoid confusing variables with names, however, it is conventional to reserve the last three letters for variables: x, y, z. It does not matter which one we use. What does matter is that the quantifier use the same letter: $(x)Px, (y)Ry, (\exists z)Qz$, etc. If the quantifier does *not* use the same letter, the result is not a statement. Thus in the formula $(\exists z)Sy$, the existential quantifier does not bind the variable y, which therefore remains free; Sy remains an open sentence; and it has no truth value because we do not know whether we are asserting the predicate S of all y or only of some.

EXERCISE 11.1B

Put each of the following statements into symbolic notation.

✱1. Everything is illuminated.
2. Something smells.
3. Everything has a purpose.
✱4. Everything is groovy.
5. Everything is edible.
6. All things change.
✱7. There's something coming for us.
8. Everything is for sale.

9. Some things are falling apart.
✱10. Everything is made of atoms.
11. There was an explosion.
12. Some things are lighter than air.
✱13. There's a reason for everything.
14. There are ghosts.
15. Some things are better left unsaid.

11.2 Categorical Statements

Now that we understand how variables and quantifiers work, let's return to the question of how to symbolize a statement about the members of a class of things—a statement such as

1a. All cities have mayors.

"Cities" is the grammatical subject of the statement, but it cannot be the subject in logical notation. The only things that can be subjects in predicate logic are (a) names or phrases that refer to a particular individual thing and (b) variables that can stand for any individual thing. But "city" is a general term referring to a certain category or class of places. It can be part of the predicate in a statement like "London is a city" (Cl). As we saw in the previous section, however, we can't take that predicate and make it the subject—MC. So how can we translate 1a into predicate notation?

The first clue is the word "all," which suggests that a universal quantifier is involved, which in turn implies that we will need to use a variable. But remember that a variable can stand for anything whatever. Statement 1a does not say that everything is a city, nor that everything has a mayor. But it does imply that *if* something is a city, *then* it has a mayor. This is the second clue to the symbolic translation. A statement of this form is treated as a conditional statement, with the same variable used as the subject in both antecedent and consequent, bound by the universal quantifier. Thus:

1b. $(x)(Cx \supset Mx)$ For all x, if x is a city, then x has a mayor.

In 1b, "is a city" is a predicate, as it has to be, and the subject of both Cx and Mx is the variable x. The translation uses both the bound variable of predicate logic and a connective from propositional logic.

The two atomic statements in which the variable occurs, Cx and Mx, are placed within a pair of parentheses immediately after the quantifier. This is to indicate that the quantifier applies to the entire statement and binds the variable in both occurrences. If we did not use parentheses—$(x)Cx \supset Mx$—the quantifier would apply only to Cx, and Mx would remain an open sentence with a free variable. To have a closed sentence, or statement, we must use parentheses to bring both variables within the **scope** of a quantifier. In this respect, a quantifier is like a negation sign. The difference between

$(x)Cx \supset Mx$ and $(x)(Cx \supset Mx)$

is like the difference between

$\sim C \supset M$ and $\sim(C \supset M)$.

In traditional syllogistic logic, the statement form "All *S* are *P*" is one of the four basic types of categorical statement. The four types are distinguished in terms of their quantity (universal or particular) and their quality (affirmative or negative):

	Affirmative	*Negative*
Universal	All *S* are *P*.	No *S* is *P*.
Particular	Some *S* are *P*.	Some *S* are not *P*.

We have just seen how modern predicate logic would deal with universal affirmative statements. What about the others? A statement such as

2a. No city is entirely fireproof

is also universal but it is negative. In traditional logic, the word "No" serves two functions: It indicates both universal quantity and negative quality. In modern predicate logic, we separate those functions, as we would in English if we had expressed 2a as "*Every* city is *not* entirely fireproof." So we use the universal quantifier, but we negate the consequent:

2b. $(x)(Cx \supset \sim Fx)$ For all x, if x is a city, then x is not entirely fireproof.

For particular statements, the word "some" suggests that we use the existential quantifier. And the connective has to be conjunction rather than the conditional. For example,

3a. Some tests are difficult

tells us that something—at least one thing in the world—is both a test and difficult. So the symbolic translation would be the existential statement

3b. $(\exists x)(Tx \bullet Dx)$ For some x, x is a test and x is difficult.

The negative statement

4a. Some tests are not difficult

would be translated in a similar way:

4b. $(\exists x)(Tx \bullet \sim Dx)$ For some x, x is a test and x is not difficult.

Why do we use different connectives for universal and existential statements? Why not use the same connective? Well, let's try it. The way to tell whether a symbolic formula is a good translation of an English sentence is to ask whether they have the same truth value. If the English sentence is true but the symbolic formula is false, or vice versa, then we don't have an accurate translation. Suppose, then, that we use conjunction for a universal statement. For example,

5. Every accountant understands arithmetic. $(x)(Ax \bullet Ux)$ [error]

This won't work because the English statement is true, but the symbolic statement is obviously false. It says that everything in the universe is both an accountant and understands arithmetic. What the English statement actually means is that if something is an accountant, then it (he or she) understands arithmetic. That's why we have to treat these universal statements as conditionals. The symbolic representation of 5 is therefore $(x)(Ax \supset Ux)$.

Conversely, suppose we try to translate a particular statement as a conditional. It's a little trickier to see why this won't work. Consider first a true English sentence:

6. Some rocks are sedimentary. $(\exists x)(Rx \supset Sx)$ [error]

The symbolic statement says that for some x, if x is a rock, then x is sedimentary. And that's true. The problem is that the symbolic statement is true not only of certain rocks (the ones that are sedimentary) but also of anything that is not a rock at all. For something that is not a rock, the antecedent of the conditional is false, which makes the conditional itself true. To see why this difference between the English and the symbolic statements is a problem, let's take a sentence that is clearly false:

7. **Some rocks are lighter than air.** $(\exists x)(Rx \supset Lx)$ [error]

Both the English sentence and the symbolic formula are false in regard to the category of rocks. For any x that is a rock, the antecedent of the symbolic formula, Rx, is true but the consequent Lx is false, which makes the conditional statement false. But for something that is *not* a rock, the antecedent of the conditional is false, which makes the conditional *true* even though the English sentence is false. So we cannot translate particular statements as conditionals; we have to use conjunction, $(\exists x)(Rx \bullet Lx)$.

For predicate logic, then, the diagram for the four statement types is as follows:

	Affirmative	*Negative*
Universal	$(x)(Sx \supset Px)$ For all x, if x is S, then x is P.	$(x)(Sx \supset {\sim}Px)$ For all x, if x is S, then x is not-P.
Existential	$(\exists x)(Sx \bullet Px)$ For some x, x is S and x is P.	$(\exists x)(Sx \bullet {\sim}Px)$ For some x, x is S and x is not-P.

Notice that in modern predicate logic we refer to "Some" statements as *existential* rather than *particular*—which is the term used in syllogistic logic. The terminology indicates that the quantifier $(\exists x)$ does double duty: It is a statement of quantity (some x rather than all x) and it is a statement of existence (there exists at least one x). The existence component raises the issue of existential import (discussed previously in Chapter 6). A categorical statement has existential import if its truth depends on the existence of objects in the subject category. Traditional logic tended to assume that all four of the standard categorical statements have existential import. Modern logic holds that particular/existential statements have existential import but that universal ones do not. One can make a case for either view, depending on which examples one chooses. On the one hand, the statement "No flying saucers were sighted over Atlanta last night" seems true even if there are no flying saucers at all; on the other hand, the statement "All of my first edition books were stolen" seems false if I never had any first edition books. Among particular/existential statements, there are similar contrasting cases. A statement of the form *Some S is (or is not) P* normally implies that the S or Ss in question exist. But what about "Some witches are good" and "Some witches are bad," as in the world of *Wizard of Oz*? If the universal statement "All witches can fly" is true despite the nonexistence of witches, why not the non-universal ones?

The point to be made here is that the modern view is built into the structure of modern predicate logic. Because universal statements are conditionals, they do not assert the existence of any Ss; all they say is that if any x is an S, then it is (or is not) a P. If there are no Ss, then any statement of the form $(x)(Sx \supset Px)$ is true by default, regardless of the consequent, because the antecedent is not true of anything. That follows from the nature of the conditional as defined by its truth table. So universally quantified statements necessarily lack existential import. By contrast, existential statements necessarily have existential import. By the nature of conjunction, any statement of the form $(\exists x)(Sx \bullet Px)$ is true only if some x is S.

If a universal statement in English seems to have existential import, then to capture this fact in a symbolic translation, we must combine a universally quantified formula with an existentially quantified one. For example, the translation of "All of my first edition books were stolen" would include two components: $(x)(Bx \supset Sx)$, and $(\exists x)(Bx)$. (In the next section, we will see how to combine two quantified statements like these into a single statement.)

The final point to keep in mind about translating into predicate notation is that English (like any other language) has many different ways of indicating universal or existential quantity. Some of the more common ones are summarized in the following table.

Universal		Existential	
Affirmative	**Negative**	**Affirmative**	**Negative**
All	No	Some are	Some are not
Any	None	There is (are)	There is (are) . . . not
A (A cat is a predator)	Not a (Not a creature was stirring)	A (A car is parked outside)	A (A student is not present)
Every, Everything	Nothing	Something	Something
Everyone (people)	No one	Someone	Someone
Always (time)	Never	Sometimes	Sometimes
Everywhere (place)	Nowhere	Somewhere	Somewhere

The table illustrates several things you need to keep in mind in translating English sentences into predicate notation.

- The indefinite article "a" can mean either universal or existential quantity, depending on the context. It can mean any instance of a category such as cats, but it can also mean some instance, as in our examples: "A car is parked outside" and "A student is not present."
- The word "there" at the beginning of a sentence normally indicates existential quantity. In a negative statement, however, it can indicate either existential or universal quantity, depending on where the mark of negation occurs, as in the following examples:

  8a. There is **not** milk in the refrigerator.
  8b. There is milk **not** in the refrigerator.

Statement 8a is a universal negative statement. It says that no milk is to be found in the refrigerator: $(x)(Mx \supset {\sim}Rx)$. Statement 8b, however, is an existential negative statement. It says that some of the milk is not in the refrigerator: $(\exists x)(Mx \bullet {\sim}Rx)$.

STRATEGY Translation into Predicate Notation

Statements in predicate logic are composed of subjects, predicates, quantifiers, and connectives. Subjects are either (a) names or phrases that refer to a specific individual thing and (b) variables that can stand for any individual thing. To translate a statement in ordinary language into predicate notation:

1. If the sentence is a singular statement, naming a specific person, place, or thing, then assign a lowercase letter to the subject of the sentence and assign an uppercase letter to the predicate describing the subject; for example, *Pa*.

2. If the sentence is a quantified statement, referring to all or some members of a class, use the device of variable and quantifier: Use a variable (*x, y, z, . . .*) as the subject of the symbolic notation, with an uppercase letter for the predicate; for example, *Px*. Next,

a. If the statement is about all members of the class, use the universal quantifier, (*x*)*Px*.

b. If the statement is about some members of the class, use the existential quantifier, (∃*x*)*Px*.

3. If the statement is one of the four standard categoricals—A, E, I, or O—then

a. For universal statements (All *P* are *Q* and No *P* is *Q*) use the universal quantifier and a conditional for the connective [(*x*)(*Px* ⊃ *Qx*) and (*x*)(*Px* ⊃ ~*Qx*), respectively].

b. For existential statements (Some *P* are *Q* and Some *P* are not *Q*) use the existential quantifier and a conjunction for the connective [(∃*x*)(*Px* • *Qx*) and (∃*x*)(*Px* • ~*Qx*), respectively].

- The last three rows of the table are quantifiers keyed to certain general classes of existents: people, times, and places. In the case of "everyone" and "someone," we would simply use a predicate for person, as in

9a. Everyone laughed.   (*x*)(*Px* ⊃ *Lx*)
9b. Someone laughed.   (∃*x*)(*Px* • *Lx*)

In the case of "always/never" and "sometimes," if the quantifier is specifically about times, then we usually need to use the more complex statement forms we will discuss later. The same is true for quantifiers keyed to places. But these quantifiers of time or place are often just variant ways of saying "all" or "some," and then we put them into symbolic form as such. For example:

10. Triangles always have three sides.   (*x*)(*Tx* ⊃ *Sx*)
11. Inflation is everywhere a monetary phenomenon.   (*x*)(*Ix* ⊃ *Mx*)

As in all issues of translating from English to symbolic notation, deciding which quantifier to use should depend ultimately on your understanding of what the sentence is about and what it is saying.

EXERCISE 11.2

Put each of the following statements into symbolic notation.

∗1. All skyscrapers are buildings.

2. Some buildings are skyscrapers.

3. Some cars are turbocharged.

∗4. Some knights wore armor.

5. All good things in life are free.

6. No fallacy is sound.

∗7. Some ketones are used as solvents.

8. No person is omniscient.

9. Some people are not sensible.

∗10. Some pitchers are good hitters.

11. No freshman can take this course.

12. All squares are rectangles.

∗13. Some rectangles are squares.

14. All of my children are home from school.

15. Some galaxies do not have a spiral shape.

∗16. Every cloud has a silver lining.

17. The quadruple axel jump has never been completed.

18. There are many thatched roofs in England.

∗19. Not a coin was found in the sunken ship's treasure chest.

20. Sometimes suspects are not perpetrators.

11.3 Quantifier Scope and Statement Forms

So far we have seen how statements of certain kinds can be translated into the standard forms of predicate logic. For singular statements, we use lowercase letters as names of particular things and uppercase letters as predicates—*Pa, Qb, Rc,* etc. Atomic singular statements like these can be combined by connectives into compound statements such as *Pa* ⊃ *Qb.* For quantified statements, we use variables instead of names as subject terms, along with a universal or existential quantifier to bind the variable. The simplest quantified statements have a single predicate: $(x)Px$, $(\exists y)Qy$, etc. For categorical statements, we use a quantifier and two predicates that are both within the scope of the quantifier: $(x)(Sx \supset Px)$, $(\exists x)(Qx \bullet Rx)$, etc. In this section, we will see how quantifiers and connectives are used in two other, more complex kinds of statements.

11.3A Compound Statements Within the Scope of a Quantifier

Categorical statements are a special case of a more general kind of statement in predicate logic: statements with a quantifier whose scope includes the entire statement. A categorical statement includes just two predicates with the same variable as subject, and one of two connectives. But a quantifier can apply to a compound sentence that has more than two predicates, linked by more than one connective. For example:

1. All banks that are chartered by the federal government $(x)[(Bx \cdot Cx) \supset Fx]$
   can borrow from the Federal Reserve System.

Statement 1 is clearly a universal affirmative statement, so we have to treat it as a conditional. Unlike the categorical statements we studied in the previous section, however, the subject category is defined by two features: being a bank (Bx) *and* being chartered by the federal government (Cx). Since these features seem independent, it is best to treat them as separate predicates rather than the single predicate "banks chartered by the federal government." So Bx and Cx must be conjoined as the antecedent of the conditional. To put 1 into predicate notation, we interpret it as saying that for all x, if x is a bank and x is chartered by the federal government, then x can borrow from the Federal Reserve System.

Here's another case of a compound subject:

2. Butter and eggs are rich in cholesterol. $(x)[(Bx \lor Ex) \supset Cx]$

"Butter and eggs" looks like a conjunction, as in 1. But the appearance is deceptive. The same substance cannot be both butter and eggs. The point is that if something falls into either category, then it is rich in cholesterol, so we translate "and" as disjunction rather than conjunction. The statement says that for all x, if x is butter or x is eggs, then x is rich in cholesterol. We would use the same form for other statements about what two different kinds of thing have in common, such as "Dogs and cats make good pets."

3. Some plants will grow only if they are fertilized. $(\exists x)[Px \cdot (Gx \supset Fx)]$

In this case we are talking about some plants, so we would expect to use an existential quantifier, with conjunction as the main connective inside the parentheses: "For some x, x is a plant and . . ." And what? The second conjunct says that x will grow only if x is fertilized. We have to remember how to represent an "only if" statement as a conditional. In our study of propositional logic, we saw that *p only if q* means *if p then q*. In the same way, Gx only if Fx is equivalent to *if Gx then Fx*. So the second conjunct is $Gx \supset Fx$. Notice that even though 3 involves a conditional element, the main connective is conjunction. We're saying of something that it has two properties: It's a plant, and if it grows then it has been fertilized.

4. All goods except foods are subject to sales tax. $(x)[(Gx \cdot {\sim}Fx) \supset Sx]$

Here we have another universal statement with a compound antecedent, but the qualifying phrase "except foods" is negative; it excludes a subcategory from the category of goods. We are saying that anything that is a good and isn't a food is subject to the tax.

5. Those who doubt the existence of God are $(x)[(Px \cdot Dx) \supset (Sx \lor Ax)]$
   skeptics or atheists.

The consequent of 5 is compound: *x is a skeptic or x is an atheist.* The subject category is defined by doubt in the existence of God, which looks like a single feature, not a compound. But the word "those" is an implicit reference to people. Remember that variables in predicate logic range over everything, so if a statement is clearly about people as opposed to other things, we should indicate that by including the symbolic predicate P in the translation: For all x, if x is a person and x doubts the existence of God, then x

is either a skeptic or an atheist. In the same way, when we are talking specifically about events, we need to include the predicate "is an event," as in the statement

6. Something happened on the way to the forum. $(\exists x)(Ex \bullet Fx)$

where Ex means "x is an event" and Fx means "x happened on the way to the forum."

11.3B Combining Quantified Statements

The examples we just discussed involved compound statements within the scope of a single quantifier. Quantified statements can also be modified and combined by connections that lie outside their scope. That is, quantified statements, like any other kind, can be put together by means of connectives into compound statements, and this often provides us with the most natural translation of a sentence in English.

Consider the statement

7. If everything is physical, then some things have mass.

Statement 7 is clearly a conditional statement. But instead of a single quantifier with a connective inside its scope, the antecedent "Everything is physical" and the consequent "Some things have mass" each has its own quantifier, and the horseshoe connecting antecedent and consequent is *outside* the scope of either quantifier.

7. If everything is physical, then some things have mass. $(x)Px \supset (\exists y)My$

Here's a more complex example, in which we have connectives both inside and outside the scope of the quantifiers.

8. Either all the gears are broken or a cylinder is misfiring. $(x)(Gx \supset Bx) \lor (\exists y)(Cy \bullet My)$

Here we have a disjunction of two separately quantified statements. Each disjunct is a compound statement with a connective within the scope of its quantifier, but the disjunctive connective is outside the scope of either.

In the examples before, we used different variables to indicate that the components of the compound statement are separately quantified. This isn't really necessary. The universal quantifier in 7 applies only to Px; its scope does not include "things [that] have mass," so we could have used x as the variable for those things. In 8, the parenthesis after Bx tells us that that is where the scope of the universal quantifier ends. Its scope does not overlap with that of the existential quantifier governing the second disjunct. So by the time we get to the misfiring cylinder, we're free to use x again to refer to it; there would be no ambiguity about which quantifier governed the variable. Later in the chapter, however, we will deal with quantifiers that *do* overlap in scope. In that case, it will be necessary to use different variables, so we might as well adopt this practice from the outset.

In both 7 and 8, there was no option about where to place each connective. By the meaning of the statement, it had to be either inside the scope of a quantifier or outside. In some cases, however, there are options.

Negation. The antecedent of 7 is

7a. Everything is physical. $(x)Px$

Suppose we wanted to deny this statement. Where would we put the negation sign, before the quantifier or after it?

9a. For all *x*, *x* is not physical.   (*x*)~P*x*
9b. It is not the case that for all *x*, *x* is physical.   ~(*x*)P*x*

Statement 9a clearly goes too far: To deny that everything is physical, we don't need to say that there are no physical things whatever. We just need to say that not everything is physical, and that's what 9b says. The general rule is that to negate a quantified statement, we put the negation sign at the beginning, in front of the quantifier. But we do have a further option. Statement 9b says that not all things are physical. We can make the same assertion by saying that some things are not physical:

9b. Not all things are physical.   ~(*x*)P*x*
9c. Some things are not physical.   (∃*x*)~P*x*

Statement 9b is the negation of a universal statement, and the negation sign is outside the scope of the quantifier. Statement 9c is an existential statement, and the negation sign is *inside* the scope of the quantifier. Statements 9b and 9c are equivalent; either would be a valid formulation.

The same principle applies to existential statements. For example:

Statement	10. Something is broken.	(∃*x*)B*x*
Negation	11a. It's not the case that something is broken.	~(∃*x*)B*x*
Negation	11b. Nothing is broken.	(*x*)~B*x*

If we deny that even a single thing is broken, we are thereby asserting that everything is unbroken; 11a and 11b are equivalent. In the next section, we will see that these equivalences are examples of a more general principle.

Conjunction and disjunction. Consider the statement:

12. Everything has a location in space and time.

Using S for "has a location in space" and T for "has a location in time," we could translate this in either of two ways:

12a. (*x*)(S*x* • T*x*)
   or
12b. (*x*)S*x* • (*y*)T*y*.

Statement 12a says that for each thing, it has a location in space and a location in time. Statement 12b says that for each thing, it has a location in space, and for each thing, it has a location in time. These are clearly equivalent.

But now consider a different statement:

13. Everything is either mental or physical.

Once again we might think of two possible translations:

13a. (*x*)(M*x* ∨ P*x*)
   or
13b. (*x*)M*x* ∨ (*y*)P*y*.

These are *not* equivalent: 13a says of each thing that it is either mental or physical and thus allows that the universe might contain two different kinds of things; 13b says that the universe is monolithic—either everything is mental or everything is physical.

Thus with a universal quantifier, it doesn't matter where we put a sign of conjunction, but it does matter where we put a sign of disjunction. The opposite is true for the existential quantifier:

14. Something is hot and cold. $(\exists x)(Hx \bullet Cx)$
15. Something is hot and something is cold. $(\exists x)Hx \bullet (\exists y)Cy$
16. Something is hot or cold. $(\exists x)(Hx \lor Cx)$
17. Something is hot or something is cold. $(\exists x)Hx \lor (\exists y)Cy$

Can you see why 14 and 15 are equivalent, but 16 and 17 are not?

SUMMARY Types of Statements in Predicate Logic

Type	Predicate Notation	Meaning	Example
Atomic singular statement	Pa	a is P	London is a city.
Truth-functional compounds of singular atomic statements	$Pa \supset Qa$ $Pa \bullet Qb$, etc.	If a is P, it is Q a is P and b is Q; etc.	If London is a city then it is large. Tom is healthy but Sue is sick.
Quantifier applied to atomic open sentence Px	$(x)Px$ $(\exists x)Px$	For all x, x is P There exists an x that is P	Everything is material. Something is on fire.
Truth-functional compounds of open sentences within the scope of a quantifier	$(x)\sim Px$ $(\exists x)\sim Px$ $(x)(Px \supset Qx)$ $(\exists x)(Px \bullet Qx)$ $(x)[Px \lor (Qx \bullet Rx)]$	Nothing is P Something is not P For all x, if x is P then it is Q Some x is P and it is Q For all x, x is P or it is Q and R	Nothing is infinite. Something is not infinite. All men are mortal. Some birds are carnivores. Everything is either scary or warm and fuzzy.
Truth-functional compounds of quantified statements. Scope of quantifiers does not cover connective.	$\sim(x)Px$ $(x)Px \supset (y)Qy$ $(x)Px \supset (\exists x)Qx$ $(\exists x)Px \lor (\exists y)Qy$, etc.	It is not the case that all x are P If all x are P, then all y are Q If all x are P, then some x is Q Either something is P or something is Q, etc.	It is not the case that everything is physical. If everything is physical, then everything has mass. If everything is created, then there is a God. There was either an explosion or a collision.

It is usually obvious which connectives to use in symbolizing a statement. But in order to tell whether they belong inside or outside the scope of the quantifiers, you need to think carefully about what the statement means and to practice putting statements of various types into predicate notation.

EXERCISE 11.3

Put each of the following statements into symbolic notation.

✱1. A building collapsed.

2. Someone got hurt, and no one helped.

3. If Mary is safe, then everything is fine.

✱4. Someone is drinking and driving.

5. Jennifer is either at the office or on her way home.

6. Any car that is turbocharged is fun to drive.

✱7. Some laws are not enforced.

8. Not every law is enforced.

9. If everyone cheated, no grades would be meaningful.

✱10. There isn't any beer in the refrigerator.

11. There's something rotten in the state of Denmark.

12. Nothing is cheap.

✱13. Some things are not explainable.

14. Some near-sighted people can't wear soft lenses.

15. Nothing is infinite.

✱16. Someone is either whistling or playing a radio.

17. Some great books are not remembered or appreciated.

18. Every great book is appreciated if it is remembered.

✱19. There are no ghosts.

20. If everything is physical, then there are no ghosts.

21. There is no such thing as a free lunch.

✱22. All trees are either evergreen or deciduous.

23. Nothing is lost.

24. Only freshmen can take this course.

✱25. Every corporation is either making money or losing money.

26. Blessed are the poor in spirit.

27. A tree, if properly cultivated, will live for a long time.

✱28. Every secret of a writer's soul, every experience of his life, every quality of his mind is written large in his works. [Virginia Woolf, *Orlando*]

29. If a photograph is black and white, it will have good contrast.

30. Dobermans and German shepherds are loyal and fierce.

✱31. If one of the tourists is late, all the tourists on the bus must wait.

32. Every physical object has a size and a mass.

33. Everyone can go home only if all the work is done.

✱34. None of my children is married or engaged.

35. Tests and homework both improve understanding and motivate study.

36. Quitters never win, winners never quit, but those who never win and never quit are idiots.

11.4 Proof

In predicate as in propositional logic, we use proofs to establish that a conclusion follows validly from a set of premises. We proceed step by step from the premises, in accordance with equivalence rules and rules of inference, until we reach the conclusion. The rules we learned in propositional logic, along with the techniques of conditional and *reductio* proof, are used for proofs in predicate logic as well. To work with quantifiers, we will also need to learn one additional equivalence rule and four additional inference rules.

11.4A Using Propositional Rules

Predicate logic deals with two sorts of statements: singular and quantified. Singular statements contain only names and predicates; quantified statements contain variables and quantifiers as well. The rules of propositional logic can be applied in a straightforward way to singular statements. Here's a simple example:

1. If Silver Blaze is lame, he will not win the derby.
   <u>Silver Blaze is lame.</u>
   Silver Blaze will not win the derby.

We could put the inference into either propositional or predicate notation:

Propositional	Predicate
L ⊃ ~W	Ls ⊃ ~Ws
<u>L </u>	<u>Ls </u>
~W	~Ws

Either way, the inference is a case of *modus ponens*. There's no need to use the predicate notation, since the validity of the inference does not depend on the internal subject–predicate structure of the atomic statements. But the point is that both versions have the same argument form:

p ⊃ *q*
<u>*p*   </u>
q

If an argument consists entirely of singular statements, moreover, we can analyze and evaluate it using only the methods of propositional logic. For example:

John's car is not an orange convertible. If his car is not a convertible, it gets hot in the summer sun. John's car is orange. So it gets hot in the summer sun.	~(Oc • Cc) ~Cc ⊃ Hc <u>Oc </u> Hc

We can prove that the argument is valid using the propositional rules of inference and equivalence:

1. ~(Oc • Cc)
2. ~Cc ⊃ Hc
3. Oc   /   Hc
4. ~Oc ∨ ~Cc   1 DM
5. ~~Oc   3 DN
6. ~Cc   4,5 DS
7. Hc   2,6 MP

The propositional rules are also sufficient for some arguments involving general statements, when the validity of the argument depends *only* on connectives outside the scope of any quantifier. An example would be the following argument:

If all actions have causes, then no action is voluntary. If no action is voluntary, then no person is either morally good or bad. So if all actions have causes, no person is morally good or bad.	(x)(Ax ⊃ Cx)	⊃	(x)(Ax ⊃ ~Vx)
	(x)(Ax ⊃~Vx)	⊃	(x)[Px ⊃ ~(Gx ∨ Bx)]
	(x)(Ax ⊃ Cx)	⊃	(x)[Px ⊃ ~(Gx ∨ Bx)]

Here we have two premises and a conclusion, each of which is a conditional statement; and in each statement, both antecedent and consequent are universally quantified. The main connectives are shaded to emphasize that they are outside the scope of the quantifiers. So despite the internal complexity of the premises and conclusion, the argument is an instance of the hypothetical syllogism inference form:

p ⊃ q
q ⊃ r
p ⊃ r

And the proof would involve a single step:

1. (x)(Ax ⊃ Cx) ⊃ (x)(Ax ⊃ ~Vx)   Premise
2. (x)(Ax ⊃ ~Vx) ⊃ (x)[Px ⊃ ~(Gx ∨ Bx)] / (x)(Ax ⊃ Cx) ⊃ (x)[Px ⊃ ~(Gx ∨ Bx)]
                                                  Premise / Conclusion
3. (x)(Ax ⊃ Cx) ⊃ (x)[Px ⊃ ~(Gx v Bx)]   1,2 HS

Most arguments in predicate logic, however, require some additional rules. The system of proof we're going to adopt uses one additional equivalence rule and four new rules of inference. We will discuss those new rules in the remainder of this section on proof—after a pause for some practice on using just the propositional rules.

EXERCISE 11.4A

Use the rules of propositional logic to construct proofs for the following arguments.

✳ 1. (x)Hx ⊃ ~(∃y)My
   (∃y)My
   ~(x)(Hx)

2. Pa ⊃ (Qa ⊃ Sb)
   ~Sb
   ~(Pa • Qa)

3. $(x)Lx \lor (y)Ny$
   $\underline{\sim(x)Lx \cdot (x)Kx}$
   $(y)Ny$

✳ 4. $[\sim(x)Bx \lor (x)Cx] \supset \sim(x)Dx$
   $\underline{\sim(x)Bx}$
   $\sim(x)Dx$

5. $(Bf \supset En) \cdot (Cf \supset Gn)$
   $Ag \lor (\sim En \lor \sim Gn)$
   $\underline{\sim Ag}$
   $\sim Bf \lor \sim Cf$

6. $\sim Fi \lor (Cd \cdot Dd)$
   $Fi \supset Cd$

✳ 7. $\underline{Cl \equiv Dt}$
   $(Cl \supset Dt) \cdot (\sim Cl \supset \sim Dt)$

8. $(\exists x)Mx \supset (y)Ly$
   $\sim(\exists x)Mx \lor [(z)Rz \lor (y)Ly]$

9. $(x)Hx \supset (\exists y)Ly$
   $(\exists y)Ly \supset \sim(Ie \cdot Je)$
   $\underline{(x)Hx}$
   $\sim Ie \lor \sim Je$

✳ 10. $\sim Ga \lor Ha$
   $Fa \supset Ha$
   $\underline{Ga \lor Fa}$
   Ha

11.4B Equivalence Rule: Quantifier Negation

In the past section, we noted that the negation of a quantified statement can be formulated in two equivalent ways.

1a. Not all things are physical. $\sim(x)Px$
1b. Some things are not physical. $(\exists x)\sim Px$

and

2a. It's not the case that something is broken. $\sim(\exists x)Bx$
2b. Nothing is broken. $(x)\sim Bx$

These equivalences are two forms of what is called the **quantifier-negation** (QN) rule in predicate logic. The rule says that we can switch the order of negation and quantifier as long as we switch quantifiers. When the negation sign passes across the quantifier, in other words, it is like a current that changes the quantifier into its opposite.

In 1 and 2, the quantified statements involve a single predicate. But the rule is true in virtue of the nature of quantifiers and negation, and therefore applies no matter how many predicates and connectives fall within the scope of the quantifier. In the previous section, for example, we discussed the statement "Those who doubt the existence of God are skeptics or atheists." If we were to deny the statement, the QN rule says that the following expressions are equivalent:

3a. $\sim(x)[(Px \cdot Dx) \supset (Sx \lor Ax)]$ It is not the case that for all x, if x is a person and x doubts the existence of God, then x is a skeptic or x is an atheist.

3b. $(\exists x)\sim[(Px \cdot Dx) \supset (Sx \lor Ax)]$ For some x, it is not the case that if x is a person and x doubts the existence of God, then x is a skeptic or x is an atheist.

Statement 3a is the direct negation of the statement; 3b makes the equivalent claim that there are exceptions to the statement.

To state the rule in its general form, we will use the notation $(\ldots x \ldots)$ to represent any expression involving x that is bound by a quantifier, where the parentheses include the entire statement within the scope of the quantifier. The quantifier-negation rule then consists of four equivalences:

~$(x)(\ldots x \ldots)$ :: $(\exists x)$~$(\ldots x \ldots)$

It is not the case that all x are...   There exists at least one x that is not...

~$(\exists x)(\ldots x \ldots)$ :: (x)~$(\ldots x \ldots)$

It is not the case that some x is...   All x are non-... OR No x is...

~(x)~$(\ldots x \ldots)$ :: $(\exists x)(\ldots x \ldots)$

It is not the case that all x are non-...   There exists at least one x that is...

~$(\exists x)$~$(\ldots x \ldots)$ :: $(x)(\ldots x \ldots)$

It is not the case that some x is non-...   For all x, x is...

Like the propositional equivalence rules, such as double negation (DN) or contraposition (Contra), QN can be applied either to a whole statement or to a component. It can therefore be used with statements in which quantified component statements are combined by connectives. For example:

4a. If everything is physical, then there are no ghosts. $(x)Px \supset (y)$~Gy

4b. If everything is physical, then it is not the case that some things are ghosts. $(x)Px \supset$ ~$(\exists y)Gy$

We can also apply QN to a component that is internally complex:

5a. All doctors are licensed but not all are competent. $(x)(Dx \supset Lx) \bullet$ ~$(y)(Dy \supset Cy)$

5b. All doctors are licensed but for some things it is not the case that if it is a doctor then it is competent. $(x)(Dx \supset Lx) \bullet (\exists y)$~$(Dy \supset Cy)$

The formulation of the consequent in 4b is strange, and the literal English translation is awkward. Since the negation sign is now inside the scope of the quantifier, however, we can use the propositional equivalence rules implication (Imp) and double negation (DN) to derive a more natural-sounding equivalent:

5b. $(x)(Dx \supset Lx) \bullet (\exists y)$~$(Dy \supset Cy)$

5c. $(x)(Dx \supset Lx) \bullet (\exists y)$~~$(Dy \bullet$ ~$Cy)$ 4b Imp

5d. $(x)(Dx \supset Lx) \bullet (\exists y)(Dy \bullet$ ~$Cy)$ 4c DN

5d says that all doctors are licensed but some doctors are not competent.

As a final point about QN, let's see how it can be combined with the propositional rules of equivalence to explain one of the relationships among the standard categorical statements. The four standard forms are often arranged in the "square of opposition," with diagonal arrows between contradictory statements:

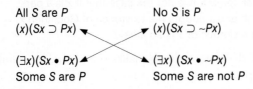

All S are P No S is P

$(x)(Sx \supset Px)$ $(x)(Sx \supset$ ~$Px)$

$(\exists x)(Sx \bullet Px)$ $(\exists x)(Sx \bullet$ ~$Px)$

Some S are P Some S are not P

The statements "All *S* are *P*" and "Some *S* are not *P*" are contradictories, which means that the negation of one is equivalent to the other. If you deny that all *S* are *P*, then you are asserting that some *S* are not *P*. So when we put those statements into predicate notation, we should be able to see *why* the negation of the A statement is equivalent to the O statement. We can prove that equivalence by the following steps (which follow the same path as the previous example about incompetent doctors):

1. ~(x)(Sx ⊃ Px)   Negation of the A statement.
2. (∃x)~(Sx ⊃ Px)   From 1, by QN.
3. (∃x)~~(Sx • ~Px)   From 2, using the propositional rule Imp: *p* ⊃ *q* :: ~(*p* • ~*q*).
4. (∃x)(Sx • ~Px)   From 3, using DN. QED.

Can you see how a similar proof could be constructed for the other pair of contradictories?

A. Which of the following pairs of statements are equivalent by QN?

Statements	
*1. (x)(Px ⊃ Qx)	~(∃x) ~(Px ⊃ Qx)
2. (x) ~(Px • Qx)	~(∃x) (Px • Qx)
3. (∃x) ~[Px • (Qx ∨ Rx)]	~(∃x) ~[Px • (Qx ∨ Rx)]
*4. ~(x) ~[Px ⊃ (Qx • Rx)]	(∃x) [Px ⊃ (Qx • Rx)]
5. (x) ~[(Px • Qx) • Rx]	~(∃x) [(Px • Qx) • Rx]
6. (x)~ [Px • Qx) ⊃ Rx]	(∃x)~[(Px • Qx) ⊃ Rx]
*7. ~(x)[Px ⊃ (Qx ∨ Rx)]	(∃x) [Px ⊃ (Qx ∨ Rx)]
8. ~(x) [(Px ∨ Qx) ⊃ (Rx ⊃ Sx)]	(∃x) ~[(Px ∨ Qx) ⊃ Rx ⊃ Sx)]

B. Use the rules of propositional logic along with QN to construct proofs for the following arguments.

*1. ~(∃x)(Sx • Rx) ⊃ Pa
  (x)(Sx ⊃ ~Rx)
  Pa

2. (∃x)~(Ax ⊃ ~Fx)
  ~(x)(Fx ⊃ ~Ax)

3. (x)Ax ⊃ (x)Bx
  (x)Bx ∨ (∃x)~Ax

*4. (x)Hx ⊃ ~(∃y)My
  (∃y)My
  (∃x)~Hx

5. (x)Ax
  (x)Ax ⊃ (∃x)~Bx
  (x)Bx ∨ (x)Cx
  (x)Cx

6. (∃x)~Dx ⊃ (x)Gx
  ~(x)Dx ∨ (∃x)Ax
  (∃x)~Gx
  (∃x)Ax

*7. [(x)Cx • (x)Dx] ∨ ~[(∃x)~Cx ⊃ (x)Dx]
  (x)Cx ≡ (x)Dx

8. [(x)(Ax • Bx) ⊃ (x)Cx] • [(∃x)Fx ⊃ (x)Cx]
  (x)(Ax • Bx) ∨ [(∃x)Fx • (∃x)Ax]
  (x)Cx

9a. <u>Pa • (Sa ∨ Se)</u>   9b. <u>Pa • (Sa ∨ Se)</u>
    (∃x)[Px • (Sx ∨ Se)]   (∃x)[Px • (Sa ∨ Se)]

In 9a, we replaced both occurrences of the name *a* with the variable *x*. The quantified statement says that someone is president and either that person is secretary or Ellen is. In 9b, we replaced only the first occurrence of *a* with a variable, and the result is the statement that someone is president and either Alan or Ellen is secretary. The conclusions in 9a and 9b are different, but both are legitimate uses of existential generalization.

Let's see how our two rules, UI and EG, work together in a proof. Consider the argument:

(x)[Px ⊃ (Qx ∨ Rx)]
<u>Sa • Pa</u>
(∃x)[Sx • (Qx ∨ Rx)]

Since the second premise is a singular statement about *a*, we will need to instantiate the universal premise using the same name. We will then have two singular statements, to which we can apply the rules of propositional logic. Our goal is to get the statement Sa • (Qa ∨ Ra), from which the conclusion will follow by generalization. The proof looks like this:

1.	(x)[Px ⊃ (Qx ∨ Rx)]	Premise
2.	Sa • Pa / (∃x)[Sx • (Qx ∨ Rx)]	Premise / Conclusion
3.	Pa ⊃ (Qa ∨ Ra)	1 UI
4.	Pa	2 Simp
5.	Qa ∨ Ra	3,4 MP
6.	Sa	2 Simp
7.	Sa • (Qa ∨ Ra)	5,6 Conj
8.	(∃x)[Sx • (Qx ∨ Rx)]	7 EG

The two rules we have just learned are natural ones, in the sense that each expresses something essential about the quantifier involved. A universal statement says something about everything, so we may naturally instantiate it with the name of any particular. An existential statement says that something is true of at least one thing, so we can naturally support the claim by inferring it from a particular example. The next two rules are less natural, and the inferences they permit are valid only if we observe certain special restrictions. (Of course, these rules are also subject to the general restrictions we've discussed: Names and variables must be interchanged consistently, and the quantifier must cover the entire statement.)

Existential instantiation (EI) is the reverse of existential generalization. It has the form:

Existential instantiation (EI):   <u>(∃x)(...x...)</u>
                                          ...a...

This does not appear to be a valid inference. The premise tells us that *something* in the world fits a certain description, but if *a* is the name of a specific individual with which we are already familiar, we cannot infer that *a* fits the description. Suppose we know, for example, that some actors are waiters: (∃x)(Ax • Wx). Does this imply that Brad Pitt is both an actor and a waiter? Obviously not. Nevertheless, it is valid to reason as follows:

At least one thing in the world is both an actor and a waiter. Let's call that thing *a*. We can now assert that Aa • Wa. Existential instantiation is valid only if we replace the variable with a name we introduce solely for the purpose of standing for the particular thing—whatever (or whoever) it may be—that makes the premise true. This means that when we use EI in a proof, the name we use must be one that has not been used previously in the proof, either in the premises or in a previous step, *and* that does not occur in the conclusion.

To see the importance of this restriction, suppose we try to prove that Devon is a knave because some people are either fools or knaves, and Devon is not a fool.

1. A($\exists x$)(Fx $\lor$ Kx)   Premise
2. ~Fd   / Kd   Premise / Conclusion
3. Fd $\lor$ Kd   1 EI [error]
4. Kd   2,3 DS

The use of existential instantiation in line 3 is invalid. The existential premise says only that some people are fools or knaves, so we cannot assume that the statement is true of Devon. To instantiate the premise in line 3, we would need to use another name like *a* that refers to some unspecified person, and then we would not be able to draw any conclusion about Devon.

The full statement of this inference rule, therefore, must include the restriction:

Existential instantiation: ($\exists x$)(...x...)
                                                     ...a...

Restriction: *a* is a name not used on any previous line of the proof nor in the conclusion.

This restriction does not apply to universal instantiation, since a universal premise is true of every instance. So if we need to instantiate both a universal and an existential statement in a proof, it's best to instantiate the existential statement first. Then we are free to use the same name when we instantiate the universal premise. An example would be the argument that some paints are health hazards because some paints contain lead, and anything containing lead is a health hazard.

1. ($\exists x$)(Px • Lx)   Premise
2. (x)(Lx $\supset$ Hx)   / ($\exists x$)(Px • Hx)   Premise / Conclusion
3. Pa • La   1 EI
4. La $\supset$ Ha   2 UI
5. La   3 Simp
6. Ha   4,5 MP
7. Pa   3 Simp
8. Pa • Ha   6,7 Conj
9. ($\exists x$)(Px • Hx)   8 EG

To obtain line 8, we had to use the same name to instantiate both premises (since Ha comes from the second premise, and Pa from the first). If we had tried to instantiate the second premise before the first (i.e., if we had tried to obtain line 4 before line 3), we would have been blocked by our restriction: The name *a* could not have been used for the existential instantiation, because it would already have been used. So we had to proceed in the opposite order.

The fourth rule of inference we need is **universal generalization** (UG), which has the form:

Universal generalization (UG):   ...a...

$$(x)(...x...)$$

We typically use this rule when the conclusion of an argument is a universal statement, as in the syllogism: All alcoholic beverages are intoxicating; May wine is an alcoholic beverage; therefore. ... The proof would be

1. $(x)(Ax \supset Ix)$		Premise
2. $(x)(Mx \supset Ax)$	/ $(x)(Mx \supset Ix)$	Premise / Conclusion
3. $Aa \supset Ia$		1 UI
4. $Ma \supset Aa$		2 UI
5. $Ma \supset Ia$		3,4 HS
6. $(x)(Mx \supset Ix)$		5 UG

We had to instantiate both premises in order to connect them by a hypothetical syllogism, and then we had to generalize to get our conclusion.

Our procedure here was legitimate because *a* was introduced as an arbitrary instance of an alcoholic beverage, so that anything we proved about it would hold for any other instance. The procedure is analogous to that of a mathematician who proves a theorem about a triangle drawn on the blackboard, and then assumes that the theorem is true of all triangles because the proof did not depend on anything distinctive about the particular example he used. But this means that universal generalization is valid *only* if the name stands for an arbitrary instance. Before we generalize from ... *a* ... to $(x)(\ldots x \ldots)$, we must review the earlier lines of the proof to make sure that ... *a* ... does not involve or rest upon any claim about *a* as a particular named example. We can do this by observing certain restrictions on UG. To understand the rationale for these restrictions, let's look at the sorts of fallacies we want to avoid.

It is clear, to begin with, that we cannot use UG on any name that already occurs in the premises. The premise that Kenya is an African nation (Ak), for example, does not allow us to infer that every country, or every thing in the world, is an African nation $(x)(Ax)$. Similarly, we cannot generalize on a name that was introduced by existential instantiation. Otherwise we could infer that everything is wet from the premise that something is wet:

1. $(\exists x)Wx$	/ $(x)Wx$	Premise / Conclusion
2. Wa		1 EI
3. $(x)Wx$		2 UG [error]

In this proof, *a* is *not* an arbitrary example of things in the world because the premise doesn't tell us that everything is wet, only that some things are, and *a* has been specially designated as one of them.

As with existential instantiation, therefore, the full statement of this inference rule must include the restriction:

Universal generalization: ...a...

$$(x)(...x...)$$

Restriction: *a* was not introduced into the proof in the premises nor by existential instantiation.

(We will need to add further restrictions when we get to more advanced forms of proof, but this one restriction is sufficient for now.)

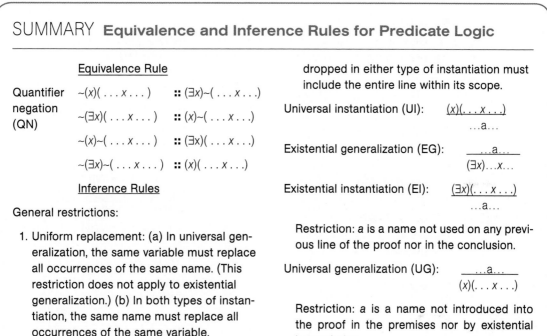

SUMMARY Equivalence and Inference Rules for Predicate Logic

Equivalence Rule

Quantifier negation (QN)

$\sim(x)(\ldots x \ldots)$ :: $(\exists x)\sim(\ldots x \ldots)$

$\sim(\exists x)(\ldots x \ldots)$ :: $(x)\sim(\ldots x \ldots)$

$\sim(x)\sim(\ldots x \ldots)$ :: $(\exists x)(\ldots x \ldots)$

$\sim(\exists x)\sim(\ldots x \ldots)$ :: $(x)(\ldots x \ldots)$

Inference Rules

General restrictions:

1. Uniform replacement: (a) In universal generalization, the same variable must replace all occurrences of the same name. (This restriction does not apply to existential generalization.) (b) In both types of instantiation, the same name must replace all occurrences of the same variable.

2. Quantifier scope: The quantifier that is added in either type of generalization or dropped in either type of instantiation must include the entire line within its scope.

Universal instantiation (UI): $\underline{(x)(\ldots x \ldots)}$
$\ldots a \ldots$

Existential generalization (EG): $\underline{\ldots a \ldots}$
$(\exists x)\ldots x \ldots$

Existential instantiation (EI): $\underline{(\exists x)(\ldots x \ldots)}$
$\ldots a \ldots$

Restriction: *a* is a name not used on any previous line of the proof nor in the conclusion.

Universal generalization (UG): $\underline{\ldots a \ldots}$
$(x)(\ldots x \ldots)$

Restriction: *a* is a name not introduced into the proof in the premises nor by existential instantiation.

EXERCISE 11.4C

A. Each of the following inferences is an attempt to apply one of the inference rules we've discussed (UI, EG, EI, and UG). Identify the rule, and determine whether it has been properly applied.

✻1. $\underline{(\exists x)(Px \cdot Qx)}$
   $Pa \cdot Qa$

2. $\underline{Pa \vee Qa}$
   $(\exists x)(Px \vee Qx)$

3. $\underline{(x)(Px \cdot Qx) \supset (y)Ry}$
   $(Pa \cdot Qa) \supset Ra$

✻4. $\underline{Pa \supset (Qb \cdot Ra)}$
   $(\exists x)[Px \supset (Qb \cdot Rx)]$

5. $\underline{(\exists x)(Px \cdot Qx) \supset (y)(Qy \supset Ra)}$
   $(Pb \cdot Qb) \supset (Qb \supset Ra)$

6. $\underline{(x)[Px \supset (Qx \vee Rx)]}$
   $Pa \supset (Qa \vee Ra)$

✻7. $\underline{(Pa \equiv Qa) \cdot (Qa \equiv Ra)}$
   $(x)(Px \equiv Qx) \cdot (Qx \equiv Rx)$

8. $\underline{(x)(Px \supset Qa)}$
   $Pa \supset Qa$

9. $\underline{Pa \supset Qa}$
   $(x)(Px \supset Qa)$

✻10. $\underline{(Pb \cdot Qb) \vee Ra}$
   $(\exists x)[(Px \cdot Qx) \vee Rx]$

11. (∃x)[(Px • Qx) ⊃ Ra]   12. Pa ⊃ Qa
    (Pa • Qa) ⊃ Ra   (x)(Px ⊃ Qx)

B. Construct a proof for each of the following arguments.

　*1. (x)Gx
　　　‾‾‾‾‾‾‾
　　　Ga • Gb

　2. (x)(Tx ⊃ Lx)
　　　~Lb
　　　‾‾‾‾
　　　~Tb

　3. Kd
　　　Bd
　　　‾‾‾
　　　(∃x)(Bx • Kx)

　*4. ~Ca
　　　(x)(~Bx ⊃ Cx)
　　　‾‾‾‾‾‾‾‾‾‾‾‾
　　　Ba

　5. (y)(Ty ⊃ Hy)
　　　Tb
　　　‾‾‾
　　　(∃x)Hx

　6. (y)(Gy ⊃ Hy)
　　　Gd
　　　‾‾‾
　　　(∃x)Hx

　*7. (x)(Hx ⊃ Mx)
　　　Hs
　　　‾‾‾
　　　Hs • Ms

　8. (x)Sx
　　　(∃y)Sy ⊃ (y)Wy
　　　‾‾‾‾‾‾‾‾‾‾‾‾‾
　　　(y)Wy

　9. ~(x)(Kx • Jx)
　　　‾‾‾‾‾‾‾‾‾‾‾
　　　(∃x)(~Kx ∨ ~Jx)

　*10. (∃x)Bx • (x)(Cx ⊃ Dx)
　　　~Da
　　　‾‾‾
　　　~Ca

　11. Fa
　　　(x)(Fx ⊃ Gx)
　　　‾‾‾‾‾‾‾‾‾‾
　　　(∃x)(Fx • Gx)

　12. (x)(Ex ⊃ Px)
　　　(x)(Px ⊃ Tx)
　　　‾‾‾‾‾‾‾‾‾‾
　　　(x)(Ex ⊃ Tx)

　*13. (x)Fx
　　　(∃y)Fy ⊃ (x)Gx
　　　‾‾‾‾‾‾‾‾‾‾‾‾‾
　　　Ga

　14. (x)[Gx ⊃ (Hx • Tx)]
　　　(x)[(Hx • Tx) ⊃ (Ix ∨ Sx)]
　　　‾‾‾‾‾‾‾‾‾‾‾‾‾‾‾‾‾‾‾‾
　　　(x)[Gx ⊃ (Ix ∨ Sx)]

　15. (x)[(Bx • Cx) ⊃ ~Dx]
　　　Da
　　　‾‾‾
　　　~Ba ∨ ~Ca

　*16. (x)Sx
　　　(∃y)Sy ⊃ (y)Wy
　　　‾‾‾‾‾‾‾‾‾‾‾‾‾
　　　Wa

　17. (x)(Ax ⊃ Bx)
　　　(∃x)Ax
　　　‾‾‾‾‾
　　　(∃x)Bx

　18. (x)~(Ax ∨ Bx)
　　　‾‾‾‾‾‾‾‾‾‾
　　　~(∃x)Bx

　*19. (x)(Lx ⊃ Mx)
　　　(y)(Mx ⊃ Nx)
　　　‾‾‾‾‾‾‾‾‾‾
　　　(x)(Lx ⊃ Nx)

　20. (x)Rx
　　　(x)(Rx ⊃ Sx)
　　　‾‾‾‾‾‾‾‾‾‾
　　　(∃x)(Sx ∨ Tx)

11.4D Strategies for Proof

We now have all the rules we need for proofs in predicate logic. So let us consider some strategies that will help us use the rules in constructing proofs. As with proofs in propositional logic, we work forward from the premises and backward from the conclusion, looking for a route that will get us from the one to the other. We will almost always need to use the propositional rules of equivalence and inference, so the strategies we learned for propositional logic are still applicable. But the rules of predicate logic require some additional strategies.

Which rules we apply, and how we apply them, depend on the type of statements we are given as premises and conclusion. We summarized these types at the end of Section 11.3. For our purpose in constructing proofs, we can simplify by reducing the classification to three kinds:

Type	Examples
1. Singular statements, whether atomic or compound	Pa $(Pa \lor Qb) \supset Rc$
2. Quantified statements (statements that are entirely within the scope of an initial quantifier)	$(x)Px$ $(\exists x)(Sx \bullet Tx)$ $(\exists x)[(Pa \lor Qx) \supset Rx]$
3. Truth-functional compounds of quantified statements	$\sim(x)(Qx)$ $(\exists x)(Px \bullet Sx) \supset (\exists y)Qy$ $Sa \bullet \sim(x)(Px \equiv Qx)$

For an argument whose premises and conclusion are all singular statements, as we saw at the beginning of this section, we do not need any of the rules for predicate logic. If the argument is valid, the proof can be constructed using only the inference and equivalence rules of propositional logic. The strategies to follow are therefore the ones we discussed in the previous chapter.

For arguments whose premises include statements of type 2, we normally need to use universal or existential instantiation (UI or EI) to derive singular statements, so that we can then use the rules of propositional logic to move toward the conclusion.

- If the premises include an existential statement with one or more universal statements, we should instantiate the existential statement first. If we instantiate a universal premise first, then the restriction on EI will prevent us from using the name we used in UI.
- If the conclusion is a singular statement of type 1, then we do not need to invoke either of the generalization rules, EG or UG. If the conclusion is an existential statement, we can generalize without restriction—for example, from $Sa \bullet Ta$ to $(\exists x)(Sx \bullet Tx)$. If the conclusion is a universal statement, however, we must be careful not to violate the restriction on UG. If the conclusion is $(x)[Px \supset (Qx \lor Rx)]$, for example, and we have derived $Pa \supset (Qa \lor Ra)$, we must check to make sure that the name a was neither contained in the premises nor introduced by EI.

If one or more premises or the conclusion is a statement of type 3, we cannot use the inference rules of predicate logic directly. Remember that the difference between statements of types 2 and 3 is whether the connectives fall within the scope of a single quantifier (2) or outside (3). The instantiation rules can be applied only to type 2 statements, in which the quantifier comes first in the statement and covers the entire statement. And the generalization rules will give us a type 2 statement, $(x)...x...$ or $(\exists x)...x...$. So with type 3 statements, we need to use other strategies.

- If a premise is the negation of a quantified statement—for example, $\sim(\exists x)(Px \bullet Qx)$—we can use the equivalence rule QN to move the negation sign inside the scope of the quantifier: $(x)\sim(Px \bullet Qx)$. Now we have a statement of type 2, and we can apply UI.

- If a premise is a conjunction of quantified statements—for example, $(\exists x)Px \bullet (\exists y)Qy$—use the propositional rule Simp to derive one or both of the statements.
- If the premise is a disjunction or conditional, look for a way to derive one of the components or a negation of a component, and then use the propositional rules MP, MT, or DS.

Example	Strategy
$(x)(Px \supset Qx) \lor (\exists x)(Px \bullet Rx)$	Look for a way to obtain $\sim(x)(Px \supset Qx)$ or $\sim(\exists x)(Px \bullet Rx)$ then use DS to derive the other disjunct.
$(\exists x)(Px \bullet Qx) \supset (\exists x)Rx$	Look for a way to obtain $(\exists x)(Px \bullet Qx)$ and use MP to derive $(\exists x)Rx$; or $\sim(\exists x)Rx$ and use MT to derive $\sim(\exists x)(Px \bullet Qx)$.

Let's work through a few examples to illustrate these strategies.

Example 1

$(x)(Px \supset Qx)$
$\underline{\sim[(\exists y)Qy \lor (\exists y)Ry]}$
$\sim(\exists x)Px$

The first premise is a statement of type 2, so we can apply UI to it. But the second premise is of type 3; both the main connective (negation) and the internal connective (disjunction) are outside the scope of either quantifier. Our first question should be what to do with this premise. The statement has the logical form $\sim(p \lor q)$, so we can apply De Morgan's law (DM) to it. The result is

$\sim(\exists y)Qy \bullet \sim(\exists y)Ry.$

Now we can use Simp and QN to derive $(y)\sim Qy$ and $(y)\sim Ry$, statements of type 2 to which we can apply the instantiation rule EI. The predicate R does not occur in either the first premise or the conclusion, so we can probably ignore it. But let's see what we can do with the first conjunct, $(y)\sim Qy$.

1. $(x)(Px \supset Qx)$ Premise
2. $\sim[(\exists y)Qy \lor (\exists y)Ry]$ / $\sim(\exists x)Px$ Premise / Conclusion
3. $\sim(\exists y)Qy \bullet \sim(\exists y)Ry$ 2 DM
4. $\sim(\exists y)Qy$ 3 Simp
5. $(y)\sim Qy$ 4 QN

We now have a universal statement that we can instantiate, and we can do the same with the first premise. Can you see that once we do that, we will be able to use MT?

6. $Pa \supset Qa$ 1 UI
7. $\sim Qa$ 5 UI
8. $\sim Pa$ 6,7 MT

Now we have a singular statement that clearly relates to the conclusion in some way, so it is time to apply a generalization rule. If we use existential generalization, the result will be $(\exists x)\sim Px$. But that is not the conclusion, $\sim(\exists x)Px$. Instead, we need to use universal generalization and then QN again to get to the conclusion.

9. $(x)\sim Px$ 8 UG
10. $\sim(\exists x)Px$ 9 QN

Finally, we need to check that the use of UG in line 9 complies with the restriction. The name *a* was introduced by instantiating two universal statements; it was not contained in either premise, nor introduced by EI. So line 9 is a legitimate inference. Notice that we used the variable *x* to replace *a*, even though *a* was used to instantiate the variable *y*. We used *x* because that is the variable in the conclusion we wanted to derive. The general point to remember is that there is no restriction on what variable we use in generalizing with UG or EG.

Example 2

$(\exists x)(Bx \supset Cx) \supset (x)(Cx \supset Fx)$
$(x)(Bx \supset Dx)$
$\underline{(\exists x)(\sim Dx \lor Cx)}$
$(\exists x)(Bx \supset Fx)$

If we ignore the quantifiers for a moment, we can see in a general way the path that the proof could take. The conclusion is $Bx \supset Fx$. If we could establish the antecedent of the first premise, $Bx \supset Cx$, we could infer the consequent, $Cx \supset Fx$. A hypothetical syllogism would then give us the conclusion. To derive the antecedent of the first premise, we will need to use the second and third premises. We can convert the third premise, $\sim Dx \lor Cx$, into a conditional, $Dx \supset Cx$, using the propositional rule implication, and then combine it with the second premise, $Bx \supset Dx$, in another hypothetical syllogism to derive $Bx \supset Cx$. The question is whether we can construct an actual proof along these lines, taking account of the quantifiers and the rules that apply to them.

We can instantiate the second and third premises but not the first, which is a type 3 statement. And we should begin by instantiating the third premise, since it is an existential statement.

1. $(\exists x)(Bx \supset Cx) \supset (x)(Cx \supset Fx)$ Premise
2. $(x)(Bx \supset Dx)$ Premise
3. $(\exists x)(\sim Dx \lor Cx)$ / $(\exists x)(Bx \supset Fx)$ Premise / Conclusion
4. $\sim Da \lor Ca$ 3 EI
5. $Da \supset Ca$ 4 Imp
6. $Ba \supset Da$ 2 UI
7. $Ba \supset Ca$ 5,6 HS
8. $(\exists x)(Bx \supset Cx)$ 7 EG
9. $(x)(Cx \supset Fx)$ 1,8 MP

From here, the proof is straightforward. We instantiate 8 and 9, use HS again, and then generalize. When we instantiate 8, however, we need to be careful not to use *a*, because that name was used in earlier lines; we will have to pick another name.

10. Bb ⊃ Cb	8 EI
11. Cb ⊃ Fb	9 UI
12. Bb ⊃ Fb	10,11 HS
13. (∃x)(Bx ⊃ Fx)	12 EG

EXERCISE 11.4D

Construct a proof for each of the following arguments.

✳1. (x)(Bx ⊃ ~Cx)
Ba
(x)(Cx ∨ Dx)
Da

2. Ba ⊃ (x)(Cx ⊃ Dx)
Ca • Ba
Da

3. (x)(Tx ⊃ Wx) • Ta
(∃x)(Wx • Tx)

✳4. (x)(Ax ⊃ Bx)
(x) (Cx ⊃ ~Bx)
(x)(Cx ⊃ ~Ax)

5. (∃y)Gy ⊃ (z)(Bz ⊃ Cz)
Gd
Bh
(∃z)Cz

6. (∃x)Kx ⊃ (x)(Lx ⊃ Mx)
Kb • Lb
Mb

✳7. (x)~(~Fx ⊃ Gx)
~(x)Gx

8. (x)[(Px ∨ Qx) ⊃ Rx]
(∃x)(Px • Sx)
(∃x)Rx

9. (x)(Px ⊃ ~Qx)
(x)(Rx ⊃ Qx)
(x)(Rx ⊃ ~Px)

✳10. (∃x)Gx ⊃ (x)~Bx
Ga
(∃x)~(Bx • Ax)

11. (x)(Px ⊃ Qx)
(∃x)(Px • Rx)
(∃x)(Rx • Qx)

12. (x)(Px ⊃ ~Qx)
(∃x)(Rx • Px)
(∃x)(Rx • ~Qx)

✳13. (x)(Ax ≡ Bx)
(x)(Bx ≡ Cx)
Ag ⊃ Cg

14. Ma
(x)(Mx ⊃ Gx)
(∃x)(Gx ≡ Mx)

15. (x)[~(~Fx ⊃ Gx) • ~(Mx • Nx)]
~(x)Gx

✳16. Fa
~(∃x)(Fx • Gx)
(∃x)(Fx • ~Gx)

17. (x)(Ix • Tx)
(∃y)Iy ⊃ (∃z)Hz
(∃z)Tz • (∃z)Hz

18. (x)(Dx ⊃ Cx)
(x)(Dx ⊃ Jx)
(∃x)Dx
(∃x)(Jx • Cx)

✳19. Ta ⊃ (y)Gy
Ia ∨ Ta
~Ia
(x)(Gx ⊃ Hx)
(x)Hx

20. (x)[Lx ⊃ (Cx • Mx)]
(x)(Mx ⊃ Vx)
(x)(Lx ⊃ Vx)

21. (x)(Rx ⊃ Sx)
(x)(Px ⊃ Qx)
(∃x)(Px ∨ Rx)
(∃x)(Sx ∨ Qx)

✳22. (x)(Bx • Ax)
    (y)(Cy ⊃ ~By)
    (∃x)(Ax • ~Cx)

23. (x)(Bx ⊃ Cx)
    (∃x)Bx
    (x)(~Dx ⊃ ~Cx)
    (∃x)Dx

24. (x)[Qx ⊃ (Tx ∨ Ix)]
    (∃x)(Qx • ~Tx)
    (∃x)(Qx • Ix)

✳25. Ta ⊃ (y)Gy
    Ia ∨ Ta
    ~Ia
    (x)(Gx ⊃ Hx)
    (x)Hx

26. (x)(Bx ⊃ Cx) • (x)(Dx ⊃ Ex)
    (x)(Dx ∨ Bx)
    (x)(Cx ∨ Ex)

27. ~(∃x)Ax
    ~(∃x)(Bx • ~Ax)
    ~(x)Bx

✳28. (x){[Bx • (Cx ∨ Dx)] ⊃ Ex}
    (∃x)(Dx • ~Ex)
    (∃x)~Bx

29. (∃z)Gz ⊃ (y)Ty
    (∃x)Ix ⊃ (x)Hx
    Gs • Ig
    (x)(Tx • Hx)

30. ~(∃x)[~Bx • (~Cx • Dx)]
    ~(x)(Dx ⊃ Cx)
    (∃x)(Dx • Bx)

11.4E Conditional Proof and Reductio ad Absurdum

In the previous chapter, we learned how the techniques of conditional proof (CP) and *reductio ad absurdum* (RA) are used in propositional logic. They can also be used in predicate logic. For some valid arguments they provide the only way to construct a proof, and for many other arguments they at least simplify the derivation.

Conditional proof is used to derive a conditional statement. We introduce the antecedent of the statement as an assumption on an indented line; from that assumption, along with previous lines in the proof, we derive the consequent; and then we enter the conditional statement on a non-indented line, with the justification CP. Here is a simple example:

1. (x)[Px ⊃ (Rx • Sx)]   / (x)(Px ⊃ Sx)   Premise / Conclusion
2. Pa ⊃ (Ra • Sa)   1 UI
   3. Pa   Assumption
   4. Ra • Sa   2,3 MP
   5. Sa   4 Simp
6. Pa ⊃ Sa   3–5 CP
7. (x)(Px ⊃ Sx)   6 UG

The use of CP gave us an easy way to extract Sa from the conjunction Ra • Sa in the consequent of 2.

In this example, we used CP with the singular statement we derived by instantiating the universal premise. But we can also use CP with quantified statements, as in the following example:

$$\frac{(x)(Px \supset Qx)}{(\exists x)Px \supset (\exists y)Qy}$$

The argument seems valid intuitively. The premise says that if anything is P, then that thing is Q. The conclusion says that if there is something that is P, then *something* is Q— a weaker claim that has to be true if the premise is true. How can we construct the proof? If we instantiate the premise, we will have a conditional statement, Pa $\supset$ Qa. But there does not seem to be any way forward from that point. Instead, we should notice that the conclusion is a conditional statement. Let's assume the antecedent, the quantified statement $(\exists x)Px$, and use conditional proof.

1. $(x)(Px \supset Qx)$	/ $(\exists x)Px \supset (\exists y)Qy$	Premise / Conclusion
2. $(\exists x)Px$		Assumption
3. Pa		2 EI
4. Pa $\supset$ Qa		1 UI
5. Qa		3,4 MP
6. $(\exists y)Qy$		5 EG
7. $(\exists x)Px \supset (\exists y)Qy$		2–6 CP

Using conditional proof in predicate logic is subject to the same restriction as in propositional logic. In the indented subproof, lines 2–6, we assume that $(\exists x)Px$ is true and we derive $(\exists y)Q\,y$ from that assumption together with the premise. But the proof is not complete until we discharge the assumption. We have borrowed $(\exists x)Px$, and now we have to pay it back. We do that on line 7. At this point in the proof, we are no longer assuming that $(\exists x)Px$ is true; we are saying that *if* $(\exists x)Px$ is true, then $(\exists y)Q\,y$ is true as well. The restriction is that once we discharge the assumption and get back to the main proof, we can no longer use any line that is part of the subproof. Any such line depends on an assumption we are no longer making. In this case, the proof ended with line 7; no further steps were required, so the restriction does not apply. But remember that a conditional subproof can be used to establish an intermediate step in a proof, and in that case we need to be careful to seal off the subproof from any further use.

There is an additional restriction on conditional proof that applies to universal generalization. We have seen that UG cannot be used to generalize from …*a*… to $(x)…x…$ if *a* was introduced into the proof in a premise or by *existential instantiation*. Now we must add that UG cannot be used within a conditional subproof if *a* was introduced in the assumption. We must discharge the assumption and return to the main proof before using UG. The following proof illustrates the fallacy we commit if we violate this restriction:

1. $(x)(Lx \supset Mx)$	/ $(x)(Lx \supset (y)My)$	Premise / Conclusion
2. La		Assumption
3. La $\supset$ Ma		1 UI
4. Ma		2,3 MP
5. $(y)My$		4 UG [error]
6. La $\supset$ $(y)My$		2–5 CP
7. $(x)(Lx \supset (y)My)$		6 UG

Let L stand for leopard, M for mammal. The premise says that all leopards are mammals, which is true. The curious-looking conclusion says that if anything is a leopard, then everything is a mammal, which is certainly false. The problem lies in step 5, where we generalized on *a* within the scope of the conditional proof. This is *not* to say that we can never use UG inside a conditional segment; it's just that we can't do it if the name occurs in the initial assumption (even if the name was introduced earlier).

The same restriction on UG applies when we use *reductio ad absurdum*. As we learned in Chapter 10, RA is a technique for demonstrating that a certain statement follows from the premises of an argument by showing that denying the statement leads to a contradiction. To establish *p*, we assume ~*p*, entering it as an assumption on an indented line. When we have derived a contradiction, *q* • ~*q*, we have completed the *reductio* subproof and we enter *p* on the next line of the main proof. Once we have discharged the assumption in this way, we can no longer use any line in the *reductio*.

Let's see how this works with an example:

1. (∃x)Px ⊃ Qa		Premise
2. (x)(Rx ⊃ Px)		Premise
3. (y)(~Ry ⊃ Py)	/ (∃y)Qy	Premise / Conclusion

We can't do anything with 1, because the quantifier does not cover the whole statement. So let's instantiate 2 and 3, using *a* for *x* so that we can eventually connect them with 1.

4. Ra ⊃ Pa	2 UI
5. ~Ra ⊃ Pa	3 UI

Now we can see that Pa must be true, given the premises. If it were not true, then we could infer both ~~Ra and ~Ra by *modus tollens* (MT), and we would have a contradiction. This suggests that we use a *reductio* proof to derive that contradiction:

6. ~Pa	Assumption
7. ~Ra	4,6 MT
8. ~~Ra	5,6 MT
9. ~Ra • ~~Ra	7,8 Conj
10. Pa	6–9 RA

Now we can go back to 1 and connect P with Q to derive the conclusion:

11. (∃x)Px	10 EG
12. Qa	1,11 MP
13. (∃y)Qy	12 EG

Conditional proof and *reductio ad absurdum* are useful techniques in predicate logic. But remember the new restriction they impose on universal generalization. The updated statement of that inference is now

Universal generalization (UG):

$$\frac{...a...}{(x)(...x...)}$$

Restrictions:

1. *a* is a name not introduced into the proof either in the premises or by existential instantiation.
2. UI is not used within a conditional or *reductio* subproof whose assumption contains *a*.

EXERCISE 11.4E

Construct a proof for each of the following arguments, using CP or RA.

✳1. (x)[(Sx ∨ Cx) ⊃ Ex]
   (x)(Cx ⊃ Ex)

2. (x)(Bx ⊃ Ax)
   (∃y)By ⊃ (∃y)Ay

3. (x)(Ax)
   (y)(By)
   ~(∃z)(~Az ∨ ~Bz)

✳4. (x)(Dx ⊃ Ex)
   (x)[(Dx • Ex) ⊃ Fx]
   (x)(Dx ⊃ Fx)

5. (x)Gx ∨ (y)Hy
   (y)(Gy ⊃ Iy)
   (∃y)~Hy ⊃ (z)Iz

6. (x)[(Gx ∨ Hx) ⊃ Ix]
   (x)Ix ⊃ (x)Tx
   (x)Gx ⊃ (x)Tx

✳7. (x)[(Ax ∨ Bx) ⊃ Cx]
   (x)[Cx ⊃ (~Ax ∨ Dx)]
   (x)(Ax ⊃ Dx)

8. (x)[Ax ⊃ (Bx ∨ ~Cx)]
   (x)(~Bx ∨ ~Ax)
   (x)(Ax ⊃ ~Cx)

9. (∃y)(x)(Lx ∨ Py)
   (x)(∃y)(Lx ∨ Py)

✳10. (x)(Px ≡ Tx)
   (x)(Tx ≡ Ax)
   Pm ⊃ Am

11. (x)(Ax ⊃ Bx) • (x)(Bx ⊃ Cx)
   (x)[Ax ⊃ (Dx ⊃ Cx)]

12. (x)(Jx ⊃ Lx)
   (y)(~Qy ≡ Ly)
   ~(Ja • Qa)

✳13. (x)[Bx ⊃ (Cx ∨ Dx)]
   (x)(Dx ⊃ ~Ex)
   (x)[(Bx • Ex) ⊃ Cx]

14. (x){[Bx • (Cx ∨ Dx)] ⊃ ~Ex}
   (x)(~Ex ⊃ ~Bx)
   Da
   ~Ba • Da

15. (x)[Px ⊃ (Qx • Rx)]
   (x)(Rx ⊃ Sx)
   (x)[(Rx ∨ Px) ⊃ Sx]

✳16. (x)[(Bx • ~Cx) ⊃ Dx]
   (x)(Dx ⊃ Cx)
   (x)(Bx ⊃ Cx)

17. (y)[(By ∨ Cy) ⊃ (Dy • Ey)]
   (y)[(Dy ∨ Ey) ⊃ (By • Cy)]
   (x)(Bx ≡ Dx)

18. ~(∃x)[Px • (Sx • Tx)]
   (x)[(Sx ∨ Qx) • (Tx ∨ Rx)]
   (x)[Px ⊃ (Qx ∨ Rx)]

✳19. (∃x)(Bx • ~Cx)
   (x){[Bx • ~(Dx ∨ Ex)] ⊃ Cx}
   (∃x)[Dx ∨ (Ex • Bx)]

20. ~(∃x)[Bx • ~(Cx ∨ Dx)]
   ~(∃y)(Dy • ~Ey)
   (x)~[Bx • ~(Cx ∨ Dx)]
   ~(∃x)~[(Bx ⊃ Ex) ∨ Cx]

21. [(∃x)Gx ∨ (∃x)Hx] ⊃ (∃x)~Ix
   (x)(Ix ∨ Qx)
   ~(∃x)(Qx • Rx)
   (x)Rx ⊃ (x)~Gx

11.5 Relations and Multiple Quantification

In addition to talking about things and their properties, we can talk about the *relationships* among things. In this section, we will learn how to represent such statements in the notation of predicate logic. Unlike the statements we have dealt with so far, relational statements often have two or more quantifiers that overlap in scope, so we need to learn how overlapping quantifiers work. Finally, we will look at arguments involving statements about relationships. We will not need any new inference or equivalence rules to construct proofs, but applying the rules to relational statements will require some new techniques and restrictions.

11.5A Relations

To understand how relationships are represented in predicate logic, let's start with singular statements. Here are some examples of relational statements about individual things:

1. Brazil is larger than Uruguay.
2. Jane married Dan.
3. Omar is president of the Stanford Chess Club.

Each of these asserts that two things are related in a certain way. Grammatically, the statements have a subject–predicate structure, and in each case the second thing named (Uruguay, Dan, and the Stanford Chess Club) is part of the predicate. And we could follow the grammar when we translate into symbolic notation. In 1, for example, the predicate would be "is larger than Uruguay," and we would translate the statement as: Lb.

But we can also break things down in a different way. We could treat Uruguay as a *subject*, alongside Brazil. The predicate would then be "is larger than," and we would interpret the statement as saying that this relational predicate is true of Brazil and Uruguay as a pair. To symbolize the statement using this approach, we need a predicate letter and *two* subject letters: Lbu. In the same way, "Jane" and "Dan" are the subjects in 2, and the predicate is "married": Mjd. In 3, "Omar" and "the Stanford Chess Club" are subjects of the relational predicate "is president of": Pos. Notice that we have to be careful about the order in which we list the subject letters. This doesn't matter much in 2 because being married is a symmetrical relationship; if Jane married Dan, then Dan married Jane. But that's a special case. If we reversed the letters in 1, we'd have the false statement that Uruguay is larger than Brazil; if we reversed the letters in 3, we'd be saying that the Stanford Chess Club is president of Omar, which doesn't even make sense. As a general rule of thumb for relational predicates, the subject letter that comes first should be the one that represents the subject of the English sentence.

Once we allow that a statement can have more than one subject, there's no reason to stop at two. Many statements assert that some relationship exists among three or more items. In symbolic form, we use a relational predicate and as many subject letters as we need. Consider the statement:

4. Lorna sold the Brooklyn Bridge to June.

Here we have a relationship among three things: two people and a bridge. It would be a little awkward to put the predicate in a phrase, as we have been doing. It's easier to think of it as a sentence structure, with slots in the positions where the subjects go:

_____ sold _____ to _____.

If we let S stand for this structure, we can symbolize statement 4 by adding letters for the subjects, in the proper order: Slbj. Lorna is the one who did the selling, so the letter *l* goes in the first slot. The Brooklyn Bridge is what got sold, and June is the one to whom it was sold, so the letters *b* and *j* go in the remaining slots. Since the structure has three slots for subjects, S is called a three-place predicate. By the same token, "is president of" is a two-place predicate, and terms for nonrelational properties such as *white* (e.g., "My car is white"—Wc) are one-place predicates. For more complex relationships, we can have predicates with a greater number of subjects—four, five, and so on indefinitely. In principle, for any number *n* we can have *n*-place predicates.

All of our relational statements thus far have been *singular* statements. Even though they are statements about more than one thing, they say something about particular items that are named as individuals. But we have seen how to form general statements by replacing names with variables. We can do the same for statements involving relations. Suppose we know that Omar is president of *something*, but we don't know what. Instead of using the letter *s*, for the Stanford Chess Club, we use the variable *x*, along with the existential quantifier:

5. Omar is president of something: (∃x)Pox.

The symbolic expression means that there is an *x* such that Omar is president of *x*.

Here are some other examples of quantified relational statements, with the subject terms underlined. Look them over carefully to make sure you understand the rationale behind each symbolic translation.

6. Lorna sold something to June: (∃x)Slxj.
7. Every thing that exists is a product of the Big Bang: (x)Pxb.
8. Some thing caused the explosion: (∃x)Cxe.
9. No South American country is larger than Brazil: (x)(Sx ⊃ ~Lxb).
10. Some thing is rotten in the state of Denmark: (∃x)(Sxd • Rx) [where S means ____ is in the state of ____].
11. I gave my dog a bone: (∃x)(Bx • Gixd) [where B means "is a bone" and G means _____ gave _____ to _____].

EXERCISE 11.5A

Put each of the following relational statements into symbolic notation.

*1. The Mets lost to the Cubs.

2. The mailman is afraid of my dog.

3. Marilyn Monroe starred in *Some Like It Hot*.

*4. I ran into Alison at Disneyland.

5. Adam ate an apple.
   Hint: Use F (fruit) for "is an apple."

6. Some people are not fans of Bruce Springsteen.

∗7. Some actions of the government are capricious.

8. A snake talked to Eve.

9. All roads lead to Rome.

∗10. Frankie loved Johnnie.

11. Anyone who marries Albert is crazy.

12. No one is a faster draw than Wyatt Earp.

∗13. There's nowhere I feel safe. (Use a two-place relational predicate S: ____ feel safe at _____.)

14. Memphis is south of St. Louis and north of New Orleans.

15. Memphis is between St. Louis and New Orleans.

∗16. I have a dream.

17. Peggy married some guy from Duluth.

18. Mary had a little lamb.

∗19. Sally borrowed a pen from Tiffany.

20. If someone enters the premises, an alarm will go off.

21. The dog was playing with a ball.

∗22. A dog ate my homework.

23. Marcy beat out Roger and won the tournament.

24. The Chrysler building has a lovely spire.

∗25. Mufasa and Sarabi adore each other.

26. Some of the passengers on the *Titanic* drowned.

27. If Susan votes for anyone, she will vote for a liberal.

∗28. Some trees have aesthetic value and should be saved.

29. Gary sent a love letter to Candace.

30. The oracle gave Neo a cookie.

11.5B Overlapping Quantifiers

The relational statements we've examined so far have a variable in one of the subject positions, bound by a single quantifier. But we can also have variables in more than one position, each bound by a separate quantifier, as long as we observe a few simple rules.

At some point in your studies, you may have had the insight that

12. Everything is related to everything.

The predicate here is

_____ is related to _____.

Since we are not talking about particular things as individuals, we need variables rather than names in both of the slots: Rxy. And since we are talking about all x and all y, we use a universal quantifier to bind each of the variables:

$(x)(y)$Rxy.

This formula is an example of multiple quantification, but it is different from earlier examples such as

13. If everything is physical, then there are no ghosts. $(x)Px \supset \sim(\exists y)Gy$

In 13, there is no overlap in the scope of the quantifiers. (*x*) applies only to P*x* and (∃*y*) applies only to G*y*. In 12, by contrast, the quantifiers do overlap; both (*x*) and (*y*) apply to R*xy*. Such overlap is typical when we have relational predicates, and it's the reason we must use different variables to represent the different subjects of these predicates. If we used the same variable in both roles—R*xx*—with the single quantifier (*x*), we would change the meaning: We would be saying that each thing is related to itself. That statement follows from 12 (if each thing is related to everything, then of course it is related to itself), but it is not equivalent.

It would not change the meaning of 12 if we switched the order of the quantifiers, as you can see by thinking through the literal meaning of the statements.

12a. (*y*)(*x*)R*xy*   For any two things, *y* and *x*, *x* is related to *y*.
12b. (*x*)(*y*)R*xy*   For any two things, *x* and *y*, *x* is related to *y*.

These are equivalent ways of saying the same thing. In general, when all the quantifiers are universal, it does not matter which we put first in the formula. The same is true when all the quantifiers are existential, as in the statement

14. Something bumped into something.

14a. (∃*x*)(∃*y*)B*xy*   There is at least one thing *x* and at least one thing *y* such that *x* bumped into *y*.
14b. (∃*y*)(∃*x*)B*xy*   There is at least one thing *y* and at least one thing *x* such that *x* bumped into *y*.

Here again, the two versions are equivalent.

When the quantifiers are different, however, order makes a difference. Suppose we wanted to symbolize the general statement,

15. Everything has a cause.

We would use a two-place predicate, _____ causes _____, in which the first slot is the cause and the second is the effect. Statement 15 asserts that for everything that exists, there's something that causes it: (*y*)(∃*x*)C*xy*. This statement does not say that everything has the same cause. It says that each *y* is caused by some *x*, but not necessarily the same *x* for all of the *y* effects. Reversing the order of quantifiers changes the meaning. (∃*x*)(*y*) C*xy* says: There is an *x* such that for all *y*, *x* causes *y*. Now we *are* saying that there is a single cause for everything.

The ability to symbolize statements about relations and to quantify variables separately makes predicate logic a very flexible and powerful instrument for analyzing arguments. But learning to use these devices properly takes practice. We have been working so far with rather simple statements. To get a better feel for the system, it will help to work through some examples that are more complex.

Consider the statement:

16. Everyone is afraid of something.

This looks like the statement about causality (15), but we can't analyze it in quite the same way. The parallel translation would be (*x*)(∃*y*)A*xy*. But this says that everything—rocks, trees, and hurricanes as well as people—is afraid of something, and we're talking only about people. The most natural way to add this information would be as follows:

$(x)(Px \supset (\exists y)Axy)$. This says: It is true of every x that if x is a person, then there is a y such that x is afraid of it. The scope of the universal quantifier is the entire statement, so it binds x in both occurrences, whereas the scope of the existential quantifier is limited to Axy. That's okay, because Axy is the only occurrence of y. All that matters is that every occurrence of a given variable fall within the scope of the corresponding quantifier.

The earlier example of Jane and Dan illustrates another important point. The statement "Jane married Dan" had two subjects and a two-place predicate. Suppose we want to say when they got married:

17a. Jane married Dan at 5:00 Saturday afternoon.

Now we can treat the time, 5:00 Saturday afternoon, as a third subject filling a slot in the three-place predicate: _____ married _____ at _____. This predicate is different from the two-place predicate M, which did not have a slot for time. So we will use a different letter, W (for wedding), to represent this predicate: Wjds. Statement 17a is still a singular statement, since 5:00 Saturday afternoon is a particular time. But now consider the statement

17b. Jane married Dan at some point in time.

Now we need a variable in the time slot, and an existential quantifier to bind it: $(\exists x)$ $(Tx \bullet Wjdx)$, where Tx says that x is a time. Bound variables for times are used to translate words like "at some time," "once," and "always." In the same way, bound variables for places are used to translate words like "somewhere" and "everywhere." (Be careful, though. These expressions are sometimes used merely as alternative ways of making ordinary universal or particular statements, as in "triangles always have three sides.")

Before we can translate a statement, we need to know how many different things we are referring to and which predicates are being asserted of them in which combinations. With complex statements, this is not always obvious, and it helps to proceed in stages. Consider the statement:

18. Any undergraduate who excels in a subject knows more about it than some graduate students in that subject.

It is immediately clear that this is about undergraduates who excel, and that it's about all of them. So we can let x stand for them and rewrite the sentence in a kind of pidgin English-symbolic form:

> (x)[(x is an undergraduate • x excels in a subject) ⊃ (x knows more about it than some graduate students in that subject)]

Because this is a universal statement, it is formulated as a conditional.

For the second conjunct in the antecedent, which refers to "a subject," we'll need another variable y, and y is also referred to in the consequent ("it" and "that subject"). The statement does not limit its claim to any particular subject or subjects, so we should use a universal quantifier for y. Now we have:

> (x)(y)[(x is an undergraduate • y is a subject • x excels in y) ⊃ (x knows more about y than some graduate students in y)]

Since the statement is also about graduate students, we need a third variable to stand for them; and because the claim is limited to some of them, we bind the variable with an existential quantifier:

(x)(y)[(x is an undergraduate • y is a subject • x excels in y) ⊃ (∃z)(z is a graduate student • x knows more about y than z does)]

We have now quantified everything that needs quantifying and used connectives to define the propositional structure of the statement. In doing so, we have isolated the predicate elements, and the only remaining task is to introduce symbols for them:

U: ____ is an undergraduate
S: ____ is a subject
E: ____ excels in ____
G: ____ is a graduate student
K: ____ knows more about ____ than ____ does

In full predicate notation,

18. (x)(y)([(Ux • Sy) • Exy] ⊃ (∃z)(Gz • Kxyz))

EXERCISE 11.5B

Put each of the following statements into symbolic notation.

*1. Someone loves me.
2. Something I ate upset my stomach.
3. Jack Sprat could eat no fat.
*4. All Wonder-Cure products are available at all drugstores.
5. What goes up must come down.
6. I don't like monkeys.
*7. I learn something new every day.
8. Every senior is older than every freshman.
9. Some freshman is older than any senior.
*10. Everyone is someone's fool.
11. A rolling stone gathers no moss.
12. If there were no evil, there would be no good.
*13. Tiffany stole a bike from someone.
14. No student may cheat at any time.
15. Something there is that does not love a wall.
*16. There are no resorts in Greenland.

17. Either everyone will go or no one will be happy.
18. Some people are lactose intolerant and can't digest milk products.
*19. Everywhere that Mary went, the lamb was sure to go.
20. Not a sound was heard by anyone.
21. If whales are mammals, then not all mammals are land animals.
*22. Rap and heavy-metal music are disturbing to some people.
23. No one can satisfy everyone all of the time.
24. Anyone who buys a used car from Mary is a fool.
*25. In any stone arch there is a stone such that, if it is removed, all the stones will fall.
26. A deciduous tree has leaves that fall from the tree.
27. If someone steals something, he has broken a law.

*28. Each man kills the thing he loves. [Oscar Wilde]

29. If you can renovate yourself one day, then you can do so every day. [Chu Hsi, *The Great Learning*]

30. If there is no god, then no action a person takes is immoral.

*31. "I would not join any club that would have someone like me for a member." [Groucho Marx] *Hint*: Use *g* to indicate Groucho Marx.

32. If the murder weapon is a revolver, then someone shot Mr. Boddy with it in the conservatory. *Hint*: Use a 4-place predicate: ____ killed ____ with ____ in ____.

33. If a tree falls in the woods and no one is there [in the woods], no sound is made.

11.5C Proof with Relational Statements

For arguments with relational statements, we use the same rules and strategies for proof that we learned in the previous section. Suppose, for example, that someone made the following inference about the 2011 National Basketball Association playoffs:

> If the Miami Heat beats the Boston Celtics in the Eastern Conference finals, then if the Dallas Mavericks beat the Oklahoma City Thunder in the Western Conference finals, Miami will play Dallas in the NBA finals. Dallas will beat Oklahoma in the Western Conference, so if Miami beats Boston in the East, it will play Dallas for the NBA championship.

This argument involves two kinds of relationship among teams and playoff finals,

B: ____ beats ____ in ____, and
P: ____ plays ____ in ____,

where the first two slots are for teams and the third is for playoff finals. So we would formulate the premises and conclusion as follows:

| 1. Bmbe ⊃ (Bdow ⊃ Pmdn) | Premise |
| 2. Bdow   / Bmbe ⊃ Pmdn | Premise / Conclusion |

Since the conclusion is a conditional statement, the simplest way to proceed is by way of conditional proof.

3. Bmbe	Assumption
4. Bdow ⊃ Pmdn	1,3 MP
5. Pmdn	2,4 MP
6. Bmbe ⊃ Pmdn	3–5 CP

In that argument, the premises and conclusion were singular statements—the atomic components referred to particular teams and particular payoff events—so we needed only the rules of propositional logic. With quantified relational statements, however, we will usually need the equivalence and inference rules for predicate logic. Since relational statements can have multiple overlapping quantifiers, we need to be careful that we apply those rules properly.

Quantifier negation. If we have more than one quantifier, we can still apply QN, but we have to do it in stages, moving the negation sign one quantifier at a time. Thus a statement of the form $\sim(x)(\exists y)Rxy$ would be transformed first into $(\exists x)\sim(\exists y)Rxy$, and then into $(\exists x)(y)\sim Rxy$. Consider the statement

19a. **Not every student owns a computer:** $\sim(x)(\exists y)[(Sx \bullet Cy) \supset Oxy]$

Statement 19a is equivalent to the statement that some student does not own any computer. We can establish the equivalence by applying QN twice and then applying the propositional equivalence rules Imp and DN:

19b. $(\exists x)\sim(\exists y)[(Sx \bullet Cy) \supset Oxy]$	19a QN
19c. $(\exists x)(y) \sim[(Sx \bullet Cy) \supset Oxy]$	19b QN
19d. $(\exists x)(y) \sim\sim[(Sx \bullet Cy) \bullet \sim Oxy]$	19c Imp
19e. $(\exists x)(y) [(Sx \bullet Cy) \bullet \sim Oxy]$	19d DN

Like an equivalence rule in propositional logic, QN can be applied either to a whole statement or to a component. That principle is especially important with relational statements, since they often have one or more quantifiers inside the statement, including only a component of the whole statement within their scope. Suppose, for example, that we have the following line in a proof:

20a. $(\exists x)[Px \bullet \sim(y)(Qy \supset Rxy)]$

QN could be applied to the portion of the statement following the conjunction sign:

20b. $(\exists x)[Px \bullet (\exists y)\sim(Qy \supset Rxy)]$

Instantiation rules. The rules for universal instantiation and existential instantiation can be used for statements with more than one variable, whether or not the statement has a relational predicate. The following are examples:

UI	EI	UI
21. $\underline{(x)(\exists y)Pxy}$	22. $\underline{(\exists x)(y)(Px \supset Qy)}$	23. $\underline{(x)[Px \supset (\exists y)(Qy \bullet Rxy)]}$
$(\exists y)Pay$	$(y)(Pa \supset Qy)$	$Pa \supset (\exists y)(Qy \bullet Ray)$

Remember that to apply UI and EI properly, we need to make sure that we replace each occurrence of the variable with the same name. Thus in 21, we replaced Pxy with Pay; in 22, we replaced Px with Pa; and in 23, we replaced Px with Pa and Rxy with Ray.

We must also remember that UI and EI are permissible only if the entire statement falls within the scope of the quantifier we instantiate. The implication is that these rules can be used only on the quantifier that begins the statement—the outermost quantifier. In 22, for example, we couldn't instantiate (y) because it is embedded within the scope of $(\exists x)$. Once we've instantiated $(\exists x)$, then (y) becomes the outermost quantifier, and we can go on to instantiate (y). In 23, however, when we have instantiated (x), we cannot go on to instantiate $(\exists y)$ because its scope does not include the entire statement. We would first need to detach the consequent—for example by deriving Pa and using *modus ponens*.

When we use existential instantiation with a relational statement, we need to be careful not to violate the restriction that EI is valid only if we replace the variable with a name we introduce solely for the purpose of standing for the particular thing—whatever (or whoever) it may be—that makes the premise true. This means that when we use EI in a proof, the name we use must be one that has not been used previously in the proof and that does not occur in the conclusion. To see the importance of this restriction, consider the following statements:

24. Everyone has a mother. $(y)(\exists x)Mxy$
25. Someone is a mother of herself. $(\exists x)Mxx$

(Strictly speaking, the symbolic formulation should include the fact that mothers and children are people: for example, 24. $(y)[Py \supset (\exists x)(Px \bullet Mxy)]$. But we will simplify by assuming that the universe consists solely of people, that is, that variables can refer only to people, so that we don't need to include Px or Py in the formula.)

Statement 24 is true, and 25 is false. Yet if we did not observe the restriction on EI, we might try to derive 25 from 24:

1. $(y)(\exists x)Mxy$ / $(\exists x)Mxx$ Premise / Conclusion
2. $(\exists x)Mxa$ 1 UI
3. Maa   2 EI [error]
4. $(\exists x)Mxx$ 3 EG

The argument is clearly invalid, and the problem in the proof occurs in step 3. We can't use *a* to instantiate *x*, because *a* has already been used to instantiate *y*. Line 2 says that someone is *a*'s mother; this does not imply that *a* is her own mother. To instantiate *x*, we need a fresh name.

Generalization rules. Existential generalization has no special restrictions, so we can use it with relational statements to replace names with variables. We just have to remember to apply EI one name at a time, as in the following proof:

1. $(\exists x)(Dx \bullet Fx)$ Premise
2. $(y)[Dy \supset (z) Gyz]$ / $(\exists x)(\exists y)(Dx \bullet Gxy)$ Premise / Conclusion
3. Da $\bullet$ Fa   1 EI
4. Da   3 Simp
5. Da $\supset (z)(Gaz)$ 2 UI
6. $(z)Gaz$ 4,5 MP
7. Gab   6 UI
8. Da $\bullet$ Gab   4,7 Conj
9. $(\exists y)(Da \bullet Gay)$ 8 EG
10. $(\exists x)(\exists y)(Dx \bullet Gxy)$ 9 EG

In line 9, we replaced b with the variable *y*, bound by $(\exists y)$. Then, in line 10, we could replace *a* with *x*, bound by $(\exists x)$, and thus complete the process of generalizing to reach the conclusion.

Universal generalization, as we saw in the preceding section, is subject to two restrictions. It is not valid (i) if the name was introduced into the proof in the premises or by existential instantiation; nor (ii) if it is used within a conditional or *reductio* subproof whose assumption contains the name. With multiple quantifiers, UI is subject to a third restriction. To understand this restriction and the rationale for it, consider the statements

26. Everyone loves someone. $(x)(\exists y)Lxy$
27. There is someone everyone loves. $(\exists y)(x)Lxy$

These are not equivalent statements. Statement 26 says that everyone loves someone (or other); 27 says that there is someone (a particular individual) whom everyone loves. Nor does 26, which may well be true, imply 27, which is almost certainly false. But consider the following "proof" that 27 follows from 26:

1. $(x)(\exists y)Lxy$	/ $(\exists y)(x)Lxy$	Premise / Conclusion
2. $(\exists y)Lay$		1 UI
3. Lab		2 EI
4. $(x)Lxb$		3 UG [error]
5. $(\exists y)(x)Lxy$		4 EI

In step 2 we used UI to replace the variable x with the name of an individual, a; 2 says that a loves someone. In step 3 we used EI to introduce b as the person a loves. Can you see why step 4 is a fallacious inference? Since b was introduced specifically as the person a loves, we can't infer that *everyone* loves b. The problem here, to put it in general terms, is that b was introduced on a line where a was already present, so we can't apply universal generalization on a until we get rid of b.

So we now have three restrictions on UI:

Universal generalization (UG): $\dfrac{...a...}{(x)(...x...)}$

Restrictions:
1. a was not introduced into the proof in the premises nor by existential instantiation.
2. UI is not used within a conditional or *reductio* subproof whose assumption contains a.
3. ...a... must not contain any other name that was introduced by EI on a line containing a.

To illustrate how to apply the equivalence and inference rules to arguments with relational statements, consider the following argument, which will require a longer proof. As we work through the proof, it might help to have paper and pencil handy so that you can keep track of where we are.

1. $(x)\{Px \supset (y)[(Qy \bullet Ry) \supset Sxy]\}$		Premise
2. $(x)(y)(Txy \supset Qy)$		Premise
3. $(x)(\exists y)Txy$	/ $(x)[Px \supset (\exists y)(Ry \supset Sxy)]$	Premise / Conclusion

The three premises and the conclusion are quantified statements, with variables in the subject position and no names. So we're going to have to instantiate all the variables in order to relate the premises and get to the conclusion. In the case of x, that won't be a problem, since it is bound in each premise by a universal quantifier, and there are no special restrictions on universal instantiation. In premise 3, however, y is bound by an existential quantifier. So let's start with that premise. The first step is to uncover the existential quantifier by instantiating the main quantifier, (x). Then we can apply EI to get a singular statement, and then go on to deal with 1 and 2 by using UI.

4. $(\exists y)Tay$		3 UI
5. Tab		4 EI
6. $(y)(Tay \supset Qy)$		2 UI

7. Tab ⊃ Qb	6 UI
8. Pa ⊃ (y)[(Qy • Ry) ⊃ Say]	1 UI

We cannot instantiate *y* in line 8 because it does not occur at the beginning of the statement. To detach the consequent from Pa, we can use conditional proof with Pa as the assumption. This is a reasonable strategy to follow because the conclusion of our proof has the internal structure of a conditional with P*x* as the antecedent, and the output of the conditional segment will be a conditional with Pa as antecedent, from which we can generalize.

9. Pa	Assumption
10. (y)[(Qy ⊃ Ry) ⊃ Say]	8,9 MP
11. (Qb • Rb) ⊃ Sab	10 UI

Now that we have instantiated all the variables, the proof is straightforward:

12. Qb ⊃ (Rb ⊃ Sab)	11 Exp
13. Qb	5,7 MP
14. Rb ⊃ Sab	12,13 MP
15. (∃y)(Ry ⊃ Say)	14 EG
16. Pa ⊃ (∃y)(Ry ⊃ Say)	9–15 CP
17. (x)[Px ⊃ (∃y)(Ry ⊃ Sxy)]	16 UG

Let's check, finally, to make sure that we used UG properly. First, was *a* introduced in a premise or by EI? No—it was introduced by UI in line 4. Did we use UG inside the conditional proof (lines 9–15)? No. So we don't have to worry about the second restriction. Did line 16 contain any other name introduced by EI? No—we got rid of *b*, which was introduced by EI, in line 15. Notice that our use of EG to get rid of *b* occurred inside the conditional segment. That's okay, because there are no special restrictions on EG.

Constructing proofs that involve relational statements, then, is amenable to the same rules and strategies that we learned earlier. There is one new restriction on universal generalization, and the need for extra vigilance in applying all the rules, but otherwise you can simply apply everything you have learned about predicate logic.

SUMMARY **Equivalence and Inference Rules for Predicate Logic**

Equivalence Rule

Quantifier negation (QN)	~(x)(... x ...)	::	(∃x)~(... x ...)
	~(∃x)(... x ...)	::	(x)~(... x ...)
	~(x)~(... x ...)	::	(∃x)(... x ...)
	~(∃x)~(... x ...)	::	(x)(... x ...)

Inference Rules

General restrictions:

1. Uniform replacement: (a) In universal generalization, the same variable must replace all occurrences of the same name. (This restriction does not apply to existential generalization.) (b) In both types of instantiation, the same name must replace all occurrences of the same variable.

2. Quantifier scope: The quantifier that is added in either type of generalization or dropped in either type of instantiation must include the entire line within its scope.

Universal instantiation (UI): $\underline{(x)(\ldots x \ldots)}$
                                         $\ldots a \ldots$

Existential generalization (EG): $\underline{\ldots a \ldots}$
                                         $(\exists x)\ldots x \ldots$

Existential instantiation (EI): $\underline{(\exists x)(\ldots x \ldots)}$
                                         $\ldots a \ldots$

Restriction: *a* is a name not used on any previous line of the proof nor in the conclusion.

Universal generalization (UG): $\underline{\ldots a \ldots}$
                                         $(x)(\ldots x \ldots)$

Restrictions:

1. *a* is a name not introduced into the proof in the premises nor by existential instantiation.

2. UI is not used within a conditional or *reductio* subproof whose assumption contains *a*.

3. …*a*… must not contain any other name that was introduced by EI on a line containing *a*.

EXERCISE 11.5C

Construct a proof for each of the following arguments.

✳1. Ca ⊃ (Mp ⊃ Hap)
 ~Hap
 ~Ca ∨ ~Mp

2. (x)~Jx
 (∃y)(Hby ∨ Iyy) ⊃ (∃x)Jx
 (y)~(Hby ∨ Iyy)

3. (x)(y)Hxy
 Hcd ⊃ Kf
 Kf

✳4. (∃y)(x)Axy
 (x)(∃y)Axy

5. (∃x)(Cx ∨ Mxx)
 (x)~Cx
 (∃y)Myy

6. (∃x)(y)Rxy
 (x)(Rxx ⊃ (∃y)Sxy)
 (∃x)(∃y)Sxy

✳7. Aa
 (x)(Ax ⊃ Bx) ⊃ (∃x)(Ax • Bx)

8. ~(∃x)(~Ax • Bxx)
 Baa
 Aa

9. (x)[Kxx ⊃ (Lx • Nx)]
 (∃x)~Nx
 (∃y)~Kyy

✳10. (x)[(~Mxa ∨ Nx) ⊃ Lxx]
 (∃y)~Lyy
 (∃x)Mxa

11. (x)(Exx ∨ Qx)
 (y)~Eyy
 (z)(Qz ⊃ Kz)
 (x)(Kx)

12. (∃x)(Nx • Sx)
 (x)[Mxn ⊃ ~(Sx ∨ Dx)]
 (∃y)~Myn

✳13. (x)(Exx ∨ Qx)
 (y)~Eyy
 (z)(Qz ⊃ Kz)
 (w)Kw

14. Cnn ∨ (Ln • Mj)
 ~(z)Nsz ⊃ ~Ln
 (∃x)[~Cxx ⊃ (z)Nsz]

15. (x)(y)[(Px • Qy) ⊃ Rxy]
 (x)(∃y)(Sxy ⊃ Px)
 (x)(∃y)[Sxy ⊃ (Qy ⊃ Rxy)]

✳16. (x)[(Hx • Gx) ⊃ Cx]
 (y)Gy • ~(x)Mxa
 (x)(Hx ⊃ Cx)

17. (∃x)[Dx ∨ (y)(Mxy ⊃ Dy)]
 (x)(Mxa • ~Da)
 (∃x)Dx

18. (x)(y)[Hxy ≡ (Ly ⊃ Dx)]
 (w)Hiw
 (∃z)Lz
 (∃x)Dx

✳19. $(z)(y)[(\exists w)Myw \supset Mzy]$
$\underline{Mba}$
$(x)(y)Mxy$

20. $(x)[Hx \supset (Sxx \supset Gx)]$
$\underline{(x)(Gx \supset Cx) \bullet (y){\sim}Cy}$
$(x)(\exists y){\sim}(Hy \bullet Syx)$

21. $\underline{{\sim}(\exists y)(Ty \vee (\exists x){\sim}Hxy)}$
$(x)(y)Hxy \bullet (x){\sim}Tx$

✳22. $(x)(Cxx \supset Sx)$
$\underline{(y)[(Sy \vee Tyy) \supset Wy]}$
$(x)[(Cxx \bullet {\sim}Kx) \supset (Wx \bullet {\sim}Kx)]$

23. $(x)(y)[Kxy \equiv (Lx \bullet My)]$
$\underline{(\exists x)(Nx \bullet Mx)}$
$(x)(\exists y)(Lx \supset Kxy)$

24. $(x)[(\exists y)Mxy \supset (\exists y){\sim}Ky]$
$(\exists y)(\exists z)Myz$
$\underline{(x)({\sim}Kx \equiv Nx)}$
$(\exists z)Nz$

Summary

Predicate logic analyzes statements in terms of names, predicates, variables, and quantifiers. The elementary unit is a singular statement consisting of a predicate attached to a name. These atomic statements can be combined into truth-functional compound singular statements. A quantified statement consists of predicates attached to variables, with the variables bound by universal or existential quantifiers. Truth-functional connectives can combine predicate-variable statements within the scope of a quantifier; and they can combine quantified statements, where the connective is outside the scope of any quantifier. The terms of traditional categorical statements are treated as predicates. Universal statements (A or E) are treated as conditionals bound by a universal quantifier; particular statements (I or O) are treated as conjunctions bound by an existential quantifier.

We can show that an argument stated in predicate notation is valid by constructing a proof.

In addition to the rules of propositional logic, a proof in predicate logic makes use of one additional equivalence rule (the quantifier-negation rule) and four additional rules of inference (the instantiation and generalization rules). The techniques of conditional proof and *reductio ad absurdum* can be used in predicate logic as in propositional logic.

Statements about relations among things can be symbolized using relational predicates. In a singular relational statement, the subjects are names for the things that are related. In a quantified relational statement, variables take the place of names. These statements typically involve more than one variable and thus require more than one quantifier. The order of the quantifiers can make a difference to the meaning of the statement and, in constructing proofs involving relational statements, to the order in which the rules for instantiation and generalization may be applied.

Key Terms

singular statement—a subject–predicate statement whose subject is a name.
variable—a symbol that stands for some, but any, unnamed individual thing.
quantifier—a function that specifies whether a statement applies to all or some of the things a variable can stand for.

universal quantifier—the quantifier that specifies that a statement applies to all the things a variable can stand for.
existential quantifier—the quantifier that specifies that a statement applies to some of the things a variable can stand for.
open sentence—a sentence with a variable not bound by a quantifier for that variable.

free variable—a variable that does not fall within the scope of a quantifier for that variable.

bound variable—a variable that falls within the scope of a quantifier for that variable.

closed sentence—a sentence in which all variables are bound.

scope—the portion of a sentence to which a given quantifier applies.

quantifier negation (QN)—an equivalence rule in predicate logic (see the Summary box).

universal instantiation (UI)—an inference rule in predicate logic (see the Summary box).

existential generalization (EG)—an inference rule in predicate logic (see the Summary box).

existential instantiation (EI)—an inference rule in predicate logic (see the Summary box).

universal generalization (UG)—an inference rule in predicate logic (see the Summary box).

Additional Exercises

A. Find statements in English that have the following logical forms.

✳1. $Pa \supset Qa$

2. Rab

3. $(x)Px$

✳4. $(\exists x)(Px \cdot Qx)$

5. $Rab \vee Rba$

6. $(Pa \cdot Qb) \supset Rab$

✳7. $(Pa \vee Pb) \cdot {\sim}Qa$

8. $(x)(Sx \supset Px)$

9. $(x)Sx \supset (x)Px$

✳10. $(\exists x)[Px \cdot (Qx \vee {\sim}Sx)]$

11. $(x)(Px \supset Rxa)$

12. ${\sim}(\exists x)(Px \cdot Qx) \supset (\exists x)(Sx)$

✳13. $(x)(y)[(Px \cdot Qy) \supset Rxy]$

14. ${\sim}(\exists x)Rxx$

15. $(x)\{Px \supset (\exists y)[Qy \cdot (Rxy \cdot Ryz)]\}$

B. Translate each of the following statements into symbolic notation, using appropriate letters as predicates and names.

✳1. Nothing is black or white; there are only shades of gray.

2. If there were no black and white, there would be no gray.

3. Every little breeze seems to whisper "Louise."

✳4. No poem is as beautiful as a tree.

5. Sticks and stones may break my bones. [Use S for "sticks" and T for "stones."]

6. People who live in glass houses should not throw stones.

✳7. "God helps them that help themselves." [Benjamin Franklin]

8. For everyone who steals and gets away with it, there are some who steal and get caught.

9. "We shall defend every village, every town and every city." [Winston Churchill]

✳10. A government is democratic if and only if all its adult citizens are eligible to vote.

11. "There never was a good war or a bad peace." [Benjamin Franklin]

12. Any object in motion continues in motion unless some force acts on it.

✳13. Every mother is someone's daughter, but not every daughter is someone's mother.

14. A nation that protects all of its citizens against failure will prevent some of its citizens from succeeding.

15. It isn't true that an authorized biography of a celebrity is always less revealing than an unauthorized biography.

✳16. "Everyone complains of his memory, and no one complains of his judgment." [La Rochefoucauld]

17. Two people are cousins if and only if they are children of siblings. [Use C for "cousin" and K for "children."]

18. "No Person except a natural born Citizen, or a Citizen of the United States, at the time of the Adoption of this Constitution, shall be eligible to the Office of President,

neither shall any Person be eligible to that Office, who shall not have attained to the Age of thirty five Years, and been fourteen Years a Resident within the United States." [U.S. Constitution]

✳19. "You may fool all of the people some of the time; you can even fool some of the people all the time; but you can't fool all the people all the time." [Abraham Lincoln]

C. Each of the following arguments can be justified by one of the inference or equivalence rules of propositional logic. Name the rule.

✳1. $(x)(Px \supset Qx) \supset (\exists y)Ry$
   $\sim(\exists y)Ry$
   $\sim(x)(Px \supset Qx)$

2. $(\exists x)Px \supset (y)[Qy \supset (Ry \lor Sy)]$
   $(y)[Qy \supset (Ry \lor Sy)] \supset (z)\sim Tz$
   $(\exists x)Px \supset (z)\sim Tz$

3. $Pa \lor (Qa \bullet Rab)$
   $(Pa \lor Qa) \bullet (Pa \lor Rab)$

✳4. $[Pa \bullet (Rab \lor Sab)] \supset Qb$
   $Pa \supset [(Rab \lor Sab) \supset Qb]$

5. $(x)(Px \bullet Qz) \lor (\exists y)\sim(Py \lor Qy)$
   $\sim(\exists y)\sim(Py \lor Qy)$
   $(x)(Px \bullet Qx)$

6. $(Pa \bullet Qb) \supset Rab$
   $(Sa \supset Pa) \bullet (Sa \supset Qb)$
   $[(Sa \supset Pa) \bullet (Sa \supset Qb)] \bullet [(Pa \bullet Qb) \supset Rab]$

✳7. $(\exists x)(Px \bullet Qx) \supset (y)(Py \supset Qy)$
   $\sim(\exists x)(Px \bullet Qx) \lor (y)(Py \supset Qy)$

8. $(x)(\exists y)[(Px \bullet Qy) \supset Rxy] \bullet (x)[Sx \supset (\exists y)Txy]$
   $(x)[Sx \supset (\exists y)Txy]$

9. $(\exists x)(Px \bullet Qx) \lor [(\exists y)(Ry \bullet Qy) \lor (Pa \bullet Ra)]$
   $[(\exists x)(Px \bullet Qx) \lor (\exists y)(Ry \bullet Qy)] \lor (Pa \bullet Ra)$

✳10. $[Pa \supset (Qa \bullet Rab)] \bullet [Pb \supset (Qb \bullet Rba)]$
   $\sim(Qa \bullet Rab) \lor \sim(Qb \bullet Rba)$
   $\sim Pa \lor \sim Pb$

D. In each of the following "proofs," one line involves an error in the use of a rule of predicate logic. Identify the error.

✳1.
1. $(x)(\exists y)(Px \equiv \sim Py)$ / $(Pa \equiv \sim Pa)$ — Premise / Conclusion
2. $(\exists y)(Pa \equiv \sim Py)$ — 1 UI
3. $Pa \equiv \sim Pa$ — 2 EI

2.
1. $(x)Px \supset (y)Qy$ / $(x)(Px \supset Qx)$ — Premise / Conclusion
2. Pa — Assumption
3. $(x)Px$ — 2 UG
4. $(y)Qy$ — 1,3 MP
5. Qa — 4 UI
6. $Pa \supset Qa$ — 2–5 CP
7. $(x)(Px \supset Qx)$ — 6 UG

3. 1. $(x)(Px \supset Qx) \supset (y)Ry$ Premise
  2. $(\exists x)\sim Rx$ / $(\exists x)(Px \cdot \sim Qx)$ Premise / Conclusion
  3. $\sim Ra$ 2 EI
  4. $(Pa \supset Qa) \supset Ra$ 1 UI
  5. $\sim(Pa \supset Qa)$ 3,4 MT
  6. $\sim\sim (Pa \cdot \sim Qa)$ 5 Imp
  7. $Pa \cdot \sim Qa$ 6 DN
  8. $(\exists x)(Pa \cdot \sim Qa)$ 7 EG

✳4. 1. $(x)(Px \vee Qx) \supset (\exists y)Ry$ Premise
  2. $(\exists y)\sim Ry$ / $(\exists x)(\sim Px \cdot \sim Qx)$ Premise / Conclusion
  3. $\sim(\exists y)Ry$ 2 QN
  4. $\sim(x)(Px \vee Qx)$ 1,3 MT
  5. $(\exists x)\sim(Px \vee Qx)$ 4 QN
  6. $\sim(Pa \vee Qa)$ 5 EI
  7. $\sim Pa \cdot \sim Qa$ 6 DM
  8. $(\exists x)(\sim Px \cdot \sim Qx)$ 7 EG

5. 1. $(x)[Px \supset (\exists y)(Q\,y \cdot Rxy)]$ Premise
  2. $(x)(Qx \supset Sx)$ /$(\exists y)(x)[Px \supset (Sy \cdot Rxy)]$ Premise / Conclusion
  3. $Pa \supset (\exists y)(Q\,y \cdot Ray)$ 1 UI
    4. Pa Assumption
    5. $(\exists y)(Q\,y \cdot Ray)$ 3,4 MP
    6. $Qb \cdot Rab$ 5 EI
    7. Qb 6 Simp
    8. $Qb \supset Sb$ 2 UI
    9. Sb 7,8 MP
   10. Rab 6 Simp
   11. $Sb \cdot Rab$ 9,10 Conj
  12. $Pa \supset (Sb \cdot Rab)$ 4–11 CP
  13. $(x)[Px \supset (Sb \cdot Rxb)]$ 12 UG
  14. $(\exists y)(x)[Px \supset (Sy \cdot Rxy)]$ 13 EG

6. 1. $(x)[Px \supset (Qx \vee Rx)]$ Premise
  2. $(\exists x)(Sx \cdot \sim Qx)$ Premise
  3. $(x)[Rx \supset (Px \cdot Sx)]$ / $(x)(Px \supset Sx)$ Premise / Conclusion
  4. $Sa \cdot \sim Qa$ 2 EI
  5. $Pa \supset (Qa \textbf{ v } Ra)$ 1 UI
  6. $Ra \supset (Pa \cdot Sa)$ 3 UI
    7. Pa Assumption
    8. $Qa \vee Ra$ 5,7 MP
    9. $\sim Qa$ 4 Simp
   10. Ra 8,9 DS
   11. $Pa \cdot Sa$ 6,10 MP
   12. Sa 11 Simp
  13. $Pa \supset Sa$ 7–12 CP
  14. $(x)(Px \supset Sx)$ 13 UG

E. Translate each of the following arguments into symbolic notation, and construct a proof.

✱1. McDonald's hypothesis about the sex life of lizards is a scientific theory, but it is not proven. For it is not consistent with some of the evidence, and a scientific theory is proven only if it is consistent with all the evidence.

2. Anyone who buys a used car from Marty is either a fool or has money to burn. Jamie bought a used car from Marty, and he doesn't have money to burn. So there's at least one fool in the world.

3. Any student who has either taken the prerequisites or received permission from the instructor may take this course. Freshmen are students, and some freshmen got the instructor's permission, so some freshmen may take this course.

✱4. The aerospace plane will have a speed of Mach 4 and will therefore have to use hydrogen fuel. That's because any plane moving at Mach 4 must use a fuel that ignites in air moving at that speed, and only hydrogen will ignite in air moving at Mach 4.

5. Anyone who passes an advanced philosophy course has a logical mind, and anyone with a logical mind can master any field of law. Gabrielle passed metaphysics, which is an advanced philosophy course, so she can master torts, which is a field of law.

6. According to Soviet law, any worker employed by a state-owned enterprise was required to cooperate with the KGB. Since anyone who worked was employed by some state-owned enterprise, all workers were required to cooperate with the KGB.

✱7. People who drink too much are either aggressive or withdrawn. Anyone who's aggressive is dangerous, and anyone who's withdrawn is boring. I don't like dangerous or boring people, so I don't like people who drink too much.

8. One is a member of a club only if the club is willing to have him and if he joins the club. But I wouldn't join any club willing to have me, so I am not a member of any club.

9. All physical things have a finite duration. If everything is physical, then the soul is physical; and the soul, if it has a finite duration, is not immortal. So if everything is physical, the soul is not immortal.

✱10. Every decision is an event, and every event is caused by something. A cause is either an event or an agent. So every decision is caused either by an event or by an agent.

11. For any number there is a number larger than it. Therefore there is no number larger than every other (assuming it is true of all numbers that if one is larger than another, the second is not larger than the first).

12. All personnel except guards left the building. No executive personnel are guards. Since everyone who left the building was safe, all executive personnel were safe.

✱13. Anyone who aids a criminal is immoral, and every dictatorial government is criminal. No moral person, therefore, would aid a dictatorial government.

14. If not all actions are determined, then people need some standard of choice, and a standard of choice is a moral code. Since some actions are not determined, every person does need a moral code.

F. Show that each of the following arguments is valid by constructing a proof.

✻1. $(\exists x)Px \supset (y)Qy$
   $(y)(\exists x)(Px \supset Qy)$

2. $(x)[(Px \lor Qx) \supset Rx]$
   $(x)Px \supset (y)Ry$

3. $(x)[Px \supset (Qx \lor Rx)]$
   $(\exists x)(Px \cdot \sim Rx)$
   $(\exists x)Qx$

✻4. $(x)[(Qx \cdot Rx) \supset Px]$
   $(x)[(Qx \cdot Sx) \supset Tx]$
   $(\exists x)[Qx \cdot (Rx \lor Sx)]$
   $(\exists x)(Px \lor Tx)$

5. $(\exists x)(y)[Px \cdot (Qy \supset Rxy)]$
   $(x)(Px \supset Qx)$
   $(\exists x)Rxx$

6. $(x)(Px \equiv Qx)$
   $(x)[Px \supset (\exists y)Rxy]$
   $(\exists x)Qx$
   $(\exists x)(\exists y)Rxy$

✻7. $(x)(Px \supset Qx) \supset (\exists y)(Ry \cdot Sy)$
   $(x)\sim Sx$
   $(\exists x)(Px \cdot \sim Qx)$

8. $(x)(Px \supset Qx)$
   $\sim(\exists x)(Qx \cdot Sx)$
   $(x)(Rx \supset Sx)$
   $(x)(Px \supset \sim Rx)$

9. $(x)[(Px \lor Qx) \supset (\exists y)Sy]$
   $(\exists x)[Px \cdot (y)(Sy \supset Rxy)]$
   $(\exists x)(\exists y)Rxy$

✻10. $(x)[Px \lor (\exists y)Rxy]$
   $(x)(Qx \supset \sim Px)$
   $(x)(y)(Rxy \supset Sy)$
   $(\exists x)Qx \supset (\exists y)Sy$

11. $(x)(Pxa \supset Rx)$
   $(\exists x)(Qx \cdot Pxb)$
   $(x)(Qx \supset \sim Rx)$
   $\sim(x)(Pxb \supset Pxa)$

12. $(x)(Px \lor Qx)$
   $(x)(\exists y)(Rxy \supset \sim Px)$
   $(x)(y)(Qx \supset Sxy)$
   $(x)(\exists y)(Rxy \supset Sxy)$

✻13. $(\exists x)\{Px \cdot (y)(z)[(Qy \cdot Rz) \supset Sxyz]\}$
   $(x)(Px \supset Rx)$
   $(y)(\exists x)(Qy \supset Sxyx)$

14. $(\exists x)(Px \cdot \sim Qx) \supset Ra$
   $(\exists x)Rx \supset (y)(Py \supset Qy)$
   $(x)(Px \supset Qx)$

15. $(x)[Px \supset (Qa \cdot Rxa)]$
   $(\exists x)(Qx \lor Sx) \supset (y)(z)(Ryz \supset Tyz)$
   $(x)(\exists y)(Px \supset Txy)$

✻16. $(\exists x)[Qx \cdot (Rx \lor Sx)]$
   $(x)[(Qx \lor Sx) \supset Tx]$
   $(x)\sim(Px \lor Tx)$
   $(\exists x)[(Qx \cdot Rx) \cdot \sim Px]$

17. $(x)\{Px \supset (y)[(Qy \cdot Ry) \supset \sim Sxy]\}$
   $(x)(y)(Txy \supset Sxy)$
   $(x)(y)Txy$
   $(x)[Px \supset \sim(\exists y)(Qy \cdot Ry)]$

18. $(\exists x)(Px \cdot Qx) \supset (y)(Ry \supset Sy)$
   $(\exists x)(Px \cdot Rx)$
   $(\exists x)(Qx \supset Sx)$

✻19. $(x)\{Px \supset (y)[(Qy \cdot Rxy) \supset (\exists z)(Sz \cdot Txyz)]\}$
   $(x)(\exists y)(Sx \equiv \sim Sy)$
   $(\exists x)(\exists y)[Px \cdot (Qy \cdot Rxy)] \supset \sim(z)Sz$

20. $(x)[Px \supset (\exists y)(z)(Qy \cdot Rxyz)]$
   $(x)(Qx \supset Sx)$
   $(x)(y)(z)(Rxyz \supset Txz)$
   $(\exists x)(\exists y)(z)[Px \supset (Sy \cdot Txz)]$

PART THREE

Inductive Logic

In Part 2, we studied deduction. The role of a deductive argument is to draw a conclusion that is contained implicitly in the premises. A deductive argument is either valid or invalid; there are no intermediate degrees of partial validity. If the argument is valid, then it is impossible for the premises to be true and the conclusion false. We turn now to *induction*, the other broad category of reasoning. In an inductive argument, the conclusion amplifies—it goes beyond—what the premises state. As a result, the truth of the premises does *not* guarantee the truth of the conclusion; there is some possibility, however small, that the conclusion is false. Inductive arguments have degrees of strength, depending not only on the relationship between premises and conclusion but also on a wider context of other available information. In the following chapters, we will learn how to analyze different types of inductive arguments and how to assess the degree of support their premises confer on the conclusion. The basic mode of inductive reasoning consists of drawing a universal conclusion about a class of things from premises about certain members of that class. We will study this process of generalizing in Chapter 12, with particular attention to generalizations about causality. In Chapter 13, we will study arguments based on analogies. Chapter 14 covers statistical inferences. In Chapter 15, finally, we'll look at the reasoning involved in giving explanations.

Inductive Generalizations

We use deductive reasoning whenever we act on the basis of general knowledge—knowledge about classes of things and the properties they share. We acquire that knowledge in various ways, but primarily by generalizing from our experience—a form of **inductive argument**. This process is captured by the old saying "Once burned, twice shy." A child who burns himself on a stove does not treat this as an isolated experience; he draws a general conclusion that will guide his future transactions with hot stoves. In the same way, all of us rely on countless generaliza-

tions we have drawn from experience: An egg will break if it's dropped; steel is stronger than wood; we can't breathe under water; shy people tend to be nervous at parties. Imagine trying to live your life without the benefit of such knowledge, treating each experience as a completely new encounter with the world, with no expectations about how things will behave or what the consequences of your actions will be.

In this chapter, we will examine the nature of inductive generalizations and the standards for evaluating them, with special emphasis on generalizations about causality.

12.1 Generalizing

In logical terms, we can see the importance of generalizing by going back to what we learned about deductive arguments. Each of the following propositions was a premise of a deductive argument in a previous chapter:

1. All of Shakespeare's plays are in blank verse.
2. No horned animal is a predator.
3. All geniuses are eccentric.

4. Uncommunicative people do not make friends easily.
5. Bill never admits he's wrong.
6. If a mass of hot, humid air collides with a high-pressure mass of cooler air, then it rains.

Each of these is a *general* proposition. It says something about an entire class: Shakespeare's plays, horned animals, masses of hot, humid air, and so on. When we studied deductive reasoning, we wanted to know what conclusions we could draw from these propositions. Now we want to know how these propositions would themselves be supported by evidence.

Each of them could be treated as the conclusion of a further deductive argument. For example, 2 might be supported as follows:

No herbivore is a predator.
<u>All horned animals are herbivores.</u>
No horned animal is a predator.

This is a perfectly good argument, but it doesn't really solve the problem, because now we have two new general premises that will need some support. In the same way, 6 might be deduced from a more general theory about the properties of air masses, but then we would have to ask what evidence we have for that theory. The implication is that we cannot support a general proposition merely by deducing it from other general propositions. At *some* point in our reasoning, for conclusions like 1–6, we have to look at the actual instances of the general propositions. We have to examine Shakespeare's plays, the different species of horned animals, the geniuses we know or have read about, and then draw the general conclusion from the particular cases.

But there are dangers here, in particular the danger of *hasty generalization*. Hasty generalization is a fallacy because a single instance doesn't necessarily prove a general rule. Suppose we have a general proposition of the form "All S are P." If an individual member of the class of Ss is P, it is called a **positive instance**, and it confirms the generalization; if it is not P, it is a **negative instance** or counterexample, and it disconfirms the generalization. But there is a logical asymmetry here. A single negative instance decisively refutes a general statement. If I say that all athletes are dumb, and you point out that the varsity quarterback is getting excellent grades, you have proved me wrong. A single *positive* instance, however, does not prove that a generalization is *true*. The fact that one athlete is a weak student doesn't prove that all of them are. How is it possible, then, to support a universal proposition merely by looking at examples?

If S stands for a small, delimited class of things, we can solve this problem by examining each member of the class individually to see whether it is P. In proposition 1 earlier, for example, the class is Shakespeare's plays—the 37 plays he wrote during his life. It would be feasible to examine each of them and to determine whether it is in blank verse. In fact, this is the *only* way to tell whether the proposition is true, because there's no particular reason why Shakespeare *had* to write all his plays in that form. This is called the method of induction by *complete enumeration,* and it is appropriate when we are dealing with small classes—an author's complete works, the members of a family, the clothes in your closet—where we know something about each member individually.

But most of the generalizations we use in everyday reasoning do not involve classes of that type. They involve classes that are open-ended: There is no limit on the number of members they may have. To claim that all geniuses are eccentric, for example, is to make a statement about the entire class of geniuses—*all* of them, past, present, and future, the obscure ones as well as the famous. Obviously, we cannot examine each member of this class individually. Even in 5, which concerns a single individual, we are still concerned with the open-ended class of occasions on which Bill is wrong. We cannot know anything about the future occasions, and even if we know Bill extremely well, we almost certainly don't know about all the past occasions. With the exception of 1, all the propositions on our list are of this type, and we cannot establish their truth or falsity by the method of complete enumeration.

So we have to rely on an incomplete survey of the class, a *sample* taken from the class as a whole, and infer that what is true of the sample is true of the class. This mode of inference is legitimate when we are dealing with classes of things that possess common traits—properties, relationships, and ways of acting. Those traits are connected in various ways, so that anything possessing a given trait will also possess another one. Members of the same biological species, for example, are alike in their basic survival needs, their method of reproduction, and many other properties. Systems of classification usually pick out classes of objects that share more than a single trait—especially when we classify in accordance with an essential principle. We find the same kind of connection in cause-and-effect relationships. Copper conducts electricity because of its atomic structure, and any substance with the same structure will also conduct electricity. Of course, an object may possess traits that are *not* connected. A given person might have red hair and a short temper, but despite popular mythology, there is no known connection between these properties and thus no reason to expect that all redheads have short tempers.

What we need, therefore, are guidelines to determine whether a sample will give us a well-supported generalization rather than a hasty one. Three rules will help us to decide. These rules are standards for assessing the strength of the inference from sample to generalization, and they are analogous to the rules for determining whether a syllogism is valid. But remember that generalizing is a type of induction, in which—unlike deduction—strength is a matter of degree. So instead of the clear-cut distinction between valid and invalid arguments that we found in studying deduction, we are now going to have to work with a continuum ranging from weak to strong. The rules should be regarded as guidelines to help us locate a given generalization along that continuum.

12.1A Three Rules for Generalizing

1. *The sample should be sufficiently numerous and various.*

A single instance is usually not enough to support a generalization. In the absence of other knowledge, the fact that a single S is P won't tell us whether S and P are connected, so generalizing that all S are P would be hasty. We need to look at a number of Ss; if all of them are P, then we have better evidence of a connection. But it is even more important to test a *variety* of Ss. If you were buying a car and were considering a Toyota, you might ask people who own Toyotas whether they are satisfied. Suppose that all of them have had problems with the car. If the people all bought cars of the same model year, from the same dealer, with the same package of options, then the problems might be due to one of these other common factors. Your conclusion that Toyotas are poor cars would be stronger if you varied these factors, checking cars of different years, with different options, bought from different dealers.

How much variety is enough? The general rule is that a sample of Ss should vary in every property (other than being S) that *might* be responsible for their being P. Consider the generalization that shy people are nervous at parties. In your sample of shy people, you would certainly want to vary such personality factors as intelligence and degree of interest in people, because these might well affect their nervousness at parties. You would also want your sample to vary in background: Are shy people with lots of social experience as nervous at parties as shy people with little social experience? In contrast, factors such as blood type, political views, or favorite movie do not seem even potentially relevant to the generalization, and there would be no need to vary them.

As the example indicates, deciding whether a given property might be relevant is a judgment call and depends on what other knowledge we have—a point we'll come back to when discussing rule 3. It also depends on how broad or sweeping our conclusion is. A given company, for example, might be classified under concepts of increasing abstractness: STEEL COMPANY, MANUFACTURING FIRM, CORPORATION. A generalization about all manufacturing firms requires a larger and more varied sample than does a generalization about steel companies, and a generalization about all corporations requires an even larger and more varied sample. In general, the more abstract the subject term of the conclusion, the more numerous and varied the sample must be.

2. *We should look for disconfirming as well as confirming instances of a generalization.*

A generalization is disconfirmed by negative instances or counterexamples: Ss that are not P, Toyota owners who are satisfied with their cars, shy people who are not nervous at parties. If we have looked hard for negative instances and haven't found any, we can be more confident of a generalization than we can if we haven't looked at all.

This rule is important for two reasons, one logical, the other psychological. The logical reason pertains to a key difference between inductive and deductive inference. A deductive argument is self-contained: The premises either do or do not support the conclusion, regardless of what other knowledge we might have. An inductive argument, in contrast, is *not* self-contained. The premises are propositions stating information about the sample, and the degree to which these premises support the conclusion depends on whether we have any *other* information about disconfirming instances. So it's important to look for such information.

The psychological reason is the phenomenon of *confirmation bias:* the tendency to look for and give weight to evidence supporting a conclusion while ignoring, downplaying, or failing to seek evidence against it. For example:

- When we are angry at someone, our minds tend to multiply examples of how that person has wronged or offended us and to forget the other times when the person was fair or kind.
- People tend to rely on sources of news—television or radio stations, Web sites, newspapers, etc.—that share their political orientation, rather than seeking news and ideas that challenge their views.
- When the economy seems to be declining, we pay heightened attention to things that confirm the trend: every house with a "For Sale" sign, every drop in the stock market, etc.
- In depression, the mind tends to obsess in a self-confirming way over one's failures, losses, and inadequacies.

In everyday contexts, we must find evidence for or against a generalization by searching our memories for positive and negative instances. In most cases, it would be impossible to remember every single experience that might be relevant. What we can extract from memory tends to be influenced by what we are looking for. If we search only for positive cases, those are probably the only ones we're going to find. To avoid this bias, we need to look for counterexamples as well.

How do we look for negative instances? There's no general rule; it depends on each particular case. But one technique is worth mentioning. When we look for instances to test a generalization that all *S* are *P*, we are looking for individual referents of the concept *S*. The easiest referents to recall are the prototypical ones, the central, clear-cut cases. But we should also look for referents close to the borderline of the concept, because many generalizations are true only of the prototypical cases, not of atypical *S*s. If you are wondering whether all birds can fly, don't think just of obvious examples like robins and crows; think also of penguins and ostriches. If you are wondering whether all democracies protect individual rights, don't look just at modern cases like England and the United States; think also of ancient Athens.

3. *We should consider whether a link between S and P is plausible in light of other knowledge we possess.*

To see the point of this rule, consider two contrasting cases. If chemists discovered a new metal, they would determine its melting point in a laboratory, and a single test would be sufficient to support the generalization that all instances of the metal melt at that temperature. However, the generalization that all swans are white was confirmed by countless instances over a long period of time, yet it was always regarded as somewhat shaky, and eventually black swans were indeed discovered in Australia. Rule 3 explains the difference between these cases. Our scientific knowledge about physical substances tells us that the melting point of a metal is fixed by its atomic structure, which defines that type of metal. So we know ahead of time that all samples of the metal will have the same melting point, whatever it might be, and a single test is enough to identify that point. By contrast, biological theory gives us no reason for thinking that all swans must have the same color, so even a great many positive instances will not make the generalization certain.

Let's look at another, more controversial example. Some people hold that men and women differ in certain mental abilities: Women, as a group, tend to be better at certain verbal skills, while men tend to be better at certain mathematical ones. There is a large body of experimental research on this question, most of it involving tests given to large numbers of people. On some of the verbal and mathematical tests, there are slight differences in average scores between men and women. But the issue is not likely to be settled solely on experimental grounds, because people interpret the results in light of their views about the bases of cognitive abilities. Those who hold that the abilities have a genetic basis find it plausible that there might be some innate differences between men and women and tend to take the test scores as evidence of such a difference. Others believe that cognitive abilities are the result of individual training. From this point of view, the experimental evidence will never be enough to show an inherent difference between men and women; it will always seem more plausible to attribute differences in test scores to nongenetic factors, such as the way boys and girls are raised and educated. In other words, we cannot treat the inductive evidence about specific verbal and mathematical abilities in isolation. We must also look at the larger issue of the sources of cognitive abilities as such. At some point, of course, we will have to settle the issue inductively, but the inductive evidence on the narrower question may not be decisive.

These three rules for generalizing, taken together, illustrate a point already mentioned: the open-ended character of induction. Unlike a deductive argument, an inductive one is not self-contained. Its strength is affected by the context of other knowledge we possess. The truth of the premises does not guarantee the truth of the conclusion, and the degree of support the premises provide for the conclusion depends on factors not contained in the argument itself. It is always possible to strengthen an inductive argument further by finding additional positive instances, especially if they increase the variety of the sample (rule 1). But the strength of the argument is dependent on our diligence in looking for disconfirming evidence (rule 2). Its strength also depends on the initial plausibility of the generalization, which is determined by the body of related knowledge we have (rule 3). This is not a defect of induction. But it does mean that inductive reasoning puts a special premium on *integration*, on looking beyond the argument itself to see how it fits with the rest of our knowledge.

The three rules we have just examined are applicable to generalizations of most kinds. Appropriately enough, they are *general* rules. But there are different kinds of generalizations, and for each kind we can formulate more specific rules. In the next section of this chapter, we will study the rules for identifying *causal* relationships. In Chapter 14, we will look at *statistical* generalizations.

SUMMARY **Rules for Generalizing**

---

1. Make sure the sample from which you generalize is sufficiently numerous and various.
2. Look for disconfirming as well as confirming instances of the generalization.

3. Consider whether the generalization is plausible in light of other knowledge you possess.

EXERCISE 12.1

A. Evaluate each of the following generalizations inductively, drawing on your own experience. If you think you don't know enough to tell whether it is true or false, identify the kind of evidence you would need in order to decide. In each case, indicate how each of the rules would guide your reasoning.

* 1. The food at restaurant X [pick one you know] is lousy.
  2. Italians are hot-tempered.

  3. The soil in my garden is highly acidic.
* 4. Dogs always go around in circles when they lie down.

5. Ms. or Mr. X [pick someone you know] works well under pressure.
6. None of the clothes in my closet is new.
* 7. Doctors have high incomes.
8. Heroes in tragic drama always have a fatal flaw.
9. All religions involve belief in a god or gods.
* 10. All geniuses are eccentric.
11. Price controls produce shortages.
12. Without antitrust laws, industries would be dominated by monopolies.

* B. The Acme Corporation has employees with different jobs—assembly-line workers, bookkeepers, salespeople, managers, etc.—with different levels of education. Each of the cards below represents an employee. On one side is the person's job; on the other side is the person's level of education. Which cards would you need to turn over to test the generalization that all the salespeople are college graduates?

Employee 1 College degree	Employee 2 Salesperson	Employee 3 Bookkeeper	Employee 4 No college degree

12.2 Causality

Generalizing is an effort to identify connections among traits. But the term *connection* is pretty vague. What sort of relationship are we talking about? In most cases, we are talking about *causality*. Causality may involve interactions among things: collisions between air masses produce rain, a lighted match will set paper on fire. Or it may be a connection between the properties of an object and the way it acts: Uncommunicative people don't make friends easily, a car's design affects its performance, a charged particle will attract or repel other charged particles. Or it may involve a causal link among properties themselves: Steel is hard because of its structure, human beings possess language because they possess reason. In one way or another, many generalizations have to do with causality, and we need to study this relationship more closely.

If you've ever skidded on an icy road, you can imagine what a world without causality would be like. That sudden loss of control, when turning the wheel or pumping the brakes has no effect on the car—imagine the same thing on a wider scale, imagine losing control over *everything*. That thought experiment shows how central causality is to our sense of the world. We expect events to follow regular patterns: Touching a hot stove leads to pain, pumping the brakes makes the car slow down, studying improves our grasp of a subject. We expect objects to act within limits set by their natures: Human beings cannot fly by flapping their arms, rocks don't engage in reasoning, dictators do not welcome opposition. And even if there is no direct causal relation between two traits that seem connected, they may both be effects of a deeper cause. A sore throat and sneezing tend to go together when you have a cold. Neither causes the other; they are both symptoms of the virus at work in your system.

As these examples illustrate, the term *causality* covers a very broad range. Different types of causality can be found in different regions of nature and human life, and the various branches of science have developed specialized techniques for studying causality in their own areas. But we are going to look at a general-purpose technique that will help us identify and analyze causal relationships of any type. The basis of this technique is a distinction between necessary and sufficient conditions.

A given causal factor *a* is a *necessary* condition for an effect *E* when *E* cannot exist or occur without *a*. Factor *a* is a *sufficient* condition for *E* when *a* is enough to guarantee that *E* exists or occurs. To see the difference, let's take a simple example: You drop an egg and it breaks. The effect—condition *E*—is the breaking of the egg. What factors are responsible for making this happen? What factors play the role of *a*? The obvious factor is (1) that you dropped the egg. We would ordinarily think of this as *the* cause, because it is the event that led directly to the effect. But there are other factors involved as well: (2) the hardness of the floor, (3) the fragility of the eggshell, and (4) the fact that the egg is heavier than air. Without 2 and 3, the egg would not have broken when it fell, and without 4 it would not have fallen in the first place. Thus 2, 3, and 4 are all necessary conditions for the effect. What is the sufficient condition? All by itself, 1 is not sufficient—because it would not have produced the effect in the absence of the other conditions. So the sufficient condition is the *combination* of all four factors.

Notice that one condition can be necessary for another condition without being sufficient. The fragility of the eggshell is necessary for it to break, but not sufficient—otherwise the egg would break even without being dropped. In contrast, a condition can be sufficient without being necessary. Together with the other factors, 1 is a sufficient condition for the effect, but there are other ways in which the eggshell could have broken: It could have been hit with a hammer, the chick inside could have hatched, and so on.

Notice also that 2, 3, and 4 are standing conditions. They are properties of the egg and its environment that endure over time; they were present all along. The act of dropping the egg, by contrast, was a stimulus or *triggering event* that occurred at a specific moment and made the egg break a moment later. In everyday speech, when we speak of *the* cause of an effect, we usually mean the triggering event. But not always. When a bridge with a structural flaw collapses during a high wind, the wind is the triggering event, but we would probably say that the flaw was the cause of the collapse. Why? Because we expect a bridge to be able to withstand winds, and most of them do. It is the flaw that distinguishes this bridge from those that do not fall in high winds. In this way, our notion of *the* cause of an event is governed partly by expectations based on our general knowledge; it is affected by what strikes us as the salient or distinctive feature of a situation. Logically, however, we would analyze this case in exactly the same way as we analyzed the breaking egg.

So far we have been talking about the cause of an *event,* but we can also talk about the cause of a *property.* The fragility of the eggshell, for example, is a standing condition that is partly responsible for its breaking. In that respect we are treating fragility as a cause. But when we ask *why* eggshells are fragile, we are considering the property of fragility as an effect of deeper causes: the shape and composition of the shell. Many of our generalizations involve causal connections of this type. When we conclude that all *S* are *P*, it is generally because we are convinced there is something in the nature of *S*s that makes them *P*: Something in the nature of steel makes it stronger than wood, something in Bill's personality makes him unwilling to admit he's wrong, something in the design of a car makes it unreliable. One of the main goals of science is to find the necessary and sufficient conditions for the properties of physical substances, social institutions, individual personalities, and other phenomena.

In short, we study causal relationships by trying to identify the factors that are necessary and/or sufficient for the effect we want to explain. This is what's wrong with the *post hoc* fallacy, the assumption that because *a* preceded *E*, *a* must have caused *E*. The fact that *a* came first is certainly relevant, but all by itself it gives us no reason to think that *a* was either necessary or sufficient for *E*.

What sort of evidence, then, *can* we use? The nineteenth-century philosopher John Stuart Mill formulated several methods for establishing evidence of a causal connection. They are known as the methods of *agreement, difference, concomitant variations*, and *residues*. Despite their formidable names, Mill's methods are used in everyday, common-sense reasoning about causality; they are also used by scientists in designing experiments.

12.3 Agreement and Difference

Suppose you were trying to figure out why you liked certain courses you've taken. You would probably start by looking for something those courses had in common. Did they share the same subject matter? Were the class discussions interesting? Did all the teachers have the same style, approach, or ability? Suppose the common factor turned out to be lively class discussions. To test the conclusion that this was the source of your enjoyment, the next step would be to look at courses that did *not* have such discussions and see whether you *didn't* enjoy them.

This example illustrates two fundamental techniques for identifying the cause of a given effect. First, we look for a common factor that is present in all the cases in which the effect occurs. When doctors are confronted with a new disease, they typically try to see whether the people who have the disease all ate the same food, or have the same virus in their blood, or are similar in some other way. A detective trying to solve a series of murders might ask whether the victims had something in common. Mill called this technique the **method of agreement**: We look for some respect in which the different cases agree.

Second, to test whether a given factor plays a causal role, we take away that factor, holding everything else constant, and see whether the effect still occurs. If your car makes a funny noise when you accelerate, take your foot off the pedal and see whether the noise goes away. If a baby is crying and you think he might be hungry, see whether the crying stops when you feed him. Scientists use the same technique when they do controlled experiments. In testing the efficacy of a new medicine, for example, they use two carefully matched groups of people. One group gets the drug, the other gets a placebo; the *only* relevant difference between the groups is the presence or absence of the drug, so that any difference in results can then be attributed to that factor. Mill called this the **method of difference**.

To understand these techniques, and to identify their use in different contexts, it helps to represent them schematically.

Method of agreement:
Case 1: $a, b, c \rightarrow E$
Case 2: $a, d, f \rightarrow E$
Case 3: $a, g, h \rightarrow E$

Therefore, a is responsible for E.

Each row represents a separate premise of the argument; it represents a case or situation in which the effect, *E*, occurs. For example, each row might stand for an individual course, and *E* would be your response to it. The lowercase letters represent the various factors present in the different situations. There will not always be exactly three cases, or exactly three factors. And it won't always happen that the factors other than *a* appear only once; *b*, *c*, and the others might be present in more than one case. What is crucial to the method of agreement is that only one factor is present in *all* the cases. The conclusion says that the factor present in all cases is responsible for the effect. Notice that this conclusion is a generalization. We are saying that *a* will cause *E* in all cases, not just those we have examined, so we are generalizing from a sample to a universal proposition. Indeed, the method of agreement is simply the first rule for generalizing, as applied to the study of causality: We identify a link between *a* and *E* by varying the other factors.

Method of difference:

Case 1: $a, b, c \rightarrow E$

Case 2: $-, b, c \rightarrow \sim E$

Therefore, *a* is responsible for *E*.

The tilde in front of *E* in the second line is a sign of negation: It indicates that *E* does not occur in this case. Once again, there may be any number of factors in each case, but this time there *is* a reason for including just the two cases. The conclusion is a generalization, as before, but we are not generalizing from a sample of positive instances. We are contrasting a single positive instance with a negative instance that is identical except for the absence of one factor, in order to isolate the causal role of that factor. It is crucial, therefore, that all the factors other than *a* be reproduced in case 2.

The methods of agreement and difference are typically combined, both in everyday reasoning and in science. This combination is called the **joint method** of agreement and difference, and we can represent its structure as follows:

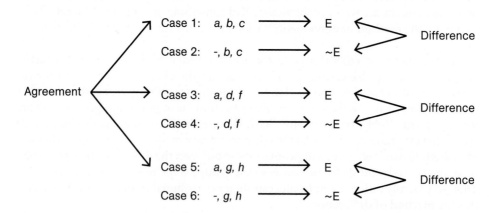

We have simply taken the method of agreement, as diagrammed above, and contrasted each positive instance with a case that is identical except for the absence of *a*. Not every use of the joint method would be this thorough. We might use the method of difference with only one of the positive instances, or only a few, especially if we have a large number of positive instances. But even a single contrasting case strengthens considerably the evidence provided by the method of agreement.

Let's look at an example of the joint method in action. In the early efforts to find the causes of AIDS, medical researchers found that the disease inhibits certain white blood cells called granulocytes. Why does this happen? Medical researchers found that the inhibiting factor is in the blood serum (the liquid part of blood) rather than in the granulocytes themselves. When they extracted the granulocytes from AIDS patients and combined them with serum from normal donors, the granulocytes were no longer inhibited. But when healthy granulocytes were combined with serum from AIDS patients, the granulocytes *were* inhibited. The effect here is the inhibition of the granulocytes, and we have two factors: the granulocyte cells and the blood serum. In AIDS patients (case 1, below), both the cells and the serum are diseased. The other two cases represent the researchers' results:

Case 1:	sick cells	sick serum	⟶	inhibition of cells
Case 2:	sick cells	healthy serum	⟶	~inhibition of cells
Case 3:	healthy cells	sick serum	⟶	inhibition of cells

Therefore, the cause of the inhibition is in the serum.

Cases 1 and 2 together constitute the method of difference: When sick cells are put into healthy serum, they are no longer inhibited. Cases 1 and 3 together constitute the method of agreement: When the serum is diseased, the granulocytes will be inhibited, regardless of whether they are themselves diseased or healthy.

To see why it is so valuable to combine the methods of agreement and difference, remember the distinction we drew between necessary and sufficient conditions. The method of agreement, by itself, provides evidence that a is *sufficient* for E. Since the effect can occur in the absence of any other factor, none of the other factors is necessary, so we have reason to think that a is sufficient. But we have less reason to think that a is *necessary*, since there may be more than one way to bring about the effect. In the case of your course preferences, you might like some courses because of class discussion and others because the subject is especially interesting. To tell whether a is necessary, we need to see whether the effect can occur in its absence—and that is what the method of difference tells us. This method provides good evidence that a is necessary. If used by itself, however, it does not support very well the conclusion that a is sufficient. Why not? Because the two cases

Case 1: $a, b, c \rightarrow E$
Case 2: $\text{-}, b, c \rightarrow \text{~}E$

leave open the possibility that b and c are necessary for the effect. (In our example of the egg breaking, b might be the fragility of the eggshell and c the hardness of the floor.) Thus the methods of agreement and difference have complementary strengths. If we are trying to show that a is necessary and sufficient for E, we need to use the methods in combination.

Agreement and difference are also used in a negative way to show that a given factor is *not* responsible for an effect. Suppose someone claimed that America's economic wealth was the result of its abundant natural resources. A counterargument would be that some countries with abundant resources, such as Sierra Leone, are *not* wealthy, and that some countries without many resources, such as Luxembourg, *are* wealthy. The first part of this argument is a negative use of the method of agreement. It says that the alleged cause is present in cases where we do not find the effect; hence that factor is not sufficient. The second part of the argument is a negative use of the method of difference. It says that we can take away the alleged cause and still have the effect; hence that factor is not necessary. In general, a negative use of agreement has the structure:

Case 1: $a, b, c \rightarrow E$
Case 2: $a, d, f \rightarrow E$
Case 3: $a, g, h \rightarrow {\sim}E$
_____

Therefore, a is not sufficient for E.

And a negative use of difference has the structure:

Case 1: $a, b, c \rightarrow E$
Case 2: $\text{-}, b, c \rightarrow E$
_____

Therefore, a is not necessary for E.

Notice that, to the left of the arrows in both cases, we have the same arrangement of factors as in the corresponding positive arguments. The difference lies solely in the arrows—in whether the effect does or does not occur.

The methods of agreement and difference can provide very strong evidence of a causal connection. If we know all the factors involved, if we have varied all of them in accordance with the methods, and if a is the only factor in whose presence the effect always occurs and in whose absence it does not occur—then the evidence may be decisive. But these are very big *ifs*. Sometimes there is more than one factor common to all the cases—and sometimes there isn't *any* single common factor. It often happens that we cannot vary all the factors exhaustively. And we are rarely if ever in a position to be sure that we know what all the factors are. Let's look at four of the more common problems in this regard.

1. *Choosing the factors.* We have been assuming so far that there is a definite number of antecedent factors, and a small number at that—perhaps three or four. Strictly speaking, however, there is always an indefinitely large number of factors in the environment of the effect, and in paying attention to only a few of them, we are making a selection. Scientists studying a chemical reaction, for example, will attend to the chemicals involved and the temperature at which the reaction occurs. They will ignore such factors as what they had for breakfast that morning or the price of gold on the London market. So the use of Mill's methods involves *plausibility* judgments. Is it plausible that a given factor could be related to the effect? Do we need to vary it or can it safely be ignored? Plausibility judgments in turn are guided by the knowledge we already possess. In the above example, chemical theory gives ample reason for ignoring the price of gold. But we need to remember that these judgments are fallible. At one time, for instance, no one realized that air pressure might affect the temperature at which water boils, so no one thought to do the experiment at different altitudes above sea level.

2. *Levels of causality.* Causal relationships exist at many different levels in the world, from the interactions of subatomic particles, to the chemical structure of a substance, to the biological activity of a single cell, to the behavior of an individual person, to the economy of an entire nation. The problem this poses is that we may look to the wrong level in selecting the factors to study. The problem can be illustrated by an old joke in inductive logic. A man says, "Last weekend I had scotch and soda and got drunk. Monday I had brandy and soda and got drunk again. Yesterday I had bourbon and soda and got drunk again. Obviously the soda is what's making me drunk." The point of the joke is that the type of hard liquor is not the level at which to look for the cause; the real causal factor, the alcoholic content of the drinks, is at the chemical level.

To take a more serious example, researchers trying to isolate the causes of cancer need to consider both genetic factors and lifestyle. These potential causes exist at different levels—the biochemistry of DNA and the behavior of the person, respectively—and require different kinds of experimental evidence. In the same way, historians trying to explain the rise of Nazism disagree about what kind of explanation to look for: economic conditions, cultural trends, or some other type of factor. In such cases, the ideal procedure would be to vary factors at all the levels in a comprehensive fashion. But this is extremely difficult to do, and often impossible; scientists typically choose some particular level to study, on the assumption that the causes will be found there. So we need to be aware of the issue, and we should try to identify those assumptions whenever possible.

3. *Conceptualization.* When we notice that a particular effect occurs in a certain situation, we know that the cause is something in that situation. Before we can use Mill's methods, we have to break the situation down into individual factors. Nature won't do this for us. The factors don't come already divided, packaged, and labeled as *a*, *b*, c, etc. We have to analyze the circumstances and isolate the factors ourselves. This is essentially a problem of classification; we try to organize the situation in terms of concepts we possess. But we have seen that there is usually more than one way to classify the same set of things, and this can affect our use of inductive methods. An obvious example is the borderline case. A sociologist studying the effects of economic status on the divorce rate will have to draw a line somewhere between the lower and middle classes. Within limits, that line can be drawn at many different places, so that a family might be treated as lower class in one study, middle class in another. This will obviously affect the results of the studies.

Let's look at a more radical case. Suppose you found that the courses you enjoy don't seem to have anything in common. They don't all have good discussions, the teachers don't give the same sorts of lectures, and so on. It may be that you need to rethink your analysis of the factors. Perhaps the real cause is something that cuts across the factors you've been looking at. Suppose the real source of your enjoyment is that, regardless of how the class is organized in terms of lectures and discussions, the teacher makes the learning process a kind of game. If so, you won't discover that fact until you step back from your original way of analyzing the situation and try to classify factors in a different way. We should also notice that the issue of conceptualization applies to the *effect* as well as to the *factors*. In biology and psychology, for example, there is a vast literature on the causes of aggression. But some people argue that aggression per se is too broad a category to study effectively; the different species of aggression should be studied separately because they may have different causes.

4. *Direction of causality.* When the methods of agreement and difference reveal a causal relation between *a* and *E*, we have been assuming that it is clear which is the cause, which the effect. But this is not always so clear. Night follows day with perfect regularity, but day does not cause night; they are joint effects of an underlying cause, the rotation of the earth. It might even turn out that *E* is the cause and *a* the effect. To use our old example one more time, suppose that the courses you enjoyed *did* all have lively class discussions. The liveliness of the discussions might be a consequence, rather than a cause, of the fact that you (and the other students) are enjoying the course. So we cannot use the methods of induction mechanically. We have to interpret the results. There is evidence that criminals have an abnormally high rate of unemployment. Does this mean that unemployment drives people to crime? Or do criminal tendencies lead certain people to avoid regular work? Or are crime and unemployment joint effects of some underlying cause? To answer these questions, we would have to make judgments about plausibility, appeal to broader theories of human nature and look for additional inductive evidence.

The problems we have just examined do not discredit induction. We can deal with them by using Mill's methods of agreement and difference. But the problems show that we have to be careful if we want to avoid hasty judgments. And these problems are interesting in a theoretical sense because they reveal once again the contextual nature of induction, the fact that inductive reasoning is affected by the context of other knowledge we possess.

EXERCISE 12.3

Analyze each of the inductive arguments below. First identify the conclusion: Is it positive or negative? Which factor is being said to be (or not to be) the cause of which effect? Then identify the method used to support the conclusion: agreement, difference, or the joint method. Use the standard schema to represent the cases. Finally, look for problems in the use of the methods.

✳ 1. ScourClean Cleansing Powder cleans best! We'll scrub half of this dirty sink with a leading cleanser, the other half with ScourClean. Look at the difference!

2. The bull markets of the 1980s and 2000s occurred throughout different phases of the business cycle. In some years unemployment was high; in others it was low. In some cases business profits were high; in other cases they were not. But during these periods interest rates were low or falling. So interest rates clearly affect stock prices.

3. We've all noticed that Monday through Wednesday, when Don is in the office, everyone works well together and a lot gets done. The rest of the week, when he is gone, the same people are not as productive. Don must be the cause of the difference in productivity.

✳ 4. I planted zinnias in a flower bed with uniform soil, and I watered them all the same, but half the bed got full sun, and the zinnias grew taller there than in the other half, which was partly shaded. So the amount of sunlight makes a difference.

5. Poverty is not the cause of crime, as there are many poor people who are not criminals.

6. Focused attention to the subject is the key to learning. Students who attend carefully improve their knowledge, regardless of differences in ability. Students who are otherwise similar in ability, but do not attend to the subject, make little or no progress.

* 7. If product safety regulations discouraged the introduction of new products, then innovation in the widget industry should have declined after the Widget Control Act was passed. But innovation continued at the same pace.

8. Self-esteem appears to be at least a necessary condition for happiness. All the happy people I've known, whatever their other differences in personality and goals, seem to have basic self-esteem, whereas people who don't have that trait never seem to be happy.

9. In a controlled study, three cars of different types, of different ages, and from different manufacturers were tested for gas mileage before and after a tune-up. In every case, mileage improved after the tune-up, which shows that a well-tuned engine affects fuel efficiency.

* 10. In the past few days I have had four e-mail messages bounce back as undeliverable. They were sent to different people. One was a new contact, one was a reply to someone who e-mailed me, and the other two were people I e-mail frequently. Of those two, one message had an attachment; none of the others did. They all had AOL addresses, though. AOL must be blocking my messages.

12.4 Concomitant Variations and Residues

So far we have been talking about causes and effects in *qualitative* terms. An effect either occurs or does not occur, a factor is either present or absent. But both sides of this equation can vary *quantitatively* as well. You may enjoy different courses in different degrees, the unemployment rate may go up and down, the current in a wire may vary continuously. Two additional methods of induction are especially useful in such cases. Mill called them the methods of *concomitant variations* and *residues*.

Despite its daunting name, **concomitant variations** is a method you have almost certainly used at one time or another. If your car makes a funny noise when you accelerate, you might take your foot off the pedal and see whether the noise goes away. As we saw, that would be the method of difference. But you might also vary the pressure on the pedal to see whether the noise varies in intensity accordingly. That would be the method of concomitant variations. If quantitative changes in the effect are associated with quantitative changes in a given factor—that is, if they vary concomitantly—then we have reason to believe there is a causal connection between them.

We can represent this method schematically.

Concomitant variations:

	Case 1:	$a-, b, c \rightarrow E-$
	Case 2:	$a, b, c \rightarrow E$
	Case 3:	$a+, b, c \rightarrow E+$

Therefore, a is causally connected with E.

As in the method of agreement, there may not be exactly three cases or three factors. As in the method of difference, however, it is important to hold the factors other than a constant, so that we can attribute the variation in E to the variation in a. Notice that I have drawn the diagram to indicate a *positive* correlation: a and E vary in the same direction, up or down. This would represent the relation between a car's speed and the pressure on the accelerator. But the correlation could also be *negative*, as in the relation between the car's speed and pressure on the *brake* pedal. Can you see how the plus and minus signs in the diagram would be changed to represent this?

The method of concomitant variations is subject to several limitations. It does not show that a is a sufficient condition for E. Since b and c are present in all three cases, one or both of them may be necessary for the effect. In our example, the car must have some gas in the tank in order to accelerate at all. Nor does the method show that a is a necessary condition. Perhaps E would occur in some degree even without a: A car on a downhill slope will gain some speed without any pressure on the accelerator. What we *can* conclude is that, given the presence of the other factors, variations in a are sufficient for variations in E. So we do have evidence that there is some causal relationship. But the relation may not be direct. Between the accelerator pedal and the movement of the car is a causal chain with many intervening links. And it is not always clear what the direction of causality is. The fact that a and E vary concomitantly does not, in itself, tell us which causes which.

Against these limitations, the method of concomitant variations has two great advantages. The first is that it can be used in cases where we cannot eliminate a factor altogether and thus cannot apply the method of difference. For example (to use one of Mill's own illustrations), how do we know that the moon causes tides in the ocean? Obviously, we cannot remove the moon and see whether the tides cease. But we *can* correlate the cycle of high and low tides with changes in the moon's position. Or suppose we wanted to establish the effect of oxygen intake on an athlete's performance. It would be out of the question to cut off the oxygen altogether, but within limits we could vary the rate of intake.

The second advantage relates more directly to the quantitative nature of causal relationships. If you take sugar in your coffee, you know that sugar makes it sweeter, but you also know roughly how much sugar will produce what degree of sweetness. An architect knows how large a beam must be to carry a given amount of weight. A doctor knows how much of a certain drug to prescribe for a patient with a certain condition. A central aim of science, finally, is to identify quantitative relationships among phenomena. Many scientific laws are expressed algebraically in the form $y = f(x)$, to indicate that one variable is a function of another: y varies in accordance with x. For example, the pressure, temperature, and volume of a gas are related by the formula $V=cT/P$ (where c is a constant).

In short, it is one thing to know that certain factors are causally related; it is another thing to know the specific way they are related quantitatively. The method of concomitant variations is especially important in the latter case. We gain our rough, everyday understanding of quantitative relationships through the experience of observing how variations in one thing cause variations in another. How else would you know how much sugar to use? In science, laws relating one variable to another are usually integrated mathematically within larger theories; they are not established solely by induction. Once a law has been formulated, however, concomitant variations are the most direct way to test it.

The last of Mill's methods, the **method of residues**, also requires that we be able to quantify the effect. In outline, the reasoning runs as follows: E occurs in the presence of certain factors a, b, and c. It has already been established that c is responsible for part of the effect and b for another part, so the remainder (the "residue") must be caused by a. This reasoning is quite different in structure from that of the other methods—so different, in fact, that it cannot be represented schematically on a par with the others. It uses only a single case, and it relies on prior knowledge about the effects of factors b and c. Instead of using several cases to bring out the role of a, we infer the role of a in a single case by subtracting the known effects of the other factors.

We use the method of residues quite often. A simple example occurs when a veterinarian weighs a dog by stepping on the scale with the dog in her arms; if her own weight is 130 pounds, and the scale reads 150, then the dog must weigh 20 pounds. Here's another, more subtle example. Suppose you agree to meet a friend at a certain time. You are 5 minutes late, and he flies into a furious rage. You might think: He's overreacting, there must be something else bothering him. Your implicit reasoning is: The fact that I was a few minutes late would make him a little angry, but not *this* angry, so the feeling must be partly due to something else. In this example, anger is the effect, your lateness is factor b, and the "something else" is factor a. In science, the classic example of the method is the discovery of radium by Marie and Pierre Curie. Working with pitchblende—one of the ores in which uranium is found—they noticed that its radioactivity was higher than could be explained by the uranium in it. They concluded that the ore must contain some other radioactive substance, later identified as the new element radium.

Notice that we have used the method of residues in two different ways. In the first example, the residual effect (the extra 20 pounds on the scale reading) was attributed to a specific factor: the weight of the dog. In the other examples, the residual effect (the friend's overreaction, the unexplained portion of the pitchblende's radioactivity) was *not* attributed to any specific factor, but merely to "something else," to some unknown, indefinite factor. This second use of the method is probably the more common and is certainly the safer of the two, because we are not going so far out on a limb. If an effect occurs in some amount that is different from what we would have expected, it's a safe bet that *some* cause is at work over and above the ones we already know about. It is riskier to claim that that cause is some particular factor, because then we are assuming that we have identified every single factor in the situation, and that we know about the contribution made by every factor but one. In some cases, this assumption is justified. The veterinarian is certainly justified in thinking that the only thing that could affect the scale reading, other than her own weight, is the weight of the dog she is holding. But we have also seen that we are rarely in a position to be sure that we have identified all the factors.

This problem is involved in the controversy over the use of statistical evidence in proving racial or sexual discrimination. The average earnings of women were reported

---

SUMMARY Mill's Methods

The following methods can provide evidence for a causal relationship between a factor *a* and an effect *E*:

Agreement   Show that *a* is the only factor common to two or more cases in which *E* occurs. (Negative use: Show that *E* does not occur in one or more cases when *a* is present.)

Difference   Show that *E* occurs when *a* is present and not when it is absent, all other factors being held constant. (Negative use: Show that *E* occurs when *a* is absent.)

Joint method   Show that *a* is the only factor common to two or more cases in which

E occurs and that *E* does not occur in one or more of those cases if *a* is removed while holding the other factors constant.

Concomitant variations   Show that quantitative variations in *a* are systematically related to quantitative variations in *E*. (Negative use: Show that variations in *a* do not correlate with any change in *E*.)

Residues   Show that in a given case where *E* occurs, the factors other than *a* explain only a part of *E*.

---

to be only 77% those of men. One factor accounting for the difference is that married women often stop working outside the home in order to raise children, so that over a lifetime they accumulate less working experience than men, and less experienced workers tend to be paid less. But when this and other factors are accounted for, some part of the earnings difference remains. Since this gap cannot be explained by other factors, some people argue that it must be the result of discrimination against women. Other people argue that we do not know all the factors affecting a person's earnings, and that some of the known factors (e.g., luck, personality) can't be measured well enough to be included in the statistical data. Therefore, they claim, it is hasty to attribute the remaining gap to discrimination in particular. Whatever your position on this controversy, it is clear that we should use the method of residues with caution and that wherever possible we should back it up by using the other methods as well.

EXERCISE 12.4

A. Analyze each of the inductive arguments below. First identify the conclusion: Which factor is being said to be the cause of which effect? Then determine whether the method used to support the conclusion is concomitant variations or residues.

✳ 1. The amount of sleep I get clearly affects my energy level. I've noticed that if I get much less than 7 hours of sleep per night, I feel tired the next day; if I get about 7 hours, my energy level is good; if I get more than 7 hours, I have extra energy.

2. My woodstove hasn't been generating as much heat as it used to. That's partly because the wood

I was burning was wet, but even when I used dry wood, the stove still wasn't up to its old level, although it was better. So something must be blocking the air flow.

3. Scientific data show that the death rate from lung cancer increases with the amount that people smoke. For those who smoke up to a pack a day, the rate is six times that for nonsmokers; for those smoking over a pack a day, the rate is about 12 times higher. Smoking is clearly a cause of lung cancer.

❋ 4. Leaving the airport in his rental car, Dexter wanted to increase the volume of the radio and reached for the knob that he thought was the volume control. He quickly established that it was not the control, because rotating it did not produce any change in the volume.

5. The ability to perceive objects in depth is due partly to the fact that we have two eyes. Each eye receives a slightly different array of light reflected from the object, and the disparity produces a sense of depth. But there must be other factors involved. If you shut one eye, you won't be able to perceive depth quite as well, but you will still have some depth perception.

B. Analyze each of the inductive arguments below. First identify the conclusion: Which factor is being said to be the cause of which effect? Then determine which of the five methods is used to support the conclusion.

❋ 1. "What's causing this traffic jam?"

"Well, traffic is always slow at this hour, from the sheer number of rush-hour commuters. But it is much slower than normal today. There must be some problem up ahead—an accident, a lane closure . . . something."

2. "I wonder why this restaurant is so hot tonight."

"They must have turned up the heat."

"But I've been here at four in the afternoon, and it isn't hot; and they wouldn't turn down the heat in the afternoon."

"Then maybe the people make the difference. It's crowded now, but there's no one here at four."

3. Iron ore is smelted and refined into different products that vary in hardness, caused by the amount of carbon they contain. Wrought iron, which is virtually pure iron, is soft and malleable. Steel is harder; its carbon content is 0.25% to 1.5%. Cast iron, with about 4% carbon, is the hardest.

❋ 4. In 1900, U.S. Army doctor Walter Reed established that yellow fever was transmitted from one person to another by mosquitoes rather than by direct contact between people. Soldiers on the Army base in Cuba who contracted the disease were exposed both to fever victims and to mosquitoes. Reed constructed two buildings on the base. In one, he had healthy volunteers sleep on beds covered with the soiled clothes and sheets used by fever patients, but carefully screened the building from mosquitoes. In the other, volunteers were kept away from any contact with fever patients but were exposed to mosquitoes. The volunteers in Building 2 got yellow fever; the volunteers in Building 1 did not.

5. Carol Johnson had a lush and healthy lawn, but there were three small areas where the grass was thin, with some bare spots. Those spots had been seeded with the same type of grass as the rest of the lawn, had received the same fertilizer, and got the same amount of sunlight. She took soil samples from those spots, and from nearby healthy areas, and had them tested for acidity. The samples from the bare spots had high acidity, while the soil from the healthy areas was not acidic.

6. It is not true that suicide bombings are always the result of mental illness, despite the seeming insanity of the act. For every suicide bomber who meets the clinical criteria for insanity, there are others who share the same political cause and religious beliefs but are not insane.

* 7. Executives at the Shermer Health Group wanted to understand why some of their clinics had exceptionally low employee turnover while others did not. The results of their investigation are indicated in the table below. They concluded that employee recognition awards were the determing factor.

	Above-Average Compensation	Employee Recognition Awards	Flex-Time Schedules		Turnover
Glenville	Y	Y	N	→	Low
Brookfield	Y	N	Y	→	~Low
Farmington	N	N	Y	→	~Low
Aster	N	Y	N	→	Low
Johnstown	Y	Y	Y	→	Low

8. A pile of sand on a flat surface has a slope at an angle of about 30 degrees to the horizontal, called the angle of repose. That angle is caused by the granular naure of the sand. You can prove this by pouring a bucket of sand on a flat surface and measuring the angle of repose. Then pour another bucket onto the pile: you will increase the size of the pile but the angle of repose will remain the same.

9. The eyes adapt to the level of illumination in our surroundings, and this adaptation affects our experience of apparent brightness. We can prove this by comparing cases. Suppose you come into a room from outdoors where the sun is shining brightly, and your eyes have adapted to a high level of illumination. The room will look much dimmer than it would if you had been there all along, with your eyes adapted to the lower level of illumination. If your eyes had adapted to an intermediate level of illumination (as on a cloudy day outside), the apparent brightness of the room would have an intermediate value.

* 10. In testing for fire-resistant factors in homes, scientists observed that 3 of 10 test houses caught on fire internally within 1 minute of exposure to high flames. House 1 had Class E windows, rose bushes in its landscaping, vinyl siding, a

roof of composition shingles, and dried leaves in its gutters. House 2 had Class E windows, buckthorn bushes, stone siding, wood shake roofing, and dried leaves in its gutters. House 3 had Class E1 windows, dogwood bushes, vinyl siding, metal roofing, and dried leaves in its gutters. The scientists inferred that dried leaves in the gutters cause houses to catch fire internally within 1 minute of exposure to high flames.

Summary

Generalization is a form of inductive inference in which we conclude that something is universally true of a class on the basis of evidence regarding a sample. To avoid the fallacy of hasty generalization, we should follow three basic rules in generalizing: (1) Use a sample that is sufficiently numerous and various; (2) look for disconfirming evidence; and (3) consider whether the conclusion is plausible in light of other knowledge we possess.

Causal generalizations are claims that a certain type of factor is necessary and/or sufficient for a certain type of effect. To establish that factor *a* is causally related to effect *E*, we may use Mill's four methods: agreement, difference, concomitant variations, and residues.

Mill's methods can also be used negatively to argue against a causal claim. To evaluate an argument that uses one or more of these methods, we should consider whether all the relevant factors have been varied appropriately.

Key Terms

inductive argument—an argument that attempts to show that its conclusion is supported by the premises even though the conclusion amplifies—it goes beyond—what the premises state.

positive instance—an item that belongs to a given class and possesses the trait attributed to the class by a given generalization.

negative instance—an item that belongs to a given class and does not possess the trait attributed to the class by a given generalization.

method of agreement—a method of identifying a cause of an effect by isolating a factor common to a variety of cases in which the effect occurs.

method of difference—a method of identifying a cause of an effect by isolating a factor in

whose presence the effect occurs and in whose absence the effect does not occur, all other factors remaining constant.

joint method—a method of identifying a cause of an effect by using the methods of agreement and difference in combination.

method of concomitant variations—a method of identifying a cause of an effect by isolating a factor whose variations are correlated with variations in the effect, all other factors remaining constant.

method of residues—a method of identifying a cause of an effect by isolating that portion of the effect not explained by known causal relationships.

Additional Exercises

A. Support each of the following statements about cause and effect by using the method indicated in brackets. Diagram the argument schematically (except for the method of residues).

❋ 1. Oxygen is a necessary condition for combustion. [Difference]

2. Sunlight causes newsprint to turn yellow. [Agreement]

3. Interest rates have a major impact on home purchases. Other things being equal, falling interest rates lead to an increase in home purchases; rising rates lead to a decrease. [Concomitant variations]

❋ 4. Moisture will condense on a surface that is colder than the surrounding air. [Joint]

5. Some of the anxiety people feel at the dentist is caused by the sight and sound of the drill, rather than the pain itself. [Residues]

B. For each of the following statements, decide whether you think it is true (a) by finding a deductive argument for or against it; and (b) by evaluating the inductive evidence for it.

✳ 1. All narrative literature (plays, novels, epic poems) involves conflict.
2. Familiarity breeds contempt.
3. People who fear confrontation are eager to forgive those who wrong them.

✳ 4. Racial or sexual harassment of any kind results in the loss of self-esteem for the victim.
5. Any stable society has a large middle class.

C. Each of the following passages presents evidence for or against a causal connection. Identify the effect (*E*), the proposed cause (*a*), and decide whether the author is supporting or rejecting the claim that *a* causes *E*. Then identify the method being used.

✳ 1. In the Clinton section of Manhattan, pigeons were roosting on many apartment buildings. Residents in three buildings put plastic replicas of great horned owls on the rooftops. Result: no pigeons on those buildings. "'The owls work,' said Sarah Weinberg. . . . 'A month ago we could not stand outside the door because of all this gook falling from the sky.'" [*New York Times*, Oct. 29, 1986]

2. When salmon are old enough to spawn, they return from the ocean to the stream in which they were born. How do they tell which stream to return to? Researchers have found that they navigate chiefly by olfactory clues. The chemical composition of each stream is distinctive, and young salmon imprint on that odor during a narrow window in their development. Fish who are caught and moved to a hatchery just before this narrow window will return to the hatchery, not their natal stream, when they are ready to spawn. Researchers have also shown that juvenile salmon exposed to synthetic chemicals, such as morpholine or beta-phenylethyl alcohol (PEA), at the time of imprinting will be attracted, when they return to spawn, into an unfamiliar stream scented with one of these chemicals.

3. ". . . decoration is not given to hide horrible things: but to decorate things already adorable. A mother does not give her child a blue bow because he is so ugly without it. A lover does not give a girl a necklace to hide her neck." [G. K. Chesterton, *Orthodoxy*]

✳ 4. "While we typically associate economic growth with technological development, organizational innovation has played an equal if not more important role since the beginning of the industrial revolution. . . .

"The development of transoceanic commerce in the fifteenth century depended on the invention of the carrack, which could sail beyond coastal waters. But it also depended on the creation of the joint-stock company, by which individuals could pool their resources and share risks entailed in funding great voyages. The extension of the railroads across the continental United States in the mid-nineteenth century required large, hierarchically organized companies with geographically dispersed managers." [Francis Fukuyama, *Trust*]

5. "As far as causing mental states is concerned, the crucial step is the one that goes on inside the head, not the external or peripheral stimulus. And the argument for this is simple. If the events outside the central nervous system occurred, but nothing happened in the brain, there would be no mental events. But if the right things happened in the brain, the mental events would occur even if there was no outside stimulus. (And that, by the way, is the principle on which surgical anaesthesia works: the outside stimulus is prevented from having the relevant effects on the central nervous system.)" [John Searle, *Minds, Brains and Science*]

6. People who commit violent crimes have a higher incidence of brain damage than other people—including seizures, head injuries, and other neurological deficits—and some theorists have claimed that such damage is the cause of their violent behavior. But as neurologist Richard M. Restak points out, "most people thus afflicted do not go on to commit violent crimes. For every Robert Harris [a convicted murderer] who may display signs of brain damage, there are many more people with similar histories who have never even thrown a punch." [Richard M. Restak, "See No Evil," *The Sciences*, July/Aug. 1992]

* 7. Snowshoe hares like to eat green alder shrubs. Both the stems and the flower buds are nutritious for the hares, but they eat only the stems. Scientists found that the flower buds contain a chemical, pinosylvin methyl ether (PME), which they suspected might be a repellent. So they prepared oatmeal, which hares like, and infused the chemical in some batches. The hares would not eat those batches. [Adapted from John P. Bryant et al., "Pinosylvin Methyl Ether Deters Snowshoe Hare Feeding on Green Alder," *Science*, Dec. 2, 1983: Vol. 222, no. 4627, pp. 1023–1025]

8. In 1896, the French scientist Henri Becquerel discovered the phenomenon of radioactivity. He had placed uranium on a photographic plate that was carefully wrapped to block light from reaching it, and then exposed the uranium to sunlight. When he developed the photographic plate, he found a silhouette of the uranium. He assumed that the sunlight had excited the uranium to emit radiation. Later, though, he left a similarly wrapped plate and some uranium in a dark place. Once again, when he developed the plate, he found an image of the uranium. The uranium itself, therefore, was spontaneously emitting radiation that caused the image.

9. During the 2006 conflict between Israel and Hezbollah in southern Lebanon, many claimed that Israel's military action increased the prestige of Hezbollah, at least within the Arab world. "Well, sure," wrote Jonathan Chait. "But Hezbullah's prestige was also boosted by Israel's 2000 withdrawal from Lebanon. If aggressive Israeli actions boost Hezbullah, and conciliatory Israeli actions boost Hezbullah, then maybe Israel's actions aren't really the prime mover here." [Jonathan Chait, "'Back Off, Israel' Doesn't Cut It," *Los Angeles Times*, Aug. 6, 2006]

* 10. "The very first point to note is that the freedom at issue (as indeed the very name 'Free Will Problem' indicates) pertains primarily not to overt acts but to inner acts. . . . We do not consider the acts of a robot to be morally responsible acts; nor do we consider the acts of man to be so save in so far as they are distinguishable from those of a robot by reflecting an inner life of choice. Similarly, from the other side, if we are satisfied . . . that a person has definitely elected to follow a course which he believes to be wrong, but has been prevented by external circumstances from translating his inner choice into an overt act, we still regard him as morally blameworthy." [C. A. Campbell, "Has the Self Free Will?"]

D. Use what have you learned about inductive reasoning to evaluate the claims made in the following chain letter. What conclusions can you draw from the information contained in the letter? What additional information would you need to have?

"KISS SOMEONE YOU LOVE WHEN YOU RECEIVE THIS LETTER AND MAKE MAGIC.

This paper has been sent to you for good luck. The original copy is in New England. It has been around the world 9 times. The luck has now been sent to you. You will receive good luck within 4 days of receiving this letter.

Send copies to people you think need good luck. Don't send money, as fate has no price. Do not keep this letter. It must leave your hands within 96 hours. An Air Force officer received $70,000. Joe Elliot received $42,000, and lost it because he broke the chain. While in the Philippines, Gene Welch lost his wife 6 days after receiving this letter. He failed to circulate the letter. However, before her death she had won $50,000 in a lottery. The money was transferred to him 4 days after he decided to mail out the letter.

Please send 20 copies of this letter and see what happens in 4 days. The chain comes from Venezuela and was written by Saul Anthony dé Croix, a missionary from South America. Since the copy must make a tour of the world, you must make 20 copies and send them out to your friends and associates. After a few days you will get a surprise. This is true even if you are not superstitious.

Do note the following: Constantine Dias received the chain in 1953. He asked his secretary to make 20 copies and send them out. A few days later he won a lottery of 2 million dollars. Andy Daddit, an office employee received the letter and forgot it had to leave his hands within 96 hours. He lost his job. Later, after finding the letter again, he mailed out 20 copies. A few days later he got a better job. Dalen Fairchild received this letter and not believing threw it away. Nine days later he died.

PLEASE SEND NO MONEY. PLEASE DON'T IGNORE THIS. IT WORKS!!!!!"

13

Argument by Analogy

Analogies are often used to express shades of meaning that would be difficult to capture in literal terms. They make our language more colorful and forceful. Analogies that are used in this way are called *explanatory* or *descriptive*. To convey a common idea of God, for example, I might say He is like a father who cares for His Children, punishes them for disobedience, etc. This analogy is descriptive: I am not saying that this conception of God is correct or even that God exists; I am merely describing one common idea of God. But analogies can also be used to *argue* for a conclusion. Arguments by analogy are inductive, for reasons we will see in a moment. In this chapter, we will learn how to analyze and evaluate such arguments.

13.1 Analogy and Similarity

To convince you that learning to reason well takes a lot of practice, I might argue as follows: "The art of reasoning is a skill, like knowing how to play tennis. And you can't learn to play tennis just by reading a book; no matter how much you know about the theory of the game, you can't acquire the skill without actually playing; so you need to practice." In this argument, I am using an analogy as a premise in an argument; I am trying to prove a conclusion. In the same way, one might argue for socialism by comparing society to a family: Since a family shares its wealth among all its members, society should do the same. You can distinguish an argumentative analogy from an explanatory analogy by the same techniques we learned in Chapter 5 for identifying arguments of any kind: Look for indicator words like "therefore," ask whether the speaker is trying to convince you of some conclusion, etc.

Arguments by analogy occur very often in everyday conversation and debate. They are frequently used in political discussions, as in the argument about socialism. Many of our expectations about people are based on analogy: John reminds us of Walter, so we expect him to have the same leadership qualities that Walter has.

What is the logical structure of these arguments? As a first step in analysis, we can state the arguments as follows:

1. Tennis and reasoning are similar.	1. Families and society are similar.	1. Walter and John are similar.
2. Tennis requires practice._____	2. Families share wealth._____	2. Walter is a good leader._____
3. Reasoning requires practice.	3. Society should share wealth.	3. John is a good leader.

The arguments clearly have a common structure, which we can represent abstractly:

1. *A* and *B* are similar.   1 + 2
2. *A* has property *P*.   ↓
3. *B* has property *P*.   3

A and *B* are the two things being compared: the family and society, skill in tennis and the art of reasoning, Walter and John. The conclusion is that *B* has a certain property: Society should be arranged so that members share wealth; the art of reasoning must be acquired by practice; John is a good leader. And the argument is that *B* has this property because it is similar to *A*, which has the property. So far, so good. But notice that the relationship between *A* and *B* is not like any of the logical relations we have studied so far. *A* is not a wider class that includes *B*, as in a categorical syllogism. Nor is *A* an instance or subclass of *B*, as in an inductive generalization. Tennis is not a species of logic, nor is logic a species of tennis. So how can a premise about one yield a conclusion about the other?

The answer obviously lies in premise 1: *A* and *B* are *similar*. The similarity may not be stated explicitly, but it is a crucial assumption. If there is no similarity between a family and a society, then the fact that families share their wealth has no bearing on society; the argument would have no strength whatsoever. But similarity per se is not enough, because with a little ingenuity we can find *some* similarity between any two things, and thus we could prove *anything* this way. I could prove that you should take your bicycle to the dentist for a regular checkup, because the gear sprockets are shaped like teeth. That's ridiculous. So we need to look more carefully at the role of similarity.

If two things are similar, they must be similar in some particular respect—in shape, color, function, or whatever. To put it differently, two things are similar because they share some property. So the first task is to identify the respect in which *A* and *B* are similar, to identify the property they have in common. There may be more than one such property, but there must be at least one. In the argument about tennis and logic, the property was stated explicitly: They are both *skills*. The argument about family and society did *not* state how they were similar, but the point might be that families and societies are both social groups whose members have shared interests. Nor were we told what Walter and John have in common. Perhaps it is charisma, or vision, or strength of character—but there must be some shared quality to sustain the analogy.

We'll use the letter *S* to stand for the property that *A* and *B* have in common, the property that makes them similar. We can reformulate the first premise in the structure of arguments by analogy as follows:

1. *A* and *B* have property *S*.

2. *A* has property *P*.

3. *B* has property *P*.

$$1 + 2$$
$$\downarrow$$
$$3$$

Our three examples can be formulated accordingly:

1. Tennis and reasoning are skills.	1. Families and society are social groups whose members have shared interests.	1. Walter and John have [charisma? vision?. . .].
2. Tennis requires practice.		2. Walter is a good leader.
3. Reasoning requires practice.	2. Families share wealth.	3. John is a good leader.
	3. Society should share wealth.	

We can now go on to ask the next—and crucial—question. What is the relationship between *S* and *P*? If there is no connection between these two properties, then the conclusion does not follow. That is the problem with the argument about bicycles. The property that gear sprockets and human teeth have in common is *shape*, but it is not because of their shape that human teeth require dental care. Indeed, two things may have many properties in common—$S_1, S_2, S_3, \ldots$—but unless there is some link between one or more of these *S*s and the further property *P*, the analogy will not work.

So the strength of the argument depends on the likelihood of a connection between the properties involved, and our goal in evaluating an argument by analogy is to estimate this likelihood. As we'll see in the next section, we can do this by using what we've already learned about inductive arguments.

EXERCISE 13.1

Each of the paragraphs below contains an analogy. First decide whether the analogy is used to make an argument or merely to describe something. If it is an argument, identify the elements in the structure of the argument: *A* and *B* (the two things being compared), *P* (the property attributed to *B* in the conclusion), and *S* (the property that makes *A* and *B* similar). If the latter property is not stated explicitly, try to find a plausible candidate.

∗ 1. Murray's mind is a cave: deep, dark, and full of bats.

2. The writing of history is like the telling of a story in that it relates events connected in time, so it must have a narrative structure.

3. Writing is a medium of communication, as air is a medium of

vision; and good writing is as crisp and clear as the autumn air in Vermont.

∗ 4. A concept is like a file folder in which we store information about a category of objects.

5. Since concepts are like file folders storing information about

categories of objects, they must be kept in a hierarchical system comparable to file drawers.

6. The layers in a crystal are spaced at regular intervals, like the floors of a building, and connected by chemical bonds, like girders; so a substance with a crystalline structure is solid and rigid.

✳ 7. A person who keeps his emotions bottled up has pressure building up inside, like a boiler with too much steam; eventually, as with the boiler, the person is going to break down.

8. For someone who has created a work of art, a book, a new discovery or idea, the creation is like a child. So it is not surprising that creators feel intensely protective about their creations.

9. Our desires provide the motive power for our actions, in the way a car's engine provides power to the wheels. But free will acts like a clutch: We can choose whether to act on a given desire, just as we can suspend power to the car's wheels by disengaging the clutch.

✳ 10. Our planet is like a ship sailing on the vast ocean of space; hence the nations of the earth, like the members of a ship's crew, can survive only if they learn to live together.

13.2 Analysis and Evaluation

Once we have identified the property that *A* and *B* are supposed to have in common—the property we're labeling *S*—we can put an argument by analogy into a standard format. This format includes an inductive step and a deductive step, and it allows us to evaluate the argument by using what we have already learned about induction and deduction. To see how this works, let's continue with the analogy between tennis and reasoning.

The common property here is that both are skills, and the relevance of this property is that skills must be learned by practice. Tennis is a particular instance in which a skill requires practice, and it serves as inductive evidence for a generalization about *all* skills; this generalization is then applied deductively to the case of reasoning. We can thus diagram the argument:

1. Tennis is a skill.
2. Tennis must be learned by practice.
3. All skills must be learned by practice.
4. Reasoning is a skill.
5. Reasoning must be learned by practice

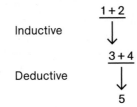

The first step in the argument is the inductive one, supporting the generalization that all skills require practice. This generalization serves as a premise in the second step, which is deductive, a categorical syllogism. That premise expresses the link between skills and practice, and without the premise we have no basis for the conclusion. Premise 4 says that reasoning is a skill—it states the property that makes reasoning similar to tennis.

Let's try this technique on another example. People who oppose government regulation of business sometimes argue that businesspeople, like journalists, have to use their minds and follow their own judgment in their work; therefore, like journalists, they should not be regulated. This is an argument by analogy: Businesspeople are being compared to journalists. The conclusion is that businesspeople should not be regulated, and the argument tells us explicitly what the professions have in common. So we can analyze the argument as follows (using a format that separates clearly the inductive and deductive steps):

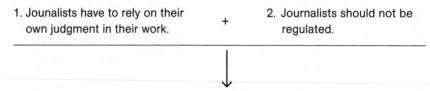

1. Jounalists have to rely on their   +   2. Journalists should not be
   own judgment in their work.   regulated.

3. No one who has to rely on his own judgment in his work should be regulated.
4. All businesspeople have to rely on their own judgment in their work.

5. No businesspeople should be regulated.

You can see that this argument fits the general pattern; the only difference is that the conclusion is negative. But it is still a generalization drawn from the particular case of journalists.

Any argument by analogy can be analyzed in this way, once we have identified the common property, S, that makes A and B similar. So an argument by analogy has the form:

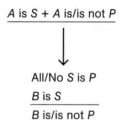

A is S + A is/is not P

All/No S is P
B is S
B is/is not P

To *analyze* an argument by analogy, the main task is to find the common property S that functions as a connecting term in the deductive step. To *evaluate* the argument, the main task is to evaluate the inductive step. You can see from the general form that the deductive step will always be valid. But the generalization that all or no S is P may or may not be based on solid inductive evidence. Let's look a little more closely at each of these tasks.

13.2A Finding the Connecting Term

In some cases, it will be easy to identify the connecting term, especially if the argument explicitly mentions what A and B have in common. This was true in both of the earlier arguments. In many cases, however, the common property will not be mentioned explicitly: There may be more than one common property, and it may not be so clear which ones are relevant to the conclusion. When we use historical analogies, we are comparing two very complex situations that have many similarities (and many differences). When we try to decide how we feel about another person, we often compare that person to others we've known in the past, and our decision usually turns on more than one personality or character trait. And in the law, the use of precedents is a kind of analogical reasoning: A lawyer will argue that the present case is like one that was decided in the past and will try to find as many similarities as possible.

The problem in such cases is not merely that A and B have more than one property in common. There is often a deeper problem as well: We may have an intuitive sense that A and B are similar without being sure exactly how to break that similarity down into distinct properties. A piece of music may sound quite similar to another one you are familiar with, leading you to infer that the first comes from the same historical period as the second; but if you don't know much about musical theory, you may be unable to say specifically what they have in common. Indeed, we tend to use arguments by analogy precisely when two things are similar in ways that are hard to analyze. Nevertheless, we must break the similarity down before we can evaluate the argument, so we'll have to do the best we can.

A useful technique is to construct a table of similarities and differences. Schematically, the table would look like this:

	A	B
Similarities	S_1	S_1
	S_2	S_2
	S_3	S_3
Differences	D_1	D_1
	D_2	D_2
Conclusion	P	P

The two columns represent the properties of A and B. Since the conclusion of the argument is the claim that B is P, we put P at the bottom and draw a line above it in the B column to indicate that it is supposed to follow from information available in the rest of the table. S_1, S_2, S_3, etc.—there could be any number—are similarities between A and B, properties that they share and that are candidates for the role of connecting term. To decide which of them is the connecting term, we ask which of them seem connected to P. If they are all relevant, then the connecting term will be a combination: $S_1 + S_2 + S_3$. . . . Usually, however, we can throw out some of the similarities as irrelevant to the analogy. It's a good idea to include any differences $(D_1, D_2, . . .)$ as well, because we'll have to consider these when we evaluate the inductive element in the argument.

Suppose someone argues that smart phones will expand individual freedom to communicate and acquire information in the same way that, earlier in the century, the automobile expanded individual mobility. This argument assumes that cars and smart phones are similar but doesn't say *how* they are similar. So let's try to find the common properties. Both cars and smart phones are products of sophisticated technology. In both cases the technology is packaged in a form that allows the average people to use it for their own purposes without being experts. Both products are cheap enough for someone of ordinary means to purchase. The automobile freed people from dependence on trains, an earlier and highly centralized form of mechanized transportation; in the same way, smart phones free people from dependence on landline telephone networks run as regulated monopolies, an earlier and highly centralized form of communication. In addition to these similarities, of course, there are differences. There's the basic difference in function: transportation versus communication. They also differ in size and the form of power they use. If you had written all this down in a table as the different points occurred to you, the result might look like this:

	Automobile	Smart Phones
S_1	Sophisticated technology	Sophisticated technology
S_2	Does not require expertise	Does not require expertise
S_3	Affordable by individuals	Affordable by individuals
S_4	Replaced centralized technology	Replaced centralized technology
D_1	Transportation	Communication/information
D_2	Uses gasoline	Uses electricity
P	Expanded individual freedom	Will expand individual freedom

We have broken down the similarity between cars and smart phones into four properties they share. We can now ask which property is linked to the question of individual freedom. That is, which property should be the connecting term in our analysis of the argument? Let's go down the list. The fact that both use sophisticated technology does not in itself seem relevant, since the same could be said of many things—from nuclear power plants to the space shuttle—that do not have the same effect for the individual, at least not in any direct way. By contrast, both the price of the machines and the fact that they don't require expertise *do* seem essential, since they imply that the average person can own and operate them. Finally, the historical point that both products replaced earlier, centralized forms of the technology does not seem crucial. It's an interesting observation, but the argument would not be any weaker without it. So we have identified two common properties to serve as a connecting term for the argument, and we can now formulate the generalization: Any technology that individuals can afford and can use without being experts expands their freedom. In our analysis of the original argument, this statement would be the conclusion of the inductive step and the first premise of the deductive step.

1. Automobiles are a form of technology that individuals can afford and can use without being experts.

$+$

2. Automobiles expanded individual freedom.

$\downarrow$

3. Any technology that individuals can afford and can use without being experts expands their freedom.
4. Smart phones are a form of technology that individuals can afford and can use without being experts.

5. Smart phones will expand individual freedom.

13.2B Evaluation

Once we have selected the most plausible connecting term and analyzed the argument accordingly, we need to evaluate the inductive step. Does the example of the automobile provide good evidence for the generalization: "Any technology that individuals can afford and can use without being experts expands their freedom"? In general, is the premise "All/No S is P" supported by the example of A? Notice that the argument gives us only a single instance to support these generalizations. We are supporting a claim about B on the basis of its similarity to A, so A is the only instance available to support the generalization. And we have seen that a single instance usually does not provide very much evidence for a general proposition. In this respect, an argument by analogy is a kind of logical shortcut, and it is a relatively weak mode of argument. Nevertheless, such arguments vary a great deal among themselves in their degree of strength, and we can assess their strength by applying our rules for evaluating inductive generalizations.

The first rule is to consider the number and variety of the positive instances. In the case of an analogy, where we have only a single instance, the key question to ask is whether increasing the number or variety would affect the argument. In the analogy between reasoning and tennis, for example, tennis is a physical skill, but the generalization is about *all* skills: physical, mental, social, etc. So we need to consider whether or not examples from the other categories would confirm the generalization. Are the differences, say, between physical and mental skills relevant to the question of whether they must be acquired by practice? (This is a crucial question for us because the art of reasoning is a mental skill.) In this case, I would say that the differences are not relevant, so the argument is a fairly strong one. But this will not always be the case. That's why it is important to include differences as well as similarities when you construct a table.

The second rule is to look for disconfirming instances. Suppose someone argued that war is like arm wrestling, so victory usually goes to the strongest. The point of similarity between war and arm wrestling is that both are contests. So we would analyze the argument as follows:

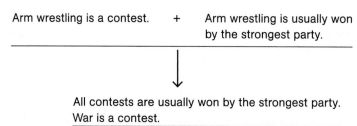

It is obvious that the major premise in the syllogism is not very well supported by the inductive evidence. Arm wrestling is a particular type of contest that happens to depend largely on strength, but other types of contests depend on other traits. Chess matches are usually won by the player with better strategy, basketball games by the side with better speed, precision, and teamwork. Both chess and basketball are negative instances that disconfirm the generalization. So you might reply to the original argument by saying "Yes, but war is also like a chess game, so victory will go to the side with the best strategy," or "Yes, but war is also like basketball, so the side with the most speed, precision, and teamwork will win." These are called *counter-analogies*, and they are one of the most effective ways of rebutting an argument by analogy.

The third rule is to consider the initial plausibility of a generalization, the plausibility that there could be a connection between subject and predicate—in this case, between S and P. In the argument about tennis and reasoning, for example, everything we know about skills makes it quite plausible to think they are acquired by practice. In the argument about bicycle gears and teeth, however, it is quite clear that the shape of our teeth has little if anything to do with their need for dental care.

An interesting case that lies between these two extremes is the analogy between the mind and a computer. Some people hold that the brain is like the hardware of a computer and that the mind is like the software, the programs that run on the machine. They use this analogy to derive various conclusions about the nature of the mind and the way it should be studied. The basis of the analogy is the fact that both computers and minds process information, and the computer is used to support the generalization that any information-processing device must have a hardware and a software component. But critics of this view find the analogy, and the generalization, completely implausible because the idea of a program doesn't make sense to them unless there is a programmer—which there isn't in the case of the mind. Whichever side you take in this dispute, the point is that people generally take sides on the basis of their general views about the nature of minds, brains, and programs.

The use of analogies in arguments, then, does not represent a fundamentally new mode of reasoning. It involves a combination of inductive and deductive elements that we can evaluate by rules we've already learned. The trick is to isolate those elements, which are normally implicit in the argument, not explicit.

STRATEGY Analyzing Arguments by Analogy

1. Identify the two things being compared (A and B) and the property (P) attributed to B in the conclusion.

2. Identify the property (S) that is supposed to make A and B similar. If this property is not stated explicitly, construct a similarity table and choose the most plausible candidate.

3. Analyze the argument into its inductive and deductive elements. The deductive step will be a syllogism with the major premise "All/No S is P."

4. Evaluate that premise as an inductive generalization:
   a. Consider its initial plausibility in light of your other knowledge.
   b. Look for additional positive instances besides A.
   c. Look for counter-analogies.

EXERCISE 13.2

Analyze and evaluate each of the following analogical arguments.

✳ 1. Jim is an intellectual, like Fred, and Fred doesn't like sports. So Jim probably doesn't like them either.

2. This bread machine was made by the same company that made my coffee maker. I've had the coffee maker for 3 years and it works great, so the bread machine should work fine, too.

3. I believe in reincarnation because it doesn't make sense that God would give us only one chance in life. You get more chances than that in baseball.

✳ 4. Like John F. Kennedy, Barack Obama is young, personable, and a Democrat. So, like Kennedy, he will be remembered by history.

5. Psychotherapies that promise instant happiness are comparable to "get rich quick" schemes in the economic realm and therefore cannot be expected to work.

6. An experiment is a question put to nature, and like a lawyer cross-examining a witness, the scientist needs to know what answer he expects.

✳ 7. The generation of Americans born in the 1990s is considerably larger in number than the generation before it. Like the "baby boomers" of the 1950s and 1960s, they will face stiffer competition with each other in school and work, and their tastes and trends will have a disproportionate influence on society as a whole.

8. A photon of light is like a billiard ball in having a definite velocity, position, and mass. A photon is therefore a particle.

9. A photon of light is like an air vibration in having a definite frequency and wavelength. Light is therefore a wave phenomenon.

*10. Efforts by the major European powers to achieve arms control, at the turn of the century and again in the 1920s and 1930s, were not successful. So arms control negotiations between the United States and other countries today are not likely to succeed either.

Summary

Analogies can be used to argue for a conclusion as well as to describe or explain. When used in an argument, an analogy purports to show that *B* has the property *P* because *A* has that property and because *B* is similar to *A*. To analyze such an argument, we must identify the respect in which *A* and *B* are similar—the property *S* that they share. To evaluate the argument, we must use inductive methods to determine whether there is a link between *S* and *P*.

Additional Exercises

A. Find an argument by analogy to support each of the following conclusions. Even if you don't agree with the conclusion, try to find the most plausible analogy.

✱ 1. Friend to potential car buyer: "That Porsche is going to cost more to insure."

2. Doctors should be allowed to advertise their services and prices.

3. The United States should not set up trade barriers against imported goods.

✱ 4. Playing the stock market is risky.

5. Children should not be overly protected against the vicissitudes of life.

B. Each of the passages that follow contains an analogy. First decide whether the analogy is being used as an argument. Then if it is, analyze and evaluate it.

✱ 1. "Prayer is like a rocking chair. It'll give you something to do, but it won't get you anywhere." [Gypsie Rose Lee]

2. Some doctors recommend that people over the age of 40 should get a physical exam every year. As one physician argued, "People take their car in for servicing every few months without complaint. Why shouldn't they take similar care of their bodies?" [*U.S. News & World Report*, Aug. 11, 1986]

3. "Absence diminishes small loves and increases great ones, as the wind blows out the candle and blows up the bonfire." [La Rochefoucauld, *Maxims*]

✱ 4. "Vigorous writing is concise. A sentence should contain no unnecessary words, a paragraph no unnecessary sentences, for the same reason that a drawing should have no unnecessary lines and a machine no unnecessary parts." [William B. Strunk, Jr., and E. B. White, *The Elements of Style*]

5. "The mode of taxation is, in fact, quite as important as the amount. As a small burden badly placed may distress a horse that could carry with ease a much larger one properly adjusted, so a people may be impoverished and their power of producing wealth destroyed by taxation, which, if levied another way, could be borne with ease." [Henry George, *Progress and Poverty*]

6. Life's but a walking shadow, a poor player,
That struts and frets his hour upon the stage,
And then is heard no more. It is a tale
Told by an idiot, full of sound and fury,
Signifying nothing.
[William Shakespeare, *Macbeth*]

✱ 7. "Taxation of earnings from labor is on a par with forced labor. Some persons find this claim obviously true: taking the earnings of *n* hours labor is like taking *n* hours from the person; it is like forcing the person to work *n* hours for another's purpose." [Robert Nozick, *Anarchy, State, and Utopia*] (You may assume from the character of the analogy that Nozick's conclusion is: taxation of earnings from labor is *wrong*.)

8. "We can follow the path taken by physics and biology by turning directly to the relation between behavior and the environment and neglecting supposed mediating states of mind. Physics did not advance by looking more closely at the jubilance of a falling body, or biology by looking at the nature of vital spirits, and we do not need to try to discover what personalities, states of mind, feelings, traits of character, plans, purposes, intentions, or the other perquisites of autonomous man really are in order to get on with a scientific analysis of behavior." [B. F. Skinner, *Beyond Freedom and Dignity*]

9. "If 'good' and 'better' are terms deriving their sole meaning from the ideology of each people, then of course ideologies themselves cannot be better or worse than one another. Unless the measuring rod is independent of the things measured, we can do no measuring." [C. S. Lewis, *Christian Reflections*]

✳10. Opponents of "guaranteed issue"—the mandate that insurance companies must insure people with preexisting conditions—argue that it will raise premiums for other policyholders. It is like selling fire insurance on a burning building.

11. Proponents of guaranteed issue argue that, since workers with company health insurance lose their insurance if they are fired, it is unfair if those who developed health problems during their employment now cannot get affordable insurance. It is like a college that cancelled all your course credits if you take a year off from school, even for a health emergency, quite possibly leaving you unable to afford starting college again from scratch.

C. The arguments below are classic arguments by analogy, which indicate how deeply analogies are woven into some of our fundamental conceptions. For each one, find a counter-analogy.

✳ 1. Anger is like steam under pressure, so you shouldn't keep it bottled up.

2. In defense of equality of opportunity: Life is a race; victory should go to the swiftest but the runners should start at the same place.

3. Human knowledge is like a building, and it must therefore rest on foundations.

✳ 4. Society is like a family, and the more productive members should provide for the needs of the less productive.

✳ D. Perhaps the most famous argument by analogy is the "argument from design," used to defend the belief in the existence of God. The passages below are from a work by the eighteenth-century philosopher David Hume. The first one is a statement of the argument itself; the second is a counter-analogy to the argument. Create a table of similarities and differences for each argument.

a. "Look round the world: Contemplate the whole and every part of it: You will find it to be nothing but one great machine, subdivided into an infinite number of lesser machines, which again admit of subdivisions to a degree beyond what human senses and faculties can trace and explain.

All these various machines, and even their most minute parts, are adjusted to each other with an accuracy which ravishes into admiration all men who have ever contemplated them. The curious adapting of means to ends, throughout all nature, resembles exactly, though it much exceeds, the productions of human contrivance—of human design, thought, wisdom, and intelligence. Since therefore the effects resemble each other, we are led to infer, by all the rules of analogy, that the causes also resemble, and that the Author of Nature is somewhat similar to the mind of man, though possessed of much larger faculties, proportioned to the grandeur of the work which he has executed."

b. "Now, if we survey the universe, so far as it falls under our knowledge, it bears a great resemblance to an animal or organized body, and seems actuated with a like principle of life and motion. A continual circulation of matter in it produces no disorder; a continual waste in every part is incessantly repaired; the closest sympathy is perceived throughout the entire system; and each part or member, in performing its proper offices, operates both to its own preservation and to that of the whole. The world, therefore, I infer, is an animal; and the Deity is the *soul* of the world, actuating it, and actuated by it." [David Hume, *Dialogues Concerning Natural Religion*]

Statistical Reasoning

Consider the following statements:

1. The population of South Carolina is about 4.5 million people.
2. The annual homicide rate in the United States is 5.6 per 100,000.
3. Ninety-seven percent of people who eat chocolate bunnies start with the ears.
4. In France before the Revolution of 1789, the median age of death was lower than the median age of marriage.
5. Other things being equal, someone who smokes is 10 times more likely to get lung cancer than is someone who does not.

Each of these statements is a *statistical* proposition. It attributes a quantitative, numerical property to some class of things: the population of South Carolina, people who eat chocolate bunnies, smokers, etc. We have not encountered this sort of proposition in our study of reasoning so far. Logic deals primarily with qualitative reasoning, while mathematics deals with quantitative. And a full treatment of statistical reasoning would require a separate book going over the relevant mathematical techniques. But the subject is too important to ignore.

14.1 Logic and Statistics

For one thing, statistical arguments are often used in connection with the kinds of topics we have been dealing with: political issues, personal decisions, generalizations about human nature. It is not unusual for a given conclusion to be supported by statistical as well as nonstatistical arguments. A proposed change in the tax laws, for example, might be supported by the claim that it will spur the economy as well as by the claim that it will be fairer. The first argument would probably involve statistical data, the second probably not. The daily paper and the nightly news offer plenty of other examples. So you need to know how to evaluate *both* kinds of argument in order to weigh all the evidence for the conclusion.

For another thing, statistical evidence is indispensable for conclusions about causality in complex systems—such as the health of a human body or a trend in the economy—where no single factor by itself is either necessary or sufficient. In this respect, some understanding of statistics is necessary to complete our study of Mill's methods.

It's important at the outset to avoid two opposite mistakes about statistics. One mistake is a misplaced worship of numbers. Statements involving numbers have a hard, clean, precise air about them; they give the impression of objectivity and expertise. For that reason, political advocates seem to think that no argument is complete without a statistic to back it up. But we should remember that a statistic is no better than the reasoning process by which it was derived. When the reasoning is fallacious, or arbitrary, or flawed in some other way, the statistic may bear no relation to reality. If someone complains that Americans represent only 8% of the world's population, but have 23% of the world's fun, you would be right to wonder how the second statistic was derived. Or if someone defends a change in the tax code on the ground that it will create 34,578 new jobs, we should be skeptical. It's extremely doubtful whether anyone could predict, with that kind of precision, the effects of legislation on something as complex as an economy. Indeed, the first and fundamental rule for evaluating a statistical claim is to step back and ask whether the phenomenon can be counted or measured at all (how could anyone measure the amount of fun in the world?), and if so, with what kind of accuracy.

The opposite mistake is to mistrust statistics entirely, an attitude expressed in the statement that "you can prove anything with statistics." This is not true. It *is* true that you can often create the *appearance* of proof by manipulating statistical information, just as fallacious reasoning can give the appearance of a strong argument. But the proper response is to learn how to identify and avoid the fallacies, not to throw the baby out with the bath water. In this chapter, we are going to cover some of the more common fallacies involving statistics. To spot them when they occur, it's a good idea to adopt a healthy skepticism about statistics in general. But you should balance that skepticism with an awareness of the value statistics can have. We rely on them in our daily lives when we make decisions about our health or our jobs, about where to live and where not to, about where to travel and how to get there. Statistical information is often relevant to political arguments. And statisticians have given us some amazingly powerful instruments for discovering patterns in nature and in human affairs that are not visible to the naked eye.

A statistic takes a mass of quantitative information about a group of objects and reduces it to a single number (or set of numbers). In the next section, we're going to look at three basic kinds of statistical information: totals and ratios, frequencies and frequency distributions, and averages. Virtually all the statistics you will encounter in everyday discussion and in the media fall into one of these basic categories or involve some combination of them. Our goal is to understand how the numbers are derived, what they stand for, and the dangers to watch out for when we use these numbers in arguments.

Before we look at the different kinds of statistical information, however, a few general points are in order. Statistics deal with *classes* of things, and for the sake of continuity with previous chapters we will use the letter S to stand for a class (and T, U, etc., if there is more than one class). Statistics also deal with the *properties* that members of a class possess, especially the measurable properties. And properties, like classes of objects, have different levels of abstractness that we can arrange in a hierarchy. Color, for example, is a more abstract, generic quality in relation to specific colors such as red or green. In statistics, a generic quality is called a *variable*, and the specific qualities are called *values* of that variable. So red and green are values of the variable *color*; A, B, AB, and O are values of the variable *blood type*; Republican and Democrat are values of the variable *political party affiliation*.

The concept of a variable is a key link between logic and mathematics, To see why, consider two variables that we might use to classify people:

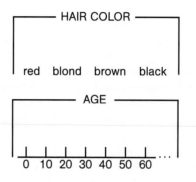

The first diagram is our familiar classification scheme, with the generic quality or variable above, and the specific qualities or values below. The same is true of the second diagram. The only difference is that hair color is a *qualitative* variable (its values differ from one another qualitatively and could have been listed in any order), whereas age is a *quantitative* variable (a specific age can be measured by number of years, and thus the values are arranged in a specific order along the numerical scale). But in either case, the variable could serve as a principle of classification, and we would group together people who have the same value. Statistics make use of both kinds of variable, but as we will see, certain kinds of statistics apply only to quantitative variables.

EXERCISE 14.1

A. For each of the following variables that apply to human beings, list three or more values of that variable.

  ✳ 1. Eye color   ✳ 4. Occupation
     2. Income   5. Intelligence
     3. Ethnicity

B. For each of the following sets of values, name the variable.

  ✳ 1. Liberal, conservative, libertarian,   2. Infant, child, adolescent, adult,
       socialist   elderly person

3. Married, single
* 4. Christian, Jew, Moslem

5. Employed, unemployed but looking for work, unemployed but not looking for work

14.2 Using Statistics in Argument

Let's turn now to the various types of statistical information and the questions to consider when we use this information in reasoning.

14.2A Totals and Ratios

The simplest operation in arithmetic is addition, and the simplest statistic, which we'll call a **total**, is the result of adding up a set of units. Examples would include:

1. Total population of the United States.
2. Total number of new jobs created in the past decade.
3. Total number of movies that Fred Astaire and Ginger Rogers made together.
4. Total number of traffic fatalities in 2005.
5. Total calories consumed in meals at the Twenty-One Club during 1956.
6. Total money spent in political campaigns in the 2008 elections.

In examples 1 through 4, the total is the number of members in some class—residents of the United States, new jobs, etc.—and we can find the total simply by counting. In examples 5 and 6, we are also concerned with classes—meals at the Twenty-One Club, political campaigns in 2008—but we are not given the number of members. We are given the sum of their values on some variable: calories and expenditures, respectively.

Totals are probably the kind of statistic we encounter most often in the media. But a simple total by itself is usually not very illuminating. In 2005, there were 16,740 murders in the United States. That's a large and frightening number. But to draw any conclusions from it, we need a standard of comparison. It would help to know, for example, whether the number has been rising or falling. So we could look up the statistics for earlier years and arrange the information in a table:

Year	Number of Murders in the United States	Homicide Rate per 100,000
1980	23,040	10.2
1985	18,980	7.9
1990	23,440	9.4
1995	21,610	8.2
2000	15,586	5.5
2005	16,740	5.6

By comparing equivalent totals (in the middle column), we can identify the trend: Murders declined during the first part of the 1980s, rose during the latter half, and have been declining since then.

An even more meaningful statistic is the **ratio** of murders to population, shown in the right-hand column. The ratio allows us to compensate for changes in population from year to year, so that we can see whether the chances of being victimized are rising or falling. You can see from the table that the murder rate has fallen even more than the total number. Such ratios also allow us to compare crime rates in different countries. Suppose you wanted to know, for example, whether the United States is a more violent country than Italy. Comparing the total number of murders, or any other crime, would be misleading because the population of the United States is much larger. But if there is a difference in the murder rate per 100,000 residents, then we have evidence that one country is more violent than the other. In general, then, a ratio is a total expressed in relative terms. It is a statistic specifying the number of items in a class or the sum of their values on a variable per unit of some other class.

When we use totals or ratios, finally, it is important to make sure that we are comparing apples to apples. People who gather statistics may use somewhat different definitions for the categories they are measuring. In some places, for example, manslaughter is included in the definition of murder, in other places it is not. You need equivalent definitions before you can draw any meaningful comparison.

EXERCISE 14.2A

For each of the following totals, give an example of (a) a related comparison and (b) a ratio.

✳ 1. Total visitors to the Jefferson Memorial in 2004
2. Fat calories you consumed yesterday
3. Hours you spent watching television last month
✳ 4. Total salmon catch in Alaska last year
5. Budget deficit of the U.S. government in 2010

6. Number of traffic fatalities in Canada in 2002
✳ 7. Number of privately owned automobiles in China
8. Number of calories in a pint of Häagen-Dazs ice cream
9. Number of shots made by Michael Jordan in 1996
✳ 10. Number of advertising pages in *Vanity Fair* magazine last year

14.2B Frequency and Distribution

A **frequency** statement says how many things in a class S have the property P; it tells us the frequency with which P occurs in that class. An *absolute frequency* statement gives the actual number of Ss that are P—for example, 2,149 students at Tiptop College are humanities majors. A *relative frequency* statement gives the *proportion* of Ss that are P—for example, 36% of the students at Tiptop College are humanities majors. As you can see, an absolute frequency is a special sort of total, and a relative frequency is a special sort of ratio. Some of the most commonly reported statistics are frequencies, such as the unemployment rate (percent of the workforce that is unemployed), the illiteracy rate (percent of adults who can't read), the poverty rate (percent of the populace living below the poverty line), or a baseball player's batting "average" (which is not an average at all, but the proportion of times at bat on which the player gets a hit).

A frequency statement divides the Ss into two subclasses, those that are P and those that are not P: humanities majors versus nonhumanities majors, employed people versus unemployed people, and so on. But we can also do a more thorough classification, dividing the Ss into those that are P, Q, R, etc., indicating the proportion that fall into each subclass. The result is called a frequency **distribution**. From a logical standpoint, a distribution is simply a classification with numbers attached and could be represented by a classification diagram. For example, the distribution of students by major might look like this:

STUDENTS AT TIPTOP COLLEGE

[major]

humanities   social science   physical science
   36%   52%   12%

It is more common, however, to see this information expressed by either a bar graph or a pie chart:

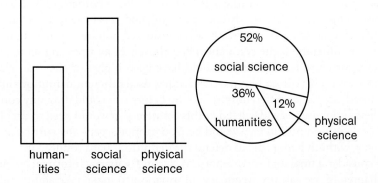

You have probably seen charts of this kind used to represent distributions such as the market share of each company in an industry, the ethnic or racial makeup of a country's population, or the proportion of government spending for military, Social Security, welfare, and other categories.

To have a meaningful distribution, we should use a single principle or a consistent set of principles—that is, a single variable or set of variables. The variable could be a qualitative one such as a student's major or it could be a quantitative one such as age, IQ, income, height, or corporate revenues. The subgroups into which the Ss are distributed are defined by specific values of the variable. With a quantitative variable, we would usually pick certain intervals on the scale—such as ages 0 to 5, 6 to 10, 11 to 15, etc. In any case, the subgroups should be mutually exclusive, so that we don't count individual things twice. If they are not mutually exclusive, the frequencies will add up to more than 100%. The subgroups should also be jointly exhaustive, so that all the Ss can be assigned to one subclass (value) or another. If they are not jointly exhaustive, the frequencies will add up to less than 100%.

Statements about frequencies and distributions also require that we define our terms carefully. If we are going to measure the proportion of Ss that are P or the distribution of Ss into subgroups P, Q, and R, we need definitions of all these groups. And unlike a definition used in ordinary reasoning, a definition used for statistical purposes can't have fuzzy borders; it must give us a clear criterion for deciding whether to include or to exclude any given thing. This usually involves an element of stipulation, and different researchers will make different decisions. One implication is that you cannot always compare statistics compiled by different researchers, even when they deal with the same subject. For example, the U.S. Bureau of Labor Statistics estimates the unemployment rate in two different ways. The figure most often reported is based on a survey of households, asking individuals whether they are currently employed. But the bureau also does a separate survey of business payrolls. Among other differences, the household survey counts people on strike as employed, while the payroll survey counts them as unemployed; so the two numbers are not comparable.

When you see a frequency statement or distribution in the media, it's important to ask what definitions were used before you draw any conclusions or use the statistic in an argument. To see why, consider the estimates that have been made about the percentage of people who are illiterate. These estimates vary enormously because different definitions of illiteracy are used. One U.S. Census Bureau study assumed that anyone with five or more years of schooling was literate; by that standard only .5% of people over 14 were illiterate. A later study used a reading and word-use test; anyone who answered 20 out of 26 questions correctly was considered literate. By that standard, 13% of adults were illiterate. If the researchers had chosen 21 as a passing score instead of 20, the number considered illiterate would have been higher; if they had chosen 19, the number would have been lower. Other studies used different definitions altogether and produced altogether different numbers. So before you could draw any conclusions about whether illiteracy is widespread in this country, you would need to decide what a reasonable definition of illiteracy would be. You cannot accept any particular number at face value, without being able to defend the definition that produced it.

Let's consider a final and very important role of frequency information. As we will see in Chapter 16, we can use frequency information to make probability judgments. In the 2012 baseball season, for example, Miguel Cabrera had a batting average of .330, the best in the American League. So on every trip to the plate, other things being equal, he had 33% chance of a hit. Similarly, if an insurance company wants to know the probability that a 35-year-old woman will die during the term of her 20-year life insurance policy, it consults a mortality table that says what proportion of 35-year-old women die before they reach 55. In general, we estimate the probability of something from its frequency in the class it belongs to, which in this context is called a reference group. (See Chapter 16 for further discussion of probability.)

EXERCISE 14.2B

Evaluate each of the following distribution statements by determining whether it uses a consistent variable and whether the subclasses are mutually exclusive and jointly exhaustive. Note any questions you have about the definitions of subclasses.

✳ 1. Book sales: adult fiction, 30%; adult non-fiction, 41%; juvenile fiction, 23%; juvenile non-fiction, 6%.

2. Land use in the United States, in millions of acres: rural, 1,374; developed, 111; forest, 406; federal, 402.

3. Nutrients in Oreo cookies (serving size: 3): fat, 7 grams; carbohydrate, 25 grams; protein, 2 grams; calories, 160.

✳ 4. 2010 expenditures by a non-profit organization: programs, 87%; administration, 8%; fundraising, 5%.

5. Matter in Earth's crust: rock, 50%; water, 10%; solids, 60%; gases, 10%.

14.2C Average and Median

We are all familiar with averages: grade-point averages, average prices of new homes, average SAT scores for this year's freshman class, average yards gained by the Green Bay Packers on third-down plays. An **average** gives us information about some class of things, S; what it tells us is the central value of Ss on some quantitative variable. It is an especially useful way of reducing a mass of quantitative information to a single number.

An average is the sum of the values of each S divided by the number of Ss. Thus, if a class of five students had the following scores on a test

Student	Score
Joan	97
Nelson	89
Harry	85
Leslie	82
Tom	80

the class average would be:

$$\frac{97 + 89 + 85 + 82 + 80}{5} = \frac{433}{5} = 86.6$$

Another common measure of the central value on a quantitative variable is the **median**: the value that lies in the middle of the range, dividing the Ss into an upper and a lower half. In our example, the median score is Harry's 85. There are two scores above his and two below. (If there had been a sixth member of the class who scored below Tom, then the median would have been halfway between Harry's and Leslie's scores—with an even number of values, the median lies halfway between the two values closest to the middle.) Notice that the average score and the median score are not the same. There was one extreme value—Joan's score—and the average is sensitive to extreme values in a way the median is not. If Joan had received a 90, the average would change to 85.2, but the median would be the same.

Even with a much larger group, an extreme value can pull the average in its direction, just as a child at the end of a seesaw can balance an adult sitting near the middle. Consider a group of 1,000 people with an average income of $35,000 a year. If we now add a single wealthy individual earning $5 million, the group average increases to nearly $40,000, whereas there would be little if any change in the median income. The reason is that income cannot get any lower than $0, but the upper end of the scale is effectively unlimited. So the figure you will often see in the newspapers is the median income, not the mean.

Both the average and the median are useful measures of the central tendency in a set of values. Which one is the better measure depends on the situation. The average is the more commonly used measure, but the median is usually better if there are extreme values only in one direction, as in the case of income. Sometimes it isn't clear whether the average or the median is the better measure, and an argument may hang in the balance. For example, doctors carry malpractice insurance; if someone sues for malpractice and wins, the insurance pays the award. Manufacturers carry similar insurance against product liability suits. In recent years, the cost of such insurance has increased rapidly, and people have argued about the causes. Some hold the courts responsible, citing the increase in the average amount of damages awarded by juries against doctors and manufacturers. Others reject this explanation on the ground that the average is pulled upward by a few "million-dollar" verdicts, whereas the median award is still quite small. Which number do you think better represents the situation (given that our goal is to understand the rise in insurance premiums)?

We have now covered the main types of statistical information that we use in everyday discussion and encounter in the media. If you understand the differences among these numbers and the dangers to watch out for in using each type of information, you should be able to understand most of the statistics you encounter in everyday contexts

SUMMARY **Kinds of Statistics**

Total: The total number of items in a class S or the sum of their values on a variable P.

Ratio: The number of Ss or the sum of their values on a variable P per unit of some other class T; a ratio is a total expressed in relative terms.

Frequency: The number or proportion of Ss that have some particular value on a variable P.

Distribution: The number or proportion of Ss that have each of the values (P, Q, R, etc.) on some variable.

Average: The sum of the values that the Ss have on a quantitative variable P, divided by the number of Ss.

Median: The middle value of the Ss on a quantitative variable P.

EXERCISE 14.2C

Identify the type of statistic contained in each of the following statements. Then evaluate how well it supports the conclusion in brackets.

✳ 1. The population of the United States is 307 million. [The United States is a large country.]

2. Between 1990 and 2008, the rate of marriage declined from 9.8 to 5.4 per 1,000 people in the United States. [Fewer people got married in 2008 than in 1990.]

3. For first marriages, the median age of the grooms was 24.1. [Grooms are getting older.]

✳ 4. Among the foreign-born population of the United States in 2009, 53% of Asians had a college degree or more, while 12% of those from Latin America had that much education. [Asians place more value on education than do Latin Americans.]

5. Foreign-born residents constitute 13% of the population in the United States, 18% in Canada, and 24% in Australia. [The United States has fewer immigrants, in relative terms, than these other countries.]

6. Population density in the United States is about 83 people per square mile. [It's crowded here.]

✳ 7. Measured in constant 2005 dollars, spending by the federal government increased from $1,832 billion in 1990 to $2,041 billion in 2000 to $3,315 billion in 2010. [Government spending increased less rapidly in the 1990s than in the following decade.]

8. The median starting salary for law school graduates in 2010 was $104,000. [Lawyers are highly paid.]

9. Completion rates within 10 years for those entering graduate school:

Humanities	49%
Mathematics and physical sciences	55%
Social sciences	56%
Life sciences	63%
Engineering	64%

[Engineering students are smarter, on average, than humanities students.]

✳ 10. In 2011, the average salary of players for the New York Mets baseball team was $4,401,752, but the median was $900,000. [A few players had much larger salaries than the others.]

and to use them intelligently in arguing for conclusions. The fundamental point to remember is that the numbers depend on the process by which they were derived and are informative only to the extent that the process is logical.

14.3 Statistical Generalization

As we saw in the past section, a statistic gives us numerical information about some class of things. In statistics, that class is called a *population* (regardless of whether or not it's a class of people). The different types of statistics—totals, frequencies, averages—tell us about certain quantitative properties of the class. And we know from our study of the basic nature of induction that there are two ways to support a statement about a class. We can examine each and every member—the method of complete enumeration—or we can study a sample of the class and then generalize our findings to the class as a whole. Statisticians use both methods. Many statistics on health, such as the frequency of various diseases or the proportion of people who die from various causes, reflect a complete tabulation of data from local public health officials around the country. And the U.S. Census Bureau issues a number of statistics based on surveys of the entire population. In contrast, opinion polls, the unemployment rate, and many other statistics are based on samples.

Samples can be used to estimate a ratio, a frequency, a frequency distribution, or an average value in a population. The unemployment rate (the *frequency* of unemployment in the workforce) is based on a monthly survey of about 100,000 people. An opinion poll tries to discover the *distribution* of voter preferences for rival candidates by interviewing a random sample of voters. *Average* values for physical and psychological variables—blood pressure, pulse rate, IQ, and the like—are inferred from samples; obviously we can't survey the entire human race. These *statistical generalizations* have much in common with the universal generalizations that we studied earlier (e.g., all *S* are *P*). In both cases, we infer that what is true of a sample is true of the entire population. And in both cases, the inference is valid only to the extent that the sample is *representative* of the population. But there are important differences in the way we try to ensure that the sample *is* representative.

For a universal generalization, as we have seen, we want a sample that reflects the qualitative diversity in the class of *S*s. We should actively seek out instances that vary in every respect (other than being *S*) that might be relevant to *P*. We should also look actively for negative instances, because even a single *S* that is not *P* would refute the generalization. But this approach would not make sense for a statistical generalization. Suppose we want to know the proportion of *S*s that are *P*—a question of frequency (similar arguments would apply to distributions and averages). There is no point in looking for negative instances. Presumably we already know that some *S*s are not *P*; the question is not whether such instances exist, but rather how frequent they are. For the same reason, the *qualitative* variety of the sample is not necessarily relevant. We are interested in a *quantitative* property of the population: the proportion of *S*s that are *P*. What we need is a method of choosing our sample so that the proportion of *P*s in the sample will reflect the proportion of *P*s in the population.

The method statisticians have devised is the use of *random* samples. The reason is that if we choose our sample randomly, then every member of the population has an equal chance of being included in the sample. Suppose that in the population at large, 17% are *P*. This would mean that every time we choose an *S* to be included in the sample, we have a 17% chance of getting one that is *P*. So in the long run, we would expect to get a *P* about 17% of the time—if our sample is large enough, it should reflect the proportion of *P*s in the population. Thus, instead of actively designing our sample by looking for certain kinds of instances, as we do for a universal generalization, we sit back and let a random process select the sample blindly.

The use of random samples has certain implications that we should be aware of. First, there is always a specific margin of error attached to the conclusion we draw about the population. Suppose you're in charge of quality control for a grain silo. You take a random sample of the grain and find that 3.2% is spoiled. Should you infer that *exactly* 3.2% of grain in the silo is spoiled? No. Your conclusion should be that spoilage in the silo is in the neighborhood of 3.2%. A sample is an instrument for measuring a quantity, and like other measuring instruments it has a specific margin of error. Second, the margin of error depends on the size of the sample. The larger the sample, the smaller the margin of error, and vice versa. For instance, when the Gallup poll reports the preferences of voters in an upcoming election, it uses a sample of about 1,000 voters, and the margin of error is about 3%. So if 56% in the sample favors candidate A, we can infer that somewhere between 53% and 59% of the entire pool of voters favors candidate A. If the sample had included only 100 people, the margin of error would have been larger—around 10%.

Finally, we should be aware that even when we take the margin of error into account, we are still only dealing with probabilities. Because the sample was randomly chosen, there is some chance, however small, that it radically misrepresents the population. In our example above, suppose that in fact only 1% of the electorate favors candidate A. That's a tiny minority, but it's still about a million voters, and it is possible that 1,120 of them were included in the sample (1,120/2,000 = 56%). In generalizing from a sample, therefore, we have to be satisfied with some degree of probability. Most people who use statistics settle for 95%. The 3% margin of error in the Gallup poll, for example, actually means that there's a 95% probability that the proportion of the voters favoring candidate A is within three percentage points of the reported figure.

There are precise mathematical techniques for computing a margin of error, given the size of the sample and the degree of probability we want. We'll leave all that to the experts. The techniques are not controversial, at least not for the types of statistics we are likely to encounter, and we can assume that if a statistic comes from a reputable source, the computations were done correctly. It is important to emphasize, however, that the margin of error refers only to the statistical relationship between the sample and the population. It does not include errors that arise in choosing and testing the sample itself. In particular, the techniques for calculating the margin of error assume that the sample was randomly chosen. This assumption is rarely true in the strict sense. A true random sample would be one chosen randomly from a complete list of the population. For a population the size of the American electorate, however, it is rarely possible to find a complete list, and it is usually too expensive to choose and test a completely random sample. So researchers typically use methods that they think will approximate randomness, but the approximation is never perfect, and there is plenty of room for biases to creep in. Let's look at some examples.

You want to know the average test score of the students in a class you're taking, so you ask the first 10 students who arrive at class one day—but that sample may overrepresent the more conscientious students, who may tend to score higher. An opinion poll uses a questionnaire distributed in airports—but people who travel by air are not a random cross section of the populace, and besides, people who fill out and return questionnaires are not a random cross section of those who receive them. A study of criminals relies on a sample of prison inmates—but criminals who are caught, convicted, and imprisoned may not be representative of criminals as a whole. All these samples are *biased* in one way or another and therefore won't tell us what we want to know about the relevant populations. Problems can also arise in testing the sample once it is chosen. A telephone interview, for example, would be a poor way to estimate the proportion of parents who abuse their children: Even if the sample was randomly chosen, you could hardly count on abusers to tell you the truth.

Another source of bias in opinion polls is the exact wording of the question. A classic example comes from the General Social Survey, which asks people whether they think the government is spending too much, too little, or the right amount on a variety of programs. One group of respondents was asked about government spending on "welfare," and another group was asked about "assistance to the poor." These two descriptions refer to essentially the same programs, but the results always differ. Here is the data from the year 2000:

Is Government Spending . . .	Welfare	Assistance to the Poor
Too little	24.0%	64.3%
About right	39.8%	24.2%
Too much	39.4%	11.5%

Source: General Social Survey, National Opinion Research Center.

It seems clear that people are responding to connotations of the terms. "Welfare" has acquired a negative connotation of dependence, whereas "assistance to the poor" has a more positive invocation of a helping hand.

An opinion poll is an especially complicated case of generalizing from a sample, because opinions are such intangible and slippery things. It's likely that some respondents make up their minds on the spot, under the influence of subtle factors like the exact wording of the question or the structure of the alternatives they're given. But opinion polls are also the kind of statistical generalization we encounter most often in the media, and they illustrate very well the kinds of biases to watch for.

Despite the problems that can arise in generalizing from a sample, this method can be a reliable way of supporting statistical claims about a population. An example is the crime rate: the number of burglaries (or other crimes) per thousand people. The FBI computes this figure by complete enumeration; it tabulates all the burglaries reported to all the police departments in the country. The National Crime Victimization Survey, however, uses a sample; it interviews about 49,000 households to see how many were victims of burglary in the previous 6 months. The NCVS runs the risks associated with any use of samples. But the FBI figures have their own flaw: Many burglaries are not reported to the police (a fact we know from the survey of victims). So the two approaches must be used to supplement one another.

As you can see, investigating the statistical properties of large populations in the real world takes a blend of common sense and specialized technique. If you need to use statistics in your studies or your work, you will need a separate course of training in the proper methods. This section is intended for the non-expert—the consumer of statistical information, not the producer. As consumers, we must rely to some extent on the authority of experts. But as in any other case of relying on authorities, we can—and should—use our own common sense to evaluate their credibility.

STRATEGY   Generalizing from a Sample

A statistical generalization is a claim about ratio, frequency, distribution, average, or median value in a population, based on information about a random sample. To assess the strength of the generalization, consider the following questions:

1. Was the margin of error reported? If so, how large is it?
2. How was the sample selected? Was the selection procedure random? Was there anything about the selection process to suggest that the sample might not be representative of the population?
3. How was information about the sample acquired? Was there anything to suggest that the process of testing the sample was unreliable? In the case of opinion polls, for example, consider whether the question used slanted language or forced respondents to choose among too small a range of alternatives.

EXERCISE 14.3

Identify potential biases and other problems in each of the following generalizations.

✳ 1. A conservative organization reports that 71% of the populace is opposed to national health insurance, based on a questionnaire sent to its mailing list.

2. To find the average salary of doctors, a reporter interviews a random sample of doctors attending a convention of the American Medical Association.

3. *Road and Track* magazine polls its readers to find out what percentage of the population favors increased speed limits on interstate highways.

✳ 4. To find the average age of Bruce Springsteen fans, researchers survey people at a Springsteen concert.

5. A poll is conducted by telephone to find the percentage of men who cannot swim.

6. Researchers telephone a random sample of households in the evening to find what percentages of families eat dinner together.

✳ 7. To assess how engaged parents are in their children's education, researchers send a questionnaire to the e-mail list of the Parent Teacher Association.

8. Two percent of apples are estimated to have pesticide residues above allowable levels, based on a sample drawn from supermarkets across the country.

9. An environmental organization uses the following question in a mail survey: "Do you believe Americans have an ethical obligation to preserve unique riverine natural systems for future generations?"

✳10. An opinion survey asks respondents: "Which of the following best represents your position on government funding of the arts:

a. Museums, symphonies, and other arts organizations should be funded by tax dollars.

b. Such organizations should rely on ticket sales to people patronizing the organizations."

14.4 Statistical Evidence of Causality

We have seen that a statistic gives us numerical information about a class, such as the total number of its members or their average values on a variable. Statistics can also tell us about *correlations* among these numerical properties. A correlation can take many forms, depending on the type of statistic involved. For example, *average* income correlates with the *total* years of education people have. The *frequency* of lung cancer is higher among smokers than among nonsmokers. A high *ratio* of high- to low-density cholesterol is correlated with a low risk (*frequency*) of heart attack. What these examples have in common, what makes them examples of correlation, is a systematic, nonrandom relationship between two variables: income and education, smoking and lung cancer, cholesterol levels and heart attacks.

14.4A Correlation and Causality

Correlations are important because they can give us evidence of causality. Medical researchers use statistical evidence to trace the causes of health and disease—the link between smoking and cancer is the best known example, but there are many others. Economists look for correlations that will explain inflation, unemployment, productivity, etc. In these and other cases, the use of correlations is required by the nature of the subject. In a complex system like the human body or the economy, a given effect is often the result of a great many factors—none of which by itself is either necessary or sufficient. Smoking, for example, is not a necessary condition for lung cancer: Some nonsmokers get the disease. Nor is it sufficient: Some smokers don't. But smoking *is* a partial or *contributing* factor, something that increases the likelihood of lung cancer, something that weighs in the balance—and can tip the balance if the right combination of other factors is also present.

To identify a contributing factor, we have to look at a large number of cases. For example, a drop in interest rates tends to cause an increase in purchases of homes. That's because individuals take the cost of a mortgage into account in deciding whether to buy. Of course, some people are going to buy a home no matter what, and others are simply not in the market. But for some individuals, a drop in mortgage costs will tip the balance. An economist, however, has no way of knowing who those particular individuals are; he can only examine the class of home buyers as a whole and see whether the class gets bigger when interest rates fall. In general, a contributing factor usually can't be identified by looking at individual cases, but it will reveal itself in the existence of a correlation among variables in the relevant class.

The existence of a correlation, however, does not prove causality—not by itself. A correlation may occur by chance or it may reflect a causal relationship quite different from the one it suggests. For example:

1. During a 19-year stretch, the stock market went up almost every year when a team from the NFC won the Super Bowl and down when the AFC team won.
2. Before the introduction of polio vaccine, investigators found a strong correlation between soft drink sales and new polio cases reported.
3. In certain areas of Europe, there is a correlation between births and the number of stork nests.
4. Arizona has one of the highest death rates in the country from bronchitis, emphysema, asthma, and other lung diseases.

It should not be surprising that some correlations, like 1, occur by chance. Think of all the variables you could measure—from the average number of Oakland A's home runs during double-headers, to the fertility rate of zebras in Tanzania. If you look long enough, you're bound to find some bizarre correlations. In other cases, variables are correlated because both reflect a third factor. Before the vaccine was developed, polio epidemics tended to occur in the summer, when soft drink sales were also high. Storks do not in fact bring babies, but they do tend to nest in buildings, and the number of buildings increases with population. Arizona's death rate from lung disease does not mean that clean air kills; it means that many people with these diseases move there to prolong their lives.

Thus inferring that variable a causally affects variable E merely because a and E are correlated is analogous to the *post hoc* fallacy. If one event causes another, the first must precede the second, but the converse does not hold; the fact that a came first does not imply that it caused E. To establish causality, as we saw, we must use Mill's methods to show that there is a connection between a and E. In the same way, a contributing factor should give rise to a correlation among variables, but not every correlation reveals a causal relation. We need a method for separating the statistical wheat from the chaff.

In the four examples earlier, you could rely on common sense to avoid drawing the wrong conclusion. But many other cases are less obvious. Does lowering a tax rate cause an increase in tax revenues? How much of a person's intelligence is due to heredity? Does caffeine cause bladder cancer? Is a murderer more likely to get the death penalty for killing a white person than for killing a black person? There is correlational evidence on all these questions, but it is not immediately obvious how to interpret the evidence, and these issues are extremely controversial. Let's take a look at some rules we should follow.

14.4B Evaluating Correlations

The rules for evaluating statistical evidence of causality rest on the same basic principle as Mill's methods, just as drawing a statistical generalization from a sample is governed by the same basic principle as universal generalizations. But there are also some important differences. Let's start by looking at an idealized case in the abstract. Then we'll look at some of the problems and issues that come up in practice.

Suppose we want to know whether some variable E is causally affected by another variable a. The ideal test would be an experiment in which we can control a and watch for corresponding changes in E; in this context, a is called the *independent* variable and E the *dependent* variable. One way to design the experiment could be diagrammed as follows:

Group 1: $a, b, c, \ldots$
Group 2: $-, b, c, \ldots$

We have two groups that are identical except that one (the *experimental* group) has the property we're testing, while the other (the *control* group) does not. You can see that this is the same basic pattern as Mill's method of difference. Alternatively, if a is a quantitative variable, we could give different experimental groups different levels of a, using the same pattern as Mill's method of concomitant variation:

Group 1: $a-$, b, $c, \ldots$
Group 2: a, b, $c, \ldots$
Group 3: $a+$, b, $c, \ldots$

Notice, however, that we are comparing two or more *groups* instead of comparing two or more *individual* cases, as we did when we studied Mill's methods earlier. We have to use groups when a is only a contributing factor, for the reason explained above. And we will also have to make an adjustment in the way we measure the dependent variable, the effect. The question is not whether the effect occurs, or in what degree, in a particular case; we are not comparing particular cases directly. We are comparing groups. So the question is whether a makes a *statistical* difference in the effect. If E is a qualitative variable, we would typically measure a frequency—for example, the frequency of tumors in mice fed a diet high in saccharine.

Group 1:   saccharine, b, $c, \ldots$ $\longrightarrow$ higher frequency
Group 2:   no saccharine, b, $c, \ldots$ $\longrightarrow$ lower frequency

If E is a quantitative variable, we would typically look at average values for experimental and control groups—for example, average SAT scores for students taking test-preparation classes.

Group 1:   test prep class, b, $c, \ldots$ $\longrightarrow$ higher average SAT
Group 2:   no test prep, b, $c, \ldots$ $\longrightarrow$ lower average SAT

But those are fairly minor adjustments to make in our use of Mill's methods. The major adjustment has to do with the other variables—b, c, etc. As we have seen, it's essential to the methods of difference and concomitant variations that we hold these factors constant. That is what allows us to infer that a is responsible for any differences in E. When we use statistical evidence, we have to meet this requirement in a somewhat different way. Consider the earlier example: We want to know whether a certain test-preparation course can raise people's SAT scores. We would have an experimental group take the course and a control group not take it, holding all other factors constant. But how are we going to do that? Individual students differ on an enormous number of variables that might affect their SAT scores: IQ, verbal ability, memory, ability to concentrate, ambition, response to stress, test-taking savvy, and so on. It would be extraordinarily difficult to find two individuals who are identical with regard to all these variables. Finding two *groups* whose members are all identical is out of the question. Fortunately, that isn't necessary. Since we are dealing with groups, what matters is that they have the same *distribution* on those variables—the same distribution by verbal ability, memory, etc. In that case, the experimental and control groups will be statistically identical except for the variable we are testing (taking the course vs. not taking it), and a statistical difference in the effect can then be attributed to that variable.

Setting things up this way is easier said than done. It takes a great deal of scientific knowledge and skill to make sure that the groups are statistically similar on these variables. In some cases, researchers try to match the groups by deliberately pairing off individuals. But this is quite difficult, especially if there are more than a few variables to keep track of. And with really complex phenomena, we simply don't know what all the relevant variables are. So it is more common to use random procedures for selecting the two groups, and the rationale is the same as in the case of generalizing from a sample. Suppose that in our pool of volunteers for the SAT experiment, 10% have IQs in the 140+ range. If we assign volunteers to groups by a random process, then every time we select someone for either group, there's a 10% chance we'll select someone in the 140+ range. So if the groups are large enough, there's a good chance that each one will have about 10% in that range. And the same would be true for values on the other variables.

Suppose, then, that we have assigned our volunteers to their groups by a random process; our experimental group has taken the cram course, and its average SAT score is higher than the average for our control group. Does this prove that the course affected the scores? It depends. Remember that we are using a random process, so we have to apply what we learned in the past section about random sampling. First, we would not expect the averages to be *exactly* the same even if the cram course had no effect whatever. The difference in averages must be of a certain size before we have evidence of causality. Second, the size of that difference depends on the size of our groups, just as the margin of error in an opinion poll depends on the size of the sample. As we increase the size of our experimental and control groups, it becomes more likely that traits such as intelligence will be distributed evenly between them, so it becomes less likely that a large difference in average scores could occur merely by chance. In general, the larger the group, the smaller the correlation has to be to count as causally significant. But third, and finally, we are still only dealing with probabilities. Even with a large sample, there is some chance, however tiny, that our random process assigned all the geniuses to the experimental group. So if the difference in average scores is x points, then to be precise we should state our result as follows: There is only a y percent probability that an x point difference could occur by chance, given the size of our groups. Most researchers consider a result *statistically significant* if y is less than 5%.

There are mathematical techniques for determining whether a correlation is statistically significant. Once again, as with generalizing from a sample, we'll leave these calculations to the experts. But once again, it's important to emphasize the limitations of these techniques. Just as the margin of error in a poll does not take account of errors in choosing the sample, a correlation that is statistically significant may not be significant in the usual sense of being important. With a large enough sample, it is possible to identify factors that play a very small causal role in contributing to an effect. This is true, for example, of many substances that have been found to "cause" cancer in laboratory animals. Or suppose a researcher found a statistically significant difference in traffic fatality rates between states with different drinking ages. That wouldn't necessarily provide an argument for raising the drinking age. Perhaps the difference was minor, and it would be more effective to impose stiffer penalties on drunk driving.

In the previous section, moreover, we saw that the techniques for computing a margin of error rest on the assumption that the sample was randomly selected—an assumption that is rarely true in the strict sense. An analogous point can be made about correlations. A statistically significant correlation is evidence of causality on the assumption that we have taken into account all the other variables that might affect our result. The idealized experiment I described earlier is an attempt to meet that standard. In practice, however, problems invariably arise that call the assumption into question. After we pause for a bit of practice, we will look at a few of these problems.

EXERCISE 14.4B

Analyze the statistical inferences below as instances of Mill's methods. First identify the independent and dependent variables and the type of statistic (frequency or average) used to measure the effect; then determine whether the method of difference or the method of concomitant variations is being used.

＊1. In a sample of pea plants grown under ultraviolet light, 80% of the seeds sprouted within a week, as against 60% of a control group, grown in normal conditions. Thus ultraviolet light fosters growth.

2. A large statistical study of doctors shows that exercise affects the risk of heart disease. Those who exercised three times a week had half the rate of heart attacks as those who exercised irregularly and a quarter as many heart attacks as those who never exercised.

3. The effects of a new gasoline additive were tested on a group of 30 automobiles of different makes, models, and model years. Each car used the same brand of gasoline for a month, measuring the miles driven on each tankful; then the same gasoline with the additive was used for a month. Average mileage for these 30 cars was 5% higher with the additive than without.

＊4. Twenty students who used appointment books to track their assignments and plan their study time each week were matched for intelligence, field of study, and year of graduation with 20 students who did not. The mean grade-point average for the first group was 3.1, versus 2.8 for the second group, a result that shows the value of using appointment books.

5. In a large study of the effects of advertising, 300 consumer-product companies were divided into four groups, depending on the size of their advertising budgets as a percent of total expenditures. It was discovered that as the size of the advertising budget increased, average profit margins increased also.

14.4C Experiments Versus Observational Studies

Suppose we want to know whether there's a significant difference in the way men and women react to stress. We can't randomly assign our volunteers to the two groups, male and female—nature has already made that decision. For a true experiment, the experimenter must be able to control the independent variable. But many variables can't be controlled: Meteorologists can't control the properties of storm systems, economists can't manipulate the economy to see what causes depressions, geologists can't decide when to have an earthquake. There are other variables that can't be manipulated for ethical reasons. You can't ask someone to smoke for 20 years for the sake of cancer research. You can't abuse an experimental group of children to see whether abuse breeds violent behavior. In all these cases, we are limited to *observational* studies. We have to observe the variables as they occur naturally, outside our control, and try to find the relevant correlations.

In the right circumstances, an observational study *can* provide evidence of causality. But it has two major drawbacks in relation to an experiment. First, it does not involve random assignment to experimental and control groups. So there's a danger that any correlation we find between two variables may be due to some third variable that is not evenly distributed among the groups. For example, it is plausible to think that a person who was abused as a child is more likely than other people to have certain problems later in life: to abuse his or her own children, engage in criminal activity, etc. And there is correlational evidence to support this hypothesis. But is the abuse actually the cause of these later problems? Parents who abuse their children are not a random sample from the population. They tend to have other traits in common: They tend to be emotionally distant and neglectful of their children, for example, and subject to economic stresses such as unemployment or poverty. Perhaps it is these traits, rather than the physical abuse per se, that contribute to the child's later problems. We can't tell from the correlation itself. In the language of statistics, the correlation we observe between two variables may be *confounded* by some other variable.

Second, an experiment allows us to control one variable and look for changes in another. If we find them, there is no question which is the cause, which the effect. But this question does arise in observational studies. Cities have higher crime rates than rural areas. Is that because urban life breeds criminals or because criminals migrate to cities to find victims? People with higher levels of education have higher average incomes. Does that mean you can boost your income by getting a college degree? Perhaps. Or perhaps the correlation is a by-product of an underlying factor—people with more intelligence or ambition may tend to do better both in school and in the job market, but for different reasons.

As a general rule, therefore, it is more difficult to draw causal conclusions from an observational study than from an experiment. But this is merely a general rule. For one thing, experiments are not immune from problems of confounding variables. Suppose you want to study the effects of political advertising on voter preferences. So you show an ad for candidate A to your experimental group and find that the proportion who say they'd vote for candidate A goes up. That may indicate that the ad had a real effect. Or it may simply mean that your subjects figured out what you were up to and were simply telling you what they knew you wanted to hear.

Careful researchers can structure experiments to avoid these problems. An observational study can also take steps to screen out confounding variables. For example, the death rate from lung cancer is about 10 times higher for smokers than for nonsmokers. That fact alone would not prove that smoking plays a causal role. The age distribution among smokers and nonsmokers may not be the same. Or perhaps the class of smokers includes a higher proportion who live in cities and are exposed to more air pollution. But cancer researchers control for such factors by comparing people of the same age, who live in the same area, and so on for many other variables—and the death rate for smokers is still higher. Among the class of smokers, moreover, the death rate varies concomitantly with the number of cigarettes a person smokes per day, the number of years that person has smoked, and the degree of inhalation. And among ex-smokers, the death rate goes down in correlation with the number of years since a person quit. When you put all this together, there is little doubt that a causal relationship does exist.

14.4D External Validity

The issues we have considered so far pertain to what is sometimes called the *internal* validity of a study or experiment. They pertain to the conclusions we can draw about cause and effect in regard to the class of things actually observed or included in an experiment. But of course we normally want to generalize from that class to a wider population. We want to know whether smoking causes cancer for people in general, not just for those who happened to be included in a particular study. And this raises questions of *external* validity, questions you should ask when a researcher claims that his findings apply to a population as a whole.

A great deal of psychological research is conducted at colleges and universities using undergraduate students as subjects. If an experiment is done properly and finds a significant correlation, we can infer that the independent variable was causally affecting the dependent variable—for the particular subjects involved. But how far can we generalize the result? To all people of college age? Perhaps—if we assume that the differences between those who go to college and those who don't are irrelevant to the outcome. Can we generalize to people of all ages? Perhaps—if we assume that age makes no difference. These assumptions may or may not be reasonable in a given case. The point to remember is that they are not supported by the experiment itself.

A similar question about external validity arose over the claim that the artificial sweetener saccharine causes bladder cancer. In experiments with rats, researchers found a significant difference between experimental and control groups in the number of tumors that developed. There does not appear to be any reason for doubting that saccharin was causally responsible. But can this result be generalized to human beings? Skeptics raised two objections. First, the experimental group was fed extremely high doses of saccharine—the equivalent of a human being drinking 1,000 cans of diet soda per day. Perhaps the high dosage was the key factor; perhaps there is a threshold below which saccharine would not have caused bladder cancer in these rats. Second, a substance that causes cancer in one species may not do so in another; we may not be able to generalize from rats to other mammals, including humans. These questions are hotly debated among cancer researchers. It may turn out that the generalization is indeed valid. The point, once again, is that it rests on assumptions that are not supported by the experiment itself.

To evaluate external validity, finally, we should remember the special importance of definitions in statistical reasoning. To establish a correlation between two variables, we must define the variables in such a way that they can be counted or measured. In some cases this is fairly easy; in others it is difficult if not impossible. Cancer researchers do not face any major difficulty in defining the category of people who smoke. Economists don't need specialized definitions of men and women to study sex differences in income. By their very nature, however, psychological traits such as intelligence, values, attitudes, or feelings cannot be observed directly. Nor is statistical information readily available for many economic and sociological categories—such as illegal aliens, entrepreneurs, fundamentalists.

To test a hypothesis involving one of these variables, therefore, a researcher must find some other variable to stand in for it, a *proxy variable* to serve as a measuring rod. Suppose you wanted to see whether some classroom exercise had any effect on racial prejudice in college students. The dependent variable you are interested in is *prejudice*. But you cannot observe what is going on in a student's mind directly, so for the purposes of the experiment you would have to measure prejudice indirectly—say, by the student's willingness to contribute to a civil rights organization. That is where the problem of external validity arises. Suppose you found a strong correlation between the classroom exercise and the willingness to contribute, a correlation strong enough to convince you that a causal relationship is involved. Does that prove the exercise affects prejudice? Only if we assume that the willingness to contribute is a good barometer of prejudice—an assumption that may or may not be true. In addition to prejudice, the willingness to contribute to a particular organization may reflect a person's level of generosity, his awareness of political issues, his agreement with the specific political goals of the organization, or simply his desire for popularity. And it may be that

---

STRATEGY **Internal and External Validity**

When statistical methods are used to support a causal generalization that factor *a* affects *E*, the chief questions to ask about the *internal* validity of the inference are

1. Confounding variables: Were there any variables, other than the ones being tested, that may have been responsible for *E*?

2. Direction of causality: Is it clear whether *a* is affecting *E* or *E* affecting *a*?

The chief questions to ask about *external* validity are

1. Extrapolation: Is the claim that *a* affects *E* being extended beyond the class of *a*'s or *E*'s or extrapolated beyond the range of the variables that were tested?

2. Proxy variables: When a causal factor or an effect cannot be studied directly, and other variables are studied as their proxies, how reasonable is it to assume a connection between the observed variable and the variation of interest?

the exercise affected one of these other variables, not prejudice per se. In general, then, when someone claims to have established a causal relationship, and one or more of the variables involved strike you as things that can't be measured or counted directly, make sure to ask what variables were actually being correlated in the study or experiment, and consider whether those stand-in variables really do reflect the variable they purport to measure.

This completes our discussion of statistical evidence of causality. Once again, we have approached this as consumers of information, not producers. If you are going to conduct experiments or observational studies yourself, you will need more training in the subject matter and relevant statistical techniques. As consumers, we must rely to some extent on the authority of those who have that expertise. But once again, we should be intelligent consumers, using the considerations we've discussed here, along with our common sense, to ask critical questions about the research results we encounter in the media and elsewhere.

✳ EXERCISE 14.4D

The paragraph below is a fictional report of research purporting to prove a causal relationship. Using what you've learned in this section, evaluate the causal inference.

Scientists at Flywheel Polytechnic have established that backseat driving can be hazardous to your health. Prior to this research, which was funded by the U.S. Department of Transportation, there had been speculation that nagging advice from passengers on how to drive might cause stress for some exasperated drivers and increase the likelihood of accidents. The Flywheel team, reasoning that spouses and other family members are the commonest source of such advice, compared traffic near Disney World, at the height of the vacation season, with commuter traffic outside New York City, consisting largely of drivers alone in their cars. Average speeds were the same in the two cases, as were driving conditions, but the accident rate in vacation traffic was 34.5% higher, a difference found to be statistically significant.

Summary

Statistics give us numerical information about a class or population of things; the information normally concerns their values on one or more variables. A total is the number of things in a class *S* or the sum of their values on a variable. A ratio is a total stated in relationship to another class *T*. A frequency is the number or proportion of *S*s that have some property *P*; a distribution is the proportion of *S*s that have each of the values (*P*, *Q*, *R*, . . .) on some variable. Frequencies and distributions are often used to estimate probability. Averages and medians are central values of *S*s on a quantitative variable.

A statistical statement about a population can be supported either by complete enumeration or by generalization from a sample. A randomly chosen sample allows us to conclude that the relevant value of the population is the same as the value of the sample, within a certain margin of error, to a certain degree of probability. Perfectly random samples are rarely used, however, and the techniques used to approximate randomness may introduce biases.

Statistical correlations among variables provide an important source of evidence for causal connections. A correlation per se, however, is not proof of causality; we must control for other variables according to the pattern of Mill's methods of difference or concomitant variations. This may be done through an experiment in which subjects are randomly assigned to control and experimental groups or through an observational study. In either case, we should watch for problems of internal validity: Are there any confounding variables? Is it clear which variable is the cause and which the effect? And we should watch for problems of external validity: Is it reasonable to generalize from the sample actually studied to a larger population? Are the variables actually measured good stand-ins for the variables of interest?

Key Terms

total—a statistic specifying the number of items in a class or the sum of their values on a variable.

ratio—a statistic specifying the number of items in a class or the sum of their values on a variable per unit of some other class; a ratio is a total expressed in relative terms.

frequency—a statistic specifying the number or proportion of items in a class that have a given property.

distribution—a statistic specifying the number or proportion of items in a class that have each of the values (*P*, *Q*, *R*, etc.) on some variable.

average—a statistic specifying the sum of the values that the items in a class have on a quantitative variable *P*, divided by the number of items.

median—a statistic specifying the middle value of the items in a class on a quantitative variable *P*.

Additional Exercises

A. For each pair of statements, determine whether the statements are compatible or contradictory.

✳ 1. (a) Thirty-six percent of seniors at Tiptop College are foreign students. (b) Eighty-four percent of students at Tiptop College are American citizens.

2. (a) The number of people employed in the U.S. economy increased 1.1% last month to 109.7 million. (b) The unemployment rate increased to 7.1% last month, from 7.0% the previous month.

3. (a) Among those who reported incomes below the poverty line in 2011, only 9% worked full-time, year-round. (b) In 2011,

only 2.6% of people who worked full-time, year-round, reported incomes below the poverty level.

✳ 4. (a) The human brain contains about 10 billion nerve cells. (b) The human brain contains about 100 billion nerve cells.

5. (a) Sixty-three percent of American voters think that taxes should be cut. (b) Twenty-seven percent of American voters think that government spending on social programs should be cut.

6. (a) Accidental Petroleum's profits this year were up 91% over last year.

(b) Accidental Petroleum's profits this year were 4% of revenues.

✳ 7. (a) In eight courses this year, Chris's grade distribution was four As, three Bs, and one C. (b) Chris's grade-point average this year was 2.2.

8. (a) Fifty percent of individuals with incomes of $75,000 or more have individual retirement accounts (IRAs), while only 25% of individuals earning less than $75,000 have IRAs. (b) Ninety percent of IRA contributions are made by people earning less than $50,000 per year.

B. Each question below is followed by references to various statistics. Which statistic would be most helpful in answering the question?

✳ 1. Has it become more expensive in the past 10 years to purchase a house?

a. The median price of houses on the market, now versus then
b. The average price of houses on the market, now versus then
c. The median price, adjusted for inflation
d. The median price as a multiple of the median family's income, now versus then

2. Has divorce become more common in the past 10 years?

a. Total number of divorces, now versus then
b. The ratio of divorces to marriages, now versus then
c. The number of divorces as a percentage of all married couples
d. The divorce rate (per unit of population), now versus then

3. Is it safer to travel by plane or by car?

a. Fatalities per vehicle mile for planes and cars
b. Fatalities per passenger mile for planes and cars

✳ 4. Has my investment in the Random Walk Fund given me a satisfactory return over the past year?

a. Dollar amount of increase in value of investment
b. Amount of increase as percent of amount invested
c. Percent of increase as compared to interest rate
d. Percent of increase as compared to increase in Standard and Poor's stock index

5. Is private education cheaper than public education? (Choose one figure from each column.)

Private Schools	Public Schools
(a) Average tuition	(d) Average expenditure per pupil
(b) Median tuition	(e) Average fee charged to pupils from outside the district
(c) Median tuition at nonreligious schools	

C. The two opinion polls below were conducted at the same time, by reputable pollsters, about the same proposed tax increase. What differences between the polls might explain the different results?

1. Q: As you may know, the tax cuts passed into law when George W. Bush was president are set to expire this year. Unless a new bill is passed, federal income tax rates will rise to the level they were at when those cuts were enacted. Which of the following statements comes closest to your view?

   Those tax cuts should continue for all Americans.   31%

   Those tax cuts should continue for families that make less than $250,000 a year, but taxes should rise to the previous level for families who make more than that amount.   51%

   Taxes should rise to the previous level for all Americans regardless of how much money they make.   18%

   [CNN/Opinion Research Corporation, August 2010]

2. Q: As you may know, the tax cuts passed during George W. Bush's administration lowered taxes by reducing the maximum income tax rate for all Americans. These tax cuts are set to expire at the end of 2010, meaning tax rates would go back to what they were before the Bush tax cuts. Congress is currently considering whether to let these tax cuts expire or extend them. Which of the following comes closest to your own view on what action Congress should take?

   Extend the tax cuts for all Americans.   49%

   Let the tax cuts expire only for people who earn more than $200,000 a year.   31%

   Let the tax cuts expire for all Americans.   15%

   [Ipsos/Reuters, August 2010]

D. Using everything you have learned in this chapter, evaluate each of the following arguments for its use of statistic claims.

❋ 1. A pharmaceutical company advertises skin rash cream to relieve the symptoms of poison ivy. For 70% of the people using the cream, it says, the rash and itching disappear within 1 week.

2. Shakespeare scholar Bernard Beckerman studied the records of Shakespeare's theater company (the Lord Admiral's Men) to determine how important new plays were for a company's bottom line, as opposed to revival of plays from previous seasons. For the 1595–1596 season, "the company gave one hundred and fifty performances of thirty different plays. Eighty-seven performances, or 58 per cent of the total, were of the fourteen new plays produced that season. Five performances, 3.3 per cent, were of one play, The Jew of Malta, revived that season. Forty-six performances, or 30.7 per cent, were given of the eight plays from the previous season, which were less than a year old. . . . Only twelve performances, 8 per cent, were of the seven plays which were more than a year old. This distribution, which is similar for all the seasons covered by Henslowe's records, emphasizes how dependent the company was on the continuous addition of new plays to its stock in order to maintain itself in London." [Bernard Beckerman, *Shakespeare at the Globe*]

3. An organization supporting research on Alzheimer's disease urges more government spending to find causes and possible treatments for the disease. After all, it argues, government-sponsored research for the millions of people with Alzheimer's comes to only $50 per victim, whereas spending on AIDS is over $10,000 per victim.

✳ 4. "Researchers at a university reported that younger wives appear to be a basis for a longer life span in men between 50 and 80 years old. The death rate for older men married to women 1 to 24 years younger was 13% lower than average for their age group. Men with older wives seemed to have a death rate 20% higher than average." [*Wall Street Journal*, January 22, 1985]

5. In defending farm programs that increase the price of products like sugar, a U.S. congressman from the Midwest asserted, "The way to determine whether or not prices of food that are from price-supported commodities are high is to go to the grocery store and compare them with those products that are not processed from price-supported products." To clinch the argument, he held up a five-pound bag of sugar costing $1.79 and a two-pound package of cat food costing $2.83. [James Brovard, "How to Think Like a Congressman," *Wall Street Journal*, August 8, 1990]

6. Psychologists Leif D. Nelson and Joseph P. Simmons conducted research purporting to show that because people like their names, they are unconsciously drawn to negative outcomes that they would consciously avoid if those outcomes reminded them of their names. In one study, they compiled the strikeout records of major-league baseball players. "For scoring clarity, strikeouts have always been recorded using the letter K. . . . Accordingly, we predicted that players whose first or last names begin with K would show an increased tendency to strike out." They analyzed the records of 6,397 players from 1913 (the first year for which there are complete data) through 2006. "Across more than 90 years of professional baseball, batters whose names began with K struck out at a higher rate (in 18.8% of their plate appearances) than the remaining batters (17.2%)," a statistically significant difference. ["Moniker Maladies: When Names Sabotage Success," *Psychological Science*, vol. 18, no. 12, 2006]

CHAPTER 15

Explanation

Compare these two statements:

1. Joan will be successful because she is bright and ambitious.
2. Joan is sad because her cat just died.

Both of these statements make a claim about Joan, and both of them offer a reason, indicated by the word "because." But there's a difference: 1 is an argument, and 2 is an explanation. In 1, my claim that Joan will be successful is a conclusion I am trying to convince you to accept on the basis of the premise that she is bright and ambitious. In 2, I am not trying to convince you that Joan is sad. We can both see that she's sad—I'm taking that fact for granted. Instead, I am trying to *explain* that fact by pointing out that her cat just died.

In this chapter, we will learn how to analyze explanations using some of the same methods we have used for analyzing arguments. We will then review the standards for evaluating explanations.

15.1 Explanation and Argument

The theoretical relationship between arguments and explanations is complex and controversial. But it seems clear that there is at least a difference in emphasis. The primary goal of an argument is to show *that* some proposition is true, while the primary goal of an explanation is to show *why* it is true. In an argument, we reason forward from the premises to the conclusion; in an explanation, we reason backward from a fact to the cause or reason for that fact. Why does ice float in water? How do salmon find their way back to the streams they were spawned in? Why did the Industrial Revolution occur when it did? Why do human beings so often make war on each other? In all these cases, we know that a certain proposition is true: Ice floats, salmon find their way, etc. This proposition is the *explanandum* (plural: *explananda*)—a Latin word meaning "that which is to be explained." What we want to know is the cause or the reason for the *explanandum*. We're looking for a **hypothesis** that will make the *explanandum* intelligible to us by explaining why it is true. Ordinarily, the word "hypothesis" suggests something tentative, an idea that hasn't been proven yet. But we're going to use the term in a broader sense, to mean any explanatory idea, no matter how well confirmed. In this sense, for example, Newton's law of gravitation is a hypothesis when it is used to explain the motion of physical objects.

Any explanation involves a hypothesis and an *explanandum*, just as any argument involves premises and a conclusion. When a doctor diagnoses a disease, the patient's symptoms are the *explananda*, and the diagnosis is the hypothesis. In a criminal trial, the prosecution tries to show that the guilt of the defendant is the only hypothesis that would explain all the evidence, and the defense tries to create doubt in the minds of the jury by arguing that some other hypothesis is possible. If you are given the assignment of interpreting a poem, the *explanandum* is the poem itself—the words, the rhythms, the images. Your assignment is to find a hypothesis about what the poet was trying to convey. The theories of philosophers and religious thinkers can often be regarded as hypotheses to explain fundamental features of the world and human experience. And of course a central goal of science is to find hypotheses that will explain observable phenomena.

Despite the difference between argument and explanation, there is also a fundamental similarity. Let's go back to our original examples.

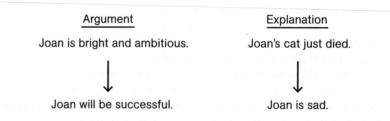

In the argument on the left, we take the premise as a given and use it to establish the conclusion. In the explanation on the right, the *explanandum* is the given, and we are trying to establish the hypothesis. Nevertheless, the arrow means the same thing in both cases. The hypothesis is related to the *explanandum* in such a way that if the hypothesis is true, the *explanandum* is likely to be true as well. Of course, we already know it's true; we know that Joan is sad. But the point is that her sadness is just what we would expect if her cat died. Had we learned about her cat before we saw her, we might have predicted that she would be sad, just as we predict her success from the premise about her character traits. An explanation, then, has the same inner structure as an argument, and we can analyze that structure with the same diagramming techniques we have used for analyzing arguments. Let's review these techniques briefly, and see how they apply to explanations. (For a fuller introduction to the diagramming techniques, see Chapter 4.)

15.1A Diagramming Explanations

It is rarely, if ever, possible for a single proposition to serve as a complete and adequate explanation of anything. In history, literature, the sciences, or any other discipline, an explanation can involve a highly complex set of propositions. Even in the earlier example, there is more than one. The death of Joan's cat is the only part of the hypothesis mentioned explicitly. But we're also assuming that Joan was attached to her cat; otherwise its death would not have meant anything to her. So the explanation includes two points that are combined additively, like dependent premises in an argument:

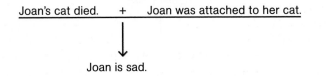

An argument can also have independent premises, which we would diagram with convergent arrows. For example:

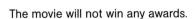

An explanation can have the same structure. Suppose a detective trying to solve a murder suspects the victim's son. The detective has to find a motive to explain why the son would do it, and as with many human actions, there may be more than one motive. Perhaps father and son had just had a violent argument, and the son also stood to inherit a lot of money. Then the hypothesis would be diagrammed:

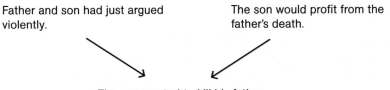

The convergent arrows indicate that the two parts of the hypothesis function independently. Even if one turned out to be false, the other could still (partly) explain the son's motive.

We have also seen that an argument can have more than one step; in fact, most of them do. The same is true of explanations. We explain something by appealing to a hypothesis, and then we can go on to ask why that hypothesis is true, and come up with another hypothesis to explain the first one. As we do so, we increase the *depth* of our explanation, and the deeper the explanation, the more fully we understand the original *explanandum*. In the early 1600s, for example, the German astronomer Johannes Kepler explained the observed motions of the planets on the hypothesis that they follow elliptical orbits around the sun, obeying certain laws that he formulated mathematically. Later in the century, Isaac Newton showed that this hypothesis is itself explained by his law of gravitational attraction. Schematically, then, we have an explanation in two steps:

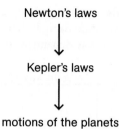

Finally, a single hypothesis can support more than one *explanandum*, a situation we diagram with divergent arrows:

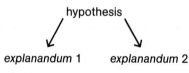

This structure is extremely important for explanations. One mark of a good explanation is that it unifies a range of phenomena: A single hypothesis explains a number of different *explananda*. A good explanation, in other words, has *breadth* as well as depth. Indeed, these two virtues are related. As we push deeper in the effort to explain something, we typically come up with hypotheses that explain a wider and wider range of things. Thus Newton's theory did more than explain the motions of the planets. It also explained the laws Galileo discovered concerning the motion of falling objects and projectiles. That is, Newton gave a unified explanation for the motion of terrestrial as well as heavenly bodies. Schematically:

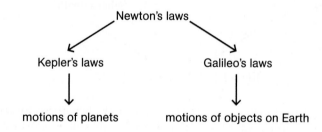

15.1B Evaluating Explanations

Explanations and arguments, then, have the same internal structure. The difference between them lies in their goals: An argument tries to show that something is true; an explanation tries to show why it is true. What about the standards of *evaluation*? Once again, there are similarities as well as differences. To evaluate an argument, we have to ask two questions: Do the premises support the conclusion, and are the premises true? In the same way, there are two basic questions to ask about an explanation.

First, is it *adequate*—would the hypothesis, if true, provide a genuine explanation of the *explanandum*? Does it provide a possible cause or reason or in some way fit the *explanandum* into a wider context that makes it intelligible? In a broad sense, adequacy is to explanation what logical strength is to argument. It pertains to the relation between the hypothesis and the *explanandum*. Indeed, it includes strength as one component. A good explanation is one in which the *explanandum* follows from the hypothesis: The relation between them is such that if the hypothesis is true, the *explanandum* has to be true as well—or at least highly likely. But strength is not the only component. To serve the purposes of explanation, as we'll see, an explanation must satisfy other criteria as well. Second, is the hypothesis *true*? False premises do not prove anything, and false hypotheses do not explain anything. To tell whether a hypothesis is true or false, we would normally use a method that is inductive in the broad sense, but different from the forms of inductive reasoning we've studied so far.

To evaluate explanations, therefore, we need to use what we've already learned about logical relationships, but we also need some additional standards that pertain specifically to explanation. In the next section, we'll look at standards for evaluating adequacy—the relation between hypothesis and *explanandum*. In the final section, we'll consider methods for determining the truth of hypotheses.

EXERCISE 15.1

For each statement, decide whether it is an argument or an explanation. If it is an explanation, identify the *explanandum* and the hypothesis, and diagram the relation between them.

*1. The stock market went up yesterday because the Federal Reserve lowered interest rates.

2. The stock market will probably rise over the next 6 months because the economy is expanding.

3. The nervous system evolved because animals, which are capable of locomotion, needed a fast and flexible means of guiding their motion.

*4. Despite her aggressive manner, Natalie is a person with very little self-confidence. That's why she is so boastful. It also explains why she rarely takes on any challenges in her work.

5. One reason for the rise of philosophical inquiry in Athens in the fifth century B.C. was that the Athenians were engaged in trade throughout the Mediterranean. Their travels brought them into contact with people of widely different beliefs and customs, which led them to pose philosophical questions about the bases of their own beliefs and customs.

6. The electrical system in a house should be grounded in order to avoid shocks and to prevent fires.

*7. Babies begin to learn language at about 1 year of age, regardless of what language their parents speak and regardless of other differences among societies and cultures. The timetable of early language acquisition is presumably to be explained by some process of physical maturation in the brain.

8. In Michael Ondaatje's novel *The English Patient*, the narrative is

layered and fragmented: He tells part of one story, involving one set of characters; then switches to another story, involving other characters; then comes back to the first story, providing more background and more of the events. The reason for this is partly to convey how the stories of the different characters intertwine, and partly to illustrate the disjointed nature of human memory.

9. The continents of the earth are located on different tectonic plates in the earth's crust. The motions of these plates in relation to each other explain the formation of new mountain ranges, the occurrence of earthquakes, and the location of zones of volcanic activity.

✳10. In her classic work *The Life and Death of Great American Cities*, Jane Jacobs posed the question: Why are some urban areas so much safer and more vibrant than others? Her answer was that the safest areas in a city tend to be those characterized by a mixture of uses—stores, apartments, businesses, restaurants. Such a mixture guarantees that people will be on the streets at all hours, and that in turn is the best deterrent against crime. The presence of people also gives these areas a vibrant feel, attracting new stores and residents.

15.2 Adequacy of Hypotheses

A hypothesis can be true without providing an adequate explanation. Suppose you notice water dripping from your ceiling, and someone ventures the hypothesis that water runs downhill. This would not be very satisfying to you. The statement is true enough, but it doesn't explain what the water is doing up there. In this section, we'll assume that the hypotheses we discuss are all true. The question is: How do we decide whether they are adequate? Every branch of knowledge has its own specific guidelines for evaluating the adequacy of explanations in that area, but there are also some general standards that apply across the board.

1. The inference from hypothesis to *explanandum* should have a high degree of logical *strength*.
2. The explanation should be *complete*: It should explain all significant aspects of the *explanandum*.
3. The explanation should be *informative*: The hypothesis should state the fundamental cause or reason for the *explanandum*.

Let's go over each of these in turn.

15.2A Strength

Explanations and arguments have different goals, but they have the same logical structure, and the *explanandum* should follow from the hypothesis in the same way that a conclusion should follow from the premises. A good explanation will show us that the *explanandum* is not mysterious, but is something we might have expected all along, something we might have predicted or inferred from the facts mentioned in the hypothesis if we had known about them.

The best way to measure strength, in this context, is a general-purpose method. We try to estimate the size of the gap between hypothesis and *explanandum*, the amount of "free play" or slip page between them. And we do this by finding the implicit assumption that would be necessary to close the gap. We explained Joan's sadness by the hypothesis that her cat died, and that she had been attached to it. The implicit assumption is that people who are attached to their pets grieve at their loss. Doubtless there are exceptions to this generalization—it's conceivable that someone would react to loss in a different way. So there is a certain gap here, but it's a small one, and the explanation seems fairly adequate. By contrast, suppose someone said he failed a course because the classroom is on the fifth floor, and he is afraid of heights. There's a sizable gap here between hypothesis and *explanandum*: To connect fear of heights with performance in a course, we would have to tell an elaborate and fairly implausible story. So this explanation is much weaker.

Let's see how this standard applies to a real example. In their effort to control government spending, legislators have found it extremely difficult to eliminate programs that give subsidies to special interests—businesses, labor unions, victims of a certain disease, schoolteachers, farmers, etc. A common explanation runs as follows. The benefits of the programs go to a small class of people, who each have a large stake in the programs and therefore lobby actively to keep them. But the costs are dispersed among all the taxpayers, who have less at stake individually. A $2 billion program, for example, would cost about $14 per taxpayer, which is not much of an incentive to organize and lobby against the subsidies. The political pressures on Congress therefore tend to favor the programs. We could diagram the explanation as follows:

1. Those who benefit from subsidies have a lot at stake individually.
2. Those who benefit lobby actively to retain the programs.
3. Those who pay for subsidies do not have a lot at stake individually.
4. Those who pay do not lobby actively against the programs.
5. The political pressures on Congress favor the programs.
6. It is difficult for Congress to eliminate the programs.

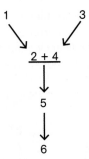

This is certainly a plausible explanation. But let's take a closer look, starting at the bottom and checking the strength of each step. The *explanandum* is that it is difficult for Congress to eliminate the programs. Does this follow from proposition 5—that the political pressures favor the programs? The implicit assumption is that the actions of Congress reflect the sum of pressures acting on it. This does not seem like a very large gap. We are not assuming that individual legislators *never* vote independently, on the basis of their own judgment and conscience. We're only assuming that a majority, on most issues, will act in response to pressure. What about the previous step, from 2 and 4 to 5? Notice that 2 and 4 tell us about the *economic* interests at stake in these programs. This implies something about the *political* pressures on Congress only if we assume that lobbying based on economic interest is the only—or at least the primary—source of political pressure. This is a more substantial assumption to make and creates a larger gap in the explanation. One might argue that in some areas, such as civil rights or abortion, Congress acts under tremendous political pressure that is rooted in *moral* rather than economic interests. Perhaps economic interests determine political pressure only by default, in cases where no one raises a moral issue. If so, we would have to amend the explanation to include the point that the press and the voters do not view the question of subsidies in moral terms.

In any case, you can see that checking for strength is an important element in evaluating an explanation. It helps us to identify hidden assumptions that should be made explicit and examined carefully.

15.2B Completeness

We can illustrate our second standard of adequacy with another example concerning money and politics. Increasing amounts of money are being spent in political campaigns. One common explanation is that campaigning has become more expensive. Candidates have to spend huge sums on television advertising, media consultants, computerized voter lists, and other "high-tech" political tools. A common criticism of this hypothesis is that it explains only part of the phenomenon. It explains why candidates need to raise larger sums of money from contributors, but it does not explain why the contributions are forthcoming. People do not part with their money without good reason. So another element in the explanation may be that as government has grown in size and importance, people are willing to invest more money to influence the political process.

1. Campaign spending on elections has increased.
2. Candidates must spend more money to afford advertising and other campaign tools.
3. Candidates must raise more money for their campaigns.
4. Government has grown in size and importance.
5. People have a greater interest in influencing the political process.
6. People are willing to give candidates more money.

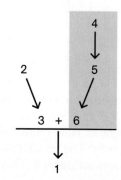

To explain the increase in campaign spending, in other words, we must explain the two major components of that *explanandum*. The left side of the diagram is our explanation for the increase in politicians' *demand* for campaign funds. On the right side of the diagram, the shaded portion is our explanation for the increase in donors' willingness to *supply* the funds. If we tried to explain 1 solely in terms of 3, our explanation would be incomplete.

This example illustrates an important point. An *explanandum* is normally complex. Whether it is a single event, a long-term trend, a fact of nature, or whatever, it will have a number of different aspects that a complete explanation must account for. In a criminal trial, the prosecution has to show that the defendant had the opportunity, the motive, and the inclination for the crime. To explain a biological trait like warm-bloodedness, we would want to know what function it serves in the animal's survival, how it arose in the course of evolution, and how it works in biochemical terms. A historical account of an event like the Civil War should explain not only why it occurred, but also why it occurred at that particular time and not 5 years sooner or later.

In applying the rule of completeness, however, there are several qualifications to consider. First, we cannot demand that a hypothesis account for absolutely everything; some points are trivial or irrelevant. The prosecution normally would not have to explain why the burglar used a red Ford instead of some other model as a getaway car. Second, we cannot fault a theory for failing to explain something it never set out to explain. Darwin's theory of evolution, for example, explains why a process of natural selection would result in traits that are favorable to survival and reproduction becoming more prevalent in a population. It is not intended to explain how the trait arose in the first place; for that we must turn to genetics and the biochemistry of DNA.

In other words, the rule of completeness is not that a *single* hypothesis must account for *every* aspect of the *explanandum*. The rule is that a *complete* explanation, which may include several hypotheses of different types, must account for every *significant* aspect. To evaluate an explanation in this respect, we should formulate each significant aspect as a separate proposition. When we draw up a diagram, we can then see whether each proposition follows from some element of the explanation as a whole. If not, then we should recognize that fact and not attribute to the hypothesis more explanatory power than it actually has.

15.2C Informativeness

An explanation should be informative. Its purpose, after all, is to make the *explanandum* intelligible, to enlarge our understanding of it. At a minimum, this means it should not be circular, as in the following "explanation":

"Why are you angry?"

"Because that's the way I feel."

Beyond that minimum standard, however, this rule becomes harder to apply because there are different patterns of explanation that are informative in different ways. In the physical sciences, we explain things in terms of the underlying properties of objects—mass, electrical charge, atomic structure—and the sum of the external forces acting on them. In this context, the more informative explanation is the one that takes us deeper into the inner structure of matter and energy. Biologists explain the traits of living organisms partly in terms of underlying mechanisms (the biochemical processes involved) and partly in terms of the function they serve in helping the organism to survive and reproduce. We explain a human action in terms of its purpose: What was the person's goal? Why did he believe this action would achieve the goal? In history, we explain an event in terms of the prior events that led up to it, within the context of the cultural, political, economic, and other conditions of the society at that time.

We could go on adding to this list—there are many different patterns of explanation. It would take a separate book to describe them all and to review the different standards they give us for telling how informative an explanation is. But there is a common element in these standards. An explanation should get to the bottom of things. No matter what pattern we use, an explanation is informative to the extent that it identifies the *fundamental* cause or reason for the *explanandum*. Newton's theory was more informative than Kepler's or Galileo's and represented an advance in human knowledge because it went deeper; it identified the laws underlying the phenomena that Kepler and Galileo discovered. Darwin's theory of natural selection was a profound insight and another major advance in knowledge because it described a basic mechanism by which organisms come to have traits that promote their survival and reproductive success. We understand a person best when we can trace his actions to fundamental goals and beliefs—the ones that are central to his character, personality, and outlook on the world. In general, the rule that an explanation should be informative is analogous to the rule that a classification or definition should use essential attributes. In both cases we are looking for fundamentality.

This is an open-ended standard. We can hardly fault Kepler or Galileo for failing to discover Newton's laws or Newton for failing to anticipate the discoveries of Albert Einstein. The fact that later theories are more informative does not imply that earlier ones are totally uninformative. But it *is* uninformative, and thus inadequate, to try to explain the *more* fundamental phenomenon by the *less* fundamental. The cause explains the effect, the essential attribute explains the superficial one, the end explains the means. In every case, an explanation that inverts the proper order is uninformative. Suppose we tried to interpret Shakespeare's *Julius Caesar* along the following lines:

> The main character is Cassius, and the basic theme of the play is that you can't trust thin people. "Let me have men about me that are fat," says Caesar. "Yond Cassius has a lean and hungry look. He thinks too much; such men are dangerous." Everything else in the play—the murder of Caesar, Marc Antony's speech, the campaign against Brutus and his suicide—are all subplots designed to emphasize just how dangerous thin people can be.

This is a ridiculous reading of the play. Cassius is not the main character, his figure is not his essential trait, and Caesar's remark does not express the central theme. These are all tangential elements in the play that would themselves have to be explained in terms of something more basic.

It is not always obvious which of two things is the more fundamental, and there are many controversies on this score. In the early part of the nineteenth century, biologists debated whether structure or function was primary in evolution One school said that structure changes first, leading a species to adopt a new way of functioning to take advantage of the new structure. Their opponents (who eventually won) said that a change in function comes first, creating evolutionary pressure for new structures that better serve that function. In the social sciences, some theorists hold that political and economic factors underlie and explain a society's intellectual–cultural life—its dominant ideology, artistic values, religious beliefs, etc. Others take the opposite view, that ideas are the fundamental factor: A society's basic values and view of the world determine the kind of political and economic institutions it will have. Debates like these indicate how difficult it can be to apply the principle of fundamentality. But they also indicate how important the principle is.

15.2D Combining the Standards

An adequate explanation should be strong, complete, and informative. To see how these standards relate to each other, let's look at one final example, a famous hypothesis whose adequacy has been questioned on all three counts. In *The Protestant Ethic and the Spirit of Capitalism*, the German sociologist Max Weber proposed that the rise of capitalism was largely the result of the Protestant Reformation in general and the doctrines of John Calvin and the Puritans in particular. Weber noted that Calvin regarded productive work as a religious virtue: One's trade or profession is a "calling," a way of serving God, and worldly success is a sign of heavenly grace. The Protestant emphasis on asceticism, moreover, discouraged consumption and thereby encouraged thrift; this in turn allowed for the savings and investment that are essential to a capitalist economy.

Some historians have argued that Weber's theory is *incomplete*. It may explain the rise of capitalism in the Protestant countries of Northern Europe and North America. And the demand for religious freedom that arose out of the Protestant Reformation may have furthered the principle of individual rights (including property rights and economic freedom) that was necessary for the full development of capitalism. But many of the early centers of commerce, such as Venice or Lisbon, were in Catholic countries, and many of the leading merchants and financiers were Catholic or Jewish. So the thesis cannot account for everything.

A different objection to Weber's theory is raised by Marxists. Weber was trying to explain an economic development in terms of religious ideas. But this, they argue, inverts the true relationship. Ideas are consequences, not causes, of underlying economic forces. The Protestant ethic in particular was a by product of class interest, a rationalization offered by the rising capitalists to sanctify their quest for control over material production. Thus, in the Marxists' view, Weber was trying to explain the fundamental phenomenon by something that was less fundamental. His explanation is *uninformative*, and ultimately circular, because to explain the Protestant ethic itself we would be led back to the very economic trends he was trying to explain.

A third criticism is that, while Weber was right to look for the historical roots of capitalism in the realm of ideas, he picked the wrong ideas. Capitalism required a secular philosophy, emphasizing happiness and prosperity in this life, the pursuit of self-interest, and the virtue of rationality. These ideas were on the rise throughout the Renaissance and the Enlightenment, but they were opposed by the early Protestant thinkers, who were other-worldly in outlook, viewed egoism as a sin, and emphasized revelation and mysticism over reason. Indeed, they went further in each respect than the Catholic Church, which they criticized for being too secular. The *explanandum*, then, simply doesn't follow from the hypothesis: The explanation is *weak*. Anyone observing the Reformation, and unaware of the other forces at work, would have expected a movement away from capitalism.

Of course, this description of Weber's thesis, and the objections to it, is vastly oversimplified. But it serves to illustrate the differences among the standards of adequacy and the way they are applied in practice.

SUMMARY Adequacy of Hypotheses

An adequate explanation should be:

1. *Strong:* The inference from hypothesis to *explanandum* should have a high degree of logical strength.

2. *Complete:* The hypothesis or hypotheses should explain all significant aspects of the *explanandum*.

3. *Informative:* The hypothesis should state the fundamental cause or reason of the *explanandum*.

EXERCISE 15.2

Each of the explanations below can be faulted as inadequate. Identify the standard (or standards) that it violates.

✳ 1. Why did the chicken cross the road? To get to the other side.

2. My term paper was late because I had to go to the dentist for a checkup the day before it was due.

3. Wolves travel in packs because they are social animals.

✳ 4. Prosecutor: "Ladies and gentlemen of the jury, you must convict Imelda Gonzales of murdering her ex-boyfriend Peter Vassili. She was furious after he broke up with her and thus had a strong motive for wanting him dead."

5. The Pythagorean theorem asserts that the square of the hypotenuse of a right triangle is equal in area to the sum of the squares of the other two sides. How was this fact discovered? The Greek geometers of antiquity learned it from the Egyptians.

6. In Western societies, people customarily wear wedding bands on the fourth finger of the left hand. That's probably because the Romans believed a vein ran from the fourth finger directly to the heart.

✳ 7. Why was George Washington admired so much, with a kind of reverence and awe, in an age filled with other great men? It was largely his height: He towered over most other men.

8. The collapse of the Soviet Union and its control over Eastern Europe in the late 1980s occurred because a socialist economic system is incapable of producing goods as abundantly as a capitalist system.

9. If the quality of education has declined, and it certainly has, the main reason is that teachers no longer enjoy the public respect and esteem once accorded their profession and are thus too demoralized to do a good job.

✳ 10. Why has art been such a pervasive feature of human life, found in every society? One theory holds that since art has no survival value, it must have evolved instead as a form of sexual display to attract mates, like the peacock's tail. An artistic achievement such as making a realistic drawing or reciting a long epic narrative requires enormous intelligence, persistence, and skill. If someone has these survival-enhancing attributes in such abundance that he can afford to waste them on creating art, that person is more attractive to potential mates.

15.3 The Truth of Hypotheses

The adequacy of an explanation does not guarantee that the hypothesis is true. A theory may be strong, complete, informative—and false. Innocent people have been convicted in cases where their guilt would have explained all the evidence. Scientists have often seen a beautiful theory murdered by the facts. How is this possible? There's a simple logical reason. The adequacy of an explanation tells us that if the hypothesis is true, the *explanandum* has to be true as well. It tells us, in other words, that we may accept the hypothetical proposition: if H, then E. And we know that E is true. But to infer from these two propositions that H is true would be to affirm the consequent—and that's a fallacy. There might well be some alternative hypothesis H' that would explain E with equal adequacy.

This point cannot be emphasized too strongly. Affirming the consequent in the manner just described is the most common error in reasoning about explanations—and indeed in all inductive reasoning. We all want things to make sense, and it's all too easy to accept the first plausible explanation we find. We hear that a medical student is going to specialize in brain surgery, and we assume it must be for the money, without considering any other possible motive. The economy falls into a recession, and we blame the president's policies without considering other factors that might have played a role. We adopt a religion or a philosophy because it offers *an* explanation of human nature and experience, without asking whether it offers the *only* or the best explanation. You can see the same thing happening in the spread of a rumor. A couple breaks up, a friend makes a guess about the reason, and by the time the gossip is repeated once or twice, speculation has become "fact."

To combat this tendency, it is crucial to consider alternatives before we accept a given hypothesis. Courts of law use the adversary system, despite its many faults, partly to ensure that the jury will hear an alternative to the prosecution's account of the crime. The canons of scientific research require that a theory not be accepted until it has proven its superiority to rival theories. In everyday life, when someone asks rhetorically, "What other explanation could there be?" the question should serve as a red flag: There almost always is some other explanation worth considering.

15.3A Testing Hypotheses

Assuming, then, that we have several hypotheses on the table, how do we decide which one is true? In some cases, we can use the methods we are already familiar with. If you think the drip in your ceiling might be caused by rain coming in through a hole in the roof, you can check this out by observation: You can look for the hole. Or suppose you want to know why the lilac bush in your garden develops mildew around midsummer. If you consult a gardening book, you will find that this happens to all lilacs. And this generalization can be confirmed by using Mill's methods.

But we can't always test a hypothesis by the standard methods of observation and induction. When you want to explain why someone is acting a certain way, you cannot manipulate the person's mind to see which factors cause the behavior. Scientists did not establish the atomic theory by generalizing from a sample—they didn't discover first that chairs are made of atoms, then that tables are, and carrots, and so on until there were enough instances to support the claim that all physical objects are so constituted. When we are trying to explain a unique individual event or when the possible causes involve things we can't observe directly, the methods of induction we have learned so far will not do the job by themselves.

Instead, we use an indirect approach. If the hypothesis is adequate to begin with, then the *explanandum* follows from it. The indirect method is to ask what *other* consequences would follow. Having first reasoned backwards from *explanandum* to hypothesis, we now reason forward, drawing further conclusion from the hypothesis and checking to see whether the conclusions are true. The process could be diagrammed schematically as follows:

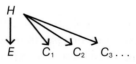

If we find that $C_1, C_2, C_3 \ldots$ are not true, we reject the hypothesis. But if they *are* true, they confirm it and become *explananda* that are themselves explained by the hypothesis.

This method of testing hypotheses should not be news; you have almost certainly used it yourself. The toaster isn't working—is the problem in the toaster itself or in the wall outlet? If the latter were the case, then the toaster should work if you plug it into a different outlet. So you try that and find that it does work, confirming the hypothesis. A friend hasn't shown up for a dinner date—did he have to work late at the office? But then he would have called, and he hasn't, so it must be something else. To a large extent, the confirmation of a scientific theory is simply a more elaborate and more refined application of the same method. Newton's theory, for example, was put to an important test when Edmund Halley used the theory to predict the next appearance of the comet named for him. Though the theory already had a good deal of evidence going for it, it gained further confirmation when the comet appeared on schedule.

If one or more of the consequences we derive from a hypothesis turn out to be *false*, then the hypothesis itself can be rejected, in accordance with the hypothetical syllogism:

If *H*, then *C*

not-*C*

not-*H*

You can see that this inference is valid even if a single consequence turns out to be false. On the positive side, however, the fact that a single consequence turns out to be *true* does not prove the hypothesis true. The inference

If *H*, then *C*

C

H

affirms the consequent and is thus fallacious. For confirmation, what counts is the number of consequences we test and their relation to the various alternative hypotheses we've considered.

We assume from the outset, moreover, that there *is* some explanation, that some hypothesis will account for the *explanandum*. The question is: which one? At the outset, there may be many alternatives, but as we test more and more consequences, we narrow down the possibilities, ideally to the point where only one hypothesis is consistent with all the evidence. Indeed, we should actively look for cases in which rival hypotheses have different implications: H implies C_x, H' implies not-C_x. Testing to see whether C_x is true or false will then rule out one of the hypotheses.

Notice that this is an inductive process. The consequences may follow deductively from the hypothesis, as may the *explanandum*. But the evidence for the truth of the hypothesis is inductive. The strength of the evidence is a matter of degree: It can always be increased by testing additional consequences. And when we accept a hypothesis because we have eliminated alternative explanations, our reasoning rests on the presupposition that we have considered all the relevant alternatives—just as Mill's methods rest on the presupposition that we have varied all the relevant factors. As we acquire more information, new alternatives may occur to us. Establishing a hypothesis is an open-ended process that depends on the context of our knowledge at a given time, and we must allow for the possibility that an explanation will have to be modified—or in extreme cases rejected—as we acquire new knowledge.

EXERCISE 15.3A

For each explanation that follows, identify (a) the hypothesis and (b) *explanandum*. Then identify (c) at least one additional implication that might be used to test the hypothesis and (d) at least one alternative hypothesis that might explain the *explanandum*.

* 1. Jim hasn't taken any science courses because he has math anxiety.

2. When a cat rubs against your ankles, it's because it wants to put its scent on you, and your ankles are the only part of your body it can reach.

3. The lawn is full of weeds because the grass is being cut too short.

* 4. I got a C on this paper because the professor is biased against people who disagree with his views.

5. My doctor says that the unusual number of colds I've had this winter may be due to a deficiency of vitamin C in my diet.

6. The basic reason why the Andersons got divorced is that he is a workaholic; she felt neglected because he was not spending much time at home.

* 7. Police investigating the murder established that the victim died from a gunshot wound in the head as he walked down Fifth Avenue in New York on the afternoon of September 7 and that the bullet came from a gun belonging to Watson. How can these facts be explained unless Watson was the killer?

8. The stock market keeps rising because people in the baby-boom generation are at the age when they are saving more for retirement and looking for places to invest their savings.

9. Acid rain produced by air pollution from factories is causing lakes in the Northeast to become more acidic.

* 10. The American Civil War was caused by a conflict over tariffs: The Northern states wanted tariffs to protect their manufacturing industries, while the more agricultural South wanted to be able to import manufactured goods from Europe without having to pay tariffs.

15.3B Plausibility

As in the other forms of inductive reasoning, testing a hypothesis requires that we make various judgments of plausibility along the way. To see why, we have to add a few complications to our picture of confirmation. For one thing, we could not hope to test every conceivable hypothesis. We have to exercise our judgment in deciding which ones are plausible enough to be worth testing, just as we have to decide, in using Mill's methods, which factors should be varied and which ones can be ignored. If we wanted to understand why a usually thrifty person suddenly splurged on a cruise in the Bahamas, there would be various hypotheses to consider, depending on what we know about the person's character and circumstances. But there are countless other hypotheses we would ignore: that cosmic rays had altered his consciousness, that he is a foreign agent living a double life, etc.

A further complication is that we can usually derive a consequence from a hypothesis only in conjunction with some additional, *auxiliary assumptions*. We need to modify our standard diagram to include this point:

$$\frac{H \; + \; A_1 \; + \; A_2 \; + \ldots}{}$$
$$\downarrow$$
$$C$$

Suppose we perform the test and find that *C* is false. This will not necessarily refute the hypothesis. It may be that one of the auxiliary assumptions was false instead. In other words, when a hypothesis fails a test, the logical structure diagrammed above allows us to save the hypothesis by blaming an auxiliary assumption. Whether it is reasonable to do so depends on a judgment of plausibility.

For example, the law of gravity implies that if I release a ball in midair, it will fall. But this consequence follows only on the auxiliary assumption that no other force is acting on the ball to counteract gravity. Suppose I release the ball and it remains motionless, floating in midair. I am certainly not going to abandon the law of gravity; it is much more reasonable to reject the auxiliary assumption and assume that some other force is at work. However, people sometimes cling to a theory in the face of overwhelming evidence against it by inventing reasons to reject auxiliary assumptions rather than the theory itself. If there were any doubt that Earth is not flat, for example, one might think the pictures taken from space would have clinched the matter. But the pictures are decisive only on the assumption that they were indeed taken from space, and some Flat Earthers argued that it was all an elaborate hoax.

What standards should we use in deciding what's plausible? The decision is not always as obvious or clear-cut as in the examples above. How do we decide whether a hypothesis is plausible enough to be considered and tested? If a hypothesis fails a test, how do we decide whether it is more reasonable to reject the hypothesis or one of the auxiliary assumptions? As in other areas of inductive logic, these judgments depend partly on one's knowledge and experience in the specific field. But there are also two general standards that apply across the board. Other things being equal, one hypothesis is more plausible than another if it is more *consistent* with the rest of our knowledge and if it is *simpler*. Let's look at these standards in more detail.

Consistency. Consider two theories that might both be said to assert the existence of a "sixth sense": (1) Certain animals such as migratory birds can perceive the earth's magnetic field; (2) certain human beings are capable of extrasensory perception (ESP). The first is a routine scientific hypothesis; most scientists would regard it as a plausible explanation for the ability of migratory birds to navigate as well as they do. By contrast, the ESP hypothesis has much less initial plausibility and would have to meet a much higher standard of evidence than the first one before it would be taken seriously. Why?

One reason is that the idea of a magnetic sense is entirely consistent with everything we know about sense perception. Perception involves a physical organ containing receptor cells that respond to various forms of energy (light waves, sound waves, etc.) and are capable of detecting various features of the environment (colors, sounds, etc.) with some reliability. A magnetic sense would fit this pattern; we need only accept the possibility of a new type of receptor that responds to a known form of energy. But ESP, as its name implies, is extrasensory. It does not involve identifiable sense organs or receptors; it is not alleged to be a response to any known form of energy; and it does not produce reliable knowledge of the environment: At best, the experiments show that certain people score slightly above chance in various guessing games. So ESP is not consistent with the rest of our knowledge about perception. To accept it as a viable hypothesis, we would have to abandon some fundamental principles derived from the study of vision, hearing, touch, taste, and smell.

We should remember that when we introduce a hypothesis to explain something, we are not operating in a vacuum. We have a vast context of background knowledge—beliefs, principles, and theories for which we have accumulated a great deal of evidence. A new hypothesis therefore starts out with a certain degree of initial plausibility that depends on how consistent it is, how well it fits, with that background knowledge. A hypothesis that conflicts with established principles and theories must meet a higher standard of evidence than a hypothesis that does not conflict. Accepting the first sort of hypothesis, after all, means giving up beliefs for which we have good evidence, so the new evidence must be strong enough and extensive enough to outweigh the old. This does not mean we should be traditionalists and reject every radically new idea just because it conflicts with the established wisdom. It does mean we should know what we're doing and be prepared to back it up.

In science, revolutions can occur when scientists discover phenomena that can't be explained by prevailing theories. But a new theory must do more than explain these anomalies; it must also explain the phenomena that the old theory explained, and it must give some coherent account of the evidence for the older view. The theory that the earth is round had to explain why it looks flat. Einstein's theory of relativity had to explain why Newton's laws describe the behavior of physical objects as well as they do. As these examples suggest, the standard of consistency applies with special force in the physical sciences, where we have a vast edifice of highly integrated and well-confirmed theories. It applies with somewhat less force in the social sciences, which are younger and less highly developed, and with less force still in the humanities. In these branches of knowledge, established views do not have the same degree of evidence as in the physical sciences, and new ideas therefore do not have as large an obstacle to overcome. But they must still take account of whatever genuine evidence there is for the older views.

The rule of consistency is especially important in evaluating claims on the fringes of science: claims about ESP and other alleged psychic powers, alien spacecraft, astrology, the Bermuda Triangle, alien astronauts who visited Earth during ancient times, etc. All of these purport to explain "the unexplained," to solve mysteries that established scientific theories cannot account for. And, as we saw in the case of ESP, the explanations conflict with, and would require us to abandon, principles or theories for which we have a great deal of evidence. Before we accept any such explanation, we should recognize that it is not, as the proponents normally claim, the only possible one. Invariably there are alternative hypotheses that might explain the phenomenon and be more consistent with our background knowledge.

One alternative hypothesis is simply that the *explanandum* isn't true, the event never occurred, and there is nothing to explain. The witnesses who claim to have seen alien spacecraft may have misidentified what they saw; the ancient texts that describe miraculous events may be mistaken; the subjects who seem to have powers of telepathy may instead be using the techniques of magicians and con artists. A second alternative hypothesis applies to amazing coincidences: the man who has a sudden feeling of dread and calls home to find his wife has had a terrible accident; the person who dreams of winning the lottery and does so the next day. These are often taken as signs of higher powers at work, but they may be just coincidences. The laws of probability make it very likely that among all the premonitions, dreams, and sudden dreads that we experience, most of which come to nothing and are quickly forgotten, a few will turn out to be accurate.

These alternative hypotheses may turn out to be false. But because they are fully consistent with our background knowledge, they must be considered and tested before we can accept any explanation that is not consistent.

Simplicity. Suppose someone on trial for burglary tries to explain away the evidence as follows:

Prosecutor:	Three witnesses said they saw you in the neighborhood the day before the crime. You don't live near there. Weren't you casing the joint?
Defendant:	No, I was just taking a walk.
Prosecutor:	Why were you loitering around the victim's building and staring at the fire escape?
Defendant:	Well, it's an old building, and the fire escape has some ornamental features that are interesting from an architectural point of view. I'm very interested in architecture.
Prosecutor:	Where were you on the night of the crime?
Defendant:	In Clancey's Bar.
Prosecutor:	Why doesn't anyone remember seeing you there that night?
Defendant:	I guess they were all drunk.
Prosecutor:	Why were the stolen goods found in your car?
Defendant:	The thief must have put them there.

A jury listening to this exchange has two hypotheses to consider. The prosecutor would explain all the evidence with a single claim: The defendant committed the crime. The defendant's explanation, by contrast, involves a string of unrelated claims. It's conceivable, of course, that they are all true. The truth is not always simple. But the jury would be justified in considering the defendant's story less plausible than the prosecutor's and in need of more evidence to back it up.

This example illustrates the principle of simplicity or parsimony. The rule is that, other things being equal, one hypothesis is more plausible than another if it involves fewer new assumptions. We have seen that an explanation rarely involves a single proposition. A full explanation usually requires a complex hypothesis, involving a number of separate propositions. If these separate propositions are new and cannot be derived from knowledge we already possess, then the fewer the better. The reason is appropriately simple. Just as an adequate explanation must account for every significant aspect of the *explanandum*, the evidence for the truth of a hypothesis must cover each positive claim it makes. The fewer the claims, the less evidence will be required. Conversely, the farther out on a limb we go, the stronger the limb must be. This is not to say that the rule is always easy to apply. It can happen that theory *A* is simpler in one respect, theory *B* in another. But if one hypothesis is obviously simpler, it is more plausible.

The standard of simplicity is particularly important in deciding what to do when we test a hypothesis and get a negative result. If the hypothesis has survived a series of tests and provides a single coherent explanation for a number of consequences that have been derived from it, it may be simpler to assume that failure on some further test is due to an auxiliary assumption. If we keep getting negative results, however, and can save the hypothesis only by a series of unrelated, *ad hoc* attempts to blame the auxiliary assumptions, the balance tips against the hypothesis.

The standard of simplicity can also be used in evaluating conspiracy theories. Conspiracies certainly do occur, and sometimes we have direct evidence for them, as when one of the conspirators confesses. But the evidence is often indirect, and in such cases the standard cuts both ways. On the one hand, the hypothesis that a conspiracy is at work may provide a single, unified explanation for a series of events that would otherwise have to be given separate explanations. As the villain in an Ian Fleming novel says, after he has encountered James Bond for the third time and infers that Bond is trying to foil him, "Mr. Bond, they have a saying in Chicago: 'Once is happenstance. Twice is coincidence. The third time it's enemy action.'"

But conspiracy theories do not always simplify. The notion that the U.S. economy and political system are governed by a secret cabal of international bankers, for example, gives only the illusion of simplicity. In fact, it raises more questions than it answers. How did this group gain so much power? Why this particular group and not some other? To control a nation of more than 300 million people, these bankers must give marching orders to hundreds of thousands of political and business leaders. How do they manage to keep all these people in line? How do they manage to keep their own role a secret? To answer these questions, the conspiracy theory would have to be spun out into an elaborate web of arbitrary claims.

As in other types of induction, testing a hypothesis—whether it is a conspiracy theory or a theory about a friend's behavior—requires that we exercise our judgment and allow for the possibility that reasonable people may disagree. That goes with the territory. But the methods and standards discussed earlier will help organize the process of inquiry and direct our attention to the relevant issues.

STRATEGY **Testing a Hypothesis Indirectly**

1. Derive consequences from the hypothesis and then see whether the consequences are true.

2. If one or more of the consequences are false, reject the hypothesis unless it would be simpler or more consistent with other knowledge to reject an auxiliary hypothesis.

3. If a number of consequences are true, the hypothesis is confirmed unless an alternative hypothesis is equally consistent with the same evidence and is as simple.

EXERCISE 15.3B

For each *explanandum*, determine which of the two hypotheses is more plausible using the standards of consistency and simplicity.

✳ 1. I get a lot of wrong-number calls at night for Shakey's Pizza.

    a. My telephone number is similar to Sharkey's.

    b. Someone is trying to harass me by waking me up during the night.

2. My dog is barking at the door.

    a. The dog was bitten by a raccoon and has rabies, which is making him delirious.

    b. There is a stranger at the door.

3. Samantha's parrot says "Hello, come in" when a guest arrives.

    a. The parrot has learned the cultural norms of politeness in our society.

    b. The parrot is imitating Samantha's greeting to guests.

✳ 4. I hear the sound of a telephone ringing.

    a. There is a telephone nearby that is ringing.

    b. I am in the Matrix and the Machines are stimulating my brain to have the experience as of a telephone ringing.

5. On September 11, 2001, two commercial airliners crashed into the World Trade Center and destroyed the towers.

    a. It was a deliberate attack planned by al Qaida terrorists in a plot to harm the United States.

    b. It was an accident.

    c. It was a deliberate attack planned by the U.S. government in order to justify war in the Middle East.

6. The Gospels of the Christian Bible (Matthew, Mark, Luke, and John) describe a man named Jesus who lived in Palestine 2,000 years ago and attracted a religious following.

    a. Religious fanatics centuries later wrote Gospels to create the myth of a founder of their religion.

    b. There was a man named Jesus who lived in Palestine 2,000 years ago and attracted a religious following.

Summary

The goal of an explanation is to show why something is true, to state the cause or reason for the *explanandum*, or to fit it into a wider context that makes it intelligible. Though an explanation differs from an argument in its primary goal, the logical relation between hypothesis and *explanandum* is the same as that between premises and conclusion, and we can use the same diagramming techniques to analyze explanations.

To evaluate a proposed explanation, we consider two basic issues: its adequacy and the truth of the hypothesis. An adequate explanation must be logically strong (the *explanandum* follows from the hypothesis), complete (the hypothesis explains all significant aspects of the *explanandum*), and informative (the hypothesis gives a fundamental cause or reason for the *explanandum*).

To ascertain the truth of a hypothesis, we should consider alternative hypotheses that would also provide adequate explanations. We decide among rival hypotheses by deriving further consequences from them and then checking to see whether those consequences are true. To decide which hypotheses to consider and to decide whether to save a hypothesis in the face of a negative test by rejecting an auxiliary assumption, we rely on the standards of consistency and simplicity.

Key Terms

explanandum—the proposition whose truth one is attempting to explain.

hypothesis—the proposition (or propositions) in an explanation that purport to show why another proposition (the *explanandum*) is true.

Additional Exercises

A. Identify the *explanandum* and the hypothesis in each of the following explanatory passages, and diagram the explanation.

✳ 1. "Here we can glimpse the mechanism of Mendelian inheritance: A zygote [fertilized egg] obtains exactly half its genes from its male parent because it receives exactly half its chromosomes from the male parent and the chromosomes bear the genes." [Philip Kitcher, *Abusing Science: The Case Against Creationism*]

2. "Many free-swimming animals, mammals, birds, amphibians and fishes, are silvery-white below in order to be invisible to enemies swimming in the depths. Seen from below, the shining white belly blends perfectly with the reflecting surface film of the water." [Konrad Z. Lorenz, "The Taming of the Shrew," in *King Solomon's Ring*]

3. "Through this flat and marshy country [the southern coast of the Baltic Sea], four historic rivers make their way to the sea: the Neva, the Dvina, the Vistula, and the Oder, all pouring freshwater into the sea, so that the prevailing current is out of the Baltic. For this reason, it is difficult for saltwater to enter the Baltic, and there are no tides at Riga, Stockholm, or the mouth of the Neva." [Robert K. Massie, *Peter the Great*]

✳ 4. "It is of interest that some eastern American azaleas are more closely allied to some eastern Chinese azaleas than they are to other eastern American azaleas. . . .
"The fact that counterpart species [similar species of plants in widely separated areas of the world] exist has been explained . . . by the existence of a flora (called 'tertiary flora') which once encircled the Northern Hemisphere before the great cycle of

glaciation. . . . In regions like the United States and China, where the mountain ranges run north and south, the vegetation simply retreated south also, only to re-colonize much of its former habitat when the ice withdrew." [William H. Frederick, Jr., *100 Great Garden Plants*]

5. "Before printing, there had been no elaborate system of censorship and control over scribes. There did not have to be. The scribes were scattered, working on single manuscripts in monasteries. Moreover, single manuscripts rarely caused a general scandal or major controversy. There was little motive for central control, and control would have been impractical." [Ithiel de Sola Pool, *Technologies of Freedom*]

6. "Mexico City . . . is built on a mixture of sand and water. Such soils settle when heavy buildings are erected, squeezing the water out of the sand. The National Theater in the center of Mexico City, origi-nally built at grade level with a heavy clad-ding of stone, in a few years sank as much as ten feet. Downward stairs had to be built to its entrance. People were amazed when later on the theater began to rise again, requiring the construction of an upward staircase. This strange phenomenon can be explained by the large number of high-rise buildings which had been erected nearby. The water squeezed out from under them by their weight pushed the theater up." [Mario Salvadori, *Why Buildings Stand Up*]

B. Each passage below is a lead paragraph from a newspaper story. In addition to the facts it reports, each offers a hypothesis to explain those facts. Identify the hypothesis, and think of an alternative.

✳ 1. "Seeking to reclaim the reform man-tle amid a series of scandals, House Democratic leaders are advocating a move that would shake up the multibillion-dollar practice of awarding no-bid con-tracts known as congressional earmarks." (Earmarks are government grants given directly to particular individuals or proj-ects, outside the general functions and programs of government.) [Paul Kane, "House Democrats seek to limit earmarks to show commitment to ethics," *Washington Post*, March 10, 2010; A02]

2. Still at pains a year after Hurricane Katrina to demonstrate his concern over the devastation it caused, President Bush said Tuesday that he took "full responsibility" for the slow federal response to the disas-ter as he made a carefully choreographed pilgrimage to the city that suffered most. [Anne Kornblut and Adam Nossiter, "Bush, Returning To New Orleans, Repeats Aid Vow," *New York Times*, August 30, 2006, Page A1]

C. Find an explanation for each of the following facts. Make sure your explanation is adequate, and indicate how you would tell whether the hypothesis is true.

✳ 1. The subject I had the most trouble with in school was_____. [fill in the blank]

2. When we spend a lot of time looking forward to something, and expect to enjoy it, we're often disappointed.

3. In midterm elections (those held midway through a president's term), the president's party usually loses seats in Congress.

✳ 4. The number of people working at home instead of at an office or a factory has been rising, both in absolute terms and as a percentage of the workforce. Some are self-employed, running their own busi-nesses; others are employees of companies, doing such work as sewing garments or word-processing.

＊ **D.** The headlines below are from a tabloid newspaper. Relying mainly on the standard of consistency, rank them in order of initial plausibility. Does the claim conflict with established principles and theories? If so, to what extent? How radical a change would we have to make in established principles and theories to accept each story as true?

1. Baby Born on Roller Coaster
2. Snake Tattoo Crawls Up Man's Arm and Chokes Him
3. Pregnancy Makes Women Able to Predict Future
4. Amazing Vitamin Keeps Skin Wrinkle-Free
5. Friendly Bigfoot Saves Dying Girl
6. Woman Adopts Own Child But Doesn't Know It

7. Woman Describes How . . . Sparks from UFO Nearly Blinded Me
8. Bat Attacks Couple Watching Dracula on TV
9. Glenn Ford Travels through Time to See His Past Lives
10. Gadget Ends Back Pain Forever

E. In a Virginia criminal case of 1882, Oliver Hatchett was accused of murdering Moses Young. The trial court found Hatchett guilty. The passage below is from the opinion of the appeals court, which overturned the conviction on the ground that Hatchett's guilt had not been proved beyond a reasonable doubt. Treating the proposition that Hatchett is guilty as a hypothesis to explain Young's death and using what you've learned in this chapter, decide whether you would side with the trial court or the appeals court.

Opinion of the Court. LEWIS, J., delivered the opinion of the Court. The plaintiff in error was indicted in the county court of Brunswick County for the murder of Moses Young, by administering to the said Young strychnine poison in whisky. . . . The facts proved, as certified in the record, are substantially these: That on the night of the 17th day of December, 1880, Moses Young died at his house in Brunswick county, and under such circumstances as created suspicions that he had been poisoned. He was an old man, 65 years of age, and was subject to the colic, and a short time previous to his death had been hurt in his side by a cart. In the afternoon of that day the father of Oliver Hatchett, the prisoner, gave him a small bottle of whisky, with instructions to take it to Moses Young; at the same time telling him not to drink it himself. The deceased lived about three miles from the prisoner's father, to whose house the prisoner at once proceeded. It seems that he was not acquainted with the deceased; or, if so, very slightly, and that he succeeded in finding the house only by inquiry of one of the neighbors. Soon after his arrival at the house of the deceased, he took supper with him, and a few minutes thereafter requested the deceased to go with him into the yard, and point out the path to him—it then being dark. After getting into the yard, the prisoner produced the bottle and invited the deceased to drink—telling him that it was a little whisky his father had sent him. The deceased drank and returned the bottle to the prisoner, who at once started on his return home. The deceased then returned into the house. In a short while thereafter he complained of a pain in his side, began to grow worse, and told his wife that the man (meaning the prisoner) had tricked him in a drink of whisky. He then got up, but fell immediately to the floor. Osborne and Charlotte Northington, two near neighbors, were then called in by his wife; and these three, whom the record describes as ignorant negroes, were the only persons present with the deceased until his death, which occurred about three hours after he drank of the whisky from the bottle handed him by the prisoner.

They described his symptoms as follows: The old man had the jerks, complained of great pain, and every now and then would draw up his arms and legs and complained of being cramped; that he put his finger in his mouth to make him vomit, and his teeth clinched on it so that one of his teeth was pulled out in getting out his finger. They also testified that his dying declaration was that the man had killed him in a drink of whisky. From the symptoms as thus described, two physicians, who were examined as witnesses in the case, testified that as far as they could judge from the statements of the ignorant witnesses, they would suppose that Moses Young died from strychnine poison. No post-mortem examination of the deceased body was made or attempted; nor was any analysis made of the contents of the bottle, which was returned about one-third full by the prisoner to his father, and was afterwards found.

After the arrest of the prisoner, and while under guard, he stated to the guard in charge of him that he would not be punished about the matter; that he intended to tell all about it; that his father, Littleton Hatchett, gave him that mess and told him he would give him something, to carry it and give it to Moses Young, and that it would fix him. He further stated that he went to Moses Young's house, called him out and gave him a drink, and returned the bottle and put it where his father had directed him to put it. The next day he made a statement on oath before the coroner's jury, and when asked by the foreman whether he was prepared, upon reflection, to say that what he had stated on the previous day was not true, he answered: "I am prepared to say that a part of what I said yesterday was true." He then made a statement in which he said that he carried the whisky to the deceased by direction of his father, who told him not to drink of it; that he went to the house of the deceased and gave him a drink, and returned the bottle as directed by his father. But he did not state that his father told him that the whisky would "fix" the deceased, or that he (the prisoner)

knew that it contained poison or other dangerous thing.

It was also proved that Henry Carroll, who was jointly indicted with the prisoner, gave to Sallie Young, wife of the deceased, about three weeks before his death, something in a bottle which he said was strychnine, and which he told her to put in the coffee or food of the deceased; and that Osborne and Charlotte Northington knew of the fact, but did not communicate it to the deceased. It was also proved that Henry Carroll was the paramour of Sallie Young, which fact was also known to Osborne and Charlotte Northington.

Such are the facts upon which the plaintiff in error was convicted and sentenced to death. Now, under the allegations in the indictment, it was incumbent upon the prosecution, to entitle the Commonwealth to a verdict, to establish clearly and beyond a reasonable doubt these three essential propositions: (1) That the deceased came to his death by poison. (2) That the poison was administered by the prisoner. (3) That he administered it knowingly and feloniously. These propositions, we think, are not established by the evidence in this case.

In the first place, there is no sufficient proof that the deceased died from the effects of poison at all. From the symptoms, as described by ignorant witnesses, one of whom at least was a party to the conspiracy to poison the deceased, and who had been supplied with the means to do so (a fact known to the others), the most that the medical men who were examined in the case could say was that they *supposed* he died from strychnine poison. Strange to say, there was no post-mortem examination of the body of the deceased, nor was there any analysis made of the contents of the bottle from which he drank at the invitation of the prisoner, and which was returned by the latter to his father and afterwards found—all of which, presumably, might easily have been done, and in a case of so serious and striking a character as this ought to have been done. . . . Great strictness should be observed, and the clearest proof of the crime required, to safely warrant the conviction of the accused and the infliction of capital punishment. Such proof is wanting in this case to establish the death of the deceased by the means alleged in the indictment.

Equally insufficient are the facts proved to satisfactorily show that if in fact the deceased died from the effects of poison, it was administered by the prisoner; and if administered by him, that it was done knowingly and feloniously. It is not shown that if the whisky he conveyed to the deceased contained poison, he knew or had reason to know the fact. It is almost incredible that a rational being, in the absence of provocation of any sort, or the influence of some strong and controlling motive, would deliberately take the life of an unoffending fellow man. Yet in this case no provocation or motive whatever on the part of either the prisoner or his father, from whom he received the whisky of which the deceased drank, to murder the deceased, is shown by the evidence. It is true that the facts proved are sufficient to raise grave suspicions against the prisoner; but they fall far short of establishing his guilt clearly and satisfactorily, as required by the humane rules of the law, to warrant his conviction of the crime charged against him. On the other hand, the facts proved show that the wife of the deceased, three weeks before his death, had been supplied by her paramour with strychnine to administer to her husband; and there is nothing in the case to exclude the hypothesis that the death of the deceased may not have been occasioned by the felonious act of his own unfaithful wife. It was not proven that the prisoner at any time procured, or had in his possession, poison of any kind; nor was the attempt made to connect him with, or to show knowledge on his part of, the poison which was delivered by Henry Carroll to Sallie Young, to be administered to her husband.

In short, the facts proved are wholly insufficient to warrant the conviction of the plaintiff in error for the crime for which he has been sentenced to be hanged: and the judgment of the circuit court must, therefore, be reversed, the verdict of the jury set aside, and a new trial awarded him. [From John Henry Wigmore, *The Principles of Judicial Proof*]

CHAPTER 16

Probability

Much of logic is concerned with methods of determining whether a statement is true on the basis of premises stating the evidence for it. But we also make judgments about probabilities:

1. There's a 60% chance of rain this evening.
2. The probability of getting two 6's on a roll of the dice is 1/36.
3 Lumberjacks have a higher probability of dying on the job than do accountants.
4. I'd say my chance of getting into a top-20 law school is 40%.

Estimates of probability are used pervasively in planning our personal lives, in business decisions, and in government policy, among many other areas. Probability plays a major role in science, especially the social sciences, and it is a basis for statistical reasoning, which we examined in Chapter 14. In this chapter, we will review the methods of supporting judgments about probability. As in the case of analogies (Chapter 12), these methods involve both inductive and deductive (mainly mathematical) elements.

These methods fall into two classes. (1) There are *direct* methods for assigning a probability to an event, by looking at the nature of the event and its circumstances, as well as the amount of evidence about whether the event will occur. (2) There are rules that give us an *indirect* method: If we have probabilities for two or more events, we can compute the probability of combinations of those events. Conversely, if we can break a complex event down into its simpler components, and if we know the probability of each component, then we can calculate the probability of the whole. These rules are known as the probability calculus. The probability calculus allows us to compute the probability of complex or multiple outcomes when we know the individual components.

16.1 Probability Measures

A probability judgment attributes a degree of probability to an event (e.g., that it will rain tomorrow), to an effect (e.g., that a roll of the dice will get two 6's), or to a thing's having some property (e.g., that a patient has the flu). It is customary to use the term "event" in all these cases: They are propositions about what might happen or turn out to be true. We are not actually asserting the proposition in question, but we are not simply confessing ignorance or abstaining from judgment altogether. Instead, we are judging *how likely* the event is. This is a quantitative judgment, a matter of degree—we are locating the event on a quantitative scale or dimension. And so we use numbers to measure the likelihood.

A probability can be expressed as an ordinary fraction (1/2), a decimal fraction (0.5), or a percentage (50%). These are mathematically equivalent, and we can use whichever form is most convenient. But whichever form we use, a probability must lie between 0 and 1 (or 100%). An event that cannot occur has a probability of 0, while an event that must occur has a probability of 1; all other probabilities lie between these extremes. If $p(A)$ stands for the probability of a certain event A, we can put this point mathematically as follows:

$$0 \leq p(A) \leq 1.$$

Finding the probability of an outcome, therefore, means locating $p(A)$ at the right point in the interval between 0 and 1—finding the right fraction or percentage.

There are two basic ways of establishing probabilities. The first is familiar from games of chance. A coin has two sides, and when you flip a coin it is equally likely to land on either one, so there's a 50% chance of getting a head on a single flip of a coin. When you are dealt a card from a full deck, the chance that it will be the ace of hearts (or any other particular card) is 1/52 because there are 52 cards in the deck. If a number from 1 to 10 is randomly selected, the chance that it is 4 (or any other number in the interval) is 1/10. The general rule can be stated as follows. To find the probability of a given event A, we count the number of possible outcomes. If that number is n, then the probability of A (or any other particular outcome) is $1/n$. This method of assigning probabilities can be called the **method of equal alternatives** because we have to consider all alternative outcomes that are possible in the situation.

The method also applies when an event A can occur in more than one way. There are four aces in a deck of cards, for example, so if A is the event of drawing an ace, there are four ways it could happen, and $p(A)$ is 4/52. The probability of an even number on a roll of a single die is 3/6. For the sake of clarity, we will use the following terms to describe probabilities:

An **outcome** is a single possible result, such as drawing a particular card from the deck.

An **event** is an outcome or a set of outcomes for which we want to know the probability, such as drawing an ace.

A **favorable outcome** is an outcome included in the event, such as drawing the ace of hearts, the ace of clubs, etc.

The term "favorable" can be a bit misleading. It does not necessarily mean that the outcome is something we would favor. If you bet $10 that the next roll of the die will be an even number, and we want to know the probability of *losing* your money, the "favorable" outcomes are 1, 3, and 5. Be that as it may, it is customary to use the term in the sense defined above.

The general rule for the method of equal alternatives is therefore

p(A) = f/n, where f is the number of favorable outcomes and n is the number of all possible outcomes.

When an event includes only a single outcome, like drawing the ace of hearts, the formula reduces to $1/n$.

An alternative way to formulate the probability of A is in terms of the odds of A versus *not-A*. The odds of getting 6 on a single roll of a die, for example, is 1:5—one favorable outcome versus five unfavorable ones. In speaking of odds, we are relating favorable outcomes not to the total set of possible outcomes but to the subset of unfavorable ones. If you bet $1 on rolling a 6, the other person should put up $5 for a bet on the remaining numbers, and the winner goes home with $6. The general rule of determining odds is

f:u, where f is the number of favorable outcomes and u is the number of unfavorable ones.

There's a simple relationship between the probability of A and the odds for it. The total number n of possible outcomes is the sum of the favorable and the unfavorable ones:

Probability of A			Odds of A
$\dfrac{f}{n}$	=	$\dfrac{f}{f + u}$	$f : u$

(In some contexts such as betting, odds are stated in the reverse order, with the unfavorable odds stated first. For example, "The odds that the Green Bay Packers will win their league championship is 7 to 1" means that the odds are 1 in favor of the Packers and 7 against. In what follows, we will use the convention that favorable odds are stated first and unfavorable second.)

The method of equal alternatives works only when certain conditions are satisfied. First, there must be a definite number of alternatives. If there isn't, then we have no n to divide by. Second, the alternative outcomes must be equally probable. Given that the coin is a fair one, or the deck of cards well-shuffled and the dealer honest, any outcome is just as likely as any other. But if one outcome were more likely than the others, we could not simply divide by n; the probability of that outcome would be higher than $1/n$, and the probability of the other outcomes would be lower.

These two conditions are satisfied in games of chance, but not often in other contexts. Suppose you want to know the probability that the next car to pass you on the street will be white. The alternative is that it will be some other color, but how many alternatives are there? Is red a single alternative or do we separate red from orange and purple? Do we treat gray as an alternative in addition to white and black? These different ways of classifying color will give us different numbers for n, so the first condition is not satisfied. Nor is the second condition. Regardless of how we classify colors, we can't assume that the next car has an equal chance of being each of the colors.

In a case like this, it is more appropriate to use what is called the **method of frequency**. To assign a probability by this method, we find the frequency with which a given outcome has occurred in a reference group of similar cases. Thus the chance that the next car that passes will be white would be estimated by finding out how many cars in your area are white as opposed to any other color. By this method, it doesn't matter how we classify the other colors or how probable it is that a given car has one of those other colors. We are comparing our outcome (a white car) not to alternative outcomes (cars with other colors) but to the class of all cars in the area. So the formula for estimating probability by the method of frequency is

f/y, where f is again the number of favorable outcomes (white cars in the area) and y is the total number in the reference class (all cars in the area).

This method is widely used in business and finance, medicine, social science, and many other areas. Here are some of the more common uses:

- *Prediction*. In situations that are complex, there are often too many factors at work for us to predict the exact outcome with any certainty. Instead, we estimate outcomes by the frequency with which they occurred in similar cases in the past. Thus, a weather forecast might predict a 60% chance of rain because it has rained 60% of the time in the past when weather conditions were similar to the current ones. If an insurance company wants to know the likelihood that a 35-year-old woman will die during the term of her life insurance policy, say 20 years, it consults a mortality table that says what proportion of 35-year-old women die before they reach 55.

- *Risk assessment*. Estimating risks is a special type of prediction that deserves special mention because numerical data are often available. Public health officials keep records based on the frequency of specific injuries and diseases among the population. Banks set interest rates, in part, by estimating the risk that people will renege on loans. Engineers have ways of calculating the risk that a mechanical system, such as a nuclear reactor, will fail. The concept of probability is implicit in these cases because a risk is the probability that some event will occur.

- *Diagnosis*. Prediction is concerned with future outcomes, but we also use the frequency method to make probability judgments about the present. A patient comes to a doctor with certain symptoms. In most cases, more than one illness can cause the same symptoms, and the doctor makes a judgment about which illness is the most likely cause. The doctor may order a diagnostic test such as a biopsy. But diagnostic tests are rarely if ever 100% accurate. In a small percentage of cases there are "false positives" (the test is positive but the patient does *not* have the illness) or "false negatives" (the test is negative but the patient *does* have the illness). So even with the tests, we can only say there is a certain probability that the patient has that illness.

To use the method of frequency, we obviously need information about the frequency of a given outcome in the relevant class of cases. If we do not already have that information, we have to acquire it by an inductive procedure of tracking the number of times the outcome occurs in that class. This is another difference between the two methods. When you flip a coin, you know that, by the nature of the coin, there are two equally likely outcomes, so the method of equal alternatives tells you that the probability of heads is 1/2. You can make that judgment before you actually flip the coin. (Because the probability is known in advance, this method is sometimes called the *a priori* method.) To use the method of frequency, by contrast, you would flip the coin many times in succession and note the proportion of heads. The result will approximate 1/2 (though it isn't likely to be exactly 1/2, and the expected deviation from 1/2 is affected by the number of trials).

As we have seen, the advantage of the method of frequency is that we need not classify all the possible outcomes or assume that they are equally probable. But it does have dangers and limitations of its own. For one thing, it has its own kind of classification problem. Before we can measure the frequency with which an outcome has occurred in similar cases in the past, we have to select the group of similar cases: We have to choose a reference group. There is usually more than one such group that could reasonably be chosen, and different groups will give us different frequencies.

Suppose we want to know the probability that a certain student will graduate from college. What is the appropriate reference group? The whole population of college students? That's awfully broad; it doesn't take account of factors that affect this particular student's chances of graduating. So perhaps we should consider the frequency of graduation in a narrower class of students. But which one? Students at the particular college? Students with the same SAT scores? The same family, ethnic, or religious backgrounds? The same personality traits? The same degree of intelligence and ambition? You can see that if we tried to find a reference group that takes account of every factor that might be relevant, we would end up with a group containing only one member—the student himself. And then there would be no frequency to measure. So between the broadest and the narrowest extremes, we have to find a reference group that takes account of the obviously relevant factors but is still broad enough to give us a reliable measure of frequency. There is no mechanical, cut-and-dried method of making this choice.

Once we have chosen a reference class, how do we determine frequency? In some cases, we can examine each and every member of the class; this would be like the method of generalization by complete enumeration. Around April 15 of each year, for example, newspapers report the probability of having your tax return audited; the frequency of audits can be calculated from IRS records on the total number of returns filed and the number it has audited in each income category. Similarly, information on mortality that insurance companies use is based on all deaths reported to local health authorities. In other cases, we can't survey the entire reference class, so we have to extrapolate or generalize from a sample of the class. Most frequency statistics are of this kind, and they require the methods of statistical generalization discussed in Chapter 14. Suffice it to say for now that the basic rules for generalizing apply here. The larger and more varied the sample, the more reliable it is: the more confidence we can have that the frequency of an event in the sample is close to its frequency in the class as a whole.

In addition to the two methods we have discussed, we also make **intuitive judgments** about probabilities, especially in regard to particular outcomes to which the methods of frequency and equal alternatives cannot be applied easily, if at all. For example:

1. You turn in a paper and think you have a good chance, maybe 60%, of getting an A.

2. A corporate executive approves a new product line based on a judgment that it has a better than even chance of being profitable.
3. A gambler bets on the Baltimore Ravens to win the Super Bowl, at 2:3 odds, judging that the probability of a Ravens win is at least 40%.

Probability judgments of this kind are often described as subjective because they reflect a person's individual judgment about the probability of a given outcome—his or her best guess—and two people may well assign different probabilities to the same outcome. But these judgments need not be subjective in the sense of being arbitrary or indifferent to evidence. In example 1, your judgment presumably reflects knowledge about the course material, the instructor's standards and expectations, and the work you put into the paper. In the same way, the executive (example 2) takes account of a large amount of information about the product line, market research, the competition, etc. And people who bet on sports events (example 3) typically know a lot about the teams. In these and similar cases, the judgment reflects the integration of relevant information to produce a kind of gestalt, a single intuitive judgment that some outcome has a certain probability, all things considered. We may not be able to spell out all the considerations in the form of explicit inferences, so this is not exactly a *method* for determining probabilities. But such intuitive judgments are common in personal and professional life and deserve recognition as a way of assigning probabilities.

Precisely because these judgments are intuitive, however, we should also recognize that they are liable to biases. Suppose I was cheated once by a used car dealer. A single incident of cheating affects the frequency of cheating by the same amount (and it's a very small amount) regardless of who the victim was. But I am more likely to remember it than if it happened to someone else, and so I may have an inflated judgment about the probability of getting cheated the next time. To guard against biases, we should try to examine the bases of our judgments and weed out the nonobjective factors as best we can.

SUMMARY Probability Measures

The probability of an event is between 0 and 1: $0 \le p(A) \le 1$.

Probabilities can be assigned to events in three ways:

1. Equal alternatives: If there is a definite number, n, of equally likely outcomes, the probability of a given outcome or set of outcomes is f/n, where f is the number of favorable outcomes. The odds of a given outcome or set of outcomes is $f{:}u$, where u is the number of unfavorable outcomes.

2. Frequency: If an event belongs to a reference class, y, of related events, the probability of a given outcome or set of outcomes is f/y, where f is the number of favorable outcomes and y is the total number in the reference class.

3. Intuitive judgment: The probability of an event can be assigned by an intuitive judgment based on integrating relevant evidence.

The three ways of assigning probabilities to outcomes are often described as different theories of probability, or as different meanings of the term "probability." That's because it isn't clear that we are talking about the same thing in all three cases. In flipping a coin or rolling a die, it is natural to think of probability as a property of the object. The method of frequency is also concerned with objective properties: We classify an outcome in a reference class on the basis the properties of the objects and actions involved. But we also have some options in choosing a reference class, and the frequency percentage is affected by the amount of inductive data we have. With intuitive judgments, finally, probability seems to be a matter of an individual's particular context of knowledge.

Probability is indeed a complex idea, and experts have put forward a range of very different theories about it. For our purposes, however, it is enough to know the different methods we use in making probability judgments. And no matter which method we use in assigning probabilities to outcomes, we use the same principles in calculating combinations of outcomes. We will turn to those principles—the probability calculus—in the next section.

EXERCISE 16.1

A. Use the method of equal alternatives to determine the probability of each of the following events.

* 1. What is the probability of getting a 4 on a single roll of a die?

2. What are the odds of drawing the queen of spades from a full deck of cards?

3. A number between 1 and 20 (inclusive) is randomly selected. What is the probability that the number will be even?

* 4. A box contains 7 blue marbles, 4 white marbles, and 10 yellow marbles. What is the probability that a marble drawn at random will be blue?

5. McDonalds has six differently colored Hot Wheels cars and five Barbie toys. What are the odds of getting the red Hot Wheels car with your Happy Meal?

B. Using the method of frequency, what reference class and frequency would you use to estimate the following probabilities?

* 1. The chance that it will rain today.

2. The probability that the next time the telephone rings it will be someone trying to sell you something.

3. The probability that the next car you see will have New Jersey license plates.

* 4. The probability that a baby will be a girl.

5. The risk of being struck by lightning.

6. The probability that a woman who is HIV positive will pass the virus to her baby.

C. Determine the probability of each of the following events. Name the method involved (equal alternatives, frequency, or intuitive judgment).

＊ 1. What is the probability that on the single role of a die, you will get a number above 4.

2. You are attending your 10-year high school reunion. You somewhat enjoyed high school. Four or five of your old friends will be there, people you still like. There is an open bar, but bad music. What are the chances that you will enjoy yourself?

3. Of 4,675 Ballista sedans sampled off the production line, 187 were found to have defective transmissions. What is the probability that a randomly selected Ballista sedan has a defective transmission?

＊ 4. What are the odds of drawing a spade from a standard deck of playing cards?

5. In 11,003 at-bats, baseball player Dave Winfield got 3,110 hits. What is the probability that, at an arbitrary at-bat, Dave Winfield would get a hit? Represent your answer as a decimal fraction to the nearest thousandths place.

6. Of 6,200 patients tested, 155 were found to have a particular recessive gene. What is the probability that Adam lacks this gene?

16.2 The Probability Calculus

Suppose we want to know the probability that the first card dealt from a full deck is *either* a heart *or* a spade. This is a complex event, which we can analyze into its components: drawing a heart, drawing a spade. If we can assign probabilities to the component events, as we can in this case, then it is possible to compute the probability of the complex event. In fact, mathematicians have developed a set of procedures, known as the **probability calculus**, for doing just this. In this section, we will review three elementary rules of the probability calculus:

Conjunction: the probability that two events will *both* occur. $p(A \text{ and } B)$
Disjunction: the probability that one or the other of two events will occur. $p(A \text{ or } B)$
Negation: the probability that an event will not occur. $p(-A)$

16.2A Conjunction

If you roll a pair of dice, what is the probability of getting "snake-eyes" (two 1's)? Since there are two dice, let's take them one at a time. By the method of alternatives, the chance of getting a 1 on the first die is 1/6, so we know that the chance of snake-eyes cannot be any greater than 1/6. But in fact it must be less, because even if the first die comes up 1, there is only a 1/6 chance that the second die will do likewise. The probability of snake-eyes, then, is $1/6 \times 1/6 = 1/36$. (You can confirm this by directly listing all the possible outcomes of rolling a pair of dice; you'll find that there are 36.) In the same way, we would use multiplication to find the probability that two unrelated people will both get the flu in the next 12 months. If person A has a 10% chance of flu and some randomly chosen person, B, has a 15% chance, then the probability that both will get the flu is $10\% \times 15\% = 1.5\%$. The rule for determining the conjunctive probability that two events will both occur is

$$p(A1 \text{ and } B) = p(A) \times p(B).$$

But there's an important qualification, which we can see by considering other cases. What is the chance of drawing two aces in a row from a deck of cards? The chance of drawing the first ace is 4/52, since there are 4 aces and 52 cards altogether. But once you've drawn the first ace, only 51 cards remain in the deck, and only 3 aces. So the probability of drawing a second ace is 3/51, and the probability of the complex event is $4/52 \times 3/51$, about 1/20. The difference from the previous cases is simple, but important. In a roll of the dice, the components are **independent events**: The outcome on the first die does not affect the outcome on the other. So we can treat the probability of each component in isolation from the other. In drawing the cards, however, the first event *does* affect the second. They are **dependent events**, and we cannot consider them in isolation. Instead, we have to consider the probability that the second event will occur *given that* the first one has already occurred. Similarly, suppose we want to know the probability of flu, not for two unrelated people but for two college roommates. Flu being contagious, B's getting the flu is not an independent event; if A gets the flu, there's a higher probability that B will also get it. If the probability that B gets the flu *given that* A did is 50%, then the probability that both get the flu is $10\% \times 50\% = 5\%$.

In the standard notation, the probability of *B given A* is written $p(B \mid A)$, where the vertical stroke "$|$" means "given that." The general rule for conjunction is therefore

$$p(A \text{ and } B) = p(A) \times p(B \mid A).$$

If two events are independent, like the dice, then A makes no difference to B. The probability of *B* given *A* is simply the probability of *B* considered by itself, and so this general rule reduces to the restricted rule that applies to independent events.

The formula $p(B \mid A)$ expresses the concept of **conditional probability**: the probability that one event will occur on condition that another event occurs. It is an important concept in many fields of knowledge and many types of planning. For example, suppose you are thinking about a career in law and want to know the probability of getting a job in a top law firm. Such firms hire chiefly from the top law schools, so you would first try to estimate your chance of getting into one of those schools by looking at their admission rates, the average grade averages and LSAT scores of those admitted, etc. The next question is the chance of a job in a top law firm given that you graduate from a top law school. You might estimate that conditional probability from the school's placement records. So the probability of getting into a top school and a job at a top firm is

$$p(\text{top school and top firm}) = p(\text{top school}) \times p(\text{top firm} \mid \text{top school}).$$

To summarize: The probability that two events will both occur is given by the general conjunction rule:

$$p(A \text{ and } B) = p(A) \times p(B \mid A)$$

In the special case where A and B are independent, $p(B \mid A) = p(B)$, and we can use the special or restricted conjunction rule:

$$p(A \text{ and } B) = p(A) \times p(B).$$

16.2B Disjunction

A disjunctive event has the structure A *or* B. To find the probability of such an event, there is once again a restricted rule and a more general rule. And, once again, let's start with the restricted rule because it is simpler.

Suppose we wanted to know the probability that a randomly chosen student at College X is either a junior or a senior. Let's say 20% of the students are seniors and 23% are juniors. Then the probability that the student is in one or the other of these two classes is

$$p(\text{senior or junior}) = p(\text{senior}) + p(\text{junior}) = 20\% + 23\% = 43\%.$$
$$p(A \text{ or } B) = p(A) + p(B).$$

Instead of multiplying the probabilities of the components, as we did for conjunction, we add them. We followed this rule implicitly in Section 16.1 when we assigned a probability of 3/6 to the event of rolling an even number because it can happen in three different ways: $p(\text{even number}) = p(2) + p(4) + p(6)$. Just as 2, 4, and 6 are favorable outcomes for that event, picking any of the individual juniors and seniors is a favorable outcome for the event of picking someone from either class.

The rule just stated is the restricted rule for disjunction, as it can be used only when outcomes are **mutually exclusive**. The die cannot come up both 2 and 4. A student cannot be both a junior and a senior. But what if we are dealing with **compatible** events—events that are *not* mutually exclusive? Suppose we wanted know the probability that a randomly chosen student is either a junior or a philosophy major. If juniors are 23% of the student body and philosophy majors are 5%, we cannot simply add the two percentages. There is obviously a subgroup that will be counted twice: junior philosophy majors. If they represent 1% of the student body, then we have to subtract 1% to correct for counting them twice:

$$p(\text{junior or philo major}) = p(\text{junior}) + p(\text{philo major}) - p(\text{junior and philo major})$$
$$= 23\% + 5\% - 1\%$$
$$= 27\%.$$

The general rule for disjunctive events is therefore

$$p(A \text{ or } B) = p(A) + p(B) - p(A \text{ and } B).$$

In the special case where A and B are mutually exclusive, we don't need to worry about any overlap between them or double-counting. If the two events cannot both occur, then $p(A \text{ and } B) = 0$. It drops out of the equation, and the general rule reduces to the restricted rule:

$p(A \text{ or } B) = p(A) + p(B)$.

This last point raises an issue that many people find confusing at first. For conjunctive events, *A and B*, we have to ask whether the components are independent or dependent. For disjunctive events, *A or B*, we ask whether they are mutually exclusive (incompatible) or compatible. These distinctions are *not* the same.

> Two events are *mutually exclusive* if and only if they cannot both occur; otherwise they are compatible.
>
> Two events are *independent* if and only if the occurrence of one does not affect the probability of the other; otherwise they are dependent.

In a strict sense, mutually exclusive events are necessarily dependent. The occurrence of one does affect the probability of the other—by reducing it to zero. But for our purposes in reasoning about probability, it is more natural to think of it this way: The question of whether two events are dependent or independent arises in a substantive way only if they are compatible. If they are mutually exclusive—if they cannot both occur—then it is really beside the point to ask whether one affects the other.

16.2C Negation

For any event A, there is an opposite event, $-A$: the nonoccurrence of A. And if we know the probability of one, we can compute the probability of the other. On a single roll of a die, the probability of getting 1 is 1/6. That leaves five ways of not getting a 1, so that probability is 5/6. In the same way, there are 51 ways of not drawing the ace of hearts, so the probability is 51/52. No matter what event we are talking about, A and $-A$ are

---

SUMMARY **The Probability Calculus**

The three elementary rules for calculating the probabilities of complex events are as follows.

	General Rule	**Restricted Rule**
Conjunction	$p(A \text{ and } B) = p(A) \times p(B \mid A)$	$p(A \text{ and } B) = p(A) \times p(B)$ Restriction: A and B are independent events, so that $p(B \mid A) = p(B)$.
Disjunction	$p(A \text{ or } B) = p(A) + p(B) - p(A \text{ and } B)$	$p(A \text{ or } B) = p(A) + p(B)$ Restriction: A and B are mutually exclusive events, so that $p(A \text{ and } B) = 0$.
Negation	$p(-A) = 1 - p(A)$	

mutually exclusive. By the restricted rule of disjunction, therefore, the probability that one or the other will occur is the sum of their individual probabilities: $p(A) + p(-A)$. In addition, they exhaust the possibilities: No matter what event we are talking about, it must either occur or not occur. The probability of its occurrence and the probability of its nonoccurrence must add up to 1, or 100%:

$$p(A) + p(-A) = 1.$$

So if we know the probability of A, we can subtract it from 1 to find the probability of $-A$, and vice versa. In mathematical terms:

$$p(-A) = 1 - p(A) \qquad \text{and} \qquad p(A) = 1 - p(-A).$$

This rule is a useful one to keep in mind because—as we will see shortly—it is sometimes easiest to figure out the probability of an event by first establishing the probability that it will not occur.

16.2D Extending the Rules

We formulated the conjunction and disjunction rules for the case of two events. But we may want to know the probability for a combination of three or more events. The rules can be extended to such cases, but there are a few complications.

Let's start with conjunction. What is the probability of getting three 6's on three rolls of the die? These are independent events, and the restricted conjunction rule can be extended in a straightforward way to give us the probability:

$$p(6 \text{ and } 6 \text{ and } 6) = p(6) \times p(6) \times p(6) = 1/6 \times 1/6 \times 1/6 = 3/216.$$

With dependent events, we have to take account of conditional probabilities. Consider the chance of drawing three face cards (jack, queen, or king) in a row from a full deck of cards. Let's call these events FC1, FC2, and FC3. There are 12 face cards, so the probability on the first draw, FC1, is 12/52, about 23%. For the second draw, the probability is FC2 | FC1 (the conditional probability of a face card given that we drew a face card on the first draw), which is 11/51. For the third draw, the probability of yet another face card is conditional upon *both* of the first two draws: FC3 | (FC1 and FC2), or 10/50. The conjunctive probability is then

$$p(\text{FC1 and FC2 and FC3}) = p(\text{FC1}) \times p(\text{FC2} \mid \text{FC1}) \times p[\text{FC3} \mid (\text{FC1 and FC2})]$$
$$= 12/52 \times 11/51 \times 10/50$$
$$= 1{,}320/132{,}600 = \text{about } 1\%.$$

You can see that the formula for three dependent events gets complicated by the need to make the probability of the third event conditional upon both of the first two. With every additional event we add to the sequence, the complications increase further because we must make it conditional upon all the previous events in the series. Notice also that when we multiply probabilities, the resulting probability can decrease rapidly—from 23% for a face card on the first draw to 1% for three in a row.

The rule for disjunction can also be extended to three or more events. If the events are mutually exclusive, we use the restricted rule for disjunction, and the extension is straightforward. We simply add the probability of the third event to the sum for the first two. Indeed, we already used this procedure implicitly in the previous example of drawing face cards. For the first draw, the probability of drawing a face card is the probability of drawing either a jack, a queen, or a king:

$p(\text{jack or queen or king}) = p(\text{jack}) + p(\text{queen}) + p(\text{king}) = 4/52 + 4/52 + 4/52$
$$= 12/52.$$

If the events are not mutually exclusive, however, the issue is more complicated. For example, suppose you are going to toss a coin three times and want to know the probability of getting at least one head. On each toss your chance of getting a head is 1/2. By the rule for disjunction, the probability so far is $1/2 + 1/2 + 1/2 = 3/2$. That's greater than 1—an indication that we are not dealing with mutually exclusive events. By the general rule for disjunction, we now have to subtract the probabilities of getting two heads (on the first and second toss, the first and third, and the second and third), as well as the probability of getting heads on all three tosses. That adds up to quite a bit of calculation. We can get to the correct answer much more quickly if we realize that there's only one way *not* to get at least one head—the outcome in which we get three tails—and then use the negation rule. Getting three tails is a conjunctive event, for which we can multiply the probabilities: $1/2 \times 1/2 \times 1/2 = 1/8$. So the chance of getting at least one head is $1 - 1/8 = 7/8$. With three or more events that are not mutually exclusive, it is almost always better to use the negation rule in this way.

Let's apply these insights to another example, this one from the criminal justice system. When a crime is committed, there is a sequence of steps from reporting the crime to the police to the arrest, conviction, and sentencing of the perpetrator, with each event having some degree of conditional probability. In the case of burglary, suppose that these probabilities are as follows:

Probability that a burglary is reported	75%
Probability of arrest, given that the burglary is reported	25%
Probability of conviction, given an arrest	80%
Probability of a prison sentence, given conviction	70%

Though the probability of arrest is low, the other probabilities are much higher. It may seem that a would-be burglar faces a good chance of ending up in prison. By the general rule for conjunction, however, we have to multiply all these probabilities to find the overall probability that the sequence will run its course:

$p(\text{report and arrest and conviction and prison})$
$= p(\text{report}) \times p(\text{arrest} \mid \text{report}) \times p(\text{conviction} \mid \text{arrest}) \times p(\text{prison} \mid \text{conviction})$
$= 0.75 \times 0.25 \times 0.8 \times 0.7$
$= 0.105.$

Our would-be burglar has only a 10% chance of prison and a 90% chance of going free. Here we see again how multiplying fractions quickly leads to much lower numbers.

Before we conclude that crime pays, however, let's consider what happens with repeated burglaries. What is the probability of getting caught and going to prison after committing 5, or 10, or 20 burglaries? That would be the disjunctive probability of going to prison the first time or the second time or the third time, etc. As with the example of getting at least one head on multiple coin-flips, however, we also have to subtract the probability of going to prison multiple times: the first and third, the second and eighth, and so on, for every possible combination. So we will use the negation rule again to find the probability of *not* going to prison for *any* burglary, and then subtract that fraction from 1 to find the probability of going to prison in *some* cases (one or more). For a single burglary, the probability of going free is 0.9. The probability for getting away with two burglaries is $0.9 \times 0.9 = 0.81$, so the chance of going to prison has increased: $1 - 0.81 = 0.19$. For three burglaries, the chance is $1 - (0.9 \times 0.9 \times 0.9) = 1 - 0.27 = 0.73$. Here is what happens as the number of burglaries keeps increasing:

Number of Burglaries	Probability of Not Going to Prison for Any Burglary	Probability of Going to Prison for One or More Burglaries
1	0.90	0.10
5	0.59	0.41
10	0.35	0.65
15	0.21	0.79
20	0.12	0.88

With 10 burglaries, the chance of prison is well over half; with 20 it is highly probable. (In the real world, each arrest will increase the probability of conviction and prison for repeat offenses, but we will ignore that point for the sake of simplicity.)

The example illustrates the difference between the conjunctive probability that *every* event in a set of events will occur and the disjunctive probability that one or more of the events will occur, and the difference has a bearing on the positive, noncriminal goals we pursue. When a goal requires a series of steps, each with only a probability of success, the probability of achieving the goal by that route declines rapidly due to the multiplication rule for conjunction and conditional probability. Perhaps that's the meaning of the old saying, "There's many a slip between the cup and the lip." The good news is that there are often multiple routes to a goal, and in that case the addition rule for disjunction *increases* the likelihood of success.

EXERCISE 16.2

A. For each of the following pairs of events, determine whether the events are compatible or mutually exclusive.

  ✳ 1. Drawing either a spade or a queen from a deck of cards.

  2. Drawing either an ace or a queen from a deck of cards.

  3. Winning first place or winning second place in the 200-meter dash.

  ✳ 4. Being the class valedictorian or winning second place in the 200-meter dash.

  5. Pitching three balls or pitching three strikes (to a single batter).

B. For each of the following pairs of events, determine whether the outcomes are dependent or independent.

❋ 1. Winning an Oscar for "Best Original Song" and winning an Oscar for "Best Picture."

2. Bench-pressing 100 pounds or being able to do a cartwheel.

3. The Stevens Point track team winning the regional competition for track & field and its swimming team winning the state competition for swimming.

❋ 4. The Stevens Point track team winning the regional competition for track & field and winning the state competition for track & field.

C. Use the probability calculus to answer the following questions.

❋ 1. What is the probability that a single roll of a fair die does not result in a 3?

2. What is the probability that a queen or king is drawn from a standard deck of playing cards?

3. Dan has applied to three law schools: Jale, Smerkeley, and SafeLaw. He estimates that his chances of being accepted are 60% at SafeLaw, 30% at Jale, and 50% at Smerkeley.

   a. What is the probability that he will be accepted at all three schools?

   b. What is the probability that he will be accepted at SafeLaw or Smerkeley?

❋ 4. An urn contains three black balls, five red balls, and seven yellow balls.

   a. If two balls are drawn sequentially, replacing the first ball before drawing the second, what is the probability that both drawn balls are black?

   b. If the balls are drawn without replacing the first ball, what is the probability that both drawn balls are black?

5. For graduation day, assume there's a 50% chance of rain and also a 5% chance that the invited commencement speaker will have to cancel at the last minute and the dean will speak instead.

   a. What is the probability that it will rain or that the invited speaker will cancel?

   b. What is the probability that the dean will speak in the rain?

6. The CEO of Wholesome Foods plans to acquire the Very Berry fruit drink company. If he acquires Very Berry Fruit Drinks, he has a 70% chance of increasing his revenue by $1 million. His investment bankers give him an 85% chance of acquiring the company. What is the probability that he will both acquire Very Berry Fruit Drinks and increase his revenue by $1 million?

❋ 7. John Q. Ball is trying to win a game of pool, and it is his turn to shoot. He estimates that he has a 90% chance of sinking the 3 ball in one corner pocket and a 70% chance of sinking the 6 ball in the other corner. If he sinks the 3, he will then have a 60% chance of sinking the 6; if he sinks the 6 first, he will have a 90% chance of sinking the 3. Which initial shot gives him the highest probability of making both shots?

8. Alice and Bob are informed by their doctor that if they have a child, the probability that it has a recessive trait is 0.22. Alice and Bob plan on having two children.

a. What is the probability that both children have the recessive trait?

b. What is the probability that at least one child has the recessive trait?

9. Students at University X received scholarships on the basis of scores on a placement test.

a. What is the probability that a randomly selected student has a scholarship of any kind?

b. If a student has a scholarship of any kind, what is the probability that he is in the 75th to 90th percentile?

c. What is the probability that a student receives full tuition?

✳ 10. Each person has a specific blood type, with either a positive or negative Rh factor. The frequency of these types in the United States is given in the table.

a. What is the probability that a person chosen at random has blood type A+ or B+?

b. Blood type B+ is compatible with types B+, B−, O+, and O−. Mary, who is type B+, has had an accident and needs a blood transfusion. What is the probability that a person chosen at random will not be a compatible donor for Mary?

Type	Rh	Frequency
O	+	37.40%
O	−	6.60%
A	+	35.70%
A	−	6.30%
B	+	8.50%
B	−	1.50%
AB	+	3.40%
AB	−	0.60%
		100.00%

Percentile	Percent in That Percentile	Scholarship
25th to 50th	15	None
50th to 75th	30	Partial tuition
75th to 90th	40	Full tuition
90th to 99th	15	Full tuition, room, and board

Summary

A probability judgment attributes a degree of probability to an event on a scale from 0 (the event definitely will not occur) to 1 (it definitely will occur). Such judgments can be made in three ways. (1) The method of equal alternatives can be used if there is a definite number of equally likely outcomes, as in games with cards or dice. The probability of a given event equals the number of ways it can occur (the favorable outcomes) divided by the total number of possible outcomes. (2) The method of frequency can be used when an event belongs to a reference class of related events. The probability of the event is determined by the frequency of similar events in that reference class. (3) The probability of an event can be assigned by an intuitive judgment, based on integrating relevant evidence.

The probability calculus is a set of rules for determining the probability of combinations of events. We use the *conjunction* rule to calculate the probability that two events, A and B, will both occur. If the events are independent, the probability is the product of the individual probabilities: $p(A$ and $B) = p(A) \times p(B)$. If the events are dependent, the probability is the product of A's probability times the conditional probability of B given that A has occurred. We use the *disjunctive* rule to calculate the probability that either A or B occurs. If they are mutually exclusive events, the probability is the sum of the individual probabilities: $p(A$ or $B) = p(A) + p(B)$. If the events are compatible, the probability is the sum of the individual probabilities minus the probability of both occurring: $p(A$ or $B) = p(A) + p(B) - p(A$ and $B)$. We use the *negation* rule to calculate the probability that an event or combination of events will not occur: $p(-A) = 1 - p(A)$.

The conjunction and disjunction rules can be extended to three or more events.

Key Terms

method of equal alternatives—a method of determining the probability of an event by finding the ratio of favorable outcomes to the total number of possible outcomes.

outcome—in probability theory, a single non-compound result among a range of possible results.

event—an outcome or set of outcomes for which we want to know the probability, such as drawing an ace.

favorable outcome—an outcome included in an event.

method of frequency—a method of determining the probability of an event by the frequency of similar events in a reference class.

intuitive judgment—a judgment about the probability of an event based on integrating relevant evidence.

probability calculus—a set of rules for determining the probability of compound events.

independent events—two events are *independent* if and only if the occurrence of one does not affect the probability of the other.

dependent events—two events are dependent if the occurrence of one affects the probability of the other.

conditional probability—the probability that one event will occur on condition that another event occurs.

mutually exclusive—two events are *mutually exclusive* if and only if they cannot both occur.

compatible—two events are compatible if they could both occur.

Additional Exercises

A. Based on what you have learned in this chapter, answer the following questions.

✳ 1. In eight coins-flips, which of the following sequences are most probable? (H, heads; T; tails.)

   a. H H T H T T H T

   b. H H H H T T T T

   c. T T T T T T T T

   d. They are equally probable.

2. You are dealt two cards from a full deck.

   a. What is the probability that the second card is a jack?

   b. You turn over the first card and it is a 7. What is the probability that the second card is jack?

3. Can mutually exclusive events be independent?

4. Create an example of a disjunctive probability with two compatible events.

B. Determine the probabilities specified in each of the following.

✳ 1. If two dice are rolled:

   a. What is the probability they add to four?

   b. What is the probability they add to seven?

2. You are interested in buying a house on a wooded hillside overlooking the ocean. The house is subject to the following risks of damage from natural disasters:

Hurricane	1 in 100 years
Forest fire	1 in 75 years
Torrential rain and mudslide	1 in 50 years

   You expect to own the house for 15 years. What is the risk that one of these disasters will occur during that period?

3. At the end of the regular season, the odds that the Giants will make it to the Super Bowl are 1:9, and the odds that the Patriots make it are 1:4. Also, over the past five years, the Giants and the Patriots have played each other six times. Of those games, the Giants won four. What is the probability that the Giants will beat the Patriots in the Super Bowl?

✳ 4. A blackjack dealer deals you two cards. Face cards are worth 10, and an ace is worth either 1 or 11, your choice. What is the probability that you are dealt blackjack; i.e., the two cards whose value adds to 21?

5. Abby is a saleswoman for a company making high-end, high-priced software. For the next month, Abby plans to pitch three prospects: iQue, a current customer, for an upgrade worth $75,000; Xenophilia, a new customer, for the complete package, worth $200,000; and DoubleDown, for a streamlined version, worth $125,000.

   Based on her knowledge of the prospect companies and her general sales experience, she estimates the probabilities of each sale as IQue, 0.9; Xenophilia, 0.6; DoubleDown, 0.7.

   a. What is the probability that Abby will make at least one of the sales?

   b. Abby has a quota of $200,000 in sales for the month. Which prospect or combination of prospects give her the highest probability of meeting the quota?

6. The Internal Revenue Service audits a certain number of tax returns each year. For returns filed in 2011, the frequency of audits by major categories of income were as follows:

Income	Number of Returns	Number Audited
Under $200,000	95,000,000	487,000
$200,000 to $999,999	4,500,000	138,000
$1,000,000 and above	337,000	41,000
Totals	99,837,000	666,000

a. Determine the probability of an audit for people in each income category.

b. What is the probability that someone's income is $1 million or more, given that he or she has been audited?

complement   a term designating the class of all things excluded by another term.

composition   the fallacy of inferring that a whole has a property merely because its parts have that property.

conclusion   a proposition whose truth an argument seeks to establish.

conditional   a compound proposition containing two component propositions (the antecedent and the consequent) and asserting that the truth of one component would be sufficient for the truth of the other. See **hypothetical proposition**.

conditional probability   the probability that one event will occur on condition that another event occurs.

conditional proof (CP)   in propositional logic, a method of proving that a conditional proposition follows from a set of premises; one assumes the antecedent and then derives the consequent from the antecedent together with the premises.

conjunction   1. a compound proposition asserting that two or more component propositions (the conjuncts) are all true; 2. a rule of inference in propositional logic (Conj) permitting inferences of the following forms:

$$p \qquad \text{and} \qquad p$$
$$\underline{q} \qquad\qquad \underline{q}$$
$$p \bullet q \qquad\qquad q \bullet p$$

connective   a logical structure that creates a compound proposition from component propositions.

consequent   the "then" component in a hypothetical proposition.

consistent   a relation between two or more statements that are both true on at least one assignment of truth values to their atomic components.

constructive dilemma (CD)   a rule of inference in propositional logic permitting an inference of the following form:

$$(p \supset q) \bullet (r \supset s)$$
$$\underline{p \vee r}$$
$$q \vee s$$

contingent statement   a compound statement that is true for some assignments of truth values to its atomic components and false for other assignments.

contradiction   a relation between two or more statements that have opposite truth values for every assignment of truth values to their atomic components.

contradictories   in the traditional and modern squares of opposition, a pair of categorical propositions that, in virtue of their logical form, could neither both be true nor both be false (A and O, E and I).

contraposition (Contra)   a rule of equivalence in propositional logic permitting the following substitution:

$$(p \supset q) :: (\sim q \supset \sim p)$$

contrapositive   the proposition that results from replacing the subject term in a categorical proposition with the complement of the predicate and the predicate with the complement of the subject.

contraries   in the traditional square of opposition, a pair of categorical propositions that, in virtue of their logical form, could not both be true but could both be false (A and E).

converse   the proposition that results from switching the subject and predicate terms in a categorical proposition.

copula   a verb of being ("is," "are," etc.) that links the subject and the predicate in a categorical proposition.

counterexample   a specific instance that proves a definition wrong.

De Morgan's law (DM)   a rule of equivalence in propositional logic permitting the following substitutions:

$$\sim(p \bullet q) :: (\sim p \vee \sim q)$$
$$\sim(p \vee q) :: (\sim p \bullet \sim q)$$

deductive argument   an argument that attempts to show that its conclusion makes explicit the information implicit in the premises, so that the conclusion must be true if the premises are.

definition   a statement that identifies the referents of a concept by specifying the genus they belong to and the essential characteristics (differentia) that distinguish those referents from other members of the genus.

denying the antecedent   an invalid mixed hypothetical syllogism in which the categorical premise denies the antecedent of the hypothetical premise and the conclusion denies the consequent.

denying the consequent   a valid mixed hypothetical syllogism in which the categorical premise denies the consequent of the hypothetical premise and the conclusion denies the antecedent. See also **modus tollens**.

dependent events   two events are dependent if the occurrence of one affects the probability of the other.

destructive dilemma (DD)   a rule of inference in propositional logic permitting an inference of the following form:

$$(p \supset q) \bullet (r \supset s)$$
$$\underline{\sim q \vee \sim s}$$
$$\sim p \vee \sim r$$

differentia   the element in a definition that specifies the attribute(s) distinguishing a species from other species of the same genus.

disjunct   a component of a disjunctive proposition—*p* and *q*.

disjunction   a compound proposition containing two or more component propositions (the disjuncts) and asserting that at least one of them is true.

disjunctive syllogism   1. a deductive argument with a disjunctive premise, other premises denying all but one of the disjuncts, and a conclusion affirming the remaining disjunct; 2. a rule of inference in propositional logic (DS) permitting inferences of the following forms:

$$p \lor q \qquad\qquad p \lor q$$
$$\underline{\sim p} \qquad\text{and}\qquad \underline{\sim q}$$
$$q \qquad\qquad\qquad p$$

distribution   1. a property of a term in a categorical proposition; the term is distributed if and only if the proposition makes an assertion about all members of the class designated by the term; 2. a rule of equivalence in propositional logic (Dist) permitting the following substitutions:

$$[p \bullet (q \lor r)] :: [(p \bullet q) \lor (p \bullet r)]$$
$$[p \lor (q \bullet r)] :: [(p \lor q) \bullet (p \lor r)]$$

3. A statistic specifying the number or proportion of items in a class that have each of the values (P, Q, R, etc.) on some variable.

diversion   the fallacy of trying to support one proposition by arguing for another proposition.

division   the fallacy of inferring that a part has a property merely because the whole has that property.

double negation (DN)   a rule of equivalence in propositional logic permitting the following substitution:

$$p :: \sim\sim p$$

enthymeme   a categorical syllogism with an unstated premise or conclusion.

equivalence   a relation between two or more statements that have the same truth value for every assignment of truth values to their atomic components.

equivocation   the fallacy of using a word with two different meanings in the premises and/or conclusion of an argument.

event   an outcome or set of outcomes for which we want to know the probability.

existential generalization (EG)   a rule of inference in predicate logic permitting an inference of the following form:

$$\frac{\dots a \dots}{(\exists x)(\dots x \dots)}$$

existential import   a property of categorical propositions; a proposition has existential import if its truth depends on the existence of things of the kinds specified by terms in the proposition.

existential instantiation (EI)   a rule of inference in predicate logic permitting an inference of the following form, subject to certain restrictions:

$$\frac{(\exists x)(\dots x \dots)}{\dots a \dots}$$

existential quantifier   a quantifier indicating that the variable it binds represents at least one thing in the world.

explanandum   the proposition whose truth one is attempting to explain.

exportation (Exp)   a rule of equivalence in propositional logic permitting the following substitution:

$$[(p \bullet q) \supset r] :: [p \supset (q \supset r)]$$

fallacy   an argument in which the premises appear to support the conclusion, but actually provide little or no support.

false alternative   the fallacy of excluding relevant possibilities without justification.

favorable outcome   an outcome included in an event.

figure   the position of the middle term in the premises of a categorical syllogism.

free variable   in predicate logic, a variable not bound by a quantifier.

frequency   a statistic specifying the number or proportion of items in a class that have a given property.

genus   a class of things regarded as having various subcategories (its species).

hasty generalization   the fallacy of inferring a general proposition from an inadequate sample of positive instances.

hypothesis   the proposition (or propositions) in an explanation that purport to show why another proposition (the *explanandum*) is true.

hypothetical proposition   a compound proposition that uses the connective "if . . . then."

hypothetical syllogism (HS)   a rule of inference in propositional logic permitting an inference of the following form:

$$p \supset q$$
$$q \supset r$$
$$p \supset r$$

implication (Imp)   a rule of equivalence in propositional logic permitting the following substitutions:

$$(p \supset q) :: (\sim p \lor q)$$
$$:: \sim(p \bullet \sim q)$$

implicit premise   a premise that is assumed by an argument but is not stated.

independent events   two events are independent if and only if the occurrence of one does not affect the probability of the other.

inductive argument   an argument that attempts to show that its conclusion is supported by the premises even though the conclusion amplifies—it goes beyond—what the premises state.

intuitive judgment   a judgment about the probability of an event based on integrating relevant evidence.

jointly exhaustive   in a classification, the property that the species taken together cover all the objects in the genus.

major premise   in a categorical syllogism, the premise in which the major term appears.

major term   in a categorical syllogism, the term that occurs in the predicate of the conclusion.

median   a statistic specifying the middle value of the items in a class on a quantitative variable P.

method of agreement   a method of identifying a cause of an effect by isolating a factor common to a variety of cases in which the effect occurs.

method of concomitant variations   a method of identifying a cause of an effect by isolating a factor whose variations are correlated with variations in the effect, all other factors remaining constant.

method of difference   a method of identifying a cause of an effect by isolating a factor in whose presence the effect occurs and in whose absence the effect does not occur, all other factors remaining constant.

method of equal alternatives   a method of determining the probability of an event by finding the ratio of favorable outcomes to the total number of possible outcomes.

method of frequency   a method of determining the probability of an event by the frequency of similar events in a reference class.

method of residues   a method of identifying a cause of an effect by isolating that portion of the effect not explained by known causal relationships.

middle term   in a categorical syllogism, the term that appears in both premises and links together the major and minor terms.

minor premise   in a categorical syllogism, the premise in which the minor term appears.

minor term   in a categorical syllogism, the term that occurs in the subject of the conclusion.

mixed hypothetical syllogism   a syllogism with a hypothetical premise, a categorical premise, and a categorical conclusion.

modus ponens **(MP)**   a rule of inference in propositional logic permitting an inference of the following form. See also affirming the antecedent:

$$p \supset q$$
$$\underline{p}$$
$$q3$$

modus tollens **(MT)**   a rule of inference in propositional logic permitting an inference of the following form. See also denying the consequent:

$$p \supset q$$
$$\underline{\sim q}$$
$$\sim p$$

mood   the order of the standard forms that make up the premises and conclusion of a categorical syllogism.

mutually exclusive   1. in a classification, the property that each species excludes the members of every other species; 2. a relationship between events; two events are mutually exclusive if and only if they cannot both occur.

negation   a compound statement whose truth value is the opposite truth value of its component statement.

negative instance   an item that belongs to a given class and does not possess the trait attributed to the class by a given generalization.

obverse   the proposition that results from changing the quality of a categorical proposition and replacing the predicate term with its complement.

open sentence   in predicate logic, a statement with a free variable.

outcome   in probability theory, a single, non-compound result among a range of possible results.

particular proposition   a categorical proposition that makes an assertion about at least one but not all members of the class designated by its subject term (I and O).

positive instance   an item that belongs to a given class and possesses the trait attributed to the class by a given generalization.

post hoc   the fallacy of using the fact that one event preceded another as sufficient evidence for the conclusion that the first caused the second.

premise   a proposition used in an argument to provide evidence for another proposition (the conclusion).

probability calculus   a set of rules for determining the probability of compound events.

proposition   the meaning or content of a statement.

pure hypothetical syllogism   a syllogism in which the conclusion and both of the premises are hypothetical propositions. See also **hypothetical syllogism**.

quality   the affirmative or negative character of a categorical proposition.

quantifier   1. in traditional logic, the element in a statement's logical form that indicates particular or universal quantity; 2. in predicate logic, the element in a statement that indicates whether a variable represents all or some of the things in the world.

quantifier negation (QN)   a rule of equivalence in predicate logic permitting the following substitutions:

$$\sim(x)(\ldots x \ldots) \quad :: \quad (\exists x)\sim(\ldots x \ldots)$$
$$\sim(\exists x)(\ldots x \ldots) \quad :: \quad (x)\sim(\ldots x \ldots)$$
$$\sim(x)\sim(\ldots x \ldots) \quad :: \quad (\exists x)(\ldots x \ldots)$$
$$\sim(\exists x)\sim(\ldots x \ldots) \quad :: \quad (x)(\ldots x \ldots)$$

quantity   the particular or universal character of a categorical proposition.

ratio   a statistic specifying the number of items in a class, or the sum of their values on a variable, per unit of some other class; a ratio is a total expressed in relative terms.

reductio ad absurdum (RA)   in propositional logic, a method of proving that a proposition follows from a set of premises by deriving a contradiction from the denial of that proposition together with the premises.

referents   the class of things for which a concept stands.

scope   the portion of a statement in symbolic notation that is governed by a quantifier.

self-contradiction   a compound statement that is false for every assignment of truth values to its atomic components.

simplification (Simp)   a rule of inference in propositional logic permitting inferences of the following forms:

$$\frac{p \bullet q}{p} \quad \text{and} \quad \frac{p \bullet q}{q}$$

singular proposition   a categorical proposition whose subject term designates a specific thing rather than a class.

slippery slope   the fallacy of arguing against a proposed action or policy by claiming, with insufficient evidence, that it will lead to a series of increasingly bad consequences.

sound   the property of a deductive argument that is valid and whose premises are true.

species   a class of things regarded as a subcategory of a wider class (a genus).

statement form   an expression using statement variables and connectives to state the logical form of an actual or possible statement.

statement variables   symbols (p, q, r, etc.) used to represent any actual or possible statement.

stipulative definition   a definition that introduces a new concept (or a new meaning for an existing concept) by specifying the criteria for inclusion in the concept.

strength   the degree to which the premises of an inductive argument support the conclusion.

subalternates   in the traditional square of opposition, the relationship between a universal and a particular proposition of the same quality (A and I, E and O): if the universal is true, the particular must be true, and if the particular is false, the universal must be false.

subcontraries   in the traditional square of opposition, a pair of propositions that, in virtue of their logical form, could both be true but could not both be false (I and O).

subjectivism   the fallacy of using the fact that one believes or wants a proposition to be true as evidence of its truth.

syllogism   a deductive argument with two premises and a conclusion.

tautology (Taut)   1. a compound statement that is true for every assignment of truth values to its atomic components; 2. a rule of equivalence in propositional logic permitting the following substitutions:

$$p \quad :: \quad (p \bullet p)$$
$$\quad :: \quad (p \vee p)$$

total   a statistic specifying the number of items in a class or the sum of their values on a variable.

truth table   a diagram displaying the truth or falsity of a compound proposition as a function of the truth or falsity of its atomic statements and connectives.

truth value   the truth or falsity of a proposition.

universal generalization (UG)   a rule of inference in predicate logic permitting an inference of the following form, subject to certain restrictions:

$$\frac{\ldots a \ldots}{(x)(\ldots x \ldots)}$$

universal instantiation (UI)   a rule of inference in predicate logic permitting an inference of the following form:

$$\frac{(x)(\ldots x \ldots)}{\ldots a \ldots}$$

universal proposition   a categorical proposition that makes an assertion about all members of the class designated by its subject term (A and E).

universal quantifier   a quantifier indicating that the variable it binds represents all things in the world.

validity   the property of a deductive argument in which it is impossible for the premises to be true and the conclusion false.

variable   1. in symbolic logic, a symbol that stands for some, but any, unnamed individual thing; 2. in statistics, a trait regarded as a generic attribute that can exist in different degrees (values).

Answers to Selected Exercises

CHAPTER 1

EXERCISE 1.1
A.

1. Genus: animal
   Species: man
   Other examples of species: cat, dog, mouse, etc.

4. Genus: sport
   Species: baseball
   Other species: hockey, football, etc.

7. Genus: countries
   Species: European
   Other species: Asian, African, etc.

10. Genus: aristocrat
    Species: duke
    Other species: baron, countess, etc.

13. Genus: burial place
    Species: mausoleum
    Other species: grave, catacomb, etc.

B.

1. Lady Gaga, singer, performer

4. Steel, alloy, metal, mineral

7. iPhone, mobile telephone, telephone, communication device

10. Brother, sibling, family member, kin

13. Cardigan, sweater, top, garment

EXERCISE 1.2

1. Not mutually exclusive (hardback first editions); not a consistent principle.

4. Not mutually exclusive (foreign pornographic) or jointly exhaustive (horror, drama); not a consistent principle.

7. Not mutually exclusive (individual aquatic); no consistent principle.

10. Not mutually exclusive or jointly exhaustive (non-leather casual shoes); no consistent principle.

13. Not mutually exclusive (clerical jobs in a service industry); no consistent principle.

EXERCISE 1.3
A.

1.

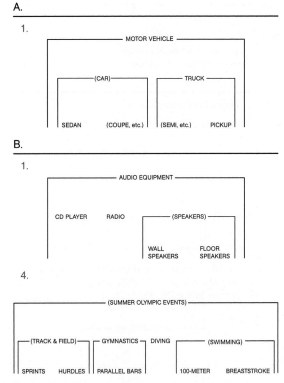

B.

1.

4.

C.

Parliamentary governments are a type of democratic government and should be classified under the latter. The three branches are not types but components of democratic governments.

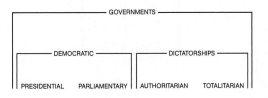

Additional Exercises

A.

1. Sauntered, strode, etc.

4. Country, domain (notice the different assumptions behind these terms); quadruped, animal.

7. Institution

10. Countless, a huge number, 57, etc.

B.

1. First genus: aircraft.
Higher-level genus: vehicle.

4. First genus: government agencies.
Higher-level genus: institutions.

C.

1. Newspaper, book, pamphlet, etc.

4. Diseases, homicide, suicide, casualties in war, . . .

D.

1.

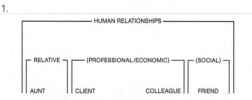

(One could treat relatives and social relationships as species of PERSONAL RELATIONSHIPS, putting the latter on the same level as PROFESSIONAL/ECONOMIC.)

4.

E.

1.

4.

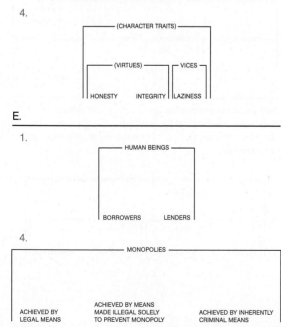

7.

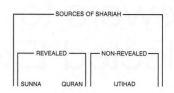

CHAPTER 2

EXERCISE 2.2A

1. Genus: precipitation
Differentia: consisting of flakes or clumps of ice crystals

4. Genus: opportunity
Differentia: to buy something at an unusually low price

7. Genus: none
Differentia: completing a run or pass across the other team's goal line

10. Genus: feeling
Differentia: of wrongful detachment from certain people or things

EXERCISE 2.2B

1. [No genus. Too narrow: light snow in a strong wind. Nonessential.]

4. Too broad—notebook

7. Too broad: radio

10. Too narrow: antidotes can counteract other toxins

13. Too narrow: calculators can be used for purposes other than those for which slide rules were used. Too broad: a computer is also an electronic instrument that could replace a slide rule. Nonessential: the definition doesn't say what calculators are for.

EXERCISE 2.2C

1. Too narrow
Genus: jewel
Differentia: worn on a pendant around the neck

4. Metaphor
Genus: rat
Differentia: wearing a fur coat

7. Vague. Too broad.
Genus: trait of a person
Differentia: playing by the rules

10. Negative. Too broad: someone who is medicated is not sober.
Genus: person
Differentia: not sober

13. Negative. No genus.
Genus: none
Differentia: not getting what you want

16. Nonessential. Too narrow.
    Genus: exercise
    Differentia: obscuring the weakness in one's own posi-
                   tion by browbeating one's opponent

19. Too broad: cape, sweater.
    Genus: outer garment
    Differentia: designed to protect the wearer from cold,
                   wind, and rain

EXERCISE 2.3
1. Published on unbound paper / information on current
   events of interest to the general public.

Additional Exercises
A.

1. Too narrow; nonessential.
   An army is the branch of a country's military whose
   primary function is to fight on land.

4. Circular.
   A genus is the broader class to which the referents of a
   given concept belong.

7. Nonessential. Too broad if taken literally (some tasks will
   be easy for anyone).
   A craftsman is a person who is skilled at creating a specific
   type of product. (One might argue that craftsmanship
   should not be limited to specific products, but should
   apply to any skill or talent; I consider that a metaphorical
   extension, but the point is certainly debatable.)

10. Too broad (all the social sciences would be included). Too
    narrow (animal studies would be excluded).
    Psychology is the science that studies the functioning
    of the mind. (Theorists of many different schools could
    accept this definition by interpreting "functioning" and
    "mind" in different ways, but the definition is still some-
    what tendentious. I don't know of a perfectly neutral one.)

13. Too narrow (a person can reform).
    To reform is to improve a person or organization by
    changing the principles on which the person or organiza-
    tion acts. (The term "principles" must be taken broadly
    here to include character, personality, and beliefs in the
    case of persons; and laws, policies, and structure in the
    case of organizations.)

B.

All of these are nonessential as stated, and either too broad
or too narrow. Most are also metaphorical. The answers given
here mention only additional faults.

1. Negative

4. Vague, metaphorical

7. Vague

10. No genus. Negative.

C.

1. Too narrow: history is concerned with past ideas, works of
   art, and other things besides events; and with the explaining as well as discovering and describing.

4. A good definition of crimes in the legal sense, as opposed
   to metaphorical extensions of the term, such as "crimes
   against nature (or nature's Law)," "crimes against
   humanity."

7. Metaphorical

10. Metaphorical

13. Good definition

16. Too narrow: payroll taxes (e.g., Social Security) are
    intended for later benefits to the taxpayer. In addition,
    "payment" would be a better genus than "contribution,"
    which suggests something voluntary.

19. Obscure. Possibly too broad: some mechanical systems
    might fit this description.

22. Nonessential: the goal is essential to an organization; the
    structure of authority is a consequence of the goal.

25. Nonessential: in Csikszentmihayli's own theory (he coined
    the concept FLOW), the features he mentions arise from a
    more fundamental pattern of attention to an activity.

D.

1. (b) is clearly a metaphorical extension, deriving from
   "headshrinker."

4. (b) and (c) seem to involve the same concept: an external force that threatens a thing's internal structure or
   functioning. (If force is regarded as something inherently
   physical, then (b) would be a metaphorical extension of
   (c).) (a) is a synonym for "emphasize," at best a metaphorical extension of the concept.

E.

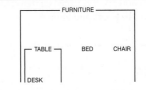

FURNITURE: movable man-made objects designed to support
and/or store other objects.

TABLE: an article of furniture designed with the primary
purpose of supporting other objects on a flat and rigid top
surface.

BED: an article of furniture with a horizontal surface designed
to support a sleeper.

CHAIR: an article of furniture designed to support a sitting or reclining person on a horizontal surface, with a vertical surface to support the back.

DESK: a table designed for work by a seated person, with a flat surface to support working materials and drawers or pigeon-holes to store them.

F.

1. an unmarried adult human male.

4. a device for processing information according to an alterable set of instructions.

7. a person who is relatively unskilled in a given activity.

10. a group of people related by birth or marriage.

G.

1. Both are types of recreation, but reflect subdivisions of the genus by different principles of classification: games are distinguished by rules from less structured activities; sports are distinguished by their physical character from less strenuous activities.

4. All three terms indicate a person's tendency—more or less deliberate and more or less habitual—to make his overt actions reflect his inner beliefs and feelings. "Sincere" is normally used for nonverbal actions and displays of feeling, "honest" for verbal ones, with frankness perhaps best seen as a species of honesty distinguished by the bluntness of the expression or the unpleasantness of what is expressed.

7. Two possibilities: (1) To adorn is to make a person more visually pleasing, to decorate is to make a nonhuman object more pleasing, with "garnish" either a synonym or a subcategory restricted to food. (2) To adorn is to add to the visual attraction of something that is already pleasing in itself, to decorate is to make pleasing something that in itself is plain or unattractive, with "garnish" as in (1).

10. Three different types of personal written communication, distinguished by length and format.

CHAPTER 3
EXERCISE 3.1A
1. Same

4. Different

7. Same

10. Same

13. Different

EXERCISE 3.1B
1. The teacher's announcement was startling.

4. The budget that the president submitted to Congress has no chance of being passed.

7. The article over-simplified or changed the information about the controversy.

10. Roger was such a good salesman; he was so persuasive that he could convince people to do things against their best interests.

EXERCISE 3.2A
A.

1. Same

4. Same

B.

1. i. He arrived in time.
   ii. He arrived out of breath

4. i. Beavers build dams.
   ii. Beavers are a type of rodent.
   iii. The dams can flood a whole valley

C.

1. Unasserted

4. Asserted

EXERCISE 3.2B
1. (a) His mind was racing.
   (a) His body was in the lead.
   Connective: "but"

4. (a) The ice storm was over.
   (a) The trees glittered in the sun.
   Connective: "After"

7. (u) Sparky hears the car in the driveway.
   (u) He runs to the back door.
   Connective: "If"

EXERCISE 3.2C
1. who live in glass houses—restrictive

4. that are waged in self-defense—restrictive

7. who was last seen wearing a Cleveland Indians baseball cap—restrictive

EXERCISE 3.2D
1. (u) Animals can talk.
   (a) The little girl thinks that animals can talk.

4. (u) Two plus two equals four.
   (a) He is convinced that two plus two equals four.

7. (u) Zack was planning a surprise birthday party for Samantha.
   (a) Samantha suspected that Zack was planning a surprise birthday party for her.

10. (a) If you buy two pairs of jeans, the third pair is free.
    (a) If your purchase is over $50, you get 30% off.
    (u) You buy two pairs of jeans.
    (u) The third pair of jeans is free.
    (u) Your purchase is over $50.
    (u) You get 30% off.
    (a) If you buy two pairs of jeans, the third pair is free; and if your purchase is over $50, you get 30% off.

13. (a) David was driving well above the speed limit.
    (a) David knew better.
    (a) David was driving well above the speed limit and he knew better.

16. (a) Professional baseball players make a lot of money.
    (u) The season is too long.
    (a) Professional baseball players should not complain that the season is too long.
    (a) Professional baseball players make a lot of money and they should not complain that the season is too long.

19. (a) The city planner called the zone developer.
    (a) The city planner wanted to find out whether the area had been marked and the architect had been chosen.
    (u) The area had been marked.
    (u) The architect had been chosen.
    (a) The city planner called the zone developer because she wanted to find out whether the area had been marked and the architect had been chosen.

22. (a) Man is a living organism.
    (a) Man is mortal.
    (a) Man is mortal because he is a living organism.
    (a) Man is rational.
    (a) Man is aware of his mortality.
    (a) Man is aware of his mortality because he is rational.
    (a) Because he is a living organism, man is mortal; [and] because he is rational, he is aware of his mortality.

25. (a) We found our seats at the racetrack.
    (a) We could hear the announcer.
    (a) When we found our seats at the racetrack we could hear the announcer.
    (a) The announcer was reporting that Pardon My Dust was already ahead of Try Me.
    (a) The announcer thought Try Me still had a chance at winning the handicap.
    (a) Pardon My Dust was already ahead of Try Me.
    (u) Try Me still had a chance at winning the handicap.
    (a) When we found our seats at the race track, we could hear the announcer saying that Pardon My Dust was already ahead of Try Me, but he thought Try Me still had a chance at winning the handicap.

Additional Exercises
A.

1. Joanne met Bob for lunch.

4. It is pouring.

7. The mail will not be delivered on Wednesday because it is a holiday.

10. I don't believe that people are innately evil, as John Calvin said.

B.

1. (a) A pedestrian hit me.
   (a) A pedestrian went under my car.
   (a) A pedestrian hit me and went under my car.

4. (a) The pedestrian had no idea which direction to go.
   (a) I ran over the pedestrian.
   (a) The pedestrian had no idea which direction to go, so I ran over him.

7. (a) A car came out of nowhere.
   (a) The car was invisible.
   (a) The car struck my vehicle.
   (a) The car vanished.
   (a) An invisible car came out of nowhere, struck my vehicle, and vanished.

10. (a) The accident happened.
    (a) The right front door of a car came around the corner.
    (a) The right front door of the car did not give a signal.
    (a) The right front door of a car came around the corner and did not give a signal.
    (a) The accident happened when the right front door of a car came around the corner without giving a signal.

C.

1. Positive—public servant, negative—bureaucrat

4. Eating to excess, pigging out

7. Delirious with joy, giddy

10. Cognitively challenged, a few bricks shy of a full load

D.

1. John has been practicing for the marathon, and did not find his 7-mile run yesterday very strenuous.

4. The law generally holds a manufacturer responsible for harm caused by its product, unless it warns the buyer that the product is dangerous or the buyer is harmed through his own negligence.

E.

1. Hamlet is always thinking about what he should do. Hamlet cannot decide what to do.

Hamlet never acts.

4. Society may restrict the liberty of the individual only if his actions would harm others.
Physical force is a way of restricting liberty.
The moral coercion of public opinion is a way of restricting liberty.
The individual is sovereign over his own mind and body.

F.

1. (a) Man is born free.
   (a) Man is everywhere in chains.
   (a) Man is born free, and everywhere he is in chains.

4. (a) The poor in spirit are blessed.
   (a) The kingdom of heaven belongs to the poor in spirit.
   (a) The poor in spirit are blessed because the kingdom of heaven belongs to them.
   (a) They that mourn are blessed.
   (a) They that mourn shall be comforted.
   (a) They that mourn are blessed because they shall be comforted.
   (a) The meek are blessed.
   (a) The meek shall inherit the earth.
   (a) The meek are blessed because they shall inherit the earth.
   (a) The poor in spirit are blessed because the kingdom of heaven belongs to them; and they that mourn are blessed because they shall be comforted; and the meek are blessed because they shall inherit the earth.

7. (a) The bourgeoisie has fashioned the weapons that bring death to itself.
   (a) The bourgeoisie has called into existence the men who are to wield those weapons.
   (a) The men who are to wield those weapons are the modern working class.
   (a) The modern working class are the proletarians.
   (a) The men who are to wield those weapons are the proletarians.
   (a) The bourgeoisie has fashioned the weapons that bring death to itself, and has called into existence the men who are to wield those weapons, and those men are the modern working class, who are the proletarians.

10. (a) All men are created equal.
    (a) All men are endowed with certain inalienable rights.
    (a) They are so endowed by their Creator.
    (a) All men have a right to life.
    (a) All men have a right to liberty.
    (a) All men have a right to the pursuit of happiness.
    (a) Governments are instituted to secure these rights.
    (a) Governments derive their powers from the consent of the governed.
    (a) We hold these truths to be self-evident, that all men are created equal, that they are endowed by their Creator with certain unalienable Rights, that among these are Life, Liberty, and the pursuit of Happiness, [and that] to secure these rights, Governments are in-

stituted among Men, deriving their just powers from the consent of the governed.

G.

Y misrepresented existing fact.
Y intended that X rely on the misrepresentation.
X did rely on the misrepresentation.
X was justified in relying on it.
X was harmed by relying on it.

CHAPTER 4
EXERCISE 4.1

1. Not an argument

4. Not an argument

7. Not an argument

10. Argument. Premise: It is rarely economical for two companies to lay cables in the same area and compete directly. Conclusion: Cable television is a natural monopoly, which should be regulated by the government.

13. Argument. Premise: In an experiment involving twins raised in different families, psychologists found that the children had significantly similar rates of depression. Conclusion: Depression is more strongly affected by one's genetics than by one's environment.

EXERCISE 4.2
A.

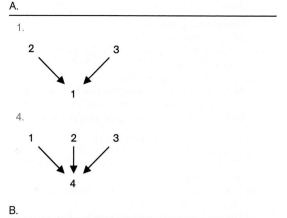

1.
2 → 1 ← 3

4.
1 → 4 ← 2 ← 3

B.

1. 3 is the conclusion, dependent

4. 1 is the conclusion, dependent

7. 3 is the conclusion, dependent

10. 3 is the conclusion, independent

C.

1. (1) Annette must be wealthy.

(2) Last week Annette bought a diamond choker for her ocelot.

4. (1) It would not be a good idea to take the American Revolution course this term.
(2) The American Revolution course conflicts with a course I need for my major.
(3) My schedule would have more balance if I took a science course.

7. (1) Business conditions will improve over the next year.
(2) When business conditions improve, corporate profits will increase.
(3) Increasing profit levels will drive up stock prices.
(4) Investing in the stock market is a good idea.

1 + 2 + 3
↓
4

10. (1) Raising the age of retirement would both decrease an expenditure for the government and generate revenue for the government.
(2) Raising the age of retirement would reduce the number of years that citizens drew money from their pensions.
(3) People would continue to pay income taxes and social security during their additional years of employment.

2 + 3
↓
1

EXERCISE 4.3
1. b
4. b
7. b
10. a

EXERCISE 4.4
1. Deductive. Valid.
4. Inductive
7. Inductive

10. Inductive
13. Inductive

EXERCISE 4.5
1. Successful salesmen are outgoing people.
4. All copper has the same melting point.
7. a. It is desirable for a recording to reproduce the spatial features of music.
   b. Most compact disc recordings do not reproduce the spatial features of music.
10. Placebos isolate physical effects from psychosomatic effects.

EXERCISE 4.6
1. (1) Within the past year you have been in fear of some personal attack.
(2) You have a stick.
(3) The stick is inscribed with a date of a year ago.
(4) You have not had the stick more than a year.
(5) You have filled the stick with lead.
(6) You have made the stick a formidable weapon.
(7) You would not have made the stick a formidable weapon unless you feared some danger.

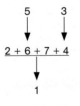

Additional Exercises
A.

1. (1) If you want to see deer in the woods, you have to be quiet.
(2) Deer tend to run when they hear noise.

4. (1) You shouldn't ask a friend to keep a secret from a spouse.
(2) Marriage is a more intimate relationship than friendship.
(3) You shouldn't ask someone to compromise a more intimate relationship for the sake of a less intimate one.

7. (1) Without welfare, some people would have no means of support.
   (2) We must not eliminate welfare.
   (3) The government has a duty to provide everyone with the essentials of life.

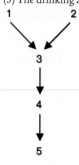

   1 + 3
   ↓
   2

10. (1) People are allowed to vote when they are 18.
    (2) Males have to register for the draft at 18.
    (3) Eighteen-year-olds are considered old enough to have these responsibilities.
    (4) Eighteen-year-olds are old enough to decide whether to drink.
    (5) The drinking age should not be 21.

    1   2
     ↘ ↙
      3
      ↓
      4
      ↓
      5

B.

1. Fairly strong.

4. Strength depends on implicit premise that keeping a secret compromises a relationship.

7. Very strong.

10. Moderately strong at best. The inference from (3) to (4) assumes: (a) that deciding about alcohol does not require a higher degree of responsibility than voting or registering for the draft; and (b) that 18-year-olds are responsible enough to vote and register—note that intermediate conclusion (3) says only that they are considered to be responsible, not that they actually are.

C.

1. If robbery had been the motive, something would have been taken.

4. A judge should not have an interest that biases his judgment.

7. A world view is a religion.

D.

1. (1) Viruses are a form of naked gene.
   (2) The best way to find out what a gene is and how it duplicates is to study the properties of viruses.

(1)
↓
(2)

4. (1) Judging people by their skin color is repugnant.
   (2) It is wrong to punish or reward people for things over which they have no control.
   (a) People have no control over their skin color.
   (3) Race is almost never relevant to a person's suitability.
   (4) We should treat people as individuals rather than as members of a group.
   (b) Judging people by skin color is treating them as members of a group.

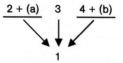

   2 + (a)   3   4 + (b)
        ↘   ↓   ↙
           1

7. (1) The methane released by the oil spill disappeared from the surrounding water.
   (2) Methanotrophs consumed the methane.
   (3) The surrounding water was depleted of oxygen.
   (4) Methanotrophs use oxygen when they consume methane.

   1 + 3 + 4
   ↓
   2

10. Not an argument

13. Not an argument

16. (1) Most of the basic elements of structure and function of all organisms are similar.
    (2) All organisms use the same sorts of proteins made of the same twenty amino acids.
    (3) All organisms use the same nucleic acids made of the same four bases.
    (4) All organisms have similar machinery for oxidizing food, producing energy, and doing cellular work.
    (5) All organisms store, replicate, and use genetic information in the same way.
    (6) The genetic code is the same in all organisms.
    (7) All organisms have a common origin.

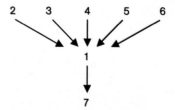

    2   3   4   5   6
             ↘ ↓ ↙ ↙
              1
              ↓
              7

19. Not an argument

CHAPTER 5

EXERCISE 5.1

1. Appeal to majority

4. Appeal to emotion

7. Appeal to force

10. Subjectivism

13. Appeal to majority

EXERCISE 5.2

1. Appeal to authority

4. *Ad Hominem*

7. *Ad Hominem*

10. *Ad Hominem*

EXERCISE 5.3

1. Hasty generalization

4. *Post hoc*

7. Hasty generalization

10. False alternative

13. Slippery slope

16. Division

19. Accident

22. *Post hoc*

EXERCISE 5.4

1. Appeal to ignorance

4. Appeal to ignorance

7. Equivocation

10. Begging the question

13. Begging the question

Additional Exercises
A.

1. Appeal to majority

4. False alternative

7. Slippery slope

10. Appeal to majority

13. Begging the question or *ad hominem*

16. Accident

19. Appeal to authority or appeal to force, depending on intent

22. Accident

25. Equivocation

28. Accident

31. Diversion

34. Division

B.

1. Either ghosts exist or Mary lied . . .

4. The popularity of entrepreneurs implies . . .

7. Capitalism squeezes out all the creative energy of workers into products sold for obscene profits, returning only a trickle to the workers . . .

10. Because logic has a lot of value and deserves your attention . . .

C.

1. *Post hoc*

4. *Post hoc*

7. *Ad hominem*

10. Equivocation, *ad hominem*

13. Diversion

16. *Post hoc*

19. Begging the question

D.

1. (1) An individual is created at conception.
   (2) Everyone was once a zygote.
   (3) No one was ever an unfertilized ovum or sperm.

   <u>(2) + (3)</u>
   ↓
   (1)

4. (1) If the task of the painter were to copy for men what they see, the critic could make only a single judgment: that the copy is right or wrong.
   (2) The critic is not limited to a single judgment.
   (3) The task of the painter is not to copy for men what they see.

   <u>(1) + (2)</u>
   ↓
   (3)

Appeal to majority or appeal to authority

CHAPTER 6
EXERCISE 6.1A

	Quantity	Subject	Quality	Predicate	Form
1.	Some	movie stars	are	good actors	Particular affirmative; I
4.	All	graduate students	are	broke people	Universal affirmative; A
7.	No	phones	are	CD players	Universal negative; E
10.	No	one who laughs at my teddy bear	is	a friend of mine	Universal negative; E
13.	Some	arguments in the works of great philosophers	are	fallacies	Particular affirmative; I

EXERCISE 6.1B

	Quantity	Subject	Quality	Predicate	Form
1.	All	human beings	are	rational beings	Universal affirmative; A
4.	Some	men	are not	people who achieve greatness	Particular negative; O
7.	All	men who seek fame for its own sake	are	foolish people	Universal affirmative; A
10.	Some	greatest authors in literature	are not	people who attended college	Particular negative; O
13.	Some	houses in the area	are not	things affected by the storm	Particular negative; O
16.		John F. Kennedy [singular]	is not	a politician who succeeded in his domestic policy	Universal negative; E
19.	Some	pieces of furniture	are not	things that are on sale	Particular negative; O

EXERCISE 6.2
1. True

4. Undetermined

7. Undetermined

10. False

EXERCISE 6.3
1. Undetermined

4. Undetermined

7. False

10. Undetermined

EXERCISE 6.4
A.

1. Some cats are friendly things

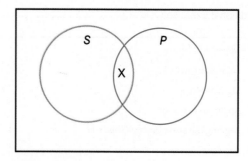

4. All police officers are people who do their best to protect us from criminals.

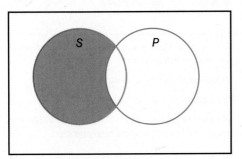

7. All clocks are things that tell time.

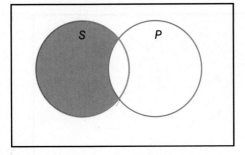

10. Some actors are people who don't know how to act.

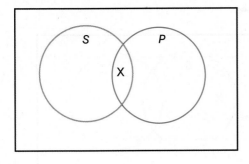

B.

1. Inconsistent

4. Consistent

EXERCISE 6.5A

1. Some leaf-shedding plants are trees.

   Equivalent

4. All things that contain beta carotene are green vegetables.

   Not equivalent

7. No adherents of Zoroastrianism were candidates for legislature this year.

   Equivalent

10. Some violent things are not video games.

    Not equivalent

13. Some safe areas are not poor neighborhoods.

    Not equivalent

EXERCISE 6.5B

1. All of the athletes are un-injured people.

4. None of Alister's friends is a nonstudent

7. Some policies are not unwise things.

10. Some companies were unprofitable enterprises this year.

13. All people in this room are nonsuspects.

EXERCISE 6.5C

1. Some non-P are non-S. Not equivalent.

4. Some S are non-P. Equivalent.

7. Some non-P are non-S. Not equivalent.

10. Some P are non-S. Equivalent.

13. No P is S. Not equivalent.

16. Some P are not S. Equivalent.

19. No P is non-S. Not equivalent.

Additional Exercises
A.

1. O. Some large corporations paid no income tax last year.

4. I. Some statistics that indicate economic growth can be misleading.

7. O. Some proponents of radical economic change have not carefully considered the consequences of their ideas.

10. E: My family never ate meat on Friday.

B.

1. All sonnets are poems that have fourteen lines. A. (No sonnet is a poem that has fourteen lines.)

4. Some fish are not carnivores. O. (Some fish are noncarnivores.)

7. No big girl is a person who cries. E. (All big girls are people who cry.)

10. You are a sweet thing. A. (You are not an unsweet thing.)

13. No real man is a person who eats quiche. E. (No person who eats quiche is a real man.)

16. All countries with the word "Democratic" in their official names are dictatorships. A. (All countries that are not dictatorships are countries that do not have the word "Democratic" in their official names.)

19. No law that forces a person to act against his judgment is a just law. E. (No unjust law is a law that does not force a person to act against his judgment.)

C. _____

1. All S are P

4. Some S are not P

7. All non-S are P; All non-P are S

D. _____

1. Subalternate. Not equivalent. Follows on traditional but not modern interpretation.

4. Subcontrary. Not equivalent.

7. Contrapositive. Not equivalent.

10. Subalternate of converse. Not equivalent. Follows on traditional but not modern interpretation.

E. _____

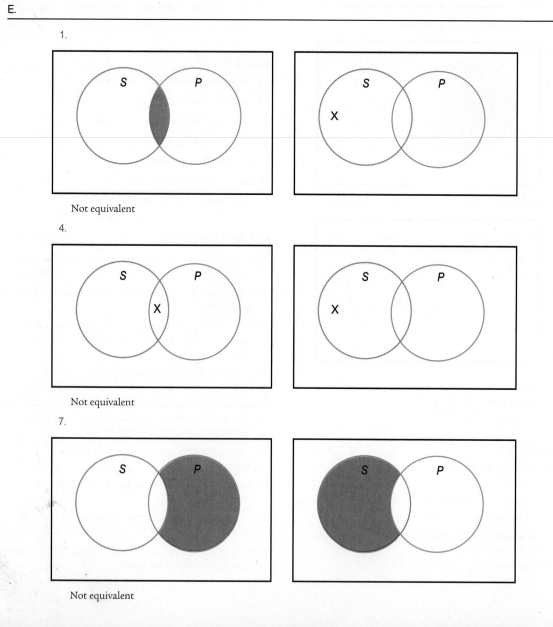

1.

Not equivalent

4.

Not equivalent

7.

Not equivalent

10.

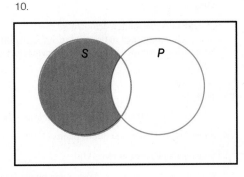 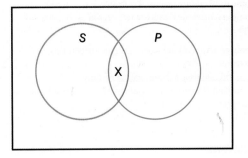

Not equivalent

F.

1. All bad events are things that have some good aspect.

4. No great work is a thing that is accomplished quickly.

7. All persons with advance warning of a threat are people who can prepare for it.

10. All suggestions or requests backed by financial inducements are things that have a good chance of succeeding.

G.

1. All great men are people who have been persecuted and derided.

   All people who have been persecuted and derided are great men.
   Illicit conversion. Conversion is not legitimate for A propositions.

4. No state that is not well armed is a state with good laws.

   All states that are well armed are states with good laws.
   Does not follow. To identify the problem here, one needs to lay out a series of steps necessary to get from the first proposition to the second; e.g., take the obverse, then the contrapositive. It is then necessary to take the converse of an A proposition, an illicit step.

H.

Legitimate
A. All S are P.
Obverse: No S is non-P.
Converse: No non-P is S.
Obverse: All non-P are non-S.

O. Some S are not P.
Obverse: Some S are non-P.
Converse: Some non-P are S.
Obverse: Some non-P are not non-S.

Not legitimate
E. No S are P.
Obverse: All S are non-P.
Converse: All non-P are S [invalid step].
Obverse: No non-P is non-S.

I. Some S are P.
Obverse: Some S are not non-P.
Converse: Some non-P are not S [invalid step].
Obverse: Some non-P are non-S.

CHAPTER 7
EXERCISE 7.1
A.

1. All *M* are *P*
   <u>Some *S* are *M*</u>
   Some *S* are *P*

4. No *M* is *P*
   <u>All *S* are *M*</u>
   No *S* is *P*

7. Some *P* are *M*
   <u>Some *M* are not *S*</u>
   Some *S* are not *P*

10. All *P* are *M*
    <u>No *S* is *M*</u>
    Some *S* are not *P*

B.

1. All ambitious people are people who can learn logic.
   <u>All people reading this book are ambitious people.</u>
   All people who are reading this book are people who can learn logic.
   AAA-1

4. No *Twilight* book is a work of great literature.
   <u>All *Twilight* books are about vampires.</u>
   Some books about vampires are not works of great literature.
   EAO-3

7. No mineral is an organic substance.
<u>Some minerals are essential nutrients.</u>
Some essential nutrients are not organic substances.
EIO-3

10. Some good poems are works that are difficult to interpret.
<u>All good poems are things worth reading.</u>
Some things worth reading are works that are difficult to interpret.
IAI-3

EXERCISE 7.2

1. Valid

4. Invalid

7. Invalid

10. Invalid

EXERCISE 7.3

1. All food that generates stomach acid is bad for an ulcer patient.
<u>All fried foods generate stomach acid.</u>
(All fried foods are bad for an ulcer patient.)
AAA-1

4. No one who trades stocks on the basis of proprietary information is an honest businessman.
<u>(Some investment bankers trade stocks on the basis of proprietary information.)</u>
Some investment bankers are not honest businessmen.
EIO-1

OR

No one who trades stocks on the basis of proprietary information is an honest businessman.
<u>(Some people who trade stocks on the basis of proprietary information are investment bankers.)</u>
Some investment bankers are not honest businessmen.
EIO-3

7. No moral movie is a violent film.
<u>(Some violent films are entertaining movies.)</u>
Some entertaining movies are not moral movies.
EIO-4

OR

No moral movie is a violent film.
<u>(Some entertaining movies are violent films.)</u>
Some entertaining movies are not moral movies.
EIO-2

10. (No democracy is an unstable nation.)
<u>Some self-determined nations are unstable nations.</u>
Some self-determined nations are not democracies.
EIO-2

OR

(No unstable nation is a democracy.)
<u>Some self-determined nations are unstable nations.</u>
Some self-determined nations are not democracies.
EIO-1

EXERCISE 7.4A

1. All (machines—D) are (manufactured objects—U).

4. Some (trees—U) are (deciduous plants—U).

7. Some (cars—U) are (lemons—U).

10. No (person with manners—D) is (a person who would clean his teeth at the dinner table—D).

EXERCISE 7.4B

A.

1. Valid

4. Valid

7. Invalid: illicit major term. Also invalid on the modern view of existential import: Universal premises, particular conclusion.

10. Invalid: undistributed middle term

B.

1. All people with things to hide are people who plead the Fifth.
<u>Tom is a person who plead the Fifth.</u>
Tom is a person with something to hide.
AAA-2
Invalid: undistributed middle term

4. No paperback book is expensive.
<u>Some paperback books are well made.</u>
Some well-made things are not expensive.
EIO-3
Valid

7. Some countries that can afford AIDS medication are capitalist.
<u>No developing nation is a country that can afford AIDS medication.</u>
Some developing nations are not capitalist.
IEO-1
Invalid: illicit major term

10. Some inspired ideas are not reasonable.
<u>All the proposals before this committee are reasonable.</u>
Some of the proposals before this committee are not things that are inspired.
IAO-2
Invalid: illicit major term

13. Some countries that can participate in the global market
are countries that flout drug patent laws.
All countries that can participate in the global market are
countries that can get the imports they need.
Some countries that get the imports they need are coun-
tries that flout drug patent laws.
IAI-3
Valid

EXERCISE 7.4C

1. (All plants are things that need water.)
All trees are plants.
All trees are things that need water.

4. All things containing coliform bacteria are things that
are unsafe to drink.

(Some water is a thing that contains coliform bacteria.)
Some water is a thing that is unsafe to drink.

OR

All things containing coliform bacteria are things that
are unsafe to drink.
(Some things that contain coliform bacteria are water.)
Some water is a thing that is unsafe to drink.

7. No creature whose actions are wholly determined by
heredity and environment is a moral agent.
(All animals other than man are things whose actions are
wholly determined by heredity and environment.)
No animal other than man is a moral agent.

EXERCISE 7.5A

1.

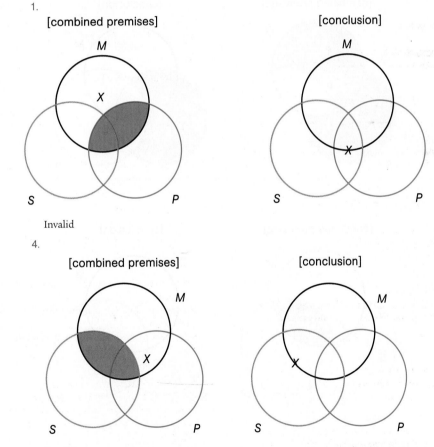

Invalid

4.

Invalid

7.

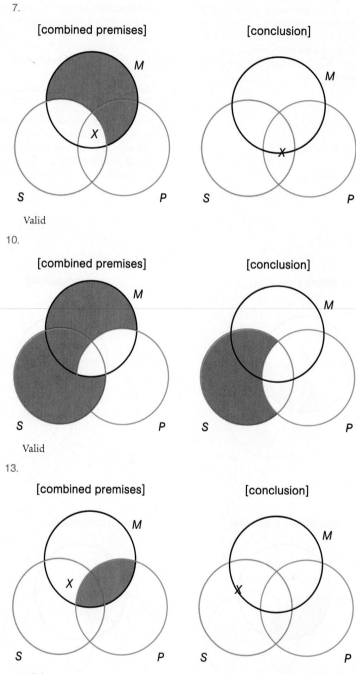

[combined premises]

[conclusion]

Valid

10.

[combined premises]

[conclusion]

Valid

13.

[combined premises]

[conclusion]

Valid

EXERCISE 7.5B

1. All *M* are *P*

4. All *M* are *P*

7. No *P* is *M* or No *M* is *P*

10. Some *S* are *M* or Some *M* are *S*

EXERCISE 7.5C

1. Modern—invalid. Traditional—valid.

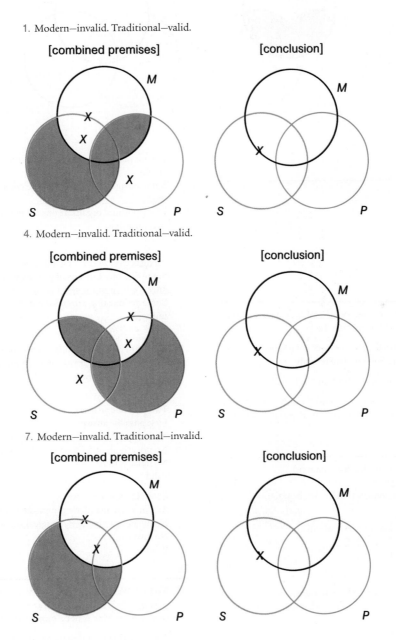

4. Modern—invalid. Traditional—valid.

7. Modern—invalid. Traditional—invalid.

10. Modern—invalid. Traditional—invalid.

[combined premises]   [conclusion]

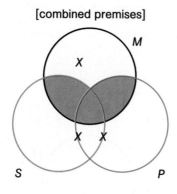

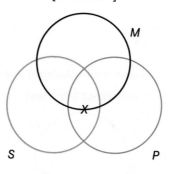

Additional Exercises
A.

1. Valid

4. Invalid

7. Valid

10. Invalid

13. Valid

B.

1. Some children are people who broke the dishes. Subject—Undistributed (U). Predicate—U.

4. Some of the president's nominees are not people who were confirmed. Subject—U. Predicate—D.

7. No question is a stupid thing. Subject—D. Predicate—D.

10. All terms in the subject position of a universal categorical proposition are distributed terms. Subject—D. Predicate—U.

C.

1. (All fish are animals that live in water.)
   All walleyes are fish.
   All walleyes are animals that live in the water.
   Valid

4. No friend of mine is a friend of Bill's.
   Mary is not a friend of Bill's.
   Mary is a friend of mine.
   Invalid

7. All countries that ignore human rights are tyrannies.
   Some democracies are countries that ignore human rights.
   Some democracies are tyrannies.
   Valid

10. No nonprofit organization is an enterprise that sells stock.
    Some hospital organizations are enterprises that sell stock.
    Some hospital organizations are not nonprofit organizations.
    Valid

13. All dishonest means of gaining wealth are immoral.
    Some dishonest means of gaining wealth are actions that are expedient in the short term.
    Some actions that are expedient in the short term are immoral.
    Valid

16. Some international conflicts arise from just motives.
    No aggressive war arises from just motives.
    Some aggressive wars are not international conflicts.
    Invalid

19. Two possible answers.
    First possible answer:
    All music is an orderly progression of sounds.
    No noise is an orderly progression of sounds.
    No noise is music.
    Valid

    Second possible answer:
    All noise is a disorderly progression of sound.
    No music is a disorderly progression of sounds.
    No music is noise.
    Valid

D.

1. No Civil War picture is a movie that made a nickel.
   Gone with the Wind is a Civil War picture.
   Gone with the Wind is not a movie that made a nickel.

4. Anything that is undeservedly forgotten is a good topic for a doctoral thesis.

Some books are undeservedly forgotten.
Some books are good topics for doctoral theses.

AND

All books that are remembered deserve to be remembered.
McGuffey's Readers are books that are remembered.
McGuffey's Readers deserve to be remembered.

E.

1. All *M* are *P*
   All *S* are *M*
   All *S* are *P*

4. No *M* is *P*
   All *S* are *M*
   No *S* is *P*

F.

1. Standard form: Some bonds are things that yield tax-free interest.

   Subject—bonds. Predicate—things that yield tax-free interest.

   Example syllogism:
   All municipal bonds yield tax-free interest.
   Some bonds are municipal bonds.
   Some bonds yield tax-free interest.

4. Standard form: Some blue-collar workers are highly paid people.

   Subject—blue-collar workers. Predicate—highly paid people.

   Example syllogism:
   All highly skilled people are highly paid.
   Some blue-collar workers are highly skilled.
   Some blue-collar workers are highly paid.

7. Standard form: Some relationships are things that last a lifetime.

   Subject—relationships. Predicate—relationships that last a lifetime.

   Example syllogism:
   All biologically based relationships are lifelong.
   Some relationships are biologically based.
   Some relationships are lifelong.

G.

1. All price controls are harmful things.
   All minimum wage regulations are price controls.
   All minimum wage regulations are harmful things.
   AAA-1.
   Valid.

4. (All people who answer every question put to them are tremendously ignorant people.)
   That man is a person who answers every question put to him.
   That man is a tremendously ignorant person.
   AAA-1.
   Valid.

7. (No one who rejoices at the expense of other men is a person who can expect to thrive in the world of men.)
   All who rejoice loudly of their victories are people who rejoice at the expense of other men.
   No one who rejoices loudly of his victories is a person who can expect to thrive in the world of men.
   EAE-1.
   Valid.

10. (All people who do not revert to normalcy after a violent episode are insane.)
    Some individuals who suffer organic abnormalities or psychoses that produce rage attacks do not revert to normalcy after a violent episode.
    Some individuals who suffer organic abnormalities or psychoses that produce rage attacks are insane.
    AII-1.
    Valid.

13. All animals are mobile.
    All observers are animals.
    All observers are mobile.
    AAA-1.
    Valid.

I.

1. The middle term in this figure is in the predicate of both premises. It will not be distributed, therefore, unless one premise is negative, in which case the conclusion must be negative.

4. If both premises are particular, then:
   In the first, second, and fourth figures, the only way for the middle term to be distributed is for a premise to be negative, which means the conclusion must be negative, which means that the major term is distributed. But it cannot be distributed in the major premise because
   In the first figure, that premise would have to be negative, but it must be positive.
   In the second and fourth figures, that premise would need to be universal.
   In the third figure, where the middle term is the subject of both premises, it cannot be distributed if both premises are particular.

CHAPTER 8
EXERCISE 8.1

1. [I'm hearing things] or [someone is out in the hall singing "Jingle Bells".]

I'm not hearing things.
Someone is out in the hall singing "Jingle Bells."
Valid; denying a disjunct

4. [We send in the troops] or [we negotiate].
We will not negotiate.
We will send in the troops.
Valid; denying a disjunct

7. [Marriage is sacrosanct] or [gays can get married].
Gays can get married.
Marriage is not sacrosanct.
Invalid; affirming a disjunct

10. [Paul wins the case] or [he is not promoted to partner].
Paul is not promoted to partner.
Paul lost the case.
Invalid; affirming a disjunct

13. [Kids cannot have access to guns] or [kids cannot play violent videogames].
Kids cannot have access to guns.
Kids can play violent videogames.
Invalid; affirming a disjunct

16. [I work hard] or [I fail this course].
I am working hard.
I will not fail this course.
Invalid; affirming a disjunct

EXERCISE 8.2A

1. Antecedent: you miss your first serve in tennis. Consequent: you get a second try. Already in standard form.

4. Antecedent: A married couple filing a joint return itemize their deductions. Consequent: They may deduct certain child-care expenses. Standard form: If a married couple filing a joint return itemize their deductions, they may deduct certain child-care expenses.

7. Antecedent: Antibodies do not exist in the patient. Consequent: Doctors cannot detect a virus. Standard form: If antibodies do not exist in the patient, then doctors cannot detect a virus.

10. Antecedent: A car does not have a cooling mechanism. Consequent: The car's engine will rapidly overheat. Standard form: If a car does not have a cooling mechanism, then its engine will rapidly overheat.

13. Antecedent: We do not have an understanding of deductive validity. Consequent: We will probably commit fallacies in our reasoning. Standard form: If we do not have an understanding of deductive validity, then we will probably commit fallacies in our reasoning.

16. Two possible standard forms:
    i. If I go out with you tonight, then you have promised not to wear your Nehru jacket. Antecedent: I go out with you tonight. Consequent: You have promised not to wear your Nehru jacket.

ii. If you do not promise not to wear your Nehru jacket, then I won't go out with you tonight. Antecedent: You don't promise not to wear your Nehru jacket. Consequent: I won't go out with you tonight.

19. Antecedent: The product is not safe. Consequent: People will not buy it. Standard form: If the product is not safe, then people will not buy it.

EXERCISE 8.2B

1. If [he had mentioned her name], then [I would have hit him].
He did not mention her name.
I did not hit him.
Invalid; denying the antecedent

4. If [I take the new job], then [I'll have a longer commute].
If [I have a longer commute], then [I will need a new car].
If [I take the new job], then [I will need a new car].
Valid; pure hypothetical syllogism

7. If [you leave the milk out of the refrigerator], then [it sours].
The milk soured.
You left the milk out of the refrigerator.
Invalid; affirming the consequent

10. If [salmon reliably return from the ocean to the streams in which they were spawned], then [they must have some means of detecting subtle differences in the chemical composition of the water of those streams at the point where they flow into the ocean.]
Salmon reliably return from the ocean to the streams in which they were spawned.
(Salmon have some means of detecting subtle differences in the chemical composition of the water of those streams at the point where they flow into the ocean.
Valid; affirming the antecedent (*modus ponens*)

13. If [Mercury's period of rotation equals its period of revolution], then [it always presents the same side to the Sun].
If [Mercury always presents the same side to the Sun] then [we can only see one side of it].
If [Mercury's period of rotation equals its period of revolution], then [we can only see one side of it].
Valid; pure hypothetical syllogism

16. If [the plan to build grocery stores in low-income areas is successful], then [deaths from heart disease will decrease].
Deaths from heart disease have decreased.
The plan to build grocery stores in low-income areas was successful.
Invalid; affirming the consequent

19. If [the lights are still working], then [the battery is not dead].

The lights are still working.
The battery is not dead.
Valid; affirming the antecedent (*modus ponens*)

OR

If [the battery were dead], then [the lights would not still
be working].
The lights are still working.
The battery is not dead.
Valid; denying the consequent (*modus tollens*)

22. If [we do not adopt this proposal], then [the company
will go bankrupt].
(The company will not go bankrupt.)
We will adopt this proposal.
Valid; denying the consequent (*modus tollens*)

25. If [the errors and distortions in television news were not
the result of political bias], then [they would be randomly
distributed across the political spectrum].
They are not distributed across the political spectrum.
The errors and distortions in television news are the
result of political bias.
Valid; denying the consequent (*modus tollens*)

EXERCISE 8.3

1. All computers that can run Microsoft Windows 7 are
computers with at least 1 gigabyte of memory.
My computer is not a computer with at least 1 gigabyte
of memory.
My computer is not a computer that can run Microsoft
Windows 7.
Valid

4. If a mechanism of natural selection did not exist, then
new species of organisms would not arise.
New species of organisms do arise.
There is a mechanism of natural selection.
Valid; denying the consequent

7. All people who can strike a log with an ax in just the right
place are people with a good eye.
All people who can strike a log with an ax in just the right
place are people who can split it with one blow.
All people who can split logs in a single blow are people
with a good eye.
Invalid; illicit minor

10. If [I am willing to take statistics], then [it is offered in the
morning].
It is not offered in the morning.
I am not willing to take it.
Valid; denying the consequent (*modus tollens*)

13. If [a new factory emits a given quantity of pollutants into
the air], then [the new factory purchased the right to
emit that quantity from some other factory].
If [the new factory purchased the right to emit that quantity from some other factory], then [the other factory is
willing to reduce its emissions by the same amount].

If [a new factory emits a given level of pollutants into the
air], then [another factory was willing to reduce its emissions by the same amount].
Valid; pure hypothetical syllogism

EXERCISE 8.4A–D

1. *a*. All criminals who leave fingerprints all over the place
are sloppy.
1. The killer left fingerprints all over the place.
b. The killer is sloppy.

2. If the killer were a professional, he would not have
been sloppy.
b. The killer was sloppy.
3. The killer was not a professional.
Valid

4. 1. All metals that can oxidize at normal temperatures
will rust.
a. No metal containing chromium is a metal that oxidizes
at normal temperatures.
b. No metal containing chromium is a metal that rusts.

b. No metal containing chromium is a metal that rusts.
2. Some steel is metal containing chromium.
3. Some steel is not metal that rusts.
Invalid; first step is illicit major

EXERCISE 8.4E

1. If a person's temperature is above 100°F, he is either sick
or has been recently engaged in some strenuous activity.
Roy is a person whose temperature is above 100°F.
Roy is sick or has been recently engaged in some strenu-
ous activity.
Roy is not sick.
Roy has recently been engaged in some strenuous
activity.
Valid

4. If the direction of time depends on the expansion of the
universe, then if the expansion stops and the universe
contracts, time will reverse direction.
(The direction of time depends on the expansion of the
universe.)
If the expansion stops and the universe contracts, then
time will reverse direction.
The expansion will stop and the universe will contract.
(Time will reverse direction.)
Valid

Additional Exercises
A.

1. Invalid

4. Valid

7. Invalid

10. Invalid

C.

1. If the Moral Law was one of our instincts, then we ought to be able to point to a particular impulse that is always good.
   We cannot point to a particular impulse that is always good.
   The Moral Law is not one of our instincts.
   Valid; *modus tollens*

4. If imitation is an important factor in language development, then it would be easy to find evidence of its importance.
   It is not easy to find evidence of the importance of imitation.
   Imitation is not an important factor in language development.
   Valid; *modus tollens*

7. If we cannot be sure of the independent existence of objects, then we cannot be sure of the independent existence of people's bodies.
   If we cannot be sure of the independent existence of people's bodies, then we cannot be sure of the independent existence of other people's minds.
   If we cannot be sure of the independent existence of objects, then we cannot be sure of the independent existence of other people's minds.
   Valid; pure hypothetical syllogism

E.

1. All occasions on which one feels pride are occasions followed by destruction.

4. All vigorous minds are curious minds.

7. If one does not know what happened before one was born, then one remains a child.

10. All occasions on which the people give up their liberties are occasions on which they are acting under some delusion.

G.

1. (If the gun had been fired from a distance of less than four yards, then there would have been powder blackening on the clothes.)
   There was not powder-blackening on the clothes.
   The gun was fired from a distance of over four yards.
   Valid; *modus tollens*

4. (Either the whole race of mankind is united into one society, or it divides into many societies.)
   The whole race cannot unite into one society.
   The whole race divides into many societies.
   Valid

7. (All opinions about things that do not interest one are absolutely valueless opinions.)

All unbiased opinions are opinions about things that do not interest one.
All unbiased opinions are absolutely valueless opinions.
Valid

10. All things necessary for one who commands are things pertaining to war.
   All things that a prince studies should be things necessary for one who commands.
   All things that a prince studies should be things pertaining to war.
   Valid

13. All clowns are people who stand before a crowd and gesture wildly to get their attention.
   All politicians are people who stand before a crowd and gesture wildly to get their attention.
   (All politicians are clowns.)
   Invalid; undistributed middle

I.

1. If appellant's conduct is a nuisance, then it is unreasonably noisy.
   If appellant's conduct is unreasonably noisy, then it produces noise out of keeping with the character of the neighborhood.
   If appellant's conduct is a nuisance, then it produces noise out of keeping with the character of the neighborhood.
   Appellant's conduct does not produce noise out of keeping with the character of the neighborhood.
   Appellant's conduct is not a nuisance.
   Valid

4. If thou never wast at court, then thou never saw'st good manners.
   If thou never saw'st good manners, then thy manners are wicked.
   If thou never wast at court, then thy manners are wicked.
   If thy manners are wicked, then thou art sinful.
   If thou never wast at court, then thou art sinful.
   If thou art sinful, then thou art damned.
   If thou never wast at court, then thou art damned.
   Then never wast at court.
   Thou art damned.
   Valid

7. Some of you are my personal enemies.
   None of you is dead.
   Some of my personal enemies are not dead.
   (All people I considered enemies of the state are dead.)
   Some of my personal enemies are not dead.
   Some of my personal enemies are not people I considered enemies of the state.
   Valid

10. All things that are mixed with one's labor are mixed with a thing that one owns.
   All things that are altered from their natural state through one's labor are things mixed with one's labor.

All things that are altered from their natural state through one's labor are mixed with a thing one owns.

All things that are mixed with a thing that one owns are things that one owns.
All things that are altered from their natural state through one's labor are things mixed with a thing one owns.
<u>   </u>
All things that are altered from their natural state through one's labor are things one owns.
Valid

CHAPTER 9
EXERCISE 9.1A

1. R: Roses are red; V: Violets are blue; conjunction; R • V

4. R: I can pay the rent; G: I can buy groceries; disjunction; R ∨ G

7. W: Jerry will win the race; S: Jerry will take second place; disjunction; W ∨ S

10. C: The Cucumber County seed-spitting contest is a world-class event; negation; ~C

13. B: The guest of honor wore brown; M: The guest of honor fell in the mud on the way to the party; disjunction; B ∨ M

EXERCISE 9.1B

1. S: These shoes go on sale; B: I'll buy two pairs; conditional; S ⊃ B

4. I: I will scratch your back; Y: You will scratch my back; biconditional; I ≡ Y

7. I: I am ready; Y: You are ready; conditional; Y ⊃ I

10. W: We will launch the new Web site next month; S: The shopping cart function passes the security test; biconditional; W ≡ S

13. L: The litmus paper in the beaker will turn red; A: The liquid is acidic; biconditional; L ≡ A

16. P: The plant will die; W: You water the plant; conditional; ~W ⊃ P or ~P ⊃ W

19. S: I'll go swimming; W: I can wear my water wings; conditional; S ⊃ W

EXERCISE 9.1C

1. H: Holly will take your call; D: Dexter will take your call; disjunction; H ∨ D

4. W: Winning is the important thing; negation; ~W

7. E: You can't hide your lying eyes; S: Your smile is a thin disguise; conjunction; E • S

10. B: The beach was beautiful; W: The water was shark-infested; conjunction; B • W

13. A: Art is long; L: Life is short; conjunction; A • L

16. L: Morley won the lottery; Q: Morley is being unusually quiet; conditional; L ⊃ Q

19. A: I'll ask his advice; S: I consider him to be a worthy sage; biconditional; A ≡ S

22. X: The doctors X-rayed my head; F: The doctors found something; conjunction; X • ~F

25. C: I will definitely come to your party; B: Something better comes along; conditional; ~B ⊃ C

EXERCISE 9.2
A.

1. (H • R) ≡ T

4. ■(B ⊃ C)

7. [(C • W) ⊃ I] ■ Q

10. ■{[(J ⊃ K) ≡ (R ∨ B)] ⊃ (R • K)}

B.

1. D ⊃ A

4. (M • C) ⊃ S

7. B ⊃ (C ∨ M)

10. ~S • P

13. (B • E) ∨ (H • D)

16. (P ∨ B) • ~S

19. ~G ⊃ (R ∨ ~C)

22. (Y ⊃ I) • (F ⊃ T)

25. (G • E) ⊃ (T ⊃ A)

28. (O ⊃ W) • (~M ⊃ ~W)

31. ~(R ∨ P) ⊃ (V ⊃ J) or ~(V ⊃ J) ⊃ (R ∨ P)

34. W ≡ [(C ⊃ F) • (H ⊃ B)]

EXERCISE 9.3
1.

A	∨	(B	∨	A)
T	T	T	T	T
T	T	F	T	T
F	T	T	T	F
F	F	F	F	F

Disjunction

4.

G	•	~	G
T	F	F	T
F	F	T	F

Conjunction

7.

(M	∨	N)	≡	O)
T	T	T	T	T
T	T	T	F	F
T	T	F	T	T
T	T	F	F	F
F	T	T	T	T
F	T	T	F	F
F	F	F	F	T
F	F	F	T	F

Biconditional

10.

[(U	⊃	V)	•	(~	V	∨	W)]	≡	(U	⊃	W)
T	T	T	T	F	T	T	T	T	T	T	T
T	T	T	F	F	T	F	F	T	T	F	F
T	F	F	F	T	F	T	T	F	T	T	T
T	F	F	F	T	F	T	F	T	T	F	F
F	T	T	T	F	T	T	T	T	F	T	T
F	T	T	F	F	T	F	F	F	F	T	F
F	T	F	T	T	F	T	T	T	F	T	T
F	T	F	T	T	F	T	F	T	F	T	F

Biconditional

13.

~	[K	∨	(L	⊃	~	M)]
F	T	T	T	F	F	T
F	T	T	T	T	T	F
F	T	T	F	T	F	T
F	T	T	F	T	T	F
T	F	F	T	F	F	T
F	F	T	T	T	T	F
F	F	T	F	T	F	T
F	F	T	F	T	T	F

Negation

EXERCISE 9.4A

1.

(A	•	B)	∨	A
T	T	T	T	T
T	F	F	T	T
F	F	T	F	F
F	F	F	F	F

Contingency

4.

~	A	⊃	(B	⊃	~	A)
F	T	**T**	T	F	F	T
F	T	**T**	F	T	F	T
T	F	**T**	T	T	T	F
T	F	**T**	F	T	T	F

Tautology

10.

(~	A	∨	B)	∨	(~	B	•	A)
F	T	T	T	**T**	F	T	F	T
F	T	F	F	**T**	T	F	T	T
T	F	T	T	**T**	F	T	F	F
T	F	T	F	**T**	T	F	F	F

Tautology

7.

(A	⊃	B)	•	(A	•	~	B)
T	T	T	**F**	T	F	F	T
T	F	F	**F**	T	T	T	F
F	T	T	**F**	F	F	F	T
F	T	F	**F**	F	F	T	F

Self-contradiction

13.

[(A	⊃	B)	•	(B	⊃	C)]	≡	(A	⊃	C)
T	T	T	T	T	T	T	**T**	T	T	T
T	T	T	F	T	F	F	**T**	T	F	F
T	F	F	F	F	T	T	**F**	T	T	T
T	F	F	F	F	T	F	**T**	T	F	F
F	T	T	T	T	T	T	**T**	F	T	T
F	T	T	F	T	F	F	**F**	F	T	F
F	T	F	T	F	T	T	**T**	F	T	T
F	T	F	T	F	T	F	**T**	F	T	F

Contingency

EXERCISE 9.4B

1.

~	(A	•	B)	~	A	∨	~	B
F	T	T	T	F	T	F	F	T
T	T	F	F	F	T	T	T	F
T	F	F	T	T	F	T	F	T
T	F	F	F	T	F	T	T	F

Equivalent

4.

~	(A	∨	B)	~	(~	A	•	~	B
F	T	T	T	T	F	T	F	F	T
F	T	T	F	T	F	T	F	T	F
F	F	T	T	T	T	F	F	F	T
T	F	F	F	F	T	F	T	T	F

Contradictory

7.

C	⊃	D		C	∨	~	D
T	T	T		T	T	F	T
T	F	F		T	T	T	F
F	T	T		F	F	F	T
F	T	F		F	T	T	F

Consistent

10.

Y	⊃	(Z	•	W)		~	(Z	•	W)	⊃	~	Y
T	T	T	T	T		F	T	T	T	T	F	T
T	F	T	F	F		T	T	F	F	F	F	T
T	F	F	F	T		T	F	F	T	F	F	T
T	F	F	F	F		T	F	F	F	F	F	T
F	T	T	T	T		F	T	T	T	T	T	F
F	T	T	F	F		T	T	F	F	T	T	F
F	T	F	F	T		T	F	F	T	T	T	F
F	T	F	F	F		T	F	F	F	T	T	F

Equivalent

13.

E	•	(F	∨	G)		(E	•	F)	∨	(E	•	G)
T	T	T	T	T		T	T	T	T	T	T	T
T	T	T	T	F		T	T	T	T	T	F	F
T	T	F	T	T		T	F	F	T	T	T	T
T	F	F	F	F		T	F	F	F	T	F	F
F	F	T	T	T		F	F	T	F	F	F	T
F	F	T	T	F		F	F	T	F	F	F	F
F	F	F	T	T		F	F	F	F	F	F	T
F	F	F	F	F		F	F	F	F	F	F	F

Equivalent

16.

(J	⊃	K)	•	(K	⊃	J)		(J	•	K)	∨	(~	J	•	~	K)
T	T	T	T	T	T	T		T	T	T	T	F	T	F	F	T
T	F	F	F	F	T	T		T	F	F	F	F	T	F	T	F
F	T	T	F	T	F	F		F	F	T	F	T	F	F	F	T
F	T	F	T	F	T	F		F	F	F	T	T	F	T	T	F

Equivalent

19.

(A	⊃	B)	∨	(C	•	A)		~	(A	⊃	B)	•	~	(C	•	A)
T	T	T	T	T	T	T		F	T	T	T	F	F	T	T	T
T	T	T	T	F	F	T		F	T	T	T	F	T	F	F	T
T	F	F	T	T	T	T		T	T	F	F	F	F	T	T	T
T	F	F	F	F	F	T		T	T	F	F	T	T	F	F	T
F	T	T	T	T	F	F		F	F	T	T	F	T	T	F	F
F	T	T	T	F	F	F		F	F	T	T	F	T	F	F	F
F	T	F	T	T	F	F		F	F	T	F	F	T	T	F	F
F	T	F	T	F	F	F		F	F	T	F	F	T	F	F	F

Contradictory

22.

(A	•	B)	⊃	C		B	•	~	C		A	≡	C
T	T	T	T	T		T	F	F	T		T	T	T
T	T	T	F	F		T	T	T	F		T	F	F
T	F	F	T	T		F	F	F	T		T	T	T
T	F	F	T	F		F	F	T	F		T	F	F
F	F	T	T	T		T	F	F	T		F	F	T
F	F	T	T	F		T	T	T	F		F	T	F
F	F	F	T	T		F	F	F	T		F	F	T
F	F	F	T	F		F	F	T	F		F	T	F

Consistent

Additional Exercises

A.

1. $q \supset p$

4. $p \cdot (q \vee r)$

7. $\sim(p \vee q)$

10. $(p \vee q) \equiv r$

13. $(p \supset q) \equiv (r \supset s)$

B.

Answers provided are examples only.

1. Either Jill is not home or I dialed the wrong number.

4. Jack fell down and either broke his crown or bruised it.

7. If Jack is at work, then either he is out of his office or he is not answering his phone.

10. Jack is at the store or he is at work, and Jill is out running or she is out riding a bicycle.

13. If the price of eggs remains constant, then it is not the case that demand has increased and supply has fallen.

C.

1. $\sim(P \supset W) \supset A$ or $\sim A \supset (P \supset W)$

4. $\{(M \supset \sim F) \cdot [\sim M \supset (F \cdot P)]\} \cdot [(M \vee \sim M) \supset (A \cdot D)]$

D.

1.

~	A	•	B
F	T	F	T
F	T	F	F
T	F	T	T
T	F	F	F

Conjunction

4.

(C	V	D)	•	~	E
T	T	T	F	F	T
T	T	T	T	T	F
T	T	F	F	F	T
T	T	F	T	T	F
F	T	T	F	F	T
F	T	T	T	T	F
F	F	F	F	F	T
F	F	F	T	T	F

Conjunction

7.

(M	•	N)	⊃	O
T	T	T	T	T
T	T	T	F	F
T	F	F	T	T
T	F	F	T	F
F	F	T	T	T
F	F	T	T	F
F	F	F	T	T
F	F	F	T	F

Conditional

10.

(V	V	W)	•	~	(V	•	W)
T	T	T	F	F	T	T	T
T	T	F	T	T	T	F	F
F	T	T	T	T	F	F	T
F	F	F	F	T	F	F	F

CHAPTER 10
EXERCISE 10.1

1.

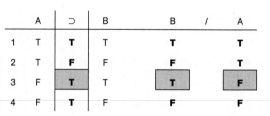

	A	⊃	B		B	/	A
1	T	**T**	T		**T**		**T**
2	T	**F**	F		**F**		**T**
3	F	**T**	T		**T**		**F**
4	F	**T**	F		**F**		**F**

Invalid

4.

F	≡	G		F	V	G	/	F	•	G
T	T	T		T	T	T		T	T	T
T	F	F		T	T	F		T	F	F
F	F	T		F	T	T		F	F	T
F	T	F		F	F	F		F	F	F

Valid

7.

G	⊃	H	/	G	⊃	(G	•	H)
T	T	T		T	T	T	T	T
T	F	F		T	F	T	F	F
F	T	T		F	T	F	F	T
F	T	F		F	T	F	F	F

Valid

10.

~	(M	∨	N)	/	~	N
F	T	T	T		F	T
F	T	T	F		T	F
F	F	T	T		F	T
T	F	F	F		T	F

Valid

13.

S	⊃	(T	•	V)		~	V	/	~	S
T	T	T	T	T		T	T		F	T
T	F	T	F	F		T	F		F	T
T	F	F	F	T		F	T		F	T
T	F	F	F	F		T	F		F	T
F	T	T	T	T		F	T		T	F
F	T	T	F	F		T	F		T	F
F	T	F	F	T		F	T		T	F
F	T	F	F	F		T	F		T	F

Valid

EXERCISE 10.2

1.

A	•	B		C	∨	B	/	~	C
T	T	T		T	T	T		F	T

Invalid. To make the conclusion false, C must be true. So it is true in the second premise, too. By making A and B true as well, both premises can be true. If the premises can be true while the conclusion is false, the argument is invalid.

4.

J	⊃	K		K	⊃	L		~	L	/	~	J
T		F		F	T	F		T	F		F	T

Valid

7.

W	⊃	Y		(W	⊃	Z)	∨	(Y	⊃	Z)		~	Z	/	~	(W	•	Y
T	T	T		T	T	T	T	T	T	T			T		F	T	T	T

Valid

10.

(A	•	C)	∨	(B	⊃	C)		~	C	∨	B	/	~	B	∨	C
	F	F		T	F	F		T	F	T	T		F	T	F	F

Valid

13.

(E	⊃	F)	∨	[E	⊃	(G	•	H)]		H	⊃	(F	∨	G)	/	E	⊃	H
T	T	T	**T**	T	F		F	F		F	**T**	T	T			T	**F**	F

Invalid

16.

~	[(A	∨	~	(B	∨	~	C)]		D	⊃	(A	⊃	C)	/	~	A	≡	~	(B
T	F	F	F	T	T				T	F	T				T	F	**F**	F	T

Invalid

19.

N	∨	O		P	∨	Q		~	Q	∨	N		P	⊃	(N	∨	R)	/	O
T	**T**	F			**T**				T		T			**T**	T	T			**F**

Invalid

EXERCISE 10.3A

A.

1. DS

4. HS

7. MP

10. MT

13. MT

16. HS

19. MP

B.

1.

4. ~A	1,3 MT
5. C	2,4 MP

4.

4. ~E	1,2 MT
5. C	3,4 MP

7.

4. ~A	1,2 MP
5. D	4,3 DS

10.

4. A ⊃ D	1,2 DS
5. B ⊃ D	3,4 HS
6. ~B	1,5 MT

OR

4. A ⊃ D	1,2 DS
5. ~A	1,4 MT
6. ~B	3,5 MT

13.

4. I ⊃ H	1,3 HS
5. ~I	2,4 MT

OR

4. ~G	1,2 MT
5. ~I	3,4 MT

16.

6. ~(A ∨ B)	2,5 MT
7. B ⊃ C	1,6 DS
8. B ⊃ ~D	3,7 HS
9. G ⊃ ~D	4,8 HS

OR

6. ~(A ∨ B)	2,5 MT
7. B ⊃ C	1,6 DS
8. G ⊃ C	4,7 HS
9. G ⊃ ~D	3,8 HS

EXERCISE 10.3B

A.

1. Simp

4. Conj

7. DD

10. CD

13. CD

16. Conj

19. Add

B.

1.

1. A / (A ∨ B) ∨ C	Premise / Conclusion
2. A ∨ B	1 Add
3. (A ∨ B) ∨ C	2 Add

4.

1. A	Premise
2. (A ⊃ B) • (C ⊃ D) / B ∨ D	Premise / Conclusion
3. A ∨ C	1 Add
4. B ∨ D	2,3 CD

7.

1. (A ⊃ C) • (B ⊃ D)	Premise
2. ~C / ~A ∨ ~B	Premise / Conclusion
3. ~C ∨ ~D	2 Add
4. ~A ∨ ~B	1,3 DD

10.

1. (D ⊃ E)	Premise
2. (F ⊃ G)	Premise
3. D ∨ F / E ∨ G	Premise / Conclusion
4. (D ⊃ E) • (F ⊃ G)	1,2 Conj
5. E ∨ G	3,4 CD

13.

1. B • C	Premise
2. ~A • D / ~A • B	Premise / Conclusion
3. ~A	2 Simp
4. B	1 Simp
5. ~A • B	3,4 Conj

16.

1. A ⊃ D	Premise
2. B ⊃ C	Premise
3. B ∨ A / C ∨ D	Premise / Conclusion
4. (B ⊃ C) • (A ⊃ D)	1,2 Conj
5. C ∨ D	3,4 CD

19.

1. (A ⊃ C) • (B ⊃ D)	Premise
2. ~C ∨ ~D	Premise
3. [(~A ∨ ~B) ⊃ E] • (~E ⊃ F) / E ∨ F	Premise / Conclusion
4. ~A ∨ ~B	1,2 DD
5. (~A ∨ ~B) ∨ ~E	4 Add
6. E ∨ F	3,5 CD

22.

1. (D ∨ A) ⊃ ~C	Premise
2. (D • B) ⊃ A	Premise
3. D • ~B / ~C ∨ A	Premise / Conclusion
4. [(D ∨ A) ⊃ ~C] • [(D • B) ⊃ A]	1,2 Conj
5. D	3 Simp
6. D ∨ A	5 Add
7. (D ∨ A) ∨ (D • B)	6 Add
8. ~C ∨ A	4,7 CD

EXERCISE 10.3C

A.

1. 1,3 MT
   2,4 MP

4. 3 Simp
   2 Simp
   4,5 Conj
   1,6 MP

B.

1.

1. A	Premise
2. A ⊃ ~B	Premise
3. B ∨ C / C	Premise / Conclusion
4. ~B	1,2 MP
5. C	3,4 DS

4.

1. D ⊃ E	Premise
2. D ∨ A	Premise
3. ~E / A	Premise / Conclusion
4. ~D	1,3 MT
5. A	2,4 DS

7.

1. (A ∨ B) ⊃ C	Premise
2. E ⊃ (A ∨ B)	Premise
3. C ⊃ D / E ⊃ D	Premise / Conclusion
4. E ⊃ C	1,2 HS
5. E ⊃ D	3,4 HS

10.

1. A ⊃ B	Premise
2. C ⊃ D	Premise
3. ~B / ~A ∨ C	Premise / Conclusion
4. ~A	1,3 MT
5. ~A ∨ ~C	4 Add

13.

1. B ⊃ C	Premise
2. B ∨ (A • E)	Premise
3. ~C / A • E	Premise / Conclusion
4. ~B	1,3 MT
5. A • E	2,4 DS

16.

1. ~(A ⊃ B)	Premise
2. (A ⊃ B) ∨ C	Premise
3. G ⊃ (A ⊃ B)/ ~G • C	Premise / Conclusion
4. ~G	1,3 MT
5. C	2,1 DS
6. ~G • C	4,5 Conj

19.

1. E ⊃ B	Premise
2. B ⊃ C	Premise
3. A ⊃ E	Premise
4. C ⊃ G / A ⊃ G	Premise / Conclusion
5. A ⊃ B	1,3 HS
6. A ⊃ C	2,5 HS
7. A ⊃ G	4,6 HS

22.

1. ~C	Premise
2. B ⊃ C	Premise
3. B ∨ C	Premise
4. A ⊃ E / E	Premise / Conclusion
5. ~B	1,2 MT
6. A	3,5 DS
7. E	4,6 MP

25.

1. (A ≡ B) ⊃ (E ∨ C)	Premise
2. (B ⊃ D) ⊃ (A ≡ B)	Premise
3. (E ∨ C) ⊃ ~G	Premise
4. ~G ⊃ A / (B ⊃ D) ⊃ A	Premise / Conclusion
5. (E ∨ C) ⊃ A	3,4 HS
6. (A ≡ B) ⊃ A	1,5 HS
7. (B ⊃ D) ⊃ A	6,2 HS

28.

1. E ⊃ A	Premise
2. B ⊃ E	Premise
3. A ⊃ ~C	Premise
4. B / ~C	Premise / Conclusion
5. B ⊃ A	1,2 HS
6. B ⊃ ~C	3,5 HS
7. ~C	4,6 MP

31.

1. A ∨ B	Premise
2. C ⊃ D	Premise
3. ~A • ~D / B • ~C	Premise / Conclusion
4. ~A	3 Simp
5. B	1,4 DS
6. ~D	3 Simp
7. ~C	2,6 MT
8. B • ~C	5,7 Conj

34.

1. (B • A) ⊃ (C • D)	Premise
2. E ≡ F	Premise
3. (~C ⊃ ~G) ⊃ [F ⊃ (D ⊃ H)]	Premise
4. [F ⊃ (D ⊃ H)] ⊃ [(E ≡ F) ⊃ (B • A)]	Premise
5. ~C ⊃ ~G / C • D	Premise / Conclusion
6. (~C ⊃ ~G) ⊃ [(E ≡ F) ⊃ (B • A)]	3,4 HS
7. (E ≡ F) ⊃ (B • A)	5,6 MP
8. B • A	2,7 MP
9. C • D	1,8 MP

37.

1. D ⊃ B	Premise
2. C ⊃ A	Premise
3. E ⊃ D	Premise
4. B ⊃ C	Premise
5. E ∨ B / (B ∨ A) • (D ∨ C)	Premise / Conclusion
6. (E ⊃ D) • (B ⊃ C)	3,4 Conj
7. D ∨ C	5,6 CD
8. (D ⊃ B) • (C ⊃ A)	1,2 Conj
9. B ∨ A	7,8 CD
10. (B ∨ A) • (D ∨ C)	7,9 Conj

40.

1. (A ∨ D) ⊃ [(B ⊃ G) • (C ⊃ E)]	Premise
2. A ⊃ ~D	Premise
3. A • ~G	Premise
4. ~C ⊃ D	Premise
5. B ∨ E / E	Premise / Conclusion
6. A	3 Simp
7. A ∨ D	6 Add
8. (B ⊃ G) • (C ⊃ E)	1,7 MP
9. B ⊃ G	8 Simp
10. ~G	3 Simp
11. ~B	9,10 MT
12. E	5,11 DS

EXERCISE 10.4A

A.

1. B • B or B ∨ B

4. ~(E ∨ N)

7. (A • K) ∨ (A • M)

10. ~(A ≡ B) ∨ ~O

B.

1. Commutation

4. Double negation

7. Commutation

10. Distribution

13. De Morgan's law

16. Commutation

19. Tautology

C.

1.

1. (A • A) ∨ ~~B / A ∨ B	Premise / Conclusion
2. A ∨ ~~B	1 Taut
3. A ∨ B	2 DN

4.

1. ~(D ∨ E) / ~D	Premise / Conclusion
2. ~D • ~E	1 DM
3. ~D	2 Simp

7.

1. A • (B ∨ C)	Premise
2. ~(A • B) / A • C	Premise / Conclusion
3. (A • B) ∨ (A • C)	1 Dist
4. A • C	2,3 DS

10.

1. C ∨ ~D / ~(~C • D)	Premise / Conclusion
2. ~~C ∨ ~D	1 DN
3. ~(~C • D)	2 DM

13.

1. (B ∨ C) ∨ D	Premise
2. ~B / C ∨ D	Premise / Conclusion
3. B ∨ (C ∨ D)	1 Assoc
4. C ∨ D	2,3 DS

16.

1. A • G	Premise
2. ~G ∨ B / B ∨ F	Premise / Conclusion
3. G	1 Simp
4. ~~G	3 DN
5. B	2,4 DS
6. B ∨ F	Add

19.

1. E ∨ F	Premise
2. ~G ∨ H	Premise
3. ~(E ∨ H) / F • ~G	Premise / Conclusion
4. ~E • ~H	3 DM
5. ~E	4 Simp
6. F	1,5 DS
7. ~H	4 Simp
8. ~G	2,7 DS
9. F • ~G	5,8 Conj

EXERCISE 10.4B

A.

1. ~B ⊃ ~A

4. ~(F • ~~G)
   or
   ~F ∨ ~G

7. [F ⊃ (G ≡ H)] • [(G ≡ H) ⊃ F]
   or
   [F • (G ≡ H)] ∨ [~F • ~(G ≡ H)]

10. ~~(F ⊃ H) ∨ (M ∨ ~N)
    or
    ~[~~(F ⊃ H) • ~(M ∨ ~N)]

B.

1. Implication

4. Biconditional

7. Implication

10. Implication

13. Implication

C.

1.

1. C ≡ D / (C ⊃ D) • (~C ⊃ ~D)	Premise / Conclusion
2. (C ⊃ D) • (D ⊃ C)	1 Bicon
3. (C ⊃ D) • (~C ~D)	2 Contra

4.

1. ~A ∨ (B ⊃ C) / (A • B) ⊃ C	Premise / Conclusion
2. A ⊃ (B ⊃ C)	1 Imp
3. (A • B) ⊃ C	2 Exp

7.

1. A • G	Premise
2. ~G ∨ B / B ∨ F	Premise / Conclusion
3. G	1 Simp
4. ~~G	3 DN
5. B	2,3 DS
6. B ∨ F	5 Add

10.

1. (F ⊃ G) • (H ⊃ J)	Premise
2. ~F ⊃ H / G ∨ J	Premise / Conclusion
3. ~~F ∨ H	2 Imp
4. F ∨ H	3 DN
5. G ∨ J	1,4 CD

13.

1. ~ (H • J)	Premise
2. ~J ⊃ K / H ⊃ K	Premise / Conclusion
3. ~(H • ~~J)	1 DN
4. H ⊃ ~J	3 Imp
5. H ⊃ K	2,4 HS

16.

1. [A • B) ⊃ C)] • (E ⊃ C)	Premise
2. (A • B) ∨ (E • A) / C	Premise / Conclusion
3. [(A • B) ∨ E] • [(A • B) ∨ A]	2 Dist
4. (A • B) ∨ E	3 Simp
5. C ∨ C	1,4 CD
6. C	5 Taut

19.

1. A ⊃ (H ∨ J)	Premise
2. J ≡ H	Premise
3. ~J / ~A	Premise / Conclusion
4. (J ⊃ H) • (H ⊃ J)	2 Bicon
5. H ⊃ J	4 Simp
6. ~H	3,5 MT
7. ~H • ~J	3,6 Conj
8. ~(H ∨ J)	7 DM
9. ~A	8,1 MT

22.

1. (J ⊃ K) ⊃ (J ⊃ L)	Premise
2. J • ~L / ~K	Premise / Conclusion
3. (J ⊃ K) ⊃ ~(J • ~L)	1 Imp
4. ~~(J • ~L)	2 DN
5. ~(J ⊃ K)	3,4 MT
6. ~(~J ∨ K)	5 Imp
7. ~~J • ~K	6 DM
8. ~K	7 Simp

25.

1. (E ∨ F) ⊃ G	Premise
2. H ⊃ E	Premise
3. ~H ⊃ F / G	Premise / Conclusion
4. ~F ⊃ ~~H	3 Contra
5. ~F ⊃ H	4 DN
6. ~F ⊃ E	2,5 HS
7 ~~F ∨ E	6 Imp
8. F ∨ E	DN
9. E ∨ F	Com
10. G	1,9 MP

28.

1. (L • C) ⊃ ~E	Premise
2. ~(C • L) ⊃ G	Premise
3. ~F ⊃ ~G / E ⊃ F	Premise / Conclusion
4. ~~G ⊃ ~~F	3 Contra
5. G ⊃ ~~F	4 DN
6. G ⊃ F	5 DN
7. ~~E ⊃ ~(L • C)	1 Contra
8. E ⊃ ~(L • C)	7 DN
9. E ⊃ ~(C • L)	8 Com
10. E ⊃ G	2,9 HS
11. E ⊃ F	6,10 HS

EXERCISE 10.5A

1.

1. H ⊃ (I • G) / H ⊃ I	Premise / Conclusion
2. H	Assumption
3. I • G	1,2 MP
4. I	3 Simp
5. H ⊃ I	2–4 CP

4.

1. D ⊃ (E ⊃ F)	Premise
2. D ⊃ (F ⊃ G) / D ⊃ (E ⊃ G)	Premise / Conclusion
3. D	Assumption
4. E ⊃ F	1,3 MP
5. F ⊃ G	2,3 MP
6. E ⊃ G	4,5 HS
7. D ⊃ (E ⊃ G)	3—6 CP

7.

1. A ⊃ B	Premise
2. (B • A) ⊃ D	Premise
3. [(B • A) • D] ⊃ E / A ⊃ E	Premise / Conclusion
4. A	Assumption
5. B	1,4 MP
6. B • A	4,5 Conj
7. D	2,6 MP
8. (B • A) • D	6,7 Conj
9. E	3,8 MP
10. A ⊃ E	4—9 CP

10.

1. ~A ∨ [~B ∨ (C • D)] / (A • B) ⊃ C	Premise / Conclusion
2. A • B	Assumption
3. A	2 Simp
4. ~~A	3 DN
5. ~B ∨ (C • D)	1,4 DS
6. B	2 Simp
7. ~~B	6 DN
8. C • D	5,7 DS
9. C	8 Simp
10. (A • B) ⊃ C	2—9 CP

13.

1. (F • G) ∨ (H • ~I)	Premise
2. I ⊃ ~(F • E) / I ⊃ ~E	Premise / Conclusion
3. I	Assumption
4. ~(F • E)	2,3 MP
5. ~F ∨ ~E	4 DM
6. I ∨ ~H	3 Add
7. ~H ∨ I	6 Com
8. ~H ∨ ~~I	7 DN
9. ~(H • ~I)	8 DM
10. F • G	1,9 DS
11. F	10 Simp
12. ~~F	11 DN
13. ~E	5,12 DS
14. I ⊃ ~E	3—13 CP

16.

1. (A ⊃ B) ⊃ ~C / ~(C • B)	Premise / Conclusion
2. C	Assumption
3. ~~C	2 DN
4. ~(A ⊃ B)	1,3 MT
5. ~(~A ∨ B)	4 Imp
6. ~~A • ~B	5 DM
7. ~B	6 Simp
8. C ⊃ ~B	2—7 CP
9. ~C ∨ ~B	8 Imp
10. ~(C • B)	9 DM

EXERCISE 10.5B

1.

1. A ∨ B	Premise
2. B ⊃ (C • ~C) / A	Premise / Conclusion
3. ~A	Assumption
4. B	1,3 DS
5. C • ~C	2,4 MP
6. A	3—5 RA

4.

1. (N ⊃ O) ⊃ P	Premise
2. (N • ~O) ⊃ P / P	Premise / Conclusion
3. ~P	Assumption
4. ~(N ⊃ O)	1,3 MT
5. ~~(N • ~O)	4 Imp
6. ~(N • ~O)	2,3 MT
7. ~~(N • ~O) • ~(N • ~O)	5,6 Conj
8. P	3–7 RA

7.

1. (A ⊃ B) ⊃ ~C / ~(C • B)	Premise / Conclusion
2. C • B	Assumption
3. C	2 Simp
4. ~~C	3 DN
5. ~(A ⊃ B)	1,4 MT
6. ~~(A • ~B)	5 Imp
7. A • ~B	6 DN
8. ~B	7 Simp
9. B	2 Simp
10. B • ~B	8,9 Conj
11. ~(C • B)	2–10 RA

10.

1. F • (G ⊃ H)	Premise
2. ~I ⊃ (F ∨ H)	Premise
3. F ⊃ G / I ∨ H	Premise / Conclusion
4. ~(I ∨ H)	Assumption
5. ~I • ~H	4 DM
6. F	1 Simp
7. G	3,6 MP
8. G ⊃ H	1 Simp
9. ~H	5 Simp
10. ~G	8,9 MT
11. G • ~G	7,10 Conj
12. I ∨ H	4–11 RA

Additional Exercises
A.

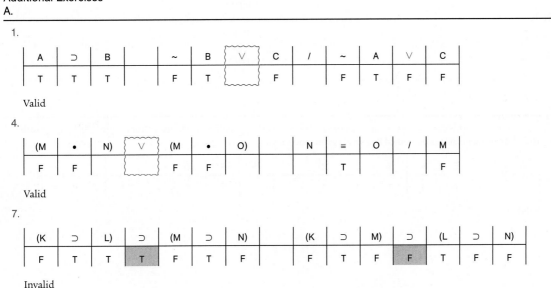

1.

A	⊃	B		~	B	∨	C	/	~	A	∨	C
T	T	T		F	T		F		F	T	F	F

Valid

4.

(M	•	N)	∨	(M	•	O)		N	≡	O	/	M
F	F			F	F				T			F

Valid

7.

(K	⊃	L)	⊃	(M	⊃	N)		(K	⊃	M)	⊃	(L	⊃	N)
F	T	T	T	F	T	F		F	T	F	F	T	F	F

Invalid

10.

E	⊃	(F	•	G)		H	⊃	(I	∨	J)		F	⊃	(~	I	•	~	J)	/	~	(E	•	H)
T	T	T	T	T		T	F	F	F	F		T	T	T	F	T	T	F		F	T	T	T

Valid

13.

[A	∨	(B	•	C)]	⊃	D		~	(D	•	E)		A	⊃	E	/	B	•	C
F	F	F	F		**T**	F		**T**	F	F	T		F	**T**	T		F		**F**

OR

[A	∨	(B	•	C)]	⊃	D		~	(D	•	E)		A	⊃	E	/	B	•	C
F	F		F	F	**T**	T		**T**	T	F	F		F	**T**	F			**F**	F

Invalid

B.

1. Simp
4. Conj
7. MP
10. Conj
13. HS

C.

1. DN
4. Imp
7. Taut
10. Exp
13. Com

D.

1. 1 Imp
   3 Com
   4 Assoc
   2,5 DS
   6 DN
   7 DM

4. 3 Simp
   2,4 MT
   5 Imp
   6 DN
   7 Simp
   8 DN
   1,9 MT
   10 DM
   3 Simp
   12 DN
   11,13 DS

E.

1. S—the earth's crust is divided into separate tectonic plates; E—earthquakes occur; M—the plates are moving; L—it's possible that the continents were once joined in a single giant land mass.

S		E	•	(E	⊃	M)		(S	•	M)	⊃	L	/	L
T		T	T	T	T	T		T	T	T	F	F		F

Valid

1. S	Premise
2. E • (E ⊃ M)	Premise
3. (S • M) ⊃ L / L	Premise / Conclusion
4. E	2 Simp
5. E ⊃ M	2 Simp
6. M	4,5 MP
7. S • M	1,6 Conj
8. L	3,7 MP

4. B—Smith is guilty of burglary; T—Smith took the goods from the Jones's residence; C—Jones consented.

B	≡	(T	•	~	C)		(T	•	C)	/	~	B
T		T	F	F	T		T	T	T		F	T

Valid

1. B ≡ (T • ~C)	Premise
2. T • C / ~B	Premise
3. [B ⊃ (T • ~C)] • [(T • ~C) ⊃ B]	1 Bicon
4. B ⊃ (T • ~C)	3 Simp
5. C	2 Simp
6. ~T ∨ C	5 Add
7. ~T ∨ ~~C	6 DN
8. ~(T • ~C)	7 DM
9. ~B	4,8 MT

7. D—human choices are determined; F—human choices are free; A—we can act differently than we do; M—we are morally responsible for our actions.

D	∨	F		D	⊃	~	A		~	A	⊃	~	M		M	/	F
F		F		F	T	F	T		F	T	T	F	T		T		F

Valid

1. D ∨ F	Premise
2. D ⊃ ~A	Premise
3. ~A ⊃ ~M	Premise
4. M / F	Premise / Conclusion
5. D ⊃ ~M	2,3 HS
6. ~~M	4 DN
7. ~D	5,6 MT
8. F	1,7 DS

10. G—Giscan is guilty of the murder of Alice Lovelace; M—Giscan had a motive; W—Giscan possessed a murder weapon; A—Giscan was with Sally Alibi; E—Lovelace ended her relationship with Giscan; T—Alibi is telling the truth; J—Alibi is jealous.

G	≡	[M	•	(W	•	~	A)]		E		A	⊃	T		J	⊃	~	T
F	T	T	F	T	F	F	T		T		T	T	T		F	T	F	T

	E	⊃	(M	•	J)		W	/	G
	T	T	T	F	F		T		F

Valid

1. G ≡ [M • (W • ~A)]	Premise
2. E	Premise
3. A ⊃ T	Premise
4. J ⊃ ~T	Premise
5. E ⊃ (M • J)	Premise
6. W / G	Premise / Conclusion
7. M • J	2,5 MP
8. J	7 Simp
9. ~T	4,8 MP
10. ~A	3,9 MT
11. W • ~A	6,10 Conj
12. M	7 Simp
13. M • (W • ~A)	11,12 Conj
14. {G ⊃ [M • (W • ~A)]} • {[M • (W • ~A)] ⊃ G}	1 Bicon
15. [M • (W • ~A)] ⊃ G	14 Simp
16. G	13,15 MP

13. B—a book repeats what is in the Bible; R—you read the book; W—you waste your time; C—a book contradicts the Bible; S—you commit a sin.

B	∨	C		B	⊃	(R	⊃	W)		C	⊃	(R	⊃	S)		~	(W	∨	S)	/	~	R
F	F	F		F	T	T	F	F		F	T	T	F	F		T	F	F	F		F	T

Valid

1. B ∨ C	Premise
2. B ⊃ (R ⊃ W)	Premise
3. C ⊃ (R ⊃ S)	Premise
4. ~(W ∨ S) / ~R	Premise / Conclusion
5. [B ⊃ (R ⊃ W)] • [C ⊃ (R ⊃ S)]	2,3 Conj
6. (R ⊃ W) ∨ (R ⊃ S)	1,5 CD
7. (~R ∨ W) ∨ (R ⊃ S)	6 Imp

8. (~R ∨ W) ∨ (~R ∨ S)	7 Imp
9. [(~R ∨ W) ∨ ~R] ∨ S	8 Assoc
10. [~R ∨ (W ∨ ~R)] ∨ S	9 Assoc
11. [~R ∨ (~R ∨ W)] ∨ S	10 Com
12. [(~R ∨ ~R) ∨ W] ∨ S	11 Assoc
13. (~R ∨ W) ∨ S	12 Taut
14. ~R ∨ (W ∨ S)	13 Assoc
15. ~R	4,14 DS

F.

1.

1. ~C / C ⊃ D	Premise / Conclusion
2. ~C ∨ D	1 Add
3. C ⊃ D	2 Imp

4.

1. B ⊃ D / B ⊃ (B ⊃ D)	Premise / Conclusion
2. (B • B) ⊃ D	1 Taut
3. B ⊃ (B ⊃ D)	2 Exp

7.

1. A ⊃ ~F / F ⊃ ~A	Premise / Conclusion
2. ~~F ⊃ ~A	1 Contra
3. F ⊃ ~A	2 DN

10.

1. (A ⊃ C) • (B ⊃ C)	Premise
2. A ∨ B / C	Premise / Conclusion
3. C ∨ C	1,2 CD
4. C	3 Taut

13.

1. E ⊃ (F ⊃ G) / F ⊃ (E ⊃ G)	Premise / Conclusion
2. (E • F) ⊃ G	1 Exp
3. (F • E) ⊃ G	2 Com
4. F ⊃ (E ⊃ G)	3 Exp

16.

1. ~C ∨ ~D	Premise
2. C / ~D	Premise / Conclusion
3. ~~C	2 DN
4. ~D	1,3 DS

19.

1. [~D ≡ E) • (B ≡ C)] ∨ (G ⊃ A)	Premise
2. ~[~D ≡ E) • (B ≡ C)]	Premise
3. G / A	Premise / Conclusion
4. G ⊃ A	1,2 DS
5. A	3,4 MP

22.

1. W ⊃ X	Premise
2. ~Y ⊃ ~X / W ⊃ Y	Premise / Conclusion
3. ~X ⊃ ~W	1 Contra
4. ~Y ⊃ ~W	2,3 HS
5. W ⊃ Y	4 Contra

25.

1. A ⊃ B	Premise
2. (C ⊃ D) • (E ≡ G)	Premise
3. A ∨ C / B ∨ D	Premise / Conclusion
4. C ⊃ D	2 Simp
5. (A ⊃ B) • (C ⊃ D)	1,4 Conj
6. B ∨ D	3,5 CD

28.

1. A ⊃ (B • C)	Premise
2. ~(A ⊃ D) / B	Premise / Conclusion
3. ~~(A • ~D)	2 Imp
4. A • ~D	3 DN
5. A	4 Simp
6. B • C	1,5 MP
7. B	6 Simp

31.

1. (H • I) ⊃ J	Premise
2. (I ⊃ J) ⊃ (K ∨ L) / ~L ⊃ (H ⊃ K)	Premise / Conclusion
3. H ⊃ (I ⊃ J)	1 Exp
4. H ⊃ (K ∨ L)	2,3 HS
5. ~H ∨ (L ∨ K)	4 Imp
6. (L ∨ K) ∨ ~H	5 Com
7. L ∨ (K ∨ ~H)	6 Assoc
8. L ∨ (~H ∨ K)	7 Com
9. L ∨ (H ⊃ K)	8 Imp
10. ~~L ∨ (H ⊃ K)	9 DN
11. ~L ⊃ (H ∨ K)	10 Imp

34.

1. (~E • F) ⊃ G	Premise
2. (H • J) ⊃ (E ∨ J)	Premise
3. ~E • (F ∨ ~J) / H ⊃ (J ⊃ G)	Premise / Conclusion
4. (~E • F) ∨ (~E • ~J)	3 Dist
5. (~E • F) ∨ ~(E ∨ J)	4 DM
6. ~G ⊃ ~(~E • F)	1 Contra
7. [~G ⊃ ~(~E • F)] • [(H • J) ⊃ (E ∨ J)]	2, 6 Conj
8. ~~(~E • F) ∨ ~(E ∨ J)	5 DN
9. ~~G ∨ ~(H • J)	7,8 DD
10. G ∨ ~(H • J)	9 DN
11. ~(H • J) ∨ G	10 Com
12. (H • J) ⊃ G	11 Imp
13. H ⊃ (J ⊃ G)	12 Exp

37.

1. [K ⊃ (L ⊃ K)] ⊃ (~M ⊃ M) / M	Premise / Conclusion
2. [K ⊃ (L ⊃ K)] ⊃ (~~M ∨ M)	1 Imp
3. [K ⊃ (L ⊃ K)] ⊃ (M ∨ M)	2 DN
4. [K ⊃ (L ⊃ K)] ⊃ M	3 Taut
5. ~M	Assumption
6. ~[K ⊃ (L ⊃ K)]	4,5 MT
7. ~~[K • ~(L ⊃ K)]	6 Imp
8. K • ~(L ⊃ K)	7 DN
9. K	8 Simp
10. ~(L ⊃ K)	8 Simp
11. ~~(L • ~K)	10 Imp
12. L • ~K	11 DN
13. ~K	12 Simp
14. K • ~K	9,13 Conj
15. M	5–14 RA

40.

1. [(A • B) ∨ C] ⊃ [D ⊃ (E • F)]	Premise
2. B • ~(A ⊃ E) / D ⊃ F	Premise / Conclusion
3. ~(A ⊃ E)	2 Simp
4. ~~(A • ~E)	3 Imp
5. A • ~E	4 DN
6. A	5 Simp
7. B	2 Simp
8. A • B	6,7 Conj
9. (A • B) ∨ C	8 Add
10. D ⊃ (E • F)	1,9 MP
11. ~E	5 Simp
12. ~E ∨ ~F	11 Add
13. ~(E • F)	12 DM
14. ~D	10,13 MT
15. ~D ∨ F	14 Add
16. D ⊃ F	15 Imp

43.

1. (A ∨ B) ⊃ [~(C • D) ⊃ E]	Premise
2. B • C	Premise
3. E ⊃ (F ∨ G)	Premise
4. (B ⊃ ~F) • (C ⊃ ~G) / D	Premise / Conclusion
5. B	2 Simp
6. A ∨ B	5 Add
7. ~(C • D) ⊃ E	1,6 MP
8. B ⊃ ~F	4 Simp
9. ~F	5,8 MP
10. C ⊃ ~G	4 Simp
11. C	2 Simp
12. ~G	10,11 MP
13. ~F • ~G	9,12 Conj
14. ~(F ∨ G)	13 DM
15. ~E	3,14 MT
16. ~~(C • D)	7,15 MT
17. C • D	16 DN
18. D	17 Simp

46.

1. H ⊃ {I • [(J • K) ⊃ (L • M)]}	Premise
2. K ⊃ ~(I • L) / J ⊃ ~(H • K)	Premise / Conclusion
3. J	Assumption
4. H • K	Assumption
5. H	4 Simp
6. I • [(J • K) ⊃ (L • M)]	1,5 MP
7. (J • K) ⊃ (L • M)]	6 Simp
8. K	4 Simp
9. J • K	3,8 Conj
10. L • M	7,9 MP
11. I	6 Simp
12. L	10 Simp
13. I • L	11,12 Conj
14. ~~(I • L)	13 DN
15. ~K	2,14 MT
16. K • ~K	8,15 Conj
17. ~(H • K)	4–16 RA
18. J ⊃ ~(H • K)	3–17 CP

CHAPTER 11

EXERCISE 11.1A

1. Bt
4. Fl
7. ~Sr • Sn
10. Cj ∨ Tj
13. Lw • ~Mw
16. Tm • Cm
19. (Ls ∨ Ei) ⊃ Ro
22. (Cs ⊃ Di) • (~Cs ⊃ Ti)
25. [(Bb ∨ Gb) ⊃ Jb

EXERCISE 11.1B

1. $(x)Lx$
4. $(x)Gx$
7. $(\exists x)Cx$
10. $(x)Ax$
13. $(x)Rx$

EXERCISE 11.2

1. $(x)(Sx \supset Bx)$
4. $(\exists x)(Kx • Ax)$
7. $(\exists x)(Kx • Sx)$
10. $[(\exists x)(Px • Hx)]$
13. $[(\exists x)(Rx • Sx)]$
16. $[(x)(Cx \supset Sx)]$
19. $[(x)(Cx \supset {\sim}Fx)]$

EXERCISE 11.3

1. $(\exists x)(Bx • Cx)$
4. $(\exists x)(Dx • Vx)$
7. $(\exists x)(Lx • {\sim}Ex)$
10. ${\sim}(\exists x)(Bx • Rx)$
13. $(\exists x){\sim}Ex$ OR ${\sim}(x)Ex$
16. $(\exists x)[Px • (Wx \vee Rx)]$
    OR
    $(\exists x)(Px • Wx) \vee (\exists x)(Px • Rx)$
19. ${\sim}(\exists x)Gx$ OR $(x){\sim}Gx$
22. $(x)[Tx \supset (Ex \vee Dx)]$
25. $(x)[Cx \supset (Mx \vee Lx)]$
28. $(x)\{[(Sx \vee Ex) \vee Qx] \supset Wx\}$
31. $(\exists x)(Tx • Lx) \supset (y)[(Ty • By) \supset Wy]$

34. $(x)[(Px \bullet Cx) \supset \sim(Mx \lor Ex)]$

    OR

    $\sim(\exists x)[(Px \bullet Cx) \bullet (Mx \lor Ex)]$

EXERCISE 11.4A

1.

1. $(x)Hx \supset \sim(\exists y)My$	Premise
2. $(\exists y)My$ / $\sim(x)(Hx)$	Premise / Conclusion
3. $\sim\sim(\exists y)My$	2 DN
4. $\sim(x)Hx$	1,3 MT

4.

1. $[\sim(x)(Bx) \lor (x)Cx] \supset \sim(x)Dx$	Premise
2. $\sim(x)Bx$ / $\sim(x)Dx$	Premise / Conclusion
3. $\sim(x)Bx \lor (x)Cx$	2 Add
4. $\sim(x)Dx$	1,3 MP

7.

1. $Cl \equiv Dt$ / $(Cl \supset Dt) \bullet (\sim Cl \supset \sim Dt)$	Premise / Conclusion
2. $(Cl \supset Dt) \bullet (Dt \supset Cl)$	1 Bicon
3. $Dt \supset Cl$	2 Simp
4. $\sim Cl \supset \sim Dt$	3 Contra
5. $(Cl \supset Dt)$	2 Simp
6. $(Cl \supset Dt) \bullet (\sim Cl \supset \sim Dt)$	4,5 Conj

10.

1. $\sim Ga \lor Ha$	Premise
2. $Fa \supset Ha$	Premise
3. $Ga \lor Fa$ / Ha	Premise / Conclusion
4. $Ga \supset Ha$	1 Imp
5. $(Ga \supset Ha) \bullet (Fa \supset Ha)$	2,4 Conj
6. $Ha \lor Ha$	3,5 CD
7. Ha	6 Taut

EXERCISE 11.4B
A.

1. Equivalent

4. Equivalent

7. Not equivalent

B.

1.

1. $\sim(\exists x)(Sx \bullet Rx) \supset Pa$	Premise
2. $(x)(Sx \supset \sim Rx)$ / Pa	Premise / Conclusion
3. $(x)(\sim Sx \lor \sim Rx)$	2 Imp
4. $(x)\sim(Sx \bullet Rx)$	3 DM
5. $\sim(\exists x)(Sx \bullet Rx)$	4 QN
6. Pa	1,5 MP

4.

1. $(x)Hx \supset \sim(\exists y)My$	Premise
2. $(\exists y)My$ / $(\exists x)\sim Hx$	Premise / Conclusion
3. $\sim\sim(\exists y)My$	2 DN
4. $\sim(x)Hx$	1,3 MT
5. $(\exists x)\sim Hx$	QN 4

7.

1. $[(x)Cx \bullet (x)Dx] \lor \sim[(\exists x)\sim Cx \supset (x)Dx]$ / $(x)Cx \equiv (x)Dx$	Premise / Conclusion
2. $[(x)Cx \bullet (x)Dx] \lor \sim[\sim(x)Cx \supset (x)Dx]$	1 QN
3. $[(x)Cx \bullet (x)Dx] \lor \sim[\sim\sim(x)Cx \lor (x)Dx]$	2 Imp
4. $[(x)Cx \bullet (x)Dx] \lor \sim[(x)Cx \lor (x)Dx]$	3 DN
5. $[(x)Cx \bullet (x)Dx] \lor [\sim(x)Cx \bullet \sim(x)Dx]$	4 DM
6. $(x)Cx \equiv (x)Dx$	5 Bicon

EXERCISE 11.4C
A.

1. EI. Valid.

4. EG. Valid.

7. UG. Invalid (second conjunct outside scope of (x)).

10. EG. Invalid.

B.

1.

1. $(x)Gx$ / $Ga \bullet Gb$	Premise / Conclusion
2. Ga	1 UI
3. Gb	1 UI
4. $Ga \bullet Gb$	2,3 Conj

4.

1. ~Ca	Premise
2. (x)(~Bx ⊃ Cx) / Ba	Premise / Conclusion
3. ~Ba ⊃ Ca	2 UI
4. ~~Ba	1,3 MT
5. Ba	4 DN

7.

1. (x)(Hx ⊃ Mx)	Premise / Conclusion
2. Hs / Hs • Ms	Premise / Conclusion
3. Hs ⊃ Ms	1 UI
4. Ms	2,3 MP
5. Hs • Ms	2,4 Conj

10.

1. (∃x) Bx • (x)(Cx ⊃ Dx)	Premise
2. ~Da	Premise / Conclusion
3. (x)(Cx ⊃ Dx)	1 Simp
4. Ca ⊃ Da	3 UI
5. ~Ca	2,4 MT

13.

1. (x)Fx	Premise
2. (∃y)Fy ⊃ (x)Gx / Ga	Premise / Conclusion
3. Fa	1 UI
4. (∃y)Fy	3 EG
5. (x)Gx	MP 2,4
6. Ga	5 UI

16.

1. (x)Sx	Premise
2. (∃y)Sy ⊃ (y)Wy / Wa	Premise / Conclusion
3. Sa	1 UI
4. (∃y)Sy	3 EG
5. (y)Wy	2,4 MP
6. Wa	5 UI

19.

1. (x)(Lx ⊃ Mx)	Premise
2. (y)(Mx ⊃ Nx) / (x) (Lx ⊃ Nx)	Premise / Conclusion
3. La ⊃ Ma	1 UI
4. Ma ⊃ Na	2 UI
5. La ⊃ Na	3,4 HS
6. (x)(Lx ⊃ Nx)	5 UG

EXERCISE 11.4D

1.

1. (x)(Bx ⊃ ~Cx)	Premise
2. Ba	Premise
3. (x)(Cx ∨ Dx) / Da	Premise / Conclusion
4. Ba ⊃ ~Ca	1 UI
5. ~Ca	2,4 MP
6. Ca ∨ Da	3 UI
7. Da	5,6 DS

4.

1. (x)(Ax ⊃ Bx)	Premise
2. (x) (Cx ⊃ ~Bx) / (x)(Cx ⊃ ~Ax)	Premise / Conclusion
3. Aa ⊃ Ba	1 UI
4. Ca ⊃ ~Ba	2 UI
5. ~Ba ⊃ ~Aa	3 Contra
6. Ca ⊃ ~Aa	4,5 HS
7. (x)(Cx ⊃ ~Ax)	6 UG

7.

1. (x)~(~Fx ⊃ Gx) / ~(x)Gx	Premise / Conclusion
2. (x)~(~~Fx ∨ Gx)	1 Imp
3. (x)~(Fx ∨ Gx)	2 DN
4. (x)(~Fx • ~Gx)	3 DM
5. ~Fa • ~Ga	4 UI
6. ~Ga	5 Simp
7. (∃x)~Gx	6 EG
8. ~(x)Gx	7 QN

10.

1. $(\exists x)Gx \supset (x)\sim Bx$	Premise
2. $Ga \; / \; (\exists x)\sim(Bx \bullet Ax)$	Premise / Conclusion
3. $(\exists x)Gx$	2 EG
4. $(x)\sim Bx$	1,3 MP
5. $\sim Bb$	4 UI
6. $\sim Bb \lor Ab$	5 Add
7. $\sim(Bb \bullet Ab)$	6 DM
8. $(\exists x)\sim(Bx \bullet Ax)$	7 EG

13.

1. $(x)(Ax \equiv Bx)$	Premise
2. $(x)(Bx \equiv Cx) \; / \; Ag \supset Cg$	Premise / Conclusion
3. $Ag \equiv Bg$	1 UI
4. $Bg \equiv Cg$	2 UI
5. $(Ag \supset Bg) \bullet (Bg \supset Ag)$	3 Bicon
6. $(Bg \supset Cg) \bullet (Cg \supset Bg)$	4 Bicon
7. $Ag \supset Bg$	5 Simp
8. $Bg \supset Cg$	6 Simp
9. $Ag \supset Cg$	7,8 HS

16.

1. Fa	Premise
2. $\sim(\exists x)(Fx \bullet Gx) \; / \; (\exists x)(Fx \bullet \sim Gx)$	Premise / Conclusion
3. $(x)\sim(Fx \bullet Gx)$	2 QN
4. $\sim(Fa \bullet Ga)$	3 UI
5. $\sim Fa \lor \sim Ga$	4 DM
6. $\sim\sim Fa$	1 DN
7. $\sim Ga$	5,6 DS
8. $Fa \bullet \sim Ga$	1,7 Conj
9. $(\exists x)(Fx \bullet \sim Gx)$	8 EG

19.

1. $Ta \supset (y)Gy$	Premise
2. $Ia \lor Ta$	Premise
3. $\sim Ia$	Premise
4. $(x)(Gx \supset Hx) \; / \; (x)Hx$	Premise / Conclusion
5. Ta	2,3 DS
6. $(y)Gy$	1,5 MP
7. Gb	6 UI
8. $Gb \supset Hb$	4 UI
9. Hb	7,8 MP
10. $(x)Hx$	9 UG

22.

1. $(x)(Bx \bullet Ax)$	Premise
2. $(y)(Cy \supset \sim By) \; / \; (\exists x)(Ax \bullet \sim Cx)$	Premise / Conclusion
3. $Ba \bullet Aa$	1 UI
4. $Ca \supset \sim Ba$	2 UI
5. Ba	3 Simp
6. $\sim\sim Ba$	5 DN
7. $\sim Ca$	4,6 MT
8. Aa	3 Simp
9. $Aa \bullet \sim Ca$	8,7 Conj
10. $(\exists x)(Ax \bullet \sim Cx)$	9 EG

25.

1. $Ta \supset (y)Gy$	Premise
2. $Ia \lor Ta$	Premise
3. $\sim Ia$	Premise
4. $(x)(Gx \supset Hx) \; / \; (x)Hx$	Premise / Conclusion
5. Ta	2,3 DS
6. $(y)Gy$	1,5 MP
7. Gb	6 UI
8. $Gb \supset Hb$	4 UI
9. Hb	7,8 MP
10. $(x)Hx$	9 UG

28.

1. $(x)\{[Bx \bullet (Cx \lor Dx)] \supset Ex\}$	Premise
2. $(\exists x)(Dx \bullet \sim Ex) \; / \; (\exists x)\sim Bx$	Premise / Conclusion
3. $Da \bullet \sim Ea$	2 EI
4. $[Ba \bullet (Ca \lor Da)] \supset Ea$	1 UI
5. Da	3 Simp
6. $\sim Ea$	3 Simp
7. $\sim[Ba \bullet (Ca \lor Da)]$	4,6 MT
8. $\sim Ba \lor \sim(Ca \lor Da)$	7 DM
9. $Ca \lor Da$	5 Add
10. $\sim\sim(Ca \lor Da)$	9 DN
11. $\sim Ba$	8,10 DS
12. $(\exists x)\sim Bx$	11 EG

EXERCISE 11.4E

1.

1. $(x)[(Sx \lor Cx) \supset Ex]$ $/ (x)(Cx \supset Ex)$	Premise / Conclusion
2. $(Sa \lor Ca) \supset Ea$	1 UI
3. Ca	Assumption
4. $Sa \lor Ca$	3 Add
5. Ea	2,4 MP
6. $Ca \supset Ea$	3–5 CP
7. $(x)(Cx \supset Ex)$	6 UG

4.

1. $(x)(Dx \supset Ex)$	Premise
2. $(x)[(Dx \cdot Ex) \supset Fx]$ $/ (x)(Dx \supset Fx)$	Premise / Conclusion
3. $Da \supset Ea$	1 UI
4. $(Da \cdot Ea) \supset Fa$	2 UI
5. Da	Assump
6. Ea	3,5 MP
7. $Da \cdot Ea$	5,6 Conj
8. Fa	4,7 MP
9. $Da \supset Fa$	5–8 CP
10. $(x)(Dx \supset Fx)$	9 UG

7.

1. $(x)[(Ax \lor Bx) \supset Cx]$	Premise
2. $(x)[Cx \supset (\sim Ax \lor Dx)]$ $/ (x)(Ax \supset Dx)$	Premise / Conclusion
3. Aa	Assumption
4. $(Aa \lor Ba) \supset Ca$	1 UI
5. $Aa \lor Ba$	3 Add
6. Ca	4,5 MP
7. $Ca \supset (\sim Aa \lor Da)$	2 UI
8. $\sim Aa \lor Da$	6,7 MP
9. $\sim\sim Aa$	3 DN
10. Da	8,9 DS
11. $Aa \supset Da$	3–10 CP
12. $(x)(Ax \supset Dx)$	11 UG

10.

1. $(x)(Px \equiv Tx)$	Premise
2. $(x)(Tx \equiv Ax)$ / $Pm \supset Am$	Premise / Conclusion
3. Pm	Assump
4. $Pm \equiv Tm$	1 UI
5. $Tm \equiv Am$	2 UI
6. $(Pm \supset Tm) \cdot (Tm \supset Pm)$	4 Bicon
7. $(Tm \supset Am) \cdot (Am \supset Tm)$	5 Bicon
8. $Pm \supset Tm$	6 Simp
9. $Tm \supset Am$	7 Simp
10. Tm	3,8 MP
11. Am	9,10 MP
12. $Pm \supset Am$	3–11 CP

13.

1. $(x)[Bx \supset (Cx \lor Dx)]$	Premise
2. $(x)(Dx \supset {\sim}Ex)$ / $(x)[(Bx \cdot Ex) \supset Cx]$	Premise / Conclusion
3. $Ba \supset (Ca \lor Da)$	1 UI
4. $Da \supset {\sim}Ea$	2 UI
5. $Ba \cdot Ea$	Assumption
6. Ba	5 Simp
7. $Ca \lor Da$	3,6 MP
8. Ea	5 Simp
9. ${\sim}{\sim}Ea$	8 DN
10. ${\sim}Da$	4,9 MT
11. Ca	7,10 DS
12. $(Ba \cdot Ea) \supset Ca$	5–11 CP
13. $(x)[(Bx \cdot Ex) \supset Ca]$	12 UG

16.

1. $(x)[Bx \cdot {\sim}Cx) \supset Dx]$	Premise
2. $(x)(Dx \supset Cx)$ / $(x)(Bx \supset Cx)$	Premise / Conclusion
3. $(Ba \cdot {\sim}Ca) \supset Da$	1 UI
4. $Da \supset Ca$	2 UI

5. ~(Ba ⊃ Ca)	Assump
6. Ba • ~Ca	5 Imp
7. ~Ca	6 Simp
8. ~Da	4,7 MT
9. ~(Ba • ~Ca)	3,8 MT
10. ~Ba ∨ ~~Ca	9 DM
11. Ba	6 Simp
12. ~~Ba	11 DN
13. ~~Ca	10,12 DS
14. Ca	13 DN
15. Ca • ~Ca	7,14 Conj
16. Ba ⊃ Ca	5–15 RA
17. (x)(Bx ⊃ Cx)	16 UG

19.

1. (∃x)(Bx • ~Cx)	Premise
2. (x){[Bx • ~(Dx ∨ Ex)] ⊃ Cx} / (∃x)[Dx ∨ (Ex • Bx)]	Premise / Conclusion
3. Ba • ~Ca	1 EI
4. [Ba • ~(Da ∨ Ea)] ⊃ Ca	2 UI
5. Ba	3 Simp
6. ~Ca	3 Simp
7. ~[Ba • ~(Da ∨ Ea)]	4,6 MT
8. ~Ba ∨ ~~(Da ∨ Ea)	7 DM
9. ~~Ba	5 DN
10. ~~(Da ∨ Ea)	8,9 DS
11. Da ∨ Ea	10 DN
12. ~Da	Assumption
13. Ea	11,12 DS
14. Ea • Ba	5,13 Conj
15. ~Da ⊃ (Ea • Ba)	12–14 CP
16. ~~Da ∨ (Ea • Ba)	15 Imp
17. Da ∨ (Ea • Ba)	16 DN
18. (∃x)[Dx ∨ (Ex • Bx)]	17 EG

EXERCISE 11.5A

1. *Lmc*

4. *Riad*

7. (∃*x*)(*Axg* • *Cx*)

10. *Lfj*

13. (*x*)(*Px* ⊃ ~*Six*) *Px* means *x* is a place

16. (∃*x*)(*Dx* • *Hix*)

19. (∃*x*)(*Px* • *Bsxt*)

22. (∃*x*)(*Dx* • *Axh*)

25. *Ams* • *Asm*

28. (∃*x*)[(*Tx* • *Ax*) • *Sx*]

EXERCISE 11.5B

1. (∃*x*)(*Px* • *Lxm*)

4. (*x*)(*y*)[(*Wx* • *Dy*) ⊃ *Axy*]

7. (*x*)[*Dx* ⊃ (∃*y*)(*Ny* • *Liyx*)]

10. (*x*)[*Px* ⊃ (∃*y*)(*Py* • *Fxy*)]

13. (∃*x*)(∃*y*)[(*Px* • *By*) • *Styx*]

16. ~(∃*x*)(*Rx* • *Ixg*) OR (*x*)(*Rx* ⊃ ~*Ixg*)

19. (*x*)[(*Px* • *Wmx*) ⊃ *Wlx*]

22. (*x*)[(*Rx* ∨ *Hx*) ⊃ (∃*y*)(*Py* • *Dxy*)]

25. (*x*)[*Ax* ⊃ (∃*y*){*Sy* • [*Ry* ⊃ (*z*)(*Sz* ⊃ *Fz*)]}

28. (*x*)(*y*)[(*Mx* • *Lxy*) ⊃ *Kxy*]   [Each man kills everything he loves]

   OR

   (*x*) [*Mx* ⊃ (∃*y*)(*Lxy* • *Kxy*)]   [Each man kills something he loves]

31. (*x*)(*y*){[(*Cx* • *Py*) • (*Lyg* • *Hxy*)] ⊃ ~*Jgx*}

EXERCISE 11.5C

1.

1. Ca ⊃ (Mp ⊃ Hap)	Premise
2. ~Hap / ~Ca ∨ ~Mp	Premise / Conclusion
3. (Ca • Mp) ⊃ Hap	1 Exp
4. ~(Ca • Mp)	2,3 MT
5. ~Ca ∨ Mp	4 DM

4.

1. (∃*y*)(*x*)A*xy*	/ (*x*)(∃*y*)A*xy*	Premise / Conclusion
2. (*x*)A*xb*		1 EI
3. A*ab*		2 UI
4. (∃*y*)A*ay*		3 EG
5. (*x*)(∃*y*)A*xy*		4 UG

7.

1. Aa	/ (*x*)(A*x* ⊃ B*x*) ⊃ (∃*x*)(A*x* • B*x*)	Premise / Conclusion
2. (*x*)(A*x* ⊃ B*x*)		Assump
3. Aa ⊃ Ba		2 UI
4. Ba		1,3 MP
5. Aa • Ba		1,4 Conj
6. (∃*x*)(A*x* • B*x*)		5 EG
7. (*x*)(A*x* ⊃ B*x*) ⊃ (∃*x*)(A*x* • B*x*)		2–6 CP

10.

1. (*x*)[(~M*xa* ∨ N*x*) ⊃ L*xx*]		Premise
2. (∃*y*)~L*yy*	/ (∃*x*)M*xa*	Premise / Conclusion
3. ~L*bb*		2 EI
4. (~M*ba* ∨ N*b*) ⊃ L*bb*		1 UI
5. ~(~M*ba* ∨ N*b*)		3,4 MT
6. ~~M*ba* • ~N*b*		4 DM
7. M*ba* • ~N*b*		6 DN
8. M*ba*		7 Simp
9. (∃*x*)M*xa*		8 EG

13.

1. (*x*)(E*xx* ∨ Q*x*)		Premise
2. (*y*)~E*yy*		Premise
3. (*z*)(Q*z* ⊃ K*z*)	/ (*w*)K*w*	Premise / Conclusion
4. E*aa* ∨ Q*a*		1 UI
5. ~E*aa*		2 UI
6. Q*a* ⊃ K*a*		3 UI
7. Q*a*		4,5 DS
8. K*a*		6,7 MP
9. (*w*)K*w*		8 UG

16.

1. (x)[(Hx • Gx) ⊃ Cx]	Premise
2. (y)Gy • ~(x)Mxa / (x)(Hx ⊃ Cx)	Premise / Conclusion
3. Hb	Assump
4. (y)Gy	2 Simp
5. Gb	4 UI
6. (Hb • Gb) ⊃ Cb	1 UI
7. Hb • Gb	3,4 Conj
8. Cb	6,7 MP
9. Hb ⊃ Cb	3–8 CP
10. (x)(Hx ⊃ Cx)	9 UG

19.

1. (z)(y)[(∃w)Myw ⊃ Mzy]	Premise
2. Mba / (x)(y)Mxy	Premise / Conclusion
3. (∃w)Mbw	2 EG
4. (y)[(∃w)Myw ⊃ Mcy]	1 UI
5. (∃w)Mbw ⊃ Mcb	4 UI
6. Mcb	3,5 MP
7. (∃w)Mcw	6 EG
8. (y)[(∃w)Myw ⊃ Mdy]	1 UI
9. (∃w)Mcw ⊃ Mdc	8 UI
10. Mdc	7,9 MP
11. (y)Mdy	10 UG
12. (x)(y)Mxy	11 UG

22.

1. (x)(Cxx ⊃ Sx)	Premise
2. (y)[(Sy ∨ Tyy) ⊃ Wy] / (x)[(Cxx • ~Kx) ⊃ (Wx • ~Kx)]	Premise / Conclusion
3. Caa • ~Ka	Assump
4. Caa ⊃ Sa	1 UI
5. Caa	3 Simp
6. Sa	4,5 MP
7. (Sa ∨ Taa) ⊃ Wa	2 UI
8. Sa ∨ Taa	6 Add
9. Wa	7,8 MP
10. ~Ka	3 Simp
11. Wa • ~Ka	9,10 Conj
12. (Caa • ~Ka) ⊃ (Wa • ~Ka)	3–11 CP
13. (x)[(Cxx • ~Kx) ⊃ (Wx • ~Kx)]	12 UG

Additional Exercises
A.

1. If Bob is sober, he is coherent.

4. Something is wet and clammy.

7. Either this apartment or the next one is available, but this one is not suitable.

10. There's a student who is either very slow or not interested.

13. Every positively charged particle attracts any negatively charged particle.

B.

1. ~(∃x)(Bx ∨ Wx) • (y)Gy

4. (x)(y)[(Px • Ty) ⊃ ~Bxy]

7. (x)(Hxx ⊃ Hgx)

10. {(x)Gx ⊃ [Dx ≡ (y)(Cyx ⊃ Vy)]}

13. (x)[(∃y)Mxy ⊃ (∃z)Dxz] • ~(x)[(∃y)Dxy ⊃ (∃z)Mxz]

16. (x){Px ⊃ [(∃y)(Myx • Cxy) • (∃z)(Jzx • ~Cxz)]}

19. (x){[Px ⊃ (∃y)(Ty • Fxy)] • (∃x)[Px • (y)(Ty ⊃ Fxy)]} • ~(x)[Px ⊃ (y)(Ty ⊃ Fxy)]

C.

1. MT

4. Exp

7. Imp

10. DD

D.

1. Line 3: a cannot be used for EI since it has been used before.

4. Line 3: QN requires a change of quantifier.

E.

1.

1. Tm	Premise
2. (∃y)(Ey • ~Cmy)	Premise
3. (x){Tx ⊃ [Px ⊃ (y)(Ey ⊃ Cxy)]} / ~Pm	Premise / Conclusion
4. Tm ⊃ [Pm ⊃ (y)(Ey ⊃ Cmy)]	3 UI
5. Pm ⊃ (y)(Ey ⊃ Cmy)	1,4 MP
6. ~(y)~(Ey • ~Cmy)	2 QN
7. ~(y)(Ey ⊃ Cmy)	6 Imp
8. ~Pm	5,7 MT

4.

1. (x){(Px • Mx) ⊃ (y)[(Fy • Uxy) ⊃ Iy]}	Premise
2. (x)(Ix ⊃ Hx)	Premise
3. Pa • Ma / (x)[(Fx • Uax) ⊃ Hx]	Premise / Conclusion
4. (Pa • Ma) ⊃ (y)[(Fy • Uay) ⊃ Iy]	1 UI
5. (y)[(Fy • Uay) ⊃ Iy]	3,4 MP
6. (Fb • Uab) ⊃ Ib	5 UI
7. Ib ⊃ Hb	2 UI
8. (Fb • Uab) ⊃ Hb	6,7 HS
9. (x)[(Fx • Uax) ⊃ Hx]	8 UG

7.

1. (x)[Dx ⊃ (Ax ∨ Wx)]	Premise
2. (x)[(Ax ⊃ D'x) • (Wx ⊃ Bx)]	Premise
3. (x)[(D'x ∨ Bx) ⊃ ~Lix] / (x)(Dx ⊃ ~Lix)	Premise / Conclusion
4. Da ⊃ (Aa ∨ Wa)	1 UI
5. (Aa ⊃ D'a) • (Wa ⊃ Ba)	2 UI
6. (D'a ∨ Ba) ⊃ ~Lia	3 UI
7. Da	Assumption
8. Aa ∨ Wa	4,7 MP
9. D'a ∨ Ba	5,8 CD
10. ~Lia	6,9 MP
11. Da ⊃ ~Lia	7–10 CP
12. (x)(Dx ⊃ ~Lia)	11 UG

10.

1. (x)(Dx ⊃ Ex)	Premise
2. (x)[Ex ⊃ (∃y)Cyx]	Premise
3. (x)(y)[Cxy ⊃ (Ex ∨ Ax)] / (x){Dx ⊃ (∃y)[(Ey ∨ Ay) • Cyx]}	Premise / Conclusion
4. Da ⊃ Ea	1 UI
5. Ea ⊃ (∃y)Cya	2 UI
6. Da ⊃ (∃y)Cya	4,5 HS
7. Da	Assump
8. (∃y)Cya	6,7 MP
9. Cba	8 EI
10. (y)[Cby ⊃ (Eb ∨ Ab)]	3 UI
11. Cba ⊃ (Eb ∨ Ab)	10 UI
12. Eb ∨ Ab	9,11 MP
13. (Eb ∨ Ab) • Cba	9,12 Conj
14. (∃y)[(Ey ∨ Ay) • Cya]	13 EG
15. Da ⊃ (∃y)[(Ey ∨ Ay) • Cya]	7–14 CP
16. (x)[Dx ⊃ (∃y)[(Ey ∨ Ay) • Cya]	15 UG

13.

1. (x)[(∃y)(Cy • Axy) ⊃ ~Mx]	Premise
2. (x)(Dx ⊃ Cx) / (x)(y)[(Mx • Dy) ⊃ ~Axy]	Premise / Conclusion
3. (∃y)(Cy • Aay) ⊃ ~Ma	1 UI
4. ~~Ma ⊃ ~(∃y)(Cy • Aay)	3 Contra
5. Ma ⊃ ~(∃y)(Cy • Aay)	4 DN
6. Ma	Assumption
7. ~(∃y)(Cy • Aay)	5,6 MP
8. (y)~(Cy • Aay)	7 QN
9. ~(Cb • Aab)	8 UI
10. ~Cb ∨ ~Aab	9 DM
11. Cb ⊃ ~Aab	10 Imp
12. Db ⊃ Cb	2 UI
13. Db ⊃ ~Aab	11,12 HS
14. Ma ⊃ (Db ⊃ ~Aab)	6–13 CP
15. (Ma • Db) ⊃ ~Aab	14 Exp
16. (y)[(Ma • Dy) ⊃ ~Aay]	15 UG
17. (x)(y)[(Mx • Dy) ⊃ ~Axy]	16 UG

F

1.

1. (∃x)Px ⊃ (y)Qy / (y)(∃x)(Px ⊃ Qy)	Premise / Conclusion
2. Pa	Assump
3. (∃x)Px	2 EG
4. (y)Qy	1,3 MP
5. Qb	4 UI
6. Pa ⊃ Qb	2–5 CP
7. (∃x)(Px ⊃ Qb)	6 EG
8. (y)(∃x)(Px ⊃ Qy)	7 UG

4.

1. (x)[(Qx • Rx) ⊃ Px]	Premise
2. (x)[(Qx • Sx) ⊃ Tx]	Premise
3. (∃x)[Qx • (Rx ∨ Sx)] / (∃x)(Px ∨ Tx)	Premise / Conclusion
4. Qa • (Ra ∨ Sa)	3 EI
5. (Qa • Ra) ⊃ Pa	1 UI
6. (Qa • Sa) ⊃ Ta	2 UI
7. [(Qa • Ra) ⊃ Pa] • [(Qa • Sa) ⊃ Ta]	5,6 Conj
8. (Qa • Ra) ∨ (Qa • Sa)	4 Dist
9. Pa ∨ Ta	7,8 CD
10. (∃x)(Px ∨ Tx)	9 EG

7.

1. (x)(Px ⊃ Qx) ⊃ (∃y)(Ry • Sy)	Premise
2. (x)~Sx / (∃x)(Px • ~Qx)	Premise / Conclusion
3. ~Sa	2 UI
4. ~Ra ∨ ~Sa	3 Add
5. ~(Ra • Sa)	4 DM
6. (y)~(Ry • Sy)	5 UG
7. ~(∃y)(Ry • Sy)	6 QN
8. ~(x)(Px ⊃ Qx)	1,7 MT
9. (∃x)~(Px ⊃ Qx)	8 QN
10. (∃x)~~(Px • ~Qx)	9 Imp
11. (∃x)(Px • ~Qx)	10 DN

10.

1. (x)[Px ∨ (∃y)Rxy]	Premise
2. (x)(Qx ⊃ ~Px)	Premise
3. (x)(y)(Rxy ⊃ Sy) / (∃x)Qx ⊃ (∃y)Sy	Premise / Conclusion
4. (∃x)Qx	Assump
5. Qa	4 EI
6. Qa ⊃ ~Pa	2 UI
7. ~Pa	5,6 MP
8. Pa ∨ (∃y)Ray	1 UI
9. (∃y)Ray	7,8 DS
10. Rab	9 EI
11. (y)(Ray ⊃ Sy)	3 UI
12. Rab ⊃ Sb	11 UI
13. Sb	10,12 MP
14. (∃y)Sy	13 EG
15. (∃x)Qx ⊃ (∃y)Sy	4–14 CP

13.

1. (∃x){Px • (y)(z)[(Qy • Rz) ⊃ Sxyz}	Premise
2. (x)(Px ⊃ Rx) / (y)(∃x)(Qy ⊃ Sxyx)	Premise / Conclusion
3. Pa • (y)(z)[(Qy • Rz) ⊃ Sayz]	1 EI
4. Pa	3 Simp
5. Pa ⊃ Ra	2 UI
6. Ra	4,5 MP
7. (y)(z)[(Qy • Rz) ⊃ Sayz]	3 Simp
8. (z)[(Qb • Rz) ⊃ Sabz]	7 UI
9. (Qb • Ra) ⊃ Saba	8 UI
10. (Ra • Qb) ⊃ Saba	9 Com
11. Ra ⊃ (Qb ⊃ Saba)	10 Exp
12. Qb ⊃ Saba	6,11 MP
13. (∃x)(Qb ⊃ Sxbx)	12 EG
14. (y)(∃x)(Qy ⊃ Sxyx)	13 UG

16.

1. $(\exists x)[Qx \bullet (Rx \lor Sx)]$	Premise
2. $(x)[(Qx \lor Sx) \supset Tx]$	Premise
3. $(x)\sim(Px \lor Tx)$ $/ (\exists x)[(Qx \bullet Rx) \bullet \sim Px]$	Premise / Conclusion
4. $Qa \bullet (Ra \lor Sa)$	1 EI
5. $(Qa \lor Sa) \supset Ta$	2 UI
6. $\sim(Pa \lor Ta)$	3 UI
7. $\sim Pa \bullet \sim Ta$	6 DM
8. Qa	4 Simp
9. $\sim Pa$	7 Simp
10. $\sim Ta$	7 Simp
11. $\sim(Qa \lor Sa)$	5,10 MT
12. $\sim Qa \bullet \sim Sa$	11 DM
13. $\sim Sa$	12 Simp
14. $Ra \lor Sa$	4 Simp
15. Ra	13,14 DS
16. $Qa \bullet Ra$	8,15 Conj
17. $(Qa \bullet Ra) \bullet \sim Pa$	9,16 Conj
18. $(\exists x)[(Qx \bullet Rx) \bullet \sim Px]$	17 EG

19.

1. $(x)\{Px \supset (y)[(Qy \bullet Rxy) \supset (\exists z)(Sz \bullet Txyz)]\}$	Premise
2. $(x)(\exists y)(Sx \equiv \sim Sy)$	Premise
$/(\exists x)(\exists y)[Px \bullet (Qy \bullet Rxy)] \supset \sim(z)Sz$	/ Conclusion
3. $(\exists x)(\exists y)[Px \bullet (Qy \bullet Rxy)]$	Assump
4. $(\exists y)[Pa \bullet (Qy \bullet Ray)]$	3 EI
5. $Pa \bullet (Qb \bullet Rab)$	4 EI
6. $Pa \supset (y)[(Qy \bullet Ray) \supset (\exists z)(Sz \bullet Tayz)]$	1 UI
7. Pa	5 Simp
8. $(y)[(Qy \bullet Ray) \supset (\exists z)(Sz \bullet Tayz)]$	6,7 MP
9. $(Qb \bullet Rab) \supset (\exists z)(Sz \bullet Tabz)$	8 UI
10. $Qb \bullet Rab$	5 Simp
11. $(\exists z)(Sz \bullet Tabz)$	9,10 MP
12. $Sc \bullet Tabc$	11 EI
13. $(\exists y)(Sc \equiv \sim Sy)$	2 UI
14. $Sc \equiv \sim Sd$	13 EI
15. $(Sc \supset \sim Sd) \bullet (\sim Sd \supset Sc)$	14 Bicon
16. $Sc \supset \sim Sd$	15 Simp
17. Sc	12 Simp
18. $\sim Sd$	16,17 MP
19. $(\exists z)\sim Sz$	18 EG
20. $\sim(z)Sz$	19 QN
21. $(\exists x)(\exists y)[Px \bullet (Qy \bullet Rxy)] \supset \sim(z)Sz$	3–20 CP

CHAPTER 12
EXERCISE 12.1
A.

1. This could be true or false, depending on the restaurant. Rule 1: Consider the quality of the different dishes served; the quality of the food at different times of day and on different days of the week, and the quality when the restaurant is crowded as well as when it is not. Rule 2: Visit the restaurant under the most favorable circumstances; ask people who patronize the restaurant regularly. Rule 3: Consider what is the most likely explanation for the quality of the food.

4. To my knowledge, this is false. Rule 1: Consider different breeds; observe their behavior indoors as well as outdoors. Rule 2: Ask dog owners whether they have seen their dogs not lying down in this manner. Rule 3: Is there any evolutionary reason why dogs might have this behavior?

7. This is true of many but not all doctors. Rule 1: Consider doctors in different specialties, regions (rural as well as urban), and institutions (hospitals, clinics, private practice, etc.). Rule 2: Consider doctors working in free clinics for the poor or in programs in poor countries abroad. Rule 3: What does the nature and value of doctors' services suggest about their expected income?

10. This is false. Rule 1: Consider geniuses in a variety of subjects, from a variety of historical periods. Rule 2: Look for geniuses who were normal in personality and mode of life. Rule 3: Is there any reason to think that exceptional mental ability necessarily has the sorts of effects on personality or mode of life that we would describe as eccentric?

B.

1. Turning over this card would provide little information. If the other side says Salesperson, it is a positive instance, but if it is some other job, it is irrelevant to the generalization

2. Turning over this card is important. If employee 2 has a college degree, it confirms the generalization; if not, it disconfirms.

3. This card is irrelevant to the generalization.

4. Turning over this card is essential: if employee 4 is a salesperson, it disconfirms the generalization.

EXERCISE 12.3

1. Cause: ScourClean. Effect: clean. Method of difference.

Case 1	ScourClean	dirty sink	→	clean
Case 2	leading cleanser	dirty sink	→	~clean

4. Cause: sunlight. Effect: tall growth. Method of difference.

Case 1	zinnias	soil	water	sun	→	tall growth
Case 2	zinnias	soil	water	~sun	→	~ tall growth

7. Negative conclusion: regulations do not cause decreased innovation. Cause: regulations. Effect: decreased innovation. Negative use of method of difference.

Case 1	~ product safety regulations	widget industry	→	innovation
Case 2	product safety regulations	widget industry	→	innovation

10. Cause: AOL. Effect: e-mails bounce. Method of agreement.

Case 1	AOL address	new contact	~ attachment	→	e-mail bounced
Case 2	AOL address	reply to received e-mail	~ attachment	→	e-mail bounced
Case 3	AOL address	frequently e-mailed	~ attachment	→	e-mail bounced
Case 4	AOL address	frequently e-mailed	attachment	→	e-mail bounced

EXERCISE 12.4

A.

1. Cause: sleep. Effect: energy. Method of concomitant variations.

Case 1	less than 7 hours of sleep	→	less energy
Case 2	7 hours of sleep	→	normal energy
Case 3	more than 7 hours	→	more energy

4. Cause: rotating the knob. Effect: radio volume. Negative use of concomitant variations.

turning knob up	→	~ change in volume
turning knob down	→	~ change in volume

B.

1. Cause: some problem up ahead. Effect: traffic jam. Method of residues.

4. Cause: mosquitoes. Effect: transmission of yellow fever.
   Joint method:
   Method of agreement: Residents of the general Army base and Building 2 both contracted the fever. Exposure to mosquitoes was the only factor they had in common.
   Method of difference: Both the Army base and Building 1 had exposure to fever victims, but the Army base residents contracted the fever while Building 1 residents did not.

Living Quarters	Exposure to Fever Victims	Exposure to Mosquitoes		Yellow Fever
Army base	Y	Y	→	Contracted
Building 1	Y	N	→	~ Contracted
Building 2	N	Y	→	Contracted

7. Cause: employee recognition awards. Effect: turnover.
   Joint method:
   Method of agreement: Glenville, Aster, and Johnstown had low turnover; employee recognition awards was the only common factor.
   Method of difference: Brookfield and Johnstown were the same except that Johnstown had employee recognition awards and low turnover while Brookfield had no awards and high turnover.

10. Cause: dried leaves in gutters. Effect: house catches fire within 1 minute of exposure to high flames. Method of agreement.

Case	Windows	landscaping	siding	roof	gutters		effect
House 1	Class E	rose bushes	vinyl	composition shingles	dried leaves	→	catches fire within 1 min
House 2	Class E	buckthorn	stone	wood shakes	dried leaves	→	catches fire within 1 min
House 3	Clase E1	dogwood	vinyl	metal	dried leaves	→	catches fire within 1 min

Additional Exercises
A.

1.

Case 1:	oxygen	flame	paper	→	paper burns
Case 2:	no oxygen (e.g., in a vacuum tube)	flame	paper	→	paper does not burn

4.

Case 1a:	colder than air	glass	window	→	condensation
Case 1b:	warmer than air	glass	window	→	~ condensation
Case 2a:	colder than air	glass	ice tea pitcher	→	condensation
Case 2b:	warmer than air	glass	ice tea pitcher	→	~ condensation
Case 3a:	colder than air	metal	bicycle	→	condensation
Case 3b:	warmer than air	metal	bicycle	→	~ condensation

B.

1. Deductive: All narrative literature has a plot, and any plot involves conflict. Inductive: Variety of instances: consider narrative literature by different authors, from different eras, etc. Disconfirming cases: Look for works that do not involve conflict. Plausibility: The plausibility of this generalization depends a good deal on our definitions and criteria for the key terms, "narrative" and "conflict." For example, would it count as a narrative if an author described a series of events without connecting them in a plot? Again, does it count as a conflict if a story presents a person overcoming challenges but without opposition from other people?

4. Deductive: All racial and sexual harassment is demeaning to the person harassed, and anything demeaning to a person lowers his self-esteem.

Inductive: Joint method: compare people subjected to harassment—do all of them have a loss of self-esteem afterward? (Comparing people who vary in other respects is the element of agreement; comparing any particular person's level of self-esteem before and after the incident is the element of difference.)

Method of concomitant variations: Compare cases of harassment that differ in degree of severity and look for corresponding differences in degree to which self-esteem is lowered.

C.

1. Effect: no pigeons. Proposed cause: plastic owls. Method: agreement, used to support the causal claim. There is also an implicit use of difference in the final contrast with conditions a month ago.

Building 1	plastic owls	→	~ pigeons
Building 2	plastic owls	→	~ pigeons
Building 3	plastic owls	→	~ pigeons

4. Effect: economic growth. Proposed cause: organization innovation. Method: agreement, used to support a causal claim.

	Cause: Organization Innovation		Effect: Economic Growth
Case 1	organization innovation: creation of joint-stock company	→	growth of transoceanic commerce
Case 2	organization innovation: hierarchically organized companies	→	extension of railroads across the United States

7. Effect: hares' aversion to eating buds. Proposed cause: pinosylvin methyl ether (PME). Joint method, used to support causal claim.

Case	PME	Nutritional Value		Effect
Stems	~PME	Y	→	eat
Buds	PME	Y	→	~ eat
Oatmeal	~PME	Y	→	eat
Oatmeal	PME	Y	→	~ eat

10. Effect: attribution of responsibility. Proposed cause: inner choice. Method: joint, used to support causal claim.

Normal case	inner choice	overt act	→ responsible
Robot		overt act	→ ~responsible
Frustrated intention	inner choice		→ responsible

CHAPTER 13

EXERCISE 13.1

1. Not an argument

4. Not an argument

7. *A*: steam boiler; *B*: person who keeps his emotions bottled up; *P*: inevitability of breakdown; *S*: build-up of internal pressure

10. *A*: ship; *B*: earth; *P*: necessity of living together; *S*: unstated. Plausible candidates for *S*: on a voyage, exposed to danger, on a fragile vessel

EXERCISE 13.2

1. Deductive element: No intellectual likes sports; Jim is an intellectual; therefore Jim doesn't like sports. The major premise is supported inductively by the example of Fred. The inductive generalization is extremely weak. Athletic and intellectual interests are not incompatible, and many intellectuals like sports.

4. Deductive element: All presidents that are young, personable, and Democrats will be remembered by history; Bill Clinton is young, etc.; therefore he will be remembered by history. The major premise is supported inductively by the example of John F. Kennedy. The inductive element is extremely weak, not only because it relies on a single example, but also because Kennedy's assassination is the more likely explanation of his being well-remembered.

7. Deductive element: Any generation that is unusually large will face stiffer competition in school and work and have a disproportionate influence on society; the generation that was born in the 1990s is unusually large; therefore, the generation born in the 1990s will face stiffer competition, etc. The major premise is supported inductively by the example of the "baby boom" generation born in the 1950s. The support is fairly strong, particularly since the generalization is very plausible, but further inductive evidence would be necessary to confirm the major premise.

10. Deductive element: No effort by rival nations to limit arms will succeed; current arms control negotiations between the United States and other countries are efforts by rival nations to limit arms; therefore current arms negotiations between the United States and other countries will not succeed. The major premise is supported by the example of efforts in Europe during the 1920s and 1930s. Since the connecting term was not given in the statement of the argument, I supplied one (efforts by rival nations to limit arms); you may have a plausible alternative. A key difference between the two cases is the existence of nuclear weapons, which may give countries today a greater incentive to control arms.

Additional Exercises

A.

1. Analogy with Jaguar, Corvette, etc.

4. The usual analogy is with gambling, but there are many significant differences (there's more to investing than money changing hands in a zero-sum game). Another analogy would be starting a business.

B.

1. Not an argument.

4. Nothing created to serve a purpose should have extraneous parts; a sentence is created to serve a purpose; thus a sentence should contain no unnecessary parts. Though an effort of persuasion is clearly being made here, the basis of the analogy may be too vague to count as an argument. No matter how florid, rococo, or redundant a sentence is, couldn't the author claim that everything in it served *some* purpose?

7. Any coercive arrangement that requires one person to work a specified amount of time for another's purposes is wrong; taxation on earnings is a coercive arrangement that requires one person to work a specified amount of time for another's purposes. Therefore taxation on earnings is wrong. The key question here is the relevance of the differences between forced labor and income taxes—for example, the conditional nature of the tax (it applies only if one chooses to work), exerting control over the product of labor versus controlling the labor itself.

10. Any policy of insuring an actual case of a potential harm will increase costs to other policyholders; insuring people with preexisting medical conditions is a policy of insuring an actual case of potential harm; therefore insuring people with preexisting medical conditions will increase costs to other policyholders. Since the major premise and the conclusion are virtually guaranteed by the mathematics of probability, the analogy with burning buildings may be better interpreted as explanatory, or else as a premise in an implicit argument about fairness.

C.

1. Anger is like a "Danger" sign, a high-voltage wire, etc.— anything that is not hydraulic.

4. Society is like a party, convention, a marketplace, etc.— anything that involves interaction but not necessarily shared interests. To an extent, 2 and 4 are counteranalogies to each other.

D.

a.)

	Machine	World
S_1	Composed of parts (at many levels of organization)	Composed of parts (at many levels of organization)
S_2	Parts are adjusted to each other with great accuracy	Parts are adjusted to each other with great accuracy
S_3	Means are adapted to serve ends	Means are adapted to serve ends
D_1	Man-made	Not man-made
P	Created by intelligent designer	Created by intelligent designer

b.)

	Living Organism	World
S_1	Continual circulation of matter	Continual circulation of matter
S_2	Constant repair of "waste" (damage)	Constant repair of "waste" (damage)
S_3	Parts act to preserve themselves as well as the whole	Parts act to preserve themselves as well as the whole
D_1	Mortal	Immortal or unknown
P	Intrinsically actuated with "life and motion" (not designed)	Intrinsically actuated with "life and motion" (not designed)

CHAPTER 14
EXERCISE 14.1
A.

1. Blue, brown, gray, etc.

4. Lawyer, banker, construction worker, etc.

B.

1. Political position

4. Religion

EXERCISE 14.2A

1. (a) Total visitors to the Jefferson Memorial in other years; (b) visitors per day, ratio of Jefferson Memorial visitors to visitors at other sites, etc.

4. (a) Total salmon catch in Alaska in other years, total catch in other fisheries, etc.; (b) ratio of salmon catch in Alaska to harvest of other fish, etc.

7. (a) Number of privately owned automobiles in other countries; (b) ratio of automobiles to population in China.

10. a) Number of advertising pages in *Vanity Fair* magazine in other years or advertising pages in other magazines; (b) ratio of advertising pages to total pages, etc.

EXERCISE 14.2B

1. Consistent variables, mutually exclusive and jointly exhaustive

4. Consistent variables, mutually exclusive and jointly exhaustive

EXERCISE 14.2C

1. Total. The premise does not give much if any support to the conclusion. "Large" is a relative term, and the premise tells us nothing about the size of the United States in relation to other countries.

4. Frequencies. The premise provides little support for the conclusion. What percentage of each group has advanced degrees depends on other factors in addition to how much they value education, such as age distribution and family incomes.

7. Totals. The premise provides strong support for the conclusion.

10. Average, median. This is a good inference. (In fact, the top six of the 27 players had salaries from $11 to $21 million).

EXERCISE 14.3

1. The mailing list overrepresents conservatives, who are more likely than those of other persuasions to oppose national health insurance.

4. People with the time and money to attend a concert are not necessarily representative of all fans. For example, they might well tend to be older.

7. Parents who sign up for the PTA's list may be more engaged than other parents.

10. The question allows only two alternatives; it does not allow people to express the view that arts organizations can or should be funded by private philanthropy.

EXERCISE 14.4B

1. Independent variable: ultraviolet light. Dependent variable: frequency of sprouting in the population of pea plants.

Group 1:   UV light,   pea plants   →   80% sprouted within week

Group 2:   no UV light,   pea plants   →   60% sprouted within week

Method of difference.

4. Independent variable: use of appointment books. Dependent variable: average grade-point average.

Group 1:   used appointment books, students   →   3.1 GPA

Group 2:   did not use appointment books, students   →   2.8 GPA

Method of difference.

EXERCISE 14.4D

Problems of internal validity: This is an observational study, subject to various possibly confounding factors. Vacationers may be more impatient to get to their destination than are those commuting to work or they may be less familiar with the road or with their route. And despite what the report says, it is unlikely that driving conditions were exactly the same in all respects, including the number of police on the road, the number of lanes, the width of shoulders, the outside temperature, etc.

Problems of external validity: Neither New York City commuters nor Disney World patrons are likely to be representative samples of drivers in general. And the presence or absence of family members is not a good variable to use for estimating the presence or absence of backseat driving. The presence of the family may distract the driver in other ways: children playing, marital squabbles, etc.

Additional exercises

A.

1. Incompatible

4. Depends on how much imprecision is allowed by the word "about." An order of magnitude seems a bit much.

7. Incompatible (assuming the 4-point system)

B.

1. The best choice would be (c). An adjustment for inflation is clearly required; but there is no reason to adjust for changes in median income.

4. Everything here depends on what kind of satisfaction one is looking for. (c) is probably the most reasonable measure for the nonprofessional investor, since everyone has the option of putting money into an interest-yielding instrument; (d) ignores the element of risk.

D.

1. The 70% improvement rate provides no evidence for the skin cream's effectiveness since we are not told how many poison-ivy victims who do *not* use any treatment also recover within a week.

4. The potential for confounding variables here is enormous: differences in health, wealth, vitality, etc., might explain both the lower death rate of men with younger wives and their attraction to younger women. And if there is a direct causal connection, it's conceivable that it runs in the opposite direction: younger women may be more attracted to older men whom they expect to live longer.

CHAPTER 15

EXERCISE 15.1

1. Explanation
   1. The stock market went up yesterday. [*Explanandum*]
   2. The Federal Reserve lowered interest rates. [Hypothesis]

4. Explanation
   1. Natalie has very little self-confidence. [Hypothesis]
   2. Natalie is very boastful. [*Explanandum*]
   3. Natalie rarely takes on challenges in her work. [*Explanandum*]

7. Explanation
   1. Babies begin to learn language at about 1 year of age, regardless of language, society, or culture. [*Explanandum*]
   2. A physical process of maturation in the brain governs language acquisition. [Hypothesis]

10. Explanation

   1. Some urban areas are safer than others. [*Explanandum*]
   2. Some urban areas are more vibrant than others. [*Explanandum*]
   3. Some urban areas have a mixture of uses. [Hypothesis]
   4. In an area with a mixture of uses, people will be on the streets at all hours. [Hypothesis]
   5. The presence of people on the streets is a deterrent against crime. [Hypothesis]
   6. The presence of people gives an area a vibrant feel. [Hypothesis]

   [5, 3, and 4 explain 1; 3, 4, and 6 explain 2.]

EXERCISE 15.2

1. Extremely uninformative. The hypothesis tells us that the chicken had some motive for crossing the road but doesn't tell us what it was. (That is presumably the point of this ancient joke.)

4. Logically weak. The prosecutor's hypothesis is based solely on alleged motive, but very few angry ex-lovers commit murder. Also incomplete. There is no explanation of how Imelda had the means, the intent, or the opportunity.

7. Logically weak. There were other tall men who were not admired as Washington was.

10. Logically weak. As stated, this evolutionary theory does not explain why sexual selection would give rise to art in particular as opposed to other "wasteful" exercises of abilities, nor does it explain the psychology of artistic enjoyment.

EXERCISE 15.3A

1. (a) *Explanandum*: Jim hasn't taken any science courses; (b) hypothesis: Jim has math anxiety; (c) additional implications: Jim hasn't taken any math courses; (d) alternative hypothesis: Jim doesn't like science or knows a lot of science already

4. (a) *Explanandum*: I got a C on this paper; (b) hypotheses: (i) I disagreed with the professor's view, and (ii) he is biased against people who disagree with him; (c) additional implications: other students who agreed with the professor got higher grades, I will get a higher grade if I write a paper agreeing with him; (d) alternative explanation: the paper deserved a C because it was poorly written, uninsightful, etc

7. (a) *Explananda*: (i) the victim died of gunshot wounds, (ii) on Fifth Avenue on the afternoon of September 7, (iii) from a bullet from Watson's gun; (b) hypothesis: Watson shot the victim; (c) additional implications: someone saw Watson shoot the victim, Watson's fingerprints are on the gun; (d) alternative hypothesis: someone else stole the gun and committed the murder.

10. (a) *Explanandum*: the occurrence of the American Civil War; (b) hypothesis: the war was caused by a conflict over tariffs; (c) additional implications: representatives from the Northern states would have introduced tariff legislation into Congress; (d) alternative hypothesis: the war was caused by the conflict over slavery.

EXERCISE 15.3B

1. Hypothesis *a* is more plausible. It is simpler than *b*, which posits a person deliberately pretending to make a deceptive call and having a malicious purpose.

4. Hypothesis *a* is obviously simpler and—skeptical arguments aside—is more consistent with our body of knowledge.

Additional Exercises
A.

1. *Explanandum*:   1. A zygote obtains half its genes from its male parent.
   Hypothesis: 2. A zygote receives half its chromosomes from its male parent.
   3. The chromosomes bear the genes.

$$\frac{2+3}{}$$
$$\downarrow$$
$$1$$

4. *Explananda*:   1. Some eastern American azaleas are more similar to eastern Chinese azaleas than to other eastern American azaleas.
   Hypotheses: 2. A tertiary species of azalea once circled the Nothern Hemisphere.
   3. The mountain ranges in China and America run north and south.
   4. When the ice-age glaciers moved south, the tertiary azalea could retreat south along the valleys.

5. The tertiary azalea survived the ice age.

6. The tertiary azalea could recolonize its former area when the glaciers retreated at the end of the ice age.

B.

1. Hypothesis: Congressional Democrats want to gain (or restore) a reputation for being concerned with ethics. Alternatives: Congressional Democrats are actually concerned with ethics, Congressional Democrats consider earmarks a genuine problem, . . .

C.

1. Hypothesis: The teachers were not good at explaining the subject. Adequacy: Logically strong, partially complete, informative. Truth: Test hypothesis by taking a course in that subject with a good teacher.

4. Hypothesis: Working at home allows working parents to care for their children during the day. Adequacy: Logically strong and informative but not complete; the hypothesis applies only to people with children and does not explain why employers accept the arrangement. Truth: Test the hypothesis by surveying parents working at home to see how much time they spend with their children, how many send their children to school or daycare, etc.

D.

Rank, from most to least consistent with current knowledge, by type:

a. Coincidences that do not involve any physical improbability: 6, 8.

b. Events that are physically unlikely but can be explained by existing knowledge: 1.

c. Events that cannot be explained by existing knowledge, but might be explained by new principles that do not conflict with existing knowledge: 4, 10, 5, 7.

d. Events whose occurrence would conflict with existing knowledge: 2, 3, 9.

CHAPTER 16
EXERCISE 16.1
A.

1. 1/6, equal alternatives

4. 7/21 (1/3)

B.

1. Reference class: Past days when meteorological conditions were similar. Frequency: Percentage of those days when rain occurred.

4. Reference class: Babies born in the same region and time period. Frequency: Percentage of girls in that class.

C.

1. 2/6, equal alternatives

4. 1:13, equal alternatives

EXERCISE 16.2
A.

1. Compatible

4. Compatible

B.

1. Independent

4. Dependent

C.

1. 5/6

4. a. $3/15 \times 3/15 = 1/5 \times 1/5 = 1/25$
   b. $3/15 \times 2/14 = 1/5 \times 1/7 = 1/35$

7. 6, then 3: $0.7 \times 0.9 = 0.63$

10. a. 44.2
    b. 46%

Additional Exercises
A.

1. D

B.

1. a. 1/13
   b. 1/6

4. $128/2{,}652 = 32/663 = 4.8\%$

Index